The Measure of a Life

THE MEASURE OF A LIFE

Diaries of a Mennonite Farm Wife 1920-2000

Ruth Martin Hostetter

Edited by Mary Alice Hostetter

ISBN:	Hardcover	978-1-4363-6647-2
	Softcover	978-1-4363-6646-5

Original cover art by Terry M. Coffey

This book was printed in the United States of America.

To order additional copies of this book, contact:
Xlibris Corporation
1-888-795-4274
www.Xlibris.com
Orders@Xlibris.com
52653

For My Parents,

Ruth Martin Hostetter and Isaac Eby Hostetter,

With Gratitude

Our lines have fallen in pleasant places.

Psalms 16:6

Prologue

My mother, Ruth Martin Hostetter, began keeping a diary in 1920 when she was fifteen and living on the family farm in Cattail, Pennsylvania with her parents and seven siblings. In those early diaries there are hints of an independent daughter trying to find her way. " . . . Had my hair combed to suit Mamma." (4/26/20) A few months later she wrote, "Hoed sweet potatoes three times till they suited Mamma, which rather insulted me." (6/10/20) And then, after getting home late from a party one evening because she had a flat tire, she noted, "I got a scolding for all my wicked deeds . . . a splendid evening." (8/5/20) The diaries she kept as a teenager reflect a keen interest in social gatherings, "crowds" they called them. She continued keeping a diary as she took jobs working for wealthy families, and when she married and started her own family. She noted the leave takings as the children grew up and left home; she kept a record of all of the visits to and from children, grandchildren and great grandchildren. Writing in her diary at the end of each day was a practice she continued until just days before her death in 2000 at the age of 95.

I doubt that my mother's life was particularly different from other Mennonite farm women in Lancaster County, Pennsylvania at that time. For most of them, I'm sure that life was defined by the demands of raising children, by involvement with the church, by births and deaths, by a passing awareness of local, national and international news events, and by the cycles of the seasons and the labor proscribed by those cycles.

A few years before she died, knowing how much I treasured her diaries, my mother entrusted them to me. When I received them, stored in two cardboard boxes, I sorted them according to decades and tied them in bundles with black velvet ribbons. The bundle for the forties contained only five volumes, the fifties only one. All of the other decades, with the exception of one volume missing in the thirties, were full sets, a diary for each year. I don't know if some diaries were lost, or if, overwhelmed by all that she had to do, she simply stopped keeping them for a few years. On one day in the only volume I have for the fifties, she writes, "I was ungraceful busy," (6/26/53), which may offer a reason for the pause in her diary-keeping.

I have often wondered why at the end of each of her busy days, days of work in the fields, in the garden, in the kitchen, with stacks of dirty laundry and dishes, eggs to gather, peas to pick, cows to milk, twelve children to feed and care for, why at the end of each of those days did she sit down at the desk and write in her diary?

I once asked her, and she answered, simply, "To keep track." And that is what she did. She kept track of dozens of this and bushels of that, and bunches and buckets and bales; and quarts and crocks and lathes and shocks. She noted how many workers she fed when they came to thresh or fill silo. She recorded what pies or cakes or puddings were made in preparation for Sunday dinner, how many gallons of milk were returned when the pole cat got in the milk house. She noted the ever-changing price of eggs, the cost of shoes, how many souls were saved at the revival and how many people attended the singing in Kennel's Woods.

She kept track of Sunday sermon topics; the games she played with her children and grandchildren; the words she misspelled at the spelling bees; designs of quilts she made; the books she read; the sizes of the rugs she braided to donate to the Mennonite Relief Sale and the amount they raised for charity at the auction.

When I was growing up, I was fascinated by my mother's diaries. I had dreams of becoming a writer, and her daily writing practice was the closest model I had. There was nothing secretive about her diary. It was always lying on the desk where anyone could read it. I often read what she had written, to see if my name was mentioned. As the tenth of twelve children, it made me feel more special if she said something about me, even though it might be a very straightforward reporting, "The children stayed home because of the snow . . . Mary Alice and Sanford worked on their quilts." Having it mentioned in the diary, no matter how mundane, made it seem more important. When I visited as an adult, I sometimes went to her desk after she and my father had gone to bed to see what she had written. "Had a nice evening with Mary Alice," she noted on one such visit. (3/25/95)

There is in her diaries limited emotional content. If she and my father had serious disagreements in their seventy three years of marriage, it is not reflected on the pages of her diaries. There were some points of friction, it seemed. On 3/4/30, she wrote, "I washed and Eby refused to hang it up, so I did it myself." His need to go to the Farm Show held in Harrisburg each January, no matter what the weather, often seemed to be a point of difference. Her protests about his going, she wrote, were "like water on a duck's back." (1/17/34).

Anyone who knew my mother during her long life was struck by her equanimity, but the diaries show that she was sometimes pushed to the limit. On one such day she wrote, "I did not feel good and could barely keep going." (12/7/39) On 1/11/37, she admitted, "My nerves are some unstrung." Of her two oldest children, she observed on 1/13/41, "Rhoda and Abram stayed at home . . . and argued till I could hardly put up with it." As a young mother to six sick children in '37, she writes, "I tried to keep the children quiet, but they were very troublesome."

Reflections on emotional highs or lows are infrequent. The birth of a stillborn baby in 1938 resulted in a rare expression of sadness. "Eby and the undertaker buried its dear little body in Hershey's Cemetery. It was a long, sad day for me." (8/17/38)

She did not write in her diary during the year after her mother's illness and death in early 1932, a time she admitted was very difficult. Her father's decline and death in 1946 was during the span of years when there were no diaries.

The births of her children, all but one of whom were born at home, were noted in the same rhythm as the rest of the day's activities, and then life went on.

1/10/40 A nice cold day. Had a big night, got up at 2:00 and Charles Lewis was born at 4:00. Eby was busy getting things ready to give him a warm reception. The children all went to school, and Eby went for the nurse, Rebecca Fisher, when he took the milk. Everything went fine today. The Dr. came.

One might wonder if it really matters that on that damp Monday in '32, "the wash didn't dry so good," and she had to bring it in to dry by the cookstove; that seventeen of the new peepies died; that she finally wrote a letter to the Maytag company letting them know that the new wringer washer was still not working right; that she had to return the shoes to Sears after six months in '34 because "they weren't wearing good." I believe it does matter. A record of the day-to-day texture of a disappearing way of life is as rare a treasure as any cultural artifact. My mother's diaries are an invitation to view that life through attentive and trustworthy eyes.

M.A.H.

Ruth Martin and Eby Hostetter wedding photo, March 24, 1927

The Twenties

1920

4/25/20 Tuesday
My fifteenth birthday. I got a card from Anna Reeser and one from Mary Hershey and a handkerchief from Albertina. The Amish men had a frolic to do Eli Beiler's work, about 52 horses there. We washed, ironed, scoured and cleaned. I was sick this morning. Landis was rolling. The lights went out. Abe Trout was here and the fish man and his wife or girl. Cloudy. Amy stuck some old onions.

4/26/20 Wednesday
Finished ironing and cleaned the spare room. Edna cleaned yard. Planted potatoes. Edna got a letter from Mae Groff. Mabel and I drove up to Intercourse this evening with a load of junk. Had my hair combed to suit Mamma. Recharged the generator.

5/1/20 Monday
Mountain still burning. Washed and tore down the machine and got it ready to paint. Mabel and I took 18 bunches of asparagus to Intercourse, the first we sold this year. Fish man was here, got 2 dozen herring.

5/8/20 Monday
Mabel and I were up at Abram Beiler's picking strawberry plants and planted about half an acre. Got the Carbide dividend for $500.

5/12/20 Friday
I swept the upstairs and cleaned the chicken houses and washed all the windows. Rained a little this morning and cleared off. Mowed and trimmed the yard. Edna has very sore arms. Scrubbed the balcony porch. Had a raccoon plaster on my corn and it pained me fierce all day. Put brush to the peas.

5/16/20 Tuesday
Finished ironing, then Mabel and I cleaned the garret and scrubbed the floor, the first time since we live here. Papa and Mamma fixed the east end of the house. Bishop Christ Brackbill was here and Mr. McClain. Mabel took Edna to the Dr. this evening. I got the machine ready to varnish.

5/19/20 Friday
Edna able to work a little. Amy and Mabel not feeling well. I put up the new stair carpet and painted peepie house and chicken house. Baked two cakes, angel and devil food. It rained showers by spells.

5/30/20 Tuesday
I helped to make flower beds and then King's came to help pull tobacco plants. Mabel and I went over and helped till 2:00. Came home and pulled here till suppertime. Then Edna, Mamma, Papa and Jay planted six rows after supper. I fixed the toilet, painted around the toilet and trimmed along the lane. Broke the scythe.

6/8/20 Thursday
Cleaned the chicken house roosts. After dinner Edna and I went down to Fenninger's to learn knitting. Miss Eby and her sister Florence were there. We were treated to ice cream and strawberries. This evening Mabel and I replanted two acres of tobacco. Edna and Amy planted 322 red beet plants.

6/10/20 Saturday
Edna, Mabel and I pulled tobacco plants at King's for Grandpap's. We washed the machine and Mabel and the three little boys and I went to Intercourse with asparagus. This evening we planted and had to hoe the sweet potatoes three times till they suited Mamma, which rather insulted me. Gusty, but we didn't have any rain.

6/22/20 Thursday
Jay and I turned hay all forenoon. This afternoon we heaped hay and then made supper. This evening we seeded the cherries that Mabel and Lloyd picked at Fenninger's. Raining this evening and windy all day.

6/23/20 Friday
Got up early and took the steers out. Edna, Mabel and I went down to Fenninger's to pick cherries. I took the machine up to Intercourse, went to the garage, bank, store and got a porch chair at Peter's. Heaped hay all afternoon and evening. A splendid day for haymaking. Got $1205.60 for steers.

6/30/20 Friday
I stirred up ginger cakes and sugar cakes. Mabel and Jay hoed tobacco. Mamma started to make a rug. Did all the Saturday work. Jay and Papa hauled in two loads of wheat. Mabel and I greased the peepies. Very warm day and a pretty evening.

7/1/20 Saturday
We washed two machine loads of wash. Mabel and Mamma helped haul in wheat till the rain came and put a stop to it. I ran the machine to Mary Houck's crowd and took Miriam Good and Elizabeth Groff along. I took the dividend to the bank and went to the store. Had a heavy gust this evening. Ira Hershey's are having a party tonight.

7/5/20 Wednesday
Had a good sleep last night, almost cold enough for frost. Agnes Loudon brought 5 quarts of huckleberries. We gave her a roaster, a box of beans, some onions and pickles and thirty cents. I picked raspberries. I cleaned the two spare rooms this

evening and we cleaned the yard and trimmed it. A very pretty evening. We are talking and planning for a social on such an evening.

7/7/20 Friday
Picked the raspberries and helped to mow wheat the rest of the day. Mabel and I harrowed the garden and cleaned some of the weeds up. We shelled peas. Papa and Mamma tried to persuade us to put off the crowd till later, but the prospects are brighter this evening.

7/22/20 Saturday
We baked pies. Henry Hershey brought A.D. Wenger here a little while. Mabel and I took Elizabeth Fenninger along to Merle Zimmerman's crowd in the machine. For supper we had: raw peaches with whipped cream, sunshine crackers, orangeade, sandwiches, crustades with corn in, cold beef, cheese, lettuce with bananas, peanuts and dressing on, orange ice, marshmallows, two kinds of cake, little candy, pretzels, olives and salted peanuts.

7/26/20 Wednesday
Edna baked pies. Mary King was here for flower slips. Mamma went to Lancaster and got each of us girls a new dress. Omar King and Jason Eckman were here putting a new roof on the barn. I mowed yard. I took the pendulum up to Beiler's. Mabel is still complaining.

7/28/20 Friday
I went up to the garage and got 10 gallons of gas and the tires pumped. Brought Mary Axe down to make a dress. I swept some of the house. Am not feeling good. Mamma fired her temper this evening. We had a gust.

8/1/20 Tuesday
We got up early and Grandpap and Grandmother and Aunt Ada went along with Papa and Mamma to Lancaster. The bishops met at Vine Street Mission to revise the conference rules. We ironed. Will Axe papered Mamma's room. We picked the blackberries. Mamma saw a woman get run down in the center square.

8/4/20 Friday
I swept some of the house. Lizzie Hershey and her family were here this evening. I scrubbed. Papa and Mamma topped tobacco. We had rain and gust this evening. Dr. Bell, the telephone inventor, was buried this evening at sunset.

8/5/20 Saturday
Mamma went to the tobacco patch and we canned blackberries, baked cakes and finished the Saturday work. Edna and I took Susan M along to Ethel Hershey's crowd. We had a good time. The rest went to Harvest Meeting. I took Susan up to Mart Hershey's and came home and had a blowout. Isaac Hershey fixed it for me. I got home safely and got a terrible scolding for all my wicked deeds. Edna

went to Daniel Kurtz's party with David Hershey. A very pretty day and splendid evening.

8/12/20 Saturday
A cloudy day. Amy and I washed the machine. Papa would not let us go to Kreider girls' crowd because we go away too much. This evening I sewed my shoes. Mamma topped tobacco this afternoon and evening. Climax reached.

8/21/20 Monday
A very cool morning with a tiny bit of frost. Henry Fox came up and said I should come down and help to cook for the threshers, but they got done and pulled out before dinner so I came home. I earned 20 cents. Edna and I succored tobacco this P.M. and Jay and Amy helped this evening. First day of school. Grandma King was here and condemned the school laws of today. She said if the children can read and cipher a little, it is enough and physiology is for doctors only.

8/27/20 Sunday
I did not feel good, so Paul, Charlie, Mabel and I stayed home. Mamma and Papa had a spat. After a good bit of argument, Mamma went along to church. A very cool and cloudy day. I wrote two letters. Edna went to church. Mabel was very grouchy.

9/7/20 Tuesday
Ironed. Put some celery in the creek. Mabel, Papa and I cut six loads of Lloyd's tobacco. Edna went to Kolb's party. A cloudy day with strong east wind.

9/20/20 Wednesday
Picked up apples for cider and snitzed three buckets this evening. The Business College man was here to get me to attend College. A nice day.

9/25/20 Monday
Washed and ironed. Papa, Mamma and Mabel went to Lancaster. I had intended going but was unexpectedly disappointed. Edna and I got new dresses. Papa made over $200 in a stock exchange.

10/6/20 Friday
I took some corn out to Zinn's. We got our pictures. Swept the downstairs, cleaned the yard. Edna scrubbed. Shelling beans this evening and cleaned a chicken for Sunday. Papa went to Conference with Landis Hershey and they went to see Galen Hostetter. A nice day.

10/18/20 Wednesday
Washed up the kitchen and powdered the flies and picked off beans. Took up the red beets and peppers and took out some celery. Mamma gave the flower pots another coat of paint. Had a tobacco buyer.

11/12/20 Sunday
We were home alone all night and we went to White Horse in the machine. I went to Mellinger's Church with Wilmer Kreider. Edna and Aaron went along. I went over the new bridge for the first time.

11/25/20 Saturday
Very cold and stormy. Papa, Mamma, Edna and I went to Mose Hershey's for dinner. Had turkey for the first time in my life. We went to Mrs. Keller for our bonnets but she would not give them to us.

12/1/20 Friday
They all took down tobacco but me. I made pies. I cut and started an everyday dress, the first I ever made. Clarence Eshleman came for roosters. Nice day with a few showers.

12/18/20 Monday
I did the washing. Papa, Mamma and Edna went to Lancaster. Jay got a new sled, and Paul and Charlie got a kiddie car. I made candy and potato chips. Mabel and I skated for the first time this year. Two barns were burned during the weekend.

12/25/20 Monday
Christmas Day. Papa, Mamma, Paul and Charlie took Grandpap's along to Uncle Emanuel's. We four girls walked to church. Amos Hershey took us part way down and brought us back. We had our dinner to ourselves which consisted of two chickens and other things. I got a handkerchief, gold box of powder, primrose, bottle of perfume and an autograph book.

1921

1/16/21
Very pleasant day. Church was full to the brim. I wasn't there. Mamma is very sick. Ate too many oysters. Papa began meetings at Chestnut Street. Edna and I went along with Papa to church.

3/19/21
Mary Axe, Elizabeth, Clarence, Landis and Morris were here. A big man was here and while Mamma was dressing and combing her hair, he got cross waiting and left. A peddler was here walking. Mamma is making paper roses. Lloyd brought his bedroom suit. Amy not feeling good. Found ten cents. Killed a mosquito.

4/10/21
Was at Hershey's Church. Mamma and Papa went to Red Well. Earl, Jere and Elizabeth Fenninger, Ross, Marian and Clair Hershey were here. We played tricks

and had great fun. Were down along the creek. Earl jumped across the creek and fell in and got wet feet. Snowed all night. Very cold and windy.

10/25/21
Carbide men were here with glowing accounts. Daniel Kaufman preached at Paradise in the evening. I was not there.

1923

1/7/23 Sunday
We all went to church at White Horse but Amy. Mamma and Papa went to John Mellinger's wife's funeral. George Axe and Albertina were here. Daniel Kurtz called and wanted to take me to Lancaster. Landis and I were skating. A very cold day.

1/11/23 Thursday
Got up late. Edna made a hair receiver for me to give to Elizabeth G. Warring in Europe. Stripped tobacco.

1/22/23 Monday
Took down tobacco and washed and ironed. Mamma stayed in bed all day. Snow on the ground this morning. Real good sledding. Clear and cold this evening.

2/1/23 Thursday
Finished stripping our tobacco. The grate broke on the school stove and the girls came home early. An entertainment at Milltown this evening. A very damp day.

2/9/23 Friday
Swept the house. Sylvia and Danny came over and we made a big snow man. Warm and the snow is melting. Edna and Mamma sewed.

2/18/23 Sunday
We four girls and Papa went to White Horse. Mabel and I went skating in the meadow and Jay went to Pequea. Amy and I went over to King's. Very cold.

2/21/23 Wednesday
Sewed and went to King's for eggs. Papa went to Intercourse. Warmer this P.M. 7 above this morning. Good skating. I lost one side of my skate.

2/22/23 Thursday
Sewed. Went to Hygiene Class this P.M. Mabel, Amy and Jay went to the Intercourse Spelling Bee. Cold and snow squaws.

2/29/23 Thursday
Edna and I went to Lancaster. I tried to live with Mrs. Dodge. Went to see Mary at the asylum. Came home with George Wenger's and stopped at the Hygiene Class. A cold cloudy day.

3/28/23 Wednesday
Felt miserable with cold in my head and neuralgia. Moved Edythe's bed upstairs and cleaned the sitting room. Wrote to Edna. A very cold day.

4/6/23 Friday
Cleaned the house and scrubbed the back porch only. Evelyn's sickness was pronounced genuine Typhoid. Dr. was here. I have a very bad cold in my head. Drank boneset tea. A nice day.

4/7/23 Saturday
Cold is very bad. I took it easy. Anna Mary Kurtz was here. Had first shot of antitoxin. Edith's father and mother were here.

4/11/23 Wednesday
Cleaned Evelyn's room and stuck onions. They put up the yard fence at home. Nice day. Mrs. Eaby is worse. Morris went fishing.

4/15/23 Sunday
Edith's earache is so bad. I could not go to church. Nursed Evelyn. Played the victrola. Mabel came up and took me home till Mamma and Papa could bring me back.

4/19/23 Thursday
Evelyn's temperature is high. I went to Hygiene Class and finished the yard. A nice day. Got last shot of antitoxin.

4/20/23 Friday
Morris and Edith went in to Lancaster to see the ear specialist. Evelyn is delirious. I did the cleaning and scrubbed. A nice warm day.

4/27/23 Friday
Washed for Evelyn. Had to get up and help tend Evelyn. She is very delirious. Dr. gave her a dose to make her rest. Very busy day. Rainy this evening.

5/4/23 Friday
Evelyn's birthday. She got 6 hankies, 9 cards, a dish, picture, a blouse and a crocinole board. Cleaned Mrs. Eaby's room. I didn't feel good. Radio installed. I listened till 12:00.

5/5/23 Saturday
Felt tough. Scrubbed. Edith went along to Lancaster. Mabel was here to see the radio and Papa and Landis and Paul. A nice day.

5/7/23 Monday
Washed and immense wash. Planted dahlias and tomatoes and cauliflower. I am very short of breath. A nice day.

5/8/23 Tuesday
Ironed all day. Nurse treated us all to ice cream. I went to the doctor's.

5/27/23 Sunday
Jay came and took me to Sunday School. Didn't feel good. Eby Hostetter and I went with Earl Fenninger and Susan M to Mt. Pleasant and to Enos Hershey's. A nice day.

6/1/23 Friday
Washed Dodge. Evelyn ate at the table. Cleaned the house. Very short of breath. A nice day. Very warm.

6/5/23 Tuesday
Fumigated the room and mowed yard. Very warm. Evelyn is improving. Edith and Morris went for pot cheese. Bill is shooting fireworks.

6/9/23 Saturday
Edith, Evelyn and Morris went to Lancaster to see the auto races. Evelyn went to her Grandma's. I went with Esther D. to Eva Ranck's crowd and down to see Lloyd's baby. Was alone till after midnight.

6/12/23 Tuesday
Last day for working here. Mowed yard and cleaned up hedge trimmings. Cleaned my room and packed up. Planting tobacco at home. Very warm.

6/19/23 Tuesday
Pulled 3000 tobacco plants. Went to Uncle Milt's and to the dentist. Amy and I had 22 cavities filled for $27.50. Very warm.

7/2/23 Monday
Hoed tobacco and washed. Uncle Thad came. Ironed a little. Party fever is increasing. Invitations nearly all written.

7/4/23 Wednesday
Went fishing with Evelyn and Edith Eaby. Had a fine time. Rained a little. Started hauling wheat. Shot fireworks.

7/8/23 Sunday
Mabel, Amy, Landis and Paul went to Sunday School. The rest of us went to White Horse. I went to Kinzer with Eby Hostetter this evening. A nice day.

7/16/23 Monday
Washed and ironed. Lizzie Hershey thought their house was afire and rang the bell. Had a very nice shower. John King's threshed. John Reeser was here for a girl.

7/24/23 Tuesday
Made ice cream and put on the finishing touches. We entertained at our home 125 guests. Had rather a wet day and a very nice shower about 11:30 when they began to take their leave. Everyone seemed to think they enjoyed themselves.

7/28/23 Saturday
Very rainy all day. I made blackberry pies. Amy went to the Denlinger girls' crowd. Edna went to Mae Groff's party with Eby Clark. I went with Eby Hostetter. Had a fine drive in the dark and mud.

8/25/23 Saturday
Went to Lancaster and out to Watt's, then to Esther Parmer's crowd at New Providence and back to Lancaster. Met Eby H and went to Susie Clark's party. End of a perfect day.

9/5/23 Wednesday
Mabel went to Beiler's. Mamma and I went to Susan Kreider's funeral and bought 6 bushels of peaches on the way home. Edna and I went to Bertha and Anna Reeser's party with M.G. and E.H. Made 8 crocks of peach butter and canned 78 quarts.

11/6/23 Tuesday
Rainy and damp. We prepared the new room. Charlie is learning to whistle. Teacher is getting ready for a big play. We had endive for dinner.

11/15/23 Thursday
Started for cousin Aaron's wedding which took place at Churchtown. Had a splendid day until we went to Stumptown in the evening and ended it in a tragedy I shall never forget. Uncle Milt's came for Granny Rogers.

11/16/23 Friday
Everyone is solemn and cross this morning. Air lightened this evening. Cleaned the sitting room. Amy's education is undecided.

12/25/23 Friday
Papa, Mamma and the boys went to Uncle Elmer's for Christmas dinner. We girls kept Sara and James Clymer. George Rhoads took the girls along to Kinzer to hear Simon Landis give a talk on his trip to Europe. I went with John W.

1924

1/1/24 Tuesday
Made 2 resolutions. Mother and Amy went to Lancaster to the New Years Meeting. Edna went in with M.G. this evening. Very stormy. Martin Wanner came this evening and learned a few new tricks. Knitted. Much colder this evening.

1/6/24 Sunday
Got up late and did not go to church. Papa, Mamma and Mabel took Landis Hershey's along to W.H. and went to John Rohrer's for dinner. Amy went down to Fenninger's. George Rhoads was over and we were skating a while. I did the

milking. Edna went to Kinzer with M.G. Mabel, George Rhoads, Eby and I went along. Very cold and clear.

1/9/24 Wednesday
Ironed. Wrote to Margaret Groff. Mysterious man parked his machine at the barn all day. Tramp stopped in for coffee. Mamma called and said I shall come home and look for a place in Lancaster. Papa came down after me, then went up to Henry Hershey's, where Russians met.

1/10/24 Thursday
Edna and I went to Lancaster in the machine. I hired with Dr. Witmer's and Edna with Harry Raub's. Went out to the hospital to see Daisy Witmer and stopped at Mae Groff's. Jay brought me down here this evening. We played with the Ouija board I bought for Nora. Warmer.

1/11/24 Friday
Rained and blowed all night. Rained a very heavy shower this morning. Cleared off this dinner time. I knitted. Edythe came in this evening and we talked to the Ouija board. Edna called and said they have another place in Lancaster for me. I put Chester's hat and coat on and scared Nora white and blue.

1/12/24 Saturday
Finished the cleaning and scrubbed the walks. Jay came down and brought me home. Daisy Witmer is on friendly terms with us at the present time. Nice day. Feels like snow. First Saturday evening I spent at home since September.

1/14/24 Monday
Papa brought Edna and I into Lancaster. I came to Dr. Witmer's. Edna hired with Raub's. Worked nearly all day. Don't like "living rich." Cleaned, dusted and cooked. Very glad for night, never felt so homesick. Mrs. Witmer went to a party. Clear and colder. Knitted 3 rows.

1/16/24 Wednesday
Got up early and worked hard all day getting ready for a bridge party of twenty. The cater was here all day and night. Mrs. McQuait did the cleaning. I didn't get to bed till 1:30 o'clock. Ruth and I are opposed to such parties. Rained all day.

1/19/24 Saturday
Got up at five. Made pot pie and rice pudding for dinner. Got through at 2:15, then had my P.M. and evening off. Did a little shopping and went out to Edna. Stayed for supper. Came along with Mae Groff to Y.P.M. John Wenger brought me here, then we went to Metzler's for grapefruit. Feeling more human.

1/21/24 Monday
Got up early. Washed and ironed for myself and 29 pieces for Mrs. W. Made potato soup for dinner. Ruth Kreider came in a while. Got a letter from Margaret Groff. Richard is better. Mrs. W. went out. Very cold. I am tired. Phoned Edna. Got my first pay. 9 one dollar bills.

1/25/24 Friday
Arthur Moyer was shot when he went out to his corn crib to see someone he heard taking corn and is in critical condition. Was busy all day. Went out to Walt's this evening with the other girls. Came back and took a bath and went to bed at 11:15. Snow turned to rain. Went downtown for shoes.

1/26/24 Saturday
Arthur Moyer died at 10:30 last night. Busy this A.M. keeping baby and answering bells this P.M. Had a card from Nora Wanner. Got all done and was ready at 7:00. Edna and Martin, Eby and I went down to Susan McGallicher's party at Mart Hershey's. 12 there. Had a very nice time. Machine nearly froze up. Went to bed at 20 of 2. Very cold.

2/1/24 Friday
Cleaned windows and kitchens, cellar and front. Took a bath. Dr. late to supper. Edna and I went to Hatville Spelling Bee with Eby H. and Martin. School House was packed. Amish boy won the $2.50. Jay, David B., Maurice Good, Amish girl and four others were winners. I misspelled "vigorous." Nice day. Mary washed the dishes for me.

2/19/24 Tuesday
Snowed first real snow all day. Mary and I cleared the pavement after 8 o'clock for the last time. Did not go to church. Eby and Martin each have new machines. Mae Groff had a beau on Sunday night. Started to sleet this evening. Cleaned medicine shelves.

2/21/24 Thursday
Cleaned silver, refrigerator, our room and windows. Very pretty day. Dr. was late to supper. Went to church and wore my black dress. Walked back with Florence Myers and a bunch of others. One confession, Elizabeth Mowery. Text was Proverbs 28-13. Mary wiped the dishes.

2/27/24 Wednesday
Made dinner, which was lemon pie, logan berries, pecans, peas, beef, mushrooms, mashed potatoes and cheese. Nora and Emma Wanner and Amy stopped in to see me. I was vaccinated after dinner. Edna and I went down to Elias Denlinger's for supper and came in for church. A big crowd. Nice day.

2/29/24 Friday

Resigned cooking and was promoted to second floor. Kathryn McCouly came and Mary Young left. Could not go to church. Papa brought me some things when he came in with tobacco and I sent some things home. Nice day. Mrs. went to a luncheon. I took my bath and went to bed at 10:30.

3/3/24 Monday

Washed and ironed a big wash. Fire nearly went out. Sent Ruth Hess' letter that we can't come. Richard was good. Mrs. Witmer went to the hair dresser's. I helped Kathryn to wash the dishes and finished my ironing. Dr. and Mrs. Witmer went to the opera and I went to bed at 12:30.

3/13/24 Thursday

Did 237 doctor bills this day. Took Richard out for an airing. Elsie Weaver and Mabel Lefever stopped for me at 7:30 and we went out to Mae Groff's. 12 girls met, got back at 11:30. We had chicken and waffles for supper. Grandma Howell is here.

3/17/24 Monday

Washed and ironed. Mrs. Witmer, Robert, Richard and I took a drive in the Cadillac out to Long's Park. Elizabeth Mosemann and I went out to see Anna Lehman. Kathryn was down at the Y.M.C.A. I came in before her. A very nice day.

3/23/24 Sunday

I went to church and S.S. for the second time this year. Eby and Martin came for us and we went up to Laura Good's for supper. We went along with Jay and Laura to Rohrerstown. Mae and Jamie seemed salty. Beautiful day.

4/11/24 Friday

Got up at 5:45 and worked all day without any stops. Richard was real good. Expected to sit up late while Mrs. Witmer was out, but a cousin of Mrs. W. came here with a heart attack and died while they carried her up to the living room. Relatives came and we had quite an excitement. I stayed with Bobbie. Nice day. Mrs. McQuate and I cleaned the halls. Mamma came in and took some of my things home. Papa was at conference.

4/12/24 Saturday

Worked as usual. Bobbie had a sudden sick spell while playing in the street and was able to get up at three o'clock. Mrs. Wilfert worked hard all day, got her discharge and wept while I was good-natured enough to wash the dishes for her. I quickly took a bath, dressed, and went to Y.P.M. with Elsie W. and walked part way home with Mabel Lefever.

4/18/24 Friday

Got a letter from Mamma. Mrs. McQuate was sick and unable to come in to clean. Clara cried all day without any relief. I had a severe pain in my left shoulder all A.M.

Cleaned the second floor. I went to church this evening as it is Good Friday. Small crowd. Rained all day. Got up from my dinner 12 times.

4/20/24 Sunday
Got up at six, slept from 3 to 6 because I had such severe pains in my shoulder. Mrs. W. rubbed it with lineament and I was able to go to church and to Elsie W. for dinner, to Paradise Bible Study in the P.M. Kitty Burkholder and Elsie stayed down for the evening and I went with Benner's and came back to church with Eby. The bunny gave me silk stockings and a 6 lb. egg.

4/22/24 Tuesday
Made up my mind to put in 3 more days. Called Elsie Weaver. Dinner went bad. Meat caught fire and the potatoes burned and were not soft, and the vinegar was all. I spilled cucumber salad juice at the Dr.'s place. Mrs. W. slept and went to market. Clara went out with her beau. Mrs. W and Flossie Mylie went to see Black Oxen, and I sat up till 10:30 when the Dr. came in.

4/24/24 Thursday
Mrs. Witmer called me, and I did usual work. Mrs. W. took Richard, Mary, Susan and I along to Neffsville when she took Robert out to Grandpa's. I took Richard out for a long walk, saw Martha Greenwalt and Elsie Weaver. Packing up. Dr. had a bunch of me in the living room this evening. John Davidson called me up. Made a mistake.

4/28/24 Monday
Washed and hoed garden. Bought herring and cleaned them. Made supper and pulled threads in handkerchiefs. Landis got up and came downstairs. Very nice day. Mamma gave my head a thorough washing.

4/29/24 Tuesday
Mabel and I ironed. Amy called and said one of us could go along with Wanners to Lancaster, so I went and did some shopping. Went back to Witmer's for the rest of my things. Mrs. Witmer is getting a new cook on Friday. She gave me a picture of Richard.

5/4/24 Sunday
Mamma was sick and stayed home all day. Papa went to Stumptown. The rest of us went to Hershey's. We three girls and Landis went to Casper's. Edna and Mart went to Paradise. Eby and I went to Easter Cantata and resolved never to go again.

5/9/24 Friday
Mamma not any better. I baked pies and a cake. Took care of Mamma, temperature stayed between 102 and 103 all day. I finished Amy's dress. Cloudy and rainy all day.

5/11/24 Sunday
Got up at five. Mamma is not any better. Temp went up to 104. Mary King, Uncle Milt's, Uncle Elmer's and Charlie were here. Amos Hershey brought Mabel home. Papa brought Amy along home this evening. I called Eby and told him not to come. Martin is here, but they did not go to church. I am nurse. Very rainy, windy and raw.

5/12/24 Monday
Mamma the same, temp. 102-103. Dr. was here. Washed a big wash. I did not feel good. Kept busy tending Mamma. Edna seems sleepy as Martin stayed late waiting till the rain was over and then he had to go home in the rain. Wash nearly all dried. Dr. pronounced Mamma's sickness influenza.

5/15/24 Thursday
Mabel and Papa went to Isaac Ramsey's funeral all day. Sometime ago Daniel Kurtz called on Marian Slaymaker and they sat on the porch swing, one in each corner. Daniel fell asleep and Marian went to bed and left him set.

6/3/24 Tuesday
Took the steers out. They averaged 1265 lbs. Andrew Hackman's brother Henry was struck by a machine while riding his bicycle on Sunday. We ironed. One duck died. Very warm. Mamma feels worse. Edna, Papa and the three little boys went to Grandpap's. Reesers came for me.

6/8/24 Sunday
John brought me home at five. I milked and did the work before the others were up. Edna and I went to Groffdale church and to Mary Musselman for dinner in the coupe. I ran it for the first time. Mary had 16 girls. We had a nice time, and it rained real hard. Edna and I went to Kinzer with Eby and Martin. John Davidson asked to bring me home. Frank Martin asked Dorothy Mellinger.

6/14/24 Saturday
Nice warm day. Very threatening, but pretty and clear this evening. Papa and I took the carriage to the community sale, and it brought $11.50. I bought three books. Had a nice time. Mabel and Amy took Edith Kurtz along to Elizabeth Fenninger's crowd and broke the glass out of door in the coupe. Eby H. took me to Merle Zimmerman's party. It was a real affair.

6/15/24 Sunday
Nice warm day. All went to church but Mamma and Charlie. We girls all went to Uncle Elmer's for dinner. Jesse Clark's came this evening. I was foolish enough to go along with Edna and Mart to Paradise, then we went to Esther Denlinger's after church, and I was obliged to go along and act as tar can.

7/7/24 Monday
Got up and Papa took me down to Reeser's before they had their breakfast. The haymakers were here for supper. I milked the four kickers that John milks. My invitation to Clara Bender's party was sent back.

7/14/24 Monday
Mabel and Papa picked a bucketful of black cherries. Jay and I hoed corn all day. Mabel and Papa helped a while. Edna fell out with Daisy Witmer. Mamma went down to Dave King's. Emanuel is a little bit better. We girls hoed some in the garden. Last night Sem Hershey and Noah Sensenig took Rhoda Hershey and Mary home. Daniel Kurtz had Mae Groff.

7/16/24 Wednesday
Mowed wheat all day at Ira Hershey's this P.M. and at 7:15 got ready to go to Myer's party. Looked rainy and we had a little sprinkle. Esther fell and broke her arm just as we started to play three deep and spoiled the evening.

7/26/24 Saturday
Edna and I hoed tobacco for Christ Beiler for 30 cents an hour. Came home for dinner. Mabel and I went to Susanna Eshelman's crowd and took Elizabeth Fenninger along. Edna went along with Esther Denlinger to Anna Esbenshade's crowd. We had a very nice time. Pretty day.

7/30/24 Wednesday
Mamma, Mary King, Becky Beiler went to Lancaster to see Maggie Wilhelm. She surprised us by entertaining us with a quilt. Did some shopping. Saw Richard Witmer. Talked with Mrs. Witmer last evening. Torrey H went out of his mind. Rained a shower.

8/8/24 Friday
I weighed 142 lbs. on Sunday at Felkers. Edna weighed the same. Mabel and I cleaned the upstairs thoroughly and did the downstairs. Edna scrubbed some this evening. I picked the blackberries. Not quite so warm.

8/18/24 Monday
Got up at four o'clock, had the washing done till 8 o'clock. Then we all went to the tobacco patch. School started and our baby Charlie went for the first. We did the ironing this P.M. Papa thrashed at Uncle Sam's. Mabel went to the butchers for thrashers meat. Amy is taking her vacation.

8/19/24 Tuesday
Very cool. Edna baked pies. Edna and Amy topped tobacco. The thrashers were here for dinner. Mary Lloyd and Rhoda had a corn roast. About 50 there. Had a delightful time. Went with Eby Hostetter.

8/23/24 Saturday
Eby and I started at 7:30 for Hershey with Minnie Felker and David Hostetter. Had a dandy time. Took a ride on the Jack Rabbit, went to Harrisburg on the way home. Stayed at Felkers a while, stopped at Maple Grove Park. I put the films in at Darmstetter's.

8/24/24 Sunday
All went to Hershey's Church. Had a lot of company from Weaverland. Alice Martin was here this P.M. Mabel, Mamma and I went away. Mamma to Clymer's and we went to Arment's, then Landis came and said Ira Hershey's were here so we came home. Eby Hostetter took Elizabeth Rohrer home. Edna went to Paradise with M.G.

8/27/24 Wednesday
Took out the potatoes and had a big crop. Uncle Milt's, Uncle Charles and their hired help went to Dupont Flower Gardens. Uncle Elmer's brought Grammy here on the way home. I went to Marian Martin's Smile Social with Eby Hostetter. A nice day. Warm.

9/3/24 Wednesday
Mamma and I went to Lancaster. I got a wine-colored charmeuse dress, Edna a marigold crepe, and Amy the same. Papa and Jay cut two loads of tobacco without any of our help. Mabel and I worked in the yard. Edna and Mabel burned all the corn we dried yesterday.

9/11/24 Thursday
Had slight frost. 36 degrees. Cut two acres of tobacco. Mabel baked a cake. Martin Hershey's wife is improving. Leopold and Loeb sentenced for 99 years imprisonment. A nice day. Wrote to Grace Stauffer.

9/16/24 Tuesday
Worked at the peaches all day. Papa and Jay cut tobacco at Uncle Sam's. Edna called and said she is walking on air. Finished sending the invitations this morning. Cloudy. King's started filling silo this morning.

9/26/24 Friday
Scrubbed everything with hot lye. Papa and Jay started cutting corn yesterday. Cleaned the back shanty. I sodded a few holes in the chicken yard. A cloudy day.

9/29/24 Monday
Rained and blowed all day. Mabel was absentminded and sleepy. Papa and Jay made pedestals. We puttered, baked three cakes and watched it raining. Sem Hershey introduced Mabel to Ivan Leaman.

10/2/24 Thursday
Felt a little blue. Papa went to Conference. Mamma went to Lancaster. Mabel and I cleaned the house. Grandpap King helped to cut corn. Sold a calf for $21. A very nice day. Myer's bull ran all over the neighborhood.

10/8/24 Wednesday
Got ready to make chow chow. Shelled a lot of beans. Mabel put them in the oven and most of them burnt. Tied 75 stalks of celery in paper. Amy and Nora came for tomatoes. A nice day.

10/20/24 Monday
Washed and ironed. Mamma planted in flowers. Papa husked corn. We canned 17 quarts or red beets. The two convicts that broke jail on Saturday night were caught last evening at Mechanics Grove. A nice day.

10/21/24 Tuesday
Cleaned the spare room, new room and sitting room. Put the flowers on the windows. Did the mending. Sent two dollars to Elizabeth Leaman's dollar donation from Eby and I. The shinerharness came and killed Topps and took her to her final resting place at the ripe old age of 26 years.

10/22/24 Wednesday
I cleaned our room. Mamma worked with the flowers. Mabel husked corn. This afternoon I took the coupe over to have the glass put in. Mamma went along as far as Trout's to talk Carbide. A nice cold day. Mabel cleaned cupboards.

10/23/24 Thursday
I cleaned the bathroom and den. Mabel went to Martin Hershey's to help clean house. Mamma helped to husk corn. This P.M. I took her to Mrs. Hine's sale and she got a wonderful clock. A nice day. Wanners offered to take us to Lyseum, but we did not dare to go.

11/4/24 Tuesday
Cleaned Harry's and Mrs. Raub's rooms. Mrs. Raub went to election all day and came home at 3 o'clock this morning. Coolidge was elected. Very nice day. David Kaufman caught fire while filling the gas tank on his truck and was badly burned.

11/11/24 Tuesday
Canned and spiced pears nearly all day. Jay and Papa hauled fodder. We did some of the ironing. Mamma did not feel good. Edna has a bad cold. Charlie is home sick. A very damp, dismal day. Agnes Loudon was married in the hospital to Howard Moore.

11/19/24 Wednesday
Mamma and I went to Clay Witmer's and sewed. It was very cold. Papa got up early and knocked down cornstalks. I wrote to Miriam Hawthorne. I think I am getting the mumps.

11/20/24 Thursday
Finished stripping the 424 lath of tobacco we had down. I finished fixing my old black coat. Mabel was sick this morning, fainted and fell down. Landis and I went to Intercourse. Nice day. Mabel cleaned the silver.

12/2/24 Tuesday
Washed and ironed. Put a wash line on the balcony. Last night someone fetched about 100 of our chickens. Papa feels very blue over it. He hauled stones this A.M. and went to anoint Henry Burkholder this P.M. Baked nut cakes and made caramels.

12/5/24 Friday
Undecided whether to go to Lancaster to do our shopping. Mabel became very wroth about it and we agreed to postpone it. It then began to rain very beautifully about two o'clock. Still at it and cold this evening. Bull is sick. Papa went to Intercourse for aconite.

12/13/24 Saturday
Mabel went to Usner's. I baked two cakes and did the rest of the work. Mamma and Papa went to John Singer's for dinner. Edna went to Esther Hershey's reception. This evening Eby and I went to "Educational" with Granville Clark and Esther Denlinger. We had an unpleasant scare at the Belmont graveyard.

12/21/24 Sunday
Most of us went to White Horse. Mabel and I took Ruth Myers along and went to Elva Kauffman's for dinner and went to the Nickel Mines and all over the Mine Hill. Walked about 5 miles. Went to Kinzer again with Eby. Very cold. The boys were skating.

12/24/24 Wednesday
Popped a lot of corn for a cake and buttered a big bag full. I got 9 greetings so far. This P.M. Landis and I went to Zimmerman's store and Eaby's, post office, Roger's, garage, Clayt Witmer's, Abe Beiler's, Mart Clymer's. Took Witmer's Xmas presents. Rainy and icy. Ran to Intercourse without any water. Results were a hot engine.

12/25/24 Thursday
Snowed last night. Uncle Elmer's and Grammy were here for dinner with little Harold Eaby. Edna came at 5 o'clock. I got a nice lot of gifts. All were excelled by a silver set from Eby. I went to Kinzer and to Elizabeth Kreider's afterward with E.H. Very cold evening.

12/26/24 Friday
Edna stayed all night and today I took her to the car and forgot to bring the battery from the garage. We made Edna a dress. I took some cakes and ice cream up to Mary Axe. She is no better and didn't sleep for two years. Very cold.

1925

1/1/25 Thursday
Mabel and I went up to Martin Clymer's and went to Lancaster to the New Year's meeting with Mart. Spent the afternoon and evening in the newly renovated gallery. Went out to Raub's with Susan and Aaron and spent the night. Went to see the demonstration at the fire engine house. Cloudy and cold.

1/2/25 Friday
Snow about a half foot deep when we got up. I took the car and went to Shand's. Mabel had just got up. We went downtown to the dentist and did our shopping and waited with lots of others on the country cars till dark. The bus did not go out. Esther Sensenig went with us to Shand's and then she stayed at Aunt Emma's all night and we went to the mission. It stopped snowing about 2 o'clock.

1/3/25 Saturday
Left the mission and stopped at Aunt Emma's for Esther, stopped at Shand's and then went to wait on the C.V. John Burky said he would try to start at 12:30. We then settled ourselves till that time when we started for Intercourse, after some narrow escapes. Lived mostly on pretzels and water. At 2:30 Landis met us. Eby called and asked to take me sleighing. I refused.

1/11/25 Sunday
All went to church but Jay and Charles. A good sized crowd. Mabel, Amy and I went to Red Hill, about 40 there and 25 sleds. Had real nice time. Mamma went up to see Mary Axe. She is miserable. Eby came but it was snowing too fast to go to church. Chilly and raw air.

1/12/25 Monday
Too cloudy to wash. We made rompers and sewed and stripped tobacco. Margie Rohrer is worse. David Hostetter, Jr. burnt his machine slightly on Friday evening when he left the engine run with the blanket on it and it caught fire. On Saturday Henry Rineer was struck and instantly killed on the railroad at Leaman Place.

1/15/25 Thursday
I finished the ironing and did the morning work. Mabel and Mamma stripped tobacco all day. I mended and made chicken and waffles for supper. About 14 bales

stripped this week. Mabel, Jay and I went to Red Hill. Sledding was great. About 17 there, got home at 10:30.

1/16/25 Friday
Cloudy, snowing and raining all day. I baked two cakes, Mamma made pies and Mabel swept upstairs. We all took down tobacco this P.M. Worked at my counterpane a little. Mamma shortened my coat. Teacher forbid about 10 boys going to the hill for disobedience.

1/17/25 Saturday
Mabel, Papa, and Mamma went to Lancaster to the dentist's. Mabel got a coat for $12.50 and a green canton crepe dress. I did the work myself, made potato chips and was done with my bath till 4 o'clock. Eby came and we went to Lancaster. It rained.

1/24/25 Saturday
Finished up the cleaning and got shined up till Edna came at 2 o'clock. She cut and started Mabel's green canton crepe dress. There was an almost total eclipse of the sun at 9 o'clock and was dark enough to light the lights to strip tobacco. Eby was here this evening, but we did not go anywhere. Pretty and clear.

1/31/25 Saturday
Felt tired and grouchy. Baked pies, boiled and peeled sweet potatoes. Swept upstairs and the back room. Baby was real good. Doctor came and Mrs. Wenger stayed in bed all day. Sara was over this P.M. Earl brought me home. Eby came and we went sleighing. Brownstown Hosiery Mill burned down. Real nice day.

2/5/25 Thursday
I swept upstairs and made dinner. Went along with Wanner's to Lancaster. Tried to find a place for Mabel. Edna and Tommy went along downtown. Martin took me along to automobile show. Saw lots of dandy machines. Mamma stripped tobacco all day.

2/6/25 Friday
Papa and Mamma stripped 225 lath of tobacco. I baked pies and oatmeal cakes. Papa put new bricks in the stove and I cleaned it up. Took the flowers out and sprinkled them and cleaned the sitting room. Oldest woman in Lancaster County died at 102 years. Nice warm spring like day.

2/9/25 Monday
Mabel and I did the washing. It is wetter this evening. Mamma helped to strip tobacco this A.M. Seed corn is $4.50 per bushel. Mabel is so sleepy she can hardly keep awake. We cleaned the shoes. Mamma started to take her herb medicine. She weighed 202 pounds.

2/15/25 Sunday
Mabel, Jay, Papa and I went to Paradise. The church was full. Papa, Mamma and the 3 little boys went to Wanner's for dinner. Mabel was grouchy nearly all day. Eby and I went to Kinzer church. Elizabeth Mellinger stopped Ivan Leaman. Very rainy and high water.

2/20/25 Friday
I went down to Wenger's to help fry up meat. Had a busy and industrious day. They took in $39.50 last night at Hatville. Program was hands only rendered. A cloudy day. Yesterday Mamma had a lump on her head treated.

2/27/25 Friday
We cleaned upstairs and down. Took the carpet out of the kitchen. Very cold and stormy. Mamma went to the Doctor's and Papa went to the dentist's. We almost went to Buyerstown Lyceum but Papa furiously objected to taking the Ford out.

2/28/25 Saturday
Baked cakes and finished the cleaning. I met Edna at 12 o'clock. After hearing some of the news Mabel and I did the scrubbing. Mart took Edna and Mabel to John Senger's Bible Study. Eby and I went along with Esther Denlinger and Granville to Pentecostal at Soudersburg. Very loud worship.

3/2/25 Monday
Cold, clear and windy. We washed and did some of the ironing. Papa took Mamma to the Dr. in Lancaster. Mabel and I crocheted a little. John Landis had Ethel Hershey last night. Ivan Buckwalter's have a baby boy. Herman Rohrer drowned yesterday while he was skating.

3/4/25 Wednesday
Sold the 9 acres of tobacco to Levy's for 15-3. Papa took Mamma to the Doctor's. She bought us lavender dresses. Mabel, Jay, Landis and I went to the Hollow Spelling Bee. Mrs. Ranck got the $2.50 in gold. David Benner, Sam Stoltzfus, Elmer Zimmerman and others won. The Nash agent was here.

3/13/25 Friday
Mabel and I cleaned up all the house. Took our tobacco away and it came to $1645.65. Mamma went along with Papa to the Dr.'s and bought us each a new dress. We cut Mabel's and got it partly done. Allen Gehman and Dave Hostetter were here with a Chevrolet.

3/14/25 Saturday
We finished Mabel's dresses and scrubbed and washed the Ford. We got a new horse, Charlie. Eby took me to Hickory Grove Spelling Bee. I tried the Spelling class, left five behind me and came down on the word "awl." Mabel and Jay went to Merle Zimmerman's St. Patrick's party and had a fine time. Real nice day.

3/26/25 Thursday
I turned the clippers while Papa clipped the mules. Mamma and I replanted some rose stalks. I went over to King's for horseradish. Jay went along with Ira Hershey to Centerville Spelling Bee and Landis and I went up to Jason Buckwalter's and took Mabel along. A big crowd. Jay won third prize.

3/27/25 Friday
Jay is walking on his ear over the success of last night. I cleaned up all the house. Papa dug garden and we planted beets, radishes, and other seeds. I washed the Ford. Chevrolet agent was here and told Papa about a prospective buyer. Papa and Mamma went to Lancaster this evening. Very rainy.

3/31/25 Tuesday
We washed and I tried to finish my dress. Had bad luck, got the belt on wrong twice. Papa dragged the road. The Chevrolet agent was here. Had open discussion this evening on touring or sedan. Cloudy, but the wash dried. Jay plowed and Mamma got the peepie house ready.

4/2/25 Thursday
The Chevrolet agent was here. Papa went to Rohrerstown to Conference. Mamma and Jay dug a flower bed on the lawn and planted some bushes. I did the ironing and mending. Papa was furiously vexed with the new flowerbed. Very rainy.

4/6/25 Monday
We washed and ironed and mended. Papa and Mamma discussed automobiles. Jay and Papa hauled about 39 loads of manure. We had chicken thieves last night and they took about 35. A very pretty day. Miriam Good didn't have any beau last night. We had a flat tire on the way home.

4/11/25 Saturday
Mabel went to Uncle Joe's. I did a little cleaning. Washed the Oakland with John King's hose. It was just like a dream. I scrubbed and went to the car for Edna. Papa went to the Brick all day. Eby took me to Lancaster. Very pretty day.

4/16/25 Thursday
Mabel and I cleaned Mamma's room and the parlor. Mamma painted the rocking chairs. Paul was sick this dinner and got worse till 2 o'clock. Temp over 104 and we sent for Dr. Ressler. Papa and Landis Hershey went visiting. I made noodles this evening. Paul is better. Nice day.

4/19/25 Sunday
We girls and Jay went to Hershey's. Papa went to Stumptown. Mabel and Amy went to Issac Hershey's and were caught in the rain. I watched Paul and read while Mamma slept. He is delirious. Eby took me to Paradise. A nice crowd. The boys tied tin cans on John Landis' Ford.

4/30/25 Thursday
Raining this morning. I cleaned the hall and stairways and hall closet. Susan cleaned the other bathroom. Mrs. Raub went for the wash, and Mr. and Mrs. Raub continued their fight and he left for Philadelphia without saying good bye. Minnie Felker is leaving Hamaker's and said we should not come this evening.

5/6/25 Wednesday
Cleaned the store room, cupboards, dining room and refrigerator. Mr. Raub was not here for dinner. This evening Susan and I walked to East Chestnut St. Church to hear Brother Keneagy from Chicago Mission. Walked back and two fellows followed and attempted to talk but we escaped. Partly cloudy and showers.

5/18/25 Monday
We washed and ironed. Mamma and Papa went to Lancaster for the Chevrolet. Mamma is just delighted with it. Mabel, Jay and I tried to operate it a little. Mamma bought us three girls each a new dress. Blind peddler was here. A pretty day.

5/19/25 Tuesday
Perfect weather. Mabel went down to Beiler's to paint the chariot. I went to help clean the church. Stayed till Fannie Hershey went, then we finished up her work that she hadn't done right. Mended this afternoon and cleaned up the paint stuff. Mabel, Jay and I went to Kinzer in the Chevrolet. It was heavenly.

5/20/25 Wednesday
Papa and Mamma went to Landis Valley in the Chevrolet and took John Singer and wife along. Mabel and I each made one of our new dresses. Amy came home this evening. Last night Herman Buckwalter, Clair Hershey, Grace Denlinger, and Aaron Newswanger's two little girls got converted. The text: The way of the transgressors is hard.

5/24/25 Sunday
Papa, Mamma and the little boys went to Red Well and to David Benner's. We kids to went to S.S. and I brought Elizabeth Fenninger along home for dinner and went to see Rachel Smoker this P.M. to make amends for the great disappointment of not going to see Miss Wilworth. Very big rain. Papa took the girls to Kinzer and Earl took Elizabeth home. Eby took me. Papa almost went into the sink hole on the Newport Road on the way home. There was a big fire somewhere north of here.

6/1/25 Monday
We got up very early as the cows broke out. Washed and did some of the ironing. Too warm to work. I took asparagus to Intercourse. Papa and Jay helped to plant tobacco at Uncle Sam's. Thief pulled plants here this evening. Mabel made a date with Ross Hershey.

6/6/25 Saturday

We baked three cakes. I took some asparagus to Intercourse. Very warm. We wore as little clothing as possible. Mabel and I picked strawberries. This evening I took Mabel and Eby along to Helen Elmer's kitchen shower. Big crowd. Edna and Mart came down from Lancaster.

6/8/25 Monday

Had the washing all done till 9 o'clock. We put the clothes away and did nearly all the ironing this P.M. Papa helped Uncle Sam's plant tobacco. Mamma went along with me to Intercourse to have Mose Hershey cure her wart when I went to Frank Hostetter's for strawberries. A little cooler.

6/10/25 Wednesday

Pulled tobacco plants. Mabel dropped. I slept an hour this P.M. Eby took me to Albertina Montgomery's Doggie Roast. About 30 there. We had lots of fun, played Bingo, Granger, Three Deep, and In the Month of May. Delightful weather and pleasant evening. Papa went to an ordination at Bowmansville.

6/22/25 Monday

Papa got up at 4 and mowed till breakfast. The rest of us followed soon. We washed and Mabel and I heaped hay from 8 till 8. Raining this evening. George Steffy helped. Elmer Buckwalter had Miriam Good last evening. I am seriously considering a month at the shore.

7/3/25 Friday

Steers went this morning, came to $1685.55. I took nearly $1800 to the bank. Bill Watson came down and helped this P.M. George Steffy was here. A nice day. We got nearly all the cleaning done and picked and canned 13 quarts of black cherries. Maggie called on John King this evening.

7/7/25 Tuesday

Very warm and sultry all day and showers and gusty this evening. Mamma has resolved to take better care of herself and did very little today. I sewed snaps on our dresses. Papa and Jay hauled manure and harrowed tobacco and corn. George went over to help Uncle Sam's.

7/11/25 Saturday

Arrived at Uncle Sam's around 6 o'clock and helped to finish their wheat. George and I quit at dinner time, and I went to Lydia and Edith Kreider's crowd. Mabel went to Esther Mellinger's. George Rhoads took Mabel to Maple Grove. Eby and I took a spin. Edna and Mart and Esther and Granville spent the evening with us. After they left we viewed the fireworks at Intercourse from the rail pile. Nice warm day.

7/16/25 Thursday
Fixed my crepe de leue dress. Cleaned Mrs. Raub's bed and bathrooms. Made red beets, carrots, scalloped potatoes, apple sauce, cup custard and raspberry strudel for dinner. Warm and sultry and very gusty this evening. Esther Denlinger called me up.

7/20/25 Monday
Got up at 4:30 and washed. Had nearly everything done when they got up at 9:15 with another machine full. Gathered it in and dampened it this P.M. and made applesauce. Got my wages, $15 per week. Had a nice shower. The Raub's went out and I'm in.

7/23/25 Thursday
Cleaned Mrs. Raub's room, Harry's and bathrooms and hall. Mrs. Raub went to Reading for the day. Yesterday I weighed 135 lbs. Mrs. Raub's mother was here for supper. I got done and dressed till 7:30. Then Eby came in and took me to Grace Denlinger's party. 72 there. Beautiful evening. 14 Hersheys.

7/30/25 Thursday
Mamma and Papa worked in the tobacco. Mabel and I canned pickles. Cleaned the upstairs. I was in bed about two hours over dinner. Very sick. Shelled peas this P.M. Edna came home at 3 o'clock. Eby took me to Mabel and Biz Rohrer's party. 150 there and we had a nice time.

7/31/25 Friday
We baked pies and a cake and prepared things for the threshers. Mamma went to Lancaster with Nora Wanner and Mabel and I fed the 13 men. Rained all day and they stopped threshing after dinner. I packed most of my things and fixed some of my clothes. Amy came home this evening.

8/3/25 Monday
Got up at 4:30 and went to Lancaster with Esther Denlinger, took the train at 6:05 for Ocean Grove. Got here at 10:30 and ate dinner with the guests. Went down to the beach all afternoon. Got partly acquainted with the other five girls and the cooks. Seems all right so far. Esther and I each wrote home this evening.

8/5/25 Wednesday
I had a table of my own with a lady and gent from Scranton for breakfast, dinner and supper. It went all right. Esther got a table with four ladies. It rained so we wrote letters. I wrote to Mae Witmer and Grammy. We went down to the beach and the water was very wild. Went to Auditorium but there was a picture and we didn't go in.

8/6/25 Thursday
Minnie praises us and Annie talks religion. I got a $.25 tip and Esther got a $1.00 tip on her guests' departure. We went up to the depot to see about our tickets and went down on the boardwalk for taffy and cards. Got 3 new guests. Esther got 5 new ones. We stayed in and wrote letters this evening. Marian kindly mailed them for us.

8/7/25 Friday
Had same guests all day. Esther got some new ones. Everything went all right, only I was fierce provoked this morning. Esther counted her money twice today. We went down to Bradley and got wet all over for the first time. Wrote home this evening. Esther crocheted. Annie left.

8/8/25 Saturday
James and Henry both left and we had to wash all the dishes, husk the corn, peel the potatoes. We got through till 10:45. I got four new guests. $.50 this dinner and $.10 this evening. We got letters from Eby and Granville and answered them before going to bed.

8/10/25 Monday
We were first in the dining room. Did our washing and ironing. Cleaned and dusted our room. We went down for a dip in the pond. We are trying for the prize in the efficiency contest. We went down for a walk on the boards and sent some taffy.

8/11/25 Tuesday
Same work and same guests. Mrs. Zelly is taking one of us girls to the temple each morning to hear the male quartet and a sermon. Thelma Brigg went this morning. Esther was in the office. Nice day. Got a getter from Aunt Cora.

8/13/25 Thursday
My three guests from N.Y. left and gave me a dollar. I was in the office and Amos Hershey, Dave Denlinger, and Frank and Sem Hershey's came very unexpectedly. Esther and I have them to serve and enjoy it. We went out with the girls this evening, walked to the end of the boardwalk and came back the other track. Took a boat through the Old Mill and some on the Whip and Merry-Go-Round.

8/15/25 Saturday
Same work and plenty of it. Got six new guests and my nice man left and gave me one dollar. I got a letter from Eby and answered it this evening. Esther wrote to Granville. We went bathing with the Lancaster kids and took some pictures. A lovely day and the water was great.

8/16/25 Sunday
Busy, beautiful day. I was disgusted this dinner with my guests and gave way to my feelings in a flood of tears. Very little time to rest. We went over to the Auditorium.

The singing was fine and sermon text was Acts 4:31. Went down to the boardwalk with the kids. Esther contracted a cold.

8/19/25 Wednesday
Esther got up early to serve Sem Eby's an early breakfast. She washed some of our clothes this P.M. and paid $.25 to have her fortune told and didn't find much out, only that she is to have two children. Marion is having a new beau. We are going to bed very early tonight.

8/22/25 Saturday
Clear and cold and some folks saw ice. We met Eby and Granville at the depot and went bathing with them. Got some new guests and three left and gave me a dollar. We took a long walk on the boardwalk and a ride on the ferris wheel and through the old mill. I have them at my table and Esther is jealous.

8/24/25 Monday
Got up early and had early breakfast and started for NY at 6:32. Had a fine ride on the water. Took a sightseeing bus and saw part of the city. Went up in the Woolworth building. Started back about 4:20 and Eby and I went to the concert and Esther and Granville stayed on the outside. Stayed in our room a while. I have a fierce cold.

8/25/25 Tuesday
Very fine weather. We went bathing with the boys, only I didn't get in on account of my cold. Took some pictures. The boys left on the 5:30 train. I got a family of four this evening. 9 in all now. Esther kept office and I wrote to Susan McGallicher and went to bed at 9:30.

8/28/25 Friday
Cooler. Got a new man. The nine plain girls spent the A.M. with us and took some pictures. Esther sewed and I wrote a letter home after ironing some aprons. This evening we went over to the Auditorium to see the communion. 1600 communed. We then walked the boardwalk and looked at the pretty things.

9/2/25 Wednesday
The one coon was very drunk and talkative and quarrelsome. Mrs. Zelly came down and discharged him. Finished our ironing. This P.M. we went to the baby parade. It was a wonderful display of vanity. We went down to see the moon come up and sat on the sand a while. Nice day.

9/3/25 Thursday
Worked the same as usual. I crocheted and Esther read and slept. The drunk man came back twice. I got a letter from Aunt Ada and she said Mary Musselman is married. Got a letter from Elizabeth Fenninger and answered it and wrote to Eby. We went down to the beach and I crocheted. Sultry and cloudy and rained a shower.

9/5/25 Saturday
We got up early and went down to the beach for shells and saw the sun come up. Very warm. Had ninety four guests this evening. Esther got a letter from Granville and it made her look 2 years younger. We slept this P.M. and went to bed this evening. Esther went down to the drugstore for pictures.

9/6/25 Sunday
Had over 100 guests. Dining room was very full. We had one hour to ourselves this A.M. and a half this P.M. Went to the auditorium and just missed the collection to our great sorrow, about 10,000 there and the text was about the rich man. "This night thy soul shall be required of thee." We were tired till bedtime.

9/8/25 Tuesday
We cleared the tables and washed the salt dips and did the ironing. We went bathing this P.M. It was very cool. We stayed in the office and the Zelly's went to the Fireman's Benefit at the Auditorium. My New Yorkers left and tipped me $3.00.

9/9/25 Wednesday
We emptied the oil and vinegar bottles and washed them. Finished the ironing which was 16 tablecloths and 165 napkins. Did our final family washing. Had a shocking surprise when Willis Byers brought Bessie Kreider here as his wedded wife. We fixed their bed.

9/12/25 Saturday
We packed. Very nice day and pretty evening for Ezra Hershey's doggie roast. We bought our gifts this A.M. Esther sewed at my dress and I cleaned our room. Had 26 guests for dinner and 23 for supper. I went out for pictures, lace and handkerchiefs. Took a last look at the Ocean.

9/13/25 Sunday
We had 20 for breakfast. Bessie and Willis left after breakfast. Very warm. Got done till eleven o'clock. We finished packing and dressed and served supper to 15 guests. Had 24 this dinner. I got four dollars and a ring. Came home through the rain and Eby and Granville met us in Lancaster.

9/19/25 Saturday
Mabel cut corn and Amy and I finished the work. Mamma sewed. This P.M. I went to the bank and brought some chairs from Brown's and met Edna. Mabel brought singing books and chairs from Hershey's. It was a beautiful day and we had about 125 at our singing. Noah Mack gave a talk.

9/23/25 Wednesday
Mabel and Mamma cut corn part of the time. We spiced cantaloupes and canned apples and made grape juice for jelly. Cleaned a chicken for supper. Had the door

shut all day to keep Mabel from freezing. Papa was able to be out again. We went down to Wanner's for bursted cabbage.

9/30/25 Wednesday
All five of us went to the cornfield. Very cloudy. We cleaned the new room this afternoon. Verna Eby and Elmer Kreider were married. Papa went to Mellinger's church this P.M. I got a letter and pictures from Mrs. Willis Byers. Took out the sweet potatoes. Had two bishops overnight.

10/3/25 Saturday
We made pies, ginger cakes, two big cakes and made things ready for company. Finished the cleaning and we all went to preparatory services at Hershey's this P.M. It's 20 of 8 and Eby isn't here. We went to Lancaster to Y.P.M. John Weaver spoke. Big crowd. Went to Shand's a while.

10/6/25 Tuesday
Mabel went to Beiler's and I washed. Clothes didn't dry very good. The McNess man was here. He lives with his wife again. I tried to fire the furnace but it leaked. Henry Herr came this evening to be anointed. Mabel and I went along with Nora and Mart to St. Paul's Reformed Church to hear one of the greatest preachers in the world.

10/9/25 Friday
Mabel went to Beiler's. Mamma, Jay and I shelled about 4 bushels of beans. Mamma sewed and I put the flowers on the windows after fertilizing them and dipping them in tobacco tea. Rained from 9:00 on till this evening when it cleared and got windy and cold.

10/25/25 Sunday
We were alone overnight. Levi King called us early for castoria. Rained and poured and blew the barn door off and the tobacco down. Had trouble starting the machine and were late to White Horse. Had Myer's three for dinner. Eby and I went along with Warren and Barbara to Mechanics Grove where Ira Hershey is holding meetings. John King came at midnight to phone for the Dr. for Susie. They thought she would die.

11/3/25 Tuesday
Mrs. Ziegler ironed. I didn't feel good. We cleaned the living room, which kept us on the move all day. I phoned to Esther and she likes her place. She came in this evening and we went to see Aunt Lil. She was out so we went to the Square to see the election. A glance was sufficient and we came back here.

11/12/25 Thursday
We canned the celery and started for Lancaster at 10:00, took Nora along. Mamma stopped at Martin Clymer's and spent the day. We hunted for a place for Mabel in vain. Mrs. Raub called and I hired Mabel to her for a trial. Very wet and rainy all day.

11/18/25 Wednesday
Nora Wanner's health is improving. Papa, the three boys and I went for the steers. Mamma brought the cabbage in and I cleaned the summer kitchen. Nice day, much warmer. I mended and pressed my batiste dress. Jay's books came. Darned stockings.

11/29/25 Sunday
We all went to Hershey's Church. David Landis preached. Papa visited the sick this P.M. Amy and Landis went to Arment's. I went to visit Christ King's. The baby is swelled very big with dropsy. Eby took Amy and I to Paradise. About 40 at Red Well. They had no preaching.

11/30/25 Monday
Amy and I washed and ironed. Mamma finished my dress and I put it upstairs already for Saturday. It was snowing this morning so we postponed the butchering. Wanner's came for Amy. Did the mending and worked at my cushion top. Agnes Souder was here.

12/5/25 Saturday
I made a cake and cleaned up the kitchen. Dressed for the reception for Susan at Martin Hershey's. 87 there. Had a very nice time, the first English reception I was ever at. We went to Groffdale this evening. It rained all day.

12/8/25 Tuesday
I did the ironing and Mamma mended. Mamma wrote some letters. Fannie Ream fell down the stair steps one week ago today, and she is still laying on the couch where they put her after she fell and did not have her dress off yet.

12/10/25 Thursday
Anna Felpel and Martin Nolt and their attendants came here to be married before Papa and Mamma were dressed and I had to let them in. They went up to Felpel's for a sumptious wedding dinner. On the way home they stopped to see Fannie Ream. I stripped tobacco.

12/12/25 Saturday
I cleaned upstairs and down. Mamma made a cake and served and made dinner. I went to the car for Edna. Eby took me to Groffdale instead of Educational. I was disappointed but went to please him as he is so down on the meeting. Lizzie Hershey was here this P.M. Rhoda Hershey died.

12/14/25 Monday
I put the clothes away and soaked the wash. We put Mrs. Witmer's comfort in and did about the half of it. Mamma bought Mabel a wrist watch for Xmas. I have the cold. Mary Houck is getting married. The Myers' cow had a calf last night.

12/21/25 Monday
We washed but did not hang it up as the weather was very damp. Mamma and Papa put more windows in the chicken house. Amy and I finished baking the sand tarts and peppernuts. We wrapped the Xmas presents and addressed our greetings. Amy went down to Wanner's this evening.

12/25/25 Friday
Christmas. We got up late and had dinner almost ready till 11:30 waiting for Uncle Milt's. They arrived at 12:00. Mabel came at 12:30 and I met Edna at 3:30. We had a much confused and very short P.M. Eby took me to Kinzer. Big crowd. John Bressler preached, his text "The Babe."

12/26/25 Saturday
Very cold and stormy. Edna went back to town this evening. She made caps. Mamma was three thirds sick. I cleaned Xmas away. I did not have a date. Amy and I went to John Senger's Bible Study. Mabel came there on the car and we brought her along home. Fierce cold.

12/28/25 Monday
We washed and ironed. It was very cold. I started to dig for a new cellar. Papa ordered a furnace this evening. Among my many beautiful gifts was a lovely ivory toilet set, a fountain pen, doily, 2 boxes of writing paper, 8 pieces of aluminum ware, promise of a cedar chest, and tea towel and 28 greetings.

12/31/25 Thursday
I made pies. Paul has not been in school all week. Papa and Jay finished digging the cellar. This P.M. Mamma helped to strip tobacco. I cleaned the sitting room. Mamma went to the stripping room this evening till John Senger and George Graham came. I phoned our store order from Ira Hershey's as our phone is out of order. Eby phoned to Ira and said he has the measles. Ira stopped and told Papa to tell me. I wrote him a letter. It is still clear and not quite so cold.

1926

1/1/26 Friday
John King called us early as Christ King's baby died. I went over before breakfast and helped till about 10:00. I cleaned up some of the house. Amy came home this evening. Jay went along with Ira to Lancaster this evening. Mamma helped to strip tobacco. Resolved not to lose my temper.

1/4/26 Monday
Amy and I went over to Christ King's before daylight and helped all day till 4:00. Everything went like clockwork. It was very damp and foggy all day. John Martin's

little boy died. I phoned to Eby this evening and to Mrs. Reeser and wrote to Prof. Getz. About 160 ate dinner.

1/6/26 Wednesday
Very foggy, cleared at dinnertime and got windy and cold. We took down tobacco this P.M., about 1200 lath. A board piece fell on Papa's head and cut it open. Little John Martin was buried this P.M. Wanner's came for Amy this evening. Wash got dry. Got a letter from Eby.

1/8/26 Friday
Papa went to Lancaster to get a smoke stack for the furnace. Mamma stripped tobacco all day. I made pies, cleaned the upstairs and cellar way. Very cold raw east wind all day. Raymond Wenger has pneumonia very bad. Made sour pickles, cranberries, dried peaches and mush.

1/14/26 Thursday
Rogers, Futer and Reno were here all day. Jay, Mamma, Nora and I went to Lancaster to the dentist's. Edna and I had our pictures taken. It was bitter cold this morning and I almost froze driving the machine. Paul did not go to school. I cleaned the side board drawers. Sledding good at Red Hill.

1/17/26 Sunday
We went to White Horse. Mamma, Landis and I went to Clayton Witmer's this P.M. The snow is melting fast. I have a wedge between my teeth and it's fierce sore. It is raining this evening. Eby took me to Kinzer. Isaac Metzler calls on Mae Groff.

1/21/26 Thursday
Papa went to Israel Zook's for a hog and we finished butchering it till 3:00 and boiled soap. They filled the heating system and it leaked all over the carpet and had to be emptied twice. I bronzed three radiators. Very rainy and damp. Rogers and Reno here.

1/22/25 Friday
It snowed and is very cold. I finished the bronzing and Sam Reno finished the heating system. Cleaned the parlor, Mamma's room, stairs, vestibule, papered the holes shut. Jay cut the boys' hair. Tobacco buyers out. Jonas Newhauser's mother was buried at the age of 101 years.

1/25/26 Monday
Mamma and I did the washing. Very cold and cloudy. This P.M. I straightened up the house and Mamma stripped tobacco. Sold to Levy's for 12-3. One-legged Negro woman was here. Hens laid 32 eggs. Jay half soled his own shoes.

1/26/26 Tuesday
I ironed and did the morning work. Stripped tobacco this P.M. and evening. Ezra Groff died at the age of 79 years. There is a verse in the Gospel Herald telling about the books of the Bible. Mamma has promised $2.00 a head for all who memorize it.

1/31/26 Sunday
Papa and Mamma started for New Providence and left the three boys at Uncle Milt's and they came back there for dinner. Amy, Jay and I went to White Horse. Slim crowd. We had oysters and ice cream for dinner. Spent a quiet P.M. Started for Kinzer church and came back as the water was too high. Very windy and rainy all day.

2/4/26 Thursday
I made doughnuts, rusk, and a coconut cake. Have the cold in my head. Milk man and mailman did not get through. Papa and Jay went out to open road with the two horse wagon. Mamma stripped tobacco all day. Had school till 2 o'clock. Landis was there.

2/7/26 Sunday
We all went to Hershey's but Jay and Mamma in the Oakland. I went along with Eby home and spent the day there. Had a nice time. Too many frog eyes and we could not go to Paradise so we sleighed to Millwood. Mabel was home a little while.

2/18/26 Thursday
We cut the meat and salted it. This P.M. Papa took the bologna meat over to Troup's. We all stripped tobacco. Amy and I stayed in this evening. I made noodles and worked at my scarf and soaked my feet. There is considerable traffic on the Cattail Road owing to a big sink hole in the road at Olie Futer's.

2/23/26 Tuesday
We put the wash up before breakfast and started for Lancaster, all of us. I rued bargains with Mrs. Raub and hired myself with Mrs. Gardener. We bought a rug for our room, mattress, coat for Amy and some smaller things. Amy went down to Wanner's this evening. Wash dried nicely.

3/5/26 Friday
Papa and Mamma went to Uncle Emanuel's and took some wool to the wool mill. We made ginger cakes, pies and cakes. We finished the cleaning. Christ Houck's mother died. Us four took Elias and Samuel Stoltzfus along to Milltown Spelling Bee. I failed on "Where are the Ural Mountains?"

3/9/26 Tuesday
I did the washing. Amy is better. Mamma patched some clothes for the blind tramp. I made two dresses. Wash dried nicely and I got it ready to iron. They spent the Spelling Bee money $13.75 for games. Cold and windy

3/16/26 Tuesday
We finished Axe's washing and I ironed it and Mamma mended some of it out of love for the little boys. Jay, Landis and I went over to Arment's expecting to go along with a bunch of 20 back to Earl Union Spelling Bee, but we 13 went in three machines, ours being one. Jammed house. Landis won a prize.

3/20/26 Saturday
Finished up. Landis and I did the scrubbing after dinner. Mamma and I went over to Arment's and down to Wanner's. Nora is better. Eby was a little late and we went to Strasburg. Took Jay along to Kinzer Spelling Bee and he got third prize. Nice day.

3/23/26 Tuesday
I went over to Ralph Arment's again. Cleaned a very dirty kitchen. I got home about 8:30 with my heart full of sympathy. Mrs. Arment was so sick she went to bed. Papa and Mamma took Mary King and baby to the Dr. in Lancaster. Rainy and cleared this evening.

3/24/26 Wednesday
Papa and Landis Hershey went to Rohrerstown. Mamma and I went to Clayton Witmer's moving. They moved to Witmer, had a fine big day. Us and three boys took Louella and Eby Leaman along to Weavertown Spelling Bee. Jay took first prize in information class. I didn't try.

3/25/26 Thursday
I took Papa over to the trolley and brought the paint along from the Station. I did the ironing and Mamma painted. Eby came up with us and went to Centerville School Spelling Bee. I went up in the Information class and came down sixth to last on Who wrote The Man Without a Country?

3/31/26 Wednesday
Stormy and rainy all day. We sewed. Cleaned the silverware. I made potpie for supper. Edna and Kitty Burkholder were down at church last evening. I had my wart pow wowed last evening. Amanda Winters was buried.

4/4/26 Sunday
All went to Hershey's communion. Mabel went to Red Well and brought Lydia Allison down. They took her down to Ramsey's and went down to Annie Grub's. We girls went down to Wanner's, then took Lydia home. Soaked the wash. Eby took me to Paradise. Big crowd. Eby gave me a 5 lb. egg.

4/19/26 Monday
Got up early and came in here to Gardener's. Barbara did a big wash and some of the ironing. Edna called up this evening. Eby gave me a five dollar gold piece for my birthday. Amy is making me two scarves. Mrs. Gardener seems very nice.

4/21/26 Wednesday
Tried to wash dishes and help all I could. It's going better. We house cleaned all day. Dr. Atlee came to see Mrs. Graham. Barbara and I went out to see Esther. Edna and Sue were there too. It was very warm. I shed my underwear.

4/24/26 Saturday
Got up at six. Cleaned the cellar and ice box. Mrs. Graham was operated on at 10:00. Had 13 oz. of ether and two hours in the operating room. Very serious, but she is as good as can be expected. I went out to Esther's and we went to Y.P.M. and came out again with Granville and Eby.

4/25/26 Sunday
My 21st Birthday. Cloudy. I was busy all morning and till 2:45 when I almost missed the C.V. for home. Mabel met me and we went to Red Well. J.W. Weaver started revival meetings. Came in with Esther and Granville at 12:30.

4/26/26 Monday
Did not have any alarm and slept till 7:00. Mrs. Heistand helped to wash an enormous wash. Ironed a few pieces. Had company for dinner. Called Edna. They sat at the supper table till 5 of 8 and I was mad xxxxx. Mrs. Graham is not any worse. Real nice day.

4/27/26 Tuesday
I got up at 4:30 and finished all my ironing till 11:30. Went to market and bought a fountain pen for Eby. Martha Greenwalt's father died on Sunday morning. A very pretty day for Mabel Rohrer and Jake Rutt's reception.

5/2/26 Sunday
Got up at seven and finished the breakfast dishes till 11:30. Made sherbet in the new Auto Vacuum Freezer. I was very mad and xxxxxxx. Soaked my clothes. Had mashed potatoes, corn, spinach, chicken and sherbert. Edna and Tommy came out here and I went back with them. Met Eby there and went to Mellinger's. Small crowd.

5/4/26 Tuesday
Made a veal pot pie which was most delicious, and I must make a pie. Did most of the ironing. Went to market. Edna called and said Papa and Mamma were in. Very much cooler. Granny is not improving very fast. I soaked my corns this evening.

5/8/26 Saturday
Got up at 5:30 and dolled up my room. Dressed before dinner and hurried faster than I could and missed the 15 of 2 by about 3 minutes. Took the next car and walked home. Had a delightful walk, very warm. Eby took me to Irvin Denlinger's. The others went to Red Well. I did the milking.

5/14/26 Friday

Did not get up till 6:30. Cleaned the ice box and cellar steps and kitchen. Had lunch this noon and went to market. It rained early this morning. Made biscuits and they were not fit to eat. Worked at my counterpane a little. Crocheted quite a bit. Talked to Edna twice.

5/16/26 Sunday

Mabel came in overnight and we went to church. I was very mad. Went down to see the Zink girls and from there out to Shand's and from there to Paradise church and Eby and Granville met us and we came in the Maxwell and spent the rest of the evening there.

5/17/26 Monday

Got up at 5:00 and had all the wash dry and in till 1:00. Ironed a few pieces. I was dead tired and went to bed at 8:30. Mrs. Gardener fell down on the stairs and is very sore. I am still looking for a decent place. Gusty and rained a shower.

5/18/26 Tuesday

I got up at 6:00 and dusted and swept and did some of the ironing. Mrs. Gardener stayed in bed till dinner time. I went to market and carried home a heavy basket. Saw Barbara Groff. Bought some stockings. Very warm and rained a few showers. Was eavesdropping.

5/19/26 Wednesday

Have fully decided to leave. Mrs. Gardener had a baby boy born to her at 1:00 at St. Joe's. I ironed all day and cooked. Very warm and gusty and lots of rain. Esther and Sue came to see me this evening. I worked at my counterpane.

5/24/26 Monday

Got up at 6:00 and started the washing. Mrs. Heistand came at 7:15 and left at 3:30. It was very rainy and we got the wash dried between showers. Ironed some. I went place hunting. Sounded real good. Marian Landis is in the hospital with appendicitis. Pretty and clear this evening.

5/25/26 Tuesday

Ironed and cooked and went to market. Esther came and we went out to see Mamie Buckwalter and stopped at Shand's and then went to Dr. Mylin's to see Park Plank as he called here and wanted me to come and live with his mother. Me brought me out here in his Jordan. My brain is whirling.

6/2/26 Wednesday

Very warm. Had late breakfast and was kept busy all morning. Cleaned the silverware this P.M. Minnie Felker called me up. I told Mrs. Gardener I was leaving and she was very reasonable and agreeable. It was very strenuous on my nerves. Edna came out this evening.

6/3/26 Thursday
I did a big wash and ironed some of it. Mrs. Heistand bid her adieu. Mrs. Graham is no better. Mr. Price was here. Edna called up. I do not feel very good. I wrote to Eby this evening. Mrs. Plank died. Nice clear day. I am tired and happy.

6/5/26 Saturday
Got up at 5:00, finished packing and made up my bed. Did all the scrubbing in the rain. Put clean papers in the drawers and cupboards. Had a big dinner at 1:30 and I was ready to leave at 3:00. Bought an umbrella and took the 3:30 car for Anna High's crowd. Had a fine time. Eby came for me and I was delighted to go home. Edna and Esther went to Educational.

6/8/26 Tuesday
Besides the dusting and cooking I did my washing and ironing which was very small. It is going real good. This evening I moved the rest of my things and Barbara and I went out to Shand's. Barbara is so sorry for Gardener's. Got to bed at 11:30. Rained.

6/11/26 Friday
I was busy most all day. Cleaned the kitchen, stove, refrigerator, laundry, steps and sun room. Mary was here. Gertrude went out. Minnie and Kathryn Hurst called me up and I went to bed early. Warm. I seem to be happy and contented.

6/14/26 Monday
Made a pie and two salad dressings. Had dinner at 12:30. This is Hartman's tenth wedding anniversary. Mr. gave Mrs. a lovely locket. I took some pictures of her in her wedding gown. Very warm, gusty and rained. I helped Mary to iron a little while. Gertrude made me a friendly call.

6/15/26 Tuesday
Had another gust in the night. Sanford Landis and another man were struck and instantly killed yesterday P.M. The storm was very severe. Five barns were struck. I did my washing and ironing. Went out to see Kathryn Hurst this evening. Much cooler.

6/20/26 Sunday
Made breakfast and corn starch and sandwiches for supper. Got dinner for Gertrude and myself. Asked Mrs. Hartman for a weekend off and she said wait till my vacation. I wept and swallowed and forgot it. I left here at 1:30 and went out to the jail to hear the male chorus. Took the 15 of 3 and went to Noah Denlinger's and from there to Kinzer church and in here. A perfect day.

6/22/26 Tuesday
Cloudy and showery all day. I managed to get my wash dry and ironed. Mary was here to iron this P.M. I had the blues before supper. Mr. Hartman left for N.Y. before breakfast. I worked at my bedspread. Talked to Edna and Esther.

7/3/26 Saturday
Very warm this morning and stayed dreadful hot all day. I was done early and took the 2:30 car to Florence Breckbill's crowd. Had a very nice time. 34 there. Eby came for me and we spent the evening. We came back here and saw a few fireworks along the way. It was dropping rain and threatening to gust all evening.

7/6/26 Tuesday
Rained all day and gusty this evening. They are not having any pageant tonight. I had my wash all hanging in the cellar till 6:30. Went down to the bank after dinner and deposited $100. Edna and I looked around a little and I came back and did my ironing. Have a cold in my head.

7/19/26 Monday
Very warm. I hurried to get my morning work done and came down on the 9:45 to take my vacation. We finished the ironing. Fixed up some of my dresses. It was too wet for any harvesting. Mamma sewed. Marvin Myers' have a baby boy last Saturday night.

7/21/26 Wednesday
Just as warm as before the rain. Mamma and I went to Lancaster to do some shopping and stopped at Clayton Witmer's on the way in and fixed Mae's dress. Brought Edna along home. Mrs. Hartman and family came down this P.M. and I promised to go with them to Atlantic City. They hauled in wheat this P.M.

7/22/26 Thursday
It was gusty from 10 till 12. Landis and I went over to Uncle Sam's to help haul wheat early this morning. It was dreadful warm. My arms got scratched and sunburned, but I stood it very well otherwise. Edna helped 7 loads and didn't care to help any more.

7/27/26 Tuesday
Cloudy but did not rain. I finished my scarf and put the initials on. Edna was in bed all forenoon. Papa and the boys were helping Uncle Sam's finish harvesting. Amy and I hoed this evening. Edna and I went to call on the King's and shocked them with the ways of the rich.

7/29/26 Thursday
Left at 3:30 for Washington D.C. I drove as far as Baltimore and part way home. Had a big day and saw a lot. Lost ourselves a few times. Got home at 12:00 P.M. It didn't rain but one shower, but rained here most of the day. We hired a colored chauffeur in a 7-passenger Cadillac sedan.

8/2/26 Monday
The girls washed. Mabel took me to meet the 9:00 car and I came back here on the job. Mary the cook is staying till Thursday when we leave for the Ocean. I wrote a

letter to Eby this evening. I am busy getting my things together. Very warm. There was a motorcycle accident here in front of Taylor's.

8/3/26 Tuesday
Mary Mail was here again this morning. I cooked and did my washing and ironing and worked at my bathing suit. Went out to Shand's this evening. It was very warm and gusty this P.M. I got in at 10:00. Mary dried the dishes for me.

8/5/26 Thursday
Did up all the work as usual. Had dinner at 11:30 and left for Atlantic City at 1:00. Arrived here at 5:00 and got ready for supper. Not as bad as I expected. Mr. Hartman, the children and I went for a walk on the boardwalk. I am staying up till they come in.

8/6/26 Friday
Helped dress the children and after breakfast we all went down on the beach till lunch time. Mr. Hartman and the children went in bathing. This P.M. I wrote to Edna and sent some cards. When the children were dressed Mrs. H. and the children and I went for a wheel chair ride. After the children were in bed I went down on the boardwalk. Got back at 9:00. Mailed salt water taffy.

8/7/26 Saturday
Dressed the kiddies and had breakfast. Went down to the beach and went bathing. I brought Bobby back and gave him his bath and dinner. Mrs. Hartman put him to bed. The three kiddies and I went down to hear a concert. Aunty Til took the kiddies out and I am staying in.

8/8/26 Sunday
Very pretty and clear all day. We all went down to the million dollar pier except Mr. Hartman to see the fish nets being pulled in. Had dinner and put the kiddies to bed and then I had off till 6:00. Read my Bible and slept a while. After supper I wrote to Eby while Aunty Til took the kids down on the boardwalk. Went to bed at 10:00.

8/9/26 Monday
A very long day. I felt very good for the condition I'm in. Went down on the beach. Mr. Hartman went in bathing with the kiddies and took the train home after lunch. I slept a while and took Bobby out for a long walk. We went down on the boardwalk for a while this evening.

8/10/26 Tuesday
I went to the beach with Bobby alone. Talked to Mr. and Mrs. Park Plank. Jack has a bad bite. This P.M. the children and I went down to the Garden Pier. This evening I went out alone and saw the baby incubators. Met Mr. and Mrs. Clarence Landis and some of their friends. Wrote to Eby and sent some cards. Got 6 letters.

8/12/26 Thursday
Took the children on the beach. This P.M. I had to myself. I took a bath in Miss Gable's tub and then slept a while and then started my cushion top. It is real warm. I put Bobby to bed and helped with the other children and then I went out on the boardwalk at 9:30. Wrote a letter to Eby while I waited for the kids.

8/14/26 Saturday
Very hot. We all went on the beach but Miss Gable. I went in for the first time and enjoyed it most immensely. This P.M. Helen, Jack, Bobby and I went down on the boardwalk. Very gusty this evening. Hartman's went out to dinner. The kiddies and I played till their bedtime. Wrote Eby.

8/16/26 Monday
Cloudy and rainy. We started from Atlantic City on a fast train at 8:55 and arrived in Lancaster at 12:15. The house was in splendid order. Mary Male was here. I did my wash and dried it in the cellar. Went out to Shand's and had a nice time. I am very glad to be back home again.

8/18/26 Wednesday
Still raining. Baked a pie and shelled a lot of lima beans. I started to work my buffet set. It rained all day and is very much cooler. I went to singing school and met Eby. He brought Esther and I out. It was very cool to sit on the sparking bench.

8/22/26 Sunday
We kids all went to Hershey's and Papa and Mamma went to Stumptown and Floyd Benner's for dinner. Edna and I went to Alice Hershey's crowd this P.M. This evening Papa and Mamma went to Fry's. We went to Paradise and came in with Esther and Granville. Cloudy and drizzly all day, but the stars and moon shone before midnight.

8/26/26 Thursday
A beautiful clear day. St. Swithin's rain ended today. Cleaned my room, darned my stockings and hemstitched around my pillowcase once. Went out to see Sue Clark. Mary Martin, Esther, Edna, Grace and her sister Mary were there. Went to bed at 11:00.

9/2/26 Thursday
Raining. Mary Male was here. Cleaned my room. Mrs. Clark and Julia Ann were here for dinner. Had hamburger, mashed potatoes, corn pudding and pineapple cake. Grace took this P.M. off. I gave Bobby his supper and set up till they came home from the movies. Made my pillow cases and a new belt for my foulard dress.

9/19/26 Sunday
Warm and partly cloudy. One of Grace's friends from Coatesville came for her about 9:45 and she has the day off. After dinner Eby came in for me and took me

to his home for supper. Elizabeth and Emma went along to Paradise church and we took them home again and came in here on the bench. Mabel stopped Clarence last Sunday night.

10/4/26 Monday
Mary was here. I was disappointed when Mrs. Hartman told me I have to stay in Saturday night and miss Grace Denlinger's party. I did my washing this P.M. Rested and sewed a little after I was through. Went out this evening and transacted some business. I have an attack of hay fever. Very warm.

10/5/26 Tuesday
Still very warm. Had lemon meringue, sweet potatoes with marshmallows, pork chops and beets. They have the Packard again. Mrs. H. went out for a water wave this P.M. I darned my stockings and put the hem in my new black dress. Did my ironing this morning.

10/9/26 Saturday
Very cold but no frost here. I made a cake, applesauce and cranberry sauce, stewed a chicken and prunes. Made sauer kraut for dinner and worked till 3:00. Took a dry bath and sewed till five. Made supper and dressed to stay in. Feeling very much disappointed that I can't go to Grace Denlinger's. Beautiful evening.

10/12/26 Tuesday
Clear and cold. Had sauer kraut and lemon meringue for dinner. Did most of my ironing this morning. Mary is ironing and complaining this P.M. The rear of the house is a wreck. Sewed. Esther, Eva Hurst and I went to hear Stough. Came back, took a bath and went to bed.

10/13/26 Wednesday
Very cloudy and rained some. Mrs. Hartman went to Philadelphia. Seven of us city girls went down home this P.M. and quilted one and part of another quilt for Edna. Had a real nice time. Sue Clark seemed grieved about something, which made me feel badly. Eby, Granville and Mart brought us back to town.

10/14/26 Thursday
Partly cloudy. Mrs. Hartman gave me the dickens for not keeping the front clean and not emptying the ash trays. Cleaned my room. Grace is off this P.M. Had French fries, Boregard eggs, cranberries, celery and chocolate Frappe. Sue Clark went to the mission to hear Raber. Walked both ways. David H. had Florence Myers.

10/30/26 Saturday
Made a Lady Baltimore cake and apple and cranberry sauce. Had a sauer kraut dinner. Took a bath and sewed this P.M. There was just the children for supper. Eby came here and took me to Y.P.M. It was very spooky downtown and everywhere. I sent some things home with Eby.

11/14/26 Sunday

Had everything to myself. Took Bobby for a walk and stopped to see Esther. Bobby and I had dinner together and I left for Shand's at 3:30 where I met Esther and we went down on the car and met the boys at Witmer turnout and went to New Providence where Ira Hershey closed a series of meetings. Had Eby in the house for the first time.

11/15/26 Monday

Cloudy and raining. Did my washing this P.M. and tried to make sand tarts. Talked to Edna. Put collar and cuffs on my black dress. Started a Xmas present. Mrs. Hartman's aunt died for the lack of breath, so she said. Helped put the kids to bed. I went to bed early.

11/25/26 Thursday

Thanksgiving Day. Pretty and clear. Got up at 5:30 and stuffed the turkey and put him in the oven. Mabel helped to get the dinner. There were fourteen with us three. Everything went real good except I spilled the cranberries. All finished till 3:15. Rested a while and Esther walked with us out to Shand's and from there to church. Went to Shand's afterward to spend the evening.

11/26/26 Friday

Very glad that yesterday is over. Mrs. H. and Helen went to Philadelphia. Mary was here. Had leavings of yesterday. Worked at Mabel's Xmas present. Rained last night and all day. Had real heavy gust this evening. Went to bed at 8:30. Hartman's came in at 2:00 A.M.

12/3/26 Friday

Cloudy, cold and raw. Did the usual cleaning. Finished before 2:00. Worked at my cushion top. This evening I went down to Bausman's to see Mabel Breckbill. Edna and Grace Clark were there too. Mrs. Shand is giving Edna silver knives and forks for wedding present.

12/6/26 Monday

Clear and very cold. Mary came and washed. I did my washing and it got dry. Worked at my hardanger cushion. I talked to Edna three times. Papa and Mamma came in and she went home for good. Amy and Mamma had an accident on Saturday. A machine ran into them sideways and damaged the Chevrolet.

12/8/26 Wednesday

I asked for two days off after Xmas and she consented. I had the afternoon off, took a bath and went downtown to do some shopping. Got a pair of black oxfords for $6.00. Brought my purchases back and took my new dress over to Neff's and Esther helped me put the sleeves and hem in. Cloudy.

12/12/26 Sunday
Pretty and clear. Had a leg of lamb and potatoes and beets, cranberries and ice cream and cake. Was busy till 11:15. Went home on the 15 of 3 and Jay met me. We had a busy time talking. Papa and Mamma were at Mart Kurtz's. The man who struck Mamma and Amy came to argue this evening. We went to Paradise. Mamma's foot is better.

12/20/26 Monday
Cloudy and snowed. Edna's wedding invitations were sent on Saturday. Helen went to Philadelphia with her Grandma Straub. Mary washed this P.M. and I did mine after she was done. Stirred up sand tarts and sewed till bedtime. Ruth Kreider was here for money for the mission workers.

12/21/26 Tuesday
Still cloudy. Grace went downtown to do some shopping. Mrs. Hartman and Helen helped to bake sand tarts. Mary was here and ironed. I did mine this A.M. Finished my friendship cushion top and feel quite relieved. Cleaned four wild ducks this evening.

12/25/26 Saturday
Christmas Day. Slept 10 ½ hours. Got up at 7:00. The children got everything imaginable. Very cloudy and damp. I got an umbrella, night gown, six handkerchiefs and a box of candy. I kept Bobby. We had chicken and ice cream for dinner. Mr. Hartman took me to the 15 of 4 and Eby met me at Hensel Road. We went to Kinzer church and then home. Raining and very icy. I stayed home all night against the boss' wishes.

12/26/26 Sunday
Very icy and I called Mrs. H. and told her we could not come in. She was displeased and I had a troubled conscience all day. Went to Hershey's and from there Eby and I went to Kathryn Hurst's for dinner and supper. Went to Lottie Snyder's in the P.M. and to Hess' church in the evening. Brought Kathryn along in. Edna and Mart were announced this morning. Stayed in the fresh air. About 20 at Hurst's. Had a nice time. Cleared off at dinner time and everything was beautiful and icy.

12/27/26 Monday
Mrs. H. was grouchy and so was I. I worked all day, did my washing and ironing and made little cakes. Mary was here and washed. Grace has the rheumatism. Very cold and clear. Clarence gave Mabel a toilet set for Xmas. Esther got a silver tea set from Granville, Kathryn a picture, and Elsie a tablecloth and napkins.

12/29/26 Wednesday
Edna's Wedding Day. All up early and busy getting things ready. The ceremony took place at 9:45 in the presence of 15 witnesses. It cleared at dinnertime and was a little

muddy. Things went as good as could be expected for the first attempt. Had about thirty for supper and everyone was gone till 6:30. We brought Edna and Mart in for the 9:20 train to Niagara Falls. Went to see the fire engine houses. Mabel and Clarence were in to see them off too.

12/31/26 Friday
Cloudy all day and began to snow about 4:30. Mrs. Hartman had a dinner party of 8 about 11:00 P.M. I helped get things ready. Grace showed me her picture album and went over to Erhart's. I took a bath and drank 3 cups of hot lemonade with whiskey in it and cured my cold but made me sick in the stomach. Esther called to see if I heard from Edna, which I did not. Hazel Fenninger is still in the hospital getting better slowly. Christ Brackbill is there yet too and is not getting along very fast. His hip was injured more than he knew it to be.

1927

1/1/27 Saturday
Everything is covered with snow and looks beautiful. I did not feel good all day. Had the party dishes to wash and Grace, Bobby and I for dinner. The others went to Clark's. Had the children for supper. Mabel came in to Keiper's for two weeks and all she has to do is keep the house locked securely.

1/3/27 Monday
Mary came this P.M. I did my washing this morning. The sink drain was stopped up and the plumbers detained me and I didn't get done till 3:00. This evening Esther, Grace and I went out to hear Gypsy Smith. Mabel was there and we went back to Keiper's a few minutes. Cloudy all day.

1/5/27 Wednesday
Very cloudy and snowing a little, but cleared off colder before dinner. Went out to Keiper's to see Mabel. Mrs. Keiper is a caution. I helped Mabel with her hardanger cushion top. Came back on the car with two plants. It snowed very fast about 5:00 and everything is white.

1/7/27 Friday
Mary was here. Bobby is not any better. Work went good. Worked at my rug. Mr. and Mrs. Hartman went out for dinner and then to a dance. I put Bobby to bed and Esther came over a little while. Worked at my rug, soaked my feet and combed my head with fine comb. Went to bed at 10:30.

1/9/27 Sunday
Got up at 8:00 and worked as fast as I could to get a three course dinner for Mrs. H's birthday. Herbert H. was here and came 15 minutes late. Hurried to get to the 15 of

3 and Kathryn Hurst went home with me. We walked to Duke St. in 10 minutes. Decided some important matters. Came in here to church and to Keiper's after.

1/10/27 Monday
I did my washing. Mary came this P.M. and sewed. I put some pictures in my album. Mrs. H. went to New York this morning. I went over to Neff's and went with Esther to Sewing Circle at Bertha Ranck's. Made a pair of sleeves. There were 80 confessions at Mellinger's. Miriam Good was one last night.

1/15/27 Saturday
Made a pie and junket and got the potatoes ready and put dried corn on and everything ready for dinner. It began to snow at 7:15 and kept it up till midnight. Mabel and I took the 10:15 car and Eby met us and we went to Edna and Mart's reception. About 41 there. Bitter cold. Eby's Ford froze up four times. He brought me in, left his Ford set and shiver and went to Ellis' all night.

1/16/27 Sunday
Got up at 8:00. 6 above zero. Was busy all P.M. We took some pictures. Eby came and had his Ford towed to a garage. He came here for me at 3:00 and we went to Elsie Weaver's for supper. 16 there. Edna and Mart did not get there as Mart had a sore throat. None of us went to church. Came out here and spent time keeping the Ford warm.

1/17/27 Monday
Not quite so cold. I did my washing this A.M. and was busy till 2:30. Talked to Mabel and Esther. Mary brought me a bundle of dandy silk patches and I am elated with them. Cloudy again this evening. Miss Gable was here for supper. I ironed my patches and went to bed.

1/19/27 Wednesday
Cleaned the silver. Grace was off. I told Mrs. H. that I'm leaving to get married. Edna brought some samples out and bought my wedding dress. Mabel came out this P.M. and went with Sue Clark to Millersville this evening. I went over to see Esther through the rain this evening.

1/20/27 Thursday
Mr. Hartman cracked up married life to me. Mary was here. Finished my rug. Worked at my cushion top that Maggie Wilhelm gave me years ago. Grace and I went over to Erhart's to help two ladies start hardanger cushion tops. Got back at 25 of 12.

1/22/27 Saturday
Rained very hard all day. I did up the work and left here at 2:00 and took the 2:30 Terre Hill and met Papa and Amy at New Holland and went home through the very muddy roads. Fit on my wedding dress. Eby came and took me down to see

the house behind the barn. Went over with Emma and Elizabeth a while and then home to eat doughnuts.

1/24/27 Monday
Did my washing and cooking. Worked at my Maggie Wilhelm cushion top. Mary was here. Yesterday Willis Buckwalter was coming home and in some way he fell from the buggy and became tangled in the lines and was dragged to death. Went to bed at 8:30. Clear, but very warm.

1/26/27 Wednesday
Cleaned all the big silver in 15 minutes. Had veal stew for dinner. For my P.M. off I went downtown to meet Edna, Mabel and Mamma, looked at the dishes and furniture. Went out to Keiper's for supper and took the 7:00 car and went to church at Millersville. Esther went too. Came back and finished my rug.

2/10/27 Thursday
Grace cleaned our room wile I made things ready for dinner. Hurried to get my work done, took the 15 of 2 and went home. Talked between times. Eby took me to Biz Rohrer's Spelling Bee. It was largely attended, big society night. Everybody had a date. It started to snow around 11:00.

2/11/27 Friday
Everything is white again but is melting fast. Did the cleaning and sewed this P.M. Grace went to hear Aimee Semple McPherson. Esther came over a while. Park Kreider had Grace Denlinger on Sunday night and Thursday night. Clarence Denlinger had Marian Hershey. Nice day.

2/15/27 Tuesday
Sprinkled Mary's wash and she came this P.M. and ironed. Mr. and Mrs. Hugh Clark were here to dinner tonight and went downtown to see Beau Geste at the Fulton Opera House. The children ate their supper early. Sue Clark and Helen Denlinger came to see me this evening. Got done till 8:00.

2/21/27 Monday
Did my washing and the cooking. Washed my head this P.M. and started more doilies. It snowed this morning but cleared at dinner time. Everything is full of snow. Mary came this P.M. and washed. I went downtown and bought a bedroom suit for $30.00. Went to bed at 9:30. It is snowing.

2/22/27 Tuesday
The girls did not have any school. Got up early and did my ironing and finished Mary's wash. Crocheted and went with Grace and Bobby sledding and made a snowman. Went over to see Alice Nissley this evening and saw Goodman's fine house. Hartman's went out.

3/2/27 Wednesday
Paul went down to Dave King's again and found Swiekert's watch. A very rough stormy day. We finished Edna's quilt and started mine. Mary King came over and brought us some spread patches. Edna made sunbonnets and my slip and bloomers. Landis got up and came downstairs.

3/4/27 Friday
Sewed and mended all day. I made some scarves. Mabel and Amy cleaned some of the house. Uncle Sam came over and helped to kill the beef. Papa, Mamma and I went to Lancaster to auction and bought ourselves rich. Got home at 12:15.

3/8/27 Tuesday
We got most of Edna's things together and went up in two machines and set her to housekeeping. It was raining and blew off and kept very stormy. We got home at 5:00 P.M. I made some bed clothing and worked till 11:00. Very nice day.

3/10/27 Thursday
We cleaned my to be green furniture and it was a big job. Boiled soap and dyed two goes of rug rags. Amy made a tub of vegetable soup. It has been a very beautiful spring day.

3/11/27 Friday
Mamma gave the furniture its first coat. We cleaned the house all but the kitchen. We three girls and Papa went down to Jake Davidson's sale and took Mary King along. I bought myself rich for $57.18. A big sale and very nice spring day.

3/13/27 Sunday
Papa and Mamma went to the Brick and to David High's. The rest of us went to White Horse and I went home with Eby and saw our future home. Nice day with balmy south winds. We went to Kinzer church. A very big crowd. The girls spent the P.M. at home.

3/15/27 Tuesday
Cleaned the good room and painted and dyed some rug rags. Sent the wedding invitations. Finished the ironing, darned the stockings. Papa and Mamma went to Uncle Charlie's to engage the cooks. Paul was not feeling good and stayed home from school.

3/16/27 Wednesday
We cleaned Mamma's room and the new room. Mamma dyed my coat and painted the kitchen chairs. Cleaned the carpet for Edna. I made pies for Grandpap King's. They were here for supper. They ate three. Lloyd came and cut Landis' hair.

3/17/27 Thursday
Mabel and Amy cleaned the parlor. I put my transfers on the bedroom suit. Mamma was sick. We cleaned around the woodpile, lawn and chicken yard. Aired the flowers.

Made some garden. Very warm and you can see things grow. Started my scarves. Amy finished inviting the neighbors.

3/20/27 Sunday
They all went to Hershey's church but me. Eby came up for dinner. Mabel went to John Groff's for dinner. I went along down with Eby and helped to milk. We took an invitation over to Mrs. Eaby and up to Martin Groff's and spent a delightful evening. It was rainy all day.

3/21/27 Monday
Washed and left it in the tubs. Rained all day. We cleaned the sitting room and parlor and set up a table in the sitting room.

3/23/27 Wednesday
Got up early and Papa, Mamma and I went to Lancaster for provisions and license to wed. Got home at 11:30. Made things ready to eat and set the tables. Fixed the papers and were very busy. Jay went for Aunt Bertha. A very pretty day and much cooler.

3/24/27 Thursday
Nice day. Cold and windy. I helped to get some things ready for dinner and then dressed to get married. Everyone was there till 11:00 and we were married before about 100 relatives and friends. After considerable rice and confetti, brothers David and Ellis brought us to the depot and we arrived in Harrisburg at 6:20. Found lodging and went for a walk to the capitol, then back and ripped some thoughtful sewing.

3/25/27 Friday
Got done sleeping till 1:00 and took the 2:10 train for Niagara Falls. It was daybreak when we got to Williamsport and we arrived in Buffalo at 11:30 A.M. Took a long walk and took the 2:20 train for Niagara Falls. Found our room and rested and went down to see the Falls illuminated.

3/26/27 Saturday
Very snowy and wet all day. We went sightseeing in a private car with a very grouchy chauffeur. Got back at 12:00. Took account of stock and went out for souvenirs and dinner and tickets. Back to our room, packed up and left for Erie. Arrived at 6:36, ate our lunch in the depot and took a taxi for Aunt Emma's.

3/27/27 Sunday
Still felt out of my element. Went to church and came back, had a stylish dinner and then went for a drive around Lake Erie and out on the peninsula and to Hillcrest. Stopped at the Cafeteria for supper. Back again and went to bed at 9:00. Pleasant and cold day.

3/28/27 Monday
Got up at 15 of 6, ate our breakfast and took the 7:00 train for home. Changed trains at Emporium Junction and rode all day. It snowed till noon. Took the 6:45 CV for Hensel and walked in to Hostetter's and Eby brought me home. Papa and Mamma went to Lancaster. Mabel Martin died at 10:45.

3/29/27 Tuesday
I washed and ironed Eby's and my clothes. The girls finished their ironing. Amy helped me hem my tablecloths. Papa went to Tobias Kreider's funeral. This evening Papa, Mamma and the three boys went up to Martin Groff's. Has been a damp day.

3/30/27 Wednesday
Got some things together and Mabel, Amy and I went down to Hostetter's and did some cleaning up. Painted, scrubbed, made garden, pulled paper off two rooms and trimmed paper for the long room. Got home at 9:30 and Mamma is sick. A wet rainy day.

4/1/27 Friday
I scrubbed off the kitchen and it was crusty. Cleaned and whitewashed the cellar way and two closets. It was very damp and cold all day. Eby, Elizabeth and I went over to Irvin's this evening. They all went to Mabel Martin's funeral but Eby.

4/4/27 Monday
Washed and ironed. I packed up my wedding presents and cleaned our shoes. Mamma and I went down to Hostetter's and painted. I planted sweet peas, pansies and flags. Papa went to a meeting at Weaverland. We did not get home till dark.

4/5/27 Tuesday
Nice day. Cold. Mabel, Mamma and I went down to my house and papered the kitchen and started the little guest room. I ate my meals in front of the barn and stayed down all night. Mamma cleaned the woodwork. Galen's baby died.

4/9/27 Saturday
Got up early and Eby and I came home and dressed. Everything went fine. It snowed nearly all day. We came home and spent the night here. Had a pleasant time. Got nice presents again. $60.00 in money with the wedding day money.

4/10/27 Sunday
Eby and I slept till breakfast. We went to Groffdale Church and to Grandpap's for dinner. Casper's, Uncle Harry's, Uncle Sam's and Mart Groff's were there too. The others went to White Horse and took Grammy home this evening. Eby and Jay washed the supper dishes and we went to Kinzer.

4/13/27 Wednesday
Eby is no better. He has a fever. I cleaned and painted. Eby got up this dinner and hung window shades. We went home tonight and ran out of gas and Eby pushed the machine from the sink hole to the mill.

4/17/27 Sunday
Went to Hershey's communion and to my home for dinner. Edna and Mart were there too. Papa went to serve communion with Landis Hershey. Came home and did the work and went to Paradise church. Emma went along. Elizabeth went for arbutus to Holtwood. Rather cold day.

4/21/27 Thursday
Did up my work and went over and cut potatoes till dinner. Did up the dinner dishes. Papa and Mamma brought some seed potatoes and some of my parlor suit. They did some jobs around the house and I went over and cut potatoes again. Charlie went along home. Had a heavy gust. Made pies.

4/22/27 Friday
Rained all day and was cold. I varnished the sitting room and scrubbed the dining chairs. Mother Hostetter came over this P.M. I cleaned up the kitchen and did the scrubbing and dusted the house. Made noodles.

4/29/27 Friday
Mabel and Papa came down and painted the peepie house, green room, put up the parlor shelf and oiled the front steps. Showery day. Eby planted the potatoes and shot a big rat. His folks went to Lancaster and brought Eby's things and a comb case and candy for us.

5/3/27 Tuesday
Painted the peepie house second coat. Elizabeth came over and we painted the porches second coat. Painted the back stairs and attic door. Washed my head. Went home for the rest of the peepies and some notions. Paul came along.

5/8/27 Sunday
The peepies are dying faster. We went to Hershey's S.S. and back here to tend the peepies and up home for dinner. Took Elizabeth along. Came home and did the work and to Hershey's for Revival Meeting. The house was filled.

5/21/27 Saturday
Captain Lindbergh sailed yesterday in his plane from New York to Paris and landed safely about 4:00 P.M., which has made him world famous. Went to church.

5/29/27 Sunday
Went to Uncle Emanuel Martin's. Had a nice time boating and singing down along the creek. Aunt Ada has a beau. We went to Paradise.

5/30/27 Monday
Eby worked till 11:00 and I did the washing and brought the clothes in and we went to Uncle Charlie's for dinner. Had a splendid dinner. Edna and Mart were very late because they were chasing chicken thieves.

6/10/27 Friday
Had first peas and new potatoes.

6/17/27 Friday
Got up early and left for Jack Fenninger's at 5:45 to pull tobacco plants, did not get enough so we went up home for 2 thousand more. Planted over 2 acres. I hauled water and planted the headlands.

No entries from 6/19-10/29

10/30/27 Sunday
Went to Hershey's Church and to John Ranck's for dinner. Got first pullet eggs. Went up home this evening.

11/1/27 Tuesday
Husked corn this P.M. and got the hay fever. Ironed this A.M.

11/2/27 Wednesday
Husked corn this A.M. and went out again this evening. My head feels as big as a bushel basket.

11/6/27 Sunday
Had ice cream to make and chickens to stuff, cranberry sauce to make and was kept real busy all the A.M. making dinner for Eby's parents, the girls, David and Irvin's. Real cold and stormy. Amy, Mabel and the three little boys came down a little while this evening for ice cream. Our first Sunday night at home.

11/7/27 Monday
Had first real killing frost. Very cold and stormy all day. Eby husked corn. I washed and ironed some this A.M. and took in some celery this afternoon and finished ironing this evening.

11/8/27 Tuesday
Went out before sunrise to husk corn. Husked this P.M. till 4:00 when it was so cold and snowing so fast I quit and dug out the rest of the celery. After Eby shot a rabbit he was willing to carry the celery to the cellar with the lantern.

11/9/27 Wednesday
Cleaned up the kitchen. Eby planted the celery in the cellar and then swept it up again. This P.M. I went down to Wanner's for information. Stopped in home on my way back. They have not found Clarence Leaman yet.

11/10/27 Thursday
Went out to the corn fields early and went out after dinner again till dark. We got 71 shocks. It was a very pleasant day, damp and cloudy and not too cold. Looked for company, but no one came.

11/12/27 Saturday
Baked pies and washed up the kitchen and went to the corn field at 8:00 A.M. Had beef and cabbage and raspberry pie which Eby's mother gave us. I dusted the house this dinner and went out again. We got 67 shocks. Came in a little before dark and scrubbed. Washed Eby's and Elizabeth's heads.

11/13/27 Sunday
I got up at 8:00, mixed pumpkin pies and baked them. Left one fall, broke the dish and smashed the pie. Eby washed and wiped the dishes. We went up home and took baths and I made dinner for the boys, Edna and Mart, and Mabel. Eby came home and did the work and brought the little boys along and came up again for me. They brought Grammy along when they came from Mechanics Grove.

11/15/27 Tuesday
Went out before sunrise and husked till after sunset. Got 62 shocks. Had vegetable soup for dinner. Edna Sensenig and Aaron Eaby have license to wed. A very balmy day.

11/17/27 Thursday
Started to rain early and Eby took out the lima bean poles. I mended and cleaned the sewing machine drawers. It kept raining all day and this evening it gusted. The streams overflowed their banks. We took the eggs up and went up home for advice about farming as Eby started bargain this morning.

11/18/27 Friday
Clear, wet and cold. We went to the cornfield. I went out again this P.M. Cleaned our bedroom this dinner. We quit early and went with Nora and Rod to Lancaster. After having a shocking experience I am well pleased. Very cold.

11/19/27 Saturday
Very cold and stormy. 12 eggs. Eby went to the cornfield and I did my work up quick and went up home and along to Lancaster with Mamma and Jay. Did some shopping and made some future arrangements on Lime Street. We spent the evening at home. Mabel is home now.

11/22/27 Tuesday
We finished husking corn till 3:00 P.M. and got 59 shocks. Eby cleaned the leaves out of the rain spouts and trimmed the hedges and helped me clean the yard. I took out the dahlia roots. This evening I did the ironing and made potato chips. Eby

and his father went to the squire's and made a written agreement. Eby went to see Earl Jones.

11/23/27 Wednesday
I was very busy. Cleaned the house, did the scrubbing, made a cake and pies, cleaned the celery and a goose which weighed 14 lbs. Eby took the eggs up to Troop's, had 6 dozen. Got 15 today. Got a letter from Mary Mehl that she is coming. Elmer Buckwalter brought Biz home from Spelling Bee.

11/25/27 Friday
Did up the morning work and went up home for the day. Started 2 quilts. Eby picked up stones and hauled in nubbins. Esther and Granville's house is going up. Cloudy and warm. Got 16 eggs.

11/28/27 Monday
Cloudy and raining. I made silk patches ready for a small comfort. Eby took up 8 bushel of turnips and I washed them. Didn't get done till 7:30. Eby went down to see Ephraim Wenger and he wants $50.00 per month. Got 19 eggs.

12/1/27 Thursday
Much colder. 26 eggs. Packed Eby's lunch and he went to fill up the graveyard. I went up home and went along with Mamma, Jay, and the little boys to Lancaster and finished my Xmas shopping and went to see Dr. Stoler. Got home at 5:00 and Eby had supper on. We ate and went with a load of turnips to see Abe Metzler's boy.

12/6/27 Tuesday
Mamma called early this morning and said that we shall both come up and help butcher today. We finished up till 9:00 P.M. and came home. Stopped on our way to pay Mart Clark for the hog. It was a very beautiful day. Got 26 eggs.

12/8/27 Thursday
Baked pies this morning. Had sauer kraut and rhubarb pie for dinner. I hemmed my new comfort this A.M. and worked at my rug this P.M. Eby took the eggs up this evening. We had 17 dozen at 50 cents. I worked at the catalogue while he was gone.

12/10/27 Saturday
Did the cleaning, worked at my rug and brought in some turnips and the rest of our cabbage. Fixed our little ice cream freezer in a bucket. We took our baths this evening and went to bed about 10:00. They hauled a load of fodder. Getting warmer. Sam Slaymaker had a wonderful fox chase. About 100 horses passed here.

12/11/27 Sunday
We slept till nine, had pork roast with baked potatoes, filling, baked beans, celery, pickles, peaches and ice cream on mince pie, and we ate till we hurt. Sleeting this

morning, but is much warmer and turned to rain. Emma and Biz were over this P.M. Bob Neff came to see Biz. We retired early.

12/13/27 Tuesday
Still foggy and cloudy and the clothes are still out. I worked at my rug, made neck ties and a lamp shade. It is very warm. Eby cleaned the chicken houses after supper, and I carried the lantern to bring over straw. Made out an order for Sears Roebuck.

12/16/27 Friday
Rained all day and I stayed in the house and kept dry as I had a poor night's rest. Cleaned up our bedroom and patched a cushion top. Got 35 eggs. Eby cleaned out the lower chicken house. It cleared about 5:00 P.M.

12/19/27 Monday
Very stormy and coldest day of winter. I washed and Eby and I left at 8:30 to help Irvin's shred fodder. Helped Mary with cooking and made Jane a dress. Got home about 4:30. Washline was on the ground, pump was frozen solid and the celery was frozen. Nothing was injured.

12/21/27 Wednesday
They hauled the fodder in. I made two little pillows and finished up my cushion for bedroom rocker. Had sauer kraut for dinner. Cleaned and made 120 bunches of celery for peddling. Still cold and stormy. Made Xmas packages.

12/23/27 Friday
Got up early and arrived in Lancaster about 8:30 with 20 rock hens and some celery and tramped and peddled till five o'clock when we had all the chickens sold and most of the celery. I went to see Dr. Stohler. We stripped tobacco this evening. Got alcohol put in the radiator.

12/24/27 Saturday
Cleaned up the house and canned 4 quarts of celery. Made preparations for company. Eby cleaned out the chicken houses and helped to carry over straw. We went over and exchanged Xmas gifts. Irvin's were there too. Came home, took our baths and went to bed.

12/25/27 Sunday
Xmas Day. We made ice cream and got things ready for dinner. Papa and Mamma came. We had roast chicken, filling, sweet potatoes, corn, celery, kippered cherries, cakes, nuts, fruit, candy, dates and figs. Had a nice quiet visit. Nice day. Cold.

12/26/27 Monday
Got up late. I did the washing and Eby stripped tobacco till it was time to go for our Xmas dinner up home. Casper's, Mart's, Uncle Elmer's and us were there. The

old blind man was there for his dinner too. Eby stripped tobacco. I went over to his home as Ellis' were still there just to be sociable. Eby was displeased.

12/28/27 Wednesday
I made pies. Mamma came along with Jay when he came to haul manure this morning. We got the two quilts over half done. Much warmer and clouding up. Got 46 eggs. I soaked my feet and read this evening.

12/30/27 Friday
Finished my white quilt. Made cold water soap. Read and took a big nap this P.M. Sold the tobacco to Pflanner and Weaver for 18-1/2 plus four. Very damp and foggy all day.

12/31/27 Saturday
Foggy and raining all day. I swept and dusted the whole house, did all the scrubbing. Made three pillowcases. Got an order from Sears and Roebuck. They took down all the tobacco but one acre. I went over and phoned home. Eby cleaned the chicken houses. Got 48 eggs. David has given up the girls entirely and retires early every night. We took our baths in the living room as usual.

1928

1/1/28 Sunday
Went up home for dinner. Jay was nursing imaginary mumps. We got home about 4:30. Were invited to Henry Denlinger's for dinner. Spent the evening around the fire eating nuts and reading.

1/2/28 Monday
Very cold. Things froze up. I did the washing and hung it on the front porch. Mother Hostetter came over this P.M. I put my little crib comfort in, and she helped me quilt it. Eby broke the corn stalks, got done about 12. Got 48 eggs again.

1/12/28 Thursday
Got up at 1:00 a.m. with a pain, put things in order and left for the hospital about 3:30. Hard day on my imagination. Read and visited and had a real nice interesting day. Eby went home at dinner time and come back this evening and brought me along home, sweet home.

1/16/28 Monday
I washed and ironed and mended. Had to dry the clothes in the house as it began to rain and freeze before dinner. Very icy. Eby's mother was over a few minutes. Got 53 eggs. Eby stripped tobacco alone this evening as it was too icy for me.

1/19/28 Thursday
Did up my morning work and helped strip tobacco. We did 110 lathe by 4 pm. Had three visitors in the stripping room, which caused me much embarrassment. Eby took the eggs up and brought Biz from the car as it was raining hard all day.

1/20/28 Friday
I swept the cellar and put the turnips in dirt, shelled the rest of my dried lima beans. Took a nap, finished reading "Barriers Burned Away." Cleared off last night and has been very stormy and much colder today. Father Hostetter has the grippe. Sewed this evening. Cleaned our bedroom.

1/22/28 Sunday
Beautiful cold day. The wind has fallen. Did not rest so good last night. Killed chicken for dinner. Eby wiped the dishes. He read, and I slept and read. Got a pain about 4 p.m. and then I got some more, and when Eby came over from doing the work we got ready and came in here about 7:00. A variety followed and finished up with a baby girl at 11:50 p.m.

1/23/28 Monday
Did not wash. Slept a little while and lay very quiet. The ward is full with Mrs. Herr, Mrs. Messerman, Mrs. Stubel, and myself. There was another baby directly after midnight last night. Mabel was here this p.m. and Eby and Mamma came in tonight. Very warm place. Had a big breakfast.

1/24/28 Tuesday
Slept about an hour last night. Two new babies came and not so quietly. Had sauce breakfast. Cereal, egg, two pieces toast, milk and tea. Soup and broth and fruit and pudding for dinner and supper. Mother Hostetter was in sewing for the hospital and came up to see me. Mary Martin, Eby, and Biz were here. Mary Martin brought baby's first gift, a comb and brush. Got my oil this morning.

1/26/28 Thursday
Had sauce breakfast and solid food for dinner. 11 visitors. Eby and Emma came in. Biz brought me a cineraria and Emma a cap and socks for the baby. The baby is doing fine. Dr. said I could have a back rest tomorrow. Eggs were 40 cents. Eby's father is no better.

1/28/28 Saturday
Snowing very fast all day. It is over a foot deep, biggest snow in twenty years. Didn't get a bit of company. Mr. Herr was the only visitor in this ward. I washed my hands, face and combed my hair. Sat up all day. Mrs. Herr gave me a magazine to read. Eby phoned he would not be in.

1/30/28 Monday
New baby girl came about 10 last night. Mrs. Herr got out for 20 minutes. Dr. Stoler said Rhoda is a real prize baby. She gained 2 1/2 oz. over her birth weight, which was 7 lbs 10 oz. Eby came in and we had a half hour to ourselves. Snow moving is a slow process.

2/1/28 Wednesday
Slept like a rock last night. Had my bath and got up and nursed the baby. Walked all around and exercised all I could and felt real strong after. I took an hours rest in bed after dinner. They came for me about 4:00 and took me up home. Stood the trip fine. Baby slept all the way. Travelling worst in Lancaster. The proud father stayed for supper.

2/2/28 Thursday
Baby slept good and so did I. Took it easy all day and felt good. Amy kept busy at her new dress. The little boys like the baby. Amy and the three boys went to Red Hill to sled. Sledding is very good. Eby came up this evening and held the baby for the first.

2/4/28 Saturday
I got up after the kitchen was cleaned and had a heap of pain all day from hemorrhoids. Eby came up this evening and went up to Dr. Sharp's for some medicine. Amy finished her new dress. Mabel, Amy and Clarence went to Kinzer this evening. The snow is melting.

2/7/28 Tuesday
Amy, Papa and Mamma took Landis and Lizzie Hershey along to ordination at Millersville. Jay and I kept house. They came home about 1:00, and Jay and Margie got here at the same time. They gave a dollar for the baby. Suffered with the piles. Rained. Eby came up. Amy, Jay, Landis and Paul went to Hickory Grove Spelling Bee. Big boys won prizes.

2/20/28 Monday
I missed my breakfast. The girls washed, Mamma painted the coach again, and went along with Papa to Lancaster and got me some things, which they brought down this evening as Eby came for Rhoda and me after dinner. We put things in order again. Nice cold day. Irvin and Biz stopped in for a while.

2/22/28 Wednesday
Eby cleaned the steer stable and went to the mill. Did the baby's wash and the usual housework. Emma brought us some beef, which was very delicious. The baby was very good this evening and sleeps well at night.

2/23/28 Thursday
Eby went to a sale over on Mine Hill this P.M. The baby did not sleep so well today, but was extra good this evening. I read a chapter in my book, "Little Women," to Eby. Elizabeth was over this P.M. She did not have any work.

2/26/28 Sunday
Baby got up when I did. Everything seemed twisted. The steers broke out. The old truck would not start. Dave came over before we had our breakfast Uncle Charlie's Grammy, Helen and Aunt Cora were coming in the P.M., and they did before we finished our lunch. Baby was just very cross from 4 to 7. Had our supper about seven. Papa, Mamma and the little boys came in the midst of it all.

2/28/28 Tuesday
Eby worked all day. I had a very big wash. Eby hung it on the line. I am taking the mumps. Baby was fussy this P.M. Eby's mother came over to see how I am. I did not tell her about the mumps, as I didn't want it to be discussed at Sewing Circle.

2/29/28 Wednesday
Mumps are more prominent. Got a half beef to put up this evening. Eby went up home to state our condition and found the three boys in bed with the mumps. Charlie came along down to help and Eby did his best, which was very good. Nice day.

3/1/28 Thursday
Baby excellent last night. Got things done up this morning, and Papa and Mamma came down to cut up the meat and took it along home to do up. Eby went to Dick Hershey's sale. Many changes have taken place since last March 1st when I came home from the Hartman's.

3/22/28 Thursday
Cloudy to begin with, then blowed, snowed, hailed, rained, thundered and lightninged, but was not so bad this P.M. Had big crowd and big dinner. Amy, Mamma and Edna kept the baby. Mary Groff and John Harsh's were in too. Biz and Ruth Hershey were over this evening.

3/24/28 Saturday
Our First Wedding Anniversary. I did the usual work. Sewed this p.m. Took Rhoda over while I milked. We took our baths and went up home to exchange two clucks at Mary King's that did not want to set. Very nice warm day.

3/26/28 Monday
Beautiful morning. Got my washing all up before Rhoda got awake at 9:15. She was good all day. I ironed this P.M. Took the baby over while I milked. Eby is counting. It cost us $2789.92 to start farming. Silas Hershey's baby died.

3/31/28 Saturday
Determined to discipline my hired girl Ruth. I began and she got sick at me. After vomiting all over the kitchen, including the dishpan, I sent her to bed and she stayed there till dinner. We decided to take her home and Mamma offered to take her so we missed preparatory and took her up. Paul came along down.

4/3/28 Tuesday
Did my morning work. Eby and Richard hauled manure all day. This P.M. I made garden. Planted peas, spinach, carrots, onions, radishes, potatoes and lettuce. A very nice day. Papa and Mamma brought Ruth back this evening. The baby was fussy.

4/4/28 Wednesday
Ruth did better, but was very tired. We cleaned the yard and I did some sewing. Tried some of the baby's clothing on her. Eby and Dick went for tobacco seed. They hauled manure. I sewed the tobacco muslin up this P.M.

4/5/28 Thursday
Cleaned the attic and made a petticoat for Rhoda. Ruth was cross and wept. Eby and Richard finished the manure, had a total of 175 loads. Had 210 lbs of milk. The baby was good. The men dug tobacco bed. A very warm, balmy day.

4/16/28 Monday
Did the washing before Rhoda got up. Washed in the kitchen. Did the ironing this P.M. and mended some this evening. Took Rhoda along to milk and she cried all the time I didn't stand beside her. Phoned my store order. Mrs. Usner was over looking for her chickens.

4/27/28 Friday
Cleaned the peepie house. 17 died so far. Cleaned the sitting room, but it rained too much to clean the rugs, so it isn't fixed up yet. Baked pies and worked at my bead bag. Very wet. Soaked my corns.

4/29/28 Sunday
Rhoda weighed 15 ½ lbs. and was good at Hershey's Church. Eby and I had our Sunday dinner together as in days of yore. We went home. Edna and Mart came too. Took some pictures. Eby and Mart went up to Witmer's for Ruth and we spent Sunday evening at home.

5/4/28 Friday
Very warm. Was busy all day doing up odds and ends. Did the scrubbing and stirred up little cakes and made rhubarb sauce. Ruth told me some back talk. The baby was fussy with the intense heat. Men are busy getting corn ground ready.

5/10/28 Thursday
Did the morning work and cleaned the cellar. White washed the basement and part of the cellar and the grape arbor. Ruth had a slow balky spell. We all went down to Galen's for the Food Demonstration in the truck. Made noodles. Got home about 11 P.M.

5/14/28 Monday
Ruth stayed up home all night and Mother took her to Lancaster and bought her a lot of new clothes. They brought her down this evening, and I got a lecture on my impatience and unkindness. I washed and ironed. Rhoda was fussy. I took her along while I milked.

5/27/28 Sunday
As our machine had wet paint and because we were not invited to go with any of the in-laws, we did not get to church. Went over to Eby's home for dinner. Ellis's and Uncle Frank's were there too. Eva gave Rhoda a dollar. Uncle Elmer's came down this evening. Aunt Minnie brought a crib blanket.

6/7/28 Thursday
I did the morning work and mowed the yard. Canned 1 pint of asparagus. Amy and mother were down this evening and brought a high chair for Rhoda, some cosmos and scarlet sage. Adrian brought me some fire branches.

6/19/28 Tuesday
Eby and Richard shot two rats this morning. I cleaned a chicken for dinner. Amy brought Mother down, and she helped me fine with the strawberries. We had a dandy shower this evening. I planted celery. We set some rat nip. Rhoda was good.

7/2/28 Monday
I washed and ironed and milked after supper. Richard jagged his arm on a nail. His brother Tom came to help haul in the hay. Eby mowed. Nice warm day. Jay's had a baby girl at noon.

7/14/28 Saturday
Took it easy, finished up the work and made a cake. Zelma was over, and Mabel and Mother came down to help me start a 7-plait rug. I washed my head and Eby's and we took our baths and went to bed. Richard went to Intercourse festival. John Rohrer's baby drowned in the creek last evening. The water was high.

7/19/28 Thursday
I helped to mow 5 loads of wheat. We finished about 7:30 and Eby went to Kinzer and bought ice cream to celebrate. Zelma was here for dinner and supper. Had chicken. Richard has a sore foot and a very bad headache.

8/6/28 Monday
Too warm to wash, so put things away and took it easy. Did not feel so spunky. Eby and Dick topped first tobacco and mowed weeds. Richard was stung with a bee. Sowed the turnip seed.

8/11/28 Saturday
Grandmother Kurtz's 95th Birthday. Did the scrubbing and canned some pickle and made a sponge cake, applesauce and dumplings. Elizabeth came over for a while this P.M. I took my bath before supper and we went up to Granville Clark's this evening. They live perfectly scrumptious. Cloudy all day. Milk check was $227.

8/19/28 Sunday
We went to Hershey's. Ira Landis preached. We went to Eby's home for dinner. They had the family for a final dinner at the farm. Mother had the Hersh reunion. Took our weekly walk to see the farm. Nice day.

9/12/28 Wednesday
Busy

9/23/28 Sunday
Went to White Horse Church and home for dinner and to Galen's this P.M. Jay's were there too, and then men folks talked church and did not agree. Got home late, did our work, and went to bed.

9/26/28 Wednesday
Eby and I got up about 4:00 and moved things over to Eby's home and got the fire made and the cider on. Had 36 gallons of cider, 11 buckets of snitz and 60 lbs. of sugar. Got 23 crocks of apple butter. Eby took Mother home after supper.

9/27/28 Thursday
The men cut corn. I tied up the apple butter and carried it to the garret over there.

10/1/28 Monday
I did the washing. The shinerhaunis gave $1.00 for the dead cow. Mother called and said I should come up and go along to see the farm. She is anxious to occupy. I did not like the place. Very nice day. I got the wash ready to iron.

10/9/28 Tuesday
Made pies and applesauce and cleaned a chicken for pot pie. The turkey buzzards got it first and ate the insides. Things seemed to go wrong all day. I picked the lima beans all off and the ripe and green tomatoes so the patch would be ready to seed.

10/18/28 Thursday
Cleaned the parlor and our bedroom. There was a peddler here who got contrary when I would not buy stockings and would not sell me anything else. Old Pete, our

mule, died last night. The men cut and husked corn. Began to rain about 5:00. Got 10 eggs. Rhoda fell out of bed.

10/26/28 Friday
Cleaned the kitchen for house cleaning. The big dirigible Graf Zeppelin from Germany has given up on its flight west over the United States and is going back to Germany before winter sets in. Clear, cold and stormy.

10/31/28 Wednesday
Spiced and canned more pears and planted the celery and some lettuce. Buried the beets and carrots. We got up early and ate our breakfast, then Eby and I milked and Dick went to the cornfield. Amy and Mother came down to help snitz pears. Mabel came on the 15 of 3 car. Made 8 buckets.

11/1/28 Thursday
Got up early and Richard gunned all day, and Eby till dinner and didn't get a rabbit. Mother and Amy came down and helped to boil pear butter and soap and wash and cook the Larro bags. Got 13 crocks of pear butter.

11/4/28 Sunday
Very rainy all day, and Eby didn't think it fit to go to church, but it was. We went up home for dinner, had chicken and pheasant. Charlie was sick and Mother had neuralgia. Rhoda has her second tooth.

11/6/28 Tuesday
Did the ironing and baked pumpkin pies. Eby and his dad hauled in corn. I tied up my pear butter and carried it to the garret. Emptied the lye. Nice mild day. Election Day. Herbert Hoover was elected instead of Al Smith for which we are glad.

11/21/28 Wednesday
Amy came down and we papered our bedroom, and it went just fine. Landis came along and kept house. Eby's mother was down and boiled soap. We got done about 5 p.m. It was very cool this morning, but the sun shone bright this p.m. Got 7 eggs.

12/24/28 Monday
I washed, ironed, and did most of the mending. Wrapped my Christmas gifts and washed up the kitchen. Papa and the little boys came down this evening and brought Dick a watch for Christmas. Eby cut his eyelid making kindling to start fire in the other house. 42 eggs. 1327 lathe of tobacco stripped.

12/25/28 Tuesday
Did up my morning work, started to read a book. We went to Eby's home for dinner. Left for my home about 3:00 and took some pictures. Very nice day. Not so cold. Came home, did the work, and went to services at Kinzers Church. Got lots of nice

presents, among them a roast pan, jardinière, candlesticks, apron, calendar, mixing bowl, linen towel, motto, milk dipper, sauce pan and bath mat.

1929

1/1/29 Tuesday
Very cloudy and rained all day. Eby and Richard were taking down tobacco here and at Clarence Weir's. I mended and made a lattice flower box. Eby and Richard both had a drink of hard cider. I had a toothache. 49 eggs. Milk check $80.98.

1/4/29 Friday
I worked at my rug, swept upstairs and made potato chips. Finished my mending. There were 23 deaths in the paper and the flu is very bad. Mother is better. Clifford is sick. Got 60 eggs.

1/7/29 Monday
I washed and ironed and Eby and Richard sorted 20 bushel sec. potatoes for his mother at $.25 per bushel and took them over this evening. Eby and I went up to his home. Eby was at the stock yards and bought a cow for $100. Had a tobacco looker this P.M.

1/8/29 Tuesday
Very cold. 12 above. Brought my begonias down in the kitchen. Did up my morning work and made the men's dinner, and Rhoda and I went up home and Mother got one comfort out and put another in. Had 30 dozen eggs at 37 cents. An airplane broke the endurance record by being in the air 7 days and nights.

1/11/29 Friday
Cloudy. Helped to strip tobacco and this evening I helped tie up as Richard went for a haircut. Rhoda was very tired and sleepy. Gave her some milk to drink for supper. She can play a mouth organ. We stripped 130 lathe.

1/13/29 Sunday
We went to White Horse. Margie invited us last evening to come down for dinner so there we went. Galen's were there this P.M. It snowed a good squall this P.M. and got fierce cold this evening. We hugged the fire. Abe Beiler died. Warren Eby's have a baby boy.

1/19/29 Saturday
Cleaned the kitchen. Washed the Ford, dressed three chickens and made things ready for Sunday dinner. Did the scrubbing. Had the outside door open most all day. It was so warm. Got done early and Irvin's came over this evening. Eby and Rhoda got haircuts.

1/21/29 Monday
Washed and it froze and dried very slowly. So I stripped tobacco this P.M. It was cloudy and cold all day. The highest price paid for tobacco was 25 x 8 to Henry Eby on Saturday. I got the clothes ready to iron this evening and hung some on the clothes rack.

1/22/29 Tuesday
Ironed this A.M. Rhoda is 1 year old. She crawled about half way up the stairs this A.M. I stripped tobacco this P.M. We had oysters to celebrate her birthday. It began to snow about 4:30 and everything was covered deep before dark.

1/23/29 Wednesday
One of our steers was dizzy this morning and after the Dr. advised butchering it and Jay and Galen didn't want to, but we decided to kill it for ourselves and sold Irvin's half. Eby's Dad butchered it this P.M. I helped strip this A.M. and cut and started a dress for Rhoda this P.M. Put a box on Eby's sled and took Rhoda sledding. Cleaned the trype.

1/24/29 Thursday
Eby's Dad came down and cut up the beef. Helped strip this A.M. Had trype cooking nearly all day. Made ginger cakes and a mince pie. Took Rhoda sledding and upset her. Eby took his new blue cow to New Holland. He got $1.00 more than cost and the hauling and commission was a loss.

1/26/29 Saturday
I made the mince meat, got 9 quarts. Galen was here for dinner, helping strip tobacco. I intended to help this P.M. but Elizabeth and Emma came down so I took off. Put the pickle on the meat. Beautiful icy day. All took our baths and went to bed. Rhoda used her chair 3 times, once for both duties.

2/3/29 Sunday
We went to Hershey's and got there for part of S.S. Edna and Mart were there and went up home for dinner, and we did too. After we came home and did our work. Mabel and Clarence were announced this morning. Had ice cream for supper. Nice cold day.

2/6/29 Wednesday
Did the ironing this A.M. and Eby took a sudden notion to buy mules and trade two old horses in on a pair of 3 and 4-year-old mules. The men brought them this P.M. I helped strip tobacco. Nice day.

2/8/29 Friday
Started to butcher about 8:00 and finished by 3:30, washing up and all. It went fine. Hog dressed 295. Got 6 crocks of pudding and a stand of lard. Took Rhoda over this A.M. and she slept this P.M. Warm and muddy day. Eby's dad was down.

2/9/29 Saturday

Put up my meat and cooked the trype. Got 7 quarts of steak, 2 quarts of ribs, a crock of back bone and nine quarts of sauer kraut. Washed up the kitchen after dinner and Mabel and Amy came before I was done. We talked a bookfull. It rained from 3:00 on till night. Took baths and went to bed.

2/10/29 Sunday

We were too lazy to go to church. Did our work and went to John Hersh's for dinner. Had a good dinner and a nice time. Went up home this evening. 71 eggs.

2/12/29 Tuesday

Mabel and Clarence were married this morning and left on a trip to Florida. I stripped tobacco and made pies and rice pudding. Ironed this P.M. Irvin helped strip tobacco. Eby and Richard made two milking stools this evening. I made scrapple and pig feet jelly. 147 lathe. 73 eggs.

2/13/29 Wednesday

I helped strip tobacco all day. Eby's dad helped this P.M. We got 240 lathe. I cleaned the milk house after dinner. The Raleigh man was here. I bought an 11 oz. bottle of vanilla for $1.00. Cold east wind all day. Made pig foot jelly this evening.

2/14/29 Thursday

Stripped tobacco this A.M. The men got things fixed to suit the milk inspector this P.M., so I had off. Mrs. Usner came over. I made Rhoda a petticoat. A nice day, springlike. Rhoda got a valentine from Donald.

2/20/29 Wednesday

Finished stripping tobacco till 5:00, had 5830 lathe. Adrian stopped in this A.M. Mabel and Clarence are having the time of their lives. Everything was covered with snow this morning and has been cold all day. Made noodles. Eby sold a hog this morning. Dressed 375 lbs. at 11 cents a lb.

2/22/29 Friday

The men cleaned the steer stable and hitched the mule when they got done. I finished a dress for Rhoda and made oatmeal cakes. It was 4 above zero this morning. I took Rhoda sledding when she got up.

2/27/29 Wednesday

Did up my work. Eby went to the freight station for Mabel's oil stove and I took it and our kitchen table up home and helped to make ready. Margie Hershey was here all day making angel food. We went over to Irvin's this evening for haircuts. Rhoda cried. Very muddy and bride and groom arrived about 2:30 with a full machine.

2/28/29 Thursday
Very muddy and raining. Eby took two dressed hogs away, 4 cents live weight. We went to the reception. Everybody got there. She got a nice lot of presents. Richard greased harness.

3/1/29 Friday
I scrubbed 3 rooms in the other house. My knees are very sore. Swept upstairs this evening. Rhoda was very good today. She is nearly weaned. Eby and Richard went to Sam Eby's sale. The highest price paid for a cow was $500.00 and her calf $180.00.

3/2/29 Saturday
Finished my cleaning and it snowed all day, a very wet snow. Eby worked at the other house this A.M. and with a lot of persuasion I got him to miss Ross Aucker's sale and to work at it this P.M. I helped too. It cleared off this evening.

3/5/29 Tuesday
Eby was carpentering at the other house. It rained all day. Eby bought nine little pigs at $2.50 per head. They went to a sale at Nine Points and bought a crib for $1.00.

3/7/29 Thursday
Very stormy all day. We butchered a porker. Jay, Mother, Amy and Mabel came down to help. Mabel painted and Amy cooked and they scrubbed up the sitting room over there. Amy stayed down all night to help with the meat.

3/8/29 Friday
Amy and I canned 8 quarts of steak, 9 quarts of sauer kraut, 1 gallon of back bone and 6 quarts of sausage. We moved the Sunday dishes and cleaned up the kitchen. Rhoda can walk real good. There was lots of damage done by the storm. Richard took Amy home. Eby dragged the road.

3/14/29 Thursday
It rained by times all day and was very damp. We moved Eby's parents. Mabel, Landis, Papa and Mother helped with everything. Went as good as could be expected. We had no water or drain closer than the barn.

3/23/29 Saturday
Cleaned up the kitchen, made a cake, pie, rhubarb sauce and red eggs and red meat. Showery all day. Went to White Horse preparatory services this P.M. and up to Eby's home this evening. Very warm. New conference rules are: No girls going to seashore to work. No Farm Women members. Not to use the term Reverend.

3/26/29 Tuesday
Did my ironing and stuck some onions, planted spinach, red beets, lettuce, carrots and radishes in the back yard bed. The men hauled manure. Mabel is busy getting her house ready to move.

4/2/29 Tuesday
Did up my work, took Rhoda up to Eby's Mother and went to Clarence Groff's setting up moving. Eby, Richard and Nelson came over for dinner. Charlie came along with me home a while till the others came by. I did my ironing this evening. Nice day. The masons were here and fixed the cistern.

4/4/29 Thursday
Washed my wedding dress. Finished painting the commode and Rhoda's bed and put up some curtains. I went out to make more garden and till I had a row of carrots planted it was raining. Eby buried the asparagus roots. We went up to Mart's this evening.

4/5/29 Friday
Made kalomine ready and cold water soap. This P.M. Eby and I kalomined the wash house. I cleaned silver ware and made pie dough this evening. It rained most all day and we got a nice lot of rain water.

4/6/29 Saturday
I cleaned up the kitchen and Emma came about 10:00 A.M. and did the scrubbing and cleaned the yard all for glory. I finished up the wash house and did the rest of the cleaning. Made a cake and pies before breakfast. We took baths and went to bed.

4/11/29 Thursday
Still cloudy and rained a few showers. I finished the painting. Had the toothache last night that I could not sleep. Mother had a sick spell, but is better today. Bought a dozen herring for 35 cents and had some for supper. Eby's Mother and Dad stopped for vinegar.

4/12/29 Friday
Rained most all night and was very showery, cloudy and cold all day. I cleaned up the house, made a pie and noodles. Put the pad on the stairs. I went up home this evening to get Rhoda's chaff bag filled. Had a flat tire on the way up at the garage.

4/17/29 Wednesday
Eby washed the breakfast dishes and I took Rhoda up home early and went along with them to Lancaster to do some shopping. Bought a Windsor rocker for $9.95 and a coat size 3 for Rhoda, but it's too small. Mabel and Clarence stopped in here on their way up home.

4/19/29 Friday
Made pies, prunes and rhubarb sauce. Eby finished filling the cesspool and put the lid on and I cleaned up the house. The Maytag man left a Maytag here and is going to wash next week for us. We all went to Irvin's this evening for haircuts.

4/23/29 Tuesday
The men cut wood all day. Sold the wool. 31 lbs. for $10.85. Sold a cow for $140.00, $5.00 more than cost. The Maytag man was here and washed for me and gave me a chance and left it here. The men were working on the milkhouse. Rhoda and I went up home for some herring fish after supper.

4/25/29 Thursday
I helped Nelson finish cutting the seed potatoes and it began to rain just as Eby was ready to start planting. I started to draw a pattern for a spread on Rhoda's crib. The men played figmill when they were done.

5/1/29 Wednesday
Started to work in the yard but the rain soon chased me in and I made potato chips. Worked at Rhoda's crib quilt.

5/3/29 Friday
Had heavy gust, rain, hail and wind last night. I made noodles and coated candy, made rhubarb sauce and chocolate cake. They moved the peepie house. Irvin came over to help and Mary and the children spent the P.M. Mrs. Usner came too. Mabel and Clarence were here this evening.

5/5/29 Sunday
I had a pain and did not get up very early and was kept very busy all morning. Had a dinner for Dave and Minnie, Eby's parents, the girls and Jay's. It rained about dinner time. Went over to Stone's a while this evening. We played jacks and went to bed early.

5/7/29 Tuesday
Finished the ironing and pressed the men's suits. The men cleaned the steer stable and chicken house and disinfected the peepie house. Eby's dad went to the fishery and brought us two shad and two dozen herring. Papa and Mother went to Downingtown and brought us two pairs of woolen blankets.

5/13/29 Monday
Washed and Mother and Papa came down and fixed my wood box. Made two out of it. I painted it, took a rest and got the wash in and cleaned the Sunday shoes. Real nice day and rained this evening. The men wed the tobacco. Eby took a calf to Lancaster for $30.00.

5/15/29 Wednesday
I was slow with my morning work and Eby's mother came walking in about 8 o'clock. She sewed for me till about 3:30 when Eby took her home. Rhoda went along. I cleaned up some of the corners.

5/18/29 Saturday
Cleaned five chickens and finished cleaning up. Made a cake and caramel pudding. Finished planting corn. Worked in the garden, planted tomatoes, beans, peas, lima beans, corn, Japanese peas, and pickles. Rained this evening. I broke my dining table.

5/19/29 Sunday
Whit Sunday. We were very busy making ready to entertain the Hersh's. Made the ice cream and Eby had to go for more ice. Mabel came early and helped with the dinner. It rained most all day. Had 28 in all. The boys were in good time this evening.

5/24/29 Friday
Cleaned up the house. Did some washing and planted beets. A fish man was here and I got a half dozen herring. The men all went to the dentist's this evening and Rhoda and I were storm stayed in the peepie house while it gusted and rained.

6/3/29 Monday
Nelson helped me wash and I did some of the ironing. Eby went to the dentist's and got $21.00 worth of work done. He bought a bull for $57.00 and got home about 5:00. I made 13 glasses of pineapple preserves. It got very nice. Hoed a while this evening.

6/20/29 Thursday
The men replanted tobacco this P.M. and all went to the fat Cattle Show this A.M. It was 3:00 till they got home. Nelson got a new suit. Zelma went along in to her home. I cleaned downstairs and worked in the yard this P.M. Rained a big shower this evening.

6/24/29 Monday
Washed and did most of the ironing. Planted some soup beans and stuck some red beets in the sweet potato row. I picked about 1 pint of raspberries. It rained a shower before supper and the men picked me some cherries, which I seeded this evening.

6/29/29 Saturday
Did my cleaning and scrubbing. Took Rhoda to Irvin's for a haircut after dinner and brought Adrian along back to help put in 4 loads of hay. He was here for supper. Picked the raspberries and hoed in the patch. Mabel came over a while this evening. I took Richard to the Gap so he would not be late.

7/1/29 Monday
We got up early and had the washing done till 8:00. I led the horses in the hook for 3 loads and made dinner. Picked the raspberries and a bucket of peas and succored the sweet corn. Had raspberry shortcake for dinner. Showery this P.M. We all hoed tobacco this evening.

7/3/29 Wednesday
Finished the ironing till 8:00 and led the horse in the hook for three loads and made a dinner of vegetables. Succored my dahlias and broke the onions, picked raspberries and picked at other jobs. Eby started to cut and Adrian was here. I helped milk. Planted some pickles.

7/4/29 Thursday
Rhoda wore panties today for the first and did fine. Led the horse in the hook and did my work between loads. Warmer today. Finished the hay. We went up home this evening for ice cream. I helped milk. Baked ginger cakes.

7/6/29 Saturday
Did my cleaning and scrubbed. Had Adrian for supper as they cut and hauled in. Mabel came after dinner and wanted me to go along to Rod Mentzer's. Had a nice time. Isaac R's wife went out of her mind. Enos Hostetter is in jail.

7/21/29 Sunday
I got up at 8:00. Had breakfast and did up my work and had Sunday. Eby sent for the Dr. for one of the steers. We went up home for dinner. Some of the married cousins were there. Had a nice time. Eby and I took a long walk to the other end of the farm. The boys kept Rhoda.

7/25/29 Thursday
I picked some beans and it began to rain about 10:00 so I got them ready. Picked the rest just before dinner. A shower came up soon after dinner and the men came in and helped me string beans. I got 13 quarts, making 35 in all. The men caught 76 biddies and took them to New Holland this evening. Came to $32.88. Eby bought a cow. They got home about 11:00 P.M. Rhoda and I were alone.

7/28/29 Sunday
I took some pictures, made fudge and caramel pudding. Spent the rest of the A.M. reading. We had our dinner and went up to Mart Groff's to find them at Camp Meeting and the Airport. Came home by way of Puddingtown and Clarence Groff's. Spent the rest of the day reading, making supper, and milking.

7/29/29 Monday
Did the washing and brought the clothes in before dinner. Had string beans. It was very hot. Nelson worked in the garden before dinner and a while after dinner till they hauled in the alfalfa and then we had a heavy gust and good rain. I wed the pickles and picked and washed them. We bandaged the cow's tail and tied it up over her back. It's been bleeding since yesterday A.M.

8/1/29 Thursday
Nelson finished harrowing corn and they all hoed tobacco. I canned 7 quarts of rhubarb and hoed the lima beans, cantaloupes and wed the sweet potatoes. Made

root beer. Had some rain this evening. I picked cucumbers and beans for market. Had electric sweeper agent.

8/5/29 Monday
Washed, boiled soap and made about 12 glasses of blackberry jelly. Mabel stopped on her way up home and on her way back and left Charlie here. Eby was looking at the Limeville farm all this A.M. The boys went to Kinzer festival this evening.

8/6/29 Tuesday
We did the ironing. Rhoda was sick last night so I had some clothes to wash out. Charlie and I gave the dining room and parlor a weekly clean. Mother came down this P.M. and sewed some notions. Eby harrowed tobacco. He went down to Limeville. Cloudy and showery.

8/7/29 Wednesday
Began making pies and Amy came along with Mother and Papa and took my place while I went with them to Limeville to see the farm. We were cured. Charlie went to Clarence Groff's this P.M. I took a bushel of onions and planted beets, celery, spinach and beans. Eby harrowed tobacco. Planted some flowers.

8/8/29 Thursday
The Hostetter-Hershey reunion was held at Long Park. It was rather warm. Charlie and I took out more onions, have a bushel and a half. Eby harrowed tobacco and fixed fence. Picked pickles. We went to Irvin's and they were not at home, so we went up to Eby's home. Charlie and I were sick in our stomachs. Cleaned the wash house with lye.

8/10/29 Saturday
Charlie went along with Eby to the creamery this morning. I cleaned up the kitchen and did the rest of the cooking. Canned some pickles. Mabel went up home this P.M., took Charlie home and Paul stayed here till she came back. Went up to Mart Groff's this evening. Heard good news.

8/11/29 Sunday
Got up at 7:00. It was sticky and damp. Had real heavy gust this morning and phone went out and Eby fixed it this evening. Had Galen's and Irvin's to dinner. Eby made the ice cream. It was warm all day. Eby and I took a walk and just got back as Clarence's got here and it began to rain. Caleb Esh's barn was struck and burned. The men all went to the fire.

8/12/29 Monday
Got up early and went to Clarence's to help thrash. Was there for dinner and supper. We got home about 5:30 and the Maytag man was here and left us a Maytag from Papa for a present. I was much delighted. Picked the pickles. Nice day. Very warm.

8/13/29 Tuesday
Mabel brought her wash over and we washed an immense load in the Maytag. It was just grand. I never could go back to arm strong again. Mabel went home about 1:30 just as it began to rain. I ironed a little, made some custards, cleaned a chicken and helped milk. Eby was helping thrash up home.

8/16/29 Friday
Canned 7 pints of elderberries. Eby fixed the water box but it leaks yet. I cleaned up the yard and did the scrubbing. Went over to Stone's for some apples. Rhoda's bowels are out of fix and she has a little fever. Nice day. Very much cooler. Eby and Nelson took the seed wheat up home and cleaned it.

8/20/29 Tuesday
Did the ironing and dried corn. It was a beautiful cool fall day. I canned 3 quarts of pickles and now have 30 quarts. Eby topped tobacco. Rhoda's bowels and appetite are still on the blink. Nelson is getting the ground ready for seeding.

8/28/29 Wednesday
Made pies and cleaned a chicken and straightened things out. Eby's mother came about 8:00 and sewed like a white head. She made two little aprons, 2 pillow cases, bound a blanket end and helped mend. Nice day. Eby and Nelson went to the woodlot for poles.

9/3/29 Tuesday
Dried a drier full of apples. Canned 2 quarts of tomatoes and boiled my peach butter again. Scrubbed up the pantry and cleaned it up again. Mabel Rohrer Rutt died of typhoid fever. Very warm.

9/13/29 Friday
I cleaned drawers upstairs and moved some things around. This P.M. I picked green limas and dry bush limas and soup beans, seed beans, tomatoes, cantaloupes and apples. The men all went to Irvin's. Our coal came. Amy, Mother and the little boys came down and brought Rhoda new shoes and rubbers.

9/15/29 Sunday
Spent the day quietly at home. Eby helped me with the beds and comfort slips. I started to read Michael O'Halleran. Very pretty cool day. David and Minnie came down a while this evening. Mabel and Clarence stopped in on their way to church as they had a flat tire.

9/22/29 Sunday
Got up at 6:30 and made some preparations for Emma and Elizabeth when they called and said they wouldn't come. We moved about slowly all day and had a nice time. I rested and read. It was cold, cloudy and windy. We took a ride up to Eby's home when Rhoda got up.

9/30/29 Monday
Did my washing and it rained all day so I dried the starched wash in the house and left the rest in the basket. The men cut corn and cleaned the big chicken house and put the pullets in this evening. I cleaned drawers and the room closet.

10/1/29 Tuesday
Still raining so I continued drying wash in the house. Cleaned a chicken for dinner. Minnie and Dave had a baby boy born to them last night at 1 A.M. Talked to Margie twice. Did not get much done. Ironed a bit this evening and cleaned medicine cabinet.

10/5/29 Saturday
Clear and frosty. Eby's Dad helped haul off corn and was here for dinner. I made 2 quarts of cherry butter and boiled tongue and made applesauce and a cake. Cleaned out some of the flowers and did all the rest of the cleaning. Nelson mowed the yard. Canned two quarts of tomatoes. Cleaned the kitchen stairway. Took late baths and went to bed.

10/7/29 Monday
I was done washing before 9:00 and picked some string beans for dinner. Ironed off all but the starched wash before dinner. Finished up the wash house. Took Mrs. Stone 10 heads of bursted cabbage and brought in 20 heads to make sauer kraut. Picked up some apples. The men began husking corn and discing for wheat.

10/8/29 Tuesday
Washed up the nursery floor. Clear and colder. Eby started seeding. I picked up some apples and some cantaloupes. Put the clothes away and cleaned the cabbage off for sauer kraut and made it this evening. Eby picked tomatoes and covered some. Mabel and Clarence stopped in on their way home with some lettuce from Mother. Amy came down this morning for some vinegar and brought my chair.

10/10/29 Thursday
Did up my morning work and canned 5 quarts of pears. Did not feel so good. Mabel and Margie called me up. I cleaned the aluminum ware this P.M. and Eby went to John Reeser's but Annie was in town so he met the 5:00 car and she came here for supper. We did the dishes and the Dr. arrived at 5 minutes after 8 and Abram at 20 of 9. Nice and clear.

10/11/29 Friday
Eby went up for Amy this morning and she set things around when she came. I felt very good. The Dr. came this P.M. Amos Hershey's and Earl Fenninger's both had baby girls last night. Eby's Daddy was here and helped to take out potatoes.

10/12/29 Saturday
Amy did up the work and prepared things for Sunday. Mabel stopped in to see the baby on their way to preparatory services and Amy went with them and took Rhoda along up home for the weekend. Eby finished seeding

10/15/29 Tuesday
Mother got lonesome at home so she exchanged places with Amy this P.M. but she is tired of being hired girl this evening. She and Annie can't work for talking.

10/18/29 Friday
Everything went about as usual. Galen's were up this evening and they gave Abram one dollar. Abram gained back his birth weight 8 lbs and 12 oz.

10/19/29 Saturday
Amy did the work up this A.M. Jay and Landis went to the dentist and mother stayed here till they came back and then Amy went along home too. Elizabeth came this P.M. about 4:00 and took Rhoda up there over Sunday. She brought her a coat and cap and sweater and mittens.

10/22/29 Tuesday
Amy ironed and got some tomatoes ready to boil down. I got up after dinner and came downstairs for the first. It blew and rained all day. The boys took Amy home this evening. The men put 25 bushels of potatoes in the cellar.

10/24/29 Thursday
Had breakfast in bed. Gave baby a bath for the first time. I got the dinner while Annie dressed to go to Lancaster. Eby took her to the 15 of 1 car and met her on the five. Got the supper most by myself. The men are busy husking corn.

10/25/29 Friday
Came down for breakfast for the first time. My right breast is gathered and I doctored it all morning. Annie made turnips for dinner and did the washing. I gave Abram his bath. Had the Dr. for my breast this P.M. and it's better this evening. Eby took Annie home and brought Amy.

11/1/29 Friday
Amy did the weekly cleaning and did some of the yard. Amy made Rhoda a pair of bloomers and Abram a petticoat. All three of the men went gunning and got 9 rabbits. I cleaned them this P.M. Nelson and Dick went out again this P.M. and got one more. Amy went home this evening. Wash dried.

11/3/29 Sunday
Did up the morning work and had late breakfast. Dick took the milk and bumped the fence and broke the windshield. Had a quiet dinner to ourselves. Rained all day and is still warm. Esther and Granville and Abner and Elam came just as we talked of retiring a little before 8:00 P.M.

11/8/29 Friday
Cloudy all day. The men hauled fodder. I worked all day and didn't get much accomplished. Spiced 4 quarts of citron. Eby shot 2 rabbits yesterday and we had them for dinner. Gave Abram catnip tea for the first time.

11/18/29 Monday

Did not wash. It rained till 12:00 and then cleared. I puttered and cleaned up the upper truck room and got things ready to wash. The men all stripped tobacco today. They have 250 done. Park Kreider has been stealing chickens. Colder.

11/19/29 Tuesday

I washed and Eby hung it up. The boys husked corn. I ironed this P.M. and Eby went to Irvin's. Abram fell off the settee, and I thought it couldn't be, and so did he. Very stormy and partly cloudy.

11/24/29 Sunday

We were going to church but Mother called and said it was too cold and snowy for little babies, so we didn't go. Went to Eby's home for dinner. My parents were there too. David and Minnie and Robert came just as we were leaving. Spent the evening at home.

11/26/29 Tuesday

I made pies. Amy came down and helped me cook. Had men for dinner and supper. We did the ironing, canned 6 quarts of apples, and I cleaned the dining room, besides having a fussy baby. Dick dug a cesspool for the wash house and took out the celery in the garden.

11/29/29 Friday

I baked crumb pies and a chocolate cake and boiled a ham end. Cleaned up the house and got the clothes ready to wash in the Maytag. Getting fierce cold.

11/30/29 Saturday

Everything froze up this morning. 6 above. I did up my work and got ready to keep warm tonight. Eby and I went to Sem Hershey's reception tonight. My breast is sore again. I was too cold last night. Rhoda caught a cold. Mabel kept the children. Mother called and invited us for Sunday dinner.

12/1/29 Sunday

Still very cold and everybody slept warm and no frozen pipes. Mother called and said we shouldn't come as she didn't think I'm fit, so we spent a quiet, peaceful Sunday at home. Somewhat warmer this evening and clouded up.

12/6/29 Friday

I cleaned the whole house. Boiled some potatoes and made cracker pudding. Congressman W.W. Griest died at the age of seventy. Mended the old coal stove and we took baths, my first bath since Abram is here. My breast is better. Very much warmer. Did up the baby wash.

12/11/29 Wednesday

Made some crumb pies and patched and finished Rhoda's dress. Called Maggie. Her father is in bed with a nervous breakdown. Jake Zook died in the hospital after an operation for his tonsils. Cold and raw. Abram and I went over to paint Mrs. Stone's flower pots.

12/18/29 Wednesday
We butchered one hog. It weighed 228 lbs. dressed. Baby was fussy. Canned some sauer kraut with ribs. 7 quarts. Boiled soap and did the baby wash. It was very damp and rainy, so I dried it in the house. Talked to Mother this evening.

12/21/29 Saturday
Did up the baby wash and scrubbing. Very cold and freezing. Eby brought furnace coal and started the fire. I cleaned celery and made final preparations. We took our baths and went to bed at 10:00.

12/22/29 Sunday
Was busy all morning. Eby and Rhoda went to church. I made dinner for some of my cousins. Mr. and Mrs. John Martin, Mr. and Mrs. George Weaver, Lena Weaver, Emma Martin and Ada Martin. Had a pleasant visit. Put Abram in short clothes.

12/23/29 Monday
I did the washing myself for the first time since Abram is here. Got done early. Kept wood fire in the furnace and dried it in the dining room. Wrapped my gifts this P.M. and did some of the ironing. Snowed all day. Sweikert kept the stove good.

12/24/29 Tuesday
I finished the ironing. Cleaned up the kitchen and straightened things out a little. Made potato chips. Amy and the little boys came down this evening and brought our Xmas gifts and stayed with Abram while we went up to Eby's home to exchange gifts. I got a white pitcher from Eby's mother.

12/25/29 Wednesday
White Xmas. Did up our work and went up to my home to spend Xmas. The others were all home and Uncle Milt's and Grammy. Had a nice time. We gave Mother a big chair. Had Abram's picture taken for the first. Spent Xmas evening at home. The White House was on fire last night.

12/26/29 Thursday
I put my gifts away and made Abram two everyday petticoats. Amy and Mother came down this P.M. and we painted Mrs. Stone's chairs first coat. Abram was fussy this evening, and Eby cut Rhoda's hair. Warmer and the ground is covered with snow.

12/30/29 Monday
Cloudy and snowed this A.M. I did not wash. Painted Mrs. Stone's chairs. Pressed and mended suits, pants and dresses. Abram was some fussy. I made a date with the dentist. Everything set to wash early and go with Mabel to Mart Groff's in the morning.

12/31/29 Tuesday

Was done washing and nearly ready to go when Mabel called and said she didn't feel able to go. So I made up my mind to stay home and work. Painted the doll bed Eby made for Rhoda. Mother and Amy stopped by on their way to Clarence's. I did the ironing and finished about 8:00. Had 9 dozen eggs at 47 cents since last Thursday evening. The chickens have worms and a few are dying. The men have stripped 3640 lath of tobacco so far and have not had a buyer yet. Warm and damp. Started Abram on orange juice.

Ruth and Eby . . . the beginning of a family.

The Thirties

1930

1/1/30 Wednesday
Did the mending and some extra patching. This P.M. I painted Mrs. Stone's chairs the third coat. Went over and painted her breakfast table and brought the mirror along back. Talked to Mother, Mabel and Mrs. Reeser. Abram can laugh loud.

1/10/30 Friday
Did up the morning work and made dinner for the men. Mabel came over, and we went up home for dinner. Mary Groff was married yesterday, and Amy stayed up to help Edna straighten up. I went up and brought her back this P.M. and saw the many beautiful and useful gifts. It was still very warm this morning, but blowed off cold and rained this P.M. Abram weighs 14 lbs. strong.

1/22/30 Wednesday
The men stripped tobacco and put the rest in the cellar. Worked at a dress for Rhoda. Did the ironing and made potato chips and candy. Went over to Stones and painted their table a second coat. Bought a 1926 Chevrolet coach from an agent that brought it here. It snowed.

1/27/30 Monday
Snowed all day. I washed and the machine stopped when I had the last go in. Eby put a new spark plug in and it worked fine and I dried the wash in the room till this evening. Galen took a cow, calf and two lambs into the stock yards and Eby went along. Eby has a sore throat this evening. We are taking tea and grease. Made Rhoda a dress.

2/11/30 Tuesday
Did the washing and it dried fine. Did most of the ironing. The men were blasting and working at the tree. We went to church this evening, took Mrs. Usner and the children along. Big crowd. He talked on Nonresistence and the text was The Unpardonable Sin.

2/21/30 Friday
I was busy with the meat. Got 9 quarts of sauer kraut, 5 quarts steak, 3 quarts ribs, 2 crocks of sausage cakes and 2 crocks back bone. Cleaned up the whole house. Very warm. Rhoda played outdoors all day. The men hauled the tobacco stalks. A few more tobacco sales reported.

3/4/30 Tuesday
Washed and Eby refused to hang it up so I did it myself. The men hauled manure. Dick went to help Irvin at New Holland. I went with Amy and Mother to see the

baby. The children slept and Eby kept an eye on them. Sold 55 dozen eggs at 23 cents.

3/13/30 Thursday
Did up my work and left for home at 8:30. Amy was at Sewing Circle. I made Abram a romper suit. Ran the Chevrolet for the second time. Put Abram in the wash basket. We went over to Clarence Groff's to see the baby this evening. Linville Hill is on fire.

3/20/30 Thursday
I sewed this A.M. and this P.M. made hot bed. Planted lettuce, radishes and sweet peas. Started my rock garden with some lilacs, lilies, flags, and winter shrubs. Eby finished Abram's pen. They plowed this P.M. Nice day.

3/30/30 Monday
Had the steamer for breakfast and dinner. I put the seed to sprout. Did the washing and part of the ironing. Talked to Mabel and Mother. Eby and Dick plowed and Nelson put manure on the garden. Eby and Rhoda went up to his home to attend to some April business.

4/12/30 Saturday
Was very busy. Made pies and peppernuts, boiled meat, did the scrubbing and scrubbed the peepie house. Had boiled cabbage for dinner. Gave the children baths and took mine, and we all went to preparatory services and baptismal services. About 18 baptized. Finished what I didn't get done this evening.

4/22/30 Tuesday
I finished the ironing and tended the peepies. 17 dead so far. Worked in the yard filling up the beds and cleaned some. Was over at the Stone's for a few minutes. Mrs. Usner sent the children an Easter basket with the baker. 300 prisoners burned to death when some of the convicts fired the prison in Ohio. Wilmer Kreider is better. Cool and windy.

5/14/30 Wednesday
Did up the morning work, mended and worked in the house while it rained a shower. Eby harrowed the garden and Nelson and I hoed it this A.M. It began raining before dinner and kept it up very nicely. Got the Dr. for Rhoda after dinner. Her glands are swollen and her temp. was as high as 103 degrees. Bought 3 pineapples.

5/22/30 Thursday
I made pies and cleaned and brushed all the winter coats and put them away. Washed for the baby. Rhoda is much better. I made her three pairs of panties. The men planted the sweet potatoes. Mabel and Mildred came over this evening and Mother and the three boys. Very nice day.

6/2/30 Monday

Got done washing by 9:30, washed the tobacco muslin to put away. Helped to pull some tobacco plants before dinner. Brought the wash in and put some away with nature's ironing. Had supper at 4:00 and I helped drop plants till sundown, then came in and washed the dishes. The children stayed in the machine.

6/7/30 Saturday

Got up at 4 and packed a lunch quickly to go to the zoo. Did up the work and took the children up home and got started about 15 of 8. Arrived about two hours later at the zoo, stopped at the new museum. We arrived home safely about 5. I went up for the children. Paul Groff went along too. It rained a little bit, but was very pleasant.

7/1/30 Tuesday

I made ginger cakes. Cleaned two chickens for dinner. Canned 3 quarts of raspberries. Sprinkled the wash. Replanted my rex begonias. It rained a big shower. Got the peas ready and cleaned off the tobacco beds and wed the flower beds and planted some flowers. Abram cut his 5th tooth.

7/20/30 Sunday

Had all the Hostetters except Ellis'. They refused our invitation. Eby went to church. It was a very hot job having company. Took Mrs. Stone some ice cream and cake and spent the rest of the day at home resting and trying to keep cool. Bathed the children.

7/28/30 Monday

I did the washing and some other odd jobs. Took the wash over to Clarence's this evening and ironed it. Not quite so hot. The men harrowed tobacco. Abram weighed 20 lbs last week and Rhoda 40 lbs and myself 139.

8/14/30 Thursday

The drought continues. Some places the corn is almost dead and the tobacco beyond help. The Susquehanna River is lower than it's been for 100 years. Prices are going up.

8/18/30 Monday

It cleared off this morning. I washed and put some of the clothes away. Finished my elderberries and have 8 quarts canned. Canned 1 quart tomatoes. Things are growing very nicely now. We went up home this evening and filled Rhoda's chaff bag. Clarence's were there too. Nice and cool.

8/20/30 Wednesday

I thought I was in a dangerous condition early this morning, so we called Dr. Hershey as Dr. Frew was on vacation. He made it worse than it was and said I must stay in bed. We sent up for Amy and she came down and did the work. Mother and the boys came down this evening and I feel fine. Mabel came over a little while.

8/21/30 Thursday

Had to stay in bed again all day. The Dr. was here and said it was the best, but I got up after supper and didn't mind it a bit. Mabel was over this p.m. and helped Amy can 23 quarts of peaches. Amy went home this evening and to Singing School. The men cut 4 loads of tobacco for the first.

9/1/30 Monday

Very cloudy this morning, so we did not wash till 9:30. Picked the tomatoes and canned 4 quarts. The Maytag balked and did not get the wash all done till after dinner. Park Davis was here all day cutting corn and tobacco. A gust came up about 4:00 and we had a dandy rain.

9/3/30 Wednesday

I made ginger snaps and pies and cleaned three chickens. Sent Mrs. Stone her dinner. This P.M. we cleaned things up a little and snitzed 12 buckets of apples and got ready to boil apple butter. Amy and Mother came down to help to snitz this evening. Eby and Mart went to the cider mill.

9/4/30 Thursday

Eby and I got up at 3:30 and put the cider on. Mabel and Eby's mother came to help to boil everything fine. Had it off by 2:00. 16 crocks. Then we canned 16 quarts of corn. Had chicken corn soup and watermelon for dinner. Very nice cool day.

9/25/30 Thursday

Did up the morning work. Mabel came over and we started for Mart Groff's about 8:30. Visited and sewed. Very hot and gusty. We got home before 5:00. We had a very heavy rain last night. Edna told me some news. Papa had our truck to go to the cider mill. He told me some news too.

10/2/30 Thursday

Paul went along to Clarence's with the creamery truck and did up the morning work and got the men's dinner. Eby's mother came down, and we left for Irvin's about 8:15 and spent a pleasant day. Got home about 5:00. Eby's mother fell down the cellar steps this evening and cut her head open. We went up to see her, and she said she didn't think she was hurt bad.

10/3/30 Friday

Canned 2 quarts of pears and stewed a crockfull to eat. Made 3 quarts of applesauce. Cleaned up the kitchen. Eby and Paul went to the cider mill and got 24 gallons of cider made. Came home by Eby's home and his mother is not so good.

10/18/30 Saturday

I made a cake and laid up the sweet potatoes. Paul left for home around 10. Eby's mother had an operation on her head this A.M. I picked lima beans and string beans, brought in some tomatoes and covered some things. It began getting colder last night. Eby took the children to the barber and bought 4 bushels of apples at Isaac Rohrer's.

10/31/30 Friday
It rained last night. I cleaned the dining room. Made turnips for dinner. I took Mabel along to Lancaster and we had the children's pictures taken at Hager's free. Much colder this evening.

11/24/30 Monday
I washed but it did not dry very fast. Did some of the ironing. Mended a little this evening. Dick has a sore finger. Abram began walking last evening over at Clarence's and he is busy at it again today.

12/2/30 Tuesday
Helped milk this morning and evening. Made pies and prepared things for supper. Had early dinner and took the children along up home and they helped make a wool comfort for Rhoda's bed. Much colder today. Snowed a little last night. Eby went up to the garage this evening. Dick was up at Dr. Leaman's. Eggs dropped from 54 cents a dozen last week to 35 today.

12/16/30 Tuesday
Did up some mending and patched. Eby killed a lamb and I cut up the meat and got it ready to can. Very cold and froze the lamb's legs. Eby went to John King's for roasters this evening. I stirred up ginger cakes.

12/17/30 Wednesday
Eby took the roasters in to A.S. Groff's to have them examined and did his Xmas shopping. Bought me a pair of scissors and a flashlight and a poinsettia. I baked ginger cakes. Rhoda took some over to Mrs. Stone. Stirred up sand tarts. Canned 8 quarts of lamb meat.

12/22/30 Monday
I overslept and missed the milking for the first time since Thanksgiving. Washed and did some of the ironing. Did my Xmas packages up. Pretty cold day and the wash didn't dry very good. Ezra Hershey's baby died on Saturday of diptheria. Made mush.

12/24/30 Wednesday
Made potato chips and stuffed some prunes. Cleaned the kitchen and made cold water soap. Got a bunch of celery ready for Mother's Xmas dinner. Helped to take down some tobacco. Gave the children baths and Rhoda set out her plate and went to bed. Had snow all morning. Got seven eggs.

12/25/30 Thursday
We did up our work and went up home a little while on our way to Galen's Xmas dinner. We had turkey and lots of goodies. All were there but Ellis'. Very nice day.

Papa and Amy came down and took Eby along to Christmas services at Kinzer and Mother stayed with me.

12/29/30 Monday
I washed and it was cloudy and had to hang most of it in the kitchen to finish drying. Papa was down this A.M. on business and we began to expand. I helped to strip tobacco this P.M. John Hess was here and advised weighing our cow feed and milk and we proceeded.

12/30/30 Tuesday
I did the ironing this A.M. and sent an order to Sears and Roebuck. Abram has two double teeth through. I helped to strip tobacco this p.m. Much colder and windy. Snowed a little last night. Sold 2 cows at $60 per head. Mended this evening. 14 eggs.

1931

1/6/31 Tuesday
Started on the meat first thing. Mabel came about 9:00 and helped till nearly 4. Got 9 crocks of pudding. Canned 11 quarts of meat and cooked the back bone for sauer kraut. Papa and Jay came down and helped to take down a lot of tobacco. Mother called and said Amos King tried to hang himself this evening about 4:00. Papa took him to the hospital. I darned stockings this evening.

2/1/31 Sunday
I made chicken and candied sweet potatoes, lima bean loaf, tomato sauce, celery and tapioca with whipped cream. We read and rested all day and went down to Jay's early this evening for ice cream. Had a nice time. One of Harry Howe's boys, 9 years old, was killed this morning when a truck upset and broke his neck. A very nice day.

2/2/31 Monday
Cloudy this morning but blowed off very nice and mild. I washed and ironed. The clothes dried very nice. The tobacco shed caught fire around the chimney and required three buckets of water to drown it out. Abram and Rhoda had a fine time playing out in the yard. Rhoda got a little broom at last. I have a toothache this evening.

2/17/31 Tuesday
Sorted about 24 dozen eggs and had 6 dozen at 17 cents for Sweigart and a bull hide at 1 ½ cents a pound. Eby went up for his mother, and we made 18 quarts mince meat, 33 quarts of steak, 62 lbs. of dried beef and 50 lbs. of bologna. Swept and washed up the kitchen and did the ironing. I was some tired this evening.

2/26/31 Thursday
Eby cut wood. I cleaned the aluminum ware. Got the eggs ready and stirred up some peppernuts. Took my rug and went over to see Mrs. Stone for a little while.

Dick is not able to work yet. Abram can say a lot of words. He is cutting his fourth double tooth.

3/16/31 Monday
I washed and dried it in the house. It snowed all day, but very wet. Eby mended horse collars. One of Usner's men was fired, and Eby took him overnight to work for his board. I did the ironing and mending and feel all right yet.

3/17/31 Tuesday
Finished up the mending. The snow is about 4-5 inches deep this morning. Everything was very pretty till the sun melted it. Eby took the children for a sled ride and mended more collars. I made rug rags and canned 2 quarts of apples. Stirred up some ginger cakes.

3/18/31 Wednesday
Got up about 5:00 with a pain. Called home and Papa went for the nurse, Mary Doutrich. Amy came along and helped get kiddies ready to take along up home. Sent for the Dr. and he came about 6:45. A ten-pound baby boy arrived at 8:20. Eby went up and told his mother and Clarence's. He went to his first sale for this year. Nice clear day. Mabel stopped in with the ginger cakes. Amy took the dough along home and mother baked them.

3/19/31 Friday
Clear. Good wash day. Mary did the cleaning. Jay came down and helped move the peepie house and was here for dinner. Rhoda came along and went home with him again. She is well pleased with the baby. I took my oil and got the piles and milk. Did not sleep very good yet. Dick was here for his society clothes.

3/23/31 Monday
Had a fine wash day. Mary washed, ironed, mended and put the clothes away. I spent the day reading and talking and resting and eating. No company. Old Ephraim Hershey and Christ Senger died. No word from Dick. Eby started to plow. Dr. made his final trip.

4/1/31 Wednesday
I have taken full charge again. Got the breakfast done and did the morning work. Bathed the baby and did the wash. It rained and stormed very hard all day, blew trees over and barn roofs and doors off. Eby attended his business affairs this A.M. and went for our girl, but she couldn't come. Started to plait a rug.

4/4/31 Saturday
I did up the morning work, lamps and mopped up the kitchen. Gave the children baths after dinner and Eby put them to bed. I was tired and laid down all P.M. Elizabeth and Robert came to spend the evening.

4/5/31 Sunday
Easter Day. I did up the morning work and the baby bath. The children slept this P.M. and so did we. Dick stopped in this A.M. to see if he should come tomorrow. Mrs. Usner came over this evening and when she went Mother and the three boys came. Adrian and Mrs. Usner brought the children candy.

4/8/31 Wednesday
Kathryn washed the dishes and swept and mopped up the kitchen. I made a custard and bathed the baby and did the wash and beds. Worked at my black dress. Took a nap and called Amy. Mother, Annie Reeser, Nora Mentzer, and Mrs. Abbie Plank were here for a few minutes. Pretty and clear. Eby was making the pigpen ready for peepies. Sold 5 steers and the old white cow.

4/11/31 Saturday
Did up the morning work and cleaned the kitchen. Kathryn scrubbed and cleaned up some of the yard. I made an angel food cake. Irvin stopped and said they have a baby boy. I bathed the children and myself. Got some of my dresses ready to wash. Eby took Kathryn home this evening and got the children haircuts. Nice day.

4/14/31 Tuesday
Did up the morning work and finished the ironing. Isaac was very good all day. I put him on the porch for the first time out. He fell off the settee this evening. I was very much scared and so was he. Eby sewed the tobacco seed and helped finish the yard fence. I cleaned some drawers and corners. Stirred some ginger snaps. Had first herring, 35 cents per dozen.

4/20/31 Monday
Did a big washing and the ironing and put the clothes away. Peepies in the pigpen are dying. The baby is good. Eby's parents and Elizabeth were here this evening and got a honeysuckle and some iris. Very nice day. The mountain is burning.

4/24/31 Friday
Eby helped take down the stove pipe and clean it first thing. We cleaned our bedroom, the bathroom and stairway. Eby harrowed and Dick plowed and they hauled some manure. The little peepies are dying with diarrhea, about 40 dead. Abram is cutting two more eye teeth. Isaac is very good.

5/3/31 Sunday
(Eby is writing now, apparently dictated by Ruth)
We all went to White Horse church and took Kathryn home. Had a bite of dinner and went over to Stone's. Amy stopped in with two of her friends and Paul on the way to the car, and Charles came over to fetch me home. Ate dinner and spent evening at home. Very nice day.

5/4/31 Monday
(Eby)
Very fine day. We washed and put nature's ironing away. We cleaned and trimmed and mowed some yard. Isaac was very good and slept on the porch all afternoon. Eby had two tobacco buyers in one hour. I got a dozen herring for 25 cents. Eby let the peepie house fire go out for the first time. Mrs. Stone is still sick. Talked to Mabel, Mother and Mrs. Usner.

5/5/31 Tuesday
(Eby)
Rhoda and Charles went out to John King's junk hole to get some tin cans for flowers. I did the ironing and put the clothes away. Eby went to Jacob Martin's funeral and took Mrs. Usner along. Eby dug the flower beds this evening and we planted the scarlet sage. Eby fixed the stone at the gate. Very nice day.

5/8/31 Friday
(Eby)
I made pies and boiled meat and made rhubarb sauce. The hay balers were here this afternoon and baled 6 tons of hay. Did not have them for any meals. Washed a big wash for the baby. Washed Rhoda's, Abram's and Charlie's hair this evening. And then I made some shampoo to put on their heads. Rhoda planted the tomatoes and cabbage just before the rain.

5/12/31 Tuesday
(Eby)
I did the ironing the A.M. and Charles helped. It rained all day. Eby brought a load of Eastern States feed from the Gap. Clarence's were here this P.M. and Eby and Clarence went up home for 25 bushel of wheat and it rained on them. I mended all P.M. Talked to Mother twice.

5/16/31 Saturday
I baked ginger cakes and took some over to Mrs. Stone. Put olive oil on her head and went over to shampoo it this P.M. It wasn't done for 9 years. Amy stopped in with my new dress on her way to Jr. Sewing Circle at John Groff's. We made ice cream this evening. I was very tired. Took baths and went to bed.

5/18/31 Monday
We did the washing and the machine did all right. We had the clothes all in till dinner and the shoes cleaned and the beds made. I went to bed and slept this P.M. as the baby has been keeping late hours. Eby planted corn all day. Nice day. Wind in the East.

5/21/31 Thursday
It was rainy and we did some odd jobs this A.M. and went up home this P.M. Eby took John King along to New Holland sale and got the hay check for $151.00.

Mabel was there too. Abram fell this evening before we went to bed and broke a tooth off. Nice evening.

5/22/31 Friday
We took Abram to the dentist, and he said his tooth was broken off. Had my teeth examined and have five cavities and two extractions. Did a little shopping and came home and had our dinner and went to Roy Hershey's wife's funeral. Worked late in the yard and it is all cleaned and trimmed.

6/1/31 Monday
Eby went for Kathryn and we washed and didn't hang it out till this evening as it rained all day. Washed 13 feed bags. The Maytag balked, so I wrote a letter to the company. The men cleaned the steer stable. Jay and Galen were here to make calls.

6/2/31 Tuesday
We canned 4 quarts of asparagus, making a total of 9 quarts. Eby's mother came about 8:00 and helped to sew and work and I took her home about 4:00. We planted some tomatoes, peppers and corn flowers. Abram upset Isaac in the coach, but there was no damage done.

6/4/31 Thursday
Did up the morning work and the service man was here and fixed the Maytag. We planted some sweet corn, Japan peas and sweet potatoes. Mabel took me along home this P.M., and Kathryn kept Mildred and Abram. Nice day.

6/17/31 Wednesday
I made pies and 11 glasses of strawberry preserves. Did a big baby wash. We sewed this P.M. The men pulled tobacco plants. Mabel and Clarence came over and Eby and Clarence kept the children while Mabel, Mrs. Usner and I went to Ron Usner's to an aluminum demonstration. Kathryn went to a party.

6/20/31 Saturday
Made cake and some jello and finished up the work. I took Charlie home about 2:30 and had a talk about some private affairs. I took Kathryn home this evening and Eby kept Isaac. Nice day. Very hot. I planted some cabbage.

7/19/31 Sunday
I got up and helped Eby with the work and took Paul home. We got ready and Clarence's came over and went with up to New Holland church and Grandpap Martin's for dinner. Mart's and the boys were there too. Irvin's had a collision with another machine on Hershey's Church road on their way over to David's. They were all bumped up and the machine wrecked.

8/5/31 Wednesday
I topped tobacco after I got ginger snaps made. I rested this P.M. We all went to Harvest Meeting at Hershey's this evening. Isaac was very unruly. Very hot and getting drier. Eby is plowing.

8/10/31 Monday
Kathryn could not come this week so I went it alone. Had a big wash and got it all dried and some put away. We went up home for Paul this evening. Had a heavy rain, wind and gust. The creek overflowed its banks. Isaac sits up alone very good.

8/11/31 Tuesday
It rained all day. I mended a big stack. Mabel brought her sewing over this P.M. and stayed for supper. Eby worked at his new chicken house and got it ready and put in 140 pullets. Ephraim Hershey committed suicide by putting coal oil on his clothes and setting it on fire.

8/16/31 Sunday
We went to Hershey's Church and home for dinner. Took a picture of the children. Rested this P.M. David's came this evening. Very nice day.

8/18/31 Tuesday
We ironed and canned 17 quarts of corn and 4 quarts of pickles. Amy and Mother were here a little while this P.M. Had Jay and Eby's Dad for supper helping cut tobacco. Grandmother Martin is not very good.

8/23/31 Sunday
It was raining very hard all morning so we did not go to church. Had our dinner and went to Frank Hostetter's this P.M. It was very rainy again this evening. Mrs. Stone is much worse. Eby and I were over several times this evening. Dr. Hershey's were up. Mother came here while the others went to church. Grandmammy is very low.

8/24/31 Monday
Kathryn could not come so I washed alone and made some chicken broth ready for Mrs. Stone. The hospital ambulance came for her about 2:30. John King helped Eby cut tobacco. I had him for supper. I canned 15 quarts of plums today and now have 27 quarts. Paul started high school and came here this evening. He walked from Paradise as the car didn't come.

8/26/31 Wednesday
I got in more corn to dry. Mrs. Stone died about 8:00 this morning. Had Galen, John King and John Wenger for supper. Kathryn picked the soup beans. Mrs. Plank came a while this P.M. I made a cake. Paul picked the Bartlett pears.

8/28/31 Friday

I helped unload two loads of tobacco and then spent most of the day at Stone's helping Mrs. Plank clean up. Eby cut tobacco alone this P.M. It is raining this evening, 60 loads of tobacco in. I cleaned Adrian's Sunday pants and pressed them.

8/29/31 Saturday

It rained fast all morning. Cleaned Adrian's Sunday shoes and took them over. Made a cake and some potato salad and 20 apple dumplings for dinner. Paul kept the boys while the rest of us went to Mrs. Stone's funeral. Took Adrian and Mrs. Usner along. It was Rhoda's first funeral. Finished yard work this P.M. Mabel went up home and took Paul along. Eby took Kathryn home.

9/4/31 Friday

Eby took Kathryn home this evening. I am going to try to do with Paul.

9/10/31 Thursday

I baked a double portion of peppernuts. Made 15 quarts of chow chow. Mrs. Plank brought me some red peppers. Eby and Dick helped Silas Hershey fill silo. Eby helped John King cut tobacco this P.M. Mowed some of the yard. Did the baby wash. Eby penned the chickens up so they would be ready to cull.

9/18/31 Friday

Isaac is six months old and weighs over 20 lbs. He pulled himself up in his pen and bed for about two weeks. Dick walked off this morning because he says he is sick.

9/20/31 Sunday

Raining. We took Amy along to Groffdale church and went to Jere Martin's for dinner and Mart Groff's for supper, then came home and did our work. Elizabeth and Bob came down a while this evening to tell us they are getting married.

9/26/31 Saturday

It rained most all day and we were busy cleaning up and making ready. I went to the Gap this evening for ice and store things. Saw a bad accident at Rising Sun where 11 hurt and 1 killed. Stopped at Weir's for the butter. Kathryn stopped on her way from David's for some clothing.

9/28/31 Monday

Had the water ready to wash and the machine refused to start so I didn't wash. Sent for a service man and did up some little jobs. Dried apples. Eby and Paul went for haircuts. Very much cooler. Eby had three men cutting corn. He started to work the wheat ground.

9/29/31 Tuesday

Dried more apples and the service man arrived just before dinner and I had the washing done till 2:30. Had a man for dinner yesterday and today cutting corn. We had early supper and took Paul and the children over to Clarence's while we went to Elizabeth's wedding. Very pretty, cool, moonlight evening.

10/1/31 Thursday
Helped Eby catch the rest of the chickens that did not stand the blood test. Eby got his tractor this P.M. and is well pleased. I went to the garage for 20 gallons of gas.

(No entries in the diary for the remaining months of '31.)

No Diary was found for 1932. Ruth's mother, Alice Martin, died after a brief illness in January '32. A son, James Landis, was born 11/29/32.

1933

1/1/33 Sunday
Clear and cold. Eby and Abram went to Hershey's Church. Rhoda and I did up the morning work and made roast chicken for dinner. Just got the dishes done when Aaron Hershey's came. Irvin's stopped in on their way home. Mrs. John King and Annie were here a little while this evening.

1/3/33 Tuesday
Paul went back to school. I did some of the ironing. Cleaned up the kitchen and got ready to butcher. Eby went to the bank and got the iron kettle mended. Clouded up. I did the baby wash. Jay is getting a cold.

1/4/33 Wednesday
We butchered a big hog which we bought from Jay. Galen brought it and helped till after dinner. Amy came down and helped too. Everything went fine. Very mild day. Amy and I cut up the meat and put it in jars this evening. She stayed all night.

1/5/33 Thursday
I tended the baby and Eby, Rhoda and Abram and I left for Lancaster about 8:00 and got home about 2:00. Got Abram an overcoat and hat for $4.95, Rhoda a tricycle for $4.95 and Isaac a kiddie kar for $1.25. We stopped at Uncle Robert's and Uncle Clarence's on the way home. Amy canned 15 cans of meat and 18 cans of sauer kraut.

1/6/33 Friday
Very mild. I did a big wash for the baby. Cleaned upstairs. Calvin Coolidge died yesterday very suddenly from a heart attack. Paul was in at Clarence's and Almeda's cold is better. Isaac and James have colds in their heads. Abram went to visit school with Charlie.

1/11/33 Wednesday
Cloudy with south wind. The children played outdoors this A.M. I was busy baking ginger cakes and late with my other work when Eby's mother came and helped me. We did the ironing and worked at Rhoda's coat. Eby's trust shares brought him $23.40, almost $10.00 more than he expected. Cleaned up the kitchen after the children went to bed.

1/15/33 Sunday
Partly cloudy and mild. The children are still coughing, so I called for the boys to come down to keep Rhoda and Isaac while the rest of us went to Warren Graham's for dinner. Eby went to church at Hershey's. Got home late. Amy was here for the boys. Spent the evening at home.

1/19/33 Thursday
Cloudy, rained last night. Baby slept good. I made oatmeal cakes this morning and did the baby wash. Mended this P.M. Dug some horseradish. The frost is out of the ground. Paul went home this evening from school and went to Mellinger's revival with Ike Ruth.

1/20/33 Friday
I overslept. A very nice day. The children played outdoors and Isaac went out after his nap. Cleaned upstairs and gave the kitchen a thorough sweep. Paul went to Clarence's for some fresh pork and down to Weir's for the butter. It is 25 cents a pound. Jay got a 69 cent watch from Sears. The baby slept good from midnight on till morning.

1/23/33 Monday
Very nice clear springlike day. Eby hung up the wash and it dried fine. The children played outdoors most all day. Got the wash ready to iron. Talked to Mrs. Usner. Horace was missing for 3 days and returned home last evening. Was hunted by a rival in a love affair and his whereabouts were unknown.

2/1/33 Wednesday
Cloudy all day and rained this P.M. I did the baby wash. Eby cleaned the horse stable and hauled tobacco stalks and we went to see Reese Worst's farm sold. It brought $110 an acre. Mabel left Almeda and Mildred here while she went to the Dr. and then her and Landis spent the P.M. here. Had another provoking shock. Did more depression mending.

2/2/33 Thursday
Foggy this morning, but cleared off before dinner and there can be no argument about the groundhog shadow. I made some soda crackers and mended. Sorted eggs for hatching and had a brush agent. Eby took Paul out to the car this morning. Abram and Rhoda helped to strip tobacco. I took a message over to David's.

2/9/33 Thursday
A very cold, stormy night and cold this morning. James was not as good as usual. I put up the meat. Made pig's feet jelly, noodles, baked a cake and made tapioca. Eby's Dad helped strip tobacco this A.M. and was here for dinner. Cleaned up the kitchen after the children went to bed. Made fire in the furnace and it did gas.

2/12/33 Sunday
Very cold this morning and the snow drifted a little bit. Abram and Issac are coughing so we did not go to church. Had ice cream, beef roast and read a book that Papa brought along for us to read. I took the children for a sled ride and helped make a snow man, but the snow is too fluffy.

2/15/33 Wednesday
Rained this A.M. and cleared and got colder this P.M. Eby ground the meat and helped peel apples for mince meat. He took Jay's scalding trough home. I made 14 quarts of mince meat and 14 quarts of vegetable soup and boiled the trype. Paul is still out of school with a sore throat. Decided Isaac and Abram have whooping cough and called the Dr. for directions.

2/16/33 Thursday
Clear and cold. Eby went to the Gap and got some things from the drugstore and did some other errands. Got the machine inspected for $2.00. Went along with David to New Holland sale. A foreigner shot at Roosevelt, the president elect, missed him and shot the mayor of Chicago. I did the baby wash, made ice cream and swept the room. Put the canned meat away and cleaned up the wash house.

2/18/33 Saturday
Nice clear day. Made a batch of ginger cakes and a chocolate cake. Eby helped me bathe the children and finish up the cleaning this P.M. Got along fine. Gave all the children a good rub and put them to bed this P.M. Put a night gown on James tonight. I read a while, took a bath and went to bed at 12:00.

2/20/33 Monday
Raining real fast this morning and I didn't wash. The children coughed quite a bit last night and I saw a fire about midnight and didn't get much sleep, so was not so ambitious today. Eby had to rebuild the waterwheel pump and it took most all day. Paul was not at school as he took the automobile exam. Put spiders around the children's necks.

3/1/33 Wednesday
Cold and stormy. I finished up the mending. Canned 2 quarts of sausage that we bought from Eby's parents. Eby was cutting small trees along the line fence. The children do quite a bit of coughing and Abram vomits. They didn't sleep so well last night.

3/3/33 Friday
Real nice day. Paul stayed home from school and helped Eby and his dad and Clarence Lefever to saw wood. They were here for dinner. I finished Rhoda's dress. The children are still coughing. Abram vomits every night about one hour after he is in bed.

3/4/33 Saturday
Partly cloudy and mild. Paul helped me with the cleaning as I had none of it done till this morning. Charlie came down when Amy went to Clarence's and spent the P.M. and stayed for supper. Made 86 doughnuts. Eby went to Gap for pipe repair and to Ellis Kramer's to hear the Inaugural Address by President Franklin Roosevelt.

3/6/33 Monday
A nice day. Got up early and the washing went good till Isaac got sick in the stomach and vomited all over himself. Eby helped his dad in the woodlot and dug the tobacco beds. Did the ironing. Rhoda did some of the easy things. Banks are closed for 4 days in U.S.

3/7/33 Tuesday
Rained all day. I didn't get much done. James was fussy. Made some clothing for Rhoda's dolls this P.M. Isaac is fine again. Got our peepies. 221 out of 540 eggs. Very poor hatch. The Mayor of Chicago died. He was shot on February 14 when a pistol shot at President elect Roosevelt hit him.

3/8/33 Wednesday
Clearing and stormy. I cleaned the cupboards and the cellar way. Washed the diapers and the vomit covers. Eby split wood. I sorted some patches and cleaned the bottom of the corner cupboard. James was fussy. Went over to David's a few minutes this evening. Edna was down home and called me up.

3/11/33 Saturday
Clear and cold and not so windy. Made a chocolate cake, raspberry mush, sweet potato croquettes and cleaned chickens. Eby took the eggs in to Groff's, and Galen and Jay went along to see John Raile at the Alms House. He has decided to live for the Lord the rest of his days. Eby turned the ice cream while I bathed the children.

3/12/33 Sunday
Cold and stormy. Did up my morning work and got everything ready for dinner and had Sunday till the company came. Mart's, Clarence's and Amy were here. Had a nice visit and lots to talk about. Aunt Mary Weaver has dropsy. Took our pictures, each family separate and all the grandchildren.

3/20/33 Monday
Still raining and blowing all day. Got up late and washed a few diapers and cut some scarves for Rhoda's room and she ripped a hem out of one of her dresses. Eby and I cleaned part of the cellar this P.M. The man who shot Mayor Cermak

of Chicago was electrocuted this morning. The Ohio River flooded and made hundreds homeless.

3/25/33 Saturday
Clouded up and began snowing about 3:00 and was about 6 inches deep when we went to bed. Everything was beautiful. Eby went to Christ Metzler's sale and bought a trough for the wash house for $.75. I made an angel food cake and it got fine. We all bathed in the kitchen and went to bed. James weighs 14 lbs.

3/27/33 Monday
I washed and it dried fine. Cold wind. Did some of the ironing. Rhoda helped. James was real fussy. His cough is not so hard. Money is scarce on every hand as April first approaches. Eby's father was here. We have lost about 24 peepies so far. Paul worked on his bicycle.

4/3/33 Monday
Cleared this morning and very nice spring day. Eby sowed his clover seed and trimmed the grapes and raspberries. I washed and ironed and sowed some cabbage, tomatoes and red beets. I am still scarce of wind. James goes to bed at 7:30.

4/4/33 Tuesday
Rained all day. The world's largest airship Akron came down in a storm last night off the New Jersey coast and was wrecked and sank with 76 men on board and all lost but three.

4/10/33 Monday
Nice day with strong east wind. I washed and put the bristles on the tobacco beds. Eby sowed the seed. I put my celery seed to sprout. Experimenting with some corn in the house, have 99 grains in a pasteboard box. Isaac walked off down to the creek.

4/13/33 Thursday
A very nice day. Eby cleaned up in general around the premises. Isaac walked off again down to the creek and gave us a scare. I cleaned the boys' room and little truck room. Paul, Rhoda and I went along with Mabel, Landis and Mildred up to Uncle Milt's and had a nice visit. Uncle Thad was there.

4/16/33 Sunday
It rained most all day. Eby went to White Horse and I kept the children at home as they all have a little cold and are coughing again. I have a sore throat. I read to the children and tried to teach them about Easter. We all slept this P.M. Esias Kling's wife died on Friday sometime.

4/24/33 Monday
A very nice day. Cool. We washed and cleaned the parlor. Landis was here helping to plow. I talked to Esther Clark this evening and she has not been well. Eby went to Mart Wanner's for feed this evening. Rhoda lost her first tooth.

4/25/33 Tuesday
A real nice day. Had a little shower this morning. I hoed the cabbage and lettuce, did the ironing and made garden, sowed some lettuce, tomato, pepper and sage seed. Transplanted my corn. Mabel and I went up home this evening and had an unpleasant time. Landis was here and plowed.

5/8/33 Monday
Cloudy and began to rain about 9:00. Did not wash. Cleaned the Sunday shoes and made Isaac a white and blue broadcloth suit, my first attempt. Talked to Mabel. James was real fussy again. I gave him 3 oz. of cows milk when I put him to bed. Eby is shooting rats this evening.

5/10/33 Wednesday
Cloudy and rained. I finished the ironing and mended and pressed dresses, suits and panties. Mabel came over this P.M. while Clarence went along with Eby to Parksburg with potatoes. I walked over to David's this evening for a necktie pattern. The first day without a paper. Can't afford it. Planted more cabbage and tomatoes.

5/16/33 Tuesday
Rained all day. I made ginger snaps and baked beans. Cut my new dress and sewed at my quilt. Eby went along with Clarence's to Lancaster to get Isaac's picture. It is good. He bought a frame for it.

5/23/33 Tuesday
A nice day. Warm. I ironed. Eby cleaned the tobacco bed paths and hoed weeds. Charlie started to white wash. Bought a shad for 25 cents. I hoed this evening. Eby's parents came for some scrap tobacco. Peepies are doing fine. Eby planted corn for David this evening. James was a good baby today, fell off the rocking chair face first.

6/1/33 Thursday
A very cool day. I had fire all day and kept the doors shut. I cleaned the house with electric cleaner. Have a sore breast. James is real good. Charlie worked in the yard. I helped this evening. Eby is working the corn. I ironed this A.M.

6/5/33 Monday
We washed and it was a fine drying day. Clouded up and sprinkled a few drops of rain. Charlie and I hoed the potatoes and lot. Eby helped after supper. There is a swarm of bees on the post up in the field. Eby would like to have them. I am giving James a bottle of milk a day.

6/6/33 Tuesday
A nice warm day. Eby went to Willis Kreider's for a bee hive and I helped milk. The bees did not go in. I did the ironing early and went with Mabel up to Mart's this P.M. Paul went along. Irene came along home. Eby and Charlie worked the tobacco patch.

6/11/33 Sunday
A nice warm day. We took the children up to Amy and we went to White Horse to communion, a big crowd. John Rohrer expressed himself in favor of Barnhouse during services. Amy had dinner ready for us. Uncle Milt's came this P.M. Eby's parents and Bob Neff's came for a while too. I helped milk and hunt the eggs. Mrs. Usner came over a little this evening hunting her ducks.

6/16/33 Friday
Cloudy and had several good showers. I made pies and sewed and cleaned some. Picked first sugar peas for supper. Paul cultivated corn and Eby cleaned out the steer stable and worked some tobacco. I had a sick dizzy spell at supper. Made 8 jars of strawberry jelly this evening. Paul picked them.

6/23/33 Friday
It was a splendid hay day. I cleaned up the house with Mabel's cleaner. The men hauled hay and it went fine. We were awakened about 2:00 A.M. by the fire whistle. The bridge over the railroad into Clarence's was badly burned. Eby went and I couldn't sleep anymore because I didn't know where it was till he came back.

7/10/33 Monday
A very nice day. I washed and ironed. Paul and Charles hoed tobacco. Paul cultivated the rest of the corn. Charles Eckman was running the highway for sport and hit and killed a bride and hurt 5 others. He is in the hospital in bad shape.

7/17/33 Monday
Not so clear. I washed and put clothes and shoes away. Eby and I went with Clarence, Mabel, Amy and Paul up on the Mt. for huckleberries. Charlie kept house. Isaac has ulcers in his mouth and is constipated. Charlie and I cleaned the huckleberries and canned 4 1/2 quarts. Eby sorted the roosters and the pullets.

7/21/33 Friday
A nice warm day. Eby got up with a bad pain in his side. I helped milk. He felt bad all day, and we went to Dr. Frew this evening and he said his appendix is out of fix. Got some medicine for Isaac's ulcers. Did all the cleaning. Planted more celery and finished planting cabbage. Have about 4000 now.

7/23/33 Sunday
A nice warm morning and got very warm. We went to White Horse church. Eby feels better. He rested and slept a lot. James could not sleep. Papa brought Paul and Charles along on his way to church. We went to Clarence's this evening.

7/25/33 Tuesday
A very hot sultry day. Got cooler toward evening. Amy came down and helped me work. Did the ironing and boiled about 25 feed bags. I mended. Eby and I replanted

cabbage this evening. Eby, Paul and Charles harrowed corn and began to hoe. Had a tramp mowing the bushes.

8/1/33 Tuesday
A very hot day again. Yesterday was the hottest in eight years. Charlie and I picked and canned 18 quarts of string beans. The road man, Pat Breslow, was here mowing. Clarence helped Eby clean the steer stable this P.M. The pump was stopped until about 4:00 P.M. I went to the garage for a leather. Charlie and I trimmed the pyrethium.

8/5/33 Saturday
A very fine cool day. Amy and Papa came down and helped to thrash. Had 24 bushel to an acre. Went to harvest services at Hershey's. John Mosemann preached. Eby is not feeling good and he is ready to go to the hospital.

8/6/33 Sunday
A nice day. Eby helped do the work and showed me how it was to be done. I layed down a while and Eby layed most all day. David's were over and Bob's, Jay's, Clarence's and Galen's stopped in to see how Eby was, and his parents came down this evening and Papa brought the boys after church. We called Dr. Frew this evening and made arrangements for Eby to go to the hospital.

8/7/33 Monday
A nice day. Did the milking and washed and ironed. A man came for pyrethium from Mt. Joy. Jay came and helped spray the cow stable. They put a window in the door. Eby was feeling worse and Clarence took him in to the hospital this P.M.

8/8/33 Tuesday
A nice day. Did up the work and got James ready and Grandpap Hostetter took me to the hospital where Eby was operated on for appendicitis at 11:00 A.M. Stayed in till 5:00 when he was about out of ether. Looked gusty but did not rain. Paul harrowed tobacco and Charlie kept house.

8/10/33 Thursday
Rained nearly all day. I dried corn. Paul picked a bucket of plums and I canned 8 quarts and some pickles. The boys pulled weeds in the corn till it began to rain. Clarence took Charlie and Rhoda and I in to see Eby, and Paul, Isaac and James stayed at Pap Hostetter's.

8/15/33 Tuesday
A very nice day. Papa Hostetter, David, Irvin, Walter, Paul and Charles picked all the corn till early dinner, then started on David's, but his was too young. Grandma was here and helped me cook. Made pies and chicken. Did the ironing. Took Mrs. Usner along up to Eby's house and they took us along in to see Eby. His blood pressure is too low to come home. Took him a pint of ice cream.

8/17/33 Thursday
Seemed clear, but had a little shower this morning. We all topped tobacco this morning and I came in when James got awake. Rhoda tapped the bell. Had early dinner and Paul and I went over for Landis' machine and Abram and I went in and brought Eby home from the hospital. Clarence's and Mart's came this evening.

8/24/33 Thursday
Strong south wind and is in the west this evening and seems clear. We pumped about 8 inches of water out of the cellar and are not done yet. Eby and Paul put a netting door on the new chicken house. I washed and rinsed out a tub full of Monday wash and it all dried nicely. Paul went for a haircut. James is much better. Biggest rain storm since 1896.

8/29/33 Tuesday
Nice day. Cooler. Charlie helped David pick corn till about 4:00. Eby helped peel pears till 4:30 and then went for the cows and out to the other end of the tobacco patch. He was very tired when he got back. He helped milk and did not lay down any for the first day. He has a little cold in his head.

8/30/33 Wednesday
A very nice clear cool day. Eby helped peel the rest of the pears and now I have 42 quarts. Charlie got in corn and I dried 5 quarts, but did not get the last on till 10:00 P.M. as Eby got worse and I tried to do for him what I could. He laid on the couch from 10:00 till dinner and then went to bed with a very bad headache and grippe. We called the Dr. and I stayed up late with Eby and the corn.

9/3/33 Sunday
A nice day. Warm. I did up the work alone. Took a walk up to see the rusty tobacco. Have about decided to leave it out and disc it down. Eby walked to the barn this evening. Amy went to Menno's home for supper.

9/7/33 Thursday
I spiced the rest of my cantaloupes and brought in all the cabbage that wasn't rotten and made 2 gallons of sauer kraut. The milk inspector was here and we must have more light in the stable and less light in the toilet vault.

9/8/33 Friday
A nice day. Eby's dad came down this morning and was very much disgusted with the inspector's orders. It caused him to order us off his farm.

9/10/33 Sunday
A very nice day. We went to Hershey's church. Spent the afternoon resting. I went over to David's this evening with James and Eby kept the rest of the children. George Graham preached. His topic was "Peace." I had to take James out and talked to Mary Axe. James fell off the high chair and got a black eye.

9/13/33 Wednesday
Cloudy and cool. The flies are miserable. Eby helped me make chow chow. Got 12 quarts. David got a half bushel of tomatoes for 35 cents. Eby started to give some to the chickens. Eby's Daddy was down mowing weeds in the meadow. I have a cold in my head and am hoarse.

9/15/33 Friday
Rained again. Eby took Charlie out for the bus. I did up some odd jobs around the house. Eby put more pullets in between showers. The children's bowels are all very loose and make a good bit of work. Rhoda does not feel good this evening. Her temperature is 102. Cold, windy and showery.

9/16/33 Saturday
A cold damp day and rained some. I was very busy, did all the cleaning and called the Dr. for Rhoda this morning. Her temperature stayed around 102 all night and her bowels moved about every half hour. He said she has something like dysentery. Eby and Charlie cleaned the horse and cow stable and all the chicken houses.

9/19/33 Tuesday
A very fine day. I did the ironing and canned some tomatoes. Cleaned two chickens this evening. Eby started to disc harrow. Clarence brought the cider, but the apple snitz were delayed because of an Amish barn burning down and Amy and Jay went to the fire and were late getting the apples.

9/20/33 Wednesday
Cloudy and showers, but cleared by 9:00. We put the cider on about 6:00 A.M. and the snitz all in by 10:30. Amy and Mabel helped and we made 16 crocks on the shares. Had it off about 2:30. We made about 24 glasses of quince honey and jelly. Eby disc harrowed. Charlie went along home as he did not go to school and feels no better.

9/22/33 Friday
It was cool and partly cloudy. I tied up the apple butter and did the baby wash. James' bowels are badly out of order and he is cutting four upper teeth. I cleaned up the kitchen and sprayed the flies. Got some squash ready for pies.

9/24/33 Sunday
A very delightful fall day. We went to Hershey's Church and had Counsel meeting. Mary Axe was not at peace. We were all at Aaron Hershey's for dinner. Had a nice visit. We did up our work and went up to Eby's home this evening. James is fussy and his bowels are bad. Ivan Hershey and Virginia were married yesterday.

9/25/33 Monday
A nice warm day. I washed and got it all ready to iron. Abram got up sick and went to bed all day. His bowels are very bad. He seems better this evening. Charlie came back again and took his bike up to the garage. Eby and I graded the eggs this evening.

9/27/33 Wednesday
A nice day, very warm. Amy came down and helped clean the cellar and white wash it. Charlie and I picked pears. Eby disc harrowed. Amy announced her intentions to wed. Our landlord is very displeased with his farmer.

10/2/33 Monday
A very nice clear cool day. Had a heavy gust in some parts and two barns were burned. We had a lot of rain. I washed and ironed. Eby had Frank Kurtz take a cow in to the stock yard this morning and paid off the fine that Dick Winters sued for and we hope we never hear from him again and that he will derive some good from it.

10/9/33 Monday
A very fine day. Eby milked and I did my washing up till 8:00 and then we took out potatoes the rest of the day. The children helped pick up good for their size. Eby subscribed for the Country Gentleman Magazine for a bushel of potatoes. Eby and I put the rest of the pullets in.

10/19/33 Thursday
A nice day. Had a white frost. Did up my morning work and went to the corn field. We picked 2 loads today. James is very good. Mary Axe is sick. I talked to Papa, Aunt Cora and Mabel. Eby set rat nip in wet mash for the rats.

10/20/33 Friday
A nice warm fall day. Eby and I picked 2 loads of corn. Rhoda did fine keeping house. Charlie took Abram along to Clarence's and walked him home as he had a flat tire. Had first turnips for supper. Granville stopped by to see if he could sell us a time switch for the chicken house. I stirred up ginger cakes.

10/21/33 Saturday
A nice fall day. I made four pumpkin pies and sprayed the flies and swept the kitchen and then went to the corn field and picked two loads. Charlie baked the ginger cakes and made dinner and cleaned the chicken roosts. I did the baby wash and washed the kitchen while Eby unloaded. Bathed the children and myself. Eight rats died so far.

11/1/33 Wednesday
Damp and foggy, but cleared up before dinner. Eby gunned till 10:00 and did not get a thing. I did up my morning work and mended. Had early dinner and took the children over to Clarence's while Eby and I went to Lancaster. He bought steers and I spent $6.80 for things we needed. Worked on Rhoda's red dress.

11/11/33 Saturday
Cloudy, cold and rough. Eby and Paul cleaned the chicken houses and manured the gardens. I cleaned up the kitchen and tried to get the boys' suits ready but James was so fussy I decided to miss church. Made drop cakes. James' temp. was 103 after supper so I called the Dr.

11/16/33 Thursday
Clear and still very cold. About 10 above zero. Cleaned the kitchen. Eby helped. Had a full day. Eby and Charlie went to church this evening. Got a can of milk back that smelled of pole cat. David clubbed one and it crawled away.

11/17/33 Friday
Very cold. I went over the house with the electric cleaner and cleaned the shanty. Cleaned some of the yard this P.M. and it was cold. Eby cut down the grape arbor and made it good as new. A fine lady was here collecting for the welfare. We sorted eggs this evening.

11/27/33 Monday
A very cold high wind. We sorted the eggs first thing this morning and washed. A very stormy wash day. Eby helped hang it up. Got the ironing all done. Eby picked out 1 quart walnut meats. Called Sue and got some candy recipes. Sold 37 old hens. 133 lbs. at 8 cents. Grammy is up home this week.

12/3/33 Sunday
A cloudy day. We went to Hershey's church and came home, had a quick dinner and took the children to Eby's home while we went to Uncle Thaddeus Brook's funeral. Rhoda and Abram went along. We spent an hour or so with Grandpap Hostetter before coming home. Spent the evening reading to the children.

12/4/33 Monday
I washed and it did not get dry so fast. Mild day. Clarence came over and helped Eby haul wood this P.M. and Mabel came along and helped me sew. Started an everyday dress for Rhoda. Planned to go to Lancaster tomorrow with the other three girls, but Galen just called and wants Eby to help him with wood, so my plan's squashed.

12/6/33 Wednesday
A rainy day. I baked my little raisin cakes. Did the mending. Eby and Jay went to Park Hornberger's funeral this P.M. He was struck and killed by a hit run on Saturday night. They went on to Parksburg sale and Eby brought oysters and fish along home. Got my Xmas fund, which was $50.50.

12/12/33 Tuesday
A very cold morning, but the wind fell and it is not so cold this evening. Had both fires going all day. I finished Rhoda's dress and mended some stockings. Eby hauled some chunks in the cellar and split wood and put a lot in the wood house. Took the reservoir off as it sprung a leak. James was fussy.

12/14/33 Thursday
Not so cold, clear and icy all day. The children tried to sled and fell a lot. Charlie had a sore throat and did not go to school. He helped me make sand tarts and flap jacks. Eby took Clarence's pudding over and got lumber started to make a wheel barrow for Jay Groff. Eby and I made toys for the children after they went to bed.

12/15/33 Friday
A damp day. I cleaned upstairs. Finished up my flapjacks. Made some walnut taffy. Charlie did not go to school as it was so very icy. He and Landis went to Hatville Spelling Bee this evening through rain and ice.

12/25/33 Monday
A very fine day. I got up late and did up the morning work. The children were pleased with their gifts. We went to Galen's for dinner. Eby's parents, Irvin's, Jay's and us were there. Emma and her friend Roy Wissler came in the P.M. Mother Hostetter gave me a dress, Mabel and Edna a food press and Amy a cream whip. I went to the Gap for ice and we made ice cream.

12/26/33 Tuesday
Snowing very fast and 8 inches fell till 2:00 P.M. We hurried through our morning work and took Isaac and James to Eby's home and Abram and Rhoda along to Amy's wedding. About 50 there, had loads left over. I shoveled snow and we sorted eggs.

12/30/33 Saturday
Not quite so cold. Cloudy and snowed a little while. We fired both stove and furnace. I finished cleaning up and stuffed the chicken and made walnut ice cream. Eby did not take a bath as he thought it was too cold.

12/31/33 Sunday
Very much warmer and the snow is melting. Eby's side is sore from cranking the machine last evening. He spent a good bit of the morning helping David to get his Auburn started, but he had to send for Ellis Kramer. We missed most of S.S. Not such a big crowd. George Graham preached on text, "I am resolved what to do." We had roast chicken and walnut ice cream and hurried to get started up to Mart Groff's. Took Amy and Menno along. Clarence's were there and Ben Kurtz's. Had a nice visit. Rhoda and Abram stayed with the boys in Intercourse. The children and I all have colds.

1934

1/3/34 Wednesday
We butchered a hog. Galen brought it from Jay's and helped butcher. Amy brought Mary Axe along down and I entertained her and Amy helped with butchering. Did a little mending after the washing up was done.

1/7/34 Sunday
Raining very fast this A.M., but drizzled and was damp for the rest of the day. Isaac was not feeling very good but we bundled him up and took Rhoda, Abram and left all three at Eby's home and met Clarence's and went to Salunga church

and they just had S.S., so we went on to the reception at Menno Hess' home. Had a good dinner and nice time. Stopped at Orville Home to see Christ Brackbill's. Isaac is better.

1/17/34 Wednesday
Very cold and windy and was snowing early this morning. Eby did his work early and went along with Galen, Jay and his daddy to the Farm Show at Harrisburg. My protesting was like water on a duck's back. I did the evening work all but watering and bedding the horses.

1/21/34 Sunday
A very nice mild day, just like spring. We went to White Horse and started for Uncle Frank Hostetter's after dinner. They had a lot of company so we drove on and visited Papa a while. He was alone and about 3:00 we went down to John King's at Cattail. Mary is better and they seemed glad to see us. Edna had a dinner for Amy.

1/28/34 Sunday
We went to Hershey's church. Ira Hershey preached. Could not decide on any place to go so we all stayed home. I read to the children and took a nap. Eby had a headache. Read more stories to the children this evening. It rained very fast about 5:00 and then began to blow off colder.

1/29/34 Monday
A very cold day with an extra high wind and some snow flurries. Had fire in the furnace and was kept real busy keeping warm. Did a little sewing, made myself a night gown for summer.

1/30/34 Tuesday
Very cold. 6 degrees below zero at Gap with high wind and no snow. I washed and dried it over the register. Ironed this P.M. and made doughnuts. Eby went to the Gap to get the sausage stuffer and rain water pump fixed. Got things ready to butcher and helped sort eggs. The children are all straightened out again.

2/7/34 Wednesday
Partly cloudy and snowed very little. Sun shone some. I mended most all day, did the baby wash. Rhoda washed up the kitchen. Eby worked to get the pump running better and opened the horse trough outlet pipe and cut wood and ranked a lot in the wash house. I sent the shoes back to Sears Roebuck that I got last September because they are not wearing good.

2/9/34 Friday
Very cold. 20 below zero with the water wheel stopped and the horse trough overflow froze this morning. I sewed and helped open the horse trough. It was very cold all day, did the baby wash. Eby started furnace fire this P.M. I had put all my flowers in the kitchen.

2/13/34 Tuesday
Snowed again last night and got much colder and stormy all day. There was a big accident up at the end of Kinzer last evening when a bus and truck struck. 3 persons were killed and 13 hurt. Air tank exploded under the bus and the oil caught fire. It was very bad. Ironed, made some ice cream for supper and helped clean and grade the eggs. The roads are drifted some and the baker just came as far as Usner's. David got stuck up the road on his way home and Eby helped shovel him out.

2/18/34 Sunday
Clear and cold. The snow melted a little. We went to White Horse, had late dinner and spent the P.M. reading and resting. Read to the children again this evening. There was an Inspiration and Farewell Meeting held at Chestnut Street church all day. John Mosemann and wife and Sister Stauffer are to sail for Africa Feb. 22. May the Lord bless the work.

2/20/34 Tuesday
Blowed the snow all night and everything is drifted shut, no milk man, no mailman, no store man, and the baker came just as far as Usner's. Water wheel was drifted shut and did not run till 5:00 this evening. I made potato chips and ironed. Did the milking this morning. Eby got a lot of wood in the cellar and split it. I mended this evening.

2/21/34 Wednesday
A nice winter day, not so cold. About 18 men were shoveling Hensel Road. It is surely very full. Cooked the bones and ground the mince meat. The store man got here about 3:00 with the salt and then we put the steak in both iron kettles and had it cooked till bedtime. Eby helped fire and ground the bologna meat. Eby helped David stuff his bologna.

2/24/34 Saturday
Still very cold. I cleaned upstairs and finished the kitchen. Made a sponge cake and coated my candy. Made sweet potato croquettes, filling and ice cream. Bathed the children. Had Emma and Roy Wissler to spend the evening. They were late getting here as Tina Weaver went to hospital with erysipelas.

2/27/34 Tuesday
Clear and very cold with the snow drifting and a high wind. Eby got up before dinner and is not feeling so good yet. I washed and dried most of it at the register. Ironed it all this P.M. Charlie did not go to school and we did all the work. Eby skinned the trype. Ivan Weaver's baby died with pneumonia and Grandpap put his sale off.

2/28/34 Wednesday
Nice clear morning. 12 below. Eby got up before breakfast and is feeling much better. He went out about 11:00 and went to Trout's sale this P.M. for a cow but they sold

above his reach. A bunch of men are shoveling Hensel Road. Charlie went to school, and I made noodles, potato chips and cleaned the trype.

3/2/34 Friday

March came in like a lamb. I made a walnut cake and a white cake and iced them, made some boiled dressing and red eggs. Cleaned the parlor and room. Had early dinner, and Eby took David on his route through Gap and Kinzer and went to Welk's sale and bought a dry cow for $45.00. Snow is melting fast and water wheel does not run as the water is high.

3/3/34 Saturday

Damp, foggy, rainy and muddy, with a little sunshine. The water is still high. I cleaned upstairs and the kitchen, boiled a ham and sweet potatoes. Amy and Paul came down to Ivan Wick's sale. After the house things were sold, Amy, Mabel and I came home and they helped me peel potatoes, salsify and get the lettuce ready. Charlie did the scrubbing and made the ice cream while we were at the sale. Ivan Wicks and Arlene came down and bargained for Arlene's board.

3/5/34 Monday

I washed and got the clothes ready to iron. Splendid wash day, very mild. Cleaned the Sunday shoes. Arlene Wicks came from school this evening to board. Charles came home from school too. Eby went to Gideon Stoltzfus' sale. The children played outdoors, it was so mild and warm. We sorted eggs this evening. The snow is melting very fast.

3/7/34 Wednesday

Cloudy. Snowed and rained. Arlene had a sore throat and did not go to school. I made pies and finished the ginger snaps. Did the baby wash and the girls washed up the kitchen. I mended this evening. Ivan Wicks brought his radio and Eby connected it, and I did not enjoy it one bit. Aunt Cora called and invited us for April 8.

3/11/34 Sunday

Still snowing and kept it up till about 12:00. We decided to go to church but not in time for S.S. Went to Uncle Charlie's for dinner. They had a fuss for Amy and Menno. Had a dandy dinner. Charlie came along with us home. Spent the evening at home. Eby had the radio turned on.

3/15/34 Thursday

Did up the morning work and Mabel took me along to Intercourse. Then we went in with Landis, stopped for Edna and went to Rheems where Amy moved to set up housekeeping. A very fine day. We got the house cleaned and things pretty well fixed up. Stopped in Lancaster a few minutes on our way home and I got a new everyday dress. Eby kept the children and got along fine. Aunt Cora called this evening.

3/19/34 Monday
A good wash day. Clouded up this P.M. Washed and did all the ironing and put the clothes away. Eby repaired his manure spreader and went to Gap for some repairs. We sorted eggs this evening. Menno has tonsillitis. Thirty-some peepies died so far. Eby sent for drivers license for me.

3/20/34 Tuesday
A nice day and warmer this evening. The children played outdoors. Isaac took a long nap. I transplanted 30 cabbage plants and sowed tomatoes, peppers and red beets. Made pies and mended and fixed one of Mother's dresses over for myself for everyday. Eby, Jay and Galen went to New Holland to help Irvin load his brooder house he bought at Alma Weaver's sale.

3/21/34 Wednesday
A real nice day. Cloudy this evening. I did up my morning work and washed the baby wash. Tended the peepies all day. They are looking better. I sewed and fixed another one of Mother's dresses over for myself and patched. Eby's mother was helping Minnie and came over for an hour this P.M. Papa is getting a housekeeper.

3/23/34 Friday
Cloudy, cold day and snowed this P.M. and is still snowing. Eby took Clarence along to the Community Sale at Intercourse and bought an engine belt for $2.00, a bucket and large enamel dipper, two screens and an iron pot, all bargains. Papa got Katie Hernley for a housekeeper. Rhoda had earache most all day. Mrs. Usner was here this P.M. We sorted eggs this evening. Got 178 today. Made two cakes and three kinds of jello.

3/27/34 Tuesday
Wet all day and began raining fast this evening with some gusts. The fire whistle awakened us for a smokehouse fire in Slaymakertown. Charlie is still in bed and does not seem much improved. I got very little done today. Hung the wash out and it is very wet now. Eby went to Phares Landis' and the mill. Clarence's were here this evening. Eby split some wood this P.M.

3/30/34 Friday
A real nice day. Eby split wood and hauled all the rest in. George Summers was here and fixed the bath tub drain where the rats had chewed a hole in the lead pipe. The Dr. was here for the last time and said Charlie can come downstairs tomorrow. He sat up this P.M. I finished the dress I bought from Mabel.

3/31/34 Saturday
It was very wet and rainy all day. I did the cleaning up in a jiffy. Ivan Wicks came for Arlene about 10:30 and took her to Lancaster. I worked on Arlene's new Easter dress all P.M. after I got the kiddies bathed. Finished the boys' suits this evening while

Eby listened to the radio. Ivan Wicks came with Arlene about 10:00 and stayed all night. Finished my Easter candy.

4/7/34 Saturday
Rained till about 4:00 and then cleared off nice. I did up the rest of the cleaning and bathed the children and made a suit and a half. Charlie went in to the hospital and had an operation for appendicitis. It was not a serious case but time to have it done. Amy stayed with him this evening and all night tonight.

4/11/34 Wednesday
Cloudy and began raining fast at dinner time. Eby plowed this A.M. I mended. Papa stopped on his way to Clarence's and left the news. We went in to see Charlie this P.M. and found him good. I took him a fern I brought from Eby's mother.

4/17/34 Tuesday
A good wash day, but clouded and is raining again this evening. I had a big wash. Paul helped me all day. Eby did odd jobs and split wood. Minnie was over and Paul and I cleaned the boys' room. Charlie is still in the hospital. Some Amish boys were caught stealing chickens. I mended the stockings.

4/20/34 Friday
A nice day. I cleaned our bedroom and the stairway. Gave the kitchen, wash house, and shanty a good sweeping. Papa and Katie brought Charlie home from the hospital and have a bed downstairs for him. Paul and I put the eggs away this evening. Eby plowed with the tractor. We had dandelion for supper.

4/23/34 Monday
Cloudy and rained a few drops with strong south wind all day. Did not wash till 5:00 and then left it in the tubs all night. I put things away and helped cut potatoes. We had dandelion for supper. Rhoda picked a big kettle full. Eby and Paul planted some potatoes. Charlie called up and is getting along fine.

5/2/34 Wednesday
A nice day. I made pies and noodles and washed up the kitchen and made butter of the milk we got back for pasture odor. Helped the kiddies set up housekeeping in the woodhouse. Started raining this evening. I cut Eby's hair. Talked to Margie and Mabel. Mabel got an electric refrigerator.

5/4/34 Friday
Showery till dinner and the sun shone most all P.M. and it is very much warmer. The children went barefoot for the first. Ground is very wet, and Eby shelled his seed corn and Paul helped me clean the cellar and the shanty. James and Isaac could not sleep this P.M. I made some cold water soap and stirred some ginger cakes and made some more butter. We got 115 lbs. of milk back.

5/6/34 Sunday
A nice warm day. Eby, Rhoda and Abram went to Hershey's church. Amy and Menno went too. The little boys and I made dinner, chicken, mashed potatoes, asparagus and raisin pie. Walked down to the creek and made the children willow whistles. I went over to see Jeanette.

5/7/34 Monday
A nice day with hot drying wind. I washed two washes, blankets, comfort slips, and bed clothes, aired the comforts and put them all away in the moth balls. Got the wash all ready to iron. Laid down a little while. Hoed the cabbage and started my rock garden. The mountain is burning and it is blue smoky. James was fussy.

5/9/34 Wednesday
A nice day, but clouded up this evening. Paul and I planted 330 strawberry plants this A.M., had rhubarb dumplings for dinner. Rhoda worked at her flower garden. I planted gladiolas and tuber roses and some seeds. Paul dug up my flower bed and I planted dahlias and put a trellis to the American Beauty rose. Eby finished plowing stalks and rolled it all. Got 300 peepies.

5/10/34 Thursday
Ascension Day. Very strong east wind and began raining about 6:00. Eby harrowed the gardens and then went to the S.S. meeting at Kinzer. The children and I made a half crock of butter. I mended and Paul and I made rock garden this P.M. Isaac broke Eby's fountain pen this evening. Got 127 eggs.

5/14/34 Monday
A showery day with warm growing weather. Eby finished planting corn. I washed and it dried between showers. Paul and I wed the tobacco bed and paths and started on the raspberries. Eby's daddy brought some plants for my rock garden and cannas, so we made a flower bed outside the yard for them. Put eggs away and fixed them so the rats could not get at them as they have been.

5/30/34 Wednesday
A nice day. Eby harrowed the gardens and Paul and I hoed them all over. Planted sweet potatoes and some cabbage in the old asparagus patch. Eby was busy listening for the president's speech this P.M. His train stopped in Lancaster a few minutes and he made a short speech which was broadcasted and David's were all over to hear it.

6/1/34 Friday
A nice hot day. I cleaned upstairs and the wash house and kitchen. Varnished the linoleum. Eby and Paul hoed thistles all day. Grandpap Hostetter has the grippe. Five baby girls were born to a woman in Canada. Paul went up to Kinzer for a straw hat.

6/14/34 Thursday

A very nice day. Cool. I pulled Irvin's some tomato plants and washed the machine. Eby and Paul put up the lima bean strings before Eby went to the ordination and the lot fell to Mart Hershey. Amy and Menno came from the ordination for dinner. Menno went home and Amy and I made 50 glasses of strawberry preserves. Planted some tomato plants and popcorn.

6/17/34 Sunday

A nice cool day. None of us went to church. Papa and Katie's nuptials were to be announced. Paul, Landis and Charlie went up to Uncle Milt's this P.M. Minnie came over for a while. We spent the day resting and reading.

6/23/34 Saturday

Partly cloudy but clear this evening. Not quite so warm. Charlie and I did the cleaning and canned 3 quarts of cherries. Charlie and Rhoda picked 6 boxes of strawberries and a few raspberries. I wed the celery plants and planted some head lettuce and peppers. Shampooed and bathed the children and put them to bed for naps. Filled James' chaff bag, took my bath and put eggs away.

6/24/34 Sunday

A warm day. Rhoda and Abram went with Clarence's to White Horse. They stopped in on their way home for about an hour. I did not feel so good all day. Took it easy and did no cooking. Landis brought Paul and Charlie back on his way home. Papa and Katie were at church in a new Plymouth.

6/25/34 Monday

A very fine wash and haymaking day. They hauled in nine loads. Charlie led the horse in the hook and picked vegetables for Dave between loads. I washed and ironed and made pies and a cake and boiled dressing. Pressed and cleaned Eby's clothes. Had a very severe toothache. Charlie picked some beans and strung them. The boys both have a grouch on.

6/29/34 Friday

A very hot sultry day. I milked and Eby dusted the potatoes. I had a very nasty toothache and called Dr. Frew and Dr. Bordner to find relief. Bordner said use iodine, which I tried. Paul went to Jay's with Eby's dad and picked about 12 quarts of sweet cherries. I milked this evening. We pulled 1000 celery plants for David. We cleaned the kitchen, wash house, and shanty.

7/1/34 Sunday

A nice day. Took it easy and had toothache. Minnie came over this A.M. Eby had radio church. Mabel had Papa and Katie to dinner and the three boys. They were over here this evening and gave the details about the machine the church donated to Papa.

7/9/34 Monday
A good wash day. I did not feel so swift, managed to do the washing and ironing. Our phone was out of order so David went up to Kinzer about 4:30 for Helen Ranck and called the Dr. and by 6:15 a 9 ½ lb. baby boy arrived. Paul took Eby's dad along down to Jay's to pick cherries and they were all spoiled. Eby mowed weeds around the premises. Paul took Isaac over to Clarence's. Rhoda, Isaac and James were at David's for supper.

7/10/34 Tuesday
Nice and cool for laying in bed. I am feeling good under the circumstances. The Dr. was here and was well pleased with baby and me. Eby went for Eleanor and she and Helen are going to do the work. Clay Hershey's wife is partly out of her mind. Eby and Paul are cleaning the corn and tobacco.

7/12/34 Thursday
Cloudy and rained some. Had my oil and got plenty of milk for baby. Guess we will call him Milton Paul. Papa, Charlie and Katie came down this P.M. and gave the baby $1.00. Charlie gave him $.25.

7/13/34 Friday
Cloudy with heavy rain in some parts. Helen and Eleanor did up the cleaning and Eleanor mowed the yard. The baby is good. The Dr. made a third trip and said it is unnecessary to come again. Galen's came this evening. Willis Hershey's and Maurice Hershey's both had baby girls this P.M.

7/18/34 Wednesday
A very nice day. The children all got up early and fought and cried a lot. Eby and Paul are hoeing the tobacco the second time. I got up about 3:30 and stayed up till bedtime. Feel good. Mabel and Charlie stopped in and took Paul along up home. Helen, Eleanor and the children went for a walk.

7/19/34 Thursday
A nice day, much warmer. I got up about 8:00 A.M. and layed down this P.M. Helen washed and cleaned things up and went along home with Grandpap Hostetter this evening. Eleanor mowed the yard this evening. Paul hoed tobacco and Eby went to John King's to thrash. Helen's bill for 10 days was $15.75.

7/30/34 Monday
A nice day. Real warm. Eby's parents came down and Grandma helped cook for the thrashers. They started about 10:00 and got done before 7:00. Had 562 bushels from 18 acres, a yield of 31 bushels per acre. Pap and Katie brought Charlie down this evening and they took Eleanor home so Eby could get to bed earlier. Last night Emma and Roy agreed to separate and discontinue their courtship and break their engagement.

8/5/34 Sunday
A very nice clear cool day. Eby's mouth, lips, chin and nose are sore and the children have colds, so no one went to church. We had a quiet restful Sunday to ourselves. I walked over to David's with the baby this evening. Menno Hess' and Elmer Shirk's came late this evening and took Abram along. He was in bed and got up again.

8/7/34 Tuesday
A very nice cool day. Charlie and Rhoda did the ironing. I did up the baby, his bath, feeding and wash. Eby and I painted our new machine. I think it looks real good. Cleaned a chicken and made drop cakes and a dish of corn starch for tomorrow. Baby was very good.

8/17/34 Friday
A real nice day, partly cloudy. David boiled 20 crocks of apple butter over here. His mother and Eleanor helped. I made pies and a chocolate cake. Charlie and I picked and hulled 3 quarts of lima beans and sold them to David for 20 cents per quart. Had a disagreeable soap peddler. Baby is very good. Got a pacifier.

8/21/34 Tuesday
A very nice cool day. Cleaned the upstairs and the dining room. Eby harrowed the gardens and Paul rolled the ground. They topped tobacco this A.M. and Eby disc harrowed his Roosevelt field. The boys cleaned up the gardens very nice. Eby, Rhoda, Milton and I went down to Jay's to see Rosa Jane.

8/22/34 Wednesday
A nice day, clouded this evening. Charlie watched the cows. I did up the morning work and baby wash. Sent Charlie over to help Mabel so I could get ready for his birthday surprise. Got the kitchen cleaned up, flies sprayed and ice cream mixed up. A vacuum-tite jar top salesman came. After a few mistakes and mishaps, we got things ready and Mart's, Clarence's, Jay and Sue came to help celebrate Charlie's sixteenth birthday.

9/1/34 Saturday
A very fine day. I finished up the cleaning, made some applesauce. Bathed the children and put them all to bed. They all slept and we hurried and got our work done and went up to see Pap and Katie and have supper with them. Got Rhoda new shoes for $1.89. We divided some things and I got the 4 yard linen table cloth.

9/8/34 Friday
Cloudy and began raining fast this P.M. I made grape juice and did the barn work as Eby was at Rutter Skiles' filling silo. Cleaned upstairs and patched this P.M. Eby took me over to Clarence's. Mart's were down and we divided Mother's dishes and some things. A very wet trip. Isaac came along home.

9/11/34 Monday
A cloudy morning and it cleared off this evening. I washed and got all the clothes dry and ready to iron. Took a rest this P.M. as the baby was awake most all last night. Charlie went up to school this A.M. and signed off for good. Education completed. Eby filled silo at Isaac Eby's. Charlie helped milk a cow this evening and did good.

9/24/34 Monday
Partly cloudy. I got the washing all done and dried and ready to iron. Eby helped to clean up and saw burnt timbers up at the mill. Charlie picked a bushel of Grimes Golden apples. I took a picture of the baby.

9/27/34 Thursday
Cloudy and damp. Had a big rain this P.M. and lots of flies. Eby took Dave's nurse home and brought his mother to help boil 24 gallons of apple butter. It is very nice. Got things in and ready for chow chow and canned some tomato juice. Charlie mowed the yard and got the wood ready. Paper is full of the Lindy kidnap case. Baby was good.

10/3/34 Wednesday
A fine fall day. Did up the morning work and Landis took Mabel, Mildred, Almeda, James, Milton and I along up to Rheems to see Menno and Amy on his way job hunting. Had a nice visit. Stopped a few minutes in Lancaster to shop. Landis and Jay are taking civil service courses. Paul hired with John Eby for winter for $20.00 a month. The plasterer was here and plastered a hole shut in the parlor.

10/10/34 Wednesday
Partly cloudy. Abram went along to visit school on his 5th birthday anniversary. Charlie took out the last ten bushel of white potatoes. We cleaned the little room and Charlie's room. Milton's rash is getting much worse.

10/18/34 Thursday
A splendid day for everything. I hurried to get ready and Mabel and I took three kiddies and went up to Intercourse and went with Pap and Katie up to Rheems while he went to Franklin County and she went to Peters. Found Amy just fine, stayed for dinner and supper and got home about 8:00. Stopped in Lancaster for a blanket for Minnie's baby and some kitchen wallpaper. Some big day.

10/19/34 Friday
A fine day. The men are busy husking corn. Charlie is hauling in. I worked fast to make up for lost time yesterday. Helped to take paper off of parlor and kitchen which was some job. Milked after supper and crated eggs. Rhoda has a boil on her back.

10/20/34 Saturday
A very fine day. Eby and Charlie husked and hauled in corn and cleaned some chicken houses and horse stable. I was busy with usual Saturday program. Washed

the woodwork in the parlor. Everything is topsy-turvy. Hope to have it better by next week. Minnie was over with David. I made 8 bottles of tomato cocktail.

11/3/34 Saturday
A very nice mild day. We did up morning work and took Abram, Rhoda and Milton along to Lancaster and did our winter shopping. I got a green silk dress for $2.76, Abram a suit, his first, for $7.95, and underwear, stockings, etc. Charlie kept Isaac and James at home. The sprayer fumigated the barn.

11/4/34 Sunday
Very warm and damp with high wind and wet rain this A.M. We all went to Hershey's church. Ira Hershey preached on Christ's second coming. Abram wore his new suit and thought he was quite a man. Spent the P.M. and evening comfortably at home. The Bishop board and bench have decided Charles Hershey shall not preach yet.

11/6/34 Tuesday
Blowing and raining very hard this A.M. but stopped and cleared. Eby went down to Jay's this P.M. to gun and Charlie went along and they did not see anything to shoot. Charlie helped me to iron and I cleaned the rabbits. Eby put a window pane in the kitchen window and fixed some doors and the swivel chair. Milton does not seem quite satisfied with me on a diet.

11/9/34 Friday
A nice day. John Plastino helped Eby haul fodder all day. I made pumpkin pies and oatmeal cakes. Charlie cleaned chicken houses. This P.M. we took out our beets and carrots and manured flower beds. Uncle David's cat went up on top of the tobacco shed and had to be brought down a ladder. Rhoda got head in the class first time.

11/15/34 Thursday
A real nice day, but cold. The drain to the kitchen sink was froze this morning. Eby and Charlie had colds and I am getting it. My right breast is sore. Did up my morning work and the baby wash and we cleaned between the house and barn and the yard. The landlord refused to let us change the garden. Milton is a good boy.

11/16/34 Friday
Not quite so cold. I did the upstairs cleaning and some down. Eby manured the gardens and plowed them. Charlie finished cleaning the yard and did the scrubbing. We popped first corn this evening. Rhoda got first head mark. Got 304 eggs.

11/17/34 Saturday
A very fine warm day. I was busy getting ready for company. Made a popcorn cake with shellbarks in and some jello. Finished cleaning. Eby and Charlie cleaned the chicken houses and horse stable. Had Dr. for sick cow. I have hemroids. Grammy came home from the hospital because she is too nervous for her operation. Gave Milton first cow's milk, about 3 oz. to go to bed on. 317 eggs.

11/29/34 Thursday
Jay's Wedding Day. Rained off and on all day and was damp, warm, and muddy. Eby got up at 4:30 and did all his work and went to Thanksgiving services while I stuffed and roasted a roaster to take along to Eby's home for their dinner. Isaac, James and Milton were good boys for Grandma while Rhoda, Abram, Eby and I went to Jay's wedding at 11:30. About ninety there. Had a very good dinner. Their plans did not work, and they had to leave on their trip in a machine decorated for the occasion. They first went to Intercourse for their untouched baggage and took Papa's new machine and went to Buffalo, Erie, Niagara Falls and Watkin's Glen. We came home wishing them all good luck.

1935

1/3/35 Thursday
A nice day. Warmer. Colds are better. My breast was sore this evening, so Eby and Charlie went to church. A big crowd with one confession. Bruno Richard Hauptmann is on trial for the murder of baby Charles Lindbergh on March 1, 1932. Milton was fussy. I cleaned the parlor and room with my new Electro Lux. Made a coconut cake.

1/12/35 Saturday
It cleared off and got much colder, and I did up my cleaning and made pies and apple dumplings for dinner. Gave Rhoda and myself shampoos. Milton is very good. Isaac and Rhoda have the itch just real bad. We have nice new calendars. 1360 lathe tobacco stripped so far.

1/18/35 Friday
A nice day. Not so cold. I did not get much done beside the usual work. We got up late and did the baby wash and made doughnuts. Eby bought some chicken powder and a gallon of buttermilk. Talked to Mabel and Papa. Milton was more or less fussy this A.M. Rhoda has been head for three days.

1/22/35 Tuesday
Still wet this morning and started to snow about 9 a.m. and is about 7 inches deep now. I washed and am drying it in the house. Made pies and boiled soap. Eby's Dad was here for dinner. My itch is very annoying. Store man did not come. Rhoda got a handkerchief for being head for 5 days.

1/24/35 Thursday
Cold and clear with everything drifted full this morning. Eby took Rhoda to the bus on a mule. It took all A.M. to get the pump going and thawed. I did the baby wash and made a white cake and a coconut cake. Had furnace fire all night and day. Milton has a second tooth. The milkman and mailman and egg man did not come. I cleaned five chickens for Sunday.

1/26/35 Saturday
A cloudy cold day. I was very busy getting ready for company. Charlie turned the ice cream. I bathed the children and put all to bed but Abram. A bunch of men finished shoveling the Hensel road open. The egg man did not get here until evening. My itch is a little better. I have decided Joshua's salve poisoned me for it was sure fierce.

1/30/35 Wednesday
A clear cold day. I did up my usual chores and the baby wash. James took a chill at dinner time and got sick and feverish and we called the Dr. and he seems a little better this evening. Made furnace fire. Rutter Skiles was here taking farm census. I borrowed Mentometzine from Minnie. Least eggs for a long time 125.

2/12/35 Tuesday
A nice day. Eby helped me wash as the wringer was broke. It dried and I got it ready to iron. Eby helped Wicks carry his furniture out to the tobacco shed. I made 8 quarts of mince meat and a very big kettle of vegetable soup. Almeda swallowed a button and Clarence took her to the Dr. and to Lancaster for an Xray.

2/17/35 Sunday
Raining and cleared this P.M. Very muddy. We did not go to church as the children were coughing and went over to Clarence's this P.M. Almeda is all right again. The Dr. charged $50 to take the button out of her throat plus Xray and hospital. Spent evening at home.

2/25/35 Monday
A very delightful wash day. I had a big wash and got it all in by 1:30. Went over to Clarence's this P.M. and Mabel is going to smock a dress for Rhoda. Eby put roof on the brooder house. Very muddy.

3/3/35 Sunday
A nice spring like day. We all went to White Horse Church and home for dinner and down to Jay's this P.M. Frank Hershey's were there too. Spent the evening at home. Milton made patty cakes for the first. 35 applicants were baptized at Mellinger's today.

3/16/35 Saturday
A very fine warm spring day. Eby and Charlie hauled manure and sweated. I cleaned up the kitchen and shanty, did the scrubbing, and made buns, a sponge cake and custards. Did the baby wash and helped wash the machine. Bathed Milton and myself and was all done by 8:00. Went over the S.S. lesson with the children. Peepies are doing fine.

3/18/35 Monday
A nice spring day. Mud about gone. I saw the first robin sitting up high in a big apple tree. Washed and got it all ready to iron. Worked this P.M. making a new hot

bed in the back of the house. Charlie helped between loads. He and Eby hauled manure all day. Sowed lettuce, red beets and radishes. Bishop Noah Landis' wife died. 224 eggs.

3/20/35 Wednesday
A very nice spring day. The things are shooting up and leaves are pushing. Had the hay balers for dinner. Seven men. Made pies and had a good-sized dinner. Eby and I went to Amanda Eaby's sale. About 1000 persons attended and some old relics were sold for very good prices. I got a half dozen silver knives and forks.

3/24/35 Sunday
A very fine clear day. Eby, Charlie and the three kiddies went to church and I made dinner for Jay and Sue, her parents, Paul Shirk's, Aldus Burkholder's and Emma, Paul and Charlie. Paul ate supper with us and then went in search of a girl. Eby and I went over to Clarence's and took them some ice cream and cakes.

3/30/35 Saturday
A nice mild day. Eby sowed his clover seed. He inoculated it, and I dried it all at the stove. Did up my Saturday cleaning and baby wash. Rhoda made her first cake, a fine chocolate. Abram and Isaac went down to Ramsey's to attend first of April business.

4/16/35 Tuesday
A very cold rough day. Snowed fast by times. Isaac went along to school. I ironed and put wash away and did my mending. Eby and Charlie hauled some of the old trolley bed in and started to pike the lane.

4/18/35 Thursday
A pretty day with drying wind. Did baby wash. Sorted my rags for the rag man and cleaned the garret this P.M. Moved the hydrangea bush and separated it along the fence. Stuck some lima beans in a box to sprout. Rhoda and Abram washed dishes three times and helped me a lot.

4/25/35 Thursday
A clear windy day. I did up the morning work and cut potatoes all day. We planted about 12 bushels. The potato planter broke and Charlie went to Gap for a new piece. Talked to Mrs. Usner and wrote Weaver Martin's wife a card as her mother died. My thirtieth birthday. The plum trees are in blossom.

5/3/35 Friday
Raining this morning. We planned to go to Lancaster this morning, then Irvin came, so we called the rest and had our frolic. Eby's mother and Margie came and helped me clean and cook chickens and make ice cream. It began raining about 3:30 and they did not get done. About 9:00 Christie called the Dr. for his Pap as he went out of his mind. Before he got home Mary met him and came back for Eby and the

machine as he got away from them, so he took Dave, and about twelve men hunted him in the rain until 1:00 and gave it up. At 2:30 he came back himself, and Christ came for Eby and to call the Dr. again. We had about an hour sleep. The Dr. took him to the insane asylum. He is very wild.

5/7/35 Tuesday
A very wet day. Rained hard this A.M. and cleared at dinner. Eby, Rhoda and I went to Lancaster to shop. I got Eby a Big Ben alarm clock for his birthday. He bought a pair of hair cutting scissors. I put my wash out and it dried good. Sawed wood. Paul came over to clean his machine with my new cleaner.

5/29/35 Wednesday
A warm day with drying wind. Had some nice showers this evening. We had frolic and hauled 39 more loads of ballask in and filled up our lane in a circle. Donald, Galens, Irvin, Clarence, John Plastino, Elmer and David helped. Grandpap Hostetter's were here too. Everything went fine.

6/10/35 Monday
A very fine day. I washed and ironed and was behind all day. John K is getting worse. They called the Dr. twice and Eby went over to stay with him all night.

6/20/35 Thursday
A very fine day. I picked the strawberries and canned 2 quarts more and made shortcake for dinner. Eby hauled Galen a load of hay. Eby and I took Abram to the Dr. to get vaccinated and then went in to Dr. Atlee's to show him the lump on my arm. I shopped a little.

7/17/35 Wednesday
A real warm day. The men dusted the tobacco, then Paul, Landis, Eby, Abram and I went to the hill for huckleberries and got about 22 quarts among us. They are not quite ripe enough. Charlie and Rhoda kept house and everything went fine. Charlie cleaned all the chicken houses. Landis mowed the yard this evening, and Eby and I went up to see Emma.

7/19/35 Friday
A very hot day. I made cakes and did some cleaning. Planted celery, spinach, corn, turnips, beets, radishes and carrots. Helped unload the last load of wheat. Charlie hoed tobacco. Eby mowed some weeds and they hauled in the rakings. Bathed the children. Abram has a boil. Lightning in the north.

8/23/35 Friday
Much cooler. I canned 28 quarts of plums. Eby succored tobacco this P.M. Grandpap had 18 tons of stone dust put on our new pike and it is sure fine. They rolled and raked it level.

8/25/35 Sunday
A very nice cool day. We all went to Hershey's church. Park Book preached a helpful sermon, text Ephesians 1. We spent the rest of the day having Sunday at home. Milton is fussy. Charlie came back this evening after helping care for Pap's chickens. Eby and I took a walk this evening.

9/10/35 Tuesday
A very clear cool day. I went with Eby when he took the milk and picked a bushel of tomatoes at Usner's and canned 18 quarts. Picked some beans for chow chow. Eby went to fill silo at Menno Eby's all day. Charlie helped cut tobacco at Clarence's. Abram is head again in his class. I did all the milking but one cow.

9/15/35 Sunday
A very fine day. Eby and I did the work and went to Paradise church and to Amos Hostetter's for dinner. The men went with Jere in to his S.S. in Lancaster and Eby attempted the devotion there for the first and was humiliated with his effort. We spent the evening at home.

9/19/35 Thursday
A nice damp day. Cleaned some chickens for supper. Mowed yard and cleaned up some weeds. Picked tomatoes and cleaned my pickle seeds. Sent some ginger cakes for the PTA chicken corn soup supper this evening. Milton can stand alone.

9/24/35 Tuesday
A nice day. Mike, Elmer, Grandpap H were here helping haul off corn. I was very busy and inclined to be some grouchy. Dried some corn on the porch roof and picked off the grapes.

9/29/35 Sunday
A stormy day, much colder. Eby and I did the work and we all went to White Horse church and to Clarence's for dinner. Aaron Hershey's and Isaac Metzler's were there too. There was a dynamite plant exploded at Lebanon last night and I heard it while getting ready for bed. Spot was killed on the highway sometime last night.

10/9/35 Wednesday
A very frosty morning. I got up before 4:00 and did up the mending till the rest got up. Eby and Charlie began husking corn. I cleaned the big truck room. Cleaned out the hot bed and sowed some spinach, radishes and onions. Abram got put in the other class. Made 8 quarts sandwich spread.

10/10/35 Thursday
Much warmer and very foggy this morning. I made apple sauce, stewed pears, made boiled dressing and cleaned two chickens. An agent was here selling Bachman's and I bought 1 lb. of cocoa and 1 lb. of candy to celebrate Abram's birthday. Eby took

a calf to Troop's for $18.10. Aunt Mary had an operation for gall stones and Papa gave her a blood transfusion.

10/13/35 Sunday
A damp morning and warm clear day. We all went to White Horse. This P.M. Eby, Milton and I slept. John Hershey's wife died. She and John were on their way to Tennessee to see John, Jr. and she fell out of the machine when the door flew open and she tried to close it.

10/25/35 Friday
A cold dry wind. I canned pears, finished them up and have 54 quarts. Helped husk corn this P.M. Eby ordered a litter carrier from George Summers. Got three chickens ready this evening. Eby took Rhoda to the Dr. for some ulcer and bedwetting medicine.

10/31/35 Thursday
We got up early to finish the corn and it began raining very fast before breakfast so we didn't get any done. Charlie helped me finish the cellar. I painted the flower pots and cleaned corner cupboard and drawers. Paul, Clarence, Charlie and Eby went to Chester to see them make Fords this P.M. I mended stockings.

11/1/35 Friday
A damp day. Eby went out for rabbits this A.M. Raleigh man was here and soap man and another extract man. Eby helped take the paper off the girls' room and it is all cleared ready for paper. Got things ready for vegetable soup. Harold left David's this evening. Poor boy came over to say good bye in tears. Very pitiful.

11/2/35 Saturday
A splendid, soft day, warm. We finished husking corn before 3:00 with sleeves rolled up. Got it all hauled in. I had to work late to get my cleaning all done. Bathed the children and we were all in bed before 10:00. Abram took out the gladiolas and Rhoda kept house just fine.

11/8/35 Friday
A nice warm day. We boiled apple butter, 21 crocks. Had 40 gallons of cider and 10 big buckets of snitz. Eby's mother helped, and Eby helped stir. She did some mending too. Cleaned some chickens for dinner. She gave me a handsome plaited rug and I am sure delighted. Got a lot of flies. Charlie and I cleaned the shanty and cellar way.

11/9/35 Saturday
A frosty morning and nice day. I made a cake, cracker pudding, marshmallows, cleaned some celery and cleaned up the kitchen. Charlie and I cleaned up the garden, put in some celery, took out the turnips, beets, and carrots. Had over 2 bushel of dandy carrots. Eby helped Clarence haul fodder all day. Bathed the children and myself.

11/20/35 Wednesday
A warm damp day. I made buns and mended this A.M. Eby and Charlie planted a post for the litter carrier. Photographer came to take Eby's picture for Agrico fertilizer ad. I finished painting kitchen first coat.

12/19/35 Thursday
Snowing this morning and partly cloudy all day. Got up earlier and finished flapjacks and made raisin cookies. Charlie and I went along with Paul and Mabel to Lancaster this P.M. and did some shopping. Charlie got a suit for $18.50. I had $5.00 and brought $.08 along home. Helped strip tobacco after I put the boys to bed.

12/24/35 Tuesday
A real nice day, cold. I finished up the wash and got sweet potatoes ready for the Christmas dinner. This P.M. Eby and Rhoda went to Zimmerman's Store to finish Xmas shopping and I went to Eby's home to help a while.

12/25/35 Wednesday
Christmas Day. A fine day, clouded up this P.M. and began snowing at dark. We got up late and all of us had a dandy dinner at Grandpap Hostetter's. All were able to be there, 46. Stopped at Clarence's to see Menno Hess'. Abram went along with them.

12/27/35 Friday
Partly cloudy. I canned 10 quarts of sauer kraut. Rhoda kept house and I helped strip tobacco. Made apple dumplings for dinner. Milton is starting to talk.

12/31/35 Tuesday
The most sunshiny day of December. The sun set a bit cloudy. I finished the ironing and put the clothes away. Charlie shoveled more paths. Eby dampened some tobacco and got 105 stripped but not all sized. I helped a while this P.M. Phares Landis was here for chick orders. Allen Rutt was here, got a $.25 box of blue bleach. Cleaned some celery.

1936

1/1/36 Wednesday
A fine winter day. Snow melted a little. I did up my work and helped strip tobacco all day. We took down 125 lath this evening. Have 1517 lath done. Abram was not feeling so good at school. Elvin B's wife died today of pneumonia. I mended stockings this evening. Milton's pacifier broke.

1/2/36 Thursday
A wet day. Rain froze and made it real icy. I helped strip tobacco all day. We took some down before supper. This evening I stirred up oatmeal cakes and made pie

dough and peeled apples. The Lindbergh's went to England to avoid American crime and get some rest and quiet. Hauptman is to die this month. Milton misses his pacifier.

1/3/36 Friday
Rained till dinnertime. Warmer, damp and foggy. I got up before the rest and made pies and cakes before breakfast. Did up my work and helped in the tobacco. Made some roasted backbone for supper. Irvin's got a warned off notice. Water was high all day and water didn't run. I put the bags on to boil that Mrs. Usner gave me. Isaac didn't feel good and vomited a lot this evening.

1/5/36 Sunday
Cloudy and sun shone this P.M. and it was pleasant. We all went to White Horse church. Mart Hershey preached. Had our dinner and went up to see Papa and Katie. She gave the boys balls, Rhoda a handkerchief, me a plate and the children candy. This evening Eby and I walked over to John King's. Pretty moonlight evening.

1/7/36 Tuesday
Still cloudy. I was busy trying to get the wash dry in the house. Got it all ironed and some mended. Eby and Charlie stripped. Eby was embarrassed in the S.S. class and set to work to learn the books of the Bible in order. Conquered the Old Testament this evening.

1/8/36 Wednesday
A mild cloudy day. We got up early to help Clarence's butcher, but Mabel had an indigestion spell and they phoned us not to come. I mended this A.M. and did some miscellaneous jobs. Went over to see Mabel this P.M. She has inflammation of the gall bladder.

1/14/36 Tuesday
The sun shone all day. Milton was some out of fix. I helped strip all day. The fertilizer men were here and took Eby's picture again. Darned stockings this evening and washed my head. The children have been very helpful this week, even Isaac.

1/15/36 Wednesday
It was damp and rained most all day. Helped strip tobacco. The children helped with the dishes and I swept and washed up the kitchen this evening. Mended some stockings. 170 eggs. Eby thinks the all night lights are a help.

1/22/36 Wednesday
A real nice morning, but got windy and clouded up and is snowing now. I got up early and did up my morning work and was all ready for Edna and she didn't come. I mended and stripped tobacco. I surprised Rhoda with chicken and ice cream for supper. 166 eggs.

1/23/36 Thursday

It blowed off cold last night and the thermometer dropped 45 degrees in 8 hours. 14 degrees below zero some places this morning with a very high wind. My flowers were nearly all frozen this morning and I stayed in the house and kept the stove wide open all day. The kiddies and I sat by the oven and mended. David went along to help Eby through the drifts with the milk and children. They were late for the first time.

1/24/36 Friday

Still some windy and 5 degrees below this morning. Not quite so cold this evening and the wind has fallen. I did up some odd jobs. The tobacco cellar is drying out. Charlie ripped my bags. People have frozen to death over the country and we hear lots of cold stories.

1/29/36 Wednesday

Real nice day for Sales Day. Eby worked on the machine this A.M. and they stripped tobacco this P.M. I made a walnut cake and cleaned the sitting room and went over the upstairs with the electric cleaner this P.M. Made some ice cream. Paul came over to sled this evening. Eby and I went out to sled a while.

2/9/36 Sunday

Snowing very fast and Charlie had trouble getting the milk out so he stayed home and kept the three little boys while Eby, Rhoda, Abram and I went to Hershey's church. There were 10 baptized. It stopped snowing about 9:30 and Paul took Charlie, Rhoda and Abram along up to Mart's for dinner. We rested and read.

2/14/36 Friday

Snowed, stormed and sleeted all night and turned to rain and froze on everything. The bus did not go so the children missed school for the first time. Eby and David rode mules to Kinzer to take Grandpap H. some chicken feed and get the mail. I sewed and made a petticoat for Jeanette's package surprise. Rhoda took it over. The sun shone this evening. Most roads are impassable.

2/19/36 Wednesday

5 below zero. Did up my work and mended all day. Charlie shoveled snow all day. Eby went to the mill and got feed for Walter and us. The baker came walking this evening with a bag of bread on his back. I taught Rhoda to knit through a spool this evening. Mary K came over to phone the Dr. for Christie.

2/27/36 Thursday

Rained this A.M., much warmer and cleared this P.M. Galen hauled a 444 lb. hog from Jay's for us and Mabel and Clarence helped us butcher. Got all done and meat cold packed till 7:30. Grandpap Martin died last night at 2:00 P.M. from a heart attack.

3/1/36 Sunday
A nice day. Snow is melting slowly. I helped with the morning and evening work. We all went to White Horse and up to Uncle Jacob Zimmerman's this P.M. and stopped at Uncle Mart's a little. Grandpap looked natural. I weigh 134 lbs. and Eby weighs 207 lbs.

3/2/36 Monday
Clear this morning and clouded up and is snowing this evening. I got up early and did the washing and got some ironing done. Isaac went along to school and Minnie kept Milton and we took James along to Grandpap's funeral.

3/9/36 Monday
A nice wash day and Charlie hung it all up and brought it in. Eby took me to Dr. Johnson to have my cyst cut off and it was not so bad. Bishop Christian Brackbill died. Had a tobacco buyer still offering 13-5.

3/12/36 Thursday
A very wet day, but cleared at dark. I made out my seed order and put things in my scrap book. This evening Eby, Charlie, Rhoda and Abram went to a Purina meeting and they are giving a picture play. I could not quite agree it was right. The 3 little boys are in bed singing themselves to sleep. Children got their pictures that were taken in school.

3/17/36 Tuesday
A very windy day and is raining in sheets this evening. Got 300 New Hampshire Reds and 300 Leghorn peeps this morning. Went to the Dr. this P.M. and he took all the stitches out and my arm feels much better. Rhoda has a swollen gland. Charlie helped me.

3/18/36 Wednesday
A very wet day. There are many flood reports in the paper. Johnstown is badly flooded and water is still rising. I made some towels and pillow cases. Eby went down to see Jay's horses and to a hardware fair down at Seller's this P.M. Isaac visited school. Aunt Cora called up this evening. Arm is better.

4/6/36 Monday
A cloudy wet day. Did not wash. Cleaned the Sunday shoes and the closets upstairs. Eby and Charlie cut wood. Eby was late getting home for dinner. He took Galen to Dr. Hostetter's after he cut his hand at Kramer's garage. I took Rhoda down to Dr. Beacher for her earache. Worked on my hooked rug.

4/9/36 Thursday
Another wet day. Eby and Charlie hauled wood till it got too wet. I finished ironing and made two batches of Easter candy this evening. Transplanted some plants and planted my ferns. Rhoda cried and fussed most all of last night with her ear. It is

better this evening. Gave a tramp a sandwich this A.M. and he threw it on the floor and said, "keep your old bread."

4/10/36 Friday
Damp and cold and began raining toward evening. Eby and Charlie took the old fence away along the road and hauled all the wood together. I did up the mending and washed diapers. Rhoda's ear opened and is better. Isaac laid all day and he had an earache last night. Coated candy.

4/14/36 Tuesday
A very fine day. Did up my work and made pies. Edna came before I was done to spend the day. We made 2 pairs of overalls for James and a suit for Isaac. Talked out. I worked at my hooked rug. Eby and Charlie blowed out the roots and stumps and got the garden finished.

4/17/36 Friday
A rough, cold windy day. I cleaned the dining room and was busy. Charlie helped me peel some apples this evening for apple dumplings. Eby and Charlie plowed the gardens and lot, took out asparagus roots and raspberry plants. School term ended and Rhoda has earache again. Eby went to a milk meeting at Gap. Rained a sprinkle about 9:00 P.M. An Amish girl was killed in an accident last night with Dr. Frew.

4/25/36 Saturday
A clear, cool day. I made a cake and prepared some eats for Sunday. Cleaned the bathroom and stairway. Took some pea seed over for Minnie. Eby plowed and disc harrowed the lot while Charlie rolled sod. Shampooed the children and bathed them. Eby sent Charlie for ice cream in honor of my birthday. Charlie gave me some nice books and Rhoda some safety pins.

5/1/36 Friday
A clear warm day. The children went barefooted. Made a walnut cake and a sponge. Rhoda cleaned upstairs and Charlie helped to clean the shanty, which finishes the house cleaning. We cut potatoes. John Bressler was here and sold me a pair of secondhand shoes for $1.00.

5/19/36 Tuesday
Rained this A.M. and cleared this P.M. Eby put the screen doors on and put the brooders away. He brought me a load of big stones to make rock garden and to put around the flower bed. Mabel had an operation for gall stones and gall bladder and appendix this P.M. She is as good as can be expected. Eby and Jay went up to Aaron Kolb's and bought a pair of year old mules for $400.00. Traded Jack in for $150.00.

5/22/36 Friday
A fine day. Charlie helped me do the cleaning and I made pies. We went in to see Mabel this P.M. and I took Rhoda and Abram to the dentist to have some teeth

pulled. Went out to Emma and borrowed $200.00 from her to help pay for the mules. Charlie went to the Dr.

5/29/36 Friday
I cleaned the upstairs. It was very cool and a little frosty this morning. Eby and I cleaned the brooder house and scrubbed it thoroughly all ready for the turkeys. Eby's daddy painted the kitchen porch. Mabel came home from the hospital and Clarence came for Mildred this evening.

6/1/36 Monday
A nice day, warmer with high wind. I washed and got it ready to iron. Mrs. Usner sent a dishpan of first strawberries over and I made about 24 glasses of preserves and each had a big dish for supper. We planted about 250 sweet potatoes.

6/3/36 Wednesday
The hottest day of the season. A gust came up about 4:00 and we had a fine rain. The lightning came in on the wires and pipes and frightened the children. I picked the strawberries and canned 8 quarts and had shortcake for dinner. Had new peas for supper. Eby fertilized corn all day.

6/9/36 Tuesday
Partly cloudy and warm. We finished planting tobacco and Eby's daddy planted his acre. Grandma was helping pull plants and spent the rest of the A.M. here helping me. Did the ironing and went over to Clarence's for sweet potato sprouts and we got them nearly all planted. The window sash blew in and killed 3 turkeys this evening and made me half sick.

6/11/36 Thursday
Had a shower this morning and it was hot until we had a gust and fine rain this evening. I trimmed and worked in the yard. Canned 3 quarts of strawberries. Cleaned up the parlor and wash house. Wed the pickle row just before dark. Cut Eby's hair this evening. He got done fertilizing the big cornfield. We got a tattooing outfit today to prevent thieves.

6/12/36 Friday
Partly cloudy all day and warm. Eby harrowed the gardens and lot and worked at the corn. I cleaned the room and upstairs and hoed in the gardens. Picked some strawberries. Scrubbed. Eby planted over 100 tomato plants. Charlie hoed the lot. His finger is better. Children worked real good. Jimmie was naughty, put 2 turkeys in a bucket with a dead one and set them in the entry. Whipped him and put him to bed.

6/13/36 Saturday
A big rain this morning and was showery all day. I finished up the cleaning and made three cakes and got things ready for company. Charlie picked the strawberries for me

and I picked the sugar peas. Eby bought 3 new cows for 3 old ones plus $125.00. The turkeys are doing real good. 5 have died and 3 were killed.

6/26/36 Friday
A dandy hay day. They hauled 8 loads in. I ran the machine to hook it off. This morning I dusted beans, cabbage, pickles, cauliflower, eggplants, melons and cantaloupes. Cleaned out two more rows of peas. Jimmie has a sore foot. Rhoda made a chocolate cake all herself.

7/9/36 Thursday
Clear and very hot. 116 in the sun. Eby helped Ross Usner this A.M. and Charlie helped Galen to thrash. Both came home after dinner. I got up at 4:30 and dusted the cabbages and beans. Hoed the new raspberry row and worked on my rug. Planted some flowers that Eby's mother sent. Helped Eby hoe tobacco. Had first tomatoes.

7/14/36 Tuesday
Warm and sultry. Did up the work and put wash away. Had early dinner and Eby took Rhoda to the dentist. I went along and had Milton's picture taken at Harold's for 39 cents each. Got a new dress for $1.00. Abram and James stayed at Grandpa H. Eby went to Clarence's to thrash after supper. I did the milking and succored corn. Gusty but no rain.

7/15/36 Wednesday
Cooled off this morning and was a fine day. Did up my work and went over to cook for Clarence's thrashers. Milton went along and Rhoda kept house. Charlie helped Walter Usner to finish harvesting. Abram is not so spry. Eby brought 3 quarts of ice cream for a treat.

7/17/36 Friday
A nice day. Warmer. We finished hoeing the tobacco for the first time this A.M. Eby and Charlie harrowed and helped hoe gardens and mowed most of the yard this evening. Yesterday Charles Lutz went wild and shot a constable dead and was desperate till a trooper shot him down, and he is in the hospital. Abram seems all right again. Had new corn for supper.

7/20/36 Monday
Had a nice shower this A.M. and seems clear this evening. I washed and hung it up at 2:00. It all dried and I got it ready to iron this evening. I helped tattoo chickens, 236 old hens and 150 pullets. All done till 8:30. I cut my new dress. Sowed the turnips.

7/23/36 Thursday
A nice warm day. Was busy all day. Did the mending. Three more turkeys smothered. I helped Eby put the wire netting fence up and put them out on the ground. Cow

kicked me upside down this evening. We all went to Irvin's. It got real gusty on the way home.

7/24/36 Friday
Started raining this morning. I canned 5 quarts of applesauce and 3 quarts of corn, 3 pickles and 5 quarts of carrots. Was some stiff from the cow's kick.

7/29/36 Wednesday
A warm rainy day, had real heavy gust and fine rain about 2:00. Cleaned the parlor and sitting room and trimmed and mowed after the rain. Eby left early this morning and went with Clarence on a poultry tour, 200 miles. He got home after 8:00. Had first lima beans. James slept very little last night with earache. It opened and seemed better this evening. Canned 5 quarts of pickles.

7/30/36 Thursday
A nice clear fresh morning after the rain and a fine cool day. Eby's parents came and took Isaac, Charlie and me along for huckleberries. We got about 20 quarts and cleaned them all this evening. Eby did the managing at home and had chicken corn soup and forgot to put the broth in.

8/25/36 Tuesday
A very hot day and was gusty and we had a good rain this evening. I made corn starch and a crock of applesauce and put a dish pan of corn on to dry on the porch roof. Rhoda picked and got string beans on for dinner and helped succor tobacco. A turkey died.

9/2/36 Wednesday
A real nice day. Had a shower this evening. I dried corn and tomatoes and got more corn this evening. Eby and Charlie helped Clarence in the tobacco and Jimmie went along to play with Almeda. Paul and Charlie went to the Mt. tent meeting and Charlie stopped to get a date with Margaret Hershey. I'm slowly improving.

9/4/36 Friday
A beautiful day. I made some grape butter and cleaned up most of the house and mended some screens. Got some corn in this evening and silked it and cleaned the eggs. I tried to get the heifer calf out of the lima beans and it threw me flat as a pancake.

9/14/36 Monday
Strong east wind and mostly cloudy. I washed and got it ready to iron. Did up 14 quarts of cantaloupes. Eby and Charlie cut corn all day. The children are very busy shelling dried beans at one cent per pound.

9/16/36 Wednesday
A very nice day. I had the water running on the garden most all day. Cleaned some corners and worked in the garden. Made about 2 gallons of sauer kraut. Cabbage is

scarce at 67 cents a lb. Eby weighed a turkey, 10 lbs. Rhoda and Abram each have 5 lbs of beans shelled and got Popsicles with their nickels.

9/23/36 Wednesday
Cloudy all morning but cleared till evening. C.V. egg auction man said our eggs are not clean enough. I worked in the garden and yard all day. The men cut corn and hauled off all day. Warm enough to sleep without covers.

9/25/36 Friday
Cleared and is very much cooler. Fire feels good with the doors all shut. I made some quince jelly and applesauce and two cakes. Picked string beans for dinner. Eby's pap got his toe under the wagon so he went home and missed the chicken pot pie for supper. Got sweet potatoes washed and apples pared for dumplings.

9/3036 Wednesday
Cold and cloudy and began raining at dinner. I helped pick the keefer pears, got 10 bushel. Finished picking the beans. Charlie cut the broom corn and hung it up and cleaned the stripping room. Eby and I laid up the sweet potatoes. I cleaned and labeled some of my seeds. The children are still working on the dry beans at one cent per lb.

10/3/36 Saturday
A splendid autumn day. I tied up and put away the apple butter. Rhoda helped to do the cleaning and scrubbing. I took a bath before dinner. Eby, Charlie and I went to preparatory services. Mildred and Almeda stayed here with the children. I cleaned 2 chickens. Papa is not so well.

10/11/36 Sunday
Partly cloudy all day and got much colder and rained a little this evening. Charlie went to White Horse and Eby and the 4 children went to Hershey's and we all went to Warren Graham's for dinner. Drove around by Galen's new farm on our way home. Charlie has a date with Margaret Hershey and Paul with Eleanor. Edna is having treatments for her lame leg.

10/12/36 Monday
Clear, colder and very stormy. I washed, boiled soap and ironed. Eby disc harrowed all day with the tractor. Charlie went with Clarence to Aunt Lizzie Martin's funeral. The children wore shoes most all day. Rhoda has not wet her bed for three nights, something very unusual.

10/24/36 Saturday
Rained a shower this morning and cleared off colder. I helped fix the turkeys in so they can't run around and we gave the sickest ones some buttermilk. Sprayed the flies and did the cleaning. The children husked the popcorn. I painted flower stands second coat.

10/26/36 Monday
A wet day. I did not wash. Cleaned the little truck room and closets upstairs. The men husked corn till about 11:00 when it rained faster. Eby put the new glass in the door at the steps and fixed two door latches. He went up to Vintage sale this P.M. Eby and David had a disagreement and he went up to his home this evening.

11/1/36 Sunday
Rained a little this morning and was cloudy all day. All went to church but Milton and I. We made roast turkey, filling, dried corn, sweet potatoes, celery, pickles, roast apples with whipped cream and cake. Paul came for dinner and he and Charlie went up to Uncle Milt's this P.M. Rested and read. Another turkey died.

11/8/36 Sunday
A very dark, cloudy, wet day. Menno Hess' were here for breakfast and went to White Horse and then home as Menno was too tired to visit. Eby and the children went to church. I helped with the evening work. Eby and the children were jumping rope this evening.

11/9/36 Monday
A damp day. I got up early and washed, cleaned the wash house and did the ironing. I feel that is enough for one day.

11/15/36 Sunday
A rough cold day. Amy and the children were here for breakfast and we all went over to Clarence's for dinner. Rhoda laid around all day and had a temperature of 103 after dinner. I helped do the evening work and cared for Rhoda.

11/16/36 Monday
A very windy cold day. Charlie hung up the wash for me. I got it all in and most of the old things ironed. Charlie took Rhoda to school in his machine this morning and I met the bus this evening and she is no better. Temp is 103 ½. Eby got Charlie to take him to town to look for a machine and get Milton shoes.

11/17/36 Tuesday
A nice cold day. Did up my morning work and got ready and went along to Lancaster with Eby to find a machine. We got a six-year-old Ford coach for $155.00 and our old machine valued at $25.00. Did a little shopping. Got a pair of part wool blankets for $3.98 and 10 yards of heavy outing for $1.00. Stopped at Dr. Frew.

11/22/36 Sunday
A cloudy, cold day. Charlie took Eby and three of the children to White Horse church. Isaac was not feeling good so Milton and I stayed home and got dinner. Had two nice big rabbits. Isaac is better this evening. Dedicated the Millwood church today.

11/26/36 Thursday
Thanksgiving Day. A nice day, cold and windy. Eby, Rhoda, James and Charlie went to church. The rest of us stayed home and roasted the turkey and made a good dinner which we all enjoyed. We have many things to be thankful for. Everything has been plentiful. Crops were all good and we have all enjoyed health the past year. I mended some stockings and cut some suits and a dress for Rhoda.

11/28/36 Saturday
A very cold cloudy windy day. Uncle Frank was here and Eby and his daddy helped finish up the window puttying. It took 16 lbs. of putty and 50 panes. I cleaned windows and did up Saturday cleaning and had myself and children all bathed till 7:00. Charlie, Abram and Isaac put a lot of chunks in the cellar.

12/2/36 Wednesday
A very wet day, good rain to fill cisterns and wells. Katie sent me a bunch of old blankets and I was very glad for them. Hemmed them and put on some patches. I made ice cream. Galen clipped the cows and was here for dinner. They started stripping tobacco. Learned the chickens are very lousy and put them all in 2 stables and treated them.

12/7/36 Monday
A good wash day. Charlie hung it up for me. Eby and his pap cut up the beef. Eby helped me to get 33 quarts cut up and in the kettles to cold pack, took it off at 7:00 and put the bones on and left them till morning. Fine cold weather for the meat.

12/10/36 Thursday
Very damp, drizzly and foggy. Made 19 quarts of mince meat and shelled some peanuts, English walnuts and grated a cocoanut and made a date and nut loaf. Finished the mending. Paul took Charlie along up to see Papa this evening. I have every jar filled again.

12/12/36 Saturday
Still wet. I finished baking the flap jacks and now have 55 dozen cakes. Did up the rest of the cleaning. Cleaned some celery and stuffed a flank for tomorrow. Bathed the children and myself and was all done by 7:00.

12/17/36 Thursday
Damp and partly cloudy. I put things in order upstairs and made some preparation. Got a cocoanut ready. Mended some everyday coats and cut some doll clothes. They took down more tobacco. Eby went to a milk meeting this evening.

12/18/36 Friday
A nice clear day, some colder. I made a walnut cake and a cocoanut cake and 4 lbs. of cocoanut bon bons. Cleaned upstairs and the corners. Made boiled dressing and chocolate syrup. They have 1400 lath of tobacco stripped. Chickens laid 54 eggs.

Eby went over to Usner's for a cow. Landis brought me a 6x9 linoleum rug for an Xmas present. It is very pretty.

12/24/36 Thursday
A fine day. I cleaned up the house, stuffed the turkey and boiled sweet potatoes. Mart and Jay came down for Irene this evening. She enjoyed her visit. They have 1700 lath of tobacco stripped. I have the toothache.

12/25/36 Friday
A very pretty mild day. We had our Xmas turkey to ourselves and all enjoyed it with good appetites. The children are well pleased with their gifts. I got the linoleum rug from Landis, table oil cloth from Charlie, flour sifter from Mabel, tea towel from Nora, pocket book, glass dish and milk pitcher.

12/28/36 Monday
A very pleasant mild day. I went to bed at 5:00 A.M. and had a baby girl at 5:30. She weighed 8 ½ lbs. Helen Ranck is taking care of us. The children have no school this week and Rhoda is very well pleased with her sister. Grandpap H. and Uncle Irvin stopped in about 7:00 and took Eby along to Galen's frolic which he expected to miss. Charlie helped with the washing.

12/29/36 Tuesday
Cloudy and damp. Busy trying to name the baby. The baby is real good and I am feeling better than usual. Eby went down to help with the barn remodeling on his new farm. The Dr. was here.

12/31/36 Thursday
Another wet day. Feeling better and baby is good enough. Eby was home today and they got 120 lath of tobacco stripped and took a lot down. We named the baby Grace. Mabel took James along home yesterday to stay a while.

1937

1/1/37 Friday
A very pretty day. Charlie helped Helen to do a big wash. Papa and Katie came early after dinner and Pap helped to strip tobacco. They did 180. Katie did some ironing. Uncle Mart came this evening. Helen cleaned upstairs. Rhoda cleaned the cellar way. Clyde Hershey died last night leaving a wife and five children.

1/5/37 Tuesday
A nice day. Eby went down to help Galen. Charlie did some odd jobs and helped Helen. The baby is very good. I got up about two hours this A.M. and two this P.M. and am feeling very good. Two Metzler girls came selling seeds.

1/6/37 Wednesday
A fine day, cloudy this evening. Helen finished up and cleaned the room and Charlie took her home after supper, making 10 days for $20. Eby went to help Galen again. I got up after breakfast and came out for dinner and supper. Took a nap this P.M. The boys are coughing.

1/9/37 Saturday
Cloudy and damp, sun shone a little. I made corn pone for dinner and helped Rhoda to make a chocolate cake. Charlie did up the cleaning. Mrs. Usner, Elsie King and Annie were here this P.M. I bathed the three little boys and Rhoda and Abram did themselves. Baby is good. Little David is doing better.

1/11/37 Monday
A very cloudy dismal day, snowed very fine this evening and is colder, way unhealthy weather. Charlie washed and it did not get dry, so he started furnace fire and hung it in the room. Little David is very much worse and the Dr. has little hope for his recovery. Talked to Mrs. Usner four times and Sue, Margie, Mabel and Minnie's mother twice.

1/12/37 Tuesday
Cloudy and damp. Eby went to tell the rest of the family of little David's death and to Lancaster for meat and new shoes and some other things. He was gone most all day. I have a stiff neck and could not sleep this P.M. and last night either. Eby was up most all night helping over at David's when their baby died. My nerves are some unstrung.

1/13/37 Wednesday
Very damp and warm. I washed and Charlie hung it up. I still have a stiff sore neck and put a mustard plaster on it tonight. Grace is very good, she began coughing a little today. I slept this P.M. Alfred Reeser died with typhoid fever. A horrible murder in New York of a former Lancaster girl married to Frank Case a year ago.

1/14/37 Thursday
A very damp foggy day. The sun came out a while this P.M. I took it easy this A.M. and went over to David's for the funeral services at the house. Charlie stayed with Milton and Grace. Irvin's came over after the funeral for Carl and Mary. Emma and Frank came this evening. Milton cried most all evening with earache. Grace is coughing. The warehouse in Kinzer burned down this A.M. about 10:00.

1/18/37 Monday
A very cloudy wet day. Did not wash, only a little for the baby. Took it easy all day. Washed dishes for the first time today. Made supper. Slept a while. The baby has slept very soundly all day and was hard to wake for feedings. Talked to Aunt Cora and Mrs. Mentzer this evening.

1/19/37 Tuesday
Cloudy, cold and damp. Charlie washed and it did not dry much. Left it out all night except some thin pieces. I cut Rhoda's waists. Slept this P.M. Charlie got butcher wood ready. Had the Dr. for baby and me and we are both improved. Milton has whooping cough. I made a cake.

1/20/37 Wednesday
Wet and cloudy. Sleeting, snowing and raining all day. Eby went to Clarence's to help butcher. Charlie and I got ready to butcher. Made fire in furnace and dried the icicles off the wash. I did hand washing and helped with ironing. Charlie cleaned rest of celery and made pies. Boiled sweet potatoes and made tapioca. Cleaned up the kitchen this evening.

1/27/37 Wednesday
A real nice day. I was busy all morning and did the ironing this P.M. Eby's Pap was here for dinner. Ed Stokes the McCormack man was here. My neck is still stiff and sore. The children have been rubbing it for me.

2/1/37 Monday
A fine wash day. Charlie helped. Got it ready to iron. Made the buttonholes in Milton's pants and have them ready to wear. Eby's Pap and Galen helped strip tobacco time P.M. Grace weighs 10 ¼ lbs. and slept all night till 5:30 and then I got up to nurse her and then she slept till after 8:00.

2/7/37 Sunday
Partly cloudy, but most pleasant Sunday we have had this year. We all went to Hershey's church and to Grandpap Martin's for dinner. The rest were all there too. Had a roast duck dinner. Grace was very good all day.

2/8/37 Monday
A cloudy day and did not wash. Delivered tobacco and Eby was gone most all day. Our share came to $534.32. Mrs. Trout is in the hospital for an operation. Abram is not feeling good this evening and managed to get a cup of boneset taken.

2/16/37 Tuesday
Snowed all day. More snow laying this evening than we had put together all winter. I did up my work this A.M. and did the ironing this P.M. Mended some this evening. David started to work in the warehouse today and goes back and forth with Eby. Charlie cleaned the manure spreader. James hung up his coat and cap without being told.

2/17/37 Wednesday
A beautiful day. The snow melted quite a lot. I did up the morning work, washed up the kitchen and made some custards. Finished the mending this P.M. Charlie cleaned the chicken houses and cleaned out some walnuts this P.M. Isaac and James

played in the snow. Rhoda missed first word in spelling this year and last year and is feeling real bad.

2/18/37 Thursday
Colder. I finished some mending and made some petticoats for Grace. Charlie made some drop cakes. Eby's Pap was here and had a lot to say about me going to the funeral.

2/28/37 Sunday
Clearest Sunday we had this year. We all went to White Horse. Park Book preached a helpful sermon, text Revelation 2.4. "Nevertheless, I have somewhat against thee, because thou hast left thy first love." Paul was here for dinner and he and Charlie went to Uncle Milt's this P.M. We spent the rest of the day having Sunday. I helped milk.

3/5/37 Friday
A cold stormy day. I helped get the stripping room and brooders ready for our peeps. Ralph Sleppy from Ephrata brought us 620 at $.12 apiece. Had a big time getting the temp of our brooder right. Granville came this evening and changed it. I made some pies.

3/15/37 Monday
It snowed very fast all day and is real deep this evening. We took the cardboard circles away from the brooders and counted the peepies. Have 599 left. Made some cold water soap and cleaned up the truck room and put jars up in the attic and watched it snow.

3/20/37 Saturday
A cloudy day and showery. They finished opening our road to the highway. Snow is melting fast. Did up the cleaning, and Eby, Charlie, Grace, James and I went to Preparatory services at Hershey's. George Graham preached and he had to say, "Where are the nine?" The crowd was not so big. Rhoda stuck a dishpan full of onion sets.

3/23/37 Tuesday
A nice day. Eby's fever broke and Dr. was here and said he could get up, but he didn't stay up more than an hour as he did not feel good up. The other children are all laying around with fever and headache. Eby feels worse this evening. I helped milk.

3/24/37 Wednesday
Real nice day. Eby got worse last night and the children are about the same. We got the Dr. again this evening and he called it flu. I am getting pretty tired and have a sore throat and some fever. I tried to keep the children quiet, but they were very troublesome. Had them all upstairs in our room.

3/26/37 Friday
We had a day of fasting. Eby came downstairs. I did just what had to be done. Read the book of Mark and wrote Mary Axe a letter. Abram went back to school. Charlie

went to Clarence's and he and Paul cleaned up their machines. Eby read his Bible and still has a headache.

3/27/37 Saturday
A nice day. I did up my work the quick way and mended this P.M. as I did not feel so good. Eby went out for the first time. He is pretty weak yet and has a poor appetite. Gave the children part baths. Rhoda is laying around with a fever. Milton is grouchy.

3/29/37 Monday
A nice day. Eby helped me wash and I got it all ready to iron. Charlie hauled manure. Eby took me up to the Dr. after dinner and got me some pills for cold in bladder. He got some more medicine for pep. Sold a cow to George Denny for $108 and a calf for $14.

4/2/37 Friday
A nice day. I was worse this morning and could hardly get around. Sent for the Dr. and he changed my medicine and we put the couch in the kitchen so I could lay down more. Mabel came over this P.M. and made a cake, boiled 2 kinds of potatoes, cleaned kitchen, and scrubbed shanty and porch. I feel better this evening.

4/5/37 Monday
A strong south wind and began raining hard toward evening. I helped separate the pullets from the biddies. We have a total 601, 316 pullets and 285 biddies. Grace weighed 14 lbs.

4/15/37 Thursday
A showery day and gusty this evening. Eby, his pap and John cut potatoes all day. I made 2 custards and finished patching and cleaned drawers this P.M. Isaac is better and took the insides all out of my old doll. Rhoda is not feeling so good. We have lost 15 of our new peepies.

4/16/37 Friday
Grace did not rest much all night and this morning her face is swelled on one side as if something stung her. I slept this P.M. so I could keep going for tonight. Put big good samaritan plaster on.

4/17/37 Saturday
A very nice warm day. I did up the cleaning and we made our garden this P.M. in a hurry. The rows are not so straight. Grace slept real good and seems better. Her eye is swelled almost shut.

4/21/37 Wednesday
Too wet to farm, so Eby helped me clean the garret and the spare room. He is a fine cleaner.

4/26/37 Monday
A very wet day. Rain blew in sheets. School closed. Rhoda and Abram each got a nice book for head mark prizes. Eby took a notion to build range shelters. I cleaned the kitchen cupboards and drawers.

4/30/37 Friday
A fine day. Margie called this morning and said Esther Clark died last evening. It was such a shock to me. Did not get much done. Cleaned the wash house, the cellar way and dish bench. Eby and John planted potatoes. Boys had earache last night. James cannot hear very good.

5/2/37 Sunday
A very pretty warm day. Eby went to church alone. I stayed home with the children. Milton kept me up most of the night with earache. Took some pictures of the children. Isaac has symptoms of the measles. Mart's stopped in a while and we went up to Granville Clark's about 4 o'clock.

5/3/37 Monday
Just a real fine day. I washed and got it all ready to iron. Eby and his pap were making a garden fence. Eby and I went to Esther Clark's funeral. The house was full. Isaac's measles are coming out today. Milton and James slept all night and seem good.

5/5/37 Wednesday
A nice warm day. I made a cake for Eby's birthday. Sue came down to help me air the comforts, wash bed clothes and do up the curtains. I cleaned the kitchen stairway this evening and packed the comforts away. Menno came this evening for the brooder. Isaac was up at the window and missed very little that was done today.

5/7/37 Friday
A fine day. Cleaned the kitchen. Eby helped me a while this A.M. to do the heavy work. I was very busy. Abram stayed in bed all day getting the measles. Last evening the giant dirigible Hindenburg exploded and burned just as it was landing at Lakehurst, N.J. 35 persons were burned. It was the first trip for this season.

5/9/37 Sunday
Partly cloudy and rained this evening. Rhoda was feeling real bad and is full of the measles. Abram is getting better. Got another can of milk back and filled up the can and made more ice cream as we had ice left. Spent the day at home. Took a walk out with the baby up to see the pullets. Read to Rhoda and Abram. Grace is fussy.

5/17/37 Monday
Clear, stormy, gusty, cool, rained and hailed. I washed and it dried fine. Eby and John cleaned chicken houses and hauled some stones off the corn field. George Summers put new leathers in the two rain pumps and two spigots. Fixed the water

wheel and bath tub leak. A woman at Christiana shot and killed her husband in a drunken quarrel. Grace was good.

5/24/37 Monday
A very nice day. The children went barefoot. I washed and ironed and cleaned the Sunday shoes. Planted some cabbage and lettuce. Eby and John hauled manure and cleaned the chicken stables. The boys caught tadpoles and picked tea and filled the horse chest and cleaned eggs.

5/28/37 Friday
A real nice day, warm and rained a good shower this evening with very little gust. We did up our morning work in a jiffy and let the 4 boys walk in to Clarence's, and Rhoda and Grace stayed at Uncle Bob's while Eby and I went to the dentist. Eby had 8 fillings and I had a bad wisdom tooth pulled and one 12 year molar. My jaw feels better this evening. Made a milk apron and a night gown for Eby this evening. Our pump motor burned out and Eby took it up to Granville this evening.

6/1/37 Tuesday
Hotter than yesterday. I replanted the pickles and did some hoeing this A.M. and went to the bank for Eby. Finished ironing this P.M. About 3:30 Sam, our new black 3-year-old mule had a heat stroke harrowing tobacco ground and died about 7:00 after the Dr., Eby and I did what we could to save him. Got $3.00 for him.

7/14/37 Wednesday
A partly wet day. Eby hoed tobacco and helped me plant about 600 celery plants. I picked raspberries and canned them and 5 quarts of rhubarb. Got 2 cans of milk back and the children helped make butter. I put the eggs away. Eby has farm fever very badly.

7/22/37 Thursday
We went up to Menno's this evening and Eby and I went over the premises and picked some blackberries. Rhoda stayed up. We came home just as a gust was coming up and just got here when it began raining fast. Eby has the farm fever real bad.

7/28/37 Wednesday
A pretty clear, cool day. I made my new dress almost done. Eby finished the manure and began plowing. The milk inspector was here and condemned the milkhouse and some other things. They stopped Walter Usner. Cleaned the eggs this evening.

8/1/37 Sunday
Just a splendid day. We all went to White Horse and had Landis, Paul, Charlie, Katie and Papa for dinner. Had some important propositions discussed. We went down to Aaron Hershey's this evening. The children were very mischievous up along the Old Road and made a lot of confusion.

8/14/37 Saturday
It was a very pretty day. Nice and cool. Landis and Josephine Hunt were married this morning. Paul and her sister Loda were attendants. They left on a honeymoon to the New England states. I did up my cleaning and got a chicken and some things ready for Sunday. We all went to Harvest services at Hershey's this evening.

9/18/37 Saturday
A fine day. I was busy getting my work done up this A.M. This P.M. Eby, Rhoda and I took Grandpap H. and Uncle Galen along to a farm sale at Smyrna. Eby bid $5400.50 and Ross Acker bought it for $5500.20. On the way home Grandpap half promised to rerent and fix up for milk shipping. I am well satisfied.

9/25/37 Saturday
A fine day. I made ice cream and finished up my cleaning and bathed the children and we all went up to Grandpap Martin's for dinner in honor of Landis' marriage. We took the ice cream. Had a nice dinner. Eby and I graded eggs. I weighed 120 lbs. after dinner.

9/28/37 Tuesday
A showery day. Eby went to Middletown to a cow sale on a free bus from Intercourse and bought 3 cows and one calf. He got home at 9:00. I did the evening work and Rhoda and I did the ironing. I canned tomatoes.

9/29/37 Wednesday
A nice day. I canned tomatoes and now have 45 quarts. Eby and John cut corn and took out potatoes. I made more quince honey and pumpkin and apple pies. Our new cows came and seem in good shape.

10/3/37 Sunday
A cloudy cold day. All went to Hershey's church. Had our communion service. Papa is not looking at all well. They went to Clarence's for dinner. I walked over to Usner's this evening. Eby and the children kept house.

11/12/37 Friday
A cloudy day. Rained and snowed. We got up at 3:45 and had our cider on at 10 of 4. Eby and I boiled alone for the first time. We had 10 fourteen quart buckets of snitz, 40 lbs. of sugar and 40 gallons of cider. Got 20 gallons of apple butter. We did not stir it till after dinner.

11/23/37 Tuesday
A nice cold day. I took the milk. I made pies and some eats. Finished the ironing and cleaned eggs. Isaac fell out of the front barn door and sprained his wrists and got his face scratched. We got the Dr. and he put a splint on one wrist. He rested real good.

11/24/37 Wednesday

A fine day. 20 this morning. I took the milk and got gas. Isaac missed his first day of school and laid most all day. He is stiff and sore but is much better this evening. I cleaned all the eggs and did baby wash and nursed Isaac. Grace is trying to pull herself up.

12/7/37 Tuesday

A very cold windy day. We did the work early and Eby went to Middletown on the free bus and bought a heifer for $31.00 and a bull for $19.00. He got a $20.00 rebate on the kicker he bought in September. I washed and tended the chickens and milked the cows and did the rest of the work. Abram is not feeling good.

12/11/37 Saturday

A cold day. Did up the work and Eby, James and I went to Lancaster to do our shopping. Rhoda and the rest kept house just fine. Grace is not feeling so good. I bathed the children and put them to bed. We sorted and put the Xmas presents away.

12/13/37 Monday

A nice wash day, very cold. I got the wash all ready to iron. The children are improving. I rubbed them all with spinol and put plasters on. Got a cocoanut ready and stirred up flap jacks.

12/14/37 Tuesday

A cold clear day. Minnie came over and offered to help to do something. I did the ironing and made the flap jacks. Eby and I cleaned all the eggs and went to bed early as we did not get much sleep last night. Milton had an earache and cried and kept Grace awake.

12/17/37 Friday

A very damp day. The men took down a lot of tobacco. I made 2 walnut cakes and some date raisin nut candy. Papered some flower pots and cleaned the room. Cleaned eggs. Milton did not rest very much last night on account of earache. We took turns rocking him at the oven door.

12/18/37 Saturday

Warm, rained and cleared this evening. Did up Saturday work and Eby, James, Grace and I went to Sem Hershey's for dinner. Rhoda had a temperature of 103 and she went to bed and Abram and Isaac kept house and did fine. I coated some candy and stuffed and sugared some dates this evening.

1938

1/1/38 Saturday

Cloudy and a cold rain. I scrubbed off the mud and the rain helped wash it off. Cleaned upstairs and the kitchen. Cut a petticoat and two night gowns and finished one. Bathed the children. Eby and I went to church, a full house.

1/3/38 Monday
A very fine day. I washed and ironed and cleaned some eggs. Eby went up to John Fisher's and down to New Holland looking for hogs. Eby went to Usner's to see about a hog this evening. Isaac is 3rd to head.

1/11/38 Tuesday
Snowed most all day, but not so much. We butchered a 455 lb. hog at 8 ½ cents. John helped and Papa came and helped too. We got all done up by 5:30. The children missed the bus for the first time because our clock was slow.

1/17/38 Monday
Cloudy, damp and rained a little. I washed and dried it in the kitchen. Eby scraped the chicken roosts. We cleaned and graded all the eggs. Grace is very good. Eby sent a fat cow to the stockyards. Isaac is head.

1/24/38 Monday
Very cloudy and damp. Began raining about 1:00. I washed it and it dried off some and I finished it in the kitchen. Grace did not rest very good last night on account of her cold and cough. She seems better today. Had a new Lloyd product dealer.

1/25/38 Tuesday
Stormy all night and just poured rain after the children left for school and Eby brought them back and they changed their soaked clothes and he took them down to school. Cleaned eggs. Got 222. Rhoda has sore throat and is not feeling good. Grace is improving. Isaac and Milton have colds too.

2/8/38 Tuesday
A beautiful mild sunshiny day. I took the milk. Eby plowed all day and is pleased with his new horse. I ironed and did some of the mending. Minnie and Jeannette were here this P.M. Jay's had a baby boy born to them this morning and named him Wilmer Leaman.

2/14/38 Monday
Just a fine day. The wash dried fine, hung it all up and took it down again without a sweater. Did the ironing and most of the mending. Eby plowed and went to Vintage this evening. He and his pap decided to farm 5 acres of peas. The children are busy looking at their valentines. I read the Bobbsey Twins to them a while.

2/17/38 Thursday
A nice day. I made doughnuts, potato chips, noodles and walnut caramels. Worked at my dress. Eby hauled manure this A.M. and plowed this P.M. The milk inspector was here and things were almost satisfactory. Rhoda's exam found her without any trouble and Abe had dirty teeth.

3/22/38 Tuesday
A warm spring day. 86 degrees. The trees are pushing their buds and leaves. I finished the ironing and put it away. Edna and Mary came to spend the P.M. while Mart and Irvin went to Usner's sale. Eby and Jay took off the P.M. for the sale. The sale amounted to $7600.00. 61 chicks have died so far. Got 179 eggs.

3/28/38 Monday
A fine wash day. My wringer is not fixed so I wrung it all by hand. Got some ironed. Eby is getting the ground ready to plant peas. 99 peeps have died so far.

3/30/38 Wednesday
A cloudy day with showers. I did up the morning work, scrubbed the kitchen, did baby wash and went to Christiana for 2 bushel more of pea seed. Took Grace along. Eby got them all planted by dinner. I cleaned and graded all the eggs. My seeds came. I sowed cabbage, cauliflower, tomatoes, peppers and radishes.

4/8/38 Friday
Very cold east wind and raining. The service man was here and fixed up my Maytag and charged $9.50. I worked at Rhoda's dress and did the other work.

4/9/38 Saturday
Cloudy and rained some. Eby quit in the warehouse at noon today and has $124.00 for his efforts. Did the cleaning and finished Rhoda's dress. Shampooed all 7 and cut Eby's hair.

4/12/38 Tuesday
A real fine day. I was sick last night and off feed all day. Took it easy this A.M. and cleaned eggs. The children just had school till dinner. Rhoda helped iron this P.M. I took the little boys along to the mill and up home, to the store and for the bolognas. Mended this evening.

4/25/38 Monday
A nice day. I did a big wash and my wringer worked very unsatisfactory. Got wash all ready to iron. Rhoda and Abram finished the school term. Rhoda got one prize and Abram got three. I cleaned up all the eggs and graded them.

4/26/38 Tuesday
A fine day. Much warmer. Eby disc harrowed with the tractor and John plowed. Rhoda and I did the ironing and made dinner. Cleaned the garret. 11 of our small peeps have died so far. Eby is taking a bath because he is so dusty. Isaac had his last day of school for the term. He did not get any prizes.

5/5/38 Thursday
A real nice day. I made a batch of ginger cakes and some pies and noodles and ice cream in the refrigerator in honor of Eby's birthday. Got all the eggs ready. Mrs.

John Hess was here for eggs for the General Hospital. Took the rugs out of our bedroom and aired and cleaned them. Started on the bathroom. Eby and John are getting ready for corn.

5/30/38 Monday
A cool windy day. I washed and did some of the ironing. Made a lot of noodles. Eby went to a sale at Middletown and got home about 9:00 and bought one cow for $11.00 and one for $20.00. Abram and Isaac planted the pumpkins.

5/31/38 Tuesday
A nice cool day. Did the ironing this A.M. and began whitewashing after dinner. Rhoda did some and likes it fine. Eby repaired and cleaned out the toilet. It took him till 3:00.

6/1/38 Wednesday
A nice day. Did up the morning work and whitewashed all day when I was not cooking. Eby disc harrowed. An airplane dusted our peas this P.M. which was quite a new event.

6/2/38 Thursday
A drying wind all day. Got things ready for dinner and the peeps and the baby wash. Whitewashed till dinner. Helped to drop 4000 of John's tobacco plants. The boys mowed the yard and cleaned the brooder houses and Rhoda cleaned eggs. Grace took a few steps.

6/7/38 Tuesday
The hottest day yet. Had a gust this evening. Eby and John finished planting tobacco. The children thinned corn. I did the ironing and mended. 11 peeps have died so far and the balance look fine. Rhoda's banties are all living.

6/18/38 Saturday
A nice day, pretty warm. Cleaned upstairs, did the kitchen and washed the shanty. Had 2 Johns for dinner and they started cutting the peas, so I had 5 men for supper. Made a white cake and got things ready for tomorrow. Eby and I went out and gleaned peas till dark and shelled some for Sunday dinner. Rhoda bathed the boys and I washed the machine.

6/28/38 Tuesday
Still cloudy and rained several showers. I washed and hung up the everyday things. Eby, Rhoda, Isaac, James and I picked about 30 quarts of black cherries this P.M. I started canning about 2:00 and we had them all seeded and canned by 10:00.

7/9/38 Saturday
A nice hot day and we had a shower this evening. Did up the cleaning and Eby put up the lima bean poles this P.M. and I hoed and tied up the vines. Bathed

the children and went out and hoed till dark when Clarence's came and caught me dirty.

7/13/38 Wednesday
A very warm day. I hoed tobacco this A.M. and evening. Rested, read and mended this P.M. Eby harrowed corn all day and hoed tobacco this evening. The boys and Rhoda cleaned the north and south end of the hog pen for the red chickens.

7/15/38 Friday
Had a gust about 4:00 A.M. and a good rain. I took out a bunch of red beets and they turned out to be white. Made 8 quarts of applesauce. John helped Eby to weed corn and Ross Usner to finish his wheat. We did some cleaning, scrubbing and hair cutting this evening. Found 16 dead pullets up by the ranges. About five men flew around the world in four days.

7/23/38 Saturday
A very wet day, rained a lot. Did up the cleaning and made some pads. Made a cake and some ice cream in the refrigerator. They finished thrashing by 8:00 and had 24 bushel per acre. Eby sat down and sympathized with himself this P.M.

7/25/38 Monday
Partly cloudy, sultry, and warm. We washed and ironed. The children pulled some weeds. I trained lima beans up the poles and planted some asters and picked lima beans. Eby and John fixed up the wheat field fence to pasture. Landis Brackbill was here talking confidentially t.o Eby.

7/31/38 Sunday
A warm partly cloudy day. Eby and the children went to S.S. all but Grace, Jim and I. Had chicken corn soup and ice cream for dinner. Rested, read and slept this P.M. and evening. They had open air singing in Kennel's Woods with about 2200 there.

8/2/38 Tuesday
A very warm day. I got in rhubarb and canned 14 quarts. Mended this P.M. Eby helped Ira Barley to thrash till 3:30. I picked pickles and put wire around the tomatoes. The tobacco is rusting all over the country and some are cutting it as fast as they can. I cut Grace's bangs.

8/12/38 Friday
A delightful day. I made pies, applesauce and a cake. Rhoda and I cleaned some cupboard and the aluminum ware and made some cold water soap. Hoed this evening. Eby plowed and put a bid on the Slack farm. Went down to Galen's this evening to take him to see the farm.

8/14/38 Sunday
A nice day, getting hotter. They all went to S.S. but Grace and me. A Russelite woman came with some phonograph speeches but I chased her off. Eby, Rhoda and Abram went to Hershey's this P.M. to the ordination for Eby Leaman who is going to Africa for Mission work. Clarence's stopped in to tell us Papa and Katie are sick with ptomaine poisoning from chicken they ate at Lois Eshleman's wedding on Thursday.

8/15/38 Monday
The hottest day yet. I washed and it dried fine and we got it all ironed and put away. Vick Kling came and stirred up farm sale and they had a little sale between Saul Stoltzfus and Eby which resulted in Eby having the last bid of $8900.00. Eby and I went up to his home and told them the step we have taken and then up to my home to see the sick. They are still pretty sick and mind the heat.

8/16/38 Tuesday
A very hot day. It was too hot to sleep last night. Did up the morning work and sat down and sewed and put quilt in the frame and started it. Eby's parents came this A.M. and did not commend us for faithful stewardship. I felt very bad, but did not help talk. Mabel stopped in on her way from seeing Papa and Katie. They say 54 out of the 60 wedding guests are sick over the chicken.

8/17/38 Wednesday
Very hot, had a shower about supper. I got up about 1:00 and Eby at 1:30. Eby helped make things ready. Everything went along fine till our baby arrived about 6:00 and to our sorrow and disappointment it was stillborn. Eby called Mabel and she came over and dressed it after the undertaker was through. After the children all saw it, Eby and the undertaker buried its dear little body in Hershey's cemetery. It was a long sad day for me. Elsie King came this P.M. and Mabel and Minnie this evening. Eby went for Aire Yoder.

8/18/38 Thursday
Much cooler and everyone is glad for the change. I slept real good. I was just tired out as I did not get much sleep the last two nights. It was a lonesome sad day again with no baby to nurse and no little bed. Time is long. Mart's came this evening. The Dr. was here again.

8/20/38 Saturday
A nice day. Rhoda helped Aire do the Saturday work. The men cut tobacco. Grandma H. was here a while this P.M. Mabel came this evening a little and brought the boys home. They took Rhoda and Abram along to White Horse harvest services. The ptomaine poisoned victims are recovering. Breasts are very uncomfortable. Mabel brought me chicken and ice cream and Grandma brought me oranges. Minnie cut a bouquet.

8/21/38 Sunday
A very pretty day. Eby, Abram and Isaac went to Hershey's church. Rhoda was not feeling able to go, so the little boys stayed at home too. The Dr. made his last visit. We all spent a quiet afternoon. Landis and Josephine came and Frank Kreider's came soon after they left.

8/28/38 Sunday
A fine fall day. It is getting very dry. They all went to S.S. but Grace and I. We made lima beans, corn, sweet potatoes and tomatoes, cake and ice cream for dinner. Eby took Walter and Ross Usner down to see our farm. Mary came over to visit me. I went out to the cow stable while Eby milked. Read to the children.

8/29/38 Monday
A nice day. The children started school. It was James' first day. Eby brought Verna to help me. We dried 10 quarts of corn and canned 12 quarts. Bishop John Moseman died yesterday. There was a man here looking at the farm.

9/8/38 Thursday
Had a good rain last night and a fine cool day. Sue came down this morning and helped Verna and I cook for the silo men. It went fine and they were done till 5:30. Verna went to a Doggie Roast this evening at Noah Denlinger's. Talked to Mabel and Aunt Cora and Grammy is in bed and not so well. Grandpap had a carpenter here to put up a new wire gate.

9/12/38 Monday
A cloudy day. We washed and ironed and I did some mending. I slept a while this P.M. Eby cut 115 shocks of corn and brought in the balance of the pullets this evening. 390 in all. James has been head in his class for 3 days and he got a book today.

9/19/38 Monday
A very wet day. Eby spent the morning on business and I spent the day mending. The children started a new program since we have no girl and did very well. I cleaned and graded all the eggs. Eby went up to his home on stale business. I shampooed my hair.

9/27/38 Tuesday
A nice day. Cooked for the potato pickers. Cooked some beets and made crumb pies and caramel pudding. Dug some sweet potatoes. Took a rest. Rhoda and I did the ironing this evening. They are making war threats in Europe.

9/30/38 Friday
A cloudy day, rained some. I cleaned upstairs and made ginger cakes and canned 11 quarts of tomatoes. Eby cleaned the horse stable and chicken roosts and picked 8 bushels of pears. The children shelled a bucket of lima beans. The Europeans have decided on a plan to avoid war at present.

10/1/38 Saturday
A nice cool day, had frost this morning. Had string beans for dinner. Did up the cleaning and laid down a while. Mabel stopped in on her way from Dr. They have a new Chevrolet Deluxe machine. I planted in some flowers. Bathed the kiddies and studied the S.S. lesson. Mrs. Weir gave Abram a duck just hatched when he went for the butter.

10/4/38 Tuesday
A very white frost. I made some pumpkin pies and boiled sweet potatoes. Papa came down from Jay's for dinner and picked up balance of the sweet potatoes. Papa has very little hope for us in our undertaking, but we are not going to give up yet. Milton and I picked 1 bushel of tomatoes and ½ bushel limas.

10/17/38 Monday
A fine warm wash day. Rhoda's teacher was sick so she was here to help me. Got the ironing all done and laid up some sweet potatoes. Peeled some pears. The boys started to take out the bean poles. Eby's pap came down to husk.

10/22/38 Saturday
A nice warm day. Paper says there is snow out west. Sprayed the flies and cleaned up the house. Rhoda washed the machine and did the scrubbing. Bathed the children and put the 3 little ones to bed. Abram and Isaac helped Eby haul in the corn. We all went to Lancaster this evening, got Abram a new gray suit for $9.75 and Abram and Isaac shoes for $1.89 and me a dress for $2.76, etc., etc.

10/28/38 Friday
A very dark, rainy day. I went along with Eby to the creamery and went and gave the house a lookover. The children kept house. I did some cleaning upstairs and put the comfort slips on. Worked on my dress this P.M. Cleaned eggs and talked to Mabel and cut Eby's hair this evening.

11/4/38 Friday
Partly cloudy. I got out the heavy underwear and did up the morning work and rested a while. Made things ready for supper. Milton went along to school and Eby, Grace and I went with Mabel and Clarence to Green Dragon at Ephrata. Eby and I went up to the Dr's this evening. He said I need building up.

11/13/38 Sunday
Cloudy. We all went to church. Eby milked alone. I did not feel so good. Went to Irvin's for dinner. Eby did the work this evening. I read to the children and rested. Raining this evening.

11/15/38 Tuesday
A real nice day. I felt pretty bad. Verna did the ironing. I mended. Eby and Paul cut wood down at John King's. Eby took me up to the Dr. again tonight.

11/26/38 Saturday
A cloudy day. Rhoda helped me do up the cleaning. We made sauer kraut for the first time. Eby and I went out to Millwood to hear Nevin Bender and Shem Peachy and George Miller. It was snowing like a real blizzard when church was over and we were glad to get home.

11/30/38 Wednesday
Fine winter day. Isaac and I took the milk. Verna canned 9 quarts of beets and I sewed. We went up to Dr. Frew's and got Isaac a certificate to go back to school and I got more medicine. The Dr. says I am better.

12/3/38 Saturday
Cold this morning and was much warmer and raining this evening. I took the milk and Verna helped clean up the kitchen and wash and dress the children and make dinner. Rhoda and I left for Lancaster about 10:30 and got her glasses and did some shopping. Got home about 4:00. I helped take down 50 lath of tobacco.

12/4/38 Sunday
A warm damp day, snow almost gone, sun shone. Eby, Abram, Rhoda and Isaac went to White Horse. I stayed home with the three little ones and their chicken pox. We rested and read. The children cut out paper dolls.

12/5/38 Monday
A very wet rainy day. I took the milk and the children to school. Cleaned and graded eggs. Helped take down a lot of tobacco. Kerr's phoned that they don't want our eggs as they did not test good enough. Planted Nora Mentzer's brown eyed Susie.

12/6/38 Tuesday
Cleared off and was stormy. I washed and got most of the ironing done. I got in one bushel more of the turnips and the rest of the cabbage that didn't freeze. Rhoda's glasses came. Kerr's came to take the bands off the chickens. I took the children and the milk.

12/8/38 Thursday
A very nice mild day. Eby went along down to John King's to plow. I took the milk this morning, got in some more celery and took out the parsnips. I let the boys play outdoors this P.M. The children took nickels to see some trained porcupines and they had movies of Holland.

12/14/38 Wednesday
Felt very bad.

12/25/38 Sunday
A nice day. We all went to Hershey's church. I tried to teach a class for the first time. We gave the children their presents when we got the dinner on. Rhoda was to have

dishes, but they did not come. Abram and Isaac tractor farm set and James and Milton each trucks. Grace a dolly and Eby and I pliers and a pair of hair clippers.

12/26/38 Monday
A real nice day, partly cloudy. We all spent the day at Grandpap Martin's and had a good Christmas dinner. I got a set of bowls, apron, posie pot and broom and a granite dish. The children got dolls, hankies, wash cloths, and the men woolen stockings.

12/28/38 Wednesday
A clear windy, very cold day. I made a cob fire in the furnace this evening. Cleaned eggs this A.M. and had turnips for dinner. Rhoda and I walked over to John King's. About ½ hour after I was there Isaac came over and said Aunt Mary was here so I cut my visit short.

12/31/38 Saturday
A real nice day. I finished up the ginger cakes. Rhoda and Isaac got up early and finished cleaning up the kitchen. I made Grace a new everyday dress and Rhoda made one for her dolly. Bathed the children this evening. Eby has 1600 lath of tobacco stripped. The year has brought many changes and new experiences, some pleasant and others not so pleasant, but we hope they have all been for our good and that through them we will be better fitted for life's journey with its problems and reverses and joys and pleasures as well.

1939

1/1/39 Sunday
Nice mild day. Partly cloudy. We all spent the morning at home and I went over to ask Minnie to go along to the Farewell services for Eby and Elva Leaman at Paradise. Had early dinner and Rhoda and Isaac went along too. The house was overflowing. They expect to sail Tuesday one minute after midnight. I read stories to the children.

1/9/39 Monday
Just like spring. Flies are coming out. I washed and got it ready to iron. Cleaned eggs. Eby plowed down at John King's all day. Minnie was over to phone for David to take Robert to the Dr. His bowels are out of order. We got milk back this morning.

1/12/39 Thursday
A nice day, some colder. Had 1 tobacco buyer before breakfast and one after 8:00. Offered 17+5. They came in again at 3:00 and Eby sold to General for 17+5. Milton went to visit school. Eggs came down.

2/6/39 Monday
A cloudy day. I washed and it did not dry so good. Hung the damp things on the rack. Cleaned the eggs and Isaac graded them. Grace was not feeling good all day.

Her stomach and appetite are not right. I got the things together for butchering and Eby took them down to Aaron Stoltzfus' this evening.

2/7/39 Tuesday
A nice day. I did the ironing and got things ready to put up the meat. Cleaned eggs. Took the paper over and visited with Minnie a little. Grace is up and down, seems about the same. I took a bath and Papa took me in to the Dr. this evening. Galen brought the meat this evening. Hog weighed almost 1000 lbs.

2/10/39 Friday
Cloudy and rained most all day. Damp and foggy. I picked the meat off the bones and canned 10 quarts of sauer kraut. Cleaned eggs. Did the work up early. The children came home from school about 3:00 as the teachers had a meeting. Eby took me in to the Dr. this evening.

2/11/39 Saturday
Rained this morning and cleared off colder this A.M. I made a cake and cleaned the upstairs room and kitchen. Did some mending and tried to get the hard wax out of James' ear. Bathed all but Rhoda and James.

2/20/39 Monday
An unusual warm day. It rained a while this morning and then cleared off. Milton and Grace were worse this morning and I called the Dr. They both laid around and slept most of the day, but seem brighter this evening. Doctored the children up and put them to bed early. Their temperatures are down this evening.

3/3/39 Friday
A nice day. Clouded up this evening. I did not feel so good. Cleaned up part of the garret and did some packing. Made some sugar cakes. Mart, Jay and Irene came this evening for clover seed.

3/9/39 Thursday
Warmer, then stormy this evening. Summers came to fix the waterwheel. Sam Zook hauled manure and plowed. I did not feel good, have a cold and cough. Milton and Grace have colds too. Irvin's little Mary has pneumonia.

3/11/39 Saturday
Snowing very fast this morning and was icy and wet all day. Did up the cleaning. Rhoda helped me good. I felt much better today. Eby finished in the warehouse and earned $160.00. The children made some fudge.

3/15/39 Wednesday
A cloudy day and is raining this evening. Mabel and Sue came and helped to cook the meat and made mince meat and vegetable soup, boiled soap and got the parlor

and spare room torn up and packed. I took the bologna meat up to butcher Lehman's after supper. The teacher sent Abram home as his one eye was a little pink.

3/17/39 Friday
A nice windy St. Patrick's Day. Did up the morning work. Mary and Irvin were here and Clarence and Donald. Ray Acker took 2 truckloads down to the new farm. Mary and I baked pies and cakes and little cakes, cleaned eggs, patched paper and packed meat and jelly.

3/23/39 Thursday
A fine day, not so warm. Margie and Sue came and helped make dinner, just had six men. We had a big crowd at our sale and things sold fairly good. Eby did some ciphering and it got late for going to bed.

3/24/39 Friday
A fine warm day. We packed and cleaned. Eby, Milton and I took a load of things down this P.M. and planted them. Put the cellar shelves up. Verna cleaned up the kitchen. Eby was busy getting things for people. The bees are out and flies too. This is our twelfth wedding anniversary.

3/29/39 Saturday
Partly cloudy. I cleaned upstairs, did the scrubbing and washed the machine. Rhoda helped and went for the butter, shampooed and bathed the children and planted some asparagus. Roy Mellinger brought a cow on trial and gave Eby a registered calf 3 days old from a cow that died of pneumonia. Eby gave the calf to the children.

5/7/39 Sunday
A warm day. We all went to S.S. Had asparagus for dinner for the first. Eby, Abram and I went to Meadville. George Lapp and wife, missionaries on furlough from India, were there. Rhoda was expecting some girls and they did not come. Spent the evening writing to Mary Axe and singing.

5/16/39 Tuesday
Partly cloudy and real cool. Rhoda, Eby and I went in to settle for the farm and got it pretty well accomplished. I went to the Dr. and took the Aunties some asparagus. I sewed this P.M. and evening. Rhoda worked on her flower garden.

5/23/39 Tuesday
Cloudy, damp and got very warm. I mended and worked in the cellar this P.M., whitewashed part of it. Lloyd products man was here. I planted more tomatoes, cabbage, lettuce, peppers and cauliflower this evening and some cantaloupe seed. Rhoda made her garden and the boys worked on theirs.

5/25/39 Thursday

A nice day. Cool. We cleaned the garret and it was really dirty. We pulled over 700 sweet potato plants and planted them before supper. Rhoda broke 4 dishes. She made dinner and supper. I hoed in the truck patch this evening and replanted the lima beans. Eby trimmed the hedge this evening. Sold 10 lbs. asparagus.

5/31/39 Wednesday

A very hot dry day. I mended and hoed and watered the tobacco plants. The children finished replanting the corn. Sent 10 bunches of asparagus to the store. We have sold 54 lbs. at 12 cents.

6/2/39 Friday

Still showery but not much rain yet. We pulled plants again. I helped drop part of the P.M. Did some hoeing and odd jobs this evening. Rhoda helped drop some plants and Abram tried it but with little success.

6/12/39 Monday

A very fine day. Things looked fresh and are growing after the rain. I pulled plants for Eby and the boys to replant tobacco. It was quite a job as lots are missing. Rhoda helped me wash and we did most of the ironing. Rhoda cleaned eggs and helped me good. My back is in bad shape.

6/28/39 Wednesday

Partly cloudy all day. Eby finished shocking wheat till dinner and he, Abram and Isaac went over to haul in at John King's. The boys built 13 loads. I cold packed 9 quarts of cherries and we picked more. I hoed tobacco this P.M. and some this evening. It is getting weedy. Rhoda cleaned eggs and we did the ironing between us. Seeded cherries from dark until bedtime.

7/21/39 Friday

A pleasant day, partly cloudy. Eby, Rhoda, Isaac and I went for huckleberries and got about 24 quarts. We got home about 6:00 and were well pleased with our berries, had a flat tire on the way home. Abram kept house and they got along fine.

7/23/39 Sunday

A nice day. Partly cloudy and warmer. We all went to Hershey's and spent the rest of the day at home. The children wrote some letters to Words of Cheer this evening. I wrote some cards and a letter to Emma Horning.

7/27/39 Thursday

A cloudy day and sprinkled a few showers here and rained a lot some places. Eby went to Riehl's barnraising all day. I picked the pickles and mended and sewed all day. Got things done up and am ready for something new.

7/30/39 Sunday
Had a fine big rain this morning and cleared off about 11:00. We all went to S.S. Had chicken corn soup for dinner and rested and read this P.M. There was a big singing at Kennel's Woods this P.M. About 2900 there.

8/4/39 Friday
A nice day, not quite so hot. We had a sprinkle last night and above Lancaster they had a heavy storm and cloudburst. I made cakes and candy. We cleaned up the house this P.M. and Rhoda finished the yard this evening. I picked lima beans, pickles, and tomatoes. Eby topped first tobacco, mowed some weeds and wed sweet potatoes. We put the Rock chickens on range this evening.

8/14/39 Monday
A warm cloudy day. Eby worked on the chicken house. We did the washing and got elderberries ready for jelly. Cooked 20 pts. in the copper kettle. Something is killing our White Rock chicks.

8/17/39 Thursday
A very hot day. Eby topped tobacco and went to New Holland and bought a cow this P.M. for $70.00. We were very busy. Canned 16 quarts of peaches, 6 quarts of applesauce and 17 glasses of crabapple jelly. Cleaned up the house. We all took baths this evening.

8/18/39 Friday
We did up our morning work and left about 7:30 for Philadelphia and Valley Forge. Clarence's took 2 of our children and we all enjoyed the trip. Got home about 5:30 and had a fine rain here. Eby and the children brought in some pullets this evening. Grace was a good girl, but very tired this evening.

8/19/39 Saturday
It rained very hard all day, and the drought is really broken. I canned peaches and made apple dumplings and did up the cleaning. Eby got ready to cut tobacco.

8/24/39 Thursday
Did up our work and took the milk down on our way to Clarence's. Rhoda, James and I spent the day there making chow chow. I got 28 quarts and so did she. Had a gust this P.M. and it burned the barn down on the farm north of Jay's. Eby helped Sam Summers fill silo. He took Abram, Isaac and Milton to see the fire this evening. Rhoda and I finished canning peaches. I now have 36 quarts.

8/28/39 Monday
Cool and partly cloudy. I did not wash and helped succor tobacco till time to get dinner. Ralph Kurtz came at 9:00 and they began cutting. They got a nice bunch cut. I cut down some this P.M. School started and the children had a lot to talk about this evening.

8/29/39 Tuesday
Cool and partly cloudy. I washed and got it all ready to iron. Made apple pies and boiled beets. Had 2 tobacco cutters for dinner and supper. Rained a little bit this evening. I planted some lettuce. War is threatening Europe.

9/2/39 Saturday
A real nice day. I helped make some cakes and apple dumplings and then succored tobacco till dinner. Eby had 3 men to help cut this P.M. I did my cleaning and was very busy and tired. Sowed some spinach and radishes. Germany declared war on Poland.

9/8/39 Friday
A very hot day. I cleaned all but the kitchen. Eby cut corn and we took out 6 bushel of potatoes for Truman Sweigart. The children had school until the last recess. The paper is full of war. Another pullet was picked to death, got 24 eggs.

9/15/39 Friday
A very fine day. I made some grape juice and canned some. Eby cut corn and disc harrowed the tobacco patch. He bought over $11.00 worth of chicken remedies. I dug some carrots and sweet potatoes. Got 50 pullet eggs and 76 big eggs.

9/18/39 Monday
A fine day, very cool. I washed and it dried fine. Got it all ready to iron. I picked the tomatoes and canned 14 quarts. Helped husk a little corn this evening. The boys picked up apples for cider. I read Uncle Tom's Cabin to the children a while this evening.

9/20/39 Wednesday
Partly cloudy and had a big shower this evening. Eby and I took out 14 bushel of potatoes this A.M. and I cleaned eggs this P.M. We emptied the vinegar barrels and filled them up with fresh. Eby sold 600 bags and some old iron to a junk man.

9/25/39 Monday
A nice day with strong south wind. I did not wash as we took out the balance of our potatoes. The three biggest children missed school to help. This morning we found 33 of our rock chickens were killed. The game warden was here investigating.

9/26/39 Tuesday
Partly cloudy and began to rain this evening and is much cooler. I washed and got it ready to iron. Picked 2 ½ bushel of tomatoes and canned 6 quarts. Cleaned eggs. Eby went to a milk meeting at the Gap this evening. We sold 116 rock chickens to Ralph Kurtz. They came to $156.00. The game warden is watching again tonight for dogs.

9/30/39 Saturday
Damp and cloudy and rained a big shower this evening. I did some baking, finished scrubbing the garret and did up the kitchen. Took my bath after dinner and went over

to Clarence's with some sewing. Made 3 aprons on Mabel's electric sewing machine. Eby paid first interest on the farm money and had $22.50 taken off.

10/13/39 Friday
A fine day. Real cool with a little frost. I cleaned the spare room and we took out half of the sweet potatoes this P.M. Isaac did not feel able to go to school this morning but was able to gather in pumpkins, got about 4 wheelbarrow loads.

10/14/39 Saturday
A cold windy, rough day. Eby and the children took out the rest of the sweet potatoes, about 31 bushel in all. I made 2 cakes and some things for Sunday. Did up most of the cleaning and Rhoda finished while we went to preparatory services. Clarence's and us went up to Uncle Milt's this evening as Grammy died early this morning.

10/15/39 Sunday
A fine day, very cool, but the wind prevented much frost. We had communion at Hershey's. Spent the P.M. resting. Rhoda had company, Muriel, Gladys and Pauline. We read Uncle Tom's Cabin this evening.

10/16/39 Monday
A nice day. Carpenters were busy working at the cow stable. I washed and got it ready to iron. I pasted the seams down in the linoleum and it was quite a job. Made grape nuts.

10/17/39 Tuesday
A nice cool day and frosty this morning. I did up the morning work and got things ready for dinner and supper. Charlie took Eby, Grace and I with Uncle Jay's along to Grammy's funeral at Strasburg. Text was Job 5:19. I did the ironing this evening. The carpenters were here.

10/19/39 Thursday
A nice day, much warmer. Made sandwich spread, a double portion. Canned 4 pints of sour celery and 8 pints of stuffed peppers. Made some applesauce and a bean supper. Cleaned eggs. Had 102 dozen for today and our check was $31.17. Clair Denlinger was here to ask Eby to go along to a corn husking contest in Mt. Joy.

10/23/39 Monday
A nice day, cold and stormy. Two Summers boys and one Umble husked corn this A.M. but it was too rough, and they quit at dinner. The chickens had a bad spell for picking and I dressed 4 of them and we had chicken pot pie for supper. Rhoda is not feeling good, has a temperature of 102 this evening.

11/3/39 Friday
A fine day. We put our cider on at 4:00 and took 27 quarts of apple butter off at 7:00. Had 40 gallons of cider, 12 fourteen quart buckets of snitz and 30 lbs. of

sugar. Mabel was helping and Papa was here husking corn. I made rabbit potpie for dinner.

11/16/39 Thursday
A fine day, very mild. Eby and I took the paper off the kitchen. Mr. Wilson came this P.M. and did the plastering. We sanded the walls this evening. Just looks like a pig pen.

11/22/39 Wednesday
Real nice day. I finished up the cleaning and bronzed the stove pipe and milk house rack. Eby was down at Jay's hauling fodder. We got a heater stove from Seller's for $14.00 and set it up and made fire. It does good. Milton is very anxious for Thanksgiving.

11/23/39 Thursday
A fine day. Eby and the boys went to church at Hershey's. We had a dinner for the whole family. Everyone was here, but Papa and Katie had to leave for a wedding right after dinner. Fannie came over and helped with the dinner. Landis brought Josephine before dinner and she helped too.

12/5/39 Tuesday
A cloudy day. We shredded fodder. Had 5 men for dinner. Made pies and was busy getting dinner. Eby helped Jay shred this P.M. I did the ironing and some mending. Did not feel so good. Grace has a temperature of 102 this evening.

12/7/39 Thursday
Did not feel good and could hardly keep going.

12/8/39 Friday
Felt very bad and took my temperature and it was almost 104, so we sent for the Dr. and he called it pyelitis. Eby brought our bed down and I went to bed. Grace went along to the Christmas party at school and she had better stayed home. It was very stormy.

12/11/39 Monday
A real good wash day. Eby took ours along and gave it to Clarence, and Mabel is going to do it. I got up for breakfast, but did not feel very good. Patched a pair of Eby's overalls.

12/15/39 Friday
Snow is still laying and the children have fun sledding. I did some mending. Eby and Paul are stripping tobacco. Grace's fever went to 105 this evening and we called the Dr. I stayed up until after 3:00 A.M. and then she rested better, so I went to bed.

12/18/39 Monday
A nice day, just like spring. Paul was here plowing. Stirred up flap jacks. Got some celery ready for Aldous Burkholders and sent it with Paul. I helped milk this evening and cleaned eggs. Grace seems much better.

12/20/39 Wednesday
A wet day. I made pies and Mabel came to help bake Christmas cookies. I cleaned eggs this evening. Sue and Jay brought the wash back all done up nicely this evening.

12/25/39 Monday
Cloudy, cold and windy. We all spent Christmas at Grandpap Martin's. Had a good dinner. Got a basin, apron, 2 tea towels, a wash line, 2 tablets. Eby got stockings and the children books, toys, etc. Eby took $.50 worth of celery to a lady in Gap this evening.

12/26/39 Tuesday
A nice day. Rhoda did some of the ironing. I washed and Rhoda hung it up. I got the wash house ready to butcher. Eby got the tools together. Paul was here stripping tobacco. The chickens are breaking off. The boys shook cream into butter. I made some things ready for tomorrow dinner.

12/27/39 Wednesday
Began snowing at daylight and kept it up till evening with a good bit laying. It was real cold. Clarence, Paul, Mabel, Papa, Katie and Maggie Hostetter helped butcher 3 hogs. It went good. We got the meat cut up and put in the cans.

12/30/39 Saturday
A cold day. Snowed more last night and blew a little. We did up rest of the cleaning. Eby, Isaac and Abram went up to Uncle Menno's sale this P.M. Gave all a shampoo but Daddy. Eby took me down to the Dr. this evening. Canned some meat off the back bone and finished it all up. 1650 lath of tobacco stripped.

12/31/39 Sunday
A clear cold day. The snow blew a little. The boys and Daddy went to White Horse. Rhoda and I made dinner. She had such a cough. Spent the day resting and reading. Took 2 pictures of the children. Fannie was away most all day. It was most too cold for the children to sled. The past year has brought many changes. We have been wonderfully blessed. May we live better lives through the coming year and be more resigned to His will.

The family farm, Gap, Pennsylvania.

The Forties

1940

1/1/40 Monday
A very cold day, below zero this morning. I washed and hung it up and got very cold and chilly. Rhoda stayed in till this P.M. when Kathleen Martin came to sled, then she went sledding and has a fever again this evening. The boys bought the wash all in and it was real dry. I made Rhoda's plaid skirt this P.M.

1/2/40 Tuesday
A cold day. The wash is all dry and I ironed it. The boys went back to school and Rhoda went back to bed after breakfast. She has a fever and no appetite. A 12-year-old girl was killed sledding on the Strasburg Pike when she ran into the path of a truck.

1/9/40 Tuesday
A nice day. Papa came down and made a cupboard under my sink in the corner. It is very nice. Landis came and was here for dinner and helped to strip tobacco for a while. The children all went to school. I did the ironing and some of the mending. Did not feel so good. Helped milk this morning and evening.

1/10/40 Wednesday
A nice cold day. Had a big night, got up at 2:00 and Charles Lewis was born at 4:00. Eby was busy getting things ready to give him a warm reception. The children all went to school and Eby went for the nurse, Rebecca Fisher, when he went with the milk. Everything went fine today. The Dr. came.

1/12/40 Friday
Cloudy and snowing. Cold. The baby is good. The nurse's daughter Rebecca came up this evening to see her mother. Mabel was here and helped to clean and bake, etc.

1/17/40 Wednesday
A cold wintry day. I am feeling good, have a good nurse and good appetite. Charlie was here this evening and gave the baby a bank with 20 quarters in it.

1/19/40 Friday
Snowed last night and the wash is still out. Fannie helped today. I got up about 10:00. Eby went to bed after breakfast and stayed in till this evening and he feels real good again. The nurse was feeling bad and Paul took her home before supper.

1/20/40 Saturday
A real nice day. Milton is laying around and the Dr. gave some medicine for him when he was here this P.M. His temperature was 105 at 3:00 but came down till bedtime.

1/22/40 Monday
A nice clear day. I took care of the sick and got the meals. Milton is better and Grace is lying around feverish. Papa and Katie came before we had dinner. Papa brought a drawer for my tea table. Katie and I did some sewing. She gave the baby $1.00.

1/23/40 Tuesday
A real nice wash day. Sue came early and got it washed, ironed and hung the underwear and heavy things in the truck room. I slept this P.M. and kept the sick ones out of the kitchen. Milton slept down on the couch last night. He is better. Rhoda went to school and they closed the school till next Monday.

1/26/40 Friday
A nice day, still cold. The children are all better, but still coughing. Eby got some pinex and they are taking that. I took care of the baby and did the wash. I slept this P.M. The children made valentines. Abram and Isaac did the chickens and put down fodder and cleaned the cow stable. Had tobacco lookers. The baby weighed 10 lbs.

1/29/40 Monday
A nice day. The baby wash dried good. The children are improving, coughs are not quite so bad. They all went out but the baby and I. Not quite so cold. Clair Denlinger was up and helped to strip tobacco. I cut some dresses and the children made valentines. Abram made some cup custards and sent them along with Paul for Mildred.

2/12/40 Monday
A nice springlike day. The baby did not sleep good last night. I did the baby wash and cleaned a bunch of celery. Eby went to John Kauffman's funeral. Charlie Hershey was here selling the Successful Farming Magazine. Baby was good. I slept till 3:00.

3/7/40 Thursday
Cloudy. Mabel brought her sewing machine early and gave the baby his bath. I did up the morning work. Sue brought her sewing machine and Edna came with hers. They made five dresses, three slips, one sheet and one apron.

4/19/40 Friday
A wet day. Eby hauled some hay from Barley's and had Ray Acker haul 2 big loads of rocks for the cesspool. I moved and divided the currant bush. The baby was fussy and I did not get much done. Finished my new dress.

5/29/40 Wednesday
A real nice day, got much cooler. I put a green stripe around the Ford. Rhoda ironed this A.M. and started the white washing this P.M. I finished ironing. Deacon John Herr's wife died. Had first head lettuce.

5/31/40 Friday
Rained hard last night and cleared partly today. Very damp. Eby took 9 lbs. of asparagus to the store at 12 cents. He took John King to Blue Ball and Mart went too, and they come home by Green Dragon, Ephrata and someone stole our shiny Ford. I cleaned the wash house and Rhoda did the wood house. Made two freezers of ice cream this evening from the milk we got back. Charles fell off the table on to the floor.

8/3/40 Saturday
A nice cool day. I finished the ginger snaps and made some pies and a pudding. Abram made a cake and washed up the kitchen. I did the baby wash and scrubbed. Eby, Charles and I took Clarence and Mabel along to Uncle Elmer's to get our inheritance from Grammy's estate. The boys kept house. Eby topped first tobacco this A.M.

8/5/40 Monday
A nice day. Eby's father sold his farm of 84 acres to Sam Zook's for $15,000 today.

8/13/40 Tuesday
Partly cloudy and we had a heavy gust and a very big flooding rain which soaked the ground and washed the lane worse than last week. Eby, Isaac, Abram, James and I went for huckleberries and got about 25 quarts. Got home before the rain.

8/17/40 Saturday
A showery day. Eby topped all the tobacco except the last 2 acres. We did up the cleaning and took baths. I cut out verses for scrap books in old papers from the garret. Eby, Abram, Isaac, James, Grace and I went to Harvest Services. Sem Stoltzfus preached, his text: "Go home and show what great things God has done for thee." Mrs. Hersh gave Grace two dresses, Rhoda 6 hankies, and the four boys pencil boxes.

10/13/40 Sunday
A very nice day. We all went to Hershey's church and communion. Grandpap Martin came here for dinner and Eby went along to Kinzer and Katie stayed here. Charles has his first tooth.

10/16/40 Wednesday
A cold day. The children did not have school on account of all men from 21 to 35 years had to register. We cleaned the garret and some of the children and I went to the apple orchard and picked up 4 bushels of apples at 40 cents. Eby was seeding and liming.

10/18/40 Friday
Cold and stormy. Eby finished the sweet potatoes, not such a good yield. I finished the 2 little rooms and planted in the geraniums and put them on the porch. Eby

picked pears. The tree is very full and makes about 13 bushel. I helped Jimmie to make some sandwich spread. It made 10 pints.

10/19/40 Saturday
Very unpleasant and began snowing this P.M. and everything is covered, celery, lettuce, endive, beets, lettuce, cabbage, and all. We cleaned three rooms upstairs, moved our room and the spare room around. Eby put some of the sweet potatoes in barrels and set up the heater stove. I cleaned a chicken for tomorrow. Eby bought a cow for $145.00. Had a busy day.

1941

1/1/41 Wednesday
A fine mild day. Eby and the boys hauled manure. Rhoda and I made a roast chicken dinner this A.M. Mrs. Hersh had a dinner for her family, 14 in all. Rhoda cleaned upstairs and played with girls. I patched the lining in Eby's Sunday overcoat. Charles can walk a little. They have about 1900 lath of tobacco stripped.

1/5/41 Sunday
Very rough and cold. Abram kept Charles at home and the rest of us went to Hershey's. Grandpap preached. Aunt Sue called and invited us up for dinner. We had a nice visit. Spent the evening at home.

1/7/41 Tuesday
A very fine day. Mabel helped to work at Uncle Milt's as Aunt Cora is sick in bed. I mended and darned stockings. Eby stripped tobacco. Charles walked almost over to Hersh's when I left him go out the door. I helped fill the tobacco cellar. We cleaned eggs all up this evening.

1/10/41 Friday
I got up with a sore breast and went to milk. Took chills when I came in and was feeling very bad all day. I laid on the couch. Rhoda was out of school with a cold and managed to do some of the work.

1/11/41 Saturday
A fine day. Rhoda has a bad cold but managed to clean the kitchen and make the meals. I was able to sit up and mended. My breast is better, but my back still aches. Rhoda and Eby took a film of pictures.

1/12/41 Sunday
Partly cloudy and cold. Eby and the three boys went to White Horse while the rest of us kept ourselves warm and were ready to go to Grandpap Hostetter's for dinner. Abram stayed home alone and is better this evening. Milton had an accident in his pants and had to go to bed.

1/13/41 Monday
A cold windy day. Rhoda and Abram stayed at home. I sewed and they worked on the scrap books and argued till I could hardly put up with it. My breast is a little better, but I feel weak. There was a young man murdered back the country on Saturday night as he went home from seeing his girl by a jealous rival.

1/14/41 Tuesday
A cold windy day. Rhoda and Eby did the washing. Milton didn't feel good and stayed home. Eby didn't feel like washing and almost froze his fingers hanging it up.

1/20/41 Monday
Windy and cold. I washed and Eby hung it up. It dried real good and we got it all ironed and some mended. I talked to Mabel, Aunt Cora and Katie. President Roosevelt began his third term today. They had a radio at school, so the children could hear the inauguration.

1/22/41 Wednesday
A real nice day. I made a birthday cake for Rhoda and cleaned 3 chickens. Eby took potatoes to Parksburg. Made a freezer of ice cream. Rhoda brought Sadie Smoker along home overnight.

1/25/41 Saturday
Everything is covered with ice and didn't melt much all day. The boys scrubbed. We did the rest of the cleaning and made some cakes and a raspberry pudding. I was surprised when Hagar's sent me a White electric sewing machine. We think Pap Martin bought it. It works fine. Shampooed all heads but my own.

1/31/41 Friday
Snowed till dinner. Not so cold. I made pies and little cakes and cleaned the kitchen. Charles is fussy. The boys went sledding this evening. Grace started to make a sewing card. We have less than one thousand lath of tobacco to strip. Jesse Beiler was offered 18 cents from Withers.

2/1/41 Saturday
A nice cold day. I cleaned upstairs and Rhoda finished the kitchen. I did the scrubbing and cleaned up the Ford. Rhoda made potato soup for dinner. Rhoda, Grace and I went up to the community sale. I got Rhoda new boots and shoes at Zimmerman's. Went to see Katie. She is sick in bed. Made a cake and washed sweet potatoes this evening and bathed the children.

2/3/41 Monday
A real nice day. Wash dried good. I brought the washing machine in the kitchen and it went fine. Isaac stayed home from school as he was sore from some carelessness yesterday. Worked on an order for Sears this P.M. Uncle Irvin's had a stillborn baby born to them yesterday morning.

2/5/41 Wednesday
A nice day. I did up the morning work and washed up the kitchen. Talked to Mabel. Mended on new sewing machine. Charles is feverish and not feeling good, seems to be his teeth. A boy was killed at Narvon sledding. His head struck a bank.

2/14/41 Friday
A nice mild damp day, rained some. I cleaned the living room and dining room. Made pies and oatmeal cakes. Landis Brackbill took Eby to see a '33 Buick and he bought it for $35.00. The children walked home through the rain.

2/23/41 Sunday
A real nice day. Eby, Abram, Rhoda and Grace went to White Horse. The other boys had colds and helped me get dinner for Uncle Menno's, Uncle Elmer's, Uncle Paul, and Uncle Charlie. Had a nice visit. Paul brought his accordion along for the children to learn to play.

2/25/41 Tuesday
A fine day. I did the mending and made a dress for Grace. Eby worked at his potato planter and trimmed some trees. Ira Barley was here a while. Eby is going to cure Grandpap Hostetter's meat and brought it this A.M. Eby, Abram, Grace and I went to Spring Garden for our Buick. I drove the Ford home.

3/2/41 Sunday
A nice day. Roads are pretty well opened. Abram stayed home with Grace and Charles as they are coughing like whooping cough. The rest of us went to Hershey's church. Had our dinner and took Abram along up to my home.

3/10/41 Monday
A fine day. Wash dried very well. Health officer put a whooping cough tag up. They are not coughing so much. Eby got the stripping room ready for the chicks and Phares Landis brought us 463 White Rocks at 9 cents this evening. Had a new calf this morning.

3/20/41 Thursday
A fine day, not quite so windy. Jesse Beiler was here and offered 16 cents for the tobacco, and Eby sold it to Jay for 16 ½ cents this evening. Had a fruit man and bought a half bushel of apples.

3/24/41 Monday
I took the milk and the children. It was wet and windy. Started to wash when I came home and it didn't dry so good. The teacher sent Rhoda home with German measles and I went for the boys and their books. Ray Acker loaded our tobacco and took it as far as Kinzer this evening. Very damp.

4/2/41 Wednesday
Cleared this morning and was a fine day. Eby and I went early to help Irvin Denlinger's to move up to Kissel Hill. Everything went fine. I took a load of women in our Buick for my first drive. Rhoda and the boys kept house.

4/6/41 Sunday
A wet day. Cleared this evening. Eby, Rhoda, Milton and I went to White Horse and the rest stayed home on account of German measles. We all went to Clarence's this P.M., the first time we were all in our Buick.

4/9/41 Wednesday
A cloudy day. I cleaned the garret. Abram helped me clean the stove pipe. Did the baby wash and washed up the kitchen. James went back to school. Isaac went to the Gap for a bamboo rake, but was too lazy to use it much when he got home.

4/22/41 Tuesday
A fine day, colder. I finished the ironing and made soap. Health officer brought James' card and took quarantine down.

5/21/41 Wednesday
Very warm. Eby finished planting corn. I thinned tomatoes and sewed this P.M. and planted 115 heads of lettuce this evening. Rhoda made a cake and pudding and she, James and Milton picked tea for market. The three boys went to Fisher's Mill for Farina and Abram went to Denlinger's. Got two loads of water.

5/23/41 Friday
A nice warm day, had a little shower this evening. Eby and I started on the Coatesville market route. It made me tired. We got home at 3:30. Rhoda kept house fine.

5/29/41 Thursday
A nice warm day, had a little rain this evening. Eby and I went to market, got home about 3:30. It went real good, sold 12 chickens.

6/4/41 Wednesday
A fine rain, showery all day. We did up our morning work and pulled 1000 tobacco plants for Ivan Umble. Took Charles over to Clarence's and started for Hershey at 8:30. Got Rhoda and Grace a coat and sweater in Lancaster. Stopped to see Landis' and ate our lunch in their kitchen. Saw the model creamery, rose garden, museum, Ice Palace, zoo and park. Stopped a little at Uncle Menno's on the way home. Got home about 6:00. All enjoyed the trip.

6/12/41 Thursday
A cloudy day and rained some showers. James and I stuck and planted the onions up in the field, quite a job. Pulled plants and planted four rows of tobacco. Picked

a bushel of beans and dressed 12 chickens. Grandpap Hostetter brought peas, beans and onions.

6/15/41 Sunday
Partly cloudy and gusty and rained some nice showers this P.M. We all went to S.S. and to Uncle Jay Martin's for dinner. The whole family was there. I took pictures of each family. Uncle Landis' came down to get two chickens for Lois.

6/24/41 Tuesday
Things are wet. Eby and the boys planted tobacco by hand til about 3:00. Rhoda ironed. I mixed a two gallon crock of pie dough rivvles and a big jar of hot cake mixture. Pulled some tobacco plants. I picked off and pulled out some peas. Planted some asters this evening.

7/19/41 Saturday
A nice day. The silo men poured the foundation for our silo. I did up the Saturday work myself. Shampooed and bathed the children. Mart's brought Rhoda home this evening. She enjoyed her vacation a lot.

7/24/41 Thursday
A nice day. Eby was home this A.M. and went to John King's to help thrash this P.M. Eby cultivated tobacco and the boys and I hoed. Rhoda cleaned yard. This P.M. we dressed 9 chickens and got things ready for market. The silo is going up fast.

7/27/41 Sunday
A real hot day. Charlie has a good many hives so I kept him at home while the rest went to S.S. Rhoda is still at Clarence's. We rested and read this P.M. and evening. Ross Usner called on Eby this P.M. There was 5000 at the Singing in Kennel's Woods this P.M. A family of four was killed at a railroad crossing in Florin yesterday while coming home from a reunion.

8/10/41 Sunday
A nice day. All went to S.S. but Abram, Charles and I. We made dinner for Grandpap Martin's, Uncle Jay's, Uncle Landis', Mother Hunt and Loda, Uncle Paul and Charlie. Uncle Menno's and Uncle Clarence's came this P.M. Had a nice visit. Last night Abram fell down the stairs in a nightmare and hurt his lip.

8/12/41 Tuesday
A real nice day. Uncle Paul and Uncle Charlie left this morning for Grottoe's Civilian Camp for conscientious objectors in Virginia for a year's free service to the Government.

8/26/41 Tuesday
A very hot day and rained late this evening. We cut first tobacco this P.M. Had 8 men and they cut over an acre. Mr. Trout called this evening and said no more school till Sept. 15 on account of the paralysis. Canned peaches with what time I had.

8/31/41 Sunday
A nice warm day. Eby and I took Uncle John Eby along to church and we all went up to Grandpap Hostetter's for dinner. Frank Kreider's were there too. Eby and I went up to the Mt. tent meetings. Noah Mack is conducting them. He is 82 years old. The children are quarantined from public on account of the paralysis.

9/4/41 Thursday
A damp showery day. Things are growing. The late tobacco is getting very nice. I canned 10 more quarts of peaches, now have 122 quarts. Made 20 glasses of grape butter. We dressed 9 chickens, got limas, corn, beans, beets, radishes, sweet potatoes, apples, tomatoes and cabbage for market and sauer kraut. Eby went for eggs this evening.

9/7/41 Sunday
A warm windy day. The children are still quarantined from public for paralysis. We made dinner and had Uncle John. Milton sprained his wrist. Read to the children and wrote to Amy this evening.

9/13/41 Saturday
A nice day. Eby and the boys succored tobacco this A.M. and Harry Kauffman and Otto Ostertag helped cut this P.M. Have 2 acres left yet. We canned 9 quarts of corn and dried 6 quarts. We did up the cleaning. Eby was moving some chickens in the range and a crate fell off and killed four so I cleaned them before I went to bed.

9/14/41 Sunday
A fine day. Eby went to church alone. The children are still under quarantine for paralysis epidemic. We all went up to Uncle Mart's for dinner. Grandpap's, Jay's, Clarence's, Charlie, Paul and his girl were there too. It was their first furlough and seemed very short. We spent the evening at home.

9/18/41 Thursday
A fine day. We filled the silo. Aunt Sue came down and helped cook and do eight chickens for market. Eby kept two of the men to help take out some potatoes for market and pick tomatoes for the rest of the day. The northern lights were visible all night and very beautiful.

9/21/41 Sunday
A beautiful cool day. Eby went to White Horse alone. The children and I spent the day at home. They took walks. I read and rested. Wrote to the boys this evening. Some of Uncle David's company got here by mistake. Mart's were up to see Menno's. They call their baby Rhoda.

9/27/41 Saturday
A nice day, cool this morning and warmed up. Eby went to Clarence's to cut corn. Rhoda and I cleaned the yard and did the cleaning. I made peppernuts and a chocolate

cake and apple dumplings. Shampooed all the children. Eby went to the store and we made ice cream to surprise him.

9/29/41 Monday
A real nice day. The children went back to school. I did the washing and got it ready to iron. Made some trellises for my posies. Eby was cutting corn for Clarence's. Emma and Frank brought the feed cart this evening.

10/8/41 Wednesday
Not quite so warm. The children picked some tomatoes before school and I finished them up till 9:00. Rhoda ironed when she came from school. I dug a bushel of sweet potatoes for market. We got things ready for sandwich spread.

10/9/41 Thursday
A nice day. I finished the sandwich spread and got 22 pints. Mrs. Hersh helped me dress the chickens. Gathered in some things for market, had a bushel of sweet corn, but the worms are bad in it. Eby took a load of tomatoes down. They graded 45% after letting them ripen in the baskets. He worked the ground for wheat.

10/10/41 Friday
A wet day. Sun came out after dinner, much cooler. We loaded up for market in the rain. I started coal fire and peeled apples to can, 8 quarts. Canned 6 quarts of red beets. Eby had a good market, eggs $.45 a dozen. Had corn, eggplant, endive, turnip, pumpkins, peppers, chickens, sweet potatoes, white potatoes, and noodles.

10/16/41 Thursday
A nice day. Eby took out the sweet potatoes, about 28 bushels. Made about 35 bu. in all. I canned 9 quarts and 5 pints of pears. Mrs. Hersh helped me dress 9 chickens. Ordered some things from Sears Roebuck and Co. Charlie came a while this evening. They came home on furlough last night to stay till Monday.

10/22/41 Wednesday
A fine day. We got up at 4:00 and put 40 gallons of cider in 2 copper kettles and had it boiling till 5:00. Started to add snitz at 7:00. Eby brought his mother and she helped to stir. We had 28 crocks done till 4:00. We boiled 12 14-quart buckets of snitz, 40 gallons of cider, 40 lbs. of sugar and put in two crocks of old apple butter.

10/24/41 Friday
A nice day. Eby went to market. Grace and I cleaned the living room. There were some Indians at school today and the children took money to see them entertain, and they were a fake. I cleaned cupboards and the rest of the drawers.

10/29/41 Wednesday
A nice day. Grandma came early and patched faithfully all day. We got a nice lot sewed. This evening we filled the sweet potato barrels and put the balance in the cellar. I finished patching Grace's everyday coat this evening.

11/1/41 Saturday
A real wet day. We got lots of rain water. Eby did some gunning and got 4 rabbits. I made a big white cake and cleaned the aluminum ware and milk buckets. We cleaned the milk house, toilet and porch. Granville Clark came to do some wiring. David Denlinger's wife was buried this P.M. I am not feeling so good this evening. Rhoda polished the furniture and cleaned the kitchen.

11/3/41 Monday
A nice day. Our baby came at 3:00 A.M. Eby did up his morning work and then went for Aire Yoder, but her mother had a stroke and she could not come but directed him to Rhoda King and he brought her. Mrs. Hersh stayed with me till he got back. The two Rhoda's got things ready to wash this evening. Had a good many pains for one day. The baby was good all day.

11/4/41 Tuesday
Eby went to Mary King's wedding. He went back for supper and came home about 9:00 and enjoyed it a lot. They sent me a box of goodies and some roast and filling. The baby slept all night. They did the washing and some of the ironing. Charlie is doing good.

11/22/41 Saturday
A fine day, much colder. Rhoda did most of the cleaning, and I made crumb pies and a chocolate cake and cracker pudding. Eby did some carpenter work and jacked the house up. All took baths this evening. Rhoda and Eby are taking colds. Mine is better. Mrs. Hersh and Walter were over, and he gave the baby a dollar and a bank.

11/27/41 Thursday
A very fine day, mild. Eby and all the children but Milton and Charles went to Thanksgiving service at Hershey's. We made roast chicken and scalloped oysters for dinner. Uncle Irvin's and Uncle Robert's were here this P.M. and Uncle Mart's came this evening. Irene Eby and Miles Nolt were married today.

12/28/41 Sunday
Cloudy and cold. We all went to White Horse. Martin Hershey preached. Text was I Peter 2:9. Went to Uncle Jay Hostetter's for dinner. Donald's were there with their new baby, Rosa Darlene. Ray could not sleep very well. We spent the evening at home. Eby has the toothache.

12/31/41 Wednesday
Partly cloudy. Eby went to Clarence's to help strip tobacco for Mabel's helping us butcher next week. I mended and patched and darned all day. Did the dinner work. Eby's jaws are healing up. Ray was good. This was a very busy year. We all enjoyed good health. Charlie is very busy, takes a big interest in my sewing machine. Eby has been named for superintendent at Hershey's, election is next Sunday, which gives him much thought. Our Country is fighting the Japanese, and most of the World is at War. We have 1650 lath of tobacco stripped so far.

1942

1/1/42 Thursday
A cloudy day and rained some. I dressed 6 chickens this A.M. and Mrs. Hersh helped me do 7 more this P.M., mostly for Jacob Miller. I got some celery ready and Eby and the boys sweet potatoes and white potatoes. Charlie spent the A.M. in the stripping room. Milton made a misstep and fell down the steps with the chamber bucket this morning. I began to read Rosanna of the Amish.

1/2/42 Friday
A very strong south wind all day. I swept the house with a broom as my cleaner is not fixed yet. Ray was very good. Eby was on market and got a late start as he had a flat tire.

1/4/42 Sunday
The snow is about 4 inches deep. We all went to Hershey's. Eby was elected superintendent and Menno Eby assistant. Amos Hershey was third after Willis Zimmerman refused to serve. Clair Denlinger came this evening.

1/5/42 Monday
Clear and cold. I washed and it dried real good. Paul left his car at Kramer's garage and came here and helped strip tobacco, and after dinner Grace, Ray and I took him over to Clarence's. We got stuck at the end of their lane on the way home, and some kind soul gave us a push out. Abram had a cold and did not go to school. He popped corn. I got the wash ready to iron.

1/6/42 Tuesday
A cold day. I started my new dress. Rhoda did some of the ironing this evening. I put a little quilt in frames for the crib. Got a card from Susan Shirk. The boys' five day furlough is ended, and they left for Grottoes at 5:00 P.M.

1/8/42 Thursday
Below zero this morning. Eby got a place ready for the chicks in the stripping room and went in to Kerr's this P.M. and bought 250 at 8 ½ cents. White

Rocks. I made a curtain for the electric brooder. Mrs. Hersh helped me dress 7 chickens and finish the mending this P.M. We cleaned the eggs this evening. Ray is good.

1/10/42 Saturday
A very cold day. I scrubbed the porch after we were done washing. Rhoda got up early and had the kitchen all cleaned before breakfast. The wash dried good, all but the underwear and overalls. I made pies and cakes. The Miller girls came to sled, but it was most too cold. Eby and the boys got the wash house ready for butchering.

1/15/42 Thursday
The 3 big boys got up at 4:00 and had the farm work all done but milking when we got up. A nice day. The snow is going very nicely, soaking into the ground. I dressed six chickens this A.M. and Mrs. Hersh helped me do 6 more this P.M. Made a big kettle of scrapple and got things ready for market. Sugar is rationed, but we could get 10 lbs. this morning. Eby is salting the meat with smoke salt.

1/18/42 Sunday
A nice mild day, snow is going very nicely. We all went to Hershey's and Eby undertook to be superintendent. This P.M. Eby took Rhoda and Abram to instruction meeting at Hershey's. I slept most all afternoon, and the children were sledding and went to see Mrs. Hersh. Spent the evening at home and retired early.

1/22/42 Thursday
A nice day. I gave Rhoda an alarm clock for her birthday. The children helped pick 15 chickens before they went to school and Grace and I worked on them till 3:00. Grace drawed a few. Mrs. Hersh was not feeling able to help.

1/24/42 Saturday
A very fine springlike day. Rhoda got up first and had the kitchen almost done before breakfast. I did some baking and finished up the cleaning, and Rhoda, Grace, Ray and I went up to Mart Groff's this P.M. I helped to make Rhoda's dress that Grandpap Martin gave her for Christmas. We all bathed this evening.

2/3/42 Tuesday
A cold windy day. Abram is home coughing. I made some bibs and Abram worked some posies on some. Did the mending.

2/4/42 Wednesday
Cold and not quite so windy. I made 2 aprons and a dress for Grace out of an old one Aunt Sue gave. Abram and Isaac were both home with coughs. They worked some bibs and Isaac popped corn.

2/5/42 Thursday
Cloudy and rained some. Mrs. Hersh helped me dress 15 chickens. Got sauer kraut, sweet potatoes and noodles ready for market. The neighborhood had a dime shower for Mrs. Trout. Last winter she spent 26 weeks in the hospital with her hip broken twice.

2/8/42 Sunday
Cold and windy. We all went to White Horse, but Abram and Grace. She had a cold. George Graham preached. Aaron Hershey's came this P.M. The clocks are all to be turned on one hour for the duration of the war. Eby, Ray and I went to see Amanda Ramsey this evening. She was in bed with a broken hip. A 15-year-old Plank boy was struck and killed by a car and died at Dr. Hostetter's while we were there.

2/10/42 Tuesday
A cold, cloudy day. I washed and it dried good. Have a real sore breast on the left side. Tried to doctor it this P.M. and darned the stockings. The children practiced coming home fast for air raid drills. The big ship Normandie was badly damaged by fire in N.Y. dock. Children are working on their Valentines.

2/11/42 Wednesday
Still cloudy. Rhoda did some ironing this morning before school and I finished it up. Finished drying the underwear at the stove. My breast is worse. Called and asked the Dr. what to do. He said use hot boric acid compresses. Was some chilly all day. We dressed 9 chickens this evening. I put a Samaritan plaster on my breast.

2/12/42 Thursday
A clear windy day. My other breast was some sore, so Rhoda volunteered to stay home and I stayed in bed all day and feel better this evening. Rhoda dressed 9 more chickens.

2/28/42 Saturday
A fine day. Got up early and took Abram, Isaac and Milton to the dentist. Abram had 11 filled at $15.00, and Isaac 3 at $4.00. Milton had an exam. Did a little shopping and got home about 12. Our date was 8:15 war time. Eby worked till dinner. Made ice cream and got supper ready for John King's and Mary and Ike and Henry and wife. Had a nice visit.

3/1/42 Sunday
A nice day. We all went to Hershey's church. Amos Sauder preached. This P.M. Eby and all the children but Charlie and Ray went to Meadville. I rested, read and wrote to the boys. Aunt Sue had her new baby Bobby at church. They got him at Millersville Children's Home yesterday.

3/9/42 Monday

Stormy and rained last night. Windy today. The current was off till 9:00 and I did not wash, but got everything ready. Did some mending. Replanted my African violets. Ray was very good.

3/28/42 Saturday

Colder, cloudy and rained. Rhoda and I went to Lancaster at 8:15 and took Mrs. Hersh along. Got Rhoda new shoes and some other things and got home at 11:00. All went to Preparatory and Baptismal services but Milton, Grace and Charlie. Rhoda and Abram and 25 others were baptized.

4/20/42 Monday

A fine day. I washed and we did the ironing this evening. Eby is still in the warehouse. The war is going on. It was reported that Tokyo was bombed, and the paper is full of awful things about war and its consequences.

4/23/42 Thursday

A nice day. Picked 18 chickens before the children went to school and Mrs. Hersh got sick while helping to dress them so I had them myself. Did dinner work and watered plants. A barn burned down on State Hill. It is getting dry. The boys in Grottoes are fighting forest fires. I picked almost a bushel of dandelion and Abram about that much water cress for market.

4/25/42 Saturday

A fine warm day. I cleaned the garret with James and Milton's help. Rhoda did the kitchen and made dinner and tended Ray. Eby and the big boys hauled manure. This evening Eby, Abram, Milton, Grace and I went to Mt. Pleasant. Mart Hershey is having revival. We had 2 shad for dinner. For my birthday, I got 3 hankies from Abram, a bucket from Daddy, a dime from James, 5 pennies from Isaac, one penny from Milton and one from Grace, and a cake from Rhoda. Granville connected our electric refrigerator.

4/29/42 Wednesday

Had a nice rain this morning. We did up the morning work and took the three boys down to school and Charlie and Ray over to Mabel. Rhoda, James and I took Grandpap and Grandma H. along to Lancaster. James had 4 teeth filled and 2 pulled. I had 3 filled and 2 pulled. Rhoda got her glasses changed for $8.00. We went out to the hospital to see Uncle Irvin, but could not go up till 3:00, so we came home and left Grandpap's in to come home on the bus. Mabel was not feeling well. Eby went to Aaron Engle's for raspberry plants.

4/31/42 Thursday

A nice warm day. Picked 18 chickens before the children went to school and I dressed them. Abram, Isaac and Grace went for water cress and tea. We bunched 25 half pound bunches of asparagus. Eby went to Galen's for potatoes and poke. We planted some raspberries this evening.

8/22/42 Saturday
A warm day, partly cloudy. Did up our Saturday cleaning. Eby, Rhoda, Abram and I went to Harvest Praise Service at Hershey's. The rest kept house. A shed burned in Gap about 1:30. We had fried chicken for supper. Made ice cream to take along to Jay's tomorrow. Milton got his hand and his arm in the wringer while playing with the washing machine.

10/8/42 Thursday
A fine sunny day. Landis and Josephine helped to finish up the potatoes. Have around 900 bushel in all. Best crop we ever had and very nice potatoes. Picked all the corn beans for market and dressed chickens and got other things ready. Made some pumpkin pies for market.

10/21/42 Wednesday
A wet day. We put our cider on at 4:30 A.M. and had 22 crocks of apple butter till 5:00 P.M. Eby, Rhoda and I did it ourselves, and it went fine.

1943

1/2/43 Saturday
A real nice day. We did up the cleaning and Eby took Rhoda, Abram, Grace and Charlie down to Dr. Beacher's for vaccinations. They all took their baths so we got done early and had a nice long evening.

1/4/43 Monday
A cold day. We washed and it got very stormy and dried it nice. Rhoda ironed it and I helped strip tobacco.

1/7/43 Thursday
Cloudy and cold. We did the chickens till 10:30, 19 of them. I cleaned some celery for market and Rhoda made potato chips and we found out this evening we can't go to market on account of smallpox. I helped strip tobacco. We have 1100 lath stripped. New gas rationing went into effect today. No pleasure driving or visiting allowed.

1/8/43 Friday
Cloudy and snowed some. Eby delivered Jacob Miller's order of chickens, potatoes and eggs, but on account of smallpox quarantine could not do his market route. I made noodles, pies, and helped strip tobacco. Rhoda made some cakes.

1/14/43 Thursday
A nice day. We dressed 18 chickens and were done till dinner. Got some celery ready for market. Had a bid of 17 cents for the tobacco from the Consolidated Company. Rhoda made potato chips.

1/16/43 Saturday
A nice mild day. Rhoda has a lot of headache and pain in her eyes. I made pies, a cake, pudding, baked beans, scrapple and boiled some potatoes. Cut Eby and Abram's hair and helped take down some tobacco. I scrubbed and Rhoda did the kitchen. Bathed and shampooed the children and studied the Sunday School lesson.

1/20/43 Wednesday
Clear, stormy and cold. Jay bought our tobacco this morning for 20+5. I did the ironing and helped strip tobacco beside the house work. We got unsliced bread this week for the first as the knives are scarce.

1/22/43 Friday
Cloudy and real cold. Eby went to market and it got warmer and he did not mind the cold so much. I mended till dinner. Cut a dress for Grace and got it partly done. Rhoda cleaned upstairs. Isaac stirred up some ginger snaps.

1/30/43 Saturday
Snowed all day. I helped do up the morning work and went to strip tobacco at 9:00. Helped all day. Had early supper and bathed and had our S.S. lesson. Put Ray and Charlie together in the little bed that Mabel loaned me of Victor's. Ray cried for his little bed. The boys did some sledding. Cutting bread is going better.

2/4/43 Thursday
A nice day. We dressed 18 chickens and 5 pigeons. I sewed and Rhoda made potato chips. Grandpap Martin helped strip tobacco all day.

2/9/43 Tuesday
A fine day. Not so cold. I helped strip tobacco all day. Rhoda went down to Landis' to keep the children while they went place hunting. He brought her home this evening and they do not have anything yet. Landis is in the stripping room talking to Eby.

2/16/43 Tuesday
Almost zero this morning and 18 above this evening. I got up early and had some wash out before breakfast and it dried nice and I got it ready to iron this evening. I helped to strip 100 lath of tobacco. Rhoda kept house and cleaned the eggs. 15 people died from the cold over the nation. Wheat is $1.50 a bushel and potatoes $1.90 a bushel.

2/23/43 Tuesday
Mild and clear. We stripped tobacco and filled the cellar. Rhoda got up early and started the ironing. She finished it till dinner. The boys were home as they are rationing down at school. We butchered a hog for Grandpap Hostetter's. It went fine. Had a Packard agent.

3/1/43 Monday
A nice day. We did our washing early and delivered the tobacco for 20 cents a pound. It came to $851.70. Eby and I left for Lancaster at 9:30 and I did some shopping and Eby attended to some business. We traded our Buick on a Packard for $350.

3/2/43 Tuesday
A cloudy cold day. Rhoda did the ironing. I did up the work and went over to see Mrs. Hersh and made her some custards and some things for dinner. Edna and Mabel came here while the men went to Ira Umble's Sale. Eby bought the truck for $262 and a bed for James and Milton. I cleaned up their room and set it up this evening.

3/19/43 Friday
Rained a lot. I took the children to school in the Packard for the first trip for me. Made 23 quarts of mince meat, 12 quarts of vegetable soup and made and roasted 7 meat loaves and four roasts. Have 134 quarts in all. Sold the Ford this evening for $40. Eby had a good market, $2.10 a bushel.

3/23/43 Tuesday
A fine day. Got up early and took the milk early. Had a quilting. Grandma Hostetter, Edna, Mabel, Sue, Josephine and Grandpap Martin's were here. Got one done and second one in and partly done. Lois got sick and Papa took Josephine home.

3/27/43 Saturday
Cloudy and rained. I dug some garden and planted 2 lbs. peas. Eby helped dig the little garden and stuck 4 quarts of onions. I went to the sale at the hotel in Gap. Eby took the children to the Spelling Bee. Rhoda, Abram and James got prizes.

3/30/43 Tuesday
A real nice mild day, dropped a little rain. I made a nut cake for Landis' moving. Josephine brought the children up here and she and Loda came for them about 6:30. Eby hauled a load up to their new home near Campbelltown. He thinks it is real nice. I did the mending and cut some aprons.

4/5/43 Monday
Cold and windy. We washed and ironed. I fixed Rhoda's blue dress. Edjol man was here. We have three calves. Rhoda has her 10th letter in answer to her Words of Cheer letter.

4/19/43 Monday
Rained and blowed all day. Blew some of the house roof off and a garret window pane out and three trees over. Blew the roof off the Millwood Church and did lots of damage. I took the boys down and went after them.

4/22/43 Thursday
Partly cloudy. Eby went to market. The carpenters were here and mended the house roof. I cleaned drawers upstairs. Mabel got a card from Paul that he is leaving for Grottoes, Va. today.

4/27/43 Tuesday
A nice windy day. We had a few showers. Had a new calf last night, the tiniest I've ever seen. Spent some time feeding it. We cleaned the garret.

5/9/43 Sunday
A fine day. We all went to Hershey's Church. Rested this P.M. and Rhoda, Grace, Charlie, Eby and I went down to see William Hurst's, the new hardware store man at the Gap.

5/11/43 Tuesday
Still cloudy and rained. I took the milk and the children to school. Grace went to visit. We cleaned the upstairs but did not get the floors all scrubbed and rugs laid. Clarence's came and brought the brooder.

5/14/43 Friday
Cloudy and the sun came out. I baked pies and ginger cakes, made rhubarb sauce and boiled sweet potatoes. Rhoda did the ironing and cleaned yard. I dug my new flower bed down in the corner of the yard. Eby had a good market. The boys came home at noon and we gave the woodhouse a good cleaning.

6/3/43 Thursday
A nice day, warm. We dressed 33 chickens and got 50 bunches of onions ready. I made noodles. Eby finished planting corn. It did not seem like Ascension Day. We had no S.S. meeting on account of the gas.

6/7/43 Monday
A showery day, but the wash dried real good. Rhoda painted some of Mrs. Hersh's kitchen and we finished planting our tomatoes. The bishops, ministers and deacons met at Rohrerstown to revise the conference rules. Abram worked at Denlinger's. Isaac went to Jay's.

6/19/43 Saturday
Nice hot day. Eby cultivated all day. Rhoda and I did all the cleaning and cooking and made a freezer of fresh strawberry ice cream.

6/26/43 Saturday
A hot day. We canned 16 qts. of string beans and prepared some things for Sunday. Eby cultivated tomatoes. I picked a basket of peas. Gusted and rained a nice shower this evening. Both cisterns were empty. Our peeps had done so good and are starting to die now.

7/21/43 Wednesday
A warm day. I mended most of the day. The children wed the potatoes out along the meadow fence. I went to start them thinning the sweet corn and Ray followed and went to the bee hives and got several dozen stings. It made a lot of excitement and we got the Dr. He was very sick and vomited for almost four hours. Rhoda got 5 stings and I got one that swelled my eye shut. Ray went to bed and slept all night.

7/22/43 Thursday
A real warm day. Had a gust and nice rain. Dressed 33 chickens. Mrs. Hersh helped finish them. Eby, Rhoda and Abram went for huckleberries. They got about 12 quarts. I did the milking, could just see out of one eye.

7/30/43 Friday
A nice day, not so hot. Eby and James went to market. I did the mending this morning. After we had our nooning we finished weeding the sweet potatoes. When we came in I got very sick and vomited. Could hardly get upstairs for giddiness and dizzy and sick.

7/31/43 Saturday
A nice warm day. I stayed in bed all day. Had Dr. Beacher up and I am still sick, dizzy and giddy. Rhoda did up the work and made apple dumplings for dinner. Rhoda, Abram, Isaac and James went to Clarence's this evening as they are having a family gathering for Paul before he goes back to camp. Eby made ice cream for the rest at home.

8/1/43 Sunday
A very fine day. Milton, Ray and I stayed home from church. I came down for dinner, but it did not go so good, so I went back to bed again.

8/3/43 Tuesday
Real nice day. I came downstairs and sat around all day. Slept this afternoon and am not feeling very good. Rhoda did the ironing and cooking. I ate very little.

8/4/43 Wednesday
A nice cool day. I did not feel any better. Dr. Beacher went on vacation so I called Dr. Hostetter. He came and examined me and could not decide what my sickness is.

8/5/43 Thursday
A nice day. Mabel came over and helped dress 35 chickens and get things ready for market. I helped a little to open chickens and get dinner. Am still very dizzy and sick. The doctor came this evening and changed my medicine. Eby harrowed tobacco.

8/8/43 Sunday
A very fine day. All went to S.S. but Ray and I. Am feeling better, but still a little dizzy.

8/12/43 Thursday
A warm day. We did 30 chickens and got things ready for market. I milked for the first time this evening. It went pretty good.

8/18/43 Wednesday
Nice day, cool. Thrashing went good and they were done till 10:00 so we gave them custard pie, cake, lemonade and crackers. Have enough eats prepared for a few days. Rhoda ironed and I did some of the mending. Eby went to Miles Harsh's after dinner to help thrash. I picked the pickles this evening.

8/21/43 Saturday
Partly cloudy and warmer. We prepared things for Sunday. Did up the cleaning. Picked pickles and limas. Abram went to Clarence's to work back the day Mabel helped while I was sick. Eby topped tobacco and burned the fence rows. We all went to harvest services at Hershey's this evening.

9/17/43 Friday
A nice day. We got things ready to feed the silo fillers. Got four tank loads of water to wet the corn in the silo.

9/30/43 Thursday
Cloudy and cold and sprinkled a little rain. Abram, Isaac and James stayed out of school and we picked about 300 baskets of tomatoes for a colored man in Coatesville at 55 cents a basket. Started to dress 28 chickens at 4:00 and got done by 10:00. Big day.

10/12/43 Tuesday
A fine day, frosty. Rhoda did the ironing. I made a six gallon crock of sauer kraut. Rhoda, Charlie, Milton and I went to Glick's apple orchard and picked up 22 bushel of apples at 50 cents a bushel.

12/7/43 Tuesday
A fine day. We got up at 4:00 and boiled 19 gallons of apple butter, making a total of 60 gallons this fall. We did peel them, but put them through the sieve. Went fine and all done by 4:00. Eby stripped tobacco most of the day and we boiled soap and cooked feed bags in the lye.

12/10/43 Friday
A nice mild day. Eby went to market alone. Rhoda and I made 6 kinds of Christmas cookies. This evening we met at Jay's and packed a box to send to Paul and Charlie.

12/25/43 Saturday
A cold day, partly cloudy. We had a nice Christmas and plenty of gifts. Eby gave me bed blankets, Rhoda a new oil cloth, Abram gloves, Isaac first aid plasters and the little ones tea towels. Mrs. Hersh gave me dishes. We all went to Uncle David's for dinner and had a very fine dinner of roast duck and chicken and all the goodies that go along.

12/29/43 Wednesday
A nice day. I did the ironing and upholstered a chair. Made a cocoanut cake. Cooked the last of our ham. This evening Eby and I went to cottage meeting up at Sylvester Patterson's. Eby and Amos Hershey had the topics. It made Eby very nervous and he did not feel good.

1944

1/1/44 Saturday
A fine day. Did up the morning work and made dinner for Sem Hershey's, Paul Shirk's, and Jay Martin's. Had a nice visit with them. This evening we made ballots to reorganize the Sunday School and read. A 6-month-old Amish baby burned to death when it pulled the table cloth and lamp with it down over it.

1/2/44 Sunday
A nice cold day. We all went to Hershey's Church. Eby and Henry Hershey were elected for the year by vote. Eby, Grace, Charlie and I took Uncle Jay and Aunt Margie along up to see Uncle Landis' new baby Esther. Got home about 6:30. It was 90 miles. Rhoda went down to Hurst's.

1/6/44 Thursday
It cleared and got colder and stormy. I did 16 chickens and popped some corn for market. Eby helped Barley take down tobacco and went out to look at some crops. Have 100 lath stripped now. Rhoda is enjoying school.

1/10/44 Monday
A real nice day. I washed and got it ready to iron. Rhoda did some of it this evening. Eby went down to help Jay Hostetter's butcher this morning. This evening Eby went to help do some repairing at Nickel Mines mission, and I went along as far as Clarence's to talk things over with them.

1/13/44 Thursday
Clear cold day. I dressed 23 chickens and they were very penny, and it took me all day as I was miserable with the piles. Cleaned some celery. The boys popped some corn. Edna called me from Uncle Sam's quilting. Had lots of school news from L.M.S. as usual.

1/22/44 Saturday
Partly cloudy. Eby, James, Milton and I stripped 150 lath of tobacco and filled the cellar. Rhoda did the housework. This evening Rhoda, Abram, the three little ones and I went to Zimmerman's Store to get Rhoda shoes and went down home for a while.

2/8/44 Tuesday
A nice day. There was an accident on Mt. Vernon Hill and six soldier boys were hurt. Jay's, David's, Bob Neff's and us met up at Grandpap Hostetter's to see the Sunotone hearing aid man give Grandma a test.

2/25/44 Friday
A nice mild day. Eby went to market. I baked ginger cakes and pies and a chocolate cake. Made vegetable soup and baked beans. Rhoda cleaned. We all went to White Horse. There was a children's meeting. Isaac and James gave their names.

2/27/44 Sunday
A nice day. We all went to Hershey's Church. Christ Lehman preached. Eby and I went up to see Katie. She is just about the same. Mart's were there too. This evening we all went to White Horse. The revival meetings closed with 14 confessions as the visible results.

2/29/44 Tuesday
A nice day. We helped strip tobacco this A.M. Barley and George came this P.M. and helped to finish it up. Rhoda ironed and I mended. Katie went to the hospital.

3/4/44 Saturday
Snowed all day and is real deep. Eby, Rhoda and I went to Lancaster. Rhoda and I each got new bonnets. We bought a mattress for our bed for $39.50. Mildred Groff, Eby and Rhoda spent the A.M. at the Sewing Circle Meeting at Chestnut St. We went to see Katie at the Osteopathic Hospital.

3/15/44 Wednesday
A nice day. Canned the balance of the meat and 20 quarts of juice. Boiled soap this P.M. and rendered the tallow. Rhoda and the boys opened 26 feed bags to boil in the lye. Eby and I went up home this evening. Katie is just about the same.

3/23/44 Thursday
A very wet day. I took the children and went for them. Eby worked. We dressed 32 chickens and got done by 12:00. Puttered this P.M. Katie does not seem any better. She is vomiting every day.

3/24/44 Friday
Real nice day. Eby went to market. Rhoda cleaned upstairs and made pies for the first time. We made some raisin cookies. I boiled a kettle of soap. Cut up the boys' old mattress and made one for the bassinet and one for the crib. The boys are busy making kites.

3/26/44 Sunday
Nice day. We all went to Hershey's church, had communion services. Spent the rest of the day at home. Katie seems to be a little worse. She knows what her sickness is. Susanna Martin is no better.

3/28/44 Tuesday
Real nice day. I took the milk and met Christ Beiler and got chickens. Finished the mending and cut and got Rhoda's dress nearly done. We got a letter from Uncle Charlie. Rhoda and Abram answered it this evening. Grandpap Martin is hunting a nurse and they are very scarce. Uncle Landis Martin's stopped in for about an hour on their way up home for the first time in almost a year. Baby Esther is growing nice.

3/29/44 Wednesday
Cloudy, cold, snowed and rained. Eby and I went along with Margie and Jay to Charles Kirtner's funeral. He being a Catholic, the services were very odd to us. I did some shopping and we all went to a sale. The children kept house OK.

4/3/44 Monday
Cold. Was a fine wash day. We got it all ironed and some mended. Eby finished working in the warehouse. I made out an order for seeds to Shumway, Ill. Cut Eby's hair this evening. They got a new nurse up home today as Mary went home.

4/6/44 Thursday
A nice cool day. We dressed 36 chickens and got done by 12:20. I got some celery in and beets ready for market. This evening 3 of the boys and I went back to the Spring Heads and got a box of water cress for market. Eby worked at Hess' Mill.

4/8/44 Saturday
Rained some this A.M. The boys hauled some manure and Eby worked at the mill till dinner and then dug the little onion garden and I stuck a few. We did the cleaning and Rhoda cleaned some yard. Eby gave me a 3 lb. box of good chocolates for Easter.

4/15/44 Saturday
Cold and rained all day except a couple hours this morning. I cleaned the wash house all but scrubbing it and boiled 14 feed bags in lye. Rhoda cleaned and kept house and painted some porch furniture. Eby took the boys to Lancaster and got Abram a new suit with conservative coat. James got two teeth pulled. I baked a cake and prepared things for Sunday.

4/24/44 Monday
A wet day. I took the children to school. Eby worked at the mill. Rhoda cleaned some kitchen cupboards. I sewed, made some pads and a slip. Eby and I went up home this evening, and Katie was real miserable, but talked some.

4/28/44 Friday
Clear and cool. Rhoda went along with Clarence's to Lancaster to get a spring coat. I did some sewing this A.M. and we cleaned the cellar this P.M. Katie passed away about 4:30, and Eby and I went up this evening.

4/29/44 Saturday
A fine spring day. The boys hauled manure and got it all out. Eby plowed the gardens and made some new fence. I did the rest of the cleaning and prepared things for tomorrow. We sowed the celery seed. I got up before 3:00 and took Rhoda down to meet Melvin Barge to go to Philadelphia market. She got home about 7:00 and liked the work.

4/30/44 Sunday
A very fine day. The blossoms are opening. Eby and all the children but Ray went to White Horse. This afternoon Eby and I went up home. Some of the uncles and aunts were there too.

5/1/44 Monday
A fine wash day. We washed and did some of the ironing. Eby helped to plant the garden and it is full. This evening Eby, James, Rhoda, Charles and Ray went up home to Katie's viewing. There were 85 there. Charlie did not like it.

5/2/44 Tuesday
Partly cloudy this morning and evening. We did our work up this morning and James kept house with the two little boys while the rest of us went to the funeral at Paradise this morning and this afternoon at Risser's. Had dinner in the basement at Paradise. It was a big day.

5/6/44 Saturday
A very strong south wind all day. I got up at 3:00 A.M. and went to bed at 11:00 P.M. Took Rhoda down to meet Melvin Barge to go to Philadelphia Market. I made things for Sunday and did up the cleaning. Eby and the boys planted cobbler potatoes and over 500 strawberries.

5/7/44 Sunday
Had some fine showers last night and today. They all went to church but Milton, Ray and I. I slept and rested and read. This evening Clarence's went along with us up home and the children stayed here. Papa seems to be getting along all right so far.

5/10/44 Wednesday
A fine day. Paul and Charlie got home this morning for their 25-day furlough. Charlie came to call on us this evening. Rhoda began whitewashing. Eby planted potatoes. I made pies. I was sick last night and didn't feel good today.

5/13/44 Saturday
A nice day, very hot. Had a real heavy gust and heavy rain this evening. I got up and took Rhoda down to meet Barges at 4:00. I did the cleaning and baking and made noodles. Was real busy. Eby and the boys finished planting potatoes. Eby took Isaac and James to White Horse baptismal services. There were 8 in the class. Charlie is in bed with the measles.

5/14/44 Sunday
A very fine day. Things look so fresh and are growing so nice. They all went to White Horse but Charlie, Ray and I. This afternoon some of us went to Clarence's to see Paul and Charlie. Eby and all but the three little children and I went to Kinzer this evening.

5/20/44 Saturday
A nice day, partly cloudy. I took Rhoda down at 4:00 to meet Melvin Barge. He gave her a $1.00 raise. I did up the Saturday work and prepared for Sunday. Made ginger snaps and sour cream cookies. Eby and the boys planted the rest of the tomatoes and 2700 cabbage plants. Ray has symptoms of the measles.

5/21/44 Sunday
A fine day. Charlie, Ray and I kept house while the rest went to church. We spent the rest of the day at home resting, reading, playing, etc. Grace has symptoms of measles. Ray was up and down all day.

5/28/44 Sunday
A fine day. They all went to church but Charlie, Ray and I. We rested this P.M. and Uncle Charlie came for supper and bid us good by. Eby and the children went to Kinzer. I read to the children and took a walk.

5/29/44 Monday
A fine morning. Our baby arrived about 5:00 this morning. The children were pleased. They had school till 10:00. Paul and Charlie left for the west at 1:20. Eby couldn't get our nurse, Aire Yoder, till tomorrow, so he got Ada Smoker. Rhoda and Ada did the washing and some ironing.

5/30/44 Tuesday

A nice warm day. I did not feel so good. Eby took Ada home after he brought Aire. Rhoda and Abram went to commencement up at L.M.S.

5/31/44 Wednesday

Nice day. I had too much pain to sleep last night. Mabel came a while this morning when she took the milk. I feel much better this evening.

6/12/44 Monday

A good wash day. I helped a little till 9:00 and then went to bed till time to get dinner. Rhoda did the ironing. I did the cooking and dishwashing. I got the wash ready to iron.

7/10/44 Monday

A hot day. We washed and ironed. I did some mending. We got done early and Eby and I went up to his home for the viewing for his father. Ellis stayed down overnight. Elizabeth could not be there as their little baby Robert is just three weeks old.

7/11/44 Tuesday

A very warm day. We did up our work and had early dinner to go to Grandpap Hostetter's funeral. Services were held at the house by George Graham and at Kinzer Church by Amos Weaver and Grandpap Martin. Mildred Groff kept Dale. I took him to the doctor this evening and he said he's doing fine.

7/26/44 Wednesday

A warm day. Mart brought Edna down this morning and she helped make a dress for Rhoda and cut and started one for me. Mabel came over this afternoon. We had a nice visit. I took Edna home this evening. Eby worked at the mill.

8/8/44 Tuesday

Cleared off and was a beautiful day. We had a frolic to put a new roof on the west side of our house. Had twelve men for dinner and supper. I took the milk and went to the store and got ice to make ice cream for supper.

8/9/44 Wednesday

A fine day. We thrashed our wheat and got done till 1:00. Sue came along with Jay and helped cook. We had 33 bushel per acre. Got along fine. I mended and Rhoda washed bed clothes, towels, table cloths and baby wash. Abram harrowed the gardens and Rhoda and I hoed this evening. James went up to help Grandma Hostetter clean up her weeds.

8/23/44 Wednesday

Very foggy this morning and was a fine day. Mabel came over here and we met Sue at Cattail and went up to see little Nathan Hess. Amy was up, but not downstairs. We canned 31 quarts of peaches and 20 quarts of chow chow. Had a nice visit too.

Stopped at Jay's on our way home to suggest Amy's nurse as a housekeeper for Papa. He consented to a trial.

8/29/44 Tuesday
A nice day. Dale is three months old and weighs 13 lbs. He is very good, sleeps all night till around 7 or 8, plays with his hands and coos.

9/10/44 Sunday
A fine, cool day. We all went to Hershey's Church. Samuel Eby from Maryland preached. We had counsel meeting. This P.M. Eby, Isaac and I went to Paradise Quarterly Bible Meeting. Eby and the three oldest took the Horst girls along. The children went to bed early to be ready for school in the morning.

10/28/44 Saturday
Clear, cold and windy. Eby and Henry Hershey took all the canned things to the Philadelphia Mission. Abram went to market. I called him at two o'clock and then stayed up and did the mending. Slept a while this afternoon. Dale weighs 17 lbs. He can almost sit alone and stands on his feet strong.

No diaries were found for the period between 1944 and 1953.

During this period, the last three children were born: Mary Alice (8/24/46); Sanford Lynn (6/29/48) and Nancy Ruth (8/14/50). Ruth's father, Abram Martin, died in 1946.

Ruth with youngest child and grandchildren.

THE FIFTIES

1950

1/1/53 Thursday
Had about 4 inches of snow that began falling yesterday. Clear this morning and the children had a lot of fun playing in the snow. Grace went with Eby to Millwood Bible School. I made pies and the boys helped make potato chips. Abram brought Jim Murphy for supper. Charlie and Ray went with James to a basketball game at Gap. Jim Murphy weighs 340 lbs.

1/2/53 Friday
Partly cloudy and warmer. Ray went with Eby to market. Grace cleaned. I washed and took Charlie to Isaac's on my way to spend the P.M. with Aunt Minnie. She is still very undecided what to do. There was a woman killed yesterday to make the first highway death for this year.

1/4/53 Sunday
A nice winter day. We all went to church. James left after S.S. to fix a pump. Took Clair Hershey along and he came here for dinner. Isaac's were here too. Abram was here and went to Jay's this evening. Grace and Charlie went to Paradise with Eby as he had a topic on God's love. Clair and Melvin Hershey were voted as superintendents.

1/8/53 Thursday
A nice lot of snow. Eby went to Millwood Bible School. They had a spelling test today. There was a fourteen-year-old girl murdered in Reading. Nancy slept this afternoon. James went to Strasburg Bible School this evening.

1/10/53 Saturday
Another wet day. Snow is almost gone. I made pies and things for Sunday. James took Ray, Dale, Sanford and I to town this P.M. Took our proofs in to Peels, got shoes for the boys and two teeth pulled for Dale. Eby, Grace and Charlie went to Kinzer to the Quarterly Bible Meeting this evening.

1/12/53 Monday
Clear, cold and windy. I washed and did most of the ironing. Mary Alice did not feel well, so she stayed home from school. Had a special letter from Abram. Farm Show started at Harrisburg today. James did not go away this evening, something rare.

1/20/53 Tuesday
Damp, cloudy and rained a little. We finished the butchering. Eby, Sanford, Nancy and I watched Dwight Eisenhower's inauguration on Mrs. Plastino's television. The children came home at noon as the teachers are having art workshop.

1/22/53 Thursday
Very mild. The children had school till dinner and came home through the rain. I washed this A.M. Cut and started Grace's green dress. Eby, Grace, Charlie and I went to Weaverland Bible School. Eby went to Strasburg. Grace and Charlie dressed 3 chickens. Weighed sausage and scrapple for market.

1/24/53 Saturday
Warm and rained a lot. Eby and I took Ray and Dale to Isaac's on our way to L.M.S. Bible Study. Went in to Lancaster on our way home and got our pictures. Grace kept house. Rhoda and Edgar got here about 9:00 P.M.

1/25/53 Sunday
Cleared off cold and windy. Clair's steers were out last night about 12:30. Eby and James put them in without waking Clair. James took Grace, Charlie and Ray to Hershey's. Eby, the little ones and I went to White Horse for the first time in years. Rhoda and Edgar went to Meadville and Grandma's for dinner. Edgar and Rhoda left after supper.

1/29/53 Thursday
A mild day, partly cloudy. Had eclipse of the moon this evening. Milton went to Penn State with Aaron Denlinger to register for second semester. He did not stop with Rhoda as it was snowing out there. He and Aaron go with sisters. Eby and Charlie went to Strasburg B.S. I went along and spent the evening with Aunt Minnie.

1/31/53 Saturday
A real nice day with strong south wind. Mary Alice and Sanford were in bed most all day. I made pies and cookies and pudding. Grace scrubbed and did the kitchen and went to a birthday party for Marian Sweigart this evening. I started an apron for Grace and finished her green dress. Eby and Ray went to Strasburg. Charlie was a busy boy.

2/1/53 Sunday
Clear, windy and getting colder. I stayed home all day. The four little ones have the grippe. Nancy was down most all day, is better this evening. I read and worked on a scrapbook page for old Mrs. Shelly.

2/4/53 Wednesday
A nice day. Dale went back to school. Mary Alice stayed at home. I sewed. Almost 2000 people have died in England, Holland and Belgium as a result of storm and floods.

2/6/53 Friday
A fine day. I washed and Eby went to market. I cleaned all day. Mary Alice went back to school. Grace went up to Isaac's to keep Joanne while they went to the

Hershey twins' reception. Eby went to the firehouse. A little girl drowned south of Strasburg.

2/7/53 Saturday
Damp and cloudy. Grace stayed at Isaac's to help with some scrapbook pages. I did up the work this A.M. Eby and I went to the firehouse from 1:30 to 10:00 to help with the turkey supper. Served over 500. Grace helped in the dining room.

2/8/53 Sunday
A fine day. Eby, Charlie, Dale, the three little ones and I went to Welsh Mountain this morning. The rest went to Hershey's. Milton led a song. I went to see Mrs. Plastino. Wrote to Abram this evening. They found the little girl's body who was drowned.

2/15/53 Sunday
A real wet day. We all went to Hershey's. Park Book preached a sermon on qualifications. We spent the afternoon at home. I wrote letters. This evening Eby, Grace, Dale, Mary Alice and Nancy and I went to William Horst's. Their new house is super deluxe.

2/16/53 Monday
A very good wash day. Washed and ironed. Isaac's came down and helped dress a hog this evening. James got $50.00 bonus from William Horst. Daddy took Grace, Charlie and Ray to the dentist this evening.

2/24/53 Tuesday
Nice day. Finished mending and put wash away. Finished Mary Alice's dress and cut another one for her. The bulldozer was here and shut up some gutters and cleared the old foundation away in the corner of the garden. Eby went to the garage this evening.

3/1/53 Sunday
A nice cold day. March came in like a lion. We all went to Hershey's. Milton was not happy to hear that we plan to raise tomatoes at Strasburg. Eby and I took Clarence and Mabel along to Meadville where Uncle Galen Hostetter was ordained to preach. Sem Hershey was in the lot too.

3/2/53 Monday
Very cold and cloudy all day. I washed and ironed all but the overalls. Eby went to the meeting at the Gap in the interest of getting Puerto Ricans to help with working this summer. It was 4:30 till he got home. He went to fire meeting this evening.

3/3/53 Tuesday
Cold, cloudy and looks like snow. Eby went to Abner Smoker's sale. I cut a print dress for myself and have it nearly done. Eby and I took some material up to Sue

for dresses for the little girls. We took Mary Alice along to P.T.A. as the first grade had the program.

3/4/53 Wednesday
Windy and rained a lot. Eby went to Rutter Skiles' sale. I cut my new summer dress and have it almost done. Joseph Stalin, a Russian dictator, had a stroke and hemorrhage. Steers are down in price.

3/5/53 Thursday
A nice day. I sewed and finished my dress. Joseph Stalin died. James took Grace to sewing circle for her first time. Sanford can write the A B C's and numbers.

3/6/53 Friday
A nice day. I washed and cleaned. We cleaned the kitchen after supper. Eby went to market. Nancy wets herself very often.

3/10/53 Tuesday
A nice day. I mended. Sanford went sledding. Eby got the potato planter repaired. The Young Peoples Group had a business meeting at Hershey's this evening. James is president of the project again. Eby took the Olds to the garage this evening.

3/27/53 Friday
Partly cloudy and rained. Eby went to market. I cleaned and made 130 large raised doughnuts for Grace's bake sale. Abram was leaving today for a tour with four foreign students through Iowa, Illinois and Indiana till after Easter. Paul White was here and bought a building lot in our field.

3/29/53 Sunday
A nice day. Cool. Mary Alice, Sanford, Nancy and I did not go to church so they would not spread the whooping cough. I wrote to Rhoda and Abram. The new chickens laid 304 eggs.

3/31/53 Tuesday
A nice day, not quite so windy. Eby brought the beef from Hartzlers and I canned 30 quarts. Did some of the mending. Mary Alice and Dale stayed home as they are coughing. Nancy vomits often when she coughs.

4/14/53 Tuesday
Cleared and was very stormy and cold. Nancy coughed and vomited last night, but seems much better today. I washed and ironed. The children went to Gospel Witness Band meeting. They are having a Bible quiz. It is new. Eby went to a milk meeting at the Guernsey Barn.

4/22/53 Wednesday
Cool and windy. I put the sweet potatoes in the hot bed. Planted radishes, beets, carrots, lettuce, spinach, corn and salsify. Eby went to Strasburg to sow the tobacco

seed. Milton is disturbed about Aaron Groff asking him to hire for $150.00 a month. Grace went to the dentist on the bus.

4/25/53 Saturday
A fine warm day. Eby and Charlie went to Isaac's, and Ray and I went along to go with Milton to Lancaster for a dental appointment. We shopped. Milton wants to hire with Aaron Groff for the summer. We stopped at Clarence's on our way home. Mabel gave me a plastic table cloth for my birthday. Issac's came this evening and gave me writing paper. I took Mary Alice and Dale to the Dr. to get permits to go back to school.

4/26/53 Sunday
Rained this morning and gusty this evening. Very warm this afternoon. We all went to church this morning. Sanford Hershey preached. Grace and Charlie went to Philadelphia to help take The Way. Milton went to help sing at the Keneagy Home. I wrote to Abram. Milton is not going with Dorothy Landis.

4/28/53 Tuesday
Cool and clear. Eby plowed a lot. I cleaned the spare room. Finished the ironing and did some of the mending. James went to Harrisburg for his physical with 103 other CO's from Lancaster County. Eby went to get Milton's chickens, and I went along to see Jay Martin's new house. Nancy is feeling better.

5/1/53 Friday
Partly cloudy and there was a gust in places this P.M. We had a few drops. I cleaned all but the kitchen. Washed and made pies. Eby came home from market about 4:30 and he, Sanford and I started for Belleville about 5:00 and took Rhoda's table and chairs along. Got there about 9:00. Aunt Minnie is disturbed.

5/5/53 Tuesday
Warm and showery. Mabel brought Aunt Minnie to spend the day. She was very much disturbed and restless. Eby went to Sam Zook's barn raising this A.M. James disced at Isaac's. Eby, Charlie and Ray went to P.T.A. Charlie won the scholarship. Grace went to prayer meeting with Clair's. I planted 2 rows of beans and did the ironing.

5/10/53 Sunday
Mother's Day. A very pretty day. We had communion this morning. Park Book was able to serve. Rhoda and Mary Alice gave me cards. Abram sent flowers, James chewing gum, Milton a pretty cake and Sanford buttercups. Charlie, Ray and Dale went for a hike in Kinzer Hill.

5/20/53 Wednesday
A nice day. Eby plowed. Ray stayed home and was able to be about. I cleaned the dining room. James came home from State College about 5:00. Eby and I went

with Clair's to cottage meeting at Flora Rutter's. William Horst sold out to George Summers. Eby plowed.

5/21/53 Thursday
A real nice day. Eby finished plowing and harrowed. I cleaned the living room. Washed the curtains when Grace came home and she put them on the stretchers. James left for his new job as dairy tester.

6/5/53 Friday
A nice warm day. Abram went to Uncle Jay's last night. I was asked to go and tell Aunt Minnie she is to go to Phil Haven and help her get ready. Mart, Edna and Charlie helped. We took her by force. I got home at 6:00. Milton and his pals got home about 8:00. Had a fine time.

6/6/53 Saturday
A very nice day. We made our lunch and cleaned up the kitchen. Left for the Martin reunion at Everly's Grove about 11:15. 135 there and we had a nice time. Came home about 4:30 and Eby, Grace and I went to the fire house to help with the ham supper. Got home at 10:00. Grace went on a rampage with Verna Sweigart and her boyfriend.

6/9/53 Tuesday
A warm day. Finished ironing and made some strawberry preserves. We hoed the lima beans and some garden and tomatoes. It rained this morning. Daddy cultivated tomatoes. He went to a P.T.A. meeting. Talked to Aunt Cora and Mabel. Ray planted pumpkins. Nellie had pups.

6/19/53 Friday
A fine warm day. I dug ½ bushel of potatoes and picked ½ bushel of peas. Got in some rhubarb for market and helped cut 2 bushel of cabbage, after which a pain shot in my back. I kept getting worse till evening. I took Ray to Isaac's after he came from Denlinger's and had early dinner to help in hay. Stopped at Clarence's on my way home. Eby went up and helped finish the hay when he came home from market. I picked sugar peas and got 6 quarts for freezing.

6/20/53 Saturday
A hot day. Isaac called and said they had a baby girl at 6:30 this morning. Eby took Grace and Ray up this A.M. and finished planting tobacco and some more corn. I did the cleaning and prepared for Sunday. Picked some peas. Bathed the children. My back is some better.

6/24/53 Wednesday
A fine day. I did the mending and put wash away. Eby and I went to see Elizabeth and little Linda. I bought 3 Christmas bundles for our S.S. class. Eby helped put Clair's hay in. Ray, Dale and I worked on the lima bean poles. Eby harrowed some corn.

6/26/53 Friday
A warm day with a south wind. They hauled the peas. Yielded 2 ½ ton to the acre. I did 44 quarts for Isaac's and 30 for us. Made pies and cooked for the men. Was ungraceful busy. Eby went to market. Jake Musser helped this A.M. Abram, Isaac, Charlie and Ray did the rest. They cut the fire company cabbage this evening.

7/7/53 Tuesday
Nice day. Cleaned and trimmed. Aunt Cora and Uncle Milt brought Aunt Minnie home from Phil Haven.

7/21/53 Tuesday
A hot day. Eby and the 4 least boys went on the Poultry Tour. I hoed the cantaloupes till dinner. Cleaned the eggs and ironed.

7/27/53 Monday
A good wash day. Warmer and a little cloudy. The peace truce was signed last evening in Korea, and the war is over. I hoed tomatoes and cleaned eggs. Eby hoed tomatoes and helped collect for the fire company this evening. Ray picked 8 quarts of blackberries. I weigh 156 lbs.

8/1/53 Saturday
A real nice day. Eby went over to help get ready for Bible School. Grace and I baked and prepared for Sunday and our reunion at Clarence's this evening. There were 60 there. I picked the first lima beans. Scrubbed and cleaned. Eby went to the community sale and bought chairs and beds for the Puerto Ricans. Canned pickles and blackberries.

8/8/53 Saturday
A cloudy day. Began raining after dark this evening. Jesse B. picked green tomatoes till noon. Grade was very poor. Grace cleaned and I scrubbed and cleaned some yard. Cleaned eggs. Milton brought Charlie home. Abram went to Ohio to see Patricia.

8/15/53 Saturday
A warm day. We did the cleaning, scrubbing and made things ready for Sunday dinner. Eby and Ray went to Strasburg and hauled some hay. Edgar and Rhoda, Ike and Elizabeth and Abram and Patricia went to John Noll's to a doggie roast. Grace kept Joanne and Linda. Eby, Ray, Dale and I went to a birthday party for Aunt Minnie. 30 there and she seemed pleased. Mary Alice, Sanford, and Nancy kept house.

8/18/53 Tuesday
A nice day. Grace picked tomatoes. Rhoda cut a dress and pattern. I finished the ironing. Eby and Edgar went to Hamburg for the Puerto Ricans, and Rhoda and I went to Isaac's to see the quarters in the stripping room and bring a load of tomatoes.

8/19/53 Wednesday
A nice day. Grace picked some tomatoes. Rhoda and I canned 45 quarts. Edgar painted the garage door. Eby went to Isaac's to haul tomatoes. We all went to Isaac's for supper in honor of Patricia's visit.

8/21/53 Friday
A nice day. Eby and Dale went to market. Isaac, the P.R.'s, Grace, Ray and I picked 335 baskets of tomatoes. Mr. and Mrs. Walter Brookhouser from Ford City came to spend the evening. They spent the night at Shaw's Cabins. Isaac, Elizabeth and the children and the P.R.'s came to help load tomatoes. A big truck came for the tomatoes for the first.

8/25/53 Tuesday
A warm day. Grandma has here and we did 18 quarts of limas and I planted 73 lettuce plants this evening. Eby went to Isaac's all day and took the boys up after supper. They picked 587 baskets in two days. Grace went on a boat ride from Phila. to Wilmington. Abram came with his microscope this evening.

9/1/53 Tuesday
Clear, hot and dry. Eby, Grace and Ray went to Isaac's this morning. I made 36 glasses grape jelly and more juice. I now have 66 quarts. Dale and Mary Alice helped me can 21 quarts of tomato juice. I picked ½ bushel limas. We all went to Red Well tent meeting but Ray. Clair Eby was evangelist. Eby had his first children's meeting.

9/4/53 Friday
Partly cloudy and not quite so hot. Eby and Dale went to market. Grace, Ray and I picked 101 baskets of tomatoes. Washed and cleaned all but the kitchen. I picked a basket of limas for Sat. dinner. The big truck came for tomatoes. Eby traded the Olds and $600.00 on a Buick.

9/5/53 Saturday
Cloudy with alternate showers and sunshine. The rain came so nicely. We filled silo and it took till 4:00. Elizabeth and the little ones came along. Had 10 men for dinner. Grace and Elizabeth picked and shelled a basket of limas for Elizabeth. Grace cleaned off the Buick and washed up the kitchen.

9/11/53 Friday
A fine day. I washed and cleaned all but the kitchen. Scrubbed. Grace and I canned 18 quarts of peaches this evening. Ray picked some lima beans. Eby was sick last night, but went to market this morning. He was pretty tired this evening. Charlie missed school to help in the tobacco.

9/18/53 Friday
A nice day. Eby went to market. I cleaned upstairs and canned 7 quarts red beets. Grace went to Green Dragon with Sweigart's. Samuel Wenger is very sick in a New York cancer hospital.

9/23/53 Wednesday
A nice day, real cool, frost some places. Eby went to White Horse with Clarence's where Richard Buckwalter was ordained deacon. I got things ready for sandwich spread. We picked a load of green tomatoes this afternoon. Eby and I went to Omar Metzler's for cottage meeting. Eby hauled tomatoes for Isaac's.

10/1/53 Thursday
A fine day. Eby and I picked 67 baskets of tomatoes. The boys got up early. The rats are getting very numerous. Donnie Ranck's have a baby girl, and Jesse Beiler's have a baby girl too.

10/5/53 Monday
A nice day. I washed and did some of the ironing. Eby went to Isaac's to fill silo. I cleaned some eggs. Nothing heard from Greenleaf kidnapping. Eby went to fire meeting, and I went to see Grandma.

10/19/53 Monday
A fine warm day. I washed and ironed and mended. Ray has a cold and stayed at home. He took out some cannas and gladiolas. Mrs. Robinson brought my Spirella. Nick and Laddie finished up the potatoes. Had a good crop.

10/20/53 Tuesday
Very foggy and cleared up at dinner. Eby took cabbage and turnips to Coatesville, and then he and Isaac went to a cow sale beyond Harrisburg and bought 9 cows averaging $400.00 a head. I cut and sold 38 bushel of cabbage. Took Charlie up to do Isaac's work. Dale and I stopped at Eby's Orchard and picked up 2 bushels of apples at $1.00 per bushel.

10/24/53 Saturday
A cloudy day. Had a nice lot of showers this P.M. Grace and Mary Alice did the house work. Daddy went to help Isaac in the corn. The boys and I cleaned the chicken houses thoroughly, washed and put the windows in. The boys hauled in the bean poles. Milton spent the evening here to escape Halloween trouble.

11/4/53 Wednesday
Partly cloudy and cool. Eby, Sanford, Nancy and I took Abram back to Phila. Ate our lunch in his apartment and walked in the shopping district a while, then went to the zoo. The children enjoyed it a lot.

11/6/53 Friday
Cold, cloudy and began snowing this morning and got faster and faster till it is quite deep this evening. Eby went to market. I cleaned the house and Charlie decided it was not fit to cut or sell cabbage. Eby did not get home till almost 9:00. Driving is treacherous. The children popped corn.

11/8/53 Sunday
Pretty and clear. Eby, Grace, and the three little ones and I went to Kinzer in the truck out through the fields. Milton came home through the fields. The children went sledding. Eby not feeling good, slept all afternoon and went to bed after supper. 13 inches of snow fell here.

11/13/53 Friday
A very foggy, cold, damp day. Coatesville was clear. Eby went to market. I washed and it did not dry. Finished cleaning the porches and windows. Got ready for our trip. Too foggy to cut cabbage.

11/14/53 Saturday
Very foggy. We got ready to leave for Belleville about 10:00, Eby, Sanford, Nancy and I. Left shoes in Lancaster to be repaired. Stopped at Marian and Ruth's and bought myself a dress and then went to Menno's. We arrived in Belleville about 2:30. Helped Rhoda with her dresses. James came for supper. No snow left around Belleville.

11/16/53 Monday
A fine mild day. I helped Rhoda with her dresses again. Eby went to help build the new piece to Belleville School and brought Edgar home for dinner. Sanford went along on the bus with Edgar. We left for home at 3:00 and got here a bit after seven. The Buick made 14 ½ miles to the gallon.

11/21/53 Saturday
Cloudy, damp and rained a little. The boys helped trench the celery in the hot bed. We took out carrots, beets, some turnips and cabbage. Wrapped cabbage in paper and put it in the hot bed covered with straw. Eby, Grace and I helped with the second annual turkey supper at the fire house. Cleared over $400.00.

11/25/53 Wednesday
A wet day. I made some icing while Eby went for the turkeys. We dressed two and four roosters. Johnny went with Eby to take them to Coatesville. I made things ready for dinner tomorrow. Eby and I went to cottage meeting for Annie Mellinger. Abram came about 10:00 without Patricia. She is coming by train.

11/26/53 Thursday
A fine Thanksgiving day. We all went to Hershey's. Park Book preached a good sermon. The children were all here but Rhoda and Edgar and James. We had roast chicken.

12/6/53 Sunday
We all went to Hershey's Church. Cloudy and began raining hard about 3:00 P.M. I took the children to the woods for some plants for winter gardens. Charlie was delighted. Eby, Grace, Charlie, Ray and Dale went to Hershey's where Alvin Martin is having revival meetings. I wrote letters.

12/15/53 Tuesday
Sunny, snowed, rained and sleeted. I washed and did most of the ironing. Eby went to Isaac's. We all went to church, but Ray, Mary Alice and Nancy. Had spinach from the garden for supper. Eva needs blood. She has been in the hospital since Friday.

12/16/53 Wednesday
Changeable. Sunny, snowy, windy and cold. Did a lot of phoning for blood donors for Eva. Eby, Milton and Isaac went into the hospital. Eby's type is AB, the boys are B. I stirred up cookies. Went to church. Dale, Sanford and Nancy kept house. Anna Mary brought Stanley products. Eby stripped tobacco, and Grace went shopping with Verna Sweigart.

12/22/53 Tuesday
A nice day. I took Charlie, Dale, Mary Alice and Sanford on a shopping trip. We got it done and were home by 3:30. Nancy went to Isaac's with Eby. Eby, Charlie, Ray, Grace and I went to the Salisbury High School Christmas Program this evening in Gap fire house.

12/25/53 Friday
A fine Christmas Day. The children all here for turkey dinner but Abram. I got candy, bowl set, address book, sheets, glasses, pitcher, towel set, cookie sheets, metal sponge and tape measure. Clarence, Harold and Mabel came over this evening.

12/26/53 Saturday
A nice cold day. I washed and Rhoda made a pair of pajamas for Mary Alice. James took his car to the garage and Eby helped carpenters. Rhoda and Edgar left for Souderton about 4:00. Bathed the children. I finished Grace's skirt.
(No diaries were found for the period 1953 until 1960.)

Taking photographs at a family gathering.

The Sixties

1960

1/1/60 Friday
A very pretty day. Eby, Sanford, Nancy, Milton, Barbara and I left at 7:25 to visit James and Patricia and little Gregory for the first time. Got home at 8:30. Grace worked at Dutch Haven. Dale hunted rabbits and they cleaned our chicken house.

1/4/60 Monday
A real good wash day. Got most of the ironing done. Grace did the morning work and made two cakes. Packed her things and left at 2:30 with Bert Weaver for E.M.C. Milton slept here last night and left at 7:40 this morning for Gordon College, Mass. Ray started repairs on the grape arbors. Had a letter from Rhoda. They are getting along good. Dale and Sanford sold seeds this evening.

1/5/60 Tuesday
Partly cloudy, not so cold. I finished ironing and mended. Ray hauled manure, delivered potatoes to school and went to the Vintage sale as weighmaster. Dale went to basketball game at Warwick. Daddy and I went to Red Well cottage meeting at Francis Buzzard's house. Eby talked on a holy life.

1/12/60 Tuesday
Partly cloudy and began sleeting this evening. Abner was called to load cinders. I finished ironing and did some mending. Ray took some packages to the post office and went to Vintage to weigh. Eby and the children culled chickens.

1/13/60 Wednesday
Very icy this morning and rained. Cloudy all day. Eby and Charlie got to work all right. Ray took eggs to Kurtz. He left for the Farm Show at 11:00 and was to be awarded the Keystone Farmers' degree with 20 other county boys. I finished M.A.'s dress and did some odds and ends sewing. Stirred up two batches of cookies. Wrote to Milton. Eby went to feed meeting. Dale popped corn.

1/16/60 Saturday
A fine day, windy. The girls and I finished up the cleaning and helped clean chicken house till dinner time. Charlie, Dale and Sanford went to market. Nancy and I went to Sewing School. Mary Alice took her dress up to Esther's for buttonholes. Charlie got a bird record from Edgar's for his birthday.

1/19/60 Tuesday
Snowing this morning but cleared cold and windy. I ironed and mended. Cut Darrell's hair. Ray painted the cultipacker and went to Vintage Sale. Had a letter from Grace. Nancy stayed home with a belly ache. Not too serious.

1/22/60 Friday
Cold and not quite so windy. Ray and I did the lard, pudding, scrapple, canned the meat, made pig foot jelly and sugar cured the meat. I made a chocolate cake and an angel food cake and some pineapple snow. Boiled dressing and chocolate syrup.

1/23/60 Saturday
Real cold, but pleasant. I cleaned the kitchen, living and dining room and upstairs. Mary Alice and Nancy did eggs and made dinner. Was very busy. Eby and I went to Ross Usner's funeral. James brought his family for the weekend. Had Abram and Patty for supper too. Little Gregory is growing. Mary Alice peeled a lot of potatoes for supper. Had sauer kraut.

1/28/60 Thursday
Cloudy, foggy and mild. Esther helped me clean 12 leghorn hens. Milton got home at 2:30 last night. He got a haircut, car inspected and went to Coy's for supper. Clair took Eby to a Calvary Hour banquet at Blue Ball this evening. Peter Shadid is to speak. Ray painted the potato planter. I varnished the cupboard. Worked on Mary Alice's dress this evening.

2/6/60 Saturday
Rained a lot last night. Cleared and got a little colder. Mary Alice did not feel well this morning. I made 2 cakes and strawberry tapioca. Finished cleaning. Milt Slaymaker was here to look at the porch. Eby worked this P.M. Ray and Sanford went to market. Charlie went to Abram's and with them to Philadelphia to see a French festival.

2/11/60 Thursday
Rained very hard last night. Cleared this morning and was very warm. Getting colder this evening. Three carpenters came to work on the porch. Ray helped. Charlie is better, but stayed in bed. I cleaned and baked 2 batches of cookies for Valentine's in Nancy and Sanford's classes. We dressed a 365 lb. hog and made it ready for cooking. Dale shot it.

2/21/60 Sunday
Cloudy and started snowing hard about 8:00 P.M. We all went to Meadville this morning and evening. We all went to Uncle Jay Martin's for a turkey dinner. Clarence's, Abram's and Aunt Jennie were there too. Abram's stopped by on their way home. Isaac's went out to see James.

2/26/60 Friday
Cold last night. Four carpenters here all day. They put the picture window in this A.M. before it got colder. I cleaned upstairs and finished my aprons. Ray cleaned the big chicken house as the fountain ran over. He moved his capons above the wash house this evening. 19 members of the Navy Band were killed in a plane accident.

3/4/60 Friday
No school. Cloudy, cold, windy and drifting. Ray and I painted the living room. At 2:00 Mr. Reedy came to the mill for the Buick and Ray took it up. Shovelled through to the end of the lane. I took the Ford and we went to Lancaster to Best and Co. to get paper for the living room. Painted again this evening. We could not get all the way in the road, so we walked through the field. Eby walked up and Charlie left his car at Melvin Martin's and came home with Abner on his digger. He opened the lane and went back out to haul cinders.

3/5/60 Saturday
Snowing and blowing and drifting. Transformer blew out just as they finished milking. Brought the peeps in the house till 2:00 P.M. when the brooders were warmed up. P.P.&L. had our Amish neighbor haul a new transformer up from Gap in bobsled. Esther helped us paper the living room. We scrubbed it and put it in order. Didn't get finished till 9:30. Boys didn't get to market.

3/12/60 Saturday
A fine day. Ray, Dale and Sanford went to market. Charlie helped with the cleaning and Daddy, Charlie, Sanford, Nancy and I left for Virginia at 6:00 to visit Grace at EMC. Saw the basketball game, my first. We slept at Poag's Motel. Nancy slept with Grace.

3/13/60 Sunday
A very nice day. Not so cold. We all went with Grace to chapel services. Had our dinner at the dining hall. Went to Grace's room a while, then to John Horst's and to Joe Leaman's. Left for home at 3:30. Came a shorter way home and got here at 9:00. The children got along fine.

3/18/60 Friday
Foggy and cleared off. I washed and ironed some. Made raisin cookies, doughnuts and sweet petals. Got Ray started for Mass. At 2:00 and he picked Mary Alice up at school and Barbara at her home. I cleaned the living room. Charlie brought shades for new window and put them up.

4/16/60 Saturday
A real warm day. We finished up the cleaning and prepared for Sunday. I made home-baked bread. Nancy and I went to Sewing School. I got lettuce and cabbage

plants on the way back and planted them. Grace went to Nancy Fisher's party with Ginny Glass. It was an old fashioned box social.

4/23/60 Saturday
A very warm day. Ninety degrees. Eby left at 2:00 with 3 Amish farmers for a sale north of Scranton. He bought 7 heifers and altogether they bought 24. Charlie and Sanford went to market. Ray, Day and Mary Alice planted potatoes here and at Usner's. I made 3 cakes, a pudding, boiled beef and tongue and sweet potatoes. Boys put the cows out for the first. Put the porch chairs out.

5/2/60 Monday
Had frost, but little damage. A fine day. I washed and ironed and did some curtains. Dug some flower beds this evening. Chessman was killed in the California gas chamber. His death sentence was postponed 8 times. Ray hauled manure. Made plans to go help clean house at Landis's. Josephine is no better.

5/15/60 Sunday
A fine day. We all went to Meadville and to Truman Coy's for dinner. Charlie went with Dick George and wife and child for a stroll on the mountain. We all went to Meadville this evening but Charlie. Dale had a short talk on the Faithfulness of Moses.

6/2/60 Thursday
A fine warm day. I went to sewing circle this A.M. Went for Dale and 1:30, and he helped Ray plant corn. I sewed at Mary Alice's dress. Went to Gap for shower gifts, and Mary Alice, Nancy and I went to a shower for Barbara at Judy Kurtz'. Charlie left for Grace from work this evening.

6/15/60 Wednesday
Cloudy, damp and rained a few showers. The boys worked at painting the milk house. Had the cow stable sprayed. Finished up the dresses after Esther made buttonholes. Grace went to Philadelphia with some Hesses to see Ben Hur.

6/16/60 Thursday
A fine sunny day. Grace baked four cakes and I washed and ironed. We cleaned this afternoon and worked in the yard this evening. The men worked on the hay. Charlie worked on Rhoda's F.M. radio. Ray and I bought a spring and mattress at the Midway trailer sale for $8.00. Made a makeshift bedroom in the garage.

6/17/60 Friday
A nice warm day with lots of rain this evening. We made up the beds and cleaned the house. Grace, Mary Alice and I went to Coy's this afternoon to help prepare food. Stopped at Rubinson's and bought a dress. Picked strawberries and onions and peas before the rain. Charlie went to Abington to bring Mr. Schauffle and Bob Snow and Bob Garner and took them to the rehearsal. Ray went too. Dressed 7 chickens. Edgar's got here at 11:15.

6/18/60 Saturday
A pretty day. Not so hot. We made chicken corn soup, salad, strawberries and cake for dinner. James and Pat came. All went to Milton's wedding this afternoon. Florence Gehman and the girls kept Darlis and Greg. Everything went along in good order. Abner and Esther took Rev. Shauffle to the train in Phila. Abner's got a piano.

6/25/60 Saturday
A fine day, windy. I finished the lima beans, ironed and scrubbed. Grace got our lunch ready for the Martin reunion at Leaman Place park. Had a nice time. Good turnout. Isaac's and Eddie Landis' managed it. Eby and the boys baled and hauled Barley's hay. I went to Suzie Zook's for Milton's rug this evening. Nancy went along. Milton and Barbara came this evening to stay all night.

6/29/60 Wednesday
A wet day. Milton and Barbara started at 7:30 for their move to Mass. Ray, Nancy, Uncle Charlie and I started for Ithaca at 8:00. Grace went as far as Lancaster and started work at Dutch Haven. We had a safe trip, stopped at Slaterville Springs on our way. I helped to pack dishes.

7/10/60 Sunday
A fine day. Warmer. All went to Meadville this morning and Eby, Charlie and I this evening. Had a song service with a short message. Paul Goodman's from Coatesville brought their twin 9-year-old sons to stay for a week. The grandparents were along. Klein Copenhaver's brought Steven's sister Rita to see him. They are very friendly folks.

7/15/60 Friday
Nice clear day. I washed a big wash. Mary Alice made 2 cakes and me 1. Made snow pudding and cracker pudding. Grace worked day shift. Charlie took the children fishing to Lapp's. Ray worked at the porch this evening. Eby worked this evening.

7/18/60 Monday
Nice warm day. Washed and took Grace to work at 11:00. Picked and canned the pickles. The children finished the straw. Men came to work on the porch. I hoed this afternoon and planted pickles, spinach, beans, endive, and broccoli. Bible School started at Meadville. 127 attended. Mary Alice made Hostetter Review.

7/30/60 Saturday
Began raining early and cleared by dinner. Charlie, Dale and Sanford went to market. Ray and Mary Alice worked on the attic. I cooked and Charlie helped me clean. Eby had a committee meeting at Meadville. Charlie, Grace, Mary Alice, Dale and Ray went to Isaac's to caponize chickens and bring Joanne and Judy along to stay for a week.

8/21/60 Sunday
Hot, sultry and rained this evening. Went to Meadville. Took Charlie, Dale, Nancy, and Uncle Mart along to Lois Martin's wedding. Mary Alice kept Greg while Jim and Pat went to a hunting party at Red Point. Isaac's came for Linda and Sally.

8/28/60 Sunday
A very warm, humid day. We went to Meadville. Grace, Ray, Dale and Mary Alice went to Philadelphia to distribute The Way. They took lunch and got home about 8:45. We rested and read this P.M. and evening. Coy's came to bring some things for Milton to take for Barbara.

9/12/60 Monday
A very rainy day, part of the hurricane. School was dismissed because of high water. I cleaned eggs and canned some plums for James. Made three portions of sandwich spread. Grace made 2 skirts for Joanne Lindecamp and a dress for Nancy. Abner and Esther have taken a baby for one week while its mother sells sandwiches at York Fair.

9/15/60 Thursday
A nice day. I boiled 2 kettles of soap and cleaned the wash house. Grace sewed on a dress for Mary Alice. Dale went to a Hi-C doggie roast. Eby and I went to David's to see Jeannette's pictures from Newfoundland. Isaac Eshleman died.

9/18/60 Sunday
A cloudy, showery day. We all went to Meadville. Had dinner quickly, and Charlie took Grace to New York to start her new job. Dale and Sanford went along. Eby, Nancy and I went to a Hostetter reunion at Long's Park. Spent the evening at home.

9/26/60 Monday
Partly cloudy and cleared by noon. Got up at 4:30 and filled silo here and at Usner's. Dale and Sanford stayed home from school to help. I washed and did some of the ironing. Gathered and cleaned eggs. Had 2 extra men for dinner. Mr. Givler came to pick out some corn for Dale.

10/4/60 Tuesday
Nice day, partly cloudy. I washed the milkers, gathered and cleaned the eggs. Helped Ray pick some corn. Finished the ironing this morning and mended this evening. Judy cow cut her teat and Dr. Bryer fixed it up and it is slow milking her. A jet plane crashed near Boston killing 52. Made apple roll.

10/14/60 Friday
A fine warm day. I made three cakes and four crumb pies and cracker pudding. I gathered and graded eggs and gathered pumpkins and cabbage. Charlie helped me clean the kitchen. Ray and Dale went to town to get Ray's suit fit, and Dale bought a gun.

10/15/60 Saturday
Fine warm day. We cleaned up outside this morning as Charlie's boss came to get him to help get dogwood trees from the woods. Elizabeth called to say that Isaac is in the hospital for an eye operation to remove a piece of metal. Eby, Mary Alice and I helped with the Ham Supper at the Fire Hall.

10/22/60 Saturday
Frosty and cooler. Charlie and Sanford went to market. The girls and I cleaned and made some pepper relish. Eby, Ray, Dale and Sanford sowed wheat. Mary Alice washed both Fords. I called Isaac and he is getting along good.

11/3/60 Thursday
Ray's 19th birthday. Windy and cold. Took Annis Denlinger along to Sewing Circle. Came home at noon. Ray picked corn. Put blankets on the beds. Sanford went to the soccer game without permission and had to go to bed without supper.

11/9/60 Wednesday
A nice day. I cleaned the cellar. Kennedy was elected president. Many people are disappointed because he is a Catholic. The corn picker sheller finished this evening. I cleaned eggs. Eby and Ray went to the mill and unloaded corn after supper.

11/12/60 Saturday
A nice day. We finished our cleaning. Washed the car. We made 3 cakes, none of them a very great success. Ray and I went to John Groff's sale. Ray bought the dough tray for $16.00. Spent the evening at home.

11/15/60 Tuesday
A nice mild day. Real Indian summer. I did the ironing and mending. Took Mary Alice and Nancy to the dentist. They each had an extra tooth pulled from the lower front jaw. Bill was $19.00. Charlie's was $35.00.

11/24/60 Thursday
Thanksgiving Day. A very fine day. Eby, Edgar and I went to services at Hershey's. Had the whole family for dinner. James and Milton left for home after supper and Abram's and Isaac's left earlier.

12/9/60 Friday
A nice cold day. 15 degrees. I cleaned upstairs. Nancy stayed home and went with Ray and I shopping this afternoon. Stirred ginger cookies and cleaned eggs. Edgar called and said they have a baby girl born at 3:30 this morning. Eby, Ray and Sanford went to a Co-op meeting at Pequea Valley. Dale is playing basketball.

12/10/60 Saturday
Cold and clouded over this evening. I washed and ironed. Mary Alice and I baked hundreds of cookies. Charlie and Sanford went to market. Charlie helped with

cleaning this afternoon. Eby and Mary Alice went to New Holland this afternoon to get his glasses mended. Bought me shoes and rubbers. I addressed some greetings. Was very busy getting ready to go to Rhoda's.

12/11/60 Sunday
Cloudy and cold and began snowing at 11:30. Eby, Sanford, Nancy and I left at 8:15 for Myerstown Church. Went to Elmer Martin's for dinner and had reservations to fly to NY at 2:32, but the flight was cancelled because of the weather. Got home safely at 5:00. Edgar called to say they found a woman to help them out, much to my relief.

12/16/60 Friday
Snowing this morning. At 10:34 this A.M. occurred the worst plane crash in history. Two passenger planes collided over Manhattan and Staten Island, killing 136 persons. Eby worked late.

12/25/60 Sunday
A nice winter day. We all went to church. The children gave a little program. Got half boxes of candy. The children were excited. We opened our gifts. Dale and Sanford went skating to Fisher's. We all went to Meadville this evening. Had a song session. Leonard Hershey spoke and his wife had a reading.

12/26/60 Monday
A fine day, but clouded this evening and rained a little. The children were all here, but the Clemens' and Grace. Had a nice time together. Daddy surprised me with an electric oven. Abram's gave us 2 aluminum folding chairs. Isaac's two towels and wash cloths, James a picture of Greg, and Milton's a wedding picture. Dale had an FFA Christmas party.

12/27/60 Tuesday
A nice cold day. I washed and cleaned eggs. We cleaned up the house and made 3 freezers of ice cream for Grace's party this evening. Sara Ann, Elsie, Ginny, Betsy, and the three Gehman girls got here. Charlie met Grace at the depot at 7:15, and she was surprised to see the girls here when she got home. Dale played basketball at Manheim.

12/30/60 Friday
Everything was glistening with ice all day. I cleaned up the garage and cellar, and the girls helped with the rest of the house. Washed and left it to hang out for the night. Abram called and told us that Aunt Jennie died very suddenly this afternoon.

12/31/60 Saturday
A very nice bright day. Finished up the cleaning. Made a cake and pudding. Packed up to go to visit Rhoda's. Eby and I left at 12:05 and arrived in Slaterville Springs at 6:05. Had good roads. Little Marcia is a nice baby and very good.

1961

1/1/61 Sunday
It began snowing early before daylight and kept it up all day until 15 inches fell. Church and SS were cancelled in this area. We spent the day in the house except Eby, Edgar and Fredric shoveled the drive open. I made rabbit potpie for dinner. Read to the children and we spent a pleasant day together.

1/2/61 Monday
Still snowing, but cleared by 8:00. I helped do up the morning work, and we left for home at 10:30 and got here at 5:30. Stopped at Bowmansville and shopped at Harry Good's store. Everything went fine. Charlie was busy baking cinnamon buns and had made pineapple ice cream. Mary Alice washed, and it dried real good.

1/5/61 Thursday
Nice cold day. I took Annis along to SC and stayed till noon. 17 there. I dressed 7 pigeons and Ray picked them. Finished Nancy's dress. There is a lot of trouble in Cuba. United States has severed all relations with her, except the Naval base. Esther made Charlie a shirt.

1/9/61 Monday
Cold and windy. I washed and ironed. Did some mending and cleaned all the eggs. Dale stayed for basketball practice. Ray made some bookshelves for their bedroom. Mary Alice had a letter from her pen pal from Germany. Sanford quit chorus today. Dale popped corn.

1/23/61 Monday
Snowed till noon. I washed and dried it in the living room. Ironed it all. Kept Darrell while Esther took her wash to the dryer. We dressed and cut up a hog this evening. Eby came home at 4:00. Everything went satisfactorily. Boys made the sausage in the kitchen, it was so cold. Clarks installed the oven. Mary Alice made gingerbread in it for supper.

1/25/61 Wednesday
3 below zero. Sunny. I mended. Went with Ray to Lancaster to have Dr. Johnson take 2 small growths off his head. We shopped for a few things. Ray bought ensilage from Usner's. I wrote to Isaac's.

2/2/61 Thursday
Very cold day. 5 to 15 degrees below zero. We finished butchering for Abner's. Esther helped. Sanford stayed home with his cough. I sewed up my dress. Wrote to Jim's. Peter Shadid's have a baby boy. His name is Kaleem. Richard Buckwalter was ordained to preach at Old Road.

2/3/61 Friday
Cloudy and began snowing at 10:30. It snowed and blew and drifted fiercely. The children came from school at 2:30 because of the blizzard. Abner went to load cinders about 3:00. Snow is sifting in at every crack and crevice.

2/4/61 Saturday
It snowed all night and stopped at 1:00. Everything is drifted full. No work, no market. By evening it stopped blowing and they shoveled a track to the barn. I cleaned the downstairs and helped Sanford start a quilt. Mary Alice worked on hers. Esther is feeling better, and Abner is on the job. Daddy and the boys looked out the window at the snow.

2/15/61 Wednesday
A nice warm day. Saw some tulips up. Ray finished Miller's lane. I sewed, gathered and cleaned eggs. Dale delivered seeds this evening. Had a letter from Rhoda.

2/22/61 Wednesday
Damp, foggy, rainy. I sewed. Ray and I went to Lancaster. Bought some fabric and a pattern for Mary Alice and Nancy. Ray started cleaning my walnut rocker. Uncle Joe Hostetter died this evening in his chicken house.

3/4/61 Saturday
Partly cloudy, warm and rained. I made doughnuts and did most of the cleaning. Got things ready to go to Jim's. We left at 4:00, Eby, Nancy, Sanford and I. Got there by 8:00. I washed this morning. Mary Alice got the wash in and finished up the work.

3/5/61 Sunday
Sunny and springlike this morning and began raining about 3:00. We all went to Spring Run Church of the Brethren. Had dinner with Jim and Pat. Went to see a pipeline milker he had installed for a 100 cow dairy barn. Started for home about 4:00 and got home at 7:30.

3/10/61 Friday
Nice day, windy. Ray and I finished the butchering by 10:00. Had the cow doctor, someone to fix the oil furnace and the brooders. Mrs. Walkhouse came to talk about Nancy. Dale came home in time to take Ray to the train in Coatesville to go to NY. Charlie went to Dr. Beacher with his side ache and we took him to the hospital where he stayed for xrays and observation.

3/15/61 Wednesday
Partly cloudy and windy. Did the morning work and helped Ray clean the top chicken house for baby chicks. Eby went to the Hog Show at Stock Yards. Jack's hogs took top prizes. Charlie called and said he is still waiting for reports. Ray, Mary Alice and Sanford went to the hospital to visit Charlie.

3/18/61 Saturday
Real nice, sunny day. Dale and Sanford went to market. Ray hauled some hay. Got 500 peeps. Eby and the boys went to Ira Barley's sale. Nancy went to Linnie's birthday party. Charlie had his appendectomy this noon. He is feeling very bad. Dale and Mary Alice went to the operetta.

4/2/61 Sunday
A nice, cold, windy day. We all went to Meadville. 113 present. Got candy crosses after each class had a part in the program. Ben Hershey's and Arno Kim and his wife Jackie were here for dinner. Mary Alice and Nancy served for the first time. Dale went with Harold to Paradise.

4/5/61 Wednesday
A nice cold day. I cleaned closets and eggs. Ray disced the asparagus and plowed the garden. We bagged 101 25lb bags of potatoes. Two boys broke out of the Rotary Home from the Welsh Mountain. One called and threatened to shoot Mr. Eshleman and Mr. Pownell. One has been caught after damaging Pequea cemetery fence and stones.

4/23/61 Sunday
A fine warm day. Brought five of my class home for dinner. Played some games with them and took them to see Mrs. Laderach, and they sang for her. Eby, Nancy and I took them home. Stopped to see Ralph Arment, but he wasn't home. Dale and Sanford played ball at Gap. Castro made a four-hour speech.

4/24/61 Monday
A very warm day. Partly cloudy and had some showers. I washed, ironed and mended. Cleaned eggs. Ray plowed. The corn and peas are sprouted. Dale wants to join the Fire Department. There is trouble in France.

5/1/61 Monday
Cloudy and rained a few showers. I washed and ironed and mended. Ray plowed. Eby and the boys sawed at the fallen apple tree this evening. I cleaned and trimmed below the milk house. A young mother of two small children was murdered in Ephrata this morning by a 13-year-old boy.

5/22/61 Monday
A nice day, very cold wind. I washed and ironed and cleaned eggs. Leroy Lapp planted our corn. Ray harrowed. Eby mowed the yard and Dale cleaned up the ash pile. Raleigh man was here. Jake Hart was killed on Friday when his chicken house fell on him. Made toll house cookies.

5/24/61 Wednesday
Real nice day. Ray mowed alfalfa. I cleaned the kitchen and finished painting the porch furniture and put a coat on the front steps. Eby, Ray, Dale, Mary Alice, Sanford, Nancy and I went to 9th grade night. Mary Alice was one of the speakers.

6/2/61 Friday
A fine warm day. We left at 8:00 for Mass. with Uncle Clarence's and Grace Clark. Arrived here at Milton's at 5:30. They left for a banquet. We ate our supper and relaxed till 9:00 when Clarence's went to Schauffle's and we went to bed.

6/3/61 Saturday
A fine day, cooler. We went sightseeing to Gloucester, Salem and saw the rocky coast. Frank Kreider's came here to Milton's for supper and went to the concert with us where the Gordon College chorus sang.

6/6/61 Tuesday
Fine weather. Left Milton's at 7:00. Came to N.H. and visited the Shaker Colony and then on to Vermont to find some Mennonites. Staying at the motels of Abram Landes. He took us to see Calvin Coolidge's grave, church, home and birthplace. I sent some cards.

6/7/61 Wednesday
A fine day. We went to the White Mountains to the Franconia Notch. Saw the Flume, Old Man of the Mountain. Took a ride on the tramway. Cooked our supper in a park near Montpelier. Called home this evening. Staying at the West End Motel.

6/9/61 Friday
Cloudy and rained some. We worked on dresses for Rhoda and Rosa. Eby and Clarence made a chicken feeder for Fredric's chickens. Edgar took us through the $4 million Ithaca High School.

6/10/61 Saturday
Had a lot of rain early this morning here in Slaterville Springs. Mabel and I finished up Rhoda and Rosa's dresses and we packed up and left for home at 10:00. Arrived here at 5:00 after driving 1800 miles on our trip. Good to be home.

7/1/61 Saturday
A fine warm day. Rained a shower this evening. Dale and Sanford went to market. Charlie, Ray, and Mary Alice went to Abram's to help move. Nancy and I did up the baking, cleaning and eggs. This evening Eby, Nancy and I went to Hummelstown to help. Dale went to see "The Shadow of the Boomerang."

7/14/61 Friday
Real nice day. Charlie left from work to get his car serviced and go to Abram's to watch after Rebel while they went to Ohio. We dressed 5 chickens. I made some pies and canned pickles. I picked beans for market. Ray and I trained lima beans. Eby worked late and Dale took his supper.

7/16/61 Sunday
A sultry, showery day. Everything is growing. We all went to Meadville with the five extra children. The boys went in the truck. Spent the afternoon and evening reading

and watching the children. Mary Alice went to Suzanne Buckwalter's and her class had a picnic at Blue Rock for dinner. Ray went to see "Exodus."

7/19/61 Wednesday
A nice warm day. Ray and Mary Alice caponized chickens for Phares Fisher. Dale harrowed garden and we hoed it and most of the truck patch. Nancy did the eggs. They postponed putting the second man into space because of the weather. We all went to Bible School except Dale and Stephen.

7/29/61 Saturday
At 4:30 a severe storm struck the County. Stephen Stoltzfus' barn was burned. Lots of rain and some hail. We had one heifer killed. 5000 trees were blown down. Sheds and roofs blown down. We did the cleaning and preparing for Sunday. Washed the car. Eby worked all day. Charlie left for NY at noon.

8/4/61 Friday
Warm day. I made cupcakes and cleaned the kitchen and dining room. Scrubbed and waxed the floors. Ray and Stephen took Sanford to Phila. for his first plane ride to Boston to visit Milton. Grace and Charlie came with the counselors and 30 fresh air children from Camp Friendship. They had their supper here and a program.

8/5/61 Saturday
A damp day with some sun. I washed and picked first limas for Jim. Ray and I picked some blackberries. Got packed for our trip and we left at 2:15 from Jay Martin's. Sandra, Stephen and Nancy went along. Took a road up the mountains for Isaac's cabin, where we spent the night. Shelled the limas and made ourselves at home. Charlie brought Grace here to spend the night.

8/6/61 Sunday
Had fog, sun and shower. All slept well in our cabin and took a hike up the mountain before breakfast. Went to Spring Run to church and to Jim's for dinner. Left for home at 3:15. Got home at 6:50 and went to Meadville, where the Puerto Ricans had the meeting. Cows were in the corn and garden when we got home. The three boys and MA went to Abram's.

8/7/61 Monday
A nice sunny day. I washed and ironed. The cow damage was not as much as we expected. Ray painted and Dale cleaned up his corn and caught his chickens for caponizing. Mary Alice left for camp at 8:15. Nancy and I did the eggs. Esther brought a picture of their house plans.

9/8/61 Friday
A hot day. Ray and Uncle Charlie took Arno and Jackie Timm along to NY and a trailer with Milton's things to Long Island. I washed and cleaned. Picked limas and we shelled 12 quarts. Abner had the water smeller, and we all witnessed the find.

9/11/61 Monday
A hot day. I washed a big wash and ironed Charlie's things, about 18 shirts. Pressed and mended his suits and coats. Eby and I went to a memorial service for Anna Breneman. Texas is having a severe hurricane. Charlie is all packed up.

9/12/61 Tuesday
Another hot day. I made dinner for the silo fillers. Dale and Sanford stayed home from school. Finished the ironing and mending. Charlie left for Goshen at 6:00. I hoed the strawberries this evening. Mary Alice took Tom Denlinger's some cantaloupes. Hurricane is letting up to 50 mph. It was 173 mph.

10/11/61 Wednesday
A fine warm day. Ray and I picked 4 rows of corn. The workmen began laying blocks for Abner's house. I washed eggs and planted the begonias into pots. Mary Alice is getting uneasy about her trip to NY. Dale is fussy about getting his teeth pulled. Sold a heifer calf for $50. Had a letter from Rhoda and one from Charlie.

10/12/61 Thursday
Ray and I picked four rows of corn. The children came home at 2:30 and picked corn. I washed. Elizabeth stopped a while. Mary Alice went to NY to see Grace by train. Ray took her to the depot. Eby, Nancy and I went to New Holland to exchange her shoes, which had a flaw. I got everyday shoes and Nancy a dress.

10/13/61 Friday
A nice warm day. Ray and I picked four rows of corn till 11:00. Gathered and washed eggs. Ray seeded the wheat. Dale came home and we took Nancy along to Lancaster. I bought her 2 coats for $14.00. Dale got four front teeth pulled and a plate put in.

10/15/61 Sunday
A cold windy day. We all went to Meadville. Dick Patterson had charge of the SS as Ben Hershey's had a fire caused by wiring in their house. I had my class of 6 home for dinner and supper. Took them to see Mrs. Laderach. Eby and I took them home on our way to church. Ray met Mary Alice at the train.

11/9/61 Thursday
Partly cloudy, cold and windy. I washed and ironed, cleaned the living room. Called Isaac's and Elizabeth came home at 11:00 with little Karen Sue. Eby went to an Interstate Meeting this evening. The boys went to bed early. I hemmed Mary Alice's choir gown. Finished a letter to Milton.

11/13/61 Monday
Partly cloudy all day. Wash dried slowly. Mary Alice did not feel well enough to go to school. I cleaned the stripping room this afternoon. Got the wash ready to iron this evening. Eby is very much excited about putting in a stable cleaner. A planed crashed in Virginia, killing 77. Had a letter from Milton.

11/28/61 Tuesday
Clear, cold and windy. I did the ironing and mended some. Grace sewed. Made a dress for Nancy from one of hers. I gathered and cleaned the eggs. Ray went to the sale. He worked on the stable. Eby, Nancy and I went to Meadville. Sanford went to the Dr. for his knee.

12/2/61 Saturday
A mild day, partly cloudy. Dale went to West Chester to take a college test. Mary Alice went to the broadcasting station in Lancaster for a recording. Ray worked on the stable cleaner. Sanford and I went to market. Grace did the work. Nancy gathered the eggs. Isaac's came this afternoon and Eby went along to look at a farm near Kirkwood. Dale went away this evening.

12/3/61 Sunday
A fine mild day. We all went to Meadville. Martin Hershey preached. After the dishes were done we walked down to see Esther's house. Kathleen stopped and invited me along to see a flower display at Wenger's greenhouses in Leacock. It was pretty, but did not seem like the thing for Sunday. Ray took Grace to the depot this evening. Wrote to Charlie. Daddy, Ray, Mary Alice and I went to Hershey's revival.

12/22/61 Friday
A real nice day. I made chicken ready for waffles for the men at the mill. Popped some corn. Washed. Ray went to the depot to meet Grace. They shopped and bought me a beautiful linen tablecloth for Christmas. The children came home at noon. We did 23 capons this afternoon. Dale went to a basketball game. Grace wrapped gifts. Cleaned and washed eggs.

12/25/61 Monday
Christmas Day. Cleared and was a real nice day. Daddy cleaned all the eggs today. I made two aprons that Esther gave me. The boys took it slow and easy. Ray, Mary Alice, Daddy and I took Milton and Barbara along to see Abram's for supper. David and Pat are both fine. Roads are very treacherous. Mary Alice stayed up to help Pat.

12/31/61 Sunday
A fine cold day. We all went to church. Had a capon dinner. Worked on my SS lessons and went down to see Abner's house. Uncle Charlie took Charlie, Nancy and Sanford up to see Abram's and to bring Mary Alice home.

1962

1/1/62 Monday
Partly cloudy. Snow melted a little. I washed and helped Charlie get his clothing ready. Washed the eggs. Eby and the boys cleaned out 13 loads of manure. Barbara

and Milton stopped in a little at noontime. Eby and I went to see Aunt Minnie Hersh this afternoon. Ray helped with the house this afternoon and evening. Charlie left for Goshen at 8:00 with five passengers.

1/6/62 Saturday
Rained, dark and foggy all day. I washed the milkers and the eggs. Made pies and a chocolate cake. Washed and hung it in the cellar. The girls helped with the work. Dale and Sanford went to market. The got wet. Sanford bought a yellow raincoat.

1/8/62 Monday
A nice day, partly cloudy. I washed and did some of the ironing. Ray helped at the house all day. I gathered and cleaned the eggs. We have burned all wood in the cookstove this winter. Nancy stayed home. She has an upset stomach. We put the concrete blocks in the cellar.

1/9/62 Tuesday
Cloudy and colder. The men put the partition in the cellar. Ray helped at the house. I ironed and mended. Nancy stayed home with cold and sore throat. I stayed home with her when Eby, Mary Alice and Sanford went to Bible School at Paradise. Ray went to the sale. His knee hurts. Dale went to a basketball game at Cocalico. I greased the cow's swollen udder.

1/12/62 Friday
Real nice day. I washed and Nancy ironed this evening. She did not go to school. I did the eggs. Made an angel food cake and salad. Ray helped at the house all day. I cleaned out the stove and mended the fire box and started a coal fire for the first time this winter. Dale, Sanford and Mary Alice went to a basketball game.

1/22/62 Monday
Cloudy and began raining at noon. I washed and had to bring it all in before it was dry. Did all the eggs. Ray helped at the house all day. Nancy and I put some wood in the wash house for butchering. I gave Nancy a choice of punishment for overstaying at Esther's. Wash the dishes herself or go to bed without supper, which she did. Dale had F.F.A. meeting. Eby, Ray and Sanford cleaned chicken roosts.

2/7/62 Wednesday
Clear and cold. 10 degrees. I cleaned the cave. Sewed and did the eggs. Willis Hershey was here to ask Ray to serve on the Gospel Witness Band. We dressed 2 hogs this evening. One cow had twin calves. Both are dead. Some cracks are showing in Esther's house. Got a load of straw. Dale stayed home and rested with a cold.

2/8/62 Thursday
Cold and just right for butchering. We were done by 10:30. I canned the meat, pudding, sausage, and sugar cured the hams, shoulders and bacons. Scrubbed the wash house and porch. Mary Alice stayed after school till 7:00 for chorus practice.

Eby, Ray, Sanford, Nancy and I took the Kauffman girls along to Bible School for the last session. John Martin spoke on The Christian and the State.

2/20/62 Tuesday
Fine cold day. John Glenn was shot into space and went around the earth three times in 4 hours and 54 minutes. Making history. I did the ironing and eggs. Ray worked at the house and went to the sale. Sanford stayed home with a stiff neck and had the radio on all day. I went with Cassy to her mother's Tupperware party. Dale had basketball.

3/3/62 Saturday
Cold, clear and sunny. Eby worked till 9:30. We were ready to start for Edgar's at 10:15. Got there at 4:00. Found them all well and happy. Gave them their Christmas gifts. Nancy and Sanford enjoyed playing with the children.

3/6/62 Tuesday
Very high wind and snowed all day. The current was off early this morning. They had no school. Ray and Dale took top off the cave. Ray went to the sale. Mary Alice helped Esther. I quilted and made dutch goose for supper. Esther quilted a while this evening. Abner was loading cinders all night and day.

3/8/62 Thursday
A nice day. I washed up the apartment kitchen and cleaned up the garage. Did the morning work and made ready for the representative from Farm Vacations and Holidays. She came at 4:00. Uncle Charlie stopped by after getting a haircut. Ray put the top on the cave and took the eggs. I quilted. Charlie called last night about 10:30. Esther came up for milk.

3/10/62 Saturday
Nice day. Snow is melting. Eby, Sanford and I went to Barry Skolnik's Bar Mitzvah. It was very interesting. Got home at 1:15 and went to help do Barbara Hilliard's quilt. Eby went to the mill to work this afternoon. Abner has a very sore throat. They were up this evening.

3/12/62 Monday
Cloudy, rainy and damp. Clearing this evening. Margie and Sue came and helped me finish my quilt. I made a sponge cake and chicken corn soup for dinner. We had a nice visit. I put the binding on the quilt after supper and finished one end. Nancy came home about 10:30 because the toilets ran over from high water. Eby had a feed meeting. Ray went to town for wallpaper.

3/13/62 Tuesday
Real nice day, had a few showers. I washed and ironed. Left before 6:00 to quilt at Ralph Hillards. Took Nora Stoltzfus and Sue along. Got home at 11:15. There were ten helping. Ray went to the Vintage Sale, biggest they ever had. Did the eggs. 7 babies died of a mistake in the Binghamton Hospital, salt instead of sugar in the formula.

3/16/62 Friday
Rough and windy. Abner called and said that little Darla Joy arrived at 3:00. I went down after the morning work and took the bassinette and helped start the baby nursing. Bathed her this evening. Washed and did most of the cleaning. Mabel came for the quilting frames.

3/17/62 Saturday
Nice windy day. Dale and Sanford went to market. I did the milkers. The girls and I went down for Darrell. He stayed till 8:00 when Sanford took him home and saw the baby. The girls and I did the rest of the cleaning. I dressed 6 chickens. Went down this afternoon and bathed Esther's baby. Made 2 chiffon cakes. Did the ironing. Eby went to Paul Nolt's open house. Got 500 baby chicks for $194.

3/18/62 Sunday
Beautiful day. We went to Meadville morning and evening. Eby and I went over to Sol Stoltzfus' this P.M. Linnie came up and Darrell came at noon. Ray got home at 5:00. Milton called at noon and told us Michael David arrived this morning. Ray spoke on Amos at Meadville this evening.

3/23/62 Friday
Nice day, like spring. Ray and I finished papering this afternoon all but two strips. Left at 12:00 to help Elizabeth clean some floors at the new place. Eby, Ray, Dale and I went to the F.F.A. Banquet this evening. Had a good speaker. Earl Wanner spoke on The Purple Curtain. Cooked tripe and rolled it up when we came home.

3/30/62 Friday
A fine day. Rhoda washed. I roasted 2 hams for Fire Supper. Rhoda helped me make 15 quarts of mince meat. Nancy spelled in the semi-final bee at Pequea Valley. Misspelled parallel. Got some stamp books ready to redeem.

4/4/62 Wednesday
Coldest April 4 on record. Cleaned the cellar way and the egg room. Ray started plowing. We all went to the Business Meeting at Meadville but Sanford. I was put on the Picnic Committee. Ray and Dale for ushers and Sign Committee. Mary Alice on the Library Committee.

4/17/62 Tuesday
Cold with ice this morning. I mended and put the wash away. Ray and I fixed up the back walks. Made some sheets and pillow cases. Charlie and Orie Clemens went to Washington to look for a summer job. Mary Alice did not get home from school until 9:30 because of practicing. Sanford and I tried to fix the sewing machine.

4/26/62 Thursday
A fine day. Real warm. I aired some comforts and the winter coats. Got ready for Bennie Fisher. He came for supper about 4:00 and spent the evening. Eby and I took

him home about 10:00. Ray plowed. Had first lettuce. Got some rug rags ready and plaited some while I visited with Bennie.

5/5/62 Saturday
A fine day. I made a tier birthday cake for Daddy. Cleaned up and got supper for Milton's, Abram's, and Isaac's. Mary Alice stayed at Esther's two hours while she went to the store. Nancy went to the Patrol Parade. I washed. Abner took his antenna off the top of our house. Karen, David, and Michael are growing.

5/18/62 Friday
Real warm day. Did up the morning work. Went down to the Gap School and made potato salad. Came home and gathered eggs and returned at 1:00 to finish it and take it to White Horse, where the Spring Fair was held. Helped with the chicken corn soup and got home at dark. Ray went to Pequea Valley for a scholarship from Kuntzler's for $500.00. He then met Grace at the train. Nancy stayed home and signed for the rug that was delivered. She went to school at noon with me. Grace mowed the yard for some tan.

6/5/62 Tuesday
A rainy day. Mary Alice and Sanford had school till noon. Ray pulled plants. Dale went with Lee Summers to register. I picked sugar peas between showers and froze 9 quarts. Ray went to the sale and the rest of us went to Dale's graduation. Had a good rain. Charlie got home about 5:00 and took Mary Alice and Sanford to Frank's viewing. Nancy went to Washington D.C.

6/7/62 Thursday
A fine day. I made 45 pts. strawberry jelly. Sanford had part of his class, 40-45, here for a picnic from 12-4. They had a nice time. Mary Alice went to a picnic for her class at Mary Jane Howe's. The boys hauled hay. Eby, Sanford, Nancy and I went to a meeting at Pequea Valley in honor of Serena Groff's and Mrs. Kauffman's retirement.

6/8/62 Friday
A fine day. The boys helped me pick the rest of the peas. Nancy picked sugar peas for market. Mary Alice did some cleaning. I finished and scrubbed and waxed the kitchen. I took Mary Alice, Suzanne and Linda to New Holland Park for their picnic in Ray's car. The boys were busy in the hay and got it all in this evening. Dale had a class party this evening.

6/24/62 Sunday
Warm, humid, with very heavy rain this afternoon. We all went to Sunday School but Ray. He stayed with the sick cow. Had the doctor 2 times, but she died this evening. We all went to Abner's for dinner. I wrote to Edgar's, Grace and Charlie.

6/25/62 Monday
A fine day. Everything is growing. Mary Alice washed and I did the ironing. Picked 5 quarts of currants. Mary Alice picked the blueberries and 8 quarts of raspberries. I canned 7 quarts. We went to Lapp's dry goods and bought two dresses for Mary Alice and one for Nancy. Got a box of apricots and canned 13 quarts. Nancy and I trained limas.

6/28/62 Thursday
A fine day. We washed and got the upstairs ready for the children. Stephen King, the Goodman twins and Barry and Judy Skolnik and Richard Evans came this evening. Mr. Goodman and Mrs. Skolnik brought them. Ray worked for Sam Yoder. We did 14 quarts beans. Milt Hershey died.

6/29/62 Friday
A nice day. We did some cleaning. I planted the celery. The boys were in high gear. Judy got on her high horse this evening. Milton and Barbara came this evening. The boys went to bed more orderly this evening. Ray worked for Sam Yoder. Dale hoed tobacco on the F.F.A. project this evening.

7/2/62 Monday
A fine day. Washed and did some ironing. Edgars came about 1:15. The girls did the eggs. Mary Alice went down to stay with Cassy and go with her to the doctor. Mrs. Skolnik and Mrs. Goodman called. The boys had words, but seem to be reconciled. The children helped Ray and Dale catch chickens.

7/3/62 Tuesday
Real nice day. Rhoda washed. I made 2 cakes, some pie shells and cooked most all day. The boys were very mischievous and disgusting. Edgar took Jeff and Richard in hand and I put Stephen to bed. Mary Alice spent the afternoon with Cassy's children and Dippner's. Chickens bought 7 cents a pound, and eggs 30 cents a dozen.

7/4/62 Wednesday
A very fine day. Had trouble with the boys and called Mrs. G. to come for three of them. Made things ready for the reunion dinner. All of our family were there but Grace and Jim's.

7/11/62 Wednesday
A nice day. I did the pickles and the mending. Worked on Mary Alice's dress. Nancy went to 4-H. Mary Alice drove tractor for hauling hay. Got all the second cutting alfalfa in. Ray sprayed. Eby hoed this a.m. Stephen left this morning. Esther dried her wash and had a talk.

7/17/62 Tuesday
Cloudy and drizzled. I hoed the sweet corn. I ironed and made Mary Alice a cape. The girls did the eggs. Mary Alice picked blackberries. Nancy pulled out some beans.

I planted a row. All went to Bible School but Sanford. Ray went to the sale and Eby took his class. Melvin Grove was murdered in Somalia working as a missionary.

8/14/62 Tuesday
A fine day. I washed and ironed. Mary Alice and Nancy got corn in to freeze, 22 quarts. Nancy's 12th birthday. Esther made her a cake. Eby and Ray went to the sale this evening. Ray and Mary Alice caponized some chickens for Hoover's. Mary Alice dug a basket of potatoes for Tom's and took them down. I planted lettuce. Train wreck at Atglen, 2 killed.

9/6/62 Thursday
A fine day. Real cool. Grace helped me can 37 quarts of peaches. Mary Alice went to school. Sanford and Nancy stayed at home. Eby painted. Grace sewed this afternoon. Eby, Nancy and I went to New Holland to the cow sale and went to Rubinson's. Charlie knitted most all day. Started seven-day pickles.

9/25/62 Tuesday
Partly cloudy and cool. I washed the bed clothes and dug some sweet potatoes for supper and planted some flowers in pots. Gary Martin came home with Sanford to spend the night. Eby went to the Vintage sales barn. Sold a cow. Started to read the Rugged Land of Gold. Wrote to Rhoda and Milton. Had a letter from Grace saying that she is coming on Saturday with a friend George.

9/29/62 Saturday
A nice day. I was busy getting Eby and Sanford off to market. Made a cake, pudding, pies and things ready for eating. Dressed chickens for corn soup. Grace came with Cecil Grove and her new boyfriend Robert (George) Weaver. Dorie slept till they came at 10:30. Kurtz's finished filling the silo. I did the ironing.

11/3/62 Saturday
Cloudy and rainy with sleet and snow. Cleared at dark. Made a chiffon cake and made a basket of sweet potato tails into croquettes. Washed and hung it in the cellar. Eby and Sanford went to market. Mary Alice went to Mike Lichty's birthday party. Oil burner smoked, and Eby, Nancy and I helped clean up the house at Meadville. Got home at 10:20. I went to bring Mary Alice and the girls home at 11:00.

11/8/62 Thursday
Warmer and mild. I finished up the garage all but scrubbing. Planted daffodils and cleaned some yard and garden. Picked balance of popcorn. Eby cleaned chicken houses. Called Clark's and they put a new unit on for $50. Cut Darrell's hair. Jim called and said they have a baby girl born at 4:30.

11/11/62 Sunday
A nice day. We all went to Meadville. Calvin Kennel talked. I wrote to Rhoda, Milton, Charlie and Ray. It was a bit smoky at Meadville this evening when we had

our communion service. The barn down at Isaac's burned this evening. Dale and I went down at 4:00, and we all went down again after church but Dale. Mary Alice and Sanford sang at Pequea Valley.

11/12/62 Monday
I washed and ironed. Helped Eby put lumber away that he bought at the relief sale. Eby went town to Isaac's to help remove the dead animals this afternoon. Mary Alice stayed at school until 11:00 working on the newspaper. Dale went to Fire Meeting.

11/19/62 Monday
A nice day. The beans were done this morning and I baked some raisin filled cookies. Daddy and I went down to Isaac's and helped with the frolic. About 100 men there and 14 women. Ironed this evening and dressed 2 capons for the man without legs. Eby went to see a carpenter barn builder. Ada Umble was hit and killed crossing the highway at Lawrence's.

11/26/62 Monday
A nice day. I washed and ironed. Dressed 6 capons. Eby put fertilizer on the alfalfa. The lump on his back is very red and sore. Seems more like it will open. Raymond Charles is to dine with President Kennedy and a Somalian ambassador in Washington tomorrow afternoon.

11/28/62 Wednesday
A nice day. I did the morning work. Cleaned up some leaves. Took out all the carrots and some endive. Eby and I covered the celery trench. Eby went down to Isaac's this afternoon. Sanford is having some discipline problems at school.

12/13/62 Thursday
Clear and cold. Stirred more cookies and baked six kinds, over 800 this A.M. Eby had a stable cleaner and a barn fan man this a.m. He went to help Isaac clip cows this afternoon. Ray took Dale to New Holland to get his car and Mary Alice, Sanford and Nancy went along to do some shopping.

12/16/62 Sunday
A nice day. We all went to Meadville. The missionary offering was $177. Ray and the girls made dinner, and I started to write my greetings. This kept me busy till 9:00. Milton's came for supper and bought the Kenyan boy. Dale went skating this afternoon. All stayed at home this evening. Not quite so cold.

12/22/62 Saturday
Icy but cleared up. Eby, Sanford and Bernard went to market. Grace and Mary Alice cleaned and I made candy and washed. Ray came home at 10:00 and coated the candy. I took Mary Alice to Kauffman's and bought her a watch for $41.50.

12/24/62 Monday
Cloudy. We dressed 12 capons. Got things ready for dinner tomorrow. Grace made a cocoanut cake. I roasted the capons and made the gravy. Cleaned the celery. Made sweet potato croquettes. Ray worked for Abner. The children all went caroling but Grace.

12/25/62 Tuesday
Snowed and rained. All the children came for dinner but Edgar's. Jim's were late because of the roads. They stayed all night after going as far as Soudersburg. Bernard is seeing plenty of snow. Esther and Elda came up to see the babies.

12/27/62 Thursday
Clouded over after sunup. We did up the morning work and left for Edgar's about 10:30. Nancy, Eby and I went. She was sick and vomiting this morning. We got to Edgar's by 4:00. Daddy got sick after supper. They are all over the measles. Ray and Mary Alice helped Abram's move to Devonshire Heights Road.

12/29/62 Saturday
Cloudy and began snowing at 10:30. I dressed four capons and two leghorns. Sold two capons. Eby and Sanford went to market. Nancy stayed with Abner's children while he went to load cinders and Esther and Elda went shopping. Charlie, Ray and Mary Alice left for New York at 10:00. I washed and ironed some. Did the eggs. Bernard went along to market.

12/31/62 Monday
It blew and drifted all day. Ray took Bernard to the Gap on the tractor to meet Milton's. Phone went out this morning. Sanford called Isaac's from Denlinger's, and Linda was hit with a barn door and had her nose injured. Eby carried water to the chickens. I ironed and worked on Ginny's quilt patches. The children all went to Abner's for a party but Nancy. Ray got his car up, but Charlie's is stuck yet.

1963

1/1/63 Tuesday
Cold and the wind is drifting the snow. Charlie got started at 1:30 with his Maryland passengers. Ray hauled him to Wise's and they shoveled him through Clair's field. The road was open by evening. Dale took eggs to Mrs. Lawrence. Had roast venison for dinner.

1/4/63 Friday.
A nice day. Dr. Westover from Penn State called and said he would be operating on Ray for appendicitis. He called this evening and said he is doing all right. We dressed 7 chickens. I did some cleaning. Elizabeth came for Karen this evening after she visited Linda. Eby finished the chicken roosts.

1/6/63 Sunday
Real nice day. We all went to Sunday School but Dale. He is sick in the stomach. I called Ray and he is still in the hospital but feeling better. Took the children to Pequea Valley for polio medicine and stopped to see Esther. Eby and I went to church this evening. Harold Book preached.

1/11/63 Friday
A foggy day with some rain. I cleaned the upstairs, living and dining rooms. Bacteria count was 360,000, and the milk inspector came to check the trouble. Eby took Sanford to Old Road for first instruction meeting. I soaked my corns.

1/13/63 Sunday
Damp and foggy and colder this evening. I had a sore throat and stayed home from church. Nancy has a cold. Miss Talbert was here to help Mary Alice with the paper. We all went up to see Larry Blatt's pictures of the World's Fair and other places. I read part of Martha Hershey's book, The Secret of the Singing Heart.

1/26/63 Saturday
Partly cloudy and began snowing at dark. Grace did the managing. We finished the cleaning, made doughnuts and ice cream. I did the eggs. Eby and Sanford went to market. Sold 14 lbs. of sausage, 21 lbs. of scrapple, 2 lbs. of pig foot jelly and 3 lbs. of lard. George called Grace and said he cannot come tomorrow.

1/27/63 Sunday
Five inches of snow fell and it cleared this morning. We all went to Meadville this morning, 78 there. The group from NY did not come, so we ate the dinner ourselves. Dale took Grace in for the 3:10 train. Mary Alice studied. Sanford played with the plastic blocks. Dale has a date with Carol Brubaker and went to Calvary Independent. My cold hangs on.

1/29/63 Tuesday
Very cold. Fifteen below zero. Calm and clear. Did the morning work and took the girls to Dr. Crandall. Bill was $24.00. Mary Alice took her driver's test and passed. They went back to school at noon. I did the eggs and sewed. I took Sanford and Nancy to Bible School. Mr. Eshleman was displeased with Mary Alice's editorial in the school paper. Robert Frost died. Eggs.35.

2/9/63 Saturday
Nice mild day. I washed and ironed. Nancy did the managing not so good. Nancy made a white cake flavored with orange and chocolate chips with walnut flavored icing. Eby and Sanford went to market. I got wood in for butchering and did the eggs. Finished my dresses.

2/17/63 Sunday
A nice day, not so cold. We all went to Meadville. Had Uncle Mart, Miriam, Uncle Charlie, Marilyn Martin and Janie for dinner. The men went down to see the new barn at Isaac's. We went to church at Meadville this evening. Dale had a topic on Requirements for Answered Prayers. Mary Alice stayed home alone. Nancy did not make a good job of entertaining her company.

2/20/63 Wednesday
Sunny and mild. Snow is melting. I did the mending. Helped unload the hay and push the wagon in the barn with tractor. Went down to see Ella Denlinger and took her an azalea for her 89th birthday. Eby and I took Clarence and Mabel along to the Ministerial Meeting at Landisville. Nancy is out of the spelling contest. She missed paralyze.

3/5/63 Tuesday
Cloudy, damp and drizzled. I did the ironing and mending. Made a pan of soap. Did the eggs. Eby went to the sale. Talked to Aunt Minnie Hersh and Esther. Dr. said we should beef the cow that can't get up if she goes 2 days longer. Mary Alice took a scholarship test today. Wrote to Ray.

3/6/63 Wednesday
Had our first thunderstorm and lots of rain. Creeks are overflowing. Eby brought the meat home for canning. I did 20 cans and sugar cured the dried beef. Sold the cow that could not get up. Eby and Sanford went to the Father and Son Banquet. Dale went to help F.F.A. to strip tobacco. Mary Alice gave me a scholarship test.

3/14/63 Thursday
Real nice day. Uncle Charlie and I left Gap at 7:30 and arrived here in Slaterville Springs at 1:30. Mrs. Reed, a neighbor, was staying with the children. I did the ironing and Uncle Charlie cleaned the back porch. The baby's name is Conrad Joel. I wrote to Grace and Ray this evening. Uncle Charlie cut the boys' hair.

3/15/63 Friday
Clear and cold. After the breakfast and hair combing were done, Uncle Charlie and I cleaned the house. The children had no school. Rhoda came home about 2:30. Conrad is a pretty little fellow, nice and fat. He is good. I started reading a book, Applesauce Needs Sugar.

3/19/63 Tuesday
Real nice day. Washed and it dried outdoors. Got a letter from home. The Running Pump Stone House has been moved across the highway to its new location. Edgar was disappointed that his visitors did not come from Wheatley. I read in my book.

3/22/63 Friday
Snowing and cold. I did the baby wash and morning work, and Daddy and I left for home at 9:00. We stopped at the Acme, Harry Good's and at Red Dan's for our bolognas. Got home at 3:00. Ray was busy cleaning. He did a big wash. I helped finish and we were all ready for Grace, George, Dorie and Cecil when they got here.

4/5/63 Friday
Real cold and stormy. Calm this evening. I finished Nancy's dress and did the eggs, 789. The stable cleaner man was here to give orders to the jack hammer driver. The children drove, and Mary Alice was inducted into the National Honor Society. She and Nancy went to the banquet this evening. Dale took his car to Sauders and went to the Tract Band Meeting.

4/15/63 Monday
A splendid wash day. Getting dry. Eby finished planting the sweet corn and got strawberry patch ready. The girls helped me do the beds and wash all the slips and blankets. They helped do the eggs. Kathy Buckwalter came this P.M. I made a sponge cake for Darrell's birthday. Eby took his income tax report to Kinzer. Did Charlie's ironing and he started for Goshen. Nancy started a bank account.

4/17/63 Wednesday
Cloudy and showery. Cleaned the egg room. Helped harrow the asparagus and picked some. Washed the eggs. The children drove to school. Eby had a meeting at Vintage Sales Barn. Sanford tried to fix the sink faucet and made it worse. He did the lavatory too and it was better. I plaited and joined a row around my rug.

4/23/63 Tuesday
Had good rain in the early morning and more showers today. I cleaned the cellar, replanted the strawberries, cleaned eggs and did the mending. Eby went to the sale. Dale stayed home with a cold. Had a letter from Jim's. The are buying at a farm. I sowed some primrose seed. Wrote to Ray.

4/25/63 Thursday
Cool and clear. I baked 2 chiffon cakes, a jelly roll and 4 lemon sponge pies. Cleaned up. Mary Alice brought Miss Talbert home to work on the paper and have supper. Before we had the dishes washed, Abner's came with a big birthday cake and Clarence's, Mildred, Clair and Tom Denlinger's, George Dippner's and Isaac's followed. I was stunned. They brought ice cream and chocolate cake and pretzels. Had a nice evening.

5/11/63 Saturday
We had a very good rain last night. It is cool and windy. Nancy made a cake. I made pumpkin pie and sliced a ham. Finished up the cleaning. Mary Alice, Sanford and Nancy went for tomato plants, corn seed and stopped at Lapp's for dress fabric. Mary

Alice could not be satisfied so came home with only skirt material. We all went to preparatory service this evening. Mary Alice mowed the yard. Nancy gathered the eggs.

5/12/63 Sunday
Nice cool day. We all went to Meadville this morning and this evening for communion. I started reading Search to Belong this afternoon. Abram's came about 3:30 this afternoon. I gave them a snack and they went to Uncle David's. Ray called, and Charlie called after we came home from church. I wrote to Grace, and Mary Alice wrote some too.

5/24/63 Friday
A fine day. Had frost that nipped beans, corn, tomatoes and potatoes. I trimmed the yard and cleaned. Eby harrowed the garden after getting the harrow repaired. This evening we had a birthday party for Galen's 68th. All the brothers and sisters were there. Miss Talbert was awarded teacher of the year.

5/29/63 Wednesday
A showery day. Jay Hostetter's, Eby and I left at 6:00 for our trip. Stopped at Jim's for a little while and came up to Erie. Found Aunt Emma in the hospital. She was recovering from a stomach ailment. We ate a cookout supper on 19 just north of Meadville. Stopped at the Jordan Motels on Route 20. The children were all going to school and Dale was going home at noon to do the eggs.

5/30/63 Thursday
Cloudy this morning but was clear till we got to Indiana. Visited some Amish folks around Nappanee and got to the outskirts of Chicago by bedtime. Have a Howard Johnson's motel. Wrote a letter to Ray and Grace. Cooked our dinner at a park in Chicago.

5/31/63 Friday
A fine day. We arrived safely at Soldier's Field soon after 7:00. Went to Board of Trade and to the Stock Yards. Had a taxi take us to the Museum of Science and Industry. Have a double room with one bath for $6.00 each. Called home and Robert this evening.

6/2/63 Sunday
Nice warm day. We went to the Bethel Conservative Church and to Goshen where we met Charlie and had our dinner. He showed us around and we attended a chorus at 3:00. Went to David Glick's for supper and back to Goshen for Baccalaureate this evening. It gave a full auditorium. Met a lot of folks.

6/3/63 Monday
A nice warm day. We left our motel and ate breakfast in a roadside park on our way to commencement at Goshen. Charlie graduated with 232 others. The speaker was

good. Packed up and ate our lunch at a restaurant before we got on the turnpike. Drove all night and stopped often. Got to Abram's at 2:30.

7/7/63 Sunday
A nice day, warmer. We all went to Meadville. Isaac's stopped for Linda and Sally and left Joanne and Judy. Helped the children play croquet. Ray met the Conover's at Gap and brought them to the apartment.

7/12/63 Friday
A nice day. Dry. Eby, Sanford and Bernard went to market. I washed and ironed. The girls cleaned and did the eggs. Ray took Sanford and the Conover's to the Cloisters and Green Dragon. Eby and Nancy went to Meadville to help get ready for Bible School. I trained the limas up the poles. The girls played ball with Bernard.

7/15/63 Monday
A nice warm day. I washed early. Eby, Nancy, Sanford, Bernard and I went to the zoo and to Independence Hall. Got home at 4:00. Mary Alice kept house and cleaned the apartment, ironed the sheets, and made the beds. We all went to Bible School but Sanford. 109 there. Ray, Mary Alice and I are teaching. Have septic tank trouble.

7/18/63 Thursday
A hot day. Eby, Sanford and Bernard worked on the septic tank and sink drain. I went to Horst's for a load of stones. I washed and Nancy went to a 4-H picnic. Mary Alice started working at Plain and Fancy. Dale worked this evening till 12:00. Nancy and Sanford mowed yard. We all went to Bible School.

7/27/63 Saturday
A hot day. Eby, Bernard and Sanford went to market. We pulled over 400 ears of corn this morning. Sold for 60 cents a dozen. I baked pies early. Mary Alice picked blackberries and left at 11:00 to stop in Gordonsville before going to work at 1:00. I scrubbed and did balance of cleaning and eggs. Ray put up new window shades in our bedroom. Nancy went to Riverside with the Dippner's all day.

7/28/63 Sunday
Another hot day. We all went to Meadville. Took Mrs. Schroder and Miss Haesler along and had them here for dinner. Bennie Fisher came to get someone to take him to Kennel's Woods to the singing. Ray took him down. Had a heavy rain and gust and some hail. Sam Smoker's barn burned. We took the NY ladies for a drive this evening and showed them some places of interest.

7/29/63 Monday
Warm and humid. I did the wash and washed the eggs. Mary Alice had a day off. Eby, Nancy and I went for huckleberries. They are very scarce. Got about three quarts. The ladies went to Hershey. Sanford continues to be very cold toward Bernard. 800 bodies were recovered from the earthquake ruins.

8/13/63 Tuesday
Showery. I washed and hung it in the cellar. Cleaned and made up the apartment beds. Mary Alice went to work at 10:00. Nancy and I kept the Smoker and Denlinger children. It was some complicated. Miss Talbert brought her mother to visit this evening. Had a nice time. Have six in the apartment. Eby went to the sale.

8/17/63 Saturday
Nice day with strong south wind. Nancy and I finished up the cleaning. Washed Dale's car. Did a big wash and some ironing. I went to sewing school. The Peter Shadid's came for supper and to spend the night. Have four in the apartment. We took Shadid's to the tent. Ray and Sanford went to Penn State and Jim's. Ray went to Tom's shop social this evening. Mary Alice went to Miss Talbert's wedding.

9/2/63 Monday
A fine day. I did a big wash. Charlie helped get the apartment ready. The teachers came in, Larry Shurr and Jere McKeen. Grace and George went to Longwood Gardens. Nancy and I canned 10 quarts of pears. Sanford went to visit Gary this P.M. Eby and the boys mowed the alfalfa.

9/3/63 Tuesday
Partly cloudy, gusty and raining this evening. I washed and ironed. Eby and I picked a bushel of limas for a Coatesville woman. Uncle Charlie dropped them off when he took Charlie to the University of Pennsylvania to start his work there. Eby went to the sale, and the children all went to the Gospel Witness Band outing at Intercourse Park. I washed the eggs. Sowed some radishes.

9/7/63 Saturday
Damp and foggy this morning. Cleared and got warm. Helped do up the morning work and got things ready for Milton's. Eby and I started at 10:15 with Bernard for Stony Brook. Stopped at Ildewild Airport and got here at 6:45. Barbara is working the evening shift at the hospital. Milton prepared a good supper for us. Canned some pickles this morning.

9/8/63 Sunday
A fine day. We all went to Centereach church. Had a good sermon. Ate lunch and went for a drive this p.m. Had dinner and heard a sermon by Billy Graham and watched Candid Camera. Boys are arriving on campus.

9/11/63 Wednesday
Nice day, warmer. I picked a basket of green beans and Eby helped pick a bushel of limas. He took both to Mrs. Johnson in Coatesville. I took Nancy to Dr. Cooper to have her teeth checked for braces. Bought material and pattern for a shift. We stopped at Aunt Minnie's on the way home. The girls hoed some garden.

9/16/63 Monday

A wet day. Ray helped me clean the living room, fixed the lights and the receptacles. I got off two baskets of grapes for Katie Beiler. Mary Alice worked at Plain and Fancy this evening. Four Negro children were killed in Alabama race troubles. Dale went to F.F.A. Eby went to look at some chickens. Ray brought radiators home for the kitchen.

9/19/63 Thursday

A nice clear day. Ironed and scrubbed the living room floor. Ray helped clean and lay the rugs and put the furniture back. The new living room suite came about 4:30. Eby and I took Sanford to Harry Good's for a new suit for $14.00. We picked up the platform rockers at Stauffers. Cassy was up to see the new furniture.

9/24/63 Tuesday

Had first killing frost. Tobacco very much spoiled. Ray finished the kitchen radiators. I did the mending and picked a bushel of limas for Jim's. Eby harrowed and went to the sale. Ray is packing up. The children drove to school and Mary Alice stayed till 6:00. Got three letters today.

9/27/63 Friday

Nice weather. An assistance caseworker was shot to death on the Welsh Mountain by Harry Millisock. Eby dug white and sweet potatoes. I got sweet corn off for market. I did some of the cleaning and washed and ironed. Eby, Nancy and I went to Harry's Auction to look for stoves and to Mrs. Swarr for my new foundation. Cost $14.00.

Mary Alice went to a Hootenanny at Long's Park.

10/12/63 Saturday

A fine day. Eby and Sanford went to market. Grace, Robert, Dale and his girlfriend left about 8:30 for Penn State to see Ray and attend a football game. Mary Alice studied, went to the store, and went to work at 12:30. Nancy and I did some cooking and baking. I washed and ironed. Had an 8:00 supper for Mr. and Mrs. Walter Funibiki from San Francisco. Eby met their bus at Gap.

10/23/63 Wednesday

Clear and warmer. I worked on Nancy's dress and washed the eggs. Eby and I hulled half the walnuts by driving the tractor over them. He worked on the corn crib. Eby, Nancy and I took Ira Hershey along to Dick Patterson's where we had our midweek service. Anna Martin showed her pictures from Tanganyika.

10/30/63 Wednesday

Cold and windy. Eby put in some windows. Sanford's capons have a cold and Dick Hershey injected them this evening. I finished the windows upstairs and did the girls' room. Got peppers and tomatoes for sandwich spread. Eby gathered the pumpkins and tomatoes all ready for frost. I brought all the flowers in. Did the eggs. Eby, Ira and Dick installed the new songbooks at Meadville. Wrote to Milton's.

11/7/63 Thursday
Rainy. I cleaned the porches, windows, and put storm windows and doors on. Eby worked on the cow stable windows. Sanford's chickens are better. I made Mary Alice a brown wool skirt after she came from school and brought more fabric from Lapp's. Mary Alice took a scholarship test at Ephrata. Dale went to New Holland for shoes and rubbers.

11/8/63 Friday
Showery and colder. I finished cleaning the kitchen cupboards and made cold soap. Did the eggs and cleaned upstairs and living room. Mary Alice left at 4:15 with her class for a trip to New York City. Got turnips, Swiss Chard, endive and sweet potatoes ready for market. Rolled pie crusts. Grandma Shirk fell down the steps, broke her neck and died.

11/13/63 Wednesday
A fine day. White frost. I made a lot of noodles. Helped Eby trench the celery and put plastic on all that we left out. Buried some beets and carrots. Did the eggs. Sanford missed the honor roll by one point. Mary Alice went to Buckwalter's from school and from there to Cassy's to babysit. Dale went on a date. I wrote to Jim's.

11/16/63 Saturday
Nice day. Eby and Sanford went to market. Made peach strusel pies and a sponge cake. Finished cleaning the kitchen. Nancy and I went for the Gable's and took them to Sewing School. Took Eby's shoes to the shoemaker. Went to Sam Bawell's for a birthday gift for Mary Alice to give Ethel Smoker. Dale's girlfriend's father came to gun. Dale and Sanford each got a bird, Sanford's first, and Dale a rabbit.

11/25/63 Monday
A nice day. Washed. Had no school because of President Kennedy's funeral. Mary Alice and Nancy made 2 trips to see it on Esther's T.V. I heard it on radio while Sanford and I did 35 capons. Dale had no work. Eby clipped cows. We all went to church this evening. On the way home we could see a barn fire. Drove till we finally came to Gordonsville where Earl Jones' barn was burning.

12/7/63 Saturday
A nice day. Eby and Sanford went to market. Dale and Mary Alice went to Conestoga Valley to take their college board exams. Nancy and I finished the work. I washed and ironed. Went to Jack Bachman's sale for a couple hours. Nancy and I went down to see Tom's little Kathy Anne. Mary Alice babysat for Abner's. Dale has a date. 63 highway deaths so far this year.

12/20/63 Friday
Very cold. 8 degrees. Water frozen in chicken houses and apartment. Children drove in truck. We dressed 10 capons. Eby and I went to New Holland to finish shopping. Eby got me Emma Jetlieb shoes. Ray backed the car into the barn. Sanford broke the milkhouse door off. Ray took the children to New Holland to finish their shopping. Dale went skating.

12/23/63 Monday
Got up at 4:30 and dressed 30 capons. Eby, Ray, Sanford and Bernard left at 7:45 for the raising of Earl Jones' barn. It began snowing at 10:30. Some people came for capons. Ray was called to load cinders.

12/25/63 Wednesday
A fine winter day. The children all came but Edgar's. Everyone had a good appetite. Milton's and Jim's stayed for supper. Eby and Bernard are playing Figmill. The older children are playing Scrabble. I wrote a letter to Esther.

12/30/63 Monday
Cold and clear. I washed and ironed. Ray hung it on the line. Made sauer kraut for dinner. Mended. Eby and Bernard went to help with Jones' barn. Charlie and Ray went to help move a dining room suit for Abram's. Nancy had a party of ten girls this evening. Milton's stopped for Bernard's clothing on their way to Stony Brook.

1964

1/3/64 Friday
A mild day. I washed and Ray ironed. Did all the cleaning but the kitchen. Ray brought Abner's tractor from Quarryville and helped Eby clean the heifer pen. Mary Alice went to Kauffman's for apples from school. Mary Alice, Sanford and Nancy took Bernard to a basketball game at Pequea Valley. Dale went to Tract Band Meeting. Ray is putting tile behind the stove.

1/6/64 Monday
A nice day. I washed, ironed and mended. Bernard visited school this forenoon. Ray brought him home. Ray laid down and used some onion poultice on his chest to help his congestion. Eby took him to the 4:27 train to go back to Penn State. Mary Alice and Sanford went to chorus practice. Dale went to Fire meeting. I wrote to Rhoda.

1/11/64 Saturday
Clear and cold. Eby and Sanford went to market. I did a big wash, finished my dress, made a cake and scrubbed the cellar and porch. Nancy finished the barn work and took Mrs. Wasson eggs. I filled up 3 baskets of potatoes. Mary Alice went to

Conestoga Valley for college tests from 1 to 5. Eby and Sanford went to Hershey's for Bible Meeting. Topic by Jacob Rittenhouse on Head Covering. Opened up the bathtub drain.

1/22/64 Wednesday
A nice mild day. I made an apron. Cassy and Kathy were here. We butchered a hog, cut it up and made the sausage. Dale had an early date. Grace called. I wrote to Charlie. Uncle Charlie thinks we should take over Aunt Minnie's business because she is not able.

1/24/64 Friday
Nice mild day. Eby went to market. I took Nancy to Paradise where Uncle Charlie met us and took her in to Dr. Cooper's to get started on her teeth. I baked four cakes this afternoon. Eby, Nancy and I went to Kinzer to Weekend Bible Studies. Dale took Sanford to the 6:35 train to visit Grace for the weekend.

1/28/64 Tuesday
Snow flurries. Cold and windy. I weighed the capons and sold 11 at $48.85. Did the ironing and mending. The oil burner gave a loud puff about 4:00 a.m. and filled the house with smoke. We quickly opened doors and windows. Called plumbers at 7:00. They worked till 1:00. This evening it clunked out again. Plumber came again. Eby went to the sale.

1/31/64 Friday
Partly cloudy. I cleaned up the house, scrubbed the cellar, gathered the eggs. Eby went to market. Uncle Charlie came to tell me that Clyde Sweigart called and told him that he is going to care for Aunt Minnie. Dale did not go away. Had Dr. Bryer for a cow. Mrs. Conger stopped by after school. Sanford stayed for detention hall.

2/7/64 Friday
A nice mild day. Eby went to market. I cleaned upstairs and the living and dining rooms. Got some celery out for Mrs. Conger and made some ready to treat the tract band which met here. Gave them Hershey assorted candies and tea.

2/10/64 Monday
Snowing this morning. It stopped by noon and started to melt. I washed and hung it in the basement. Dressed six capons. Dale and Sanford went to a basketball game. Mary Alice is disturbed about finishing the yearbook.

2/15/64 Saturday
Partly cloudy. Finished up cleaning, made pies, a cake, tapioca and boiled dressing. Mary Alice and Sanford went to chorus practice this forenoon. Eby went to the hog sale and to John Reeser's sale. I took Mabel to Aunt Minnie's to make some dresses for her. Mary Alice went to Judy Miller's this evening. I mended. Grace sent an engagement announcement.

2/20/64 Thursday
A fine cold day. Eby took Nancy to Dr. Cooper's. Mary Alice went to Dr. Crandall's and had a tooth extracted and some filled. I canned the meat, made pig feet jelly, sugar cured the big meat and put some in the freezer. The children had no school because the buses could not get through. Eby and I went to Ella Denlinger's 90th birthday celebration this evening. Dale skidded into a car in Quarryville and damaged both cars and got a hard bump on his chin.

2/21/64 Friday
A nice day. Eby went to market. He sold 25 lbs. of scrapple and 16 lbs. of sausage. I made doughnuts and a jelly roll. The Watkins man was here. I washed and did some of the cleaning. Worked on my rug this evening. Played a game of Scrabble. Eby did not let Sanford go to the game.

3/4/64 Wednesday
Cloudy and foggy. I started cleaning the attic. Eby went to Aaron Groff's sale. I went along and visited Aunts Cora and Minnie. Carried ashes and coal and wood for Aunt Minnie. Mary Alice and Sanford had chorus practice this evening. I called Ray to get information about Dale's college acceptance.

3/12/64 Thursday
Snowed a wet snow all day. We finished up the butchering. Eby took Mary Alice to the Iris Club where she received her D.A.R. award. He signed for government corn and visited Ellis. I canned the meat, made pig feet jelly, sugar cured the hams, weighed the sausage and scrapple.

3/13/64 Friday
Nice mild day. Eby went to market. I cleaned. Some Stony Brook teachers brought David Arch, an exchange student from Scotland. Mary Alice, Sanford and David went to a Hootenanny at the Guernsey Barn.

3/28/64 Saturday
Fine day. We finished the cleaning. Charlie came for lunch. He washed some things and I mended them. Mary Alice worked at Plain and Fancy. Grace and Robert went shopping. I prepared some food. We did some cleaning. Went to Pequea Valley this evening to see the movie, "The Devil's Pit." It was on dope addicts. Milton took David to see some places and gave him dinner and supper.

4/5/64 Sunday
Fine day. Warmer. We all went to Meadville this morning except Dale. We rested this afternoon. Mary Alice had her three friends here this afternoon to study. They came in their shorts. Dale went to spend time with Linda. General McArthur died.

4/6/64 Monday

A wet day. I made 17 quarts of mince meat. Cut and made a dress all but finishing for Mary Alice. I washed the eggs. The plumbers were here to fix the pump. Nolt's men were here to fix the manure spreader. The children were home early for Teacher's Meeting. Sanford went to Garden Spot with Mr. Givler for a speech contest. Dale went to a Fire Meeting.

4/7/64 Tuesday

A wet day. I washed and it hung in the rain all day. I finished Mary Alice's dress. Made a jumper for Nancy from one of Grace's dresses. Eby went to the sale. Mary Alice worked on her scholarship questionnaire. Had letters from Grace and David Arch.

4/18/64 Saturday

A fine day. Dorie helped carry milk morning and evening and helped clean the top chicken house. I made pies and dressed the last two capons. Helped finish the chicken house. Eby plowed Smoker's, Dippner's and Tom's gardens. He disced ours and we put in the sugar peas and 7 lbs. of hull peas. Went down to help with the ham supper at the Fire Hall. Fed about 600. Grace and Robert went to Downingtown.

4/19/64 Sunday

A wet day. We all went to Meadville. I wrote to Milton's. Dorie took a nap. Grace and Robert courted. Mary Alice studied and Nancy loafed. Sanford rested and Dale went to see Linda. Robert took Grace and Dorie to meet the 10:15 train. I called Abram's. They got home this morning. Flew from San Francisco to Baltimore in 4 hours.

4/20/64 Monday

A very wet day. I cleaned the windows upstairs and washed the woodwork. Washed the eggs. Uncle Charlie cut Eby's hair. Mary Alice is in a rage about going to a movie with Buckwalter's. She went without our consent. Eby and I went to Millwood where Jacob Rittenhouse is having meetings.

4/21/64 Tuesday

Another wet day. I cleaned the cave and Grace's room. Cut a dress for myself and a blouse for Nancy. Eby went to the sale till supper when Dick Hershey took his place so he could go to the F.F.A. banquet. We had a good ham supper. Dale received the Kuntzler scholarship for $500.00. Roy Mentzer was honored as star farmer.

5/13/64 Wednesday

Partly cloudy and rained a good shower this evening. I planted the cantaloupes in the potato row. Hoed the strawberries and cleaned the flower bed. Planted the dahlias and some Chicago fires. Gathered and washed the eggs. Eby plowed. Nancy harrowed.

Mary Alice worked this evening. She did not win the speech for commencement. Worked on Nancy's dress.

5/16/64 Saturday
A fine day. I made pies and Nancy made a cake. Washed and ironed. Eby went to the hog sale. I went to sewing school this p.m. Nancy did the eggs. Milton called last night and told us little Douglas Arthur arrived at 8:05. Put the pea wire up. Mildred Groff came for Chicago fires and had car trouble.

5/23/64 Saturday
A real summer day (in Stony Brook). I did some washing and ironing. Cleaned the kitchen, bath and bedroom. Milton and David Arch took Mike and I to the train in New York and we got to Lancaster before dark. Daddy met us and Mike was very good the entire trip without a nap. Dale crimped the hay and Eby mowed. Charlie came by bus this evening.

5/26/64 Tuesday
Nancy stayed at home to crimp hay. I hoed garden and watched Mike outdoors. Ironed this P.M. and filled some dirt on flower beds. Mike helped. Eby went to the sale. Milt's called and Mrs. Coy.

6/4/64 Thursday
A fine cool day. I took Annis along to Sewing Circle. Brought Sanford's picnic table home from school. Washed two days' eggs. The children had school till noon. The Raleigh man was here. Mr. Conner got 3 cases of eggs. Nancy picked 4 quarts of strawberries. I watered some this evening. Mike hates his bath.

6/16/64 Tuesday
Clear with drying winds. Mary Alice and I took Nancy in to have her braces tightened. I bought her a girdle, bra, slip and stockings. Mary Alice picked strawberries and sugar peas. I mended and did the ironing. Dale had a ball game and late date. Mary Alice and Sanford went to Hershey's Bible School.

7/2/64 Thursday
A very hot day. I washed and ironed and cleaned. Eby and I went to town to meet Grace and her train was 2 hours late because of a death on the train. We took her to Columbia to buy her crystal. It is an engagement gift from Robert. Eby and Sanford worked at the corn and potatoes.

7/4/64 Saturday
Cleared and got cooler. I made some pies and things for lunch and supper. We had things ready to go soon after 11:00 and had our reunion at Paradise Park. There were 176 there. We had charge of the program. The children were all here for supper but Isaac's and Dale. We spent a pleasant day today. Ellis and his family were not there. Five of Grace's friends picked her up and took her back to the city.

7/9/64 Thursday
I did two washes and it dried real good. Things are growing fast. Did some ironing for the apartment. Took Nancy, Sally and Linda up to Aunt Minnie's to look for her lower plate which she lost about three months ago. Eby, Jimmie and I went to Harry's auction and bought a Hotpoint refrigerator for $29.40. Grace may want it.

7/18/64 Saturday
Nice warm day. I went out at 6:00 to hoe and train limas. Nancy got up before breakfast for the first time in weeks. Eby went to the sale. Sanford, Nancy, Jimmie and I went to Clair Hershey's ordination. Mary Alice stayed and got dinner. Finished the kitchen and made a cake, two puddings and two dressings. Washed eggs and Nancy helped haul bales and crimp hay. Jim's left the children while they went to wedding in Reading.

7/25/64 Saturday
Cool and cloudy. Ray caponized Sanford's chickens. 38 smothered while they were crated. I helped to harrow the sweet potatoes. Eby went to the hog sale. I did the scrubbing and cleaning. Gathered and washed the eggs. Washed and ironed this p.m. Got 6 in the apartment. Dale and Don Eisenberger cleaned up their cars. Nancy washed the truck and made a cake.

8/3/64 Monday
A wet day. I washed and it was nearly dry before it rained. Ironed all but the pants. Mary Alice had club for the neighbor children this afternoon. They started making rugs. I got up early and mended. Picked a half bucket of pickles. Suzanne took Mary Alice to Plain and Fancy to show her cousin and Kathy stayed with Nancy. Got tourists in apartment and in our room.

8/9/64 Sunday
The weather was pleasant. We all went to Meadville but Dale. He went to Monument and to a reunion with Linda. We spent the afternoon reading. We went to Hershey's this evening where the Literary Fellowship gave the program. It was interesting. Mary Alice was aroused to action. Eby went for Jimmie after the service.

8/17/64 Monday
Partly cloudy and warmer. I washed and Nancy and I did most of the ironing. Picked and canned pickles. Made 2 crocks full. Charlie fixed the mixer, clock, door latch, etc. He met Grace at 4:00 at the depot. We did 2 baskets of peaches over supper time. David Arch came about 5:00. Got tourists for the apartment and our bedroom. Mary Alice worked 1:00 to 9:00.

8/24/64 Monday
A warm day. I washed and ironed some. Did the apartment and have two couples in. Rhoda washed for Charlie and her family. Mary Alice went to work at 1:00. Edgar's

left with the three oldest children and Charlie at 6:15 for New York. The other three went to bed nicely. Eby left at 10:30 for Rock Hall with five Amish men to fish. It is 11:30 and he is not home yet.

8/28/64 Friday
A nice warm day. I washed, ironed and did the apartment. Picked some limas for supper. Helped Eby get corn and things for market. Canned 8 quarts of peaches. Rhoda washed and ironed and they left about 7:00 for Grandpa Clemens. They got here about 12:00 last night. Mary Alice went to a Pajama Party at Phyllis Eshleman's.

8/31/64 Monday
Cloudy and raining a little this morning. I washed and hung it in the cellar and one the porch. Milk inspector was here and found trouble and I was in an uncomfortable flurry for about three hours cleaning up to please him. Eby picked limas and cleaned eggs. We canned 28 quarts of pears. Sold three bushels. Eby and the children helped shell limas. Eby sold 200 ears of corn and a bushel of limas.

9/6/64 Sunday
A sunny dry day. We all went to Meadville. Rested and read and fixed the beds for tourists. We took a Jewish man and his Lutheran wife to church this evening to hear Omar Stahl and see his slides at Ben Hershey's after the service. Mary Alice went with Tom Denliger's to see Ray at Abram's. Charlie left on the 5:00 bus for a second term at the University of Pennsylvania.

9/8/64 Tuesday
Clear, warm and dry. I picked three baskets of limas. Put most of them in freezer. Filled trench silo, had two extra men for dinner. Eby went to the sale. I made pudding and pies. Dale and Mary Alice are packing up for college. Mary Alice worked her last day at Plain and Fancy. Grace called this evening. Nancy is making herself a loose dress.

9/13/64 Sunday
A cloudy, cool day. We all went to Meadville but Dale. He brought Linda for dinner and supper. Clarence's went with us to Charles Horning's for supper. Mary Alice left for Abram's about 1:30 and stopped to see Mrs. Conger.

9/20/64 Sunday
Cloudy and rained all night. We went to Spring Run Church of the Brethren. Left to take Dale to Altoona for college from church. Ate our lunch on the way. Stopped at Jim's on our way home and ate supper. Got home at 9:30. Uncle Charlie helped Sanford with the work this morning. Clair's took Sanford and Nancy to church at Hershey's. Dorie and Cecil came to get things to take for Grace.

9/22/64 Tuesday

Clear day, warm. I did the morning work and picked almost a bushel of limas for Harry Diller and for chow chow. Picked and canned tomatoes and made catsup. Eby went to the sale and I did the eggs and took Sanford to the F.F.A. meeting and brought him home. Wrote to Charlie and Mary Alice.

9/24/64 Thursday

Cooler, windy and dry. I wrote to Dale this morning and we got our first letter from him. I did 20 quarts of grape juice. Got things in for market. Dug first sweet potatoes. Eby harrowed all day. I took Sanford to the barber and he walked home. Eby took car to the garage. Anna Slaymaker got potatoes. Nancy had a severe belly ache this evening.

9/28/64 Monday

A fine rain fell all day, almost an inch. Eby swept webs. I made hedge pear and currant jelly. Helped Nancy with a dress from one of Grace's old ones. Nancy stayed home from school with a cold and cramps. We made toll house cookies and I took some along to treat when we went to clean the church this evening. There were 12 who helped. Sanford went to Ephrata Fair with Mr. Givler.

10/2/64 Friday

Real nice day. Eby went to market. I cut some weeds. Cleaned most of the house. Did the chickens and eggs. Cut up the last ham. Mary Alice came about 8:30. Grace, Dorie and Cecil came from New York about 10:30 and Robert arrived about the same time. Nancy made graham cracker fluff.

10/3/64 Saturday

Nice day. Did up the morning work. The guests slept late, had their breakfast and left for Harry's Auction. They bought some bargains. They went out for supper and bowled late. Mary Alice went to see Mrs. Conger and Cassy. Filled silo this afternoon.

10/5/64 Monday

Partly cloudy and colder. I washed and ironed. Cleaned drawers in boys' room. Picked and canned 21 quarts of tomato juice for Edgar's. Helped Eby chop some corn for cows. Got 250 leghorn hens at fifty cents each. Nancy has her hair cut almost short.

10/16/64 Friday

A fine day, real warm. I did the morning work and filled 4 bushel of potatoes for ham supper. Cleaned upstairs. Gathered and washed the eggs. Put cows in the alfalfa. Eby went to market. I washed the milk tank. Took Sue along to Mart Hershey's to finish the quilt for the evangelist's wife. Got up at 4:00 and took Sanford to Pequea

Valley to go by bus with his class to the World's Fair in New York. Roasted hams for ham supper. Made 2 cakes, pies and snow pudding.

10/31/64 Saturday
A fine sunny day. Sanford went hunting with Gary but got nothing. Made pumpkin pies. Did up the morning work and the eggs. Eby went to the hog sale. Grace, Nancy and I went shopping to Harry Good's and on back to Emma Horning's to pick a quilt for Grace. I bought a top for $10.00. We stopped in New Holland and got an ironing board for Grace. Abram called and said Charlie is in the hospital at the University of Pennsylvania.

11/1/64 Sunday
A pretty day, mild. Sanford and I went for Bonnie and Nora. Bonnie was disappointed that she couldn't come here, because Abram's took Eby and I down to see Charlie. They think he may have gall bladder trouble. Abram's stayed here for supper and we did not go to church. Grace and Nancy kept David and Andrew. Grace went home with Abram's to spend a couple days.

11/3/64 Tuesday
Damp and foggy. Nancy stayed home with a sore throat. She read most all day. I did some mending and finished my dress. Lengthened two of Nancy's dresses. Eby went to the sale. Uncle Charlie brought Grace home from Abram's. Lyndon B. Johnson was elected president for the next term.

11/4/64 Wednesday
A fine mild day. I helped Eby trench some celery and went to Sadsburyville for turnips. We put some carrots and beets in for winter. Grace cut and started a dress for Nancy. I did the eggs. Grace and Sanford went to Abner's for supper. Nancy stayed out of school. Charlie called and said he will have an operation on Friday.

11/16/64 Monday
Cloudy and sprinkled a few showers. I washed and finished drying it in the cellar. Helped Sanford clean up the woodpile and got the furnace cleaned out for boiling apple butter. Grace and Robert went for marriage license and did some shopping. He left at 5:00 and took Grace's chest. Eby put windows in cow stable and went for apples.

11/17/64 Tuesday
Clear and a little colder. Did the morning work and ironing. Grace, Sanford and I started to snitz apples at 10:00. Uncle Charlie came for lunch and helped to snitz the balance of the 7 baskets. Clair Weir sprayed the stables. Sanford got the cider made this P.M. Sanford and I went to church. Eby went to the sale. Grace went to get her dress fit.

11/27/64 Friday
A fine mild day. Eby went to market. I washed and Grace ironed. I washed and waxed the kitchen. Grace, Robert and Charlie did the living and dining room. Charlie took the center light from the living room ceiling. Sanford did the outside cleaning. I scrubbed the porch and did the bouquets. Vance and his girlfriend came at 7:30.

11/28/64 Saturday
Partly cloudy. Had 8 Virginia folks for the night. A carload came early this morning. Grace and Robert were married at 11:00 with about 50 guests present. Martha Hershey came and stayed with Rhoda's four children. Had the reception at Plain and Fancy for 119 guests. Had 30 for supper. Grace and Robert left at 5:30 for their honeymoon to Florida and the Bahamas.

12/3/64 Thursday
Cloudy and mild. Rained a little. I went to Sewing Circle. Brought Sanford along home from school and he helped dress 30 capons. Nancy made supper and washed eggs. Had a card from Grace and Robert. We got the end of the dining room ready for Aunt Minnie.

12/5/64 Saturday
Cloudy, damp and rainy. I made a sponge cake. Clarence and Mabel brought Aunt Minnie about 8:00. Eby went to the hog sale and to a sale in Kinzer. He bought a window fan for $3.00. Sanford and Nancy went shopping to New Holland. Nancy made some gum drop cookies. The Congolese rebels shot and killed Dr. Paul Carlson in Stanleyville. Aunt Minnie did real good.

12/22/64 Tuesday
Nice mild day. Charlie and I went shopping and Mary Alice stayed with Aunt Minnie and spent an hour at Pequea Valley addressing the guidance class. Eby went to the sale. Charlie and I took Aunt Minnie to the Dr. Sanford, Nancy and I went to the Christmas program.

12/25/64 Friday
Mild sunny day. We had a roast capon for dinner for Ray, Sanford, Nancy, Bernard, Daddy and I. Aunt Minnie went with Dale to Uncle Milt's when he went to Linda's for dinner. Mary Alice came home at 5:00 from Abram's. Daddy, Ray, Sanford, Nancy and I went to Isaac's in the truck to see the farm they bought. Eby and I went to Ralph Arment's viewing with Clarence's.

12/27/64 Sunday
Real nice day, but rained and was cloudy. I went with Sanford in the truck to get Bonnie. Ray kept Aunt Minnie. Grace and Robert helped him with the dinner. The men went to see Isaac's farm. The children gave us a set of Noritake china.

12/31/64 Thursday
A fine day. I cleaned upstairs and the living room. Washed and ironed and got things ready for the trip to Edgar's. Weighed up the capons and Sanford took them to the locker plant. Eby and Bernard went to market. Charlie got home from Florida this evening. They drove home in 26 hours. Mary Alice went back to Abram's.

1965

1/1/65 Friday
Partly cloudy. We got started for Edgar's about 9:00. Linda and Judy came last evening to go with us. Had a good trip to Edgar's and they are all fine and have their house about fixed up. Making some rooms in basement. Charlie is helping Nancy with the housework and looking after Aunt Minnie.

1/2/65 Saturday
Snowing fast till noon. We spent the forenoon visiting and Eby helped Edgar with a basement room. Fredric is recovering from his operation. We left for home at 1:15 and had snowy roads and 35 m.p.h. speed limits most of the way home. Got here at 10:00. Linda and Judy stayed overnight. Aunt Minnie is very much disturbed because we went away.

1/6/65 Wednesday
A fine mild day. I ironed 20 sheets and pillow cases. Helped paint the new window. Washed the eggs, 449. Eby painted and cleaned up the window scraps. Cassy called for manure and a seed catalogue. Signs of spring. I wrote to Rhoda and Grace. Sanford played basketball this evening.

1/11/65 Monday
A pretty day. Everything is snowy. Eby opened the lane with the manure loader. I washed and dressed 10 capons. We dressed a 350 lb. hog this evening. Aunt Minnie is disturbed and does not want to go to bed. Daddy did not get frustrated scalding the hog.

1/23/65 Saturday
Damp rain, sleet, ice and snow. Eby went to the hog sale. Dale and Sanford tore out the chimney and put the cupboard in. They met up with some problems, a sloped sewer pipe, uneven floor and bulged plaster board. I made some food ready for Sunday. Nancy baked tollhouse cookies after she got up at 10:30.

1/24/65 Sunday
Raining and freezing. Eby, Sanford and I went to Meadville. Very icy and we slipped in the gutter and were late. 49 there. Nancy got dinner. We sang with Aunt Minnie this P.M. a while.

1/29/65 Friday
Cold and clear. I cleaned the dining and living room. Did the chickens and eggs. Eby went to market. Mary Alice went to the dentist and the store. Dr. Prowell was here to see Aunt Minnie and talked a long time to Mary Alice about Lebanon Valley. I washed and ironed. Sanford played basketball and Mary Alice went to the game.

1/30/65 Saturday
Cloudy. We did our morning work and Mary Alice took Daddy and I to Abram's. We left for Staunton to visit Grace and Robert at 10:00. Got to Ingleside Motels at 3:30 where we are staying for the night. Went on to get supper at Robert's. Franklin Weaver's came after supper. Katie gave me a rug.

2/17/65 Wednesday
A fine mild day. Eby took the scalding trough home and trimmed the grapes. I sewed and did the eggs and a small wash and ironing. Eby had an offer to be an assistant mail carrier. Sorted some recipes. Aunt Minnie is sleepy. Eby talked to George Dippner about mailman.

2/24/65 Wednesday
Cold east wind. Did up the morning work. Did the eggs and chickens. Eby went on the mail route with George Dippner. Aunt Minnie was drowsy all day. Worked on my rug. Got letters from Grace and Eunice Hess. Eby and I went to midweek at Montgomery's. His topic was Hannah's Song.

2/26/65 Friday
Cold and windy. Eby went to market. I did most of the cleaning. Aunt Minnie was drowsy and walks very poorly. Sanford and Nancy went reluctantly to a Taffy Pull at Marty Martin's for the Meadville teenagers. Finished a scarf I was working on. Transplanted some sage. Washed and ironed.

2/27/65 Saturday
Clear and not so cold. I washed up the kitchen, made a cake and pudding. Was very much provoked at Nancy. She got up at 9:30 and washed breakfast and dinner dishes without putting them away and put eggs in the crate. She slept this P.M. and went to Leon Stoltzfus' to babysit. Eby went to the P.O. and the hog sale. I went to Dr. Prowell's for pills for Aunt Minnie. Oil burner went empty. Tom came, and Zimmerman's filled tank.

3/2/65 Tuesday
A nice day. Eby went with John Eby to take our beef to the locker plant. Milk inspector and cow doctor came to score the barn and examine the cows. I cleaned and cooked the trype. Put liver in the freezer. Cut and made an apron. Sanford and I caught 60 chickens for relief. Aunt Minnie fell and bumped her head and hip. She had a dizzy spell. I am going to sleep downstairs.

3/3/65 Wednesday
Mild and partly cloudy. Eby went to the P.O. and brought the hog this afternoon. We dressed it and made the sausage. Called Dr. Prowell for Aunt Minnie and he is sending her to the hospital for xrays. Eby took Nancy to the dentist this forenoon and went to the bank for my pay.

3/4/65 Thursday
A fine warm day. We finished our hog by 12:00. I got Aunt Minnie ready for the ambulance trip to the hospital for xray. Mabel went along to take her in and Charlie went along to bring her home. She is not supposed to have a broken bone. I canned the meat and rubbed the big pieces with sugar cure. Dressed 3 capons and weighed the sausage. Clyde came to make arrangements to take Aunt Minnie to a home.

3/6/65 Saturday
A real nice day. Eby helped at the P.O. and went to the hog sale. Sanford went with Weir's to get hay at Uncle Milt's. I did the cleaning, made a cake and rice pudding. Got Aunt Minnie ready to take to the Oregon Nursing Home. I went along in the ambulance and Eby followed and we went to Mart Nolt's and got a set of stainless steel knives and forks. Nancy did not feel well. The White Chimney's was on fire. Cleaned up the dining room.

3/14/65 Sunday
Nice day, cold. We all went to Meadville. Had council meeting. Clyde called and said Aunt Minnie died at 9:15 in the nursing home. Eby and I met Clyde at Bachman's and made plans for her funeral. Went to Uncle Milt's afterward. Wrote to Charlie, Ray, Abram's and Mary Alice.

3/16/65 Tuesday
A windy day. I left at 7:00 with Uncle Charlie for Isaac's place. Uncle Charlie painted and I worked on the cupboards and drawers. Eby hauled manure and went to the sale. Sanford, Nancy and I went to the viewing for Aunt Minnie. A good number of people came out. We have the odor of dead mouse or rat in house.

3/24/65 Wednesday
38th Anniversary. Nice day. Eby, Uncle Charlie and 2 Amishmen left at 6:00 A.M. for Vermont to buy cows. Ray and I went with Uncle Jays to Issac's. Jay papered closets and put some ceiling on the kitchen. Ray helped wall up the cesspool. Mary Alice took Nancy to the dentist and visited some schoolmates. Dale hauled manure and did the eggs. Clyde Sweigart came this evening to get some pictures and Aunt Minnie's gold watch. I got a splinter and Ray took it out.

3/28/65 Sunday
A real nice day. We all went to Meadville. Dale went to Paradise Communion. Rested and read after dinner. Eby, Nancy and I went to Clarence's at 3:00. All of

my family were there for supper to help celebrate our anniversary. Got nice gifts and a pretty bouquet.

3/31/65 Wednesday
A fine day. Cold. I did the ironing. Eby and I went to Lancaster to Sam Wenger's law office on business. Rhoda had dinner ready when we got home. Eby took Rhoda and the children to Isaac's after dinner. Conrad went to bed. Edgar and Fredric went to help move Isaac's cows. I made cakes and things for supper tomorrow evening.

4/1/65 Thursday
Nice day, not so cold. We cleaned the house. Rhoda washed and we prepared food for supper this evening. Made buns. Charlie came at 2:15, Jim's at 3:45 and Abram's and Isaac's. Had a pleasant evening together. Served cafeteria style. Made chicken pies. We called Ray and he had been in the hospital for 3 days with a virus plus his ailment.

4/2/65 Friday
Everything white and still snowing. Edgar's packed up and started for home at 9:35. It got very quiet with Daddy at market and no one but me. I went over the house and did the eggs. F.F.A. Banquet at Pequea Valley this evening.

4/9/65 Friday
Cleared off cool. Eby went to market and I cleaned the closets upstairs. Did the eggs. Sanford went to the store and to play tennis at Paradise. Eby got a call to haul mail tomorrow so I wrote the box names off for him. Ray called and said his xrays show that he has an ulcer. He is accepted at Cornell. Nancy made kisses. I boiled some meat.

4/21/65 Wednesday
Partly cloudy and warmer. I sewed on my dresses. Made up the apartment beds. Did the eggs. Eby plowed. I took Nancy in to Dr. Cooper. Her braces are to come off next time. Bought her a girdle. Got my quilt from the lady who marked it. Got cabbage and lettuce and tea from Sam Summers and planted all of it.

4/25/65 Sunday
A cloudy cool day. Rained. We all went to Meadville. We went to Abner's for dinner. Esther had a good dinner, with birthday cake and with gifts. Eby, Sanford and I went to the Mt. where Meadville gave the program. Nancy stayed home. Abram, Grace, Mary Alice and Charlie called to say Happy Birthday.

4/27/65 Tuesday
Cloudy and showery. I washed and ironed, did the eggs. Eby cleaned the back barnyard and went to the sale. I sewed on my dresses. There was racial trouble in Parkesburg last evening. A Negro boy was shot dead by a white boy. Sanford is studying meat cuts with a slide projector.

5/7/65 Friday

Cloudy, cold and wet. Did the morning work and went to Pequea Valley to the Honorary Induction program. Sanford was inducted into the National Honor Society. Stopped on the way home to see Ella Denlinger. Finished cleaning living and dining room. Did the eggs. Nancy and I bunched 45 lbs. of asparagus. Eby got home from Indiana at 10:00 with lots of stories to tell.

6/13/65 Sunday

A fine cool day. We all went to Meadville. Ben Hershey's were there. I got things ready to go with Jay's to Jim's. Left at 4:00 from Uncle Jay's. Stopped at Abram's for supper and to take Mary Alice along. Arrived about 8:30 and went to bed at 11:00.

6/14/65 Monday

A cloudy cool day. We started on our job at Jim's farm house and papered three rooms and the hall. Jim was busy with the carpentering. Pat cooked good meals for us. Beth went to Grandma Deeg's.

6/15/65 Tuesday

Cloudy and cool and dropped a little rain. Jay and Sue papered the dining room and Mary Alice and I scrubbed floors. Had late dinner and left for home at 4:30. Stopped a few minutes at Abram's. Milton's came at 1:00. They are staying all night and leaving the boys.

6/21/65 Monday

A hot sunny day. I washed and made space in the wash house for wood. The boys cleaned around the woodpile and helped Eby get the trailer park ready for the Twigg's. Nancy made ice cream for Cassy's birthday. Eby and I took Mike and Douglas down this evening and we shared it with some of her friends. She is 35. Nancy has a bad cold.

6/22/65 Tuesday

A hot day. I did the ironing and washed again this afternoon. Mended and started a dress for Nancy. Eby and the boys worked on the orchard fence and water line for the trailer park. Nancy went to Cassy's for cauliflower and stayed all evening. Eby went to the sale and Ray went up to relieve him at 9:00. Richard King fell from a silo and was killed in Indiana.

6/25/65 Friday

Nice day. Cool. Got things together for Milton's and Nancy. They left about 8:15. Ray and Dale started to renovate the boys' room, tore out the little closet and put in a bigger one. Eby went to market. I did the eggs and cleaned and cooked. Mary Alice and David came and Charlie came this evening. The Twigg's brought their trailer and parked it in the orchard.

7/1/65 Thursday

A warm day. I went to Sewing Circle. 11 there. Dale and I hoed and trained lima beans. Eby and Sanford went to Shenk's to pick cherries this afternoon. Picked 73 lbs. and took most of them to market. I picked beans and bunched beets and rhubarb. Esther came up with some papers of the Dodge City flood. Grace called and said Steven Eric was born Wednesday.

7/9/65 Friday

Hot and humid. I washed 18 sheets, etc. and ironed. Canned 3 quarts of sour cherries, 13 qts. raspberries, 8 qts. of blueberries and froze 10 qts. Eby brought some back from market. Scrubbed and cleaned. Dale worked for John Haldeman a couple hours. Sanford harrowed corn and took out pea wire. Our $800 cow died after a long illness. Had a dead calf. Elizabeth brought Joanne. Abram's Rebecca was born.

7/12/65 Monday

Clear, pleasant day in Stony Brook. We packed up about 8:30. Took Milton to his school on our way to the World's Fair. Got there about 9:30 and walked around with the thousands of others looking at the exhibits. Saw a lot and left with more unseen at 7:30. Got home safely at 11:30. Sanford and Dale did a good job. Had tourists Sunday and Monday who want to stay till Thursday.

7/27/65 Tuesday

Pleasant weather. Dropped a little rain. Sanford baled the stubble, 129 bales, and Nancy helped to haul it in. Dale helped mow it. Ray went to the sale. I canned 7 qts. of pickles and put a bucket of beans in the freezer. Did some mending. Gathered and washed eggs. Eby carried the mail. We went to Bible School. Tourists stayed a second night.

7/28/65 Wednesday

Real nice day. I picked pickles, gathered eggs, washed, ironed and cleaned the apartment. Made 2 rooms ready for tourists upstairs. Ray, Sanford, Nancy, Tommy and Lawrence Twigg baled and hauled 600 bales of hay. Have one man in Grace's room. The Swiss people are coming back. The war in Viet Nam is getting serious. Nancy stayed home from Bible School. Eby carried mail.

8/2/65 Monday

A real nice day. I washed and ironed. Eby worked on the manure spreader and went to Isaac's to paint. Nancy, Fredric and Rosa went along. Dale rested today. He is thinking of the Peace Corps. Have a Dr. Mayer and his wife for tourists. I picked a bucket of pickles and put them in to process.

8/3/65 Tuesday

A fine cool day. I washed and ironed. Nancy started a club with Tommy, Heidi, Ricky, Rosa and Fredric. I canned pickles, picked pickles, green beans, corn and limas. Eby and Sanford plowed and harrowed. Eby went to the sale. Nancy and Rosa mixed four kinds of cookies. Have a tourist family of four.

8/7/65 Saturday
A hot humid day. We finished the morning work and left for Edgar's at 10:00. Ray, Sanford, Nancy, Rosa, Fredric and I shelled a basket of limas enroute and we got there about 4:00. Had a cookout supper and Edgar took us for a drive to see the area where they live and Cornell University. Eby kept house alone and did the work. He had five tourists. The cows broke out into the corn because Sanford did not turn on the fencer.

8/11/65 Wednesday
A fine day. I ate and left for Black Rock Camp from Clarence's at 7:40. Helped Sue with the meals. Went for some walks to see the grounds. Got home at 6:55 and left with Eby for midweek services. Nancy and Rosa did the wash, apartment, and made the meals. Got a basket of peaches. Have five tourists. Sanford's capons are sick.

9/16/65 Thursday
Partly cloudy. Eby worked on the stables and dug potatoes and picked limas. I helped and picked 2 baskets of pink tomatoes and put 14 qts. of corn in the freezer. Nancy mowed yard and went to Twiggs a short time. Helped get corn off for market, endive, beets and green beans. Helped put the balance of the chickens out of the top house. Eby deloused all the roosts.

9/18/65 Saturday
A very warm humid day. I did the scrubbing and picked limas and got some corn in and things ready for going to Abram's. Nancy went with Twiggs shopping. Eby and I went to Lancaster and bought him a Stetson, looked at carpet, bought a shirt, socks and belt. Went to Abram's for supper. Noah Shrock's and John Lerch's were there for the weekend.

9/24/65 Friday
Partly cloudy with heavy rains this evening. I cleaned the house and mowed some of the yard. Canned 11 qts of applesauce. Eby went to market. Took eggs, sweet potatoes, white potatoes, apples, tomatoes, corn, limas, beets, spinach, endive, pumpkins, cauliflower, cantaloupes and grapes. I gathered the eggs. Eby, Sanford and I went to preparatory service. A convict broke out of Lancaster jail.

9/27/65 Monday
A nice clear cool day. I washed and ironed. Gathered and cleaned the eggs. Made 14 qts. of applesauce. Eby worked on the stable. Nancy babysat for the Twiggs. Sanford went to an F.F.A. meeting at Penn Manor. The convict was caught in Baltimore.

10/2/65 Saturday
A very fine day. I did the morning work. Washed Dale's clothing and ironed it. Made cake, pudding, meat and got vegetables and potatoes ready. Nancy got up at 10:00. Washed eggs and finished the cleaning. Took Nancy to New Holland for shoes and she insisted on spikes so she had to pay for them herself. Were held up with the Baby and Pet Parade from the Fair. Abram called and said they are coming.

10/13/65 Wednesday
A fine day. We managed to get the milking done by 8:00. We plowed some potatoes and I picked them up. Eby worked on the stable. Elizabeth and Karen came for linoleum paste. I gathered and washed all the eggs. Fed the chickens. Made quince honey and 8 qts. of grape juice. The end of the grapes. Got the family letter, the first one edited by Milton.

10/25/65 Monday
Nice day, colder. I washed and did most of the ironing. Did all of the eggs. Eby worked on the stable. I put supper on and left at 3:30 for Abram's. Took Cassy, Annis, and Nora Denlinger to Jay Martin's, and he and Sue took us all to Abram's. Pat took us to the Flower Show at Harrisburg. It was very pretty. Got home safely at 12:45.

10/29/65 Friday
Coldest morning. 24 degrees. Chicken and cow water frozen. I carried water to hens and capons today. Eby went to market. Ten of the new hens smothered. I cleaned the garage and made applesauce while I warmed up. Did the eggs, 463. Cleaned and waxed the kitchen after supper. Eby has a feeder sale. Sanford and Nancy went to John Hershey's to help shell the project popcorn. Wrote to Rhoda.

11/1/65 Monday
Windy and colder. I washed and Nancy ironed. She came home early. Cleaned 3 days eggs. Made apple sauce and canned apples and quinces. Made sauer kraut. Eby worked on the stable. I made an appointment for Nancy's tonsillectomy. Sanford has been asked to do some "special" singing.

11/20/65 Saturday
A fine day. Got up at 3:30 and Uncle Charlie picked up Joanne and we left for Jim's at 4:00 to help them move to their farm house. Everything went good and we got home at 8:00. Some neighbors helped. Mr. Deeg is still critical. Eby carried mail and Nancy did the washing for Dale and cooked. Eby and Sanford went to church. Isaac's came for Joanne.

11/22/65 Monday
A rainy wet day. I washed and hung it in the cellar. Did the eggs. Eby went to a milk hearing in Philadelphia with Charlie Colon. I made cakes, cranberry sauce and fudge.

Eby, Nancy and I went to Meadville. Sanford had an F.F.A. meeting and game. Called Pauline S and got an unpleasant lecture on the cows being on her lawn.

11/27/65 Saturday
Mild and rainy. Cleared this p.m. I took Nancy to the hospital for a 7:30 appointment. She had a tonsillectomy at 10:00. I did some shopping and went back to the hospital before coming home. Ray did the cooking. Eby went to the hog sale and put windows in stable. We went to Nora and Joe's reception at Blue Ball Fire Hall. They seemed happily married. Washed the eggs and swept up. Ray did some washing and ironing.

12/1/65 Wednesday
A fine mild day. I took a truck load of dirt and sod to patch Polly's lawn. She was not at home and it took very little. Got stuck and had to be tractor towed. I washed and cleaned out the truck. Helped clean up outside and put the stable scraps in the wash house for firewood. Did the eggs. Nancy kept very low in bed today. Eby and I went to midweek at Ed and Tillie Reams.

12/4/65 Saturday
I did the morning work. Cleaned the woodhouse. Sanford went to Conestoga Valley for a test. Eby went to the hog sale and had a cyst removed from his back. I took Nancy to Dr. Walsh in Lancaster. Eby got sick and rested a while before we went to Plain and Fancy, where Mart had our family for a supper. All were there.

12/7/65 Tuesday
A nice cold day. Did the eggs. Made some date and rice krispie candy. Had Jay Ranck for dinner. He finished clipping the cows. Helped Eby get potatoes ready for the school. Nancy babysat for Twiggs. Eby went to the sale. I made 39 croquettes. I went with Sanford to have Dr. Lancaster check his hand and the xray that Dr. Beacher took. He played basketball and Pequea Valley won. Wrote the family letter.

12/15/65 Wednesday
Cloudy and damp. I worked on the cookies, got a lot baked. Nancy wrote Sanford's topic, "What Christmas means to me as a Teenager" for tonight at the Samaritan Home. He had to play basketball till 6:45. Dale did not have a date for the first night since he is home. Eby worked at the P.O.

12/22/65 Wednesday
A fine day. Eby worked at the P.O. Two of Elam Smoker's grandchildren died in Africa from taking pills. Eby and I went to Lancaster this afternoon. I got a new corset and some gifts for the grandchildren. Mary Alice got up late and took it easy. I weighed up the capons. Sanford and Mary Alice went to a ball game. Nancy babysat for Twigg's.

12/25/65 Saturday

Damp, cloudy, rainy and gusty this afternoon. One half of the children were here for dinner. Isaac's, Milton's, Charlie, Ray, Sanford and Nancy. 17 in all. Had capon, filling, sweet potato croquettes, limas, celery, cranberries, carrot salad, rice pudding, cakes, cookies, nuts, candies and raw fruit. Abram's sent me 2 bedroom lights, Isaac's towels and wash cloths, the girls gave 8 glasses, Jim's sent towels and wash cloths, Milton's a lawn lounge chair, Charlie Today's Health subscription, Dale a paper dispenser, Mary Alice a wooden tub flower stand, and Sanford a Mennonite cookbook.

12/28/65 Tuesday

A fine day. Sanford worked for Horst. Eby went to the sale. Nancy washed the eggs. She and Mary Alice went to Lapp's to buy corduroy to make jumpers. We have Mary Alice's almost done. Sanford and the girls went to a basketball game at Pequea Valley. I called Aunt Cora and did the ironing. Ray went back to Philadelphia.

1966

1/1/66 Saturday

Cloudy, damp, mild. Stable cleaner broke and the welder came and mended it. Eby, Nancy and I left at 8:30 for Virginia and arrived at Robert and Grace's new home at 3:00. Grace had a roast turkey supper and had Franklin Weaver's for supper too. We had a nice visit with them. Cassy invited Dale, Linda and Sanford for supper.

1/5/66 Wednesday

Partly cloudy and mild. I cut and made a dress for myself all but hems and snaps. Eby bought a new cow and had Ed Miller haul it today. $400. I did the eggs. Sanford went to a basketball game. Nancy went to visit Mrs. Twigg. Eby worked on some bills and sent forms to the hospital to pay the tonsil, cyst and hand bills.

1/6/66 Thursday

Cloudy, damp and rainy. I went to Sewing Circle alone. This afternoon Eby and I went to Coatesville to look for carpet. Isaac called from the General Hospital to tell us he had a broken leg because of an accident with the power take off on his tractor. It is broken above and below the knee. I called and told Abram's and Jim's. Eby and I went to Bible School at Paradise. Sanford played basketball.

1/11/66 Tuesday

A fine day. Colder this evening. We finished cooking the hog and washed up by 11:30. Ben and Alice Ranck came for capons and stayed for an hour. Eby went to the sale. I rubbed the meat and canned 8 quarts. Put balance in freezer. Isaac went home from the hospital. Sanford went to Pequea Valley to see Mr. Givler about missing the Farm Show. Nancy stayed for F.H.A. and I went to bring her home.

1/13/66 Thursday
Cold and gave a little bit of snow. I washed and hung it in the cellar. Did some mending. I carried water to the chickens all day. Convinced Eby of a way to improve the chicken fountains. Cleaned up the stripping room. Eby carried mail. Nancy visited Twigg's. Sanford went to a basketball game.

1/17/66 Monday
Cold and windy. I washed and ironed. Did the eggs and some mending. Eby bagged 15 bushel of potatoes and took them to the elementary school. We laid the new carpet in our bedroom. A 77-year-old Amish woman was killed when her carriage upset going around a corner in the road.

1/21/66 Friday
Partly cloudy but nice and mild. Eby went to market. I did the eggs and most of the cleaning. Pasted the woodoleum in our room. Nancy washed the eggs. Eby took her to Susan Brackbill's to spend the night at 9:30. Some girls are going by bus to the Library. Sanford played basketball at Garden Spot. He made 7 points.

1/24/66 Monday
Clear and roads are full of snow. Our road was plowed open before dark. No school. Eby brought Ray from Newport Road by tractor. Eby and Larry opened the lane. Sanford and I dressed 20 capons. Nancy got up at 11:45. Eby met the mill truck at the Newport for feed. Ray, Sanford, Nancy and I played Scrabble this evening. Copied some recipes.

1/27/66 Thursday
Cold and snowed five more inches. They had no school. I made a double portion of doughnuts and Nancy glazed some. I made 2 aprons. The neighbor children came to sled on the lane and came in to warm, eat doughnuts and popcorn, and play hockey. Eby went to market because he wants to attend a cow sale in Bradford County tomorrow.

1/30/66 Sunday
Snowed all night and most all day. Temperature is 16 degrees and snow is drifting fiercely. Nothing is moving. Everything is cancelled. We rested, read and did the chores. I called Rhoda, Abram's, Isaac's and Grace. Nancy and Sanford went to Twigg's. Nancy stayed from noon till 11:15. Abram's are storm-stayed on their way home from a trip to New York City.

1/31/66 Monday
About 10 degrees and snow kept blowing and drifting till late afternoon. No school. Ray and I shelled balance of pecans, 3 pints. Eby shelled a pint of black walnuts. Sanford sorted some books and papers from the attic. Nancy made a little dress for Karen. Ray left after dinner walking to Lawrence's with his suitcase on a homemade

toboggan. He called at 10:00 and said he was back in his room after waiting in Lancaster five hours for a train and standing all the way in a crowd. Abram's got home, part way by bobsled.

2/3/66 Thursday
Had three inches of snow. Warmer and roads are being opened. Did some sewing. Made a sunbonnet and worked on a dress for Nancy. She babysat for Esther and worked on her little dresses. Potato chip man was stuck in the lane for about two hours. He gave Sanford $3.00 for helping. Eby worked on the chicken house fountains. The Vermont cow went for beef.

2/5/66 Saturday
A fine winter day. I did the morning work. Slipped on the chicken house steps and hurt my hip and one finger. Broke 11 eggs and cracked more. Washed and waxed the kitchen. Nancy got up at 11:00 when Mrs. Twigg called her to babysit at 11:30. Nancy got home at 6:30. Sanford took Gary Martin to a basketball game at Pequea Valley.

2/9/66 Wednesday
Mild day. I did some sewing. Eby and I went to Lancaster to Fulton Bank to continue our will proceedings and to Sam Wenger's. Redeemed the green stamps and King Korn stamps. Got hair clippers, sheet, blanket, dresser set and some toys. Took a coat to get dyed. Got dog license and made dental appointments. Sanford played basketball. Bought a new Bible for myself for $8.95.

2/10/66 Thursday
Cloudy, mild and snow is melting. I took Annis to Sewing Circle. Eby was struck by a car enroute to the garage and our car was badly damaged. I took Sanford to basketball. He worked for Summers Plumbing today, a new school project. Larry took us down to the garage to see the car. It has a bad bump.

2/13/66 Sunday
Very wet and rainy. Eby, Nancy and I went to church in the truck. Sanford went to Hershey's with Clair's. Nancy went to Twigg's for Dwayne's birthday dinner. We rested and read this afternoon. Nancy babysat for Twigg's this evening. Esther came up and showed us her Kansas pictures. William Horst died in Ethiopia yesterday and was buried today.

2/17/66 Thursday
Cold and windy, sunny too. A cow got loose in the night and rubbed the spigot open and flooded the cow stable. I helped Daddy bail out the water with the sump pump. I made a double portion of doughnuts and glazed half of them. Did the eggs, 225. Eby went to Melvin Stoltzfus' sale. I wrote to Charlie and Mary Alice. Cut some patches. Sanford went to Pequea Valley for practice.

2/18/66 Friday
Partly cloudy with chilly south wind. I did the morning work, scrubbed the porch, cleaned upstairs and down. Gathered and washed the eggs. Made a cake and pudding. Eby went to market. Sanford went to a game at Solanco without supper. Nancy went with Joan Burkholder. Barbara Fisher got herself ready to go to the Ice Capades in Hershey in Twiggs' trailer. 8 young Amish met her and left not looking like Amish.

2/19/66 Saturday
A fine day with a little snow this evening. Dale came home so I washed and ironed. Nancy kept house while I cleaned attic. Eby went to the hog sale. Sanford hauled manure. Nancy babysat Twigg's and Leon Stoltzfus wanted her before she was through at Twiggs, so they brought Linette and Brian here, and Sanford took them down with Nancy. On the way he struck the bridge abutment and a big evening followed, anxiety, ambulance, Drs., hospitals, stitches, good neighbors and all thankful that it wasn't worse.

2/21/66 Monday
Clear, cold and windy. I washed and ironed and got things together for butchering. Leon Stoltzfus took Sanford along to the Dr. to have his head dressed. He and Nancy went to school. Larry took them. Leon Stoltzfus gave us his truck to use. I washed the eggs and did some mending. Nancy babysat and Sanford went to basketball. Eby went to see the insurance man.

2/25/66 Friday
Have seven inches of nice wet snow. Eby went to market in Leon's truck. I did the cleaning. Leon and Nancy took Sanford along to Dr. Witmer. He took some of his 23 stitches out. I fixed my dress over where it did not fit. Gathered the eggs. Nancy went to Twigg's as soon as she got home from school.

3/8/66 Tuesday
Nice cold day. I did the eggs, ironed and mended. The barn on Paul Slaymaker's farm burned last night in Kinzer. Many fire companies turned out to save the town. Eby and Sanford went. We are making plans to have a reception for Dale. I did not sleep much last night. The fire broke out at 1:30. Nancy stayed for F.H.A. and Sanford went to chorus practice.

3/12/66 Saturday
Real nice day, had a few showers. I made doughnuts, rice pudding, red eggs and sweet potatoes for Sunday. Made pig stomach for supper. Mary Alice came in her new Volkswagen. She went down to meet Ray in Gap at 7:45. Eby carried mail. Sanford sang with the chorus at Holiday Inn for Cedars of Lebanon.

3/13/66 Sunday
Nice day with a few showers this morning. We all went to Meadville. Mary Alice took me for a ride in her new car. Abram's came this afternoon. He took Ray back to Philadelphia in Mary Alice's car. Nancy babysat for Twiggs.

3/20/66 Sunday
Fine day, cooler. Milton's left for New Holland Church and the Coy's after breakfast. Sanford went with Clair's to Hershey's. The rest of us went to Meadville. Spent the rest of the day resting and reading. Karen played nicely by herself. Isaac's named their baby Kimberly Louise.

3/26/66 Saturday
Cold and partly cloudy. Dale slept late, then went for a haircut and the wedding cake and to get Clarence Lefever to marry them as the other pastor got sick. Did the cleaning and eggs. Sanford sold 20 capons. Eby went to hog sale. Eby and I went to the wedding at the Monument and to Linda's grandfather's for supper. Got home in time to take Nancy and two other's to Debbie's birthday party.

3/29/66 Tuesday
Nice day, not so cold. I washed the sweet potatoes and put them in pots. Sowed peppers and sage. Made 2 cakes, cleaned the stove, filled the kettle for dressing capons, made snow pudding. Worked on Nancy's dress and took the skirt apart twice. Gathered and washed the eggs. Got second prize of $100.00 for a Necci sewing machine at Garvin's.
Nancy babysat.

4/2/66 Saturday
Partly cloudy, cold. I got up early, made up the flowers and cut off the capons. Edgar took us to the Fire Hall with all the food at 9:15. Mary Alice, Nancy, Ray and I got things on the way for Mary Groff, Alice Crouse, Effie Reeser, Mrs. Twigg and Kathleen Denlinger to take over and serve the dinner at 12:30. Mary Alice, Joanne, Linda and Nancy helped serve. All but 5 of the 80 invited were there. Had 32 for supper. Sanford took Ray and Charlie to Philadelphia and stayed overnight when they missed the bus.

4/5/66 Tuesday
Partly cloudy and cold. Had a snow flurry. Eby and I leveled off lower part of the yard. This afternoon we went to Lancaster for the Easter candy for Sunday School. Eby had the last 11 teeth pulled and 2 plates put in for $344.00. Bought some grass seed. I babysat for one hour at Twiggs while Nancy stayed for F.H.A. after school. Eby went to Vintage to buy a lamb.

4/7/66 Thursday
Partly cloudy with some light showers. I sowed the grass seed on ours and Twigg's lawns. Cleaned most of the house and did some mending. Sowed the sweet peas. Eby carried mail. Sanford got a haircut. Nancy went to an Easter party at Christ's Home and had to be brought home at 5:30. Eby complains of a sore jaw and eats very carefully. Abe and Pat and David left by plane for Switzerland.

4/14/66 Thursday
Clear and cool. I cleaned out one end of the freezer for the beef. Got soap fat ready to sell and packed up the chicken fat. Finished sweeping the attic. Kathleen brought Nancy's dress and I sewed it up ready to fit. Made a sponge cake. Brought Nancy home from school. She and Sanford went to Honor Roll banquet. Jim called last night and said Greg is in the hospital with pneumonia. Wired Greg some flowers.

5/3/66 Tuesday
A fine day, frosty and cool. Eby plowed and took potatoes out to school and went to the sale. I cleaned the big bedroom. Nancy stayed after school till after 8:00. I fixed a dress for Nancy. We had a supper valued at six cents each to save and share with the hungry in Viet Nam and India. I made chicken rice soup, small homemade buns, beets, tea, peach juice and mints. No butter or sugar.

5/7/66 Saturday
A very fine day. I fixed Larry's trousers. After Nancy's party ended at 10:00 we washed the bed clothes and towels. Nancy went to bed after dinner and slept till 9:00. I did the ironing and cleaning. Gathered the eggs. Eby finished washing them. I wrote a letter to the family and to Milton's. Felt very badly about Nancy's party.

5/16/66 Monday
Nice day and started raining this evening. I washed and ironed and did the mending. Did the eggs. Eby and I went to Ira Barley's funeral, about 25 there. Eby finished plowing. Sanford tested milk. Nancy picked up some corn from the corn crib. Sanford had F.F.A. and Nancy went with Mrs. Twigg and Mrs. Campbell to Harry Good's and I stayed with the children and sewed on my dress.

5/20/66 Friday
A fine warm day. Cut spinach and asparagus for market. Also lettuce. Helped with the milking and did most of the cleaning. Eby went to market. I went to Aaron Gehman's funeral and to Flaud's for plants. Planted petunias, alyssum, egg plant and sage. Nancy went to Twiggs three times this evening and is still there at 10:30.

5/23/66 Monday
A fine warm day. I washed and ironed and mended and did the eggs. Got 487. Eby carried mail. Sanford stayed home from school and harrowed. Leroy Lapp planted most of the corn. Bugs are at the pickles. I dusted them. Hoed some flower beds.

Sanford helped me tear out the forsythia bush. Eby went to a D.H.I.A. meeting. Minnie called and said Ellis is not very well. Milk house cesspool is full again.

5/27/66 Friday
Partly cloudy and sprinkles. I did the cleaning, raked, trimmed and mowed yard. Did the eggs. Sanford went to market. Eby carried mail. Nancy stayed home sick and spent most of the day babysitting at Twigg's. Eby and Sanford went to New Holland for the truck. Clair Weir sprayed the corn field for weeds and where I planted the limas.

5/30/66 Monday
A fine day. I washed and did the eggs. Helped clean two years accumulation of manure from the capon house. Washed the windows. Eby set up the brooder and put in the windows. Eby and Sanford mowed a field of grass. Nancy crimped it and did some of the ironing. Nancy slept till12:00 after being out with Twiggs till 11:00. I went to bed early.

5/31/66 Tuesday
Partly cloudy and cool. Snowballs are blooming. I finished the ironing. Replanted the pickles and thinned the cantaloupes. Got 300 silver cross cockerels. Eby went to the sale. He sowed Sudan grass this morning. Talked to Mabel.

6/6/66 Monday
A warm day and dropped a little rain. Washed, ironed and helped haul hay. Mrs. Twigg helped with one load till Sanford came from school. Mary Alice had a dental appointment at 1:30 and came home and helped bale and load. I washed eggs and made more room for the peeps. Sanford went to his first Fire Meeting. I dug some tulips and daffodils.

6/7/66 Tuesday
A warm day. Mary Alice was here. I did some planting and hoeing. Fixed Charlie's plants. Sanford took Gary Martin and his motorcycle to near Philadelphia to have it repaired. We all went to Sanford's graduation this evening. 87 in the class. Mary Alice spent part of the night visiting Suzanne Buckwalter.

6/13/66 Monday
A bit showery but sunny and hot. I did some mending for Charlie this a.m. and washed after dinner. Eby harrowed corn and fixed the stable cleaner. Nancy came home at noon and did some ironing. Sanford, Nancy, Eby and I took Charlie to Philadelphia airport for a 10:00 jet to Miami. Got home at 12:00.

6/17/66 Friday
A nice warm day. We picked and froze 2 bushels of peas. Milton and Mike went visiting friends far and wide. Eby went to market. Eby and I went with Milton's to Clarence's for supper. Victor's were there too. Nancy babysat for Esther. Barbara

shelled peas all day. Charlie called by short wave radio from Nicaragua and said he is happy and doing fine.

6/28/66 Tuesday
Another hot sultry day. Began raining so nicely this evening. Eby carried mail and worked at Vintage sale this evening. I cleaned up a half crate of eggs that dumped on the floor for Nancy. Hoed asparagus patch and some garden. Nancy answered phone for Twigg's till noon and finished ironing and cleaned part of the pea patch and shelled all the peas. Sanford went to Bible School.

6/30/66 Thursday
Clear and hot with a heavy dew. I got sick in my stomach and laid down between jobs. Vomited when I gathered the eggs. I helped Eby finish the top chicken house. Washed tank and put milkers together. Nancy answered phone for Twigg's. Froze the last 2 quarts of peas. Nancy and I planted the pea patch almost full of beans, corn, beets, carrots, etc. Eby went for Bible School supplies. Had a letter from Charlie.

7/3/66 Sunday
A very hot day, 100 degrees in the shade and 120 in the sun. We went to Meadville, Sanford to Hershey's. Amos Hershey and Eby were nominated for minister by 7 who went out to vote. Eby and I went to Hettie Kurtz's funeral this p.m. and Sanford and Nancy tried to keep cool. Sanford went to Old Road this evening, and Eby and I went to Meadville to a song service. Nancy stayed home. The capons are warm.

7/5/66 Tuesday
Partly cloudy and sultry. I cleaned off some garden and planted pickles and flower plants. Tommy Denlinger came to spend the day while his mother worked. Helped to gather eggs and hoe lima beans. Eby pulled weeds from the potatoes. Clair Eby's and Galen's were here this p.m. We went to Meadville this evening where some bishops met with us. Nancy spent the evening at Twigg's.

7/10/66 Sunday
Real nice day. Had a good shower this evening. Sanford went to Hershey's. We went to Meadville. This afternoon was the ordination. We were well satisfied to have the Lord choose Amos Hershey by lot. The church was filled. I read and Eby slept this evening. Nancy stayed with the Twigg's children.

7/14/66 Thursday
Partly cloudy and not quite so hot this evening. I hoed the garden and planted beans and some flower plants. Nancy got up at 10:00 and mowed the yard and made dinner and supper. I helped Eby weed potatoes till 3:00 when the sprayer came and we had to quit. We cleaned along the lane and I trimmed the yard. Got six chickens for the freezer. Eby went for blueberries and raspberries. Eight nurses were murdered in Chicago.

7/20/66 Wednesday
Clear, windy, day. Nancy slept late and washed and ironed. I hoed the garden and did the mending. Made vegetable soup and tapioca for supper. Took some air blisters from the capons. Eby carried mail. Verna Gockley came for eggs. Mike and Karen rested. Sanford went to a ball game in Baltimore with the F.F.A.

8/1/66 Monday
A fine day. Washed and harrowed the garden partly. I consented reluctantly to go with Eby and Fredric and Tommy Denlinger to an Interstate picnic at Lenape Park. The boys rode free on the amusements. We got there about 12:30 and got home at 4:00. We had our Sunday School picnic at Dick Patterson's. The young people played Flying Dutchman and Nancy came home disgusted.

8/8/66 Monday
Nice warm day. We left Edgar's at 6:45 and got home at 12:45. Nancy and Sanford got along fine at home. She washed and went with Linda King on some school paper business. I did the ironing and some eggs. Fixed a shirt for Eby. Got the beds ready. Watered some garden. Had three lady guests. Eby went to a D.H.I.A. meeting and Nancy went to Twigg's.

8/14/66 Sunday
Cloudy and cool with some showers. Went to Meadville, had a Harvest Sermon. Text was Psalms 103. Had a birthday dinner for Nancy. Mary Alice brought David and Andy this afternoon. Isaac's came all but Joanne and Kim. Mary Alice visited friends this evening, and Nancy kept the boys.

8/19/66 Friday
A hot day. Eby carried mail. The Clemens family slept on the porch in their sleeping bags. They left for home about 9:00. Fredric stayed here. Nancy babysat for Twigg's most of the day. Fredric and I mowed yard, and I did some of the trimming and harrowed and watered the garden. Picked beans for supper. Some folks came to see about a cow. Got a letter from Charlie in Corn Island, Nicaragua.

8/20/66 Saturday
Fine day. I washed and Nancy ironed and made a cake and pudding. I picked limas and Fredric shelled them. Made vegetable soup and washed up the kitchen. Eby carried mail. Sanford overhauled the milker and did a repair job for Horst. Henry Beiler's house caught fire last night and we did not call Sanford. He was disgusted. Eby and Fredric went to Elmer Lapp's for ice cream. Nancy went to a drama at the Ephrata Cloisters with Linda King.

8/26/66 Friday
Pleasant weather. Did the morning work. Picked a bushel of limas. Daddy, Fredric and I left at 10:10 for Jim's. Got there at 1:15. Shelled the limas and had supper

with them. Spent the evening with Dale and Linda. Back to Jim's for the night. Pat has everything spic and span. Eby, Jim, Fredric, Greg and Beth went to spot deer and saw some.

8/31/66 Wednesday
Hot and dry. I mixed up some cookies. Washed eggs and picked a bushel of limas. Eby carried mail. Sanford left at 12:30 to get Ray and meet Charlie at Philadelphia Airport. He got home at 4:30. This afternoon Nancy and Fredric and Charlie helped shell 2 bushel of limas. I put 13 quarts in the freezer. Nancy is feeling a little better. I helped Charlie to clean off his desk with liquid sandpaper.

9/2/66 Friday
A real nice day. Eby went to market. I made pies. Nancy is almost bed fast. Rhoda cleaned the living room and kitchen. I did the yard and porches. Fredric mowed. We prepared most of the food. Sanford worked his last day at Horst's. I picked a basket of limas. Edgar and Fredric picked the Bartlett pears. Robert and Grace and Stevie came this evening.

9/3/66 Saturday
A fine warm day. Had all the family here, and Edgar's were in charge of the food preparation. All were here but Joanne. She went to Youth Retreat. Charlie left early and Abram, Pat and Becky came after dinner. Jim's and Milton's left after supper, and the others stayed all night. Nancy is not so good.

9/8/66 Thursday
Clear and cool. Got up early and Eby carried mail. Sanford helped milk and he and Mary Alice left for Abram's about 8:30. He started to Goshen with him. Nancy went with Linda King to Pequea Valley from 9:15 to 2:00. I canned pickles and pears. Picked a bushel of limas and went to Beiler's for 4 baskets of peaches and to Glick's for 3 baskets of tomatoes. We took the car to the garage and got cantaloupes.

9/16/66 Friday
Clear and cool. 42 degrees. I helped milk twice. Eby went to market. I did the cleaning and eggs. Got grapes in and made 14 quarts of juice. Nancy stayed after school for F.H.A. and I babysat for Twigg's till she came home. Had milker trouble. I planted in some geraniums and other plants. Had first letter from Sanford at Goshen and he is fine.

9/18/66 Sunday
A fine day. We went to Meadville. Amos' text was Making Choices. Had a temperance lesson. Spent the rest of the day reading and resting. I wrote to Grace and Sanford. Jim called and said Clair Fisher went through the ensilage wagon and is in critical condition. Dale is doing his work.

9/20/66 Tuesday

Raining and blowing all day. I cleaned up the cellar, did the eggs. Eby got parts for the plow and painted the toilet. I went to a luncheon at the Fire Hall. 125 women attended. Nancy babysat and went to an F.T.A. meeting. I wrote to Mary Alice. There is contention in many of our churches. Put the electric heater up for Miss Horrmann.

9/29/66 Thursday

Mild, foggy and rainy. I cleaned the cellar way and shelves and some drawers. Mr. Harry Wonder came to check the capons. They have lucosus. Eby went to look at Clarence Denlinger's yearlings. We had early lunch and went to look at some near Mt. Joy. I went to Miriam and Ruth and got a bonnet and some notions. Eby had a dairy meeting and I went for tomatoes. Nancy babysat. Got peaches for market.

10/4/66 Tuesday

Fine day, warmer. I cleaned closets, drawers and corners. Eby harrowed the wheat ground. Sold a cow that was bought in New York State. Tommy and Frank helped a while to catch the old chickens. Caught and crated 660. Nancy babysat. Mrs. Barr called and said Dale has not yet heard from the draft board and Clair Fisher had his leg amputated.

10/8/66 Saturday

A fine warm day. We dressed the first 2 capons. Nancy made a birthday cake and washed the car and helped milk this evening. Also cleaned her room. Cleaned some celery. Did the downstairs and waxed the kitchen. Eby mowed alfalfa and broke the mower. Our new dairy tester is from Virginia, and his parents were here. Had a call from Dr. Amstutz that Sanford must have an appendectomy. Sanford called about 9:00 and said he felt fine.

10/23/66 Sunday

A very mild day. We went to Meadville through dense fog. Galen preached. His text was "Do all things without murmuring and complaining." Made chicken pie for dinner. Wrote to Sanford and Dale. Daddy slept. Nancy read and slept. Called Jim's and heard that Dale is deferred and is moving to York.

10/24/66 Monday

Mild and damp. Sprinkling this evening. I washed and ironed. Brought the milkers in and boiled the metal parts. Cleaned them thoroughly. Eby carried mail. I did the chickens and cows. Nancy carried milk this evening. She said she is not going to be a stupid farmer's wife. She stayed after school. Eby weaned the two little heifers.

11/5/66 Saturday

Clear and cold. I dressed 4 capons. Charlie came at 9:00. He showed the slides he took in Nicaragua. Clarence's, Jay's, Uncle Charlie and Abner's were here. Nancy babysat for Leon and Nancy. Eby went to eye doctor and bought a new Ford Galaxie.

11/10/66 Thursday

Cloudy and rainy. I cleaned cupboards and drawers. Dressed 5 capons and got turnips, beets, Swiss chard and onions ready for market. Eby went to Meadville to help with the cementing. Bought a new garage door from the salesman this p.m. Nancy stayed after school for a Faculty Banquet. Rented the big room to two teachers.

11/16/66 Wednesday

Partly cloudy, cool. Eby carried mail. I did up the barn work. Cleaned rug for Nancy's room. Mended and did the eggs. The two teachers, Al and Bill, moved in. Ordered beef for Edgar's. Nancy went to play practice. Eby and I went to Meadville. Text was parable of the husbandman.

11/24/66 Thursday

A fine mild day. I helped with the chores. Made croquettes, filling and oysters ready for Thanksgiving dinner. Daddy and I went to Kinzer church. Isaac's, Robert's, Dale's and Milton's were here for dinner. Milton's left at 4:00 and Dale's at 7:00. Isaac's went home in time to do their work. Abner's and Elda Friesen came up a while after dinner.

11/28/66 Monday

A very wet day, rained 2 inches. I washed two washes and hung it in the cellar. Took care of Stevie. Eby worked on the garage doors. I washed the eggs. Went to Anna Mary Lapp's Stanley party. Eby had an Interstate meeting here. Nancy is getting ready for an interview with A.F.S. to be an exchange student. Kept cows in for the first night.

12/3/66 Saturday

A cold day, windy. Had some frozen pipes. Dressed 4 capons. Nancy and I went to Abram's to see little Samuel. It was 7:45 till we were done with the work. I looked after the Twigg children till Nancy was through babysitting at Abner's at 10:00.

12/4/66 Sunday

Clear and cold. Eby and I went to Hershey's for the first time in years. Mart Hershey preached. Nancy babysat for Twigg's. She stayed in bed with a headache till noon. Three ladies came to interview us about Nancy as an exchange student. We all went to Meadville this evening. Henry Ruth and a quartet from Harleysville gave the program.

12/12/66 Monday

Clear and cold. I washed and stirred up three kinds of cookies. Dressed 7 capons. Eby worked at the Post Office this morning. Nancy came home at 1:30 because of a teacher's meeting. I took Nancy to the doctor for a physical for her driver's permit and if she should go as a foreign exchange student.

12/16/66 Friday
A fine day. Eby worked at the P.O. until 9:00 and went to market. I finished up the work. Did the eggs and cleaned the house. The oil burner stopped and the plumbers came and fixed it and cleaned it. I went to bed at 9:00 and got up at 10:00 to meet Sanford in Ephrata at 11:00. We got there at the same time. Nancy went to a basketball game at Solanco.

12/24/66 Saturday
Began snowing at 6 a.m. and is still snowing and blowing a real blizzard. Eby worked at the P.O. We dressed 8 capons. Dale and Linda came about 10:30 and went to her home through the snow for supper. Charlie fixed the kitchen table and worked on the mixer. Cut Daddy's hair this evening and made sweet potato croquettes.

12/25/66 Sunday
We were snowed in till evening when Abner opened our lane. Charlie, Sanford, Nancy and I went down to see the Smoker gifts and they made ice cream for us. We spent a quiet Christmas eating, reading and resting. There were very few churches having services. Grace called and said they are snowed in too.

12/28/66 Wednesday
Partly cloudy and started snowing about 3:00. Sleeted and gave some ice. A tractor trailer got in the gutter by mistake in our lane while making a delivery to Abner's. Ray and Sanford worked for over 2 hours helping get him out. Milton's came this p.m. for a while. We did not go to midweek because of the ice. Nancy helped Mrs. Twigg clean trailer this p.m. and evening.

1967

1/2/67 Monday
Real nice day. I washed and Nancy ironed. We covered and knotted an old wool comforter and I cleaned Bill's room and the bathroom. Ivan Yost was injured last evening when he was milking a heifer. Started reading the Old Testament.

1/4/67 Wednesday
Partly cloudy and mild. Eby had some major repairs done on the stable cleaner. I made suits for relief. We dressed 14 crippled capons this afternoon. Nancy carried milk and gathered eggs. Jack Ruby, who killed Oswald, died. Esther sent a loaf of her good rye bread.

1/7/67 Saturday
Cloudy and rainy. Finished the cleaning. Made a lot of sweet potato croquettes for the freezer. Alfred got 6 gallons of capon fat. Nancy got up at 10:45. I did the eggs.

Eby went to a sale and took Isaac along. He bought a cow for $420. I made some pumpkin pies and crusts. Larry's check bounced. Had Dr. for heifer's teat.

1/9/67 Monday
A fine day. I washed and Nancy and I did the ironing. Gathered and washed the eggs. Nancy came home an hour earlier. Eby took Nancy to the Dr. for a signature and then to school. He worked on the manure. An Amishman came to rent the farm. Offered $2500.

1/10/67 Tuesday
A fine day. I did some mending. Made 8 quarts of applesauce. Eby went to New Holland to a lawyer to have a paper made up to sell his Vintage Sales stock to Harold Hess. Nancy missed the bus and I took her to school. A man came to advise us that our method of dressing capons is not lawful.

1/14/67 Saturday
Damp, rainy and foggy. Eby carried the mail. I gave the milkers a 2-hour cleanup. Did the eggs. Made a cake and finished the suits for relief. Nancy got up at 11:00 and had a backset this afternoon. She went to Twigg's to babysit at 4:00. Leroy Lapp has 4 heifers at large. Aldus brought the groceries and got 20 dozen eggs.

1/19/67 Thursday
Clear and cold. I canned the meat. Weighed up 25 lbs. sausage and 23 lbs. scrapple. Dressed 5 capons. Did the eggs. Eby and I went to Bible School. Nancy went to Twigg's. The Amish church had a divide. 80 families have decided on some labor-saving farm equipment.

1/24/67 Tuesday
A fine warm day. No heat is needed. Eby worked on the stable cleaner. Ray took Nancy to the orthodontist for a checkup. She went back to school and they left at 2:00 for Abram's. Abram and Pat are taking them to a Symphony Orchestra. I did the eggs and chores. Nancy has been wearing eye shadow.

1/27/67 Friday
A very wet day. Rained over an inch. Eby went to market and got wet. I did most of the cleaning. Nancy went to Evie Herr's to help with some invitations. Charlie called from Gap and I went down for him. Three astronauts were killed in a test flight.

2/1/67 Wednesday
A mild day. Got up at 4:00. Eby carried mail. I mended and worked on my dress. Finished a seed order. Helped with chores as usual. Did the eggs, fed the cows, cleaned the stable, helped milk, fed and watered calves, gave cows hay and bedded them. Took Nancy to Dutch Town and Country for a $25.00 reward for the Peace essay she wrote.

2/19/67 Sunday
A fine day. We went to Meadville. Richard Buckwalter preached. Mary Alice brought Barbara, the German girl, for dinner and they stayed till 9:45. This afternoon the girls went to Esther's and Tom's and took a drive. Nancy did some driving. The children are planning to have a celebration for our 40th anniversary.

2/21/67 Tuesday
Snowing and blowing, but cleared. I did the ironing and mending. I scrubbed and waxed the stair steps. Eby made some pegs for chicken house windows. Sold 3 cows for beef. Eby went to the sale and cows brought over $700. Helped Nancy bake a cherry pie, her first.

2/22/67 Wednesday
A fine day. Roads are dry. Eby finished the work and I took Nancy and her pie to school on my way to Mart Hershey's to help quilt Kathryn Huyett's quilt. Cleaned up this p.m. Had midweek service here. Charlie came and showed his slides of Nicaragua. Nancy got 2nd prize in pie contest.

2/25/67 Saturday
Very cold and windy. 10 degrees. Pipes were frozen and got done late with chores. Took Nancy to Pequea Valley for National Merit Scholarship test at 7:45. Made buns, ice cream, sweet potatoes, roasted capon and other things ready for company tomorrow. Nancy went from school to Twigg's and came home at 5:30. Sue Barge called and asked to take Nancy to the Y in the cold. I refused to let her go.

3/2/67 Thursday
A fine day. Warmer. I canned the meat. Put some in the freezer. Made pig foot jelly. Weighed up 37 lbs. of sausage and 34 lbs. of scrapple. Eby carried mail. We got up at 4:00. Clifford called at 1:00 a.m. and said turn the water off as he had a bursted pipe. Nancy went to school with her stocking tops showing. It made me sick.

3/9/67 Thursday
A mild day. I washed a small wash and sewed my dresses. Worked on Nancy's this evening. She did not go to school because of infirmities. Worked on her term paper when she was able to be up. Eby went to Sam Dunn's sale at East Petersburg and bought a cow for $750.00. Eby gathered the eggs and Nancy washed them.

3/25/67 Saturday
A fine day. We were busy adding the last minute details for the celebration of our anniversary. Edgar's, Dale's, Robert's and Jim's came this p.m. We did the work early and all got to Dutch Town and Country by 6:00. Had some pictures taken and were served a good meal. 42 of us. Had an interesting program and visited for a while. The children gave us a camera, projector, and screen.

3/26/67 Sunday
A beautiful warm day. We all went to Meadville but Nancy and Stevie. We added 15 to the attendance. Had a handy lunch of chicken corn soup, buns, cole slaw, rice pudding and cake. Had a drop-in for our anniversary. About 80 came. It was an unusual and happy experience to see so many friends and relatives in so short a time. All the children were here but James and family.

3/27/67 Monday
A real nice day. Eby took Sanford to the hospital for a knee operation. Edgar's left about 10:30. Rosa and Jonathan stayed here. I washed and Rosa hung it up. Rosa and Jonathan started to clean the chicken house where the capons were. Milton and Barbara and boys were here for supper. Milton showed us some slides.

3/29/67 Wednesday
A nice day. I did up the work and put things in order. Rosa and Jonathan finished cleaning the capon house. Eby took some orchard fence out. Nancy was late getting home from school, 7:15. She, Rosa and I went in to see Sanford. He is feeling better.

4/1/67 Saturday
A fine spring day. I cleaned up the house. Nancy was sick from her big night. She made 2 lemon sponge pies and babysat for Leon and Nancy all night till 1:00. Cleaned some yard and stuck some onions. Kathleen called and said Mabel was in a bad accident with three cars and eleven injured. She was driving and struck a Cadillac coming home from a Sewing Circle meeting.

4/3/67 Monday
A warm day, cooled off this evening. I washed and did some ironing. Did the eggs. Had quite a few calls to ask about Mabel. Nancy came home at 1:00 and rolled the lawn with Summer's roller. The Coy's came to see Mike. Sanford and I went to the hospital to see Mabel. He then met his load at Norman Reeser's to start for Goshen.

4/6/67 Thursday
Partly cloudy and warmer. I took Annis along to Sewing Circle. Nancy stayed home with Mike and this P.M. we went to take her driver's test, which she failed. She was disappointed. Put a trype on to cook. Nancy washed the eggs. The bulldozer finished the trees and covered the holes.

4/7/67 Friday
A damp day. Hurried to get to Pequea Valley by 8:05 to Nancy's induction to the National Honor Society. Eby took Mike to Esther when he went to market. I picked him up at 10:00. Cleaned this afternoon and started the work early as we had our preparatory service this evening. Mike went along.

4/15/67 Saturday
A warm day. Nancy slept late. I scrubbed the porch. Did the eggs. Hershey Kurtz was here and plowed 13 acres. Eby hauled manure. Nancy, Mike and I went to retake her test. She failed again. Went to General Hospital for a form to pay Sanford's bill. Stopped at Dutch Wonderland with Mike. Abram and boys were there with the Robert Lerch family. Got done with work late.

4/21/67 Friday
Partly cloudy and began raining this evening. Eby went to market. Mike and I did the cleaning and scrubbed the porch. We went for oil for stable cleaner and some tomato plants for Milton. Mike was in the calf pen and I gave him water in a bucket. Nancy went to Leon's to babysit after she came home from school. The Meadville young people came here to have a meeting and show a film.

4/22/67 Saturday
Fine day. Eby took eggs to the Burkholder store and bought some of the "going out of business" specials. I got things ready for our trip to Stony Brook and finished up the work. Nancy got up soon after 10:00 to help. Dale and Linda got here for lunch and took over the work. Nancy cooked. We started at 1:00 and arrived at 6:00. Had our supper and went to see the new house. Mike was happy to get home.

4/23/67 Sunday
Very cool and windy after a good night's rest and breakfast. We went with Milton's to an old Presbyterian church for worship. Went again to the new house and looked it over by daylight. Saw the lawn with all the pretty flowers. Had dinner in the dining hall with the boys. Had tea with the faculty and visited some of them. Relaxed and talked till 3:00 and started for home. Arrived at 8:00. Dale and Linda left for home at 10:00.

4/25/67 Tuesday
A fine day. I finished the ironing. Went to Bylers for the canning meat and did 16 quarts. Cooked the meat for mince meat. Eby worked on the manure. Esther brought a pretty cake for my birthday and they came up this evening with ice cream and we had a party. Abram and Mary Alice called. Nancy stayed after school and I went for her.

4/27/67 Thursday
Snowed this morning and rained. I took Annis along to Sewing Circle. Went with Nancy for her driver's test, which she passed. Went to pottery store to look about a job for her. Made 14 quarts of mince meat when I got home. Got a half beef for freezer. Mabel's inquest exonerated both drivers.

5/6/67 Saturday
A wet cool day. Nancy got up for breakfast. We cleaned her room, the bathroom and finished our room. Eby took eggs to Lawrence's and worked on the orchard fence. I

picked a bucket of asparagus. Nancy made her first driving trips to take Mrs. Wasson asparagus and to meet Charlie at Gap. She spent the evening with Ellen.

5/9/67 Tuesday
A cold day. Rained a little. I finished weeding the strawberries. Eby worked on the stable cleaner. I mended and did the eggs. Suzette came for flowers for the banquet. Nancy and I went at 7:00. A lot of mothers and daughters were there. Eby went to help at Meadville. Robert called and said Grace had an appendectomy at 6:00.

5/16/67 Tuesday
A wet day here in Staunton. I did a load of wash and ironed. Swept the house and cleaned the bathrooms. Swept basement, garage, and rec. room. Made rhubarb sauce and put some in freezer. Grace's incision opened this evening and she felt scared and sick. A little later she was much relieved and was able to sit up and look at Charlie's slides of Nicaragua.

5/17/67 Wednesday
Had a few showers but it was clear when we got home at 9:30. Left Staunton at 5:00. I washed and ironed two loads and mopped the kitchen. Grace is feeling much better. Mrs. Lester Hershey came to see her. Stevie is contented and cooperative. Robert is very busy with Valley Paving. Daddy and Nancy managed to get things done all right.

5/22/67 Monday
Fine day. Had our work done before 8:00 and Abram's took us to Charlie's graduation at Philadelphia Civic Center. Governor Schafer spoke. It was the largest class of the University of Pennsylvania. Charlie got a $220.00 award. We ate at Bookbinder's. Charlie is leaving by plane for Nicaragua at 11:00 tonight. Got home at 5:00. Eby went to a D.H.I.A. meeting and Nancy to a show at the Fulton.

5/24/67 Wednesday
Very cool with high winds. Ironed and mended. Eby carried mail. Cleaned some flower beds. Did the eggs. Got the pictures that were taken at our anniversary party. Had a letter from Rhoda. Nancy has been chosen of the two for exchange student.

6/4/67 Sunday
A fine day. We went to Meadville this morning and Eby and I went this evening. Mary Alice brought two girls from Hershey for dinner and supper. Ray took them to New Bolton Center and Longwood Gardens. I entertained David. We left the truck at Gap for Ray to come home at 11:00.

6/10/67 Saturday
A fine day. I watered some this morning. Did the morning work and went out to Flaud's for tomato and sweet potato plants. We planted them this afternoon. Eby cleaned the cow stable and upset the tractor when he hauled the wagon load of old

siding from the house to the thicket. Nancy slept till noon. Sanford cleaned some fence row and the barn hill. He took the car to go out tonight.

6/11/67 Sunday
A fine warm day. We went to Meadville and Sanford went with Clair's to Hershey's. We rested this afternoon and this evening. Sanford, Nancy and I played croquet, scribbage and sang.

6/14/67 Wednesday
A cloudy day. Eby took the cow stable windows out and raked the hay. Sanford worked for Horst's. Nancy and I made her bathing suit. I thinned the pickles and cantaloupes. Picked sugar peas and strawberries. Eby and I went to midweek service.

6/16/67 Friday
A hot day. Eby went to market. Nancy slept till 10:00. I got big room ready for Milton's. Cleaned and mowed some yard. Nancy stirred up some cookies. Milton's got here about 6:00. He and Sanford left about 8:30 to pick up a load of furniture and take it to Long Island tonight while traffic is lighter. Barbara and Nancy did their hair. The peeps are doing good.

6/17/67 Saturday
A warm day. Nancy, Barbara and Mike picked sugar peas for Abrams and themselves. Abram's came about 10:00 and took Nancy along to the shore to help with the children. Milton and Sanford got back from Long Island about 1:00. Barbara and Milton left at 4:00 for the Nurse's banquet at Harrisburg. Sanford went away this evening. I put the boys to bed after bathing them.

7/7/67 Friday
Fine day. I did a big wash after the tourists left about 7:30. Eby carried mail. Fredric and I mowed the yard. I made deviled clams for supper. Did the ironing. Sanford finished the milking this morning and started it this evening. Fredric hoed weeds from the asparagus.

7/9/67 Sunday
A fine day. Sanford went to Hershey's and Eby, Fredric and I went to Meadville. Eby and I went to Abram's. It was Becky's birthday. Mary Alice went to Dale's, so we didn't get to see her. Sammy started pulling himself up. Sanford and Fredric did the work.

7/15/67 Saturday
A fine day with some showers after dark. Nancy made 2 cakes and some mints and helped with the cleaning. I scrubbed and cleaned the kitchen and waxed the floor. Got capons and food ready for the Dr. Wallace family from Nicaragua for supper. Sanford met Charlie and Ray at Coatesville depot at 2:15. Things went off fairly well considering our inefficiency.

7/26/67 Wednesday

Bright hot day. Eby worked on shed doors. I trained the limas and hoed balance of sweet potatoes. Nancy and Fredric picked 1 ½ bushels of beans. Tommy came to help crate eggs. Sanford has some pain in his bad knee. Eby, Nancy, Fredric, Tommy, Heidi and I went to Bible School. Violence continues in Detroit. Had first corn.

7/28/67 Friday

Sultry and partly cloudy. Extra! Extra! Nancy got up at 7:00 to make an apple pie for Jeff. She made four for us. Isaac and three girls, Linda, Sally, Judy and Karen, came to help bale the straw. Nancy helped bale. Eby went to market. I cooked dinner and did the eggs. Karen stayed. We all went to Bible School but Sanford. Got candy and did not stay to help clean up.

8/4/67 Friday

Had showers this morning and a heavy gust with lots of wind and rain. Shirk's garage burned after being struck by lightning and a plane crashed in Lancaster and killed the three passengers. Nancy got up early and made a blackberry pie for Jeff. I washed while the sun came out at noon and mowed the yard. We went to Isaac's after the storm to bring Judy. Sanford went to the fire.

8/8/67 Tuesday

Sultry and warm. Eby worked on his silo room. Nancy and I worked on her room and gave the furniture first coat of paint. She babysat for Judy Thurban this evening and Sanford collected for the Fire Company. Melvin Groff sent us six tourists and Mabel sent three. I got the big room and our room ready in a jiffy.

9/2/67 Saturday

A beautiful clear day. Mary Alice and Nancy came here and went with us to Isaac's where the whole family got together for a delicious dinner that Isaac's prepared. Everything was very well panned. Sanford went to Philadelphia for Charlie and his bed and Ray. They all came here for supper but Isaac's and Dale's. I took some slides.

9/4/67 Monday

A fine day. Sanford painted on the barn. I went to Harry Good's for a gallon of paint. Robert picked a basket of limas and we took out a bushel of potatoes and 5 dozen sweet corn for Robert's. They left for home at 12:30. Eby mowed alfalfa and Nancy crimped. Milton's came for supper and then went to Coy's. We went down to Abner's for homemade ice cream in honor of Sanford's leaving for college.

9/7/67 Thursday

A pretty day. Mary Alice, Sanford and Nancy started for Goshen at 6:45. Janet has milk fever. Dr. came early. I cleaned Sanford's drawers and did some mending. Helped haul balance of hay this p.m. Clifford helped. Picked green and yellow beans, pickles, beets, tomatoes, potatoes and 400 ears of corn. Did the eggs. Eby went to Lapp's for apples, peaches, and red and blue plums.

9/12/67 Tuesday
A fine day. Frost in some places. Mabel and Mildred come for corn. I put 8 qts. in freezer and canned 9 qts. of pickles. Molly had twin calves. Picked a basket of limas. Mary Alice brought her friend Lois for supper and they shelled the beans. Nancy went with them to do some antique shopping.

9/19/67 Tuesday
A warm day. I did 15 qts. end-of-the-garden relish. Made some grape jelly. Did the eggs. Eby cleaned the cow stable and mowed some weeds. We took Molly's twins to Vintage to sell this evening. I cleaned some yard. Five capons died last week. A New Holland branch bank was robbed of $40,000. Nancy went back to school this evening and damaged the chrome on our car in the parking lot.

9/21/67 Thursday
Warm and rained this evening. I cut a half bushel of grapes for Mrs. Beiler and one to make juice. Canned plums and made jam. Made grape jelly. Eby and I picked a bushel of limas. Got corn, pickles, beets, cabbage, rhubarb, cauliflower, potatoes and tomatoes for market. Did the eggs. Had a new calf. Three men held up an armored truck and took $50,000. They were soon caught in a Host Motel.

10/1/67 Sunday
A real October day. Partly cloudy and windy. We went to Meadville. Nancy is babysitting for Judy Thurban contrary to our wishes. I read and wrote letters. Nancy came home at 6:00.

10/2/67 Monday
A fine day, warmer. I washed and Nancy ironed when she came from school at 1:15. I picked a bushel of limas and Eby helped shell them this evening. Sanford had one of his friend's mothers call from Akron to ask us to send him food. Nancy made whoopie pies and we got a big box ready and I took it back to Akron this evening.

10/29/67 Sunday
A fine day. Frosty. Had an extra hour this morning. We went to Meadville this morning and had our communion service. Had a capon dinner. Spent the afternoon reading and resting. David and I played some games. He and Mary Alice left about 7:00. Earlier Nancy and Mary Alice went to the Spring Heads for cattails.

11/1/67 Wednesday
Nice mild day. Eby cleaned a load of manure from the big chicken house and repaired the fountain. I cleaned the hi fi. Did the eggs. Cleaned part of the attic and mowed most of the yard. The tramp who came last evening is still in the barn and

is not feeling well. I gave him two trays of food and two aspirin. Eby and I went to midweek at the Samaritan Home. Nancy stayed after school till 6:30.

11/2/67 Thursday
A very wet day. I went to Sewing Circle along. Housecleaned the bathroom this afternoon. The tramp is still in the barn, but says he is feeling better. Eby went to Dutch Town and Country for a dairy meeting. Nancy returned to school twice this evening. I worked on scrapbook page till Kathleen came.

11/4/67 Saturday
Clear and cold. Three of Nancy's friends came and they decorated cupcakes for American Education Week to give to the township teachers. Two of them were here for lunch. I cleaned some celery. I washed all the stable windows and Eby put them in. He met Charlie at the Coatesville depot. The tramp is still here and I am carrying him food.

11/6/67 Monday
Coldest morning. Fountains frozen. I washed and ironed. Did the eggs. The tramp left at 4:00. I gave him some underwear. Ellen Hermann came home sick at noon and Dr. Beacher asked me to look after her till her mother came this evening. Nancy drove to school and went to Albright College and stayed for play practice this evening.

11/8/67 Wednesday
A cold day. Joe Bechtold was here helping make a place for the corn. I cleaning the living room and dining room windows inside and out. Did the eggs and kept chickens in water. Rev. Wright came for an interview about Nancy's A.F.S. prospects. Nancy went to play practice and Eby and I went to midweek services.

11/16/67 Thursday
Clear and cold. Left at 8:15 to go to St. Joseph's Hospital to sew. They kept us till 3:30 and got home at 4:30. Eby was in a bad mood because it was late and he had picked 8 capons after finishing the chicken house. I dressed them and helped finish up the chores. Nancy helped before going to play practice. We went to Meadville. The text was the Prodigal Son's elder brother.

11/17/67 Friday
Cloudy with snow and rain. Eby went to market. I baked pumpkin pies and got ready to go to Abram's but it looked like bad traveling so I stayed home and did the chores and cleaned the dining room. Called Abram's at 3:00 and he had just brought Pat home while I was talking to Grace. Nancy went up to school and home again and then to the play. Uncle Charlie came for things to take for Abram's and Grace.

11/23/67 Thursday
A damp, cloudy day. After doing the chores, cutting up the capons, making 5 pumpkin pies, 1 mince pie and 2 puddings, Eby and I went to Thanksgiving services

at Hershey's. Edgar's all went too. The others got things ready for dinner. All were here but Jim's, Milton's and Robert's. Uncle Charlie was here and took Charlie and Ray to the Coatesville depot. Sanford went to visit Dale's.

11/28/67 Tuesday
Cold and windy. After the morning work I cleaned some drawers and made blackberry mush. Helped Eby clean chicken house this afternoon. This evening I had an appointment with Dr. Beacher for a driver's physical. It was the first doctor's appointment I had since Nancy was born. Got a few things at the store. Kinzer's P.O. was robbed.

12/2/67 Saturday
Cold and partly cloudy. Nancy took her college boards at Conestoga this forenoon. She washed the car and babysat for Abner's this evening. Eby took some water to Meadville to flush the toilets till the pump is installed. I prepared some food and finished sweeping the attic. The Conestoga Bank in Lancaster at the Square burned this afternoon.

12/9/67 Saturday
Mild and cloudy. Nancy took Suzette and Missy along shopping to Lancaster. I mixed 4 kinds of cookies and finished the cleaning. Eby helped sort mail this morning. Joe Myers died of a heart attack. Maple Grove Church burned this evening. There is evidence of foul play.

12/11/67 Monday
Damp and rainy. Eby helped at the Post Office morning and evening. I stirred more cookies and Nancy baked the oatmeal cookies this evening. I put some window panes in the capon house sash. The Palmyra Electrolux agent delivered a sweeper from the children and grandchildren. We were stunned. It is very nice.

12/13/67 Wednesday
A fine warm sunny day. I trimmed the bush at the porch and raked some yard. Eby helped put the porch furniture in the garage. I did the eggs and scrubbed the egg room and cellar. Eby worked at the P.O. We did things up fast and got to the Christmas party at the Fire Hall by 7:00. Had a good supper. Nancy went to see "Gone With the Wind" in Philadelphia with the National Honor Society. Had as her first date James Brackbill. Took three hours to get ready.

12/15/67 Friday
Clear and colder. Eby worked at the P.O. till 9:00 and then went to market. I mixed up flap jacks and got a cocoanut ready. Did most of the cleaning. Elizabeth and Kim came and ate lunch with me while the butcher processed their deer. Nancy is having a party in the apartment and they have gone to a ball game at Pequea Valley. Made a plucket for Nancy's party.

12/17/67 Sunday
Fine cold day. We all went to Meadville. Harold Book preached on the axe that floated. I wrote letters and cards this p.m. Eby and Nancy slept. After helping with the work I met Sanford at the Lancaster depot. He waited inside and I waited outside for 45 minutes. One of us should have made a move sooner.

12/25/67 Monday
A real fine day and raining this evening. Eby did the chores alone and I got things ready for dinner. Had all the children but Edgar's, Jim's and three of Isaac's girls, who were sick. Ray and Mary Alice left for Edgar's about 3:30. They all went before supper but Charlie. Had a nice time together. Nancy started knitting this evening.

12/30/67 Saturday
A fine day. Dressed 3 capons. We finished up the cleaning. Eby went to an Amish sale near Coatesville. Sanford took car to the garage. Nancy folded Sanford's clothing and he packed. Nancy, Sanford and I went to Lancaster and bought her a coat for $29.00 at Adler's. Took Sanford to the depot to get the train to Harrisburg where he is going to Abram's.

12/31/67 Sunday
Cloudy and began snowing at 10:30 and is still snowing. Galen preached. His text was covetiousness. He has resigned. Spent the afternoon reading and resting. I called Esther and got a report on their trip to Kansas. Our gas water heater is not working. We have had a lot for which to be thankful in 1967.

1968

1/1/68 Monday
Have about 6 inches of snow. Clear and cold. I washed and ironed. Did the eggs. Mended a clothes pole. Cleaned Sanford's room. Eby shoveled snow and put more paddles on the stable cleaner. Nancy finished a dress and made over a skirt. I called Aunt Cora this evening. Had our sauer kraut for supper.

1/7/68 Sunday
Clear and cold. Snow is drifting. Put chains on and got to church without trouble. Services cancelled many places this evening. Nancy and I played Scribbage. Sue, Esther and Mabel called and we talked about an hour and a half. An accident near Harrisonburg, Va. killed 8 persons. Snow plows have been busy today. There has been another heart transplant.

1/11/68 Thursday
A pretty day. Temperature into low twenties. Eby carried mail. I did the chores. Nancy and I milked all but four cows. She put down ensilage again. I took Lawrence's a

crate of eggs. Sewed on my dress this afternoon. Popped corn and made some into a cake and caramelled some. Nancy borrowed Esther's typewriter this evening. Sold a capon. Kathleen saw a red light in the sky this evening.

1/15/68 Monday
Snowed this morning and was cloudy all day. Got up at 4:00, did the chores, and Eby helped kill and pick 16 capons before leaving for the Farm Show at 9:00. I did the capons, washed and hung it in the cellar. Washed the eggs. Nancy went with Phyllis Brown to sell ads for the yearbook. She and I did all the chores with Tommy's help. Sadie had a calf. Kathleen brought me a good sauer kraut dinner. Nancy's appetite is gone. Nancy has quilt fever.

1/26/68 Friday
A real nice cold day. Eby went to market late. Artificial inseminator came to breed a heifer and Dr. Bryer came to treat the new cow for giving bad milk. Nancy went back after school in the quest for a scholarship. Tommy came to help with the chores. I started the milking and did the eggs. Sorted some magazines.

1/31/68 Wednesday
Cloudy and mild. I left at 8:15 and stopped at Tom Denlinger's to see Andy on Romper Room. Picked Sue up at 9:00 and we helped quilt for Doris Moore at John Yost's. Eight of us Meadville women had it done by 1:00 and I stopped at Aaron Glick's to have a family record written. Nancy stayed after school and babysat for Leon's this evening. I made out my vegetable seed order. Had a hog butchered at Glick's.

2/1/68 Thursday
Cloudy all day and drizzling. I took Annis along to Sewing Circle. 14 there. Eby opened the new silo. Nancy went to Gap for nylons to wear to the Fashion Show at Dutch Town and Country this evening. She finished her dress to wear. I did the eggs, canned pork and sugar cured the meat.

2/24/68 Saturday
A fine day. Eby carried mail. I went for Benuel at 7:15 and took him home at 4:00. I made a jelly roll, sour cream cake, Lord Baltimore cake, and snow pudding. Nancy slept till 11:00 and took a nap this afternoon after being out late for 2 nights. Esther came up while Nancy and I were milking. Tommy helped.

3/1/68 Friday
Cleared cold and windy. No school because of snow. Eby carried mail. Nancy slept till 11:00. I did the cleaning. Nancy made cookies and a big supper. Mary Alice came at 1:00 after an interview near Philadelphia.

3/8/68 Friday
Fine mild day. Eby carried mail. I did the cleaning, scrubbed the porch and got things in shape for having the Meadville young people for a covered dish supper.

Eby and I took eggs to Coatesville and ate early. A cow laid on our nice big calf and smothered it.

3/19/68 Tuesday
A fine warm day. Eby carried mail. I finished cleaning the cellar. Did the eggs. Washed and it dried slowly. Sold Fad, our oldest cow. Mrs. Coy called and said Milton's had to postpone their trip because of Milton's jury duty. Nancy has been chosen to be an A.F.S. exchange student.

3/29/68 Friday
Nice warm day. 75 degrees. Eby carried mail. I took Nancy to Intercourse at 5:40 to go with Mrs. Hoover to meet the bus for Pittsburgh for an F.H.A. conference for three days. I cleaned the back yard and did most of the cleaning. Sanford came at noon. He had a dental appointment and did the milking this evening. Benuel was here all day hauling manure and harrowed the garden.

3/30/68 Saturday
A pleasant day. Eby carried mail. Sanford and I planted peas, onions, spinach and radishes. I did the eggs. Mended some of Sanford's clothing and washed for him. Mrs. Twigg called for Nancy to babysit, but she is in Pittsburgh. Grace called and said she is to go to the hospital at 11:00 a.m. tomorrow.

3/31/68 Sunday
A mild day with a shower. Sanford went with us to Meadville. We rested this p.m. Sanford left for Abram's at 4:00. Eby went to the depot for Nancy and the other girls. Robert called at 1:00 and said their baby girl was born at 1:18 A.M.

4/2/68 Tuesday
A fine day. Eby carried mail. I went for Benuel and he did the eggs and hauled manure. Nancy and I left at 9:00 for Lebanon Valley College to attend Mary Alice's induction into Phi Alpha Epsilon honor society. We went out for lunch to a good restaurant in Palmyra. At 1:00 we left for Uncle Landis' and stayed a short time. They are very busy with store, chicken house, dairy and jobs. Got home in time to start work.

4/3/68 Wednesday
A fine day. Eby carried mail. I gave Benuel some orientation. I did the eggs this a.m. Benuel is cleaning up the lane banks and gutter. Mended my old coat. Esther took me to the bus depot at 12:15 to come to Staunton, Virginia to help Grace with her new baby, Jennifer Ruth. Had a good trip, and Robert and Stevie met me at 11:00 p.m. in their new car.

4/4/68 Thursday
Partly cloudy. Stevie and I slept till 8:00. Robert brought Grace home from the hospital at 11:00. She stayed up till bedtime. The baby was good. I washed and

ironed and did some mending. Two of the neighbor ladies came in a short time. Martin Luther King was shot and died at 8:00 this evening.

4/5/68 Friday
A nice day with a shower this evening. Grace and the baby are good. Baby slept till 4:00 a.m. Washed and did some ironing. There is much disturbance with Martin Luther King's murder. Violence, lootings and burnings. Stevie likes the baby more each day.

4/8/68 Monday
Partly cloudy with showers. I washed, ironed and mended. Did the dishes and some brushing up. Called Aunt Katie Weaver. Saw some of the procedure for Martin Luther King's funeral and memorial marches on T.V. Wrote to the Shadid's. The baby is sleeping nearly all night.

4/9/68 Tuesday
Fine day. I cleaned up my room. Washed and ironed the bedding. Dusted and mopped and packed to go home. Had our lunch early and Robert and Stevie took me to the bus at 12:25. Had a good trip back with 2 bus changes. Eby met me in Lancaster at 9:15. Baltimore had a 7:00 curfew and everything was deserted and quiet.

4/19/68 Friday
A fine warm day. Eby carried mail. I cleaned the kitchen for weekly clean and mowed the yard. Dug the flower bed and planted the geraniums. I did the evening work alone till Eby came. Nancy came to the barn in shorts and refused to dress otherwise and did not help. Eby had a D.H.I.A. meeting here with the new tester.

4/24/68 Wednesday
A fine rainy day. Eby carried mail. I did some mending and did the eggs. Nancy went to a banquet at Millersville State. Abner, Esther and the children came with a swan cake, gold medal flower, detergent, calgon, mints, jelly eggs, saran wrap and mayonnaise for my birthday. We took Andy along to Meadville for preparatory service.

4/25/68 Thursday
Cold and windy. Eby carried mail. Andy and I went for Benuel and took him home. I cleaned the cupboards and did the eggs. Esther was up to see how I was celebrating my birthday. Nancy stayed after school for detention hall and then went to Art Rohrer's for Hi-C.

5/14/68 Tuesday
A fine day. Eby carried mail. I washed and ironed. Did the eggs. Planted some cabbage. Nancy stayed after school. Came home with Rene and got ready to go back for the Mother Daughter Tea. She took Suzette and Mrs. Hoover picked me up.

5/16/68 Thursday
A wet day, over an inch of rain. Eby carried mail. I cleaned the kitchen. Did the eggs. Nancy finished her pants dress and set her hair for Hi-C. She went bowling and to Ricky Martin's. Eby went to Meadville to help with painting the new doors. I sorted some magazines.

5/23/68 Thursday
A wet showery day. Eby carried mail. I tried to fix up the sugar peas. Put cows in the pasture for the first time. Picked asparagus. Nancy helped put the cows in the stable for milking. Nancy cut a yellow polka dot dress for herself.

5/28/68 Tuesday
A very wet day. Eby carried mail. I did up the chores and Nancy and I went to Lancaster. I bought a pair of special shoes and got Nancy a pair at Foot so Port for $28.00 and $11.95. Had parking problem and we both got very wet. Mary Alice came at 2:30 and Charlie at 6:30 to go to Nancy's graduation. She got a $25.00 award from New Holland Machine. She went to a class party at Dr. Crandall's.

6/2/68 Sunday
Had some showers in the A.M. and it got nice and warm. Rhoda helped me get things ready for our dinner at Abram's. We all left about 9:00 for Lebanon Valley College and Abram's. Mary Alice graduated. Dale's, Charlie, Ray, Fredric, Rosa, Sanford, Abram, Andy, David and Nancy attended. All were at Abram's for dinner but Robert's. We went to Meadville this evening for services.

6/5/68 Wednesday
A fine warm day. Eby carried mail. Hershey Kurtz cut one field of alfalfa. Horst worked on paving the lane. Nancy washed a small wash. I did the eggs. Doug sat in a basket and broke a lot. Milton and Barbara came about 4:00 and left the boys stay on till tomorrow. Nancy went driving with Linda King. Put the small heifers in the orchard. Robert Kennedy was shot.

6/6/68 Thursday
Fine warm day. Eby carried mail. Did the chores and filled up 7 baskets of potatoes for Dan Kurtz. Took Nancy to Pequea Valley and went for her. She picked strawberries and went to a baseball game at Paradise this evening. Milton's came and stayed for supper and took the boys to Coy's. I hoed the flower bed. Horst finished paving the lane. Kennedy died last night.

6/16/68 Sunday
Nice day with heavy rain this evening. We went to Meadville. Marvin Eshleman preached. His text was "Chariots." We went to Donald Hostetter's for dinner. All the Hostetter family was there but Ellis. Had a delicious dinner. Nancy rested and lay in the sun.

6/27/68 Thursday
Weather fine. Eby carried mail. I picked the currants, blueberries and raspberries. Cut a dress for myself to keep Nancy sewing. Charlie left for Abram's, then Dale's, then Jim's and on to South Dakota to serve his two years in the Public Health Service.

7/3/68 Wednesday
Damp and partly cloudy. Eby carried mail. Kim, Brian, Mike and I went to pick cherries at Elmer Beiler's. Canned 22 quarts by evening and 11 quarts of raspberries. Nancy got her A.F.S. letter with an invitation to go to Zurich, Switzerland.

7/6/68 Saturday
A fine day. Eby carried mail. Grace called at 9:00 and said she is ill and must go to the hospital by 10:30. I promised to help her. By evening Sanford promised to take me down for the children on Sunday. Worked to get things in order for my trip.

7/7/68 Sunday
A fine day. We got around early and went with Clarence's to Mt. Joy church and Menno's for dinner. Sanford came for me at 3:00 and took me to King's Daughter's Hospital in Staunton to see Grace. Her Dr. says she has an infection of the chest tissue. Went to Robert's for the night.

7/8/68 Monday
A fine day. We washed and packed things for the children. Talked to Grace twice and started for home at 12:25. Arrived home at 5:00. Had a good trip in Pat's air conditioned station wagon. Children did well.

7/24/68 Wednesday
A hot day with thunder showers this evening. Eby carried mail. I hoed some garden. Benuel and Harold were here and harrowed the garden, mowed some yard, cleaned the stable and bed the chickens. I made snow pudding, chocolate syrup, a spice chiffon, meat loaf and new corn. Had two Vietnamese army officers for supper. Eby took them along to Bible School. Joe painted. Race riots in Cleveland killed ten.

7/26/68 Friday
A fine day. Eby carried mail. I canned 14 quarts of bean. Did the eggs. Hoed celery and strawberries. Joe painted and Benuel mowed some yard after supper. I gave the chickens oyster shells. Grace wrote that she is feeling better. Eby took eggs to market. Had a pain in my neck.

8/3/68 Saturday
A warm day. Eby carried mail. I did the scrubbing, eggs, and mowed some of Benuel's skippers. Worked on my dress and ripped some of Nancy's mistakes. Cyrus Reed was here to ask if we would let them wash our eggs for a half cent per dozen. Our new D.H.I.A. tester was here this evening. Tommy helped me get the cows in. Eby washed the car.

8/9/68 Friday

Fine day. Eby carried mail. I was busy with cleaning and mowing and getting things ready for company. Cooked chicken. Took a bath and Larry Twigg called at 10:00 and said their 5th boy was born at home and they want me to come and stay till Mother Lee can come. Eby objected to my going.

8/10/68 Saturday

Nice day. Eby carried the mail. I hurried the chores and left for Twigg's at 7:45 to stay with Beverly and the new baby till her mother came from Waverly. Had to miss the Martin reunion for the first time. Robert's got here about 3:30. I went to Beiler's for peaches.

8/14/68 Wednesday

Warm day with some showers. Eby carried mail. I washed, did the eggs, picked pickles and made root beer. Benuel could not help with work so Nancy and I did it. We got lunch ready and went to Paradise Park by 6:30 for our supper. Abram and Sanford brought chicken delight. A party was held for Nancy, the new A.F.S. student from Argentina, officers and families. I ironed when we came home.

8/15/68 Thursday

A fine day. Eby carried mail. I took Nancy to do her final shopping in Lancaster. I helped Benuel to milk. Linda King came for Nancy at 7:15 to take her to Paradise Park for a surprise farewell party. A good number came out. I made a milk can of punch and took five gallons of root beer. The band was so loud that we came home at 9:30.

8/18/68 Sunday

A nice warm day. We all went to Meadville. Willis Kling preached. Text was Judgment. We took Nancy to the 3:10 train in Lancaster and Milton will meet her in New York City. Esther brought us some sandwiches and potato salad for supper. I read this evening.

8/21/68 Wednesday

A fine warm day. We did our chores and packed up to leave for Stony Brook to spend a few days with Milton's. Got here about 3:00 and Mary Alice drove all the way. Barbara went to work at 3:30. Nancy called this evening and seems to be enjoying her orientation. We played croquet with Mike's new set.

8/23/68 Friday

A fine day, cooler and partly cloudy. Milton's got started on their way to Lancaster County about 10:00. I made an apple pie, dumplings for supper and some apple sauce. Mary Alice worked on her scrap book and read. Daddy and I took a drive this afternoon. There is war in Czechoslovakia. Listened to some records and wrote some letters.

8/24/68 Saturday
Partly cloudy. I cleaned up the house. Mary Alice slept late. Eby got the car filled with gas and went to a sale nearby. Mr. Gillette drove us to Kennedy Airport to see Nancy off to Switzerland. Left at 3:15 and returned at 7:45. Traffic was not too bad. Made late supper and read for a while.

8/25/68 Sunday
A warm day. We left Milton's at 8:00 and got home by 12:00. Mary Alice drove all the way. She left at 1:30 for the Layser's in Myerstown. We slept and read. Yesterday afternoon there was a violent storm here with wind and rain. Two barns in the county were struck and burned.

8/26/68 Monday
Much cooler and pleasant. Eby mowed alfalfa. I got up at 3:00 because I could not sleep. Did the washing and washed the eggs till time to milk. Canned 20 quarts of tomato juice by lunch time. Eby and I each picked a basket of limas. Esther and the children helped shell them. Eby went to a meeting at the Farm and Home Building. Kinzer siren blew.

8/29/68 Thursday
A fine cool day. I canned ten quarts of peaches. Did the eggs. Eby mowed the yard and cut off the sweet corn in the garden. Had a card from Nancy and she is fine in Switzerland. I trimmed and raked some yard this evening. Esther came for noodles and pickles.

8/31/68 Saturday
A very fine sunny day. We did the chores. I made buns and Rhoda helped get things ready for our dinner. Made chicken and other foods for Edgar's, Isaac's, Dale's, Sanford, Mary Alice and Abram's three oldest children. Eby and Isaac went for Ray after dinner, and he stayed till the 5:00 bus. Edgar's and Mary Alice went to see "Strangers at the Mill." Milton's took us to see it this evening after they all insisted and persuaded us to go. Mary Alice moved her things in our truck.

9/4/68 Wednesday
Nice day, warmer. I washed and did most of the ironing. Did three days eggs. There was an earthquake in Iran that killed 8000 persons and injured many. Miss Kramer called and offered a student teacher. She moved in after school. I got Sanford's room ready for her. Judy Martin helped her move from Mrs. Pownall's. Her house had too many cats. We went to mid-week.

9/15/68 Sunday
A very fine day. We went to Meadville. Amos Weaver preached. The text was Romans 8:1. Mary Alice came for dinner. Her friend Lois Weil came for supper and Jean

ate with us too. Eby read and slept. A new cow had a deformed bull calf. The girls helped bring it from the pasture.

9/19/68 Thursday
Fine weather. I cleaned more of the garden and helped Eby fix the garden tractor. He helped John Eby cut tobacco this afternoon. I washed a crate of eggs and took them to Lawrence's and went to Eshleman's for nylons for Nancy. Packed Nancy's boots and some nylons with a cookbook for mailing to her in Switzerland.

9/21/68 Saturday
A fine warm day. We overslept because the clock was not wound. I scrubbed the porch and made 2 cakes and gathered the eggs. Eby cleaned the stable. I cut his hair. This afternoon Jay Martin's took us to New Bolton Center and Ray showed us all around the place. Mary Alice called and said she may come home tomorrow and she is going to the annual picnic at New Bolton Center this evening.

10/1/68 Tuesday
A fine day. Eby is not feeling well. He laid down this p.m. I did the eggs and finished the ironing. I made 8 quarts of apple juice. Helped with chores. Esther came up this evening to tell me a ditch had caved in on Abner today.

10/2/68 Wednesday
A fine warm day. Eby is feeling better and the sick cow is eating a little. Dr. Breyer made his 3rd visit. I made sandwich spread and 7 quarts of chow chow. Dressed the first capon. Abner is fine and went to work at 6:00 a.m. Got first letter from Sanford.

10/5/68 Saturday
A fine day with light frost. I canned 15 quarts of applesauce and we left at 11:30 for Kitchen Kettle where we joined the A.F.S. group and had a free lunch. We went to the community sale for a while and then came home. I planted some flower slips and we did our work early and then went to the Amos Stoltzfus farm where we had our dinner with the A.F.S. group, about 25 in all. Mary Alice called about 9:30 and gave an account of her day on the Chester County tour.

10/14/68 Monday
A damp foggy day. I washed and hung it out but it did not get dry. Benuel came at noon to help clean the top chicken house. Eby was feeling quite miserable today. He ate no supper. Menno and Amy and Gary Jones and Eunice came with their new baby Amy for a little while. Eby went to bed early after we tried home remedies. I wrote to Nancy.

10/15/68 Tuesday
Cloudy all day and cleared up this evening. I ironed and did the eggs and the milking by myself this evening. Eby was not able to be up all day. Dr. Beacher came and

said he has pyelitis. Joe Bechtold came and got the stable ready for white washing. I took Jean to Gap for her car and brought her home again. Abram called from Miami, Florida.

10/16/68 Wednesday
Clear. Larry Twigg helped to milk this morning and Tommy and Benuel did it this evening. I did the eggs and cared for Eby this A.M. Dr. Beacher came at 1:00 and advised that he go to the hospital. The ambulance came and took him in and I drove in and stayed till 6:45. He seemed to be resting a little better. Mary Alice came at 5:00. I called Rhoda, Isaac's, Grace and Milton's. I feel very much alone.

10/17/68 Thursday
Clear and warm. I called Jim's and Dale's to tell them about Daddy. Had quite a few calls. Larry milked morning and evening. Tommy helped this evening. I left at 1:15 for the hospital. Eby was feeling very sick. He ate a little ice cream for lunch. Made supper for Jean and me. I slept very little last night. Eby had Xrays this morning.

10/19/68 Saturday
Showery and cleared this evening. I did up the eggs. Had calls from John Eby, Galen, Abram, Mary Alice, Mabel and Aunt Cora. Esther and Kathleen were here. I sent a letter to Nancy. Sanford came this forenoon and took me to see Daddy. Ray came up on the train this evening. Dale and Linda were in for a wedding and came for the night. Eby's kidneys seem better but his breathing is not so good. My heart is so heavy.

10/22/68 Tuesday
Fine day. Joe Bechtold, Isaac, Clarence and Hershey Kurtz picked the corn. Esther helped get dinner for them. I did some ironing. Mary Alice came for supper and took me in to see Daddy. Joanne and Linda were there too. He is feeling real good and has no pain. Abram's were in to see him. I made some checks ready to pay bills. Charlie called.

10/30/68 Wednesday
Had a white frost. Mabel came over and we cleaned the dining room windows and gave it a good sweeping. Put on the storm doors in the kitchen and did the eggs. Jay Hostetter took me along to the hospital to bring Eby home. He feels real good and ate a hearty supper of rabbit that Tommy Denlinger shot. The children were trick or treating. Mary Alice came for supper. Jean was not here.

11/1/68 Friday
Fine mild day. I did all the eggs. Saw some signs of rats in the egg room. Galen and Sue came this p.m. I worked on Jean's room, patched plaster and paper. Called vet for a heifer that was freshening this morning. Eby still has some pain in his one leg. Rhoda called this evening and Abram too. Clifford sold his trailer to Fox and they rented our trailer park.

11/3/68 Sunday

Cloudy and mild with showers. Ray milked morning and evening. I missed church for the third Sunday. Landis' and Paul's were here. Mary Alice came at 4:00 and took Ray back to Philadelphia after supper. Eby got a weak spell this evening. Clair and Annis came this evening.

11/6/68 Wednesday

A cloudy day. Joe was here till noon. Paul visited Eby this forenoon and Richard Patterson's this afternoon. Called Dr. Beacher about Eby's leg. He said it is a blood clot and sent him to the hospital in the ambulance about 3:30. Clair and Annis took me in this evening. He must hold his leg very still. Benuel Glick and his friends demolished his car on the way home from Indiana. I wrote to Nancy and washed some of Eby's things this evening.

11/7/68 Thursday

Cloudy and showery. Did up the chores and eggs. Cleaned up the big bedroom. Ironed Eby's things to take to the hospital. Esther came up and brought me supper. I went to Glick's to pick up Nancy's family record and on in to the hospital to see Eby. He feels good. Abram was in a couple hours this morning. I wrote to Sanford and took a bank deposit down. Abram called and said he called Rhoda, Grace, Jim's, Milton's, Dale's and Sanford. Charlie called him last evening. Eby Hershey was here to ask about buying the cows.

11/8/68 Friday

Cleared colder. I did most of the cleaning. Esther took me in to see Eby. He is about the same. He had a pain in his leg at noon. Benuel helped milk this evening. I did the eggs. Diane went home. Mary Alice called. I am all alone tonight.

11/15/68 Friday

Cloudy and damp. Joe was here. I took out some of the celery, carrots, beets, turnips and put some in a hole. Grace got my brown dress almost done. Grace and Mary Alice cleaned. They started for the hospital but had car trouble and came back. Isaac came with a badly cut hand from a nose hook for a heifer. Uncle Charlie took Grace and I to the hospital this evening. Mary Alice had Kramer's fix her car. Larry milked.

11/17/68 Sunday

Cloudy, damp and mild. I did up the chores and took a nap. Mary Alice met Ray and his girlfriend at the depot. It was our first meeting with her. After dinner Ray, Jane and I went to the hospital and Mary Alice did the dishes. I stayed till evening when Jay and Sue brought me home. Ray helped with the work and Mary Alice took them back to Philadelphia.

11/19/68 Tuesday
Had some sunshine today and a little snow this evening. Joe was here. I did the ironing and Esther came at 12:15 to take me in to bring Eby home. He is feeling real good. Marty Martin's came and Larry and the boys stopped in a few minutes. The mechanic was here to fix the stable cleaner.

11/22/68 Friday
Real nice day. Joe was here. I cleaned and scrubbed the porch and washed the car. Scrubbed the kitchen and waxed it. Eby's leg was swollen so I called the doctor and took him down this evening. He is to keep it up and have more bandage. Milton called and I had a letter from Nancy.

12/4/68 Wednesday
Cloudy and raining some. Joe was here. Benuel helped milk this morning and I did it this evening. Eby carried some of the milk. Dressed five capons. Wrote to Charlie and he called this evening. Tom Denlinger got a deer. Eby had a jittery spell this forenoon.

12/7/68 Saturday
A fine cold day. I finished the cleaning, did the eggs. Joe was here. Levi Stoltzfus was here to talk about renting the farm. Had 2 capon buyers. Eby and I did the milking.

12/8/68 Sunday
A fine day, colder. Eby and I went to church. Mary Alice came for a capon dinner. Abram's, Isaac's and Robert Neff's were here this afternoon. Tommy helped with the chores. Eby talked to the boys about buying Horst's house and renting the farm.

12/9/68 Monday
Clear and cold. Some chicken water frozen. Larry milked this morning and Eby and I this evening. I did the eggs and washed. Eby went to the bank and doctor. He did not need his blood checked this week. We looked at the Horst house this afternoon. Joe was here and the stable cleaner broke. I wrote to Nancy.

12/14/68 Saturday
A wet mild day. Joe was here till noon and Larry was here before I was up. I did five capons. Stirred more cookies and baked some. Did some cleaning. Isaac, Karen and Kim came this afternoon. Levi Stoltzfus called to say that he will farm for us. Eby called Ella Horst to say that we will take her house.

12/16/68 Monday
Very cold and windy. Joe was here. Uncle Charlie took Eby to Lancaster for blood work. I did five capons and the eggs. Levi Stoltzfus and his family came to make a bargain for farming for us. Esther came up with a sob story and stirred up my emotions. Addressed some cards again this evening.

12/18/68 Wednesday
A fine day. Larry milked and I paid him. Joe was here. I baked a lot of cookies and Eby put the icing on a lot of them. Eby made a down payment on the Horst house. We showed Diane some pictures and talked this evening. Called Dale.

12/24/68 Tuesday
Cold and windy. Joe was here and took capon signs down. All orders were filled and we turned some away. Eby helped clean up and I roasted 3 capons, washed and waxed the kitchen. Eby helped set the table. Dale and Linda came in time for supper. We had a nice visit this evening. Linda knit a sweater for Dale and I peeled the sweet potatoes and oranges.

12/25/68 Wednesday
Nice cold day. We did up the work and got things ready for dinner. Because the trains were not dependable, Eby got Abner to drive to Philadelphia for Ray and Jane. Abram's, Isaac's and Sanford were here for dinner. We recorded a tape for Nancy. David came out with the chicken pox. I wrote to Grace this evening. Charlie called. I gave Daddy a Bible.

12/26/68 Thursday
Real nice cold day. Clouded this evening. Joe was here. Eby took Sanford to the hospital for his knee surgery and tooth extraction. Jim's came for dinner and left at 3:45. Had a nice visit. Tommy helped and Eby and I are doing the milking. Got a package from Nancy. Seems like candy. Spent a quiet evening. Eby took a bank deposit down.

12/28/68 Saturday
Foggy, damp and rained. Cleared this evening. Joe was here. Eby did the eggs. I worked on my dress that Grace did when she was here. We went in to the hospital to see Sanford this afternoon. He is resting comfortably. Tommy did the chores. Glen Hershey bought the cows for $575. each. The three space men came safely back from the moon. Plane crash in Chicago killed 30 persons.

1969

1/1/69 Wednesday
Very cold and windy. Joe came till 10:00. Eby did the eggs. I made a sauer kraut dinner. Ray, Jane and Mary Alice came from Abram's about 12:15. Sanford is getting better. I played Probe with him this evening. Mary Alice left at 4:30 for her room in Berwyn. Ray and Jane ate early and went to Isaac's.

1/2/69 Thursday
A bit warmer and not so windy. I wrote to Dale's. Ray, Jane and Sanford slept late. Eby did the eggs. Joe was here till 10:00. Had early dinner and Ray and Jane went on a shopping tour. Ray bought three chairs. I made a chicken pie for supper. Ray took Jane to the Coatesville depot after supper. Eby, Diane and I played Scribbage and Probe.

1/3/69 Friday
Partly cloudy and warmer. Uncle Charlie brought Sanford some nuts and was here for dinner and took Sanford to Dr. Lancaster for a knee checkup this afternoon. Ray got our cane seated rocker repaired. Esther brought Sanford a $3.00 gift. I dusted and Eby did the sweeping. Ray did the milking this evening. I got the capon fat ready. No letter from Nancy for 2 weeks.

1/6/69 Monday
A good wash day. It started snowing this evening. I did the ironing and some eggs. Eby went to Dr. Beacher and to the hospital for a blood check. He went to Meadville to help fix the oil burner this P.M. Joe was here and Tommy this evening. Had a letter from Nancy. She had been sick with sore throat, earache and headache.

1/12/69 Sunday
A beautiful cold day. Diane stayed in bed and we went to Meadville. Just as we were starting for a drive to show Diane the County, Frank and Emma came so we took them along. They stayed here a short while. Ray called and announced his engagement to Jane. Wrote to Nancy. Mary Alice visited Ray and Jane and I talked to her when they called.

1/18/69 Saturday
Cloudy and damp with rain. Joe was here till 2:00. Eby did the eggs. I made 2 rice krispie cakes. Linda and Dale came for supper and overnight. Charlie called. He was cooking trype and has made plans for two weeks in Nicaragua.

1/20/69 Monday
Mild with increasing cloudiness. Joe was here. I washed and ironed. Eby took eggs to Viola and a package to the P.O. for Nancy. It was rice krispie cake. He went to Dr. Beacher for a check up. I read this evening. Nixon was inaugurated president.

1/23/69 Thursday
Cloudy with some rain. I worked on the attic this forenoon. Eby did the eggs. Jay was here for eggs. Eby helped get two gallons of vinegar from the barrel. I pickled the trype. Carolyn, the new student teacher, came out to the stable. Eby had a spell while we were milking. I wrote to Emma Horning.

2/3/69 Monday

Rained, damp and cleared this evening. Joe and Robin came and left before dinner. I washed this afternoon. Hung it in the cellar. Mary Alice called and said she broke a bone in her foot getting out of bed to answer the phone.

2/9/69 Sunday

Snowing and covered over about 3 inches. Cleared this evening. Got things ready for dinner and went to Meadville. Amos preached on the evils of our day. Isaac Metzler's, Maurice Hershey's, Granville Clark's, Clarence's, Mart and Miriam were here for dinner. Had a nice time visiting. Carolyn came at 5:30. New York had 15 inches of snow and is tied up the worst in years. 6000 persons at the airport.

2/15/69 Saturday

Clear and cold. Joe was here. Eby Hershey came for one calf. I roasted the meat and got things ready for Sunday dinner. Finished the cleaning. Eby took eggs to Lawrence's. He did the eggs. I made buns. Ray, Jane and Mary Alice came for supper about 7:15. Ray has a cold and Mary Alice is wearing a cast.

2/21/69 Friday

A fine mild day. Joe was here. The Clemens children helped carry things from the attic. Rhoda did some supervising. Edgar kept the trash fire going. Eby and Edgar took some things to Harry's Auction and a load of junk to the dump. Had a letter from A.F.S. that Nancy has been moved.

2/28/69 Friday

A mild day. Joe and Robin were here till 11:15. Eby helped with cleaning and went with Jay to Green Dragon and bought a load of straw. I worked on the jars and garage and trunk in the attic. Had a second letter from A.F.S. saying that Nancy has been moved with another family because of unsatisfactory relations at Hans Greuter's.

3/1/69 Saturday

Cloudy and began snowing this evening. Eby went to the store. I made a dessert and a cake. Washed up the kitchen and the porch. Ray, Jane and Mary Alice came about 4:30 and went to Tom Denlinger's this evening. We put a heifer in the stable. Mary Alice tried to assure me that Nancy would be cared for.

3/4/69 Tuesday

A fine day. Isaac came and helped get the woodhouse ready to cement and clean out the wash house. Eby took a load of junk to the dump. They loaded Abner's truck with wood from the wash house. I cleaned the cave and worked on the cellar and jars. Worked on my dress and wrote to Rhoda. Sold the tractor for $850.00.

3/5/69 Wednesday

A fine sunny cool day. Joe cut down a picture frame for our family record and I varnished it. Made mince and cherry pies, a jelly roll, tapioca and noodles. No word from Nancy, so I called A.F.S. in New York City and they think she is all right. Eby went to the garage and the hardware store.

3/6/69 Thursday
Fine, mild day. Joe and Robin were here. Isaac and Kim came to help cement the woodhouse for Levi's horse. Isaac helped Daddy to clean out some corners. I had to stick around with the little girls and did some drawers and corners. We had a letter from Nancy. She is happy with her new family and we feel better. Had Dr. Breyer to treat Tillie for mastitis. Carolyn left for the weekend.

3/8/69 Saturday
Real nice day. Eby did the eggs and went to the store. I cleaned up the kitchen and made a rice pudding. Invited Uncle Charlie for Sunday dinner. Charles Crawford and his wife Nancy brought Mary Alice and after being here for a while they went to Annie Newhauser's sale. Came here to see us milk and then went to Plain and Fancy for supper and back here for a while.

3/10/69 Monday
Clear, cold and windy. I washed and ironed. Eby did the eggs and got his income taxes all ready. A colored man was stabbed to death in Lancaster in a fight. We went down to Horst's and Ella promised to let us move in March 31.

3/12/69 Wednesday
Clear and not so cold. Eby had an appointment with Dr. Beacher and is discharged. Is overweight at 214 lbs. I made 3 chicken pies. Went with Mabel, Mildred, Sue and Pauline to Uncle Milt's for our annual visit. Had a big letter from Nancy.

3/13/69 Thursday
Fine day. Eby painted a milk can for a mailbox and a little trough. I made Spanish cream and crumb pies. Eby took the truck for inspection and did the eggs. I bagged and sorted rags. I sorted Dale's school box this evening. Abram called and said he has accepted job at Phil Haven.

3/14/69 Friday
Fine day. Truck came for 300 bales of hay. I dusted and Eby swept. I scoured the outside of the copper kettle. Esther came up this evening. Eby started for the Fisher sale and was struck by a car and then spent the evening with accident procedures. Space men came back to earth safely. We got a pretty Swiss calendar from Nancy.

3/28/69 Friday
A nice day. Joe came this afternoon. Uncle Charlie came and helped clean windows and woodwork. I packed all the dishes from the dining room. Esther came up. President Eisenhower died. Mary Alice came this evening all ready to help.

3/30/69 Sunday

Cold with some snow flurries. Mary Alice went along with us to Meadville communion. Ray and Jane went to Paradise where Myron Augsburger preached. We saw some of Eisenhower's funeral on Mary Alice's television. Ray and Jane took some pictures of the farm and Mary Alice dropped them off at the Coatesville depot.

3/31/69 Monday

Clear and cold. Joe came all day. Isaac's, Jim's, Milton's, Uncle Jay and Charlie, Mary Alice and Esther helped us to move to our new home in Gap. Mary Alice took food to Tom Denlinger's and she and Aunt Mary served us in elegant style. Everyone worked with willing heart and hands and much was accomplished. Milton helped milk in my place and I got supper ready.

4/1/69 Tuesday

Clear cold day. Had a poor night. We slept in an empty farm house and did the milking this morning. The cows went this forenoon. Isaac, Uncle Charlie, Milton and Daddy helped load them. The Amish folks started coming about 7:15 and it gave a big crowd. Milton, Uncle Charlie and Isaac helped here to get things in order. Also Mary Alice, Barbara and the boys.

4/2/69 Wednesday

Cloudy and rained. Eby went to the bank, Keen's and the dump. Mary Alice went to Paoli for some clothing. We moved the drapes to the bedroom and put up some curtains. I made some pies and pudding. Found places for things. Eby and I went to midweek service.

4/7/69 Monday

Nice sunny day. Eby started on his new job at Keen's. I washed and ironed. Uncle Milt's and Helen stopped in this afternoon a short time. Mary Alice got here with Grace and the children about 4:00. She then went to Coatesville for Ray.

4/11/69 Friday

Clear and colder. I made buns. Uncle Charlie came this forenoon for a visit. Edgar and the boys played ball and he planted 25 asparagus roots this afternoon. Edgar's left for Souderton about 7:00. Had first letter from Nancy in three weeks. Ray and Jane called to invite us to Perkasie. Grace bathed her children. Eby went to the bank, for gas and to Abner's to order dirt.

4/15/69 Tuesday

Partly cloudy. I wrote to Landis' and to Dale's. Sent for my license. Cleaned the windows upstairs and swept the floor. Varnished the back door and the front doorstep. Felt lonely. A plane to Cuba was hijacked. We went down to Isaac's this evening. They were busy milking, sewing, discing and washing dishes.

4/21/69 Monday
Clear, cool day. I washed and ironed. Put a second coat of varnish on door and sill. Raked up some of the grass and cleaned the flower bed across the drive. Eby harrowed the garden this evening and I uncovered some of my plants. He went for milk. I wrote a big letter to Nancy. Saw a big flock of wild geese.

4/23/69 Wednesday
Partly cloudy, cool and showery. I left at 10:00 for Lancaster and got the curtains exchanged for longer ones. Visited Aunt Cora the rest of the day. Was shocked to hear of Mrs. Twigg's death when the tractor upset on her. We went down to offer our help and share our sympathy.

4/24/69 Thursday
Cool and partly cloudy. Esther went with me to Twigg's to bring the baby here. Larry and the others went to Bradford County. Little Dennis was real good. Larry called this evening to ask how he is doing. Dan Kurtz came to pay for the iron.

4/25/69 Friday
Fine clear day. I did baby wash. Esther came and brought me birthday gifts, sugar, ice cream, foil, napkins, nuts, $3.00 and a card. Charlie sent flowers. Got nine cards. Kathleen brought a suit for Dennis. We took him up to Esther at 9:00 all ready for bed. I mowed the back yard and Eby did the front and washed the car. Had an appointment with Dr. Beacher for myself.

4/26/69 Saturday
We started at 7:00 from Jay Martin's with Uncle Charlie driving our car to Athens for Beverly Twigg's funeral. Arrived at 12:15 and attended the service from the funeral home and the burial. Then we went to Larry's home for a snack and short visit before leaving for Edgar's and arriving by 5:30 for supper.

4/27/69 Sunday
A fine day, warmer. Uncle Charlie could not find his way back from the motel, and it made us a bit late for Sunday School at Bethel Grove. Had a good turkey dinner and a relaxing visit with Edgar's. Left for home at 4:00 and arrived safely at 8:45. Uncle Charlie did all the driving. Called Esther and she is having some problems with little Dennis.

4/28/69 Monday
Fine day, warm. I washed, ironed and mended. Esther brought the baby at 11:00. He slept all afternoon. I made a lemon pie. Eby harrowed the garden and planted cabbage, lettuce and peppers.

4/29/69 Tuesday
Partly cloudy. Did the baby wash. Planted some corn and beans. Pulled weeds. The baby was real good. Esther took LeVon to the doctor for his ears and stopped a while.

She took a package to the P.O. for me for Nancy's host family. Larry came for the baby at 8:30. Seems like a lot missing.

5/11/69 Sunday
Cool and partly cloudy. We went to Meadville. Ray and Mary Alice came for dinner. We all went up to Abram's for supper. They are all well. They are considering selling their house and buying something closer to Phil Haven. Got home by 9:00. Aldous Burkholder is having heart trouble.

5/21/69 Wednesday
Clear and cooler. Ray went to look for work in New Jersey. I washed his clothing and ironed them. Naomi Beiler brought my Stanley things. Kathleen brought the rug she is making to show me. The astronauts are circling the moon in Apollo 10. We had a letter from Sanford and I wrote to him. Eby harrowed the garden and I hoed it.

5/23/69 Friday
Partly cloudy and cool. I dusted the house till the boys got up. Galen stopped in to see Charlie. Charlie went for tuxedoes for the wedding and I went along and ordered a bra from Mrs. Swarr and got Eby a white shirt. Charlie and Gary did some shopping and sightseeing. Ray got his things ready for going. I swept and washed and got things ready for the Weaver's.

5/24/69 Saturday
Partly cloudy all day. We had early dinner. Everyone got off to Ray's wedding by 12:45. Isaac's came here and drove our car to Perkasie to St. Andrew's Lutheran Church where Ray and Jane were married at 3:00. Had reception at the church and went to Jane's home afterward. All our family were there except Sanford, Nancy, Joanne, Linda and Kim. Ray and Jane went to Virginia for their honeymoon.

6/6/69 Friday
Partly cloudy and had a gust and heavy rain this evening. I went up to Levi's and picked 24 boxes of strawberries. Made jam and put some in freezer. Eby went to the Samaritan Home this evening. Isaac and Elizabeth and Karen and Kim came to spend the evening. A plane crashed, killing 76 persons. Birds are after the peas. We have them covered with muslin.

6/11/69 Wednesday
Partly cloudy. Ray and Jane left at 6:30 so he could take some tests in Philadelphia. Jay and Sue came for us at 7:30 and we started on our trip to South Dakota. Came as far as Bremen, Indiana and we are staying at the Knotty Pine Motel. We stopped real often and had a good trip.

6/13/69 Friday
Clear this morning when we left Midway Motel. We drove through rain and snow and stopped often at rest areas and arrived here in Wanblee, South Dakota about

3:00. Saw the clinic and Charlie took us for a drive this evening. He made us a good roast chicken supper. John and Judy Blackfeather came to call this evening. Got some cards ready for mailing.

6/14/69 Saturday
A beautiful day. Frosty with snow on the high places. We saw much of the Badlands, Wounded Knee Memorial, Mt. Rushmore, Gold Mine, Marine Land and stopped at an Indian Dance at the Wounded Knee Museum. Ate at the Mt. Rushmore Cafeteria and at a restaurant where we got Kentucky fried chicken. Stopped at a shopping center for food and got back to Wanblee about 11:00. Took a lot of slides.

6/15/69 Sunday
A fine cool day. Charlie was called from breakfast when a girl was bitten by a snake and then for a sick baby. After lunch we started for the National Bad Lands Monument. It was just so terrific and majestic. Some Indian boys came to visit and three stayed for lunch. We had a late lunch. Ralph Barr, the school teacher, and his wife came to use the phone.

6/17/69 Tuesday
Beautiful day. Spent this day in Yellowstone and Teton National Parks. Saw the Grand Canyon Lake, gorges, falls, geysers and Old Faithful erupted two times while we were there. Sue did not feel good for a while this afternoon and Eby did not feel good this a.m. We are in a motel in Dubois this evening.

6/18/69 Wednesday
Fine weather. Left Dubois and started for Boulder across Wyoming. Arrived at Daniel Hess' about 6:30 and had a nice visit with Dan, Jane, Stevie and Jimmie. They took us for a drive high up on the Boulder Mountain and we saw some climbers in action climbing and repelling. Came back to our Lazy J Motel after Dan showed us his moving pictures. We have two rooms with a shared bath for $20.00.

6/19/69 Thursday
Fine day. We left Boulder about 8:00 and drove to Meade after eating dinner at Garden City where the restaurant lady told us she knew the Friesen's. We got to Esther's home about 6:00 and visited late. They are in wheat harvest.

6/20/69 Friday
A fine day. Had a good day at the Friesen's and they took us for a drive through Meade and the country. Jay and Sue drove the truck and we all went to the wheat field where Eby drove a couple rounds on the huge combine and I went along. Jay and Sue rode on a second one while they gleaned about 1000 bushels. Ate dinner on the road. We left for Inman where we are spending the night with Wilbur's. We seeded cherries after they took us for a drive through Inman.

6/22/69 Sunday
Cloudy with some sunshine and rain. Left our motel to look for the little church near Potosi. Did not know where to look so we attended service at a Baptist Church. Asked for Harry Nichols and one of his neighbors asked us to follow him home from church to the Nichols home which was a rare place of interest, a beautiful garden and orchard with fruit, berries, pretty yard, chickens and a hearty welcome. Ate a bite and found Floyd Sutterfield's. They served us a barbecue and entertained us royally. Took us to St. Louis and we went up in the Gateway to the West. Left in a pouring rain and are in a motel in Greenville, Illinois.

6/24/69 Tuesday
Clear and pleasant but got warmer as we neared home. Left our motel about 8:30 and started for home. Jay drove real fast and we stopped off to see Frank Kreider. He is able to be around and manage again. Got home about 3:30. Ray and Jane are here and she had beans ready for supper.

7/9/69 Wednesday
I washed more sheets and bed spreads. Canned some pickles. Cleaned up and made up the beds. Made raspberry and blueberry pies. Wrote to Nancy. Abram's came for supper and brought Fredric along. Becky and Sammy are staying here while they go west to see Charlie and relatives.

7/15/69 Tuesday
Fine day. The children are doing well. Abram called this forenoon from Rapid City. They are traveling with Charlie and seeing a lot. Becky and Sammy talked to them. They have bought a farm east of Campbelltown. Picked some blueberries. Did six quarts of beets. Went to Bible School.

7/17/69 Thursday
Very hot and humid. I did 4 quarts of pickles. Washed and did the beds. Picked 2 quarts of blueberries. Becky, Sammy and I went to see Uncle Milt's. We helped pick off some green beans. Stopped at IGA Store and came home early and put the children to bed after they had a shower. Nancy is to arrive at New York at 8:15. Ray and Mary Alice are meeting her.

7/18/69 Friday
A hot day with heavy gust and lots of rain in some places this evening. I did the cleaning and washed some things for the children. Mary Alice brought Nancy home about 4:00. She was detained at the airport and did not land until 3:30 a.m. Made a pie. Went to Bible School. Nancy talked and stayed up late even though she was tired. She looks the same.

7/19/69 Saturday

Not so warm. Mary Alice washed the car. Nancy slept late. I made a pudding and did some pickles. Ray and Jane came this afternoon for a class reunion at Dutch Town and Country. They helped us pick some blueberries. Nancy showed us a lot of her slides. They are real good.

7/20/69 Sunday

Showery and damp. Ray and Jane went to her family reunion. Mary Alice and Nancy went with us to Meadville. Mary Alice brought her T.V. and we watched the men land on the moon till midnight. I showed Nancy our slides. Charlie called. Senator Kennedy had a car accident and his passenger was drowned.

7/24/69 Thursday

Cloudy and cool. The children slept late. We went to Harry Good's and bought a Sunbeam Mixer for $29.95 and two dresses for Nancy. She cut one out and started it this evening. I picked blueberries and pickles. Had corn on the cob for supper. Went to Bible School and we had 13 in the nursery. Dale called this evening. Moon men landed safely.

7/28/69 Monday

A very wet day, over two inches of rain. I picked the pickles and did 5 quarts. Nancy packed up and we met Mary Alice at Exton. They then went on to meet Nancy's Swiss girlfriend at the airport at 6:15. The highway was flooded in some places. Had a safe trip. Minnie called and Larry Twigg. Pete Brown called for Nancy. No word from Sanford.

7/29/69 Tuesday

Cloudy with some showers. I washed and got the children's things all packed up. Put the oven on to dry some. Made vegetable soup and tapioca pudding. Abram's came at 5:30 from their trip and after supper they took Becky and Sammy home. Had four tourists upstairs.

7/30/69 Wednesday

A bit cooler and the sun shone. I washed and ironed. Made up the beds and got rooms ready. Put 33 pints in the freezer. I picked green beans and pickles. I missed the children.

8/3/69 Sunday

A damp, sultry day. Sanford, Daddy and I left about 8:15 to pick up Nancy and Esthi in Wayne and we went to Doylestown for services. They had preaching first, so we were soon on our way to visit Ray and Jane. Ate our lunch by the roadside and arrived there soon after 12:00. Ray got home at 2:00. Had a nice visit and a good supper, our first visit with them. Nancy showed her slides.

8/11/69 Monday
A fine day. I washed and ironed. Picked the pickles and cut off the sweet corn. Nancy and Esthi went to the shopping center and the wax museum. They had a flat tire and took it to Kramer's and then stopped at Levi's to see the farm. They made bread and an angel food cake. Have our rooms filled with 9 tourists. Wrote to Sanford.

8/13/69 Wednesday
Fine day. Had four tourists for breakfast. Did the washing and ironing for upstairs beds. Nancy, Esthi and I went to Harry Good's and we stopped for a bucket of mountain dirt for my philodendron. We went to Clarence's to see the chicken house and Mildred's pretty quilts. Nancy and Esthi went to Landis Valley Museum and to Mr. Martin's at Manheim for supper.

8/15/69 Friday
A warm day. I made some snow pudding and chicken pie. Nancy and Esthi slept late and did some work on their quilts. Mary Alice brought Nancy Crawford for dinner and they took Nancy and Esthi along. Esthi was not ready to leave the States and I was sorry to see her go.

8/19/69 Tuesday
Real fine day. Showers this evening. I washed and ironed sheets. Mary Alice and Nancy came about 10:00 and Mary Alice left about 8:15. They both worked on their quilts. Gulf Coast had its worst hurricane. Hundreds dead. Nancy is considering a job without college. I crocheted this evening.

8/27/69 Wednesday
Fine day. I put five pints of corn in the freezer. Cleaned the flower bed and hoed the celery. Nancy got her slides and speech ready for the party at Leaman Place Park this evening. She took a lunch for herself and Pete Brown.

8/31/69 Sunday
A warm day. Eby and I went to Meadville. Milton's stayed here till noon and went to Coy's. Robert's, Ray and Jane, Mary Alice, Nancy and Fredric all stayed home and said they had a discussion on church. Nancy made dinner. She is very much disturbed about what to do about college, going to Abram's or otherwise. Bonnie Woomer and her boyfriend came about 5:45 to spend the evening.

9/1/69 Monday
A hot day. Eby had off and helped some with getting Mary Alice's furniture cleaned up. Nancy was busy getting things packed up for school. I washed and ironed and helped the girls. Lester Howerter moved into Nancy's room. Grace and family left at 9:00 and Mary Alice this evening. Eby and I went to Abner's to say good by to the Friesen's.

9/2/69 Tuesday
A hot day. I did up the work and Nancy and I packed up and went to Abram's and set her up in Mary Alice's room. After lunch and packing some things for Mary Alice, I started home. Eby and I went to Akron to help dry corn. A lot there.

9/3/69 Wednesday
Fine rain all day. I canned 16 quarts of tomato juice and put 16 pints of corn in the freezer. Nancy got her $800.00 scholarship. We went to midweek service. Charlie called and said his is going to the hospital for minor surgery. Trouble in Parksburg and one Negro man was shot.

9/6/69 Saturday
Rained a shower and was warm and sultry. I picked a box of limas and made a basket of vegetables ready for Mary Alice. Made apple pies and sauce. Finished the cleaning. Eby and I took her things down to her apartment in Wayne. Had some trouble with the truck but got home safely. Mary Alice has a nice apartment for $125.00 a month to share with another teacher. Eby finished mowing. Many police around Atglen where the Negro is to be buried.

9/10/69 Wednesday
A fine cool day. I started my new cleaning job with Mrs. Kelchner in New Holland. It went real good. Two planes crashed in Indiana, killing all 83 passengers. Eby and Clair collected for the Fire Company this evening. I canned 8 quarts of peaches and cut a lot of rug rags with the cutter I borrowed from Kathleen.

9/12/69 Friday
A fine day. Uncle Charlie came for me at 7:00 and took me to Abram's where he did the lawn and I helped Pat make 54 quarts applesauce. Everything went fine. We stayed for supper and I helped Nancy fit her dress for the hem. We got home about 9:15.

9/15/69 Monday
A fine warm day. I washed and ironed. Hoed the garden. Got some vegetables in for chow chow. Cut some rug rags this evening. Edgar called at 6:30 and said their baby girl Andrea Luanne was born at 10:00 this morning.

9/19/69 Friday
Fine day, cooler. I made 7 hours at my job in New Holland and got my first paycheck for $60.00. Did 15 quarts of tomato juice and a batch of catsup this evening. Had a long talk with Mabel. Richard Buckwalter is improved from getting silage gas.

9/23/69 Tuesday
A fine day, warmer. I did 9 quarts of grape juice. Went to Harry Good's and stopped at Beiler's for apples. Ordered a piece of red linoleum for the apartment. Went on to

Ebersole's for Ray's chairs, four walnut with acorn trim. I picked a bucket of limas and Eby helped shell them.

10/7/69 Tuesday
Partly cloudy. I cleaned closets and drawers. Took Anna Mary to see the doctor with the baby. Watkins man came. Sanford called. He wants information about his Grandfather Martin. I started sorting some old letters this evening. Ben Stoltzfus, a Mennonite missionary, was shot in Honduras.

10/18/69 Saturday
A fine day. I did the ironing. Washed and waxed the kitchen and Nancy took me to the Fire Hall and I helped till noon when she came from the dentist. She had no cavities. Eby finished mowing and cleaned up some leaves. We got ready for the Meadville folks to come to see Nancy's slides this evening. About 45 came. I went and helped at the Ham Supper from 6:00 to 7:00. Mary Alice, Nancy Crawford and her mother and grandmother came.

10/26/69 Sunday
Fine day. The folks all went to Bethel Grove Church but baby Andrea and I. She was good and I read and watched the pot roast for dinner. We enjoyed our visit and started for home at 2:00. Stopped to see Mary Alice in Wayne and brought Sanford along home. Spent the evening looking through old letters of Grandpa's.

10/27/69 Monday
Partly cloudy all day. I washed and ironed. Did some mending. Charlie went to Washington. Sanford took Eby to work after they took the truck to the garage. Sanford went to the Information Center for research. This evening he went to Uncle Jay Martin's. Eby and I went to the Interstate Banquet at Plain and Fancy.

10/28/69 Tuesday
Had a heavy frost. Sanford went to Salunga and to the cemeteries. Got a lot of material. Charlie went to Conestoga High School to talk to Mrs. Brown's class. He had lunch with her and Mary Alice and she took them out for dinner. He got home late. I cleaned kitchen cupboards and drawers. We took Jay and Margie along to an antique sale. Had car trouble on the way home and had to be towed.

11/7/69 Friday
Damp and partly cloudy. I went to Kelchner's and did all the cleaning. Both Mr. and Mrs. are miserable and he went to the Dr. Went to Rubinson's and got some birthday cards. We went to Meadville and took Levi's along. I called Abram's and invited Nancy to go with us to Dale's.

11/14/69 Friday
Cloudy with some showers. I picked up my shoes on the way to Kelchner's. Cleaned the up and downstairs and shopped a little in New Holland and got 3 plants at the greenhouse on my way home. Mary Alice came for supper and we went to Fisher's sale. She got a lamp, waffle iron, glasses and rug samples. Apollo 12 took off today for the moon.

11/25/69 Tuesday
A nice day. I cut the filling bread, cleaned the celery, raked some leaves, painted some of the laundry room. Made a rice krispie cake. Washed sweet potatoes. Eby helped open the table. I wrote to Pat and wired her some flowers. Called Jim this evening and she is resting better.

11/28/69 Friday
A fine mild day. I washed the tea towels, tablecloths, sheets and some diapers for baby Andrea. Edgar's left to stop to see Mary Alice and Nancy and go on to Edgar's home. I cleaned up the house and ironed. Cleaned the meat from the chicken bones. Milton's were here for supper and a short visit. Charlie is leaving for an Epidemiology course in Arizona.

12/1/69 Monday
Cold and windy with snow flurries. I washed and ironed. Made up the upstairs beds. Put the stamps in books. Called Jim and Pat's fever is less but she is too sick to talk on the phone. Draft lottery has been televised. We saw it on Lester's T.V.

12/4/69 Thursday
Clear and cold. I took Annis along to Sewing Circle all day. I called Jim this morning and they started treatment for Pat's heart on Monday. She is feeling a little better. I stirred up some sand tarts. Our bed broke down last night and we brought one down from upstairs till it is fixed.

12/5/69 Friday
Clear and cold. I made a pie. Mrs. Kelchner called and said she has a house full of company and I was not to come. I cleaned Lester's room and wrote the family letter. Went to the store. Robert Weaver's came about 3:30. Jennie is real friendly. Grace and I shelled peanuts while we talked. Eby and Robert went for milk and eggs.

12/6/69 Saturday
Fine day. I called Jim and Pat is better. Her mother came for the weekend. Grace, Robert and Stevie left at 9:00 to go to see Mary Alice and then on to Tennessee. Jennie is doing very well for me. Mabel took me along to Kathryn Kreider's funeral. Eby raked some leaves.

12/7/69 Sunday

Cloudy with sleet, snow and rain. We went to Meadville this morning and evening. Had a Christmas program. Eby's part was "Christmas Get-Togethers." Jennie was good in church and at home. We rested and read this afternoon. Abram called and said they visited Pat yesterday and she is feeling better with the treatment for heart infection. Grace called from North Carolina.

12/9/69 Tuesday

Partly sunny. I put the rest of the wash outdoors and it got dry. Made cookies and caramels. Baked sand tarts, Taylor cakes, peppernuts, and stirred up some raisin filled. Jennie helped me wrap caramels. Dressed 4 capons this evening. Eby went to Board Meeting. Grace called from Knoxville to see how Jennie is doing.

12/10/69 Wednesday

Cloudy, damp and rained a lot this evening. I made cookies and candies. Jennie and I went to the store. She fell off a chair three times. I bathed her after dinner and dried the diapers in the basement. Iced a lot of cookies. Mary Alice called and said she has been sick and not in school for three days. We went to midweek through the rain.

12/11/69 Thursday

Cleared off mild. I washed for Jennie. Put the cookies away. Pressed Eby's suit and my dresses. Cleaned and waxed the kitchen. Robert and Grace got here at 4:15. Made the deer hamburger that Kathleen gave us. Eby, Robert and Stevie went to Meadville to see about doing the basement. I called Jim and Pat is feeling better.

12/17/69 Wednesday

Had some sunshine and snow flurries. I made some date balls and stirred up taylor and peppernut cookies. Finished cleaning upstairs and did the living room and laundry room. Made rabbit potpie for supper. Made tapioca and peanut brittle. Jim went to the hospital and took the children to see Pat before they move her to Harrisburg. Baked the cookies and was very busy. Called home.

12/19/69 Friday

Snowing a little. I made a pumpkin pie and cracker pudding and more date balls. Put things in order and had early lunch. Jim took his two deer to the butcher in Belleville. We left for the hospital in Harrisburg at 12:15. Found Pat feeling good, but still getting tests. Isaac's came to see Pat and brought me home in time to go to the Christmas supper at Dick Patterson's. 56 there.

12/24/69 Wednesday

Cleared and is cold. Mary Alice left for Abram's and Virginia. I did the capons, sweet potatoes and pudding and Nancy made popcorn balls and caramel popcorn. Filled up cookies and candy and set the table. I did the ironing. Nancy did some decorating. Eby took a capon to Melvin Groff's and one to Abner's. Nancy is full of cold.

12/25/69 Thursday
Sunny and started snowing about 3:00 and is making time. Nancy is feeling better. We put things in order and had dinner at 12:15. Abram's, Isaac's, Sanford and Nancy were here. I called Mabel this evening.

12/30/69 Tuesday
Cloudy with some rain. I worked on my rug. Sanford came about 1:00 after stopping at Uncle Jay Martin's for some information. He left for Salunga about 3:00. I cleaned up the old aluminum pan.

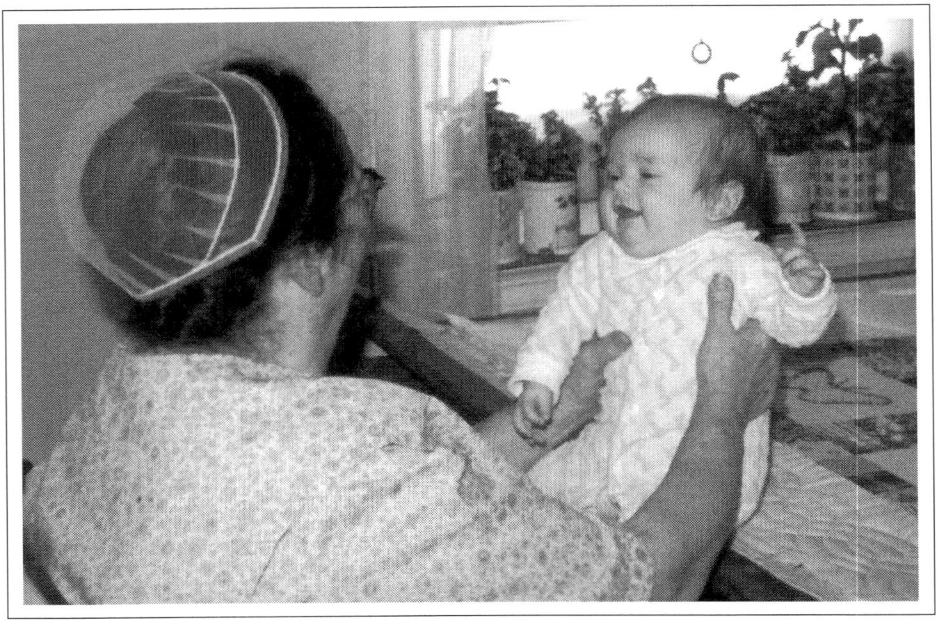

Ruth with granddaughter and quilt, 1972.

The Seventies

1970

1/1/70 Thursday
A cloudy day, cold. I did the dusting and sweeping. We went to Jay Martin's for dinner. Mart and Miriam, Clarence's, Menno's, Landis', and Paul's were there. We had a good dinner and a nice visit. Eby took an Amish carpet man to Meadville and he looked at the floors. I started reading Hex. Kathleen laced some of my rug.

1/4/70 Sunday
A fine sunny day. We went to Meadville, 53 there. This afternoon we took Jay and Margie to Paradise to hear Tom Skinner. The reporters were there and the T.V. cameras. It was standing full. We went to Meadville this evening to hear the Manheim chorus. 45 sang.

1/5/70 Monday
Sunny and not so cold. I wrote to Ray and Jane and worked on my rug. It measures 22x48 inches. Mine Worker president Joseph Yablowski, his wife and daughter, were murdered in Clarksville, Pa. Sledding has been very good and many children have brush burns, one a ruptured liver and one an injured spleen.

1/7/70 Wednesday
Snowed all night and most all day. Light and soft and it may blow and drift. I wrote the family letter and Charlie's birthday letter. There was no school. I did the ironing and worked on my rug. A runaway horse with a bobsled ran down the road and safely crossed the highway and went on out the State Road. Midweek service was cancelled. Uncle Charlie went to Florida last Friday morning.

1/10/70 Saturday
About zero and got up to twenty degrees. I made blueberry and pumpkin pies, rhubarb sauce and roast venison. Abram's brought Sammy about 9:00 and left for the plane at Baltimore to go to Nassau for a psychiatric convention. Eby went to a sale at Leola and bought a rug for the dining room for $140.00. Sammy was a good boy.

1/12/70 Monday
Snowed most all day. I did not wash. Did some sewing. Wrote to Sanford and sent him a book. A Philadelphia truck driver was killed in a collision with another truck in front of the hotel on the highway. Eby went to Levi's for milk. I started reading Sam Levenson's Everything But Money.

1/22/70 Thursday
Fine sunny day. Three above this morning. Nancy went to Pequea Valley this morning and again this afternoon. She got some wool for my rug at Tom's. They are having drug problems at Pequea Valley. I worked on my rug this evening. Uncle Charlie came home from Florida this evening.

1/24/70 Saturday
Clear and sunny. We packed up and left for Ray's at 9:00. Stopped in Wayne and left Nancy with Mary Alice. She gave us tea and buns. Arrived at Ray and Jane's by lunch time. They took us for a drive to see some places of interest, ski lift and lots of skiing, a furniture place where antique reproductions are made and the surrounding countryside. Had Cornish hens for supper.

1/25/70 Sunday
A cloudy day and warmer. We went to the Princeton chapel for services. A Jewish rabbi preached the sermon in the beautiful huge chapel to a lot of people. We saw the Walker-Gordon dairy barns and milking in progress. Had a good dinner of roast lamb and got home at 6:30. Daddy complained of poor vision coming home.

2/6/70 Friday
Partly cloudy and warmer. I did most of the cleaning and quilted. Eby worked till 8:00. Joe Weaver's little adopted two-year-old girl was killed when she was run over by a tractor this morning. Sam Stoltzfus died of a head injury this morning. He was hurt last Saturday while working at Young's. Five houses were robbed on Wednesday night in Gap.

2/14/70 Saturday
Snowed all day. Nancy went to Pequea Valley to help with a carnival all day. Mary Alice went for a few hours. I did some cleaning and quilted. Mary Alice and Nancy helped for a while this evening. We took it out with a little to finish. Looks real good. Eby seems a little better. We played Foil a while this evening.

2/24/70 Tuesday
A fine day. I took Anna Hershey along to Old Road to help with a quilt for the Relief Sale. There were 18 there. This evening we got 3 capons at Levi's and dressed them. Some women had a shower for Larry Twigg's bride-to-be this afternoon. Mrs. Kelchner called and said she is getting a woman to come in each day.

2/27/70 Friday
Real nice day. I washed and ironed. Did the cleaning. Made a cake and doughnuts. Washed the car. Took some doughnuts to Kauffman's. I went to Herr's for Nancy at 6:00. Milton brought Doug and seven foreign students. Got a job at Harvest Drive. Snowed this evening.

3/12/70 Thursday

Cloudy, rained and sleeted. Some ice on trees and wires. I saw some wild geese. Did some sewing. Started a five-braid rug from old corduroy from Rhoda. A woman called and asked how much education we have and offered us a free course. Burglars robbed a store in Lancaster.

3/17/70 Tuesday

Clear day, cold. I washed and ironed. Worked on rug. Kansas had two feet of snow, which will help the wheat crop. Some places in Pa. had eight inches. Eby got tires filled up. Trouble in Laos, Cambodia, Vietnam, Israel, Jordan and with the Arabs.

3/18/70 Wednesday

Snowing and raining all day. I finished the rug for Rhoda. Ripped some coats for rug rags. Cut a dress for myself A jet flying from Newark to Boston was hijacked and the co-pilot shot dead and the pilot shot in both arms. He landed the plane safely. We went to midweek service.

3/20/70 Friday

A rainy day. I did most of the cleaning and sewed. Fixed the chime clock. Mary Alice should be on her way to London by this time. A 19-year-old girl was killed on 501 near the airport. Mail strike is growing.

3/30/70 Monday

Clear and snow is melting. Milton and Edgar went to Atglen for lumber. Nancy made lunch. Mary Alice came about 1:30 and gave us some highlights from her London trip. Uncle Charlie came to take Nancy to meet Abram at Phil Haven. Milton's left for Coy's and after supper were driving home. Edgar and Rhoda went shopping at Good's Store this evening. I kept the baby and played with the children.

3/31/70 Tuesday

Cloudy with some rain. Edgar's left at 10:30. I put things in a little order. Sent Rhoda the baby spoon that she forgot. Started work at 2:00 at Harvest Drive Restaurant. Four of us served a full meal to a bus of sixty students. Got home at 9:45. Martha Hershey called and said Bonnie came with her boyfriend and said she is leaving home.

4/11/70 Saturday

A fine day. We planted the peas and stuck the onions. I went to work at 11:00 and worked till 10:30. We were very busy with two buses and a wedding reception for 95. A lot of others came in for meals. I cut two of my fingers, one on a ladle and one on the saran wrap box. Eby raked garden. Space craft #13 took off today.

4/17/70 Friday

Fine day. I roasted two hams for the Ham Supper. Cleaned the house and got things ready for our trip. Went to the store and to Tom's for rug wool. Nancy came at 4:00

and left for Mary Alice's at 6:30. Charlie called this evening and said they have 24 inches of snow and it's still snowing. Space men got down.

4/18/70 Saturday
Fine day. Uncle Charlie came for us at 6:45 and he took us to meet Abram at Olmstead Airport and he drove us to Goshen by 5:00. We went out for supper and then went to the dedication service for the new pipe organ donated by the Jacob Rupp family. Daddy and I stayed at the Holiday Inn and Abram and Charlie stayed at Sanford's apartment. Mabel and Clarence helped at the Ham Supper in our place.

4/19/70 Sunday
A very wet day. We attended church services at the Chapel and baccalaureate at 11:00. Had lunch in the dining room. Sanford's commencement was at 3:30. Uncle Charlie took Abram to South Bend for a plane and we ate supper with Sanford. We are staying at the Western Motel in Ohio.

4/20/70 Monday
Started out in the rain and got to Erie by 12:00. We drove out on the peninsula for a while and got to Aunt Emma Ray's soon after 1:00. Had a nice visit and left for home about 3:00. Got to Abram's about 12:00 and got home by 1:00. The children are sending me 12 rose bushes for my birthday.

4/25/70 Saturday
A fine warm day. I did the cleaning. Went to work at 12:00 and quit at 8:00. Jay Ranck was here visiting Eby when I got home. Esther came with a lot of useful gifts and a pretty cake for my birthday. We treated Jay to ice cream, cake, drink and nuts. The children each gave me a rose bush from Star Roses.

5/2/70 Saturday
Real warm day and rained this evening. We finished the new rose bed and planted the 12 fine rose stalks the children gave me for my birthday. I washed the car. Mary Alice came for dinner and supper and washed her rugs. I went to work at 12:00 and quit at 10:00. Very busy. Eby got chicken barbecue at the Elementary School for supper.

5/15/70 Friday
Partly cloudy and cool. I worked from 8:00 to 5:00. Made 50 dishes of jello salad, 12 gallons of shredded cabbage, 10 gallons of orange drink, dished 5 gallons of applesauce and breaded 470 pieces of chicken. Hemmed a dress this evening. Charlie and Sanford called from Wanblee for the snow pudding recipe. Sanford is having banking problems. I wrote him a letter.

5/18/70 Monday
A fine cool day. I washed, ironed and mended. Had calls from Mabel, Aunt Cora and Rebecca. We put the pea wire up this evening. I scrubbed the porch and glider. Hoed and pulled some weeds. Sanford does not yet have a job. He is staying with Charlie.

5/23/70 Saturday
Real nice day. Jay and Sue came for us at 8:30 and we started for Edgar's. Stopped at Star Roses, Marian and Ruth's in Mt. Joy and to eat our lunch. Got there about 3:00. Went to a picnic supper with the Mennonite Fellowship in a park in Ithaca. Sue and I each hemmed a dress for the girls. The children were all home but Fredric, Rosa and Jonathan. Went up the new Route 81.

5/26/70 Tuesday
Partly cloudy with gusts and heavy rain this evening. I did the ironing and left for work from 12:00 to 8:30. We were not busy and I wrote to Rhoda. Called Charlie. Sanford is working with the Indians and trying to find a job.

6/15/70 Monday
A cool rainy day. I picked about a bushel of peas and four boxes of strawberries before it rained. I did the peas and put them in the freezer. At 2:00 I left for Lancaster to get sheets with my stamp books. At Orange and Broad Streets, when I went on a detour I got bumped by a car in the intersection because I did not yield the right of way, thinking the detour had the right of way. Damage to our car is about $400. Trained the lima beans.

6/19/70 Friday
A fine fresh day after all the storm and tornado damage all over the country. I worked from 8:00 to 4:30. Stopped at the store after taking Elsie home. Made a chicken pie, apple pie and dumplings for Abram's moving. Had a letter from Sanford and he has a job in Montana with retarded children.

6/22/70 Monday
A fine day. I got up early and drove to Abram's new house to help with moving preparations. Went back and forth and packed and unpacked dishes. Ate dinner and supper at Devonshire Heights. Uncle Charlie was busy helping too. Stayed and slept with Nancy. Mrs. Allison took the three youngest children to the pool this afternoon.

6/23/70 Tuesday
A fine day. Uncle Charlie locked himself out this morning so Nancy and I left at 6:30 with our load and to take a key. I unpacked things, cleaned bathrooms, washed windows and kitchen floors. A Philhaven doctor's wife brought supper complete with fried chicken, French fries, salad, fruit cocktail, cookies and lemonade. Got home before dark.

6/24/70 Wednesday
A fine day. I washed and planted the garden where the peas came out, corn, beans, celery and flowers. Mary Alice brought her friend Joanne Townsend and her mother, Mrs. Eckert. They helped pick 4 boxes of strawberries. I picked green and yellow beans and two quarts of blueberries. Trained up the lima beans.

6/29/70 Monday
A fine day. I went to Isaac's early to help paper the kitchen. Linda, Sally and Elizabeth helped all day and Judy some with the ceiling. I got home at 8:30. Mrs. Nixon went to Peru to see the earthquake damage and sympathize.

7/12/70 Sunday
A fine day with some showers this evening. Went to Meadville, Ray and Jane to Paradise. Amos preached on the Potter. Ray and Jane were here for dinner and Mary Alice came at 1:30. We went up to the farm and walked up the hill. Ray's left at 5:00 and were stopping at Mary Alice's place.

7/14/70 Tuesday
Nice day. I made some soap and did some cleaning. Picked 3 quarts of blueberries. Charlie called from Abram's and said he is coming this afternoon. He arrived and is very thin and has a mustache. He and Daddy had supper at Harvest Drive. I worked from 5:00 to 10:30. Had two rooms of tourists.

7/18/70 Saturday
A fine harvest day. Eby worked most all day. I picked and canned pickles. Washed the cars. Charlie was here for lunch. He picked some blueberries and left for Abram's this afternoon. I worked from 1:00 till 10:30. Had two rooms of tourists. Had a busy day with 8 buses.

7/21/70 Tuesday
A fine day. Had an inch of rain last evening and night. I worked from 8:00 to 8:30. Had some buses. We have three rooms of tourists. Mary Alice called and is busy with the classes she is taking. A 16-year-old Kirkwood boy drowned in the bath tub from a fainting spell.

7/29/70 Wednesday
Hot and sultry with some showers this evening. I picked four quarts of blueberries and went to work at 11:00 and worked till 10:00. Nancy and Becky came before 5:00 and made supper for Daddy. Nancy and I talked until after 12:00.

8/4/70 Tuesday
A fine cool day. I went to the Samaritan Home early and helped all day. Eby made up the beds and was ready for the tourists. We have a full house, fourteen tourists.

8/16/70 Sunday
A warm day. We packed our suitcase and lunch and went to Mt. Joy church for services. Left there for Jim's and stopped to eat on the way. Got there about 3:00. They attended a picnic and got home by 5:00. We had a delicious cookout when Jim got done milking. Enjoyed the quiet and peaceable farm atmosphere. Jim took Daddy and the children to the woods to see some deer.

8/18/70 Tuesday
A fine day. I washed and made up the beds. Worked from 10:00 to 5:00. Had three buses. Melvin sent us eleven tourists. Eby picked 2 quarts of blueberries. Four armed robbers took over $12,000 from Gap Bank yesterday. They have not been caught.

9/6/70 Sunday
A beautiful day. We took it easy this morning and left for Abram's at 10:00. All were there soon after 11:00 and we had a service with music, singing, prayer, and talk from Joanne and a tape from Sanford. We had a very enjoyable time together.

9/10/70 Thursday
Warmer with showers. I finished canning the tomatoes and made some crabapple jelly. Worked from 12:00 to 9:30. Made 135 meat loaves and 21 jello salads. Planes are being hijacked by Arabs and they are threatening to bomb them.

9/12/70 Saturday
A beautiful day. I did some cleaning and went to work at 11:00 and worked till 10:00. Very busy day. Had 19 buses. Becky was in a fret at times. Eby worked till noon and worked on the drain system at Levi's. He had some truck trouble. The Arabs blew up some planes in Jordan.

9/13/70 Sunday
A fine day. We went to Meadville. Rested and read all day. Sanford called and we had a nice phone visit. I called Isaac's to see how Judy's feet are. They are healing from blisters after playing basketball at Abram's. Jim called for cow information as he sold a cow and heifer for $2800.00.

10/27/70 Tuesday
Partly cloudy. I finished ironing. Made chicken corn soup for supper. Went to work at 11:30 and got done at 8:30. I made 42 meat loaves and Annie and I cleaned under and behind the kitchen tables and cleaned the two big ovens. Had no one in the dining room but the help. Eby went to a D.H.I.A. banquet at Plain and Fancy.

10/31/70 Saturday
Cloudy with some rain. We left with Jay and Sue for Virginia at 8:30. Stopped at Duff's in Winchester for dinner and got to Robert's at 2:00. Found them all well. Jay and Sue went to Park View to spent the night with Jesse Byler's. We had a good steak dinner.

11/2/70 Monday
Partly cloudy and cleared this evening. I washed and brought it in to finish drying before I went to work at 4:00. Worked till 8:00. Had a bus of 57. Ruth Meck, Elsie and Dorothy Martin helped. Took Ray's aquarium to Mary Clark to have a winter garden planted. A theater fire in France burned 142 persons.

11/13/70 Friday
Cloudy with rain. Went to work at 8:00 and quit at 7:00. Had Ivan Martin Stone Company employees, wives and children, about 240. Things went off well. Eby went to church and I made up the beds and bathed and packed. We went to the Samaritan Home for the weekend. A tidal wave killed thousands in India.

11/20/70 Friday
Cloudy and rainy. I worked from 8:00 to 3:00. Becky and I got food ready for Saturday. It is believed that nearly a million may have drowned last Friday in Pakistan. I sorted some papers and magazines.

11/28/70 Saturday
Nice day. I got things together for dinner. Eby went to the store. Edgar's, Isaac's, Jim's, Dale's, Robert's, Mary Alice and Nancy came. Had a good time together. Looked at some slides that some had taken here and there.

12/1/70 Tuesday
Mild and sunny. Robert and the children went to Keen's a while this morning. At 10:00 they all ate a snack after getting packed up and left at 10:30 go to Glen Burnie, Maryland to spend the evening and night with Charlie. I got on the job and called Aunt Mabel and we were soon on our way. Stopped at Harry Good's Store and got things for quilts and on to the Parkside Rest Home in Reamstown to visit Albertina Montgomery, then to Charles Horning's to get a quilt done. Left at 5:00.

12/5/70 Saturday
Real nice day. We finished up and started for Ray's about 8:00. Ate an early lunch of good vegetable soup, relish, buns and ice cream. Started for Milton's in Ray's V.W. and arrived about 2:15 and found them well and ready for our visit. Doug likes someone to help him with his games.

12/6/70 Sunday
Cold, windy and some snow flurries. Went with Milton's to Setauket Presbyterian Church. Had a good ham dinner. Eby had one of his weak spells at dinner time. We started home at 2:30. Got to Ray's at 5:45 and came on home. I called Ray to report a safe trip. Wrote a letter to Sanford.

12/13/70 Sunday
Cloudy and damp with fog and ice on high places. I made two blueberry pies to take along to Abram's for lunch. Went to Abram's from church and enjoyed the afternoon visiting with about 110 of the staff and personnel from Phil Haven Hospital. Things went off very orderly and the food was delicious. We got home at 9:30.

12/14/70 Monday
Clear and windy. I did the washing and ironing. Uncle Charlie came this forenoon to share the Paradise problems about having recorded music to assist with their worship. I called Mabel this evening.

12/19/70 Saturday
Fine mild day. I baked some cookies and cleaned up. Charlie came at 9:30 and Mary Alice at 11:00. Eby worked till noon and cut bushes off this afternoon. I worked from 10:00 till 6:30. Charlie and Mary Alice visited Uncle Jay Martin's and shopped and made a delicious supper for us as part of their Christmas present.

12/21/70 Monday
Cloudy and started snowing about 2:30. I washed and did some ironing. Made two kinds of cookies and some caramels. Went to work at 4:30 and worked till 9:30. Uncle Joe's celebrated their 49th anniversary at Harvest Drive. Good's Dairy had a banquet. Just had six people to do the job. I called Abram's to see how Nancy is doing. She had all her wisdom teeth taken out.

12/24/70 Thursday
Clear, cold and windy. Mary Alice left at 10:00 for Abram's and then on to Virginia to spend Christmas with the Weaver's. I did the cleaning. Took a gift to Abner's and some cookies to Tom's. I cleaned the rest of the celery and baked the ham. Charlie went to South Dakota.

12/25/70 Friday
A very nice day. We took it easy. Went to Isaac's for dinner. Had fruit cocktail, ham, sweet potato croquettes, noodles, corn, scalloped oysters, molded salad, pickles, mince pie, ice cream and nuts. They took us for a drive to see the southern end of the County. This evening I made sherbert, caramel sponge cake and got the raw vegetables and oranges ready.

12/30/70 Wednesday
Clear and cold. I sewed and made an apple pie. Joe was here and finished painting the bedroom ivory. I went to work at 4:00 and worked till 7:00. Worked on the Samaritan Home record book this evening. Got the quilt in the mail that the children worked in cross stitch for our Christmas gift.

1971

1/2/71 Saturday
A fine day. Abner opened our drive. Eby brought the desk from the apartment and repaired it for our student teacher's room. Dusted, cleaned and framed some post cards. Charlie called and said he returned from his South Dakota vacation last night.

1/11/71 Monday

Nice mild day. Joe came about 8:00 and painted the hallway. I had a pain this morning. Esther called about her quilt. I took the frames and props and some trays this afternoon and Mrs. Glick and I helped to put it in and quilted a little. Washed and ironed. I called Kathleen to congratulate her for winning a prize for her rug at the Farm Show in Harrisburg. 15,000 at the Farm Show.

1/15/71 Friday

Cloudy and cold. Ice is melting. I made a chocolate cake and washed windows. Gave the cane seated rocker first coat of shellac. Cleaned the upstairs and down. Made a whimsie. Eby worked late. Miriam Hershey called me to help nurse at the Samaritan Home.

1/18/71 Monday

I washed and got it ready to iron. Put things in order. Worked on my scrap books. Rested and got things on for supper and worked at the Samaritan Home from 4-12. Helen Ranck gave me my instructions and it went real good. Vandals burned the covered bridge at Soudersburg.

1/21/71 Thursday

Cloudy and warmer. Wrote to Charlie and Mike. Did some sewing on my dresses. Took Sue and Eleanor along to Baker's to quilt this afternoon. Eby took Amos Hershey to Carpenter's to teach Bible School this evening and I stopped at Abner's to help Esther quilt. Got a card from Ray and Jane on their Windjammer cruise.

1/31/71 Sunday

Very cold and windy. Went to Meadville. Amos preached about Hell. Eleanor taught our class on God's rewards. We went in to see Ellis this afternoon. He is better after a sick spell. Worked at Samaritan Home from 4-12. Helen R. was on. Apollo 14 went to the moon this evening.

2/4/71 Thursday

Cloudy and cold with some snow. I was not brave enough to go to Sewing Circle. I took a snooze and quilted. Made sauer kraut and gingerbread for supper. Milton called this evening. Mike has been out of school with the grippe. I called Isaac's. Joanne came home from North Carolina on Tuesday after a year in voluntary service.

2/6/71 Saturday

Sunny and snow is melting. I made a pie and things ready for lunch. Mary Alice brought Joanne Townsend to help quilt. She did not like it so well. Got almost two rows done. Eby went for milk and eggs and got some potatoes at Leroy Kreider's and the groceries. Mary Alice and Joanne left about 5:15. Daddy worked the table top down again and varnished it and the rocker. Got some ant traps.

2/10/71 Wednesday
Did up work and ironed. Quilted a lot. Took Anna Mary to the new fabric shop in Intercourse. Worked from 4-12. Death toll from California earthquake reached 52. Fine weather.

2/13/71 Saturday
A very wet day with high waters. I made chicken corn soup and things for lunch and for tomorrow. Mary Alice came with Mrs. Brown and the Riggios for lunch. Eby took them for a drive. Mary Alice and Suzanne went to Kitchen Kettle and I kept little Charlotte. Quilted this evening.

2/18/71 Thursday
Sunny and mild. I quilted this forenoon and evening. Went to Marcus Byler's for four tongues and put them in sugar cure. Twelve pounds for $8.25. Some L.M.S. boys are being paid $25.00 for getting haircuts.

2/20/71 Saturday
Fine mild, sunny day. I made buns, a walnut cake, sweet potatoes, caramel sponge pudding, applesauce, jello salad and raw vegetables ready for Sunday dinner. Eby went to the store and washed the car. I worked from 4-12. Eby set the table for 10. Salted the tongues.

3/14/71 Sunday
Mild day. Went to Meadville. 81 there. The Patterson children were baptized. Galen had a stroke at the beginning of the service and was taken to the hospital in the ambulance. I rested and worked from 4-12. Very foggy coming home.

3/18/71 Thursday
Real nice day. I made a birthday cake for Mike and Barbara. Got things cleaned up and was busy getting supper ready for Milton's and the Coy's. Judy Kurtz and the children also came this evening. We saw some of Coy's Christmas slides and showed some of ours.

3/21/71 Sunday
A fine day. We took Mike and Doug along to church. Rested after dinner and took the boys to Clarence's while we went to Paul and Pauline's 25th wedding anniversary. Saw Landis' and Menno's there. Stayed at Clarence's a little while and came home. Played scribbage and cubic with Mike. Had some stories and put Doug to bed before Milton's got here at 8:45. They had a good trip.

3/23/71 Tuesday
Nice day with snow this evening. I went to Lancaster to apply for Medicare. Quite a job. Got things ready for supper and worked at the Home from 4-12. Helen was working. Carrie Buckwalter was back and thinks her eye is better.

4/4/71 Sunday

Galen died early this morning. Went to Meadville. Glen Yost was our Sunday School teacher and Miriam Hershey's class gave the program. It was good. An accident by Levi Stoltzfus' house where a pole was hit and broken in three places shut off our power for seven hours. A Daniel Stoltzfus was taken to the hospital with injuries. We rested this afternoon and I worked from 4:00 to 12:00.

4/24/71 Saturday

Made a cake and pudding and cleaned up. Eby harrowed the garden. The peas are up. Eby got a new suit at Rubinson's made to order. I worked at Harvest Drive from 10:00 to 9:00. A hectic day. Lots of buses and people

5/2/71 Sunday

We went to Meadville, and the old people, six of them, quizzed against that many young people and the old ones won. Did not seem like a worship service with laughter and clapping of hands. It was our host Sunday and we did not get any guests. This afternoon Eby slept and I wrote letters. We went to Meadville this evening where the Millmont and Buffalo young people gave a program, mostly of song.

5/8/71 Saturday

Did some cleaning and wrote the family letter. Eby went to Lancaster for his teeth. He had car trouble. Had early lunch. Jay and Sue picked us up and we started for Ray's at 12:10. Had a good trip and a nice visit. Eby and Jay went along with Ray on calls.

5/9/71 Sunday

Mother's Day. Cloudy with drizzle. We went to Lambertville for service at the Mennonite Church. Went to Washington's Crossing afterward and then back to Ray's about 1:00. We were very much surprised to see Abram's, Isaac's, Jim's, Milton's, Charlie, Dale's, Mary Alice, Sanford, Nancy, Uncle Charlie, and Jane's mother and brother. They all brought some food and we had plenty for all. They gave us a nice radio. We got home at 8:30. I wrote to Grace and Rhoda.

5/24/71 Monday

I went to work at 9:00 and quit at 3:30. Had a group of 90 at noon. Becky was real good. I stopped at Flaud's for plants and planted them. Also some corn, beans and beets. Had a yak yak meeting at Meadville this evening. Not many there and some new ideas about the home meetings for young couples.

6/11/71 Friday

A fine day. Went to work at 8:00 and worked till 5:00. Had a hectic day. Becky's leg hurt. Came on an accident in Buyerstown on the way home where a 13-year-old Amish boy was struck and killed. Another 15-year-old was struck and killed on Strasburg Road while catching some runaway mules. Nancy called this evening and said she is coming on Sunday. I made a chocolate cake and picked out some shell barks.

6/27/71 Sunday
A warm day. We went to Meadville. Clair Eby was there to council about ordaining a deacon. Not all were in favor, so time will tell the results. Rested a while and went to the Home from 4:00 to 12:00. Miriam and I had a long talk.

6/29/71 Tuesday
Cloudy and sultry. I wrote to Grace and went up and papered the apartment bathroom. Cleaned it and some more of the dirty place. Eby and I went up again this evening and brought some things down here. Charlie called and said he is in the Baltimore Hospital with hepatitis. Came there from San Juan, Puerto Rico. Mary Alice came back to Abram's from Robert Weaver's. Elizabeth called and offered to help with the apartment.

6/30/71 Wednesday
A hot day. I went to work at 6:15 and finished up at 9:15. Becky was off. Had a busy day, but not frustrating. Eby brought more things from the apartment and picked a quart of blueberries. Eleven men escaped from the Lancaster prison and one guard died of a heart attack.

7/2/71 Friday
Cleared cooler. I worked from 8:00 to 2:00. Becky had the others cook the chicken and pour the broth down the drain. Edna Baker quit last Saturday and Sue Herr was fired. Called Mabel to say good bye as they are leaving in the morning for a trip to Colorado.

7/4/71 Sunday
A beautiful day. Went to Meadville. John Yost taught our class. Abram and Nancy came for dinner and took us to Baltimore to see Charlie in the Public Health Hospital where he is resting with hepatitis. Had a good trip. Had a bite of supper with them before they left for home and we went to Meadville. Tourists are staying a second night.

7/7/71 Wednesday
Nice warm day. I went to work at 6:15 and worked till 9:15. Made 130 meat loaves, roasted beef briskit and made jello. Abner's left for Kansas this morning. The governor has allowed Sunday liquor sales.

7/8/71 Thursday
A hot day. I cleaned Steve and Lester's rooms and made a chocolate cake. Hoed some garden and flower beds. Planted some marigolds. Talked to Margie and Kathleen. Went up to the apartment to meet Petersheim's man to pick some cover for bathroom siding. Joe is putting down the floor covering. Went to the Home. Called Milton's at Coy's. They were at Abram's for supper and got Mike after his vacation at Uncle Abram's. Abram called Charlie and he is back in bed today, but his tests show that he is getting better.

7/11/71 Sunday
A wet day with steady rain. We went to Meadville and Amos preached about Moses' call. Jay and Margie came here and we took them along to Frank Kreider's for dinner. All were there but Sue and Ellis. Elizabeth had been in the hospital for eight days and Minnie is still limping. Milton's came at 5:00 and had supper and spent the evening. A vote is to be taken next Sunday to have or not have Grant Stoltzfus show his Russian slides on August 1.

8/1/71 Sunday
Sunny and showery. Went to Meadville. Luke Horst preached and votes were taken for deacon. Fifteen persons went out to vote or wish the Lord's blessing. Richard Patterson, Glen Martzell and Glen Yost were named. We were invited to Clair Eby's for dinner. Went to Meadville this evening where Grant Stoltzfus showed pictures of his trip to Russia and gave a talk. We were called to Harvey's where the thieves broke in and stole a lot of his watches. Had a cop interview.

8/6/71 Friday
A fine day. I went to work at 8:00 and worked till 4:30. Becky was not so happy and Mae was worried. Ruth Overpeck was puzzled. Charlie cooked up a good supper of steak, succotash, tossed salad and lemon pie. He mowed some lawn and washed his car. Charlie and I planned the menu for our family reunion.

8/8/71 Sunday
Fine sunny day. We went to Meadville and Charlie went to Hershey's and Clair Denlinger's took him along to Meadow Valley for dinner. Went to the ordination this afternoon where Glen Martzell was ordained deacon. I went from there to the Samaritan Home. Charlie came back and ate a snack before leaving for Washington where he plans to start work in the morning. Barn at Intercourse was burned this evening when children were playing with matches.

8/19/71 Thursday
Some showers. I washed and ironed some sheets and pillowcases and towels. Hoed garden. Made up the beds and cleaned the rooms. Rested and worked at the Home from 4-12. Got a basket of Golden Jubilee peaches. Charlie was flying to Seattle, Washington today.

9/3/71 Friday
Warm day. Nancy and I took the car to Kramer's for inspection. Nancy made pies and I did some cleaning and roasted a 12 pound beef roast for Charlie's portion of our family dinner. Mary Alice came about 10:30 and she and Nancy bought the car home and got ice cream at Elmer Lapp's. Edgar's got here about 8:00 and brought sleeping bags. They brought Jimmie Lee along.

9/4/71 Saturday
Fine day. We got things lined up to have an outdoor lunch. The children all came but Sanford and he sent a letter. Mary Alice brought Mrs. Esther Groff to spend the day with us. She taught all twelve of the children. Nancy had some free fabric and Grace had some dresses from Mrs. Richey. We all had a nice time and each brought plenty of food.

9/5/71 Sunday
Nice day. We went to Meadville. Robert's, Ray's, Charlie and Mary Alice stayed home and blamed it on the leak in the kitchen cupboard from upstairs toilet. Had a relaxing afternoon. Robert's took Mary Alice's table down to Wayne.

9/6/71 Monday
Very warm and sultry. Had breakfast for Robert's, Ray's and Charlie. Robert's left at 10:00. The others shopped at Harry Good's and went to Isaac's for dinner. Ray's were taking Charlie to the Philadelphia Airport to fly to Wisconsin this evening. I washed tablecloths, tea towels, and some sheets. Went to Harvest Drive from 1:00 to 4:00. Had some buses. Canned seven quarts of pears. We went to Kinzer revival meeting, where Harold Fly is the minister for the week.

10/15/71 Friday
Fine warm day. I worked from 8:00 to 5:00. Cooked 400 pounds of chicken and breaded most of it. Made 30 dishes of jello. Mabel was working and helped bread chicken and wash dishes. I roasted two hams for the fire company. Made quince jelly.

10/21/71 Thursday
Fine warm day. Went to work at 8:00 and worked till 1:30. Made 55 dishes of jello and Florence and I did five large tubs of cabbage. Did some chicken. Mabel was helping. Stopped at Byler's Store and came home. Made some sherbet and things for supper. Eby had a hearing aid salesman this evening. This evening I went to the Lancaster School of the Bible for the Homebuilder's Meeting. Abram was the speaker. The topic was "What are Mothers Good for?" Went with Edith Hoover, Mabel and Ruth Clark.

10/23/71 Saturday
Nice mild day. Did some cleaning and made sweet potato croquettes. Set up the table for Progressive Supper appetizer. Eby worked till noon. I went to work at 11:00 and quit at 6:00. Made a lot of potatoes for buses and the restaurant was very busy, making lots of dishwashing. Got home at 6:15 and dished up the fruit cup and raspberry sherbet with cookies and crackers. Daddy got some pretty oak leaves for the table in time for the group of 13 young people in Tommy Martin's truck. They arrived at 6:45. Had three rooms of tourists.

11/8/71 Monday

Clear and cold. I went to the Home for the first day shift. It went all right. Eby took tile off the back of shower to dry it off for a new job. Jane called and said she came home with the baby today and they are both fine. Boys in the apartment at the farm are disturbing Levi's very much and Eby called Gordon Kling to put them out.

11/14/71 Sunday

A fine day. We went to Meadville and Edgar Denlinger preached. He drew the face of a clock on the black board and talked about us numbering our days. We came home and ate a snack. Left for Ray's and picked Mary Alice up in Wayne and she drove. Had a nice visit with them and Jane's mother. We took supper along. Baby Laura is a very sweet little girl and has all a baby needs. On the way home we were detained by an accident and got home at 9:00.

12/2/71 Thursday

I took Annis along to Sewing Circle. 14 there. Did one quilt and started another. Five on the sewing machines. Came home at 1:30 and went to the Home from 4-12. Lizzie Messer was bumped on the head when Katie Donley opened the toilet door on her head and knocked her on the floor. Joe stopped in and Eby showed him what I want made for Christmas.

12/12/71 Sunday

A fine day. We went to Meadville. Had an oyster stew for dinner and went up to Jay's and Charlie took us along to Abram's. He took us to see the new Medical Center and to see the Founder's Memorial. Also the Millard quarries. Had our supper and went to Derry Presbyterian Church to hear the Christmas program in song. Got home at 10:30 and Daddy is tired.

12/14/71 Tuesday

Cloudy with rain. I ironed. Wrote letters and cards. Started baking cookies and the oven went out. Painted some spools for sewing boxes. Mary Alice came for supper and to pick up her sheep hides. Eby had a Board meeting.

12/25/71 Saturday

Fine mild day. I got the morning work in order and Eby washed the car before I left for the Home at 7:30. Had a good Christmas with the old folks. Alice Snyder was not able to go to the dining room. Eby came up for the dinner. We gave the capons and they had all the extras. Very good. Eby and Willard went for a drive and we got things ready for dinner this evening. Ray, Jane and Baby Laura came.

1972

1/3/72 Monday
A fine day. I washed and ironed. Cut a dress from the seersucker fabric Nancy brought me in the summer. Sewed it up this evening. Had phone calls from Becky, Margie, Mabel, Aunt Cora, Esther and Mrs. Elam Kauffman. Put Christmas card list in my diary. Ruth Mellinger died at University of Pennsylvania Hospital after heart surgery.

1/11/72 Tuesday
Some rain and foggy. I washed and hung it on the porch. Stamped one of Elsie Martin's scarves for Bertha Denlinger to embroider. Took Helen Ranck along to Mart Hershey's where Doris Hershey took us to Bird-in-Hand Motor Inn for a 1:30 dinner for all 15 of the workers at the Home, an annual treat of J.B. Sauder. Enjoyed a good meal. Stopped for butter and at Marcus Byler's. Eby has Board meeting this evening.

1/18/72 Tuesday
Clear and not so cold. I cut patches and cleaned up the bedroom for Dale. He came to spend the night from a two-day Agway meeting. Worked at the Home from 4-12. Maggie Herr was real weak when I left her with Miriam. Eby weighs 230 lbs.

1/21/72 Friday
Cloudy and damp. I worked on my scrap book this morning. Took a bath and went to the doctor for a physical for my job at the Home. A pretty thorough job for $15.00. I sewed patches on Mary Alice's butterfly quilt. Eby worked late.

1/24/72 Monday
A fine day. I washed and ironed. Made soap. Stamped two scarves for Elsie Martin. Cut two aprons. Rested this afternoon for a while. A barn burned last evening in Hempfield Township. Arson suspected. Mary Alice called and is coming home for nursing care.

1/26/72 Wednesday
A fine day. Made cracker pudding for supper. Worked at the Home from 8-4. Maggie Herr was real low. Mary Alice took it easy and Nancy Crawford came for her and ate supper and they left by 6:00. Mary Alice is feeling better. A 17-year-old boy confessed to firing two of the barns that burned this month. We did the Home report this evening.

1/30/72 Sunday
A fine day. Good sledding. Went to Meadville. Ethel taught our class and Amos preached on Love. Had Aaron Hershey's, John and Wilmer Reeser, Mart and Miriam for dinner. I put the capon in at 4:00 A.M. Levi called at 11:00 last night and said the boys in the apartment were having a beer party for about 24 people. Eby called police.

2/6/72 Sunday
Cloudy and started to snow this evening. Cinder trucks are out. We went to Meadville. 68 there. Spent the afternoon and evening at home. Read Christy. Called Rhoda, Abram, Isaac, Jim, Dale, Milt, Grace and Mary Alice. Told them all of Uncle Ellis' death at 12:00 A.M.

2/9/72 Wednesday
Clear and cold. I made a peach pie and rhubarb sauce. We left at 9:15 for Ellis Hostetter's funeral at the Lutheran Church on East Orange Street at 10:00. The burial was at Paradise Presbyterian. Abram's and Isaac's came here for lunch. I quilted this afternoon and marked some border.

2/15/72 Tuesday
A fine mild day. Got things done up early to be ready for quilting. Martha Hershey and Aunt Sue Hostetter came about 7:45. Aunt Mabel, Aunt Margie, Anna Hershey, Alice Crouse, Margie Kauffmann, Amy, two Stoner girls, and Mrs. John Hess were here and did most all of it. I worked some this evening. Kathleen came to see the quilt and talk a while.

2/16/72 Wednesday
Fine weather. I went for eggs and to the Widow Fisher's store in Salisbury Heights for quilt supplies. Made rhubarb custard and finished the quilt. Charlie came about 11:00 and spent the day. We went up to Jay Martin's this evening. Charlie showed some of his slides. I made Dutch goose for supper.

2/17/72 Thursday
Cloudy and began snowing at 3:00. I had a big job putting Mary Alice's butterfly quilt in the frames. Had a lining problem. Went to the Home at 3:30. Charlie left for the Hershey Medical Center and to Abram's from there.

2/19/72 Saturday
Snowed and blowed all day with things filled up. No traffic. Ray walked to the farm down at the corner for milk. Could not get to the store. Power off about three hours. We did some quilting. Ray made ice cream this evening.

2/20/72 Sunday
Real winter day. Snow plows slowly opening roads. Drifting continued all day. Spent the day leisurely. Sanford called. They have fifty degrees in Montana. Ray and Jane and I played some games.

2/21/72 Monday

Clear and not so cold. Eby washed Ray's and Mary Alice's cars and hosed the porch and drive with hot water. I made a chicken pie and Waldorf salad for lunch. Mary Alice brought Nancy Crawford for lunch and to help quilt a few hours. Ray took me to the store after Abner opened the drive. He made some ice cream and quilted. Eby went to the Amish neighbors for milk. Ray's and Mary Alice and Nancy left at 3:30 and I quilted. Did report on Home this evening. Roads are getting opened.

2/23/72 Wednesday

Cloudy and snowed this evening. Cold. I did the ironing. Quilted a lot. Made a blueberry pie. Seven boys escaped from Barnes Hall. Two were captured. Called Ray about our trip to Nicaragua.

2/25/72 Friday

Very foggy with ice and lots of accidents. I cleaned a trype and put it in salt water. Quilted a row of patches. Called Mabel. Had two little girls selling Girl Scout cookies. We went to Lee Hoar's and had our pictures taken for passports. I slipped and fell on the ice.

2/26/72 Saturday

Very foggy till noon. Eby worked and went to store and for milk this P.M. I made a pie, did the cleaning, popped corn and made cracker jack. Mary Alice came about 12:15 and helped quilt. Got a row of patches done. There were 100 auto crashes yesterday due to ice and fog.

3/1/72 Wednesday

Fine day. 70 degrees, a record. I quilted most all day. Brought the beef from Marcus Byler's. Sugar cured a tongue and two dried beefs. Freezer is almost full. Mabel came and helped quilt this afternoon. We went to Bible Study this evening. Dale called and said he is going to the hospital to have all his teeth pulled tomorrow.

3/6/72 Monday

Clear, cold and windy. I washed and it dried nicely. Quilted part of the day. Nancy wrecked her car when the front tire blew out as the rim caught a water pipe and hit a pole so that she could not steer. We went to Dr. Beacher's for our shots this evening.

3/7/72 Tuesday

Nice weather. I quilted most all day and did not get done all I wanted to. Wrote a letter to Nancy. The soldier who held up a Millersville cop on Sunday also killed a young Mt. Joy farmer whose body was found yesterday at Pine Grove. Eby went to a meeting at Salunga.

3/9/72 Thursday

Fine day. I finished Mary Alice's quilt by 9:00. Eby came home at 9:30 and we went to Lancaster to apply for our passports. I got two shirts and a wallet for Eby and some underwear for myself. Rested a short time and worked at the Home from 4-12. Eby went to Meadville. Planes are being bombed.

3/10/72 Friday
A fine day. I hemmed Mary Alice's quilt and put it on her bed to sleep in tonight. Did the cleaning and made supper for Milton's. They came at 5:30 and Mary Alice soon after. Eby worked late. Milton's are on their way to Virginia to spend a week. We went to the Home for bedtime.

3/22/72 Wednesday
Rained with some gust, very wet. Joe was here painting. I did some odd jobs. Cleaned closets and drawers. Made some pillowcases. Mary Alice, Nancy Crawford and David left this morning for Nicaragua. I cut Eby's hair.

3/24/72 Friday
Cloudy and cold. I had severe abdominal pains and vomiting last night. Slept from 2:00 till 6:00. After morning work was finished I slept till 12:00. Joe was here and finished painting by noon. I cleaned the windows and washed bedroom floor and cleaned bathroom. Worked at the Home from 4-12. Our 45th anniversary.

3/28/72 Tuesday
A fine day. I did up the morning work and left at 9:30 for Lancaster. Got a sweater for Eby and a handbag for myself. Got our certificates signed at the Health Center. Stopped for butter and cheese. We went to Paradise this evening for the first Passion Week service.

4/11/72 Tuesday
Rained this morning and cleared. Worked from 12-8. Cleaned up the house. Got things packed up. Esther was here and brought me a birthday gift and to say good bye. Aunt Cora made a sunbonnet for Elizabeth Hall and I went up for it. Went to the bank for traveller's checks.

4/12/72 Wednesday
Got up early, ate breakfast and finished packing. Isaac and Elizabeth picked us up at 7:00 and we met Ray and Jane in Wayne where they left their car and went on to the Philadelphia Airport where we flew on Northwest to Miami and changed planes for Guatemala. Daddy's first flight. It went fine. Stayed at the Biltmore Hotel.

4/26/72 Wednesday
Left Managua at 11:00 and arrived in Philadelphia at 6:55. Isaac, Elizabeth and Kim met us and we got home by 9:00. Mary Alice called at 11:00. Uncle Charlie had everything in fine shape. He went home. Charlie, Jane and I shopped at the outdoor Managua Market this morning. I bought some beans and dress fabric. Charlie took us to the airport.

4/27/72 Thursday
A pretty day, cool. I washed, ironed and mended. Aunt Cora called. I talked to Margie, Esther and Mabel. Abram called to ask about our trip. They are leaving for a four-day convention in Dallas, Texas tomorrow. Daddy has diarrhea and chills this evening.

5/15/72 Monday
Partly cloudy with rain this evening. I washed, ironed and mended. Pulled some weeds. Started cleaning the basement. Eby helped put up the pea wire and put on the balance of the screens. Esther was here to bring me a Mother's Day gift. Kathleen called and said Kathy found a balloon with a card that was sailed off this morning from Maryland. Went to bed early.

5/16/72 Tuesday
Cleared. I worked from 12-8. Still having doughnut problems. I made whoopie pies. Rested and Bennie Fisher came at 2:00. He had trouble finding us. I took him home on my way to Harvest Drive. Had buses. Worked from 3-8. Brought a can of ice cream along. Eby went to Salunga. Governor Wallace was shot while campaigning in Maryland.

5/20/72 Saturday
Cold, cloudy and rainy. I worked from 12-8. Helped with breakfast for Mike and Doug. Milton made sandwiches and I helped get a lunch ready for them. They left at 10:45. Eby worked till noon. He went to New Holland to see about the projector and it was beyond repair, so he bought a new one for $99.00. We worked on our slides till bedtime. I bathed, took a nap and went to work at 11:30.

5/24/72 Wednesday
A fine day. I worked from 8-4. Had a good day. I stopped at Flaud's for some plants on my way home and planted them this evening. Eby treated the lawn for dandelions. Dr. Beacher was married today. Nixon and his wife are in Russia.

6/14/72 Wednesday
Cleared warm. I worked on my dress. Cleaned up for our company who came this evening to see our slides. Jay and Sue brought Uncle Milts, Uncle Charlie, Mart and Miriam. Served a snack of ice cream, cookies, pretzels, chips and drink. Last evening Aaron Denlinger's wife shot him four times in their $100,000 home. Big ball game this evening.

6/19/72 Monday
Sultry and showery with some sun this evening. Called Mabel and Clarence was not feeling good yesterday. I picked and put a bushel of peas in the freezer. Also some asparagus, sugar peas and strawberries. Got family letter and Judy is not supposed to work so hard. She had a spell while helping in the hay. Kim was a flower girl at her neighbor's wedding on Saturday.

6/22/72 Thursday
Rained hard all day. Flooding in many places. Roads closed and some power failures. Many events are cancelled. Worked on my scrap books. Water is coming in the basement, and we blocked the freezer up a bit. Could not get Abram's or Isaac's by phone. 10 inches of rain in 24 hours. An Amish man and his baby and horse drowned at Pequea on Belmont Road. A man was electrocuted in his basement at New Holland.

6/24/72 Saturday
Partly cloudy and rainy again this evening. I picked a bushel of peas and Eby shelled most of them. Prepared supper for our guests. Had a pleasant evening and showed our slides. Eby took some Amish men to Paradise to search for the body of Samuel Kauffman, who drowned on Thursday in the Pequea. It was found near Gordonsville Road at the Park. Flooding is still bad in Harrisburg. Mary Alice and her friend Cynthia cancelled their trip because Cynthia's house was flooded.

6/26/72 Monday
Had some sunshine and fresh air. I put all the dishes in place and washed and ironed. Cleaned the peas off the garden. Clark's greased the freezer fan. Clarence came home from the hospital. I mowed yard till the mower stopped. Eby mowed this evening. Flood waters are lowering and the clean-up has begun. The curious were very much unappreciated on the roads yesterday.

7/5/72 Wednesday
A wet day. I worked from 8-4. Had a good day. Alice Snyder is getting real feeble, but spunky. Stopped for 50 celery plants on my way home and planted them after supper. Also got a dozen zinnias. Went to Bible Study. Got a letter from Florence Guthries in Puerto Cabezas, Nicaragua.

7/25/72 Tuesday
Not quite so hot, with a gust and rain this evening. I worked from 12-8. Came home and rested. Nancy, Sammy and I went to New Holland and to Harry Goods to do some shopping. Stopped to show Sammy how to pick blueberries on the mountain. Made some applesauce and picked some pickles. Mrs. Westman washed. They went to see their son. I bathed Sammy and put him to bed.

7/30/72 Sunday
Fine day. Went to Spring Run Church and had dinner at Jim's. Beth leads her heifer Adele and plays with her mouse. Pat worked from 3-11 Saturday night. We left for home at 4:30. Saw a lot of flood results along the rivers and in Harrisburg, Highspire, and Middletown. Got home after 8:00.

8/2/72 Wednesday
Fine weather. I got up at 4:00 and met Dorcas M., Rhoda Yost and Clyde Metzler's at Mart Hershey's where Miriam went with us to Bird-in-Hand to meet our driver

who took us to Wilkes Barre where we helped clean flooded houses. Worked with folks from Franconia in two houses. The damage is indescribable. The city looks terrible. Many people are helping to clean. Got home at 7:00 and went to Prayer Meeting.

8/22/72 Tuesday
A fine day, warmer. Worked from 12-8. Stopped for two baskets of Golden Jubilee peaches @ $3.00 a basket and at Salisbury Heights for tubing and embroidery cottons. Canned 14 quarts peaches and 4 quarts of pickles. Slept from 1-5. Watered garden this evening. Have 11 tourists. Some Amish women were coming to help can 25 baskets of peaches at the Home.

8/23/72 Wednesday
Clear and warm. I canned 8 quarts of peaches. Washed all the beds and ironed and made them up. Cleaned the rooms. Pat, her mother, Greg, Beth, her sister Judi, husband and children stopped about 2:45 on their way from four days at Cape May. I left for work at 3:45 and arrived at 3:59.

8/26/72 Saturday
Our first reunion at Black Rock. Fine warm day. Got breakfast over and all ready to go to Black Rock at 10:00. Jay, Sue and Charlie entertained all of us except Charlie and Sanford. Their jobs hindered them. Had a full program. Brain teasers, trail hunt, swimming, boating, plenty of food, old slides, skit, speech by Isaac on Old Mother Hubbard, reading class, spelling class and information class. We had sandwiches, buns, red eggs, pickles, cookies, bologna, cheese, soft drinks, baked beans, rice pudding, salad trays, bananas, peaches, popsicles, etc.

9/1/72 Friday
Sunny and cooler. Joe finished painting the house. His bill was $194.00 for scraping and painting. I watered some garden and canned 3 quarts of peaches. Did the cleaning. Anne Caldwell, our student teacher, came to set up her room. Nancy made the Dean's List at Lebanon Valley.

9/8/72 Friday
Clear and sunny. I met Isaac's at Mellinger's Church and went with them to Linda's graduation from her Practical Nursing training. 39 in the class. Got home at 11:45. Canned 4 quarts of peaches and made some preserves. Did the cleaning. Watered garden and picked and shelled a basket of limas. Paul called and said he is out of work.

9/9/72 Saturday
Light showers and clearing. I put some corn and limas in the freezer. Went to Harvest Drive from 11:00 to 4:00. Stopped at Priscilla Fabrics for coverings and stockings. Eby took truck to garage and helped appraise Jake Martin's farm this afternoon. It went to Melvin for $80,000.

9/12/72 Tuesday

Showery and cloudy. Warmer. Worked from 12-8. Linda had an interview at Samaritan Home and she brought two baskets of tomatoes. I did one. I stopped for plums, apples and eggs. Made some applesauce. Nancy called and said that Mrs. Hans Greuter died in Switzerland. She was one of her A.F.S. mothers.

9/23/72 Saturday

A beautiful day. Worked from 12-8. Got things ready for supper. I worked at Harvest Drive from 10:30 to 4:00. Charlie and Stern got here before 10:00. They waited for Mary Alice and did some touring and came here for supper and left about 7:00 for Washington. Nancy called and said she was involved in an accident last night and escaped unhurt. She was with Beaver.

9/29/72 Friday

Cloudy and drizzly. Isaac and Elizabeth picked me up about 8:00 to take me to help Ray and Jane move to Amwell Road. Everything went fine. A neighbor brought supper in so the corn soup was left for tomorrow. Jane's mother helped too. Got home at 9:30. Two drug pushers were caught in Lancaster. Sally likes her work at the Osteopathic Hospital.

10/2/72 Monday

A fine day with frost in some places. I washed and ironed. Rested this afternoon. Picked a bucket of beans. Canned two quarts of tomatoes. Linda stopped a few minutes on her way from her first day of work at the Samaritan Home. Said it went real good. Mabel called. We went to a Historical Meeting at L.M.S. It was in the interest of the Hans Herr House restoration.

10/13/72 Friday

Fine day. Warm. I did the cleaning and worked at Harvest Drive from 11:30 to 6:30. Eby worked late. I rested and read Black Like Me this evening.

10/19/72 Thursday

Cloudy and snowed till late afternoon. Plumbers and electricians were here and installed the unit for the upstairs apartment. I got things ready for end-of-garden relish. Made a strawberry pie. Cleaned the hair clippers. I had a severe group of abdominal pains from 8:00 to 10:00.

11/4/72 Saturday

Partly cloudy and mild. Worked from 12-8. Eby and Milton went to see the horses bathe at Christiana. I made breakfast. They left for shopping and to Coy's for supper. I made sweet petal, a sponge cake, applesauce, jello, sweet potatoes, etc. Rested a while and went to Sue Hostetter's for supper. She had all the others.

11/6/72 Monday
A fine day. I washed and ironed and mended. Cleaned some of the attic. Ray called at 3:00 and said that baby Martha Alice arrived at 2:00 today, just one day after Sister Laura's first birthday. Eby sent an order for some trousers.

11/8/72 Wednesday
Rained all day. I wrote family letter. Richard Nixon was elected our 37th president. I cleaned some closets and worked on freezer room. Boxed some relishes for Christmas gifts. Linda stopped in for some clothes.

11/9/72 Thursday
Clear, windy and colder. I polished the woodwork, scrubbed and waxed the kitchen and cleaned the ovens. Made a burnt sugar cake. Went to Harold Eby's for chickens. Went to a sale at the Guernsey Barn and bought a refrigerator for $30.00, a table top for $3.00 and a gallon of paint for $2.00.

11/17/72 Friday
Cloudy and warmer. Worked from 12-8. I stopped for eggs and at Spring Heads for water cress on the way home. Cleaned the living and dining rooms and the basement room. Rested a while. Linda stopped and went on to a banquet at Rhodes Restaurant for Mechanics Grove Church. Eby worked late. John Kennel's son stabbed his mother to death. Sorted some slides.

11/21/72 Tuesday
Real nice day. Worked from 12-8 and Alice was not very good. Linda overslept and came late. I stopped for eggs and tubing. Went to the store, Elmer Lapp's for ice cream and Harold Eby's for turkeys. Cleaned the celery. We went to Meadville. Not so many there. Ray and Jane and the little ones were here when we got home.

11/23/72 Thursday
Thanksgiving Day. Fine weather. Got things ready for dinner. Jane rested after helping with breakfast. Daddy set the tables, one in the living room and one in the dining room. Abram's, Isaac's, Jim's, Ray's, Charlie, Mary Alice and Nancy were here. Edgar's got here about 2:15.

12/2/72 Saturday
Fine day. I washed the car and kitchen floor. Bagged the popcorn. Eby brought a load of horse manure from Levi's for roses, asparagus, strawberries and flower beds. He painted basement second coat. I worked at Harvest Drive from 2:00 to 7:00. Woman hit and killed on New Holland Pike last evening. Josephine called and said they can't come for dinner.

12/9/72 Saturday
A cloudy day. I finished the quilt and made a mattress slip. Finished up cleaning. Mary Alice came at 11:00 to make winter gardens. We went to hardware store and to farm attic for some treasures. Made up 8 gardens. Mary Alice left about 9:00. Plane crashed in Chicago.

12/21/72 Thursday
Foggy, dark and rained. Did some cleaning. Painted woodwork in basement. Eby helped take the bed down this evening. I planted the terrarium that Mary Alice gave. Esther came and brought a sweet petal and a pound of pecans. I cleaned up the desk this evening. War is raging in Viet Nam.

12/23/72 Saturday
Cloudy and damp. Eby worked till noon. I made cranberry jelly, Spanish cream, sweet potato croquettes, filling, roast duck and made ready for Dale's tomorrow. An earthquake killed 10,000 in Managua today and the city is burning. I wrapped my gifts. Saw a large flock of wild geese flying south.

12/25/72 Monday
Christmas Day. Cloudy and mild. We had breakfast for Dale and Linda and they left for Linda's home. Milton's came here and we went to Isaac's for dinner. Abram's were there too. Had a good dinner and a nice time. Got home at 7:00. We brought Mike and Doug here while Milton and Barbara went to Serena Groff's husband's viewing at Strasburg.

1973

1/1/73 Monday
A fine mild day. Charlie, Mary Alice and Nancy came for a sauer kraut dinner. Had a nice relaxing visit. Nancy stayed till 9:15. Abram is starting private practice in Hershey tomorrow. Linda came and went for the evening.

1/7/73 Sunday
Cold and sunny. Ten degrees. Worked from 12-8. Had Uncle Milt's and Clarence's for dinner. Aunt Cora wanted to see our Christmas cactus in bloom. Over 100 are open. Eby had charge of Sunday School. Harvey Kauffman's came home from two weeks in Florida.

1/8/73 Monday
Cold and partly cloudy. I washed and ironed. Took Harvey's key home. They gave us 6 oranges and 2 grapefruits. I finished my dress. Earl Clark bought Hitler's deluxe car for $153,000 at a sale in Arizona. Eby went to Joe Bechtold's to make up a Sunday evening program for Feb. 4.

1/15/73 Monday
Partly cloudy. I was sick from 12:30 on till morning. Put breakfast on and went back to bed till Mabel called at 12:00. Worked on my rug this afternoon. Margie called to chat. Ray called this evening and said they may come this weekend. Eby spent his evening in the basement. Went to bed early.

1/23/73 Tuesday
Partly cloudy. Worked from 12-8. Read and slept till 11:30 and took Helen Ranck and Miriam Hershey along to Bird-in-Hand Restaurant for the annual dinner for the Home workers. Got home at 3:00. Made some wool ready for cutting into rug strips. Started working the picture Ray's gave for Christmas. Nixon has declared peace.

1/27/73 Saturday
Worked from 12-8. Linda followed me. Anna Good in bed. I finished cleaning and worked on my rug. Eby took washline poles to Joe Ruth. Uncle Charlie brought some cut patches. Linda came and went again. The peace treaty was signed today and the draft is done. Took a bath and went to bed early.

2/2/73 Friday
Dark and cloudy with lots of rain. I cleaned and sewed up some braids on rug. Went to the store and for milk. I made doughnuts. A car went into Lake Octorara and drowned a 10-year-old girl. Milton came at 5:00 with Dougie and two Islam boys from Iran. They were here for supper and he took them to Fisher's Auction.

2/5/73 Monday
Fine mild day. I washed and ironed. Braided some rug. Called Aunt Cora. Uncle Charlie called and said he will cut more patches and wants a picture of Grandpa Martin. Anne gave Eby her T.V. to watch the news. I bathed and went to bed early.

2/9/73 Friday
A fine day, colder. I cleaned. Anna Mary asked me to take her to the doctor, but the car did not run so I did not take her. George Kramer came and started it. I did some painting and cleaned paint brushes. Mr. Goldberg from Stony Brook School called from Host Motel where he was attending a convention just to be nice and friendly. Said he appreciates Milton so much.

2/10/73 Saturday
Cold and partly cloudy. Worked from 12-8. I finished cleaning and started on another rug. Eby went to Kauffman's for cider for mince meat and to John Eby's to pay for our beef. Talked to Mary Alice about an A.F.S. move to bring some Conestoga High School foreign students to the County in March. Called Mabel.

2/13/73 Tuesday
Fine weather. Worked from 12-8. Slept 1 ½ hours, ate a bite and then went with Mabel, Sue, Mary Ellen, Rodney and Almeda to Landis' to buy fabric. Spent $31.86 for two dress lengths and 20 yards of quilt binding and three buttons. Eby went to Board meeting at the Home. I got a twenty cent raise and my check was $163.54 for 180 hours. I worked on a quilt patch for Francis Nolt.

2/14/73 Wednesday
Had sleet and rain. I worked on rug. Made a rhubarb custard. Trimmed the winter garden and terrarium. Eby is talking about developing the farm.

2/22/73 Thursday
Things are white with a light snow. Worked on rug. Made two mince pies. A plane was shot down over Sinai Desert and 105 people were killed. I went to bed early.

2/25/73 Sunday
Pleasant. Went to Meadville. Miriam was our teacher. Amos preached counsel meeting sermon, "A little leaven leaveneth the whole lump." A few things were brought up. One was for more discipline and one for less. Joe Kerschner brought his parents this afternoon and we had a nice visit. Read this evening.

3/3/73 Saturday
A wet day. I worked from 12-8 and helped with cooking. Rested this afternoon. Worked on my cross stitch motto. Blanche was on day shift. A barn was burned at Irishtown and arson is blamed. Two Americans were killed in Israel. There is trouble at Wounded Knee, S.D. with the Indians.

3/9/73 Friday
Sunny and warm. I did the cleaning. School opened two hours late because of the fog. I had an appointment with Dr. Beacher for a complete physical. He said I have a closed tube in my right ear and a cystaseal. Painted this P.M. and worked on my dress. Mabel called. Wrote to Bernard Mumo in Kenya and Elizabeth Hall in Puerto Cabezas.

3/17/73 Saturday
Rained and cleared windy and colder. Had a late breakfast. I made pies and peeled potatoes before breakfast. Got things ready for dinner. Put Rosa's quilt in and started on it. Rosa, Marcia, Jonathan, Conrad and Rhoda all helped. Eby, Edgar and the girls went to the sale and got nothing. They left after supper for Edgar's home.

4/14/73 Saturday
Sunny and mild. I made doughnuts, rhubarb sauce, blueberry pie and sauer kraut for dinner. Finished cleaning. Charlie got here about 11:00 and went to the Reeser sale and for water cress. He bought a drop leaf table for $45.00. Eby harrowed up

the garden and we planted the peas and potatoes. Charlie called at 10:30 and said he has cleaned his table top and it is beautiful.

4/21/73 Saturday
A fine day. Worked from 12-8 and got things ready for dinner. Robert Weaver's came about 11:00. Eby cut ham at the Fire Hall this A.M. and finished mowing yard. We went to the Fire Hall for supper. Eby and Robert helped with serving from 4:00 to 7:00. Grace and I finished Joanne's quilt patches this afternoon. Peeled potatoes this evening.

4/24/73 Tuesday
A fine day. Worked from 12-8. Stopped at Amos Martin's for strawberry plants for $1.00. Planted them this evening. I took a nap and woke up to find Bennie Fisher here. He stayed for dinner and supper. Eby took him home. Linda stopped to get the balance of her things. Amy and Menno stopped with two marble rollers for Mrs. Brown.

5/11/73 Friday
Shower this forenoon and blustery. Francis called me to work at 12:30 as I was not planning to work. I got there at 1:05. This morning I did the cleaning and painted the laundry room with some leftover paint. Planted some tea that Willie gave me. Our Washington bus trip is off because the bus company has bus problems. Annis and Clair suggested going somewhere else, and I called Dale's.

5/12/73 Saturday
A variety of weather. Clair and Annis came at 8:30 and picked us up and we went to Dale's Agway Store first and then to their new home. Had a good dinner and then we visited till 3:30 when we started for Jim's. We spent a couple hours there and came home, stopping at Good and Plenty for supper. Ate too much of their delicious food. Got home at 9:30 and had a note to call Abram. He said "Happy Mother's Day," and said they had a good trip to Honolulu.

5/20/73 Sunday
A very wet rainy day. I worked from 12-8. Had a quiet morning. I rested an hour and then we left for Abram's. Met Charlie, his Chinese friend, Mary Alice and Mrs. Brown and we went to Nancy's graduation at Lebanon Valley College. 205 graduated. Had dinner at Abram's and a snack for supper. Beaver came this afternoon. Nancy got a $57.00 award. Got home at 7:30. Still cloudy and raining.

5/21/73 Monday
Cloudy, windy and cleared this evening. I washed, ironed and mended. Hoed the bulb beds and planted some marigolds. Talked to Mabel for an hour. Called Aunt Cora. We did the report for the Samaritan Home. Watergate scandal keeps making the news. Had letters from Rhoda and Elizabeth Hall.

6/6/73 Wednesday
A fine warm day. Anne had last day of school and moved out. We packed up and left for Edgar's at 8:00 and got there at 2:00. Had a good trip. They are all well and busy with adding an additional room to their house. Fredric has finished his first year at Goshen and does not have a job yet. Rosa does some cleaning two days a week. Jonathan has promise of a job with a truck gardener. Rhoda has kept an afflicted Mother's two children for a few days.

6/7/73 Thursday
A fine day. Edgar hoed some of the garden. I helped Rhoda with some mending. This afternoon we went to an antique store to look for some used furniture and found some prospects. This evening we planted some flower plants around the patio.

6/8/73 Friday
Clear and warm. I helped with ironing and mending. Eby hoed the garden. We went to see the renovations at Bethel Grove. Left at 1:00 and drove beyond Carlisle to the Valley Motel. Ate supper in the restaurant. I did some of the driving. Eby turned on the T.V.

6/9/73 Saturday
A warm day. Started out about 8:00 and took turns driving. Stopped for gas and a snack in Harrisonburg. Got to Grace's at 1:30. After supper they took us to see Aunt Katie Weaver and to the Springdale cemetery. Had a nice visit with Aunt Katie. Had a watermelon treat before going to bed.

6/11/73 Monday
A warm day. We slept comfortably in the Weaver's air conditioned house. Left at 9:00 and got home at 2:15. Stopped for a snack. A little rain fell as we got home. Unpacked and got some supper. Eby mowed yard. Bathed and went to bed early. Donald put an air conditioner in his room while we were gone.

6/12/73 Tuesday
Very warm, in the nineties. Worked from 12-8. All were fine. Linda came on to work. I washed and ironed. Rested a while. Finished Sanford's letter. Mary Alice called as they were not having school because of the heat. Eby harrowed and hoed and finished mowing yard. I helped put up lima bean poles. Eby went to Board meeting.

6/20/73 Wednesday
Partly cloudy, clearing and warmer. I washed and ironed. Had a bad pain spell with vomiting from 12:30 to 4:30. Got up at 9:15. I wed the canna row. Trained the limas. Had our midweek service. Eby talked and had to lead in our prayer group.

6/25/73 Monday
Partly cloudy and warm. Milton and I left at 6:00 to pick 41 lbs. of cherries at Elmer Beiler's. After our breakfast Milton's left for a day of sightseeing with Treichler's and

Soderstrom's. I canned the cherries and did the washing. Milton's came for supper and the Treichler's came here and took Daddy and Milton's to the tent meeting at Intercourse. I kept the four children. We served watermelon when they came home.

6/29/73 Friday
Had a gust and lots of rain all night and cleared up around noon. I washed and ironed. Did the cleaning. Picked a quart of blueberries. Doug picked some potato bugs and I finished. Milton's came for Doug about 2:30. I went to Leon Summers' for bread and Stoltzfus' for eggs for Ray's. Eby worked late. I got two yellow jacket stings.

7/2/73 Monday
Hot and sunny. I washed and ironed. Hoed garden and Eby harrowed it again. I planted corn, pickles, carrots, beans, radishes, beets and some flower plants. Did two buckets of green beans for freezing. Eby went to a meeting to plan the Hostetter reunion. Rhoda called that Jonathan is in the hospital with osteomyelitis. Galen Buckwalter broke his neck when he dived in the Susquehanna River.

7/10/73 Tuesday
A hot day. Worked at the Home 12-8. Hoed and dusted and picked one gallon of blueberries. Canned six quarts of beets. Talked to Aunt Cora. Eby went to Board meeting. Have a couple tourists. Sanford called and said he's in love.

7/12/73 Thursday
A beautiful clear day. Much cooler. I ironed the sheets. Made a blueberry pie and a chicken pie. Nancy brought Ursula, a Swiss girl who is at Abram's for two weeks. Mary Alice came at 11:00 and after dinner they all left. Mary Alice and Nancy went to get Swiss money for their trip. Mary Alice left after supper, and Nancy, Ursula and I went for a drive before they went home.

7/17/73 Tuesday
Partly cloudy and not so hot. Worked from 12-8. Things are mixed up because Betty is on vacation. Sara Fisher is not happy and E. Ressler has problems. I did some ironing last night. I was much disturbed about Dale. Called Mary Alice and Nancy before they left for Switzerland. Picked four gallons and a pint of blueberries. Went to Bible School. Got two rooms of tourists from Fox Motel.

8/1/73 Wednesday
Cloudy with showers. I went to Hershey's to help with a quilt for the sale to benefit Galen Buckwalter's hospital expenses. Eight persons helped. We went to Sue's for our Bible study. Airplane crash in Boston killed 88 people.

8/5/73 Sunday
A beautiful day. I worked from 12-8. Had a sick spell and am feeling all right again. Took a nap when I got home. Took Carl along to Meadville. Isaac and Elizabeth came this afternoon. I rested and worked on a scrapbook page for Anna Good.

8/8/73 Wednesday
Hot and sunny. Worked from 12-8. Had a quiet night. I washed and ironed. Rested. Made meat loaf and tapioca. Mrs. White wants cooking privileges. I cleaned up the rose bed. Nancy and Mary Alice called when they arrived back from Switzerland about 10:00. Called Mabel.

8/17/73 Friday
Rain some places, but it is getting dry here. I watered this evening. Finished the limas and canned 14 quarts of tomatoes and did some corn for freezer. Got up at 8:00. I worked at the home from 1:00-4:00 for Linda as she went to a wedding. E. Ressler is not in a good mood yet. I called Dale this evening. He is working on his basement and is getting used to living alone. Is proceeding with a divorce.

8/25/73 Saturday
A beautiful day. The children gathered here and we packed up the food and all met at Black Rock Retreat for our reunion. All were there but Sanford, who sent a telegram. Had a very nice time together. Linda and her boyfriend came for supper. Also Uncle Jay Martin's brought Uncle Milt's. Rhoda had some things for adults and Grace for the children.

9/3/73 Monday
A hot day with more breeze. I was sick from 3:00 to 7:30. Slept till 10:00. Eby had the day off. Nancy and I made eight cushions from fabrics she brought and she made drapes for her and Michelle's apartment. White's came and went. I went to bed early and Nancy and Eby got the T.V. out.

9/4/73 Tuesday
Had a good rain last night and an inch this afternoon. Worked from 12-8 and did a lot of ironing. Nancy left at 9:30. I washed and got a bad spell of pain that lasted a half hour. Finished washing and went to bed. Had a glass of milk for dinner. Was wakened by the thunder at 3:00 and the wash was all wet. I let it hang. Went to the store for cheese and crackers. Went to Tel Hai for supper where the Home staff had a picnic. Still have a gnawing pain.

9/6/73 Thursday
Partly cloudy and cooler with showers this evening. I took Annis along to Sewing Circle. Fourteen there. I did not feel very good most of the day. Did the ironing and took a rest. Got grapes in and made 11 pints of jelly. Mrs. White went to a urinologist and is feeling very badly. Eby harrowed some garden and sowed turnips and radishes.

9/11/73 Tuesday
A fine day. Worked 12-8 and shelled limas till 5:15. Got apples on way home and did 12 quarts of sauce and made sandwich spread and canned 5 quarts of

plums. Had an appointment with Dr. Beacher at 12:00 and he wants me to have an Xray tomorrow. Eby went to a Board meeting this evening. I am feeling real good.

9/12/73 Wednesday
Weather pleasant. I went up to the farm for a bushel of grapes. Took a bath and Eby came home for lunch and took me to the General Hospital for an Xray. I did one basket of grapes into 21 quarts of juice. Eby mowed the yard. We did the record in the Home book and sent it to the Mission Board. Kathleen called to see if I had surgery. A report got out.

9/15/73 Saturday
Fine day. Worked 12-8. Stopped for apples and made them into sauce. Picked the limas and got things ready for Sunday dinner. Took some naps. Made apple dumplings for dinner. Eby swept out front and shelled the limas. Has an urge to fix up the basement room. White's moved out. Dr. Beacher called and said my Xrays show a malfunctioning gall bladder. Sandy went back to the hospital with a convulsion. I bathed and went to bed early.

9/18/73 Tuesday
Fine day. Worked 12-7. Had a sick night and came home before breakfast. Had pain all day and was very miserable. Talked to Mabel, Ray and Charlie. Had a little relief this evening. Eby got his own supper. Charlie told me to take a hot bath. It gave some relief.

9/19/73 Wednesday
Fine day. Eby served the breakfast and I got up at 8:00. Laid down till Nancy came and felt sore and washed out and weak. We went to some used furniture places to look for a chest of drawers for Nancy. Got eggs and some bread at Leon Summer's. Linford Horst came to see about putting a toilet in the basement.

9/21/73 Friday
Partly cloudy. Eby came home to take me to Dr. Davidson for a checkup. He said my gall bladder is not bad enough to remove. Wants me to try a diet for three weeks. I did some cleaning and rested. Went to Fisher's auction and bought an iron pan for Ray. Did not get Nancy's chest of drawers. It brought $16.00, and she said $15.00.

9/30/73 Sunday
A beautiful sunny day. Worked 12-8. We went to Meadville. Had our communion service. Clair preached and Amos served. Edna Simmons had a spell while washing feet. Slept a while and visited Mary Hershey. We went to a viewing for Sandy Rissler at Terre Hill. Abram's, Isaac's and Dale were there.

10/4/73 Friday
Very foggy morning. I trimmed the dried beef and had it sliced at Marcus Byler's. Went to Sewing Circle and left at 2:00 to get a bonnet at Intercourse, but my kind has gone out most places. Got the groceries. Anne Caldwell came to visit this evening.

10/7/73 Sunday
Fine weather. I got things ready for dinner and made Richard's lunches ready. Tourists left before we went to church at Meadville. 50 there. Abram and Pat came for dinner and we left for Williamsburg a little after 1:00. Arrived at 6:00. Ate our supper in the Lodge dining room @$6.25 each. Room $27.00 per night. Took a walk to see some of the town. A lot of people here for the Psychiatric Convention.

10/8/73 Monday
Partly cloudy and sprinkled a little rain. We ate breakfast and lunch in the cafeteria and supper at the Christiana Campbell house. We looked around on our own till 3:00 when Abram and Pat took us to Jamestown and to see the Glass Works. Abram had a psychiatric meeting and Pat had a meeting for ladies on antiques. Bill for four at the Christiana Campbell Tavern was $36.00. I had Virginia fish.

10/10/73 Wednesday
A fine warm day. We ate breakfast together in the cafeteria and they took us to the capitol for a tour and then went through the governor's mansion. Went back to the Lodge and checked out and bought a gift for Abram's and they came at 12:30 and we left for home. Stopped for a carryout snack and got home at 5:30. They started home. Vice President Spiro Agnew resigned because of income tax evasion.

10/12/73 Friday
Fine day. Worked 12-8. Very easy. Had an appointment with Dr. Davidson at 8:30. He said no operation and to stay on my diet. Stopped for bread and to see about getting carpet made at Mose Stoltzfus'. Did the cleaning. Talked to Aunt Cora and Abram.

10/13/73 Saturday
Beautiful day. Got up at 5:00 and left at 6:30 from Gap Fire Hall on a bus trip to Washington D.C. Had a friendly group and saw White House, Capitol, Smithsonian, Wax Museum, Arlington Cemetery, Tomb of the Unknown Soldier and Kennedy's Grave.

10/17/73 Wednesday
A fine day. I got things lined up for dinner and went up to the Home to bring three of the ladies and Mabel brought two. They all said they enjoyed their visit very much. Mabel helped take them back at 3:30. We went to midweek service this evening. Had a silly spell with Nora's story today.

11/3/73 Saturday
Sunny and mild. Got up late. Worked at Harvest Drive from 10:00 to 2:00. Made a lot of mashed potatoes. Stopped for bread. We went to make a survey on Meadville Road and invite folks to the meetings. Did eight stops. Most seemed friendly. Four are Baptists. Eby dug the cannas and we put them in. Made vegetable soup.

11/14/73 Wednesday
Nice mild day. Forty degrees. I was sick and vomiting from 1:00 to 5:00 and slept till 10:00. Did the mending and cleaned. Raked leaves and covered the strawberries and flower beds with leaves and dirt. Eby went for milk. Mabel called and said Ruth Clark is interested in teaching the quilting class at Conestoga High School. Finished the needlepoint motto that Ray's gave. Got a package from Charlie with English walnuts and fruit cake.

11/15/73 Thursday
Nice and mild. I made nine cushions and filled seven. Packed up ten boxes of jelly for Christmas gifts. Sent birthday cards to Karen, Beth and Sammy. Mary Alice called and said she has some students with serious problems. She has given up her trip to see Mrs. Conger over Thanksgiving.

11/22/73 Thursday
A fine mild day. Got our things ready for dinner. Had a nice group. Edgar's, except Fredric, Abram's, Isaac's, except Joanne, James and the children, Dale, Ray's, Mary Alice, a friend of Sally's and Alfred Gerhart. All stayed for supper except for Isaac's and Jim's. Some used sleeping bags.

11/24/73 Saturday
A cloudy day with some rain. Edgar's left for Souderton about 10:30. I washed the car and worked at Harvest Drive from 12:00-4:00. Eby worked till noon. Did a little cleaning this evening. There are many places saving power by using less lights. Gasoline stations are closing in places because of shortage.

11/27/73 Tuesday
Damp and foggy. I worked 12-8. Did some ironing. Wrote to Sanford. I rested a while and did some cleaning. I put the slides in order and sent an order for Child Life magazine for Christmas gifts for grandchildren.

12/1/73 Saturday
A fine day. We started for Milton's at 5:00 and had good traveling. Had a nice visit and went with Barbara to the Fair that is held for their scholarship fund. Dougie and I visited in their new basement room where he enjoyed turning off the lights.

12/2/73 Sunday
A pretty day. We went with Milton's to the Setauket Church. By the end of the service I was feeling quite sick. I left the dinner table and spent from 12:15 to 4:30

vomiting and staying in bed. I made a nest in the back seat and rested and slept on the way home. Everything went well here while we were away. Came home in four hours. Traffic was light due to gas problems.

12/8/73 Saturday
Partly cloudy and not so cold. Jay and Sue came at 10:00 and we started for Ray's. Had a good trip and food. Went to a museum in Hopewell. Looked over the premises and hot bed. Saw slides of their Kentucky trip and lots of the little girls. Ray has a pretty collection of flowers under a lamp. Saw deer out the window.

12/9/73 Sunday
A wet day in New Jersey. Slept late and went to the Presbyterian Church in Hopewell. Good attendance and a good sermon. Had a snack and dinner at 3:00. Beef made on a rotisserie. I felt good on the food. Started home at 5:20 and helped a girl out who had slipped in a ditch.

12/15/73 Saturday
Partly cloudy and cold. Worked 12-8. Mary Alice and Nancy came and helped make a lot of cookies. Eby took junk to the dump. Had Glen Clark fix the water heater. Sink drain is leaking. Bathed and went to bed early.

12/24/73 Monday
A fine day. I washed and ironed and scrubbed Mary Alice's chicken crate. Made buns for Aunt Cora's Christmas dinner. Eby had off. He went to New Holland for the horse sale and it was a hog sale and too cold for him. Mary Alice stopped on her way to Virginia to Robert Weaver's. She gave us three books, a diary and a handmade picture.

12/30/73 Sunday
Fine day. Worked 12-8. Had a messy night. Milton's came early and visited with Ray's and Jim's, Isaac's, Abram's, Mary Alice and Nancy. Dale and Robert came too. Had a nice time. Served on trays and had cow in the garden, baked corn, escalloped spinach, chicken salad, trype, pudding, fruit salad, cookies and candy.

1974

1/1/74 Tuesday
Foggy, rained and cleared. Worked 12-8. Still some have the bug. Florence Shaub is down. I stopped for apples on the way home. Washed and made some cushions this afternoon. Eby had off and watched rose parade on T.V. and slept most all day. Got some turnips out for supper. Charlie called. He and Ed had a good trip to Mexico.

1/2/74 Wednesday
A fine day. Joe was here all day. I did the ironing and mending. Made 37 apple dumplings and a chicken pie. Want to send some to Dale. Margie Kauffman brought me a loaf of homemade bread. Went to midweek service. Had a pain last night.

1/8/74 Tuesday
Fine day. Worked 12-8. Willard started car with jumper cables. I washed and rested. Cleaned heater room in basement. Sorted nails, bolts, screws, etc. and put them into jars. Plane crash at Johnstown killed 11 persons. Eby went to Board meeting. Willard's are to have one day a week off. They want Linda to stay on. Nurses are to have a raise.

1/10/74 Thursday
Cloudy and rainy. I was sick all day with vomiting, diarrhea and pain. Took a sitz bath for more than an hour. Felt better this evening. Called Miriam to exchange shifts with me. Eby took George Summers along to Board meeting at The Medical Center.

1/19/74 Saturday
Sunny and mild. Worked 12-8. Got home before Robert Weaver's were up. After breakfast Grace and I quilted till lunch. Mary Alice and Nancy came and we all went shopping to Harry Good's. Got Eby a white shirt. The Weaver's went to Isaac's for supper. Ray's and Dale's came this afternoon. Daddy washed some cars.

1/27/74 Sunday
Sunny and mild. People walking and riding bikes. Took Carl and Sue along to Meadville. 43 there. Emma taught our class and Amos preached on Psalms 119. I did not feel very well and got worse this afternoon when we went to visit Uncle Harry Felpel's. Went to bed when we got home and feel better now at 10:30.

1/30/74 Wednesday
Fine mild day. Helen Ranck, Elizabeth, Mrs. Mohler and Linda came to help quilt. Elizabeth brought chicken corn soup. Got a lot done. I did not feel so good and started on a vomiting spree 15 minutes after they were gone and kept it up till 10:00. Eby got his own supper.

2/4/74 Monday
Cold and ice-covered. I washed and it dried real good. Hemmed one side of the quilt. Helen and Mabel called. I called Dr. Beacher about my problem. Eby went for milk. We did the Home record this evening.

2/8/74 Friday
Cloudy and started snowing at 11:00 and is still snowing. I went to Dr. Davidson's and am scheduled for the hospital Feb.26. Stopped at Uncle Milt's on the way home and washed up their kitchen. Got gas and groceries. Got a lot of things ready for carpet. Worked on dolls this evening. Snowmobiles are traveling.

2/11/74 Monday
Sunny and not so cold. I washed and did some mending. Cleaned my drawer. Made a nightie from some old shirts. Linda stopped in on her way from work. Said she will work till November if she gets a raise. Went to bed early.

2/12/74 Tuesday
Clear, cold and sunny. I worked 12-8. Told Ruth my hospital plans. Cleaned my drawer and did the ironing. Made some mayonnaise. Eby went to Board meeting. We all got raises. Mine is $2.40 an hour. Linda and her boyfriend came for her check. I called Aunt Cora. Uncle Milt gets weak spells.

2/22/74 Friday
Very mild and sunny. I finished the quilt and cleaned the house real thorough. Washed the car and went for gas, but did not get any. A plane was hijacked in Washington D.C. and three were killed. Dale came this evening on his way to Isaac's with his organ. Gas situation is worse.

2/26/74 Tuesday
Fine day. Worked 12-8. Linda got stuck in the snow and was fifteen minutes late. Finished packing, bathed and Eby came home at 10:00 to bring me to the hospital. Was admitted and arrived in Room 777 at 12:00. Had the usual procedures and Xrays. Called Amy. Read The Blue Nile. It is very quiet. Went to bed at 9:00.

2/27/74 Wednesday
Fine weather. No breakfast or water. Xrays at 7:30. Bathed and finished reading The Blue Nile. The book is a description of what is in man. Amos and Eleanor were in for a few minutes. Got first card. More Xrays. Light liquid supper. Drinks of thick white, pink and a pint of clear citrate of magnesia at bedtime. Joanne took Eby supper and brought him in this evening.

3/1/74 Friday
No food or water and went for surgery at 2:10 and got back to room at 6:00. Eby and Abram were here when I came back. Felt very uncomfortable coming back to reality. Got oxygen at intervals during the night.

3/2/74 Saturday
Very sore and got a light diet and oxygen. Abram and Pat and Eby and Joanne were here. Mary Alice and Nancy brought Eby in. Flowers are coming and some cards. Went for a walk in the hall.

3/5/74 Tuesday
Not so sore and had normal B.M. Bathed myself. Food tastes a little better. Lots of visitors. Jay and Margie had Eby for supper and then brought him in.

3/6/74 Wednesday
Partly cloudy and raining this evening. Eleanor Hershey called this forenoon. Took my bath and combed hair. Still on soft diet. Dr. Davidson took out some stitches and redressed the incision. I watered my flowers and picked out the dead ones. Charlie brought Eby in. Got four more bouquets and plants. Got 16 cards and letters. Linda made supper for Eby. Mary Alice came earlier. Visited a lady up the hall.

3/8/74 Friday
Partly cloudy and pleasant. Hospital maintenance man fixed the heat and the room is more comfortable. The room was cool and pleasant. Went for walks and got all the stitches out and bottle off. Called Johnnie Plastino, Florence Gehman, Bertha Martin, Sue and Uncle Charlie. Aunt Mary, Aunt Cora, Abram, Mary Alice and Emma called. Talked with a young woman up the hall with back surgery. Her 19th hospital stay.

3/9/74 Saturday
Cloudy, colder and drizzling. I got all ready to leave and rested. Milton, Barbara and Daddy came for me at 2:30. They helped get the flowers in and placed. Dale came and Daddy went for hams and bacons. Stopped for fresh oysters and we had soup for supper.

3/10/74 Sunday
Windy day. I was up most all day. Eby went to church. Dale and I got dinner. Milton's, Mary Alice and Nancy came this afternoon and evening. Esther came. Food tastes better and I feel stronger.

3/11/74 Monday
Sunny and cloudy by evening. I spent the day resting, writing, reading. Showered and dressed my incision. Talked to Mabel. Wrote some thank you notes. Eby slept most all evening.

3/19/74 Tuesday
Nice day. I rested till Helen Ranck came on way from work. Watered flowers and ate lunch and Rhoda called. Emma and Martha Horning came about 1:15. Had a nice visit. Emma brought some quilts and fabrics. Eby burned the brush and trash on the garden. He lost his glasses and missed them when he came in. He will use mine.

3/20/74 Wednesday
Fine weather. Bathed and dressed my incision. Sewed some doll clothes. Cleaned sewing machine drawers. Found Eby's glasses. They were in the fire and plastic was melted and the glass brown. I cleaned them up and put the glass in his old frames. They are all right. He went to midweek service.

4/8/74 Monday
Cloudy with some rain. The Clemens family worked on house cleaning. Swept down, washed windows, cleaned floors and baseboards. Edgar brought tongues and I sugar cured three. Linda stopped on her way from work and was here for supper. Eby got TV out for Edgar and the children.

4/17/74 Wednesday
A fine day. Frosty. I cut some quilt patches. Rubbed the cupboards. Went for eggs and lettuce and cabbage, which we planted this evening. Aunt Cora called and I called Helen Ranck and Ray. John Stoltzfus was here to get Ray's address to order horse medicine. Wrote to Gary Bluelegs.

4/18/74 Thursday
Weather fine. I did most of the cleaning. Made doughnuts. Finished the second Laura Ingalls Wilder book. Sanford sent me a pretty bouquet of cut flowers for my birthday. Eby went to Board Meeting at the Medical Center. Got letters from Rhoda and Grace.

4/24/74 Wednesday
Partly cloudy and cool. Mabel came and brought me dress fabric for a birthday gift. Went to Byler's and picked up the canning meat, dried beef and mince meat. Cured dried beef and got meat cooked and ground for mince meat. Cleaned things up and Mrs. Brown and Mrs. Rose Ordille took Daddy, Mary Alice and me out to dinner at Plain and Fancy. We all had an enjoyable evening. Mrs. Brown gave me a fern, notes and a cactus. Rose gave me a yarn box and scissors, Mary Alice a flower book.

4/30/74 Tuesday
Sunny and warm. I put the flowers out of the kitchen and cleaned the windows and put the screens in. Planted the geraniums and larkspur. Gave the roses a soaking. Rested a while. Aunt Cora and Mary Alice called. Eby put strings up for passion vine and mowed yard. Planted thumbergia.

5/3/74 Friday
Rained all night and cloudy. Worked 12-8. Had a good night. Everyone said it was good to have me back. Went to Harry Good's, Shady Maple, Provident Bookstore, the Silk Mill, to Ezra King's and for bread. Rested and ate and took Louise Poole along to Leon Summer's to help ice cupcakes for the Fire Hall. Got home at 4:30. Rested. Eby worked late. Had a long talk with Mabel.

5/6/74 Monday
Sunny with some showers. I washed and ironed. Aunt Cora and Sue called. Mrs. Charlotte Brown stopped to take me along to take the Swiss A.F.S. student to Victor's and the Australian A.F.S. student to Harold's. Talked to Mabel.

5/17/74 Friday
A hot day. Worked 12-8. Stopped for watercress, eggs and bread. Made a shell bark chiffon cake and got things ready to take along. Left at 5:00 for Milton's with Coy's.

5/18/74 Saturday
A pretty day. Slept late and we all went for brunch at 10:00 at the school dining room. Spent the afternoon visiting and the Coy's showed their slides of the tornado in Ohio in April. I had story time with Dougie. Barbara cooked us a good supper in honor of Dougie's birthday. The men went fishing. Peter Haile was in charge of the dining room.

5/19/74 Sunday
Fine day. Slept late. Had a good omelet for breakfast. Went to services at the chapel. Mrs. Simons gave a talk, a senior gave a talk, and Peter Haile a message. Had dinner in the school dining room and met a lot of the faculty. Left for home about 3:00 and got home at 8:45. Truman is a very good driver and we had a nice trip.

5/20/74 Monday
Fine weather. I cleaned and ironed. Rested a while. Made cream puffs and filled them with ice cream to serve with raspberry sauce. Cooked supper for Mary Alice and Nancy, who brought the foreign students staying with Victor's and Harold's. Had a nice evening. They left at 10:00. Daddy went to start the car and it was dead because he left the glove compartment open. He took me to work. Helen and I had a long gab session.

6/3/74 Monday
A fine sunny day. I washed, ironed and mended. Wed the iris and cannas row. Picked two boxes of strawberries. Washed two rugs and rebound one. Elizabeth called to see if it suits to bring Mrs. Kohler to see Kassy's rug tomorrow. Eby dusted potatoes, beans, pickles, eggplant and cantaloupes. I read in Abram's surgery book about ganglion, which Mary Alice may have. Went to bed early.

6/6/74 Thursday
A fine day. Took Annis along to Sewing Circle. Stayed all day. Pressed some dresses this evening. Put four pints of strawberries in the freezer. Eby is full of going on Social Security. Becky called and wants me to help June 15. There are problems in some schools about teaching the Occult.

6/30/74 Sunday
Real nice day. Worked 12-8. Milton's took us to Meadville and to Abram's for dinner. Had an outdoor dinner. Isaac's, Jim's and Dale were there too. Had a nice time. Stopped at Uncle Landis' on the way home. Ben Clark has been voted in for deacon at Kinzer. Had a treat of ice cream when we came home. Had a card from Mary Alice where she is spending a week in Helvetia, West Virginia.

7/1/74 Monday
Gusty night with rain. Cleared warm. Milton and I went for cherries at 6:30. Got white sweet at 28 cents a pound and sour at 18 cents. Milton, Mike, Barbara and I seeded and canned all of them till dinner except what I put in freezer. Milton and Barbara went to Flaud's after lunch for plants and then to New Holland shopping. I slept and mended and washed up Dougie's Zippy.

7/4/74 Thursday
A hot day. We froze two freezers of ice cream for the picnic at the Home at noon today. The 31 guests were all able to be outdoors to eat. Eby mowed the yard and I hoed some garden and planted more corn after we got home. I cleaned up the ice cream freezers. Sanford called and is leaving Montana in August.

7/13/74 Saturday
Fine day. Worked 12-8 and got gas on my way home. Rested a little and dropped off Aunt Cora's buns at Clarence's. Went on to Harvest Drive and worked till 2:00. Got bread on way home. Slept till 6:00. Picked a half bucket of pickles. Got a card from Mary Alice. She enjoyed her visit with Sanford in Montana and is now in California with Charlie.

7/21/74 Sunday
Beautiful day. Took Sue and Mary Horst along to Meadville. Nora taught our class. Dan Leaman preached a harvest sermon. 56 there. Uncle Milt Barge died last night. The Weaver's did not go to church. Nancy came about 11:00 and stayed till 9:00. Robert's left at 3:15. We went with Clarence's to see Aunt Cora. She seems resigned. I called Landis, Paul and Charlie to be pallbearers.

7/24/74 Wednesday
Cloudy with some good showers. I did some searching for pictures for the reunion. Washed the car. Eby came home for lunch. We went to Uncle Milt Barge's funeral at Strasburg. Text was Micah 6:8. No singing. Had lunch for most everyone. Stopped to visit with Aunt Cora's six boys and their wives. Took our load to Bible School.

7/27/74 Saturday
Sunny and hot. I made drink for the reunion. Elizabeth furnished chicken and sandwiches and lots of good things. 130 were there. Had a tug of war, two pig chases and baby pictures guessing. Dale, Robert and Terri came to spend the night. They went to Good and Plenty for supper and to a play at the Guernsey Barn, "Isaac Takes a Wife." I picked the pickles.

8/6/74 Tuesday
Sunny and warm. I finished the first corn and put 8 quarts in the freezer. Made and the beds and cleaned. Boiled some ham and beef. Made a baked shad and blueberry

buckle for supper. Did some mending and wrote the family letter. Went up to sleep at Aunt Cora's. She is lonesome and talked till 10:00.

8/7/74 Wednesday
Rained this morning. I ate breakfast with Aunt Cora and got home at 8:45 to find that Eby had all the beds filled with tourists. I made a cake for Black Rock, washed and ironed. I picked a gallon of blackberries, a bucket of limas, pickles and canned 7 quarts. Took Sue along to Bible Study.

8/24/74 Saturday
A fine warm day with showers in the evening. Had Milton's, Weaver's and Nancy for the night. We gathered the food and spent the day at Black Rock for our third reunion there. All attended but Charlie and Greg. Uncle Charlie, Uncle Clarence's and Aunt Cora were our guests. Had a quiz made up of questions from the family. 86 questions.

8/30/74 Friday
Hot and sultry with showers. Worked at Harvest Drive from 8:00 to 2:00. Slept till 6:00. I picked pickles, a half bushel of limas and wed the flower bed by the white birch tree. Got a letter saying that Dale was named Outstanding Man of the Year.

8/31/74 Saturday
Warm day. Worked 12-8 at the Home. Rested an hour, ate lunch and worked at Harvest Drive 12:00-3:00. Made apple dumplings for supper and picked pickles. Bathed and went to bed early. Eby mowed lawn and stayed up for tourists. Have two rooms. Copes dried corn plant burned and Mr. Cope burned to death.

9/3/74 Tuesday
Sultry and cloudy with lots of rain this evening. I picked the pickles, some corn, limas, peppers, tomatoes and foods for Mary Alice and Grace. Made three apple pies. Mary Alice stopped for lunch on her way to Grace's and then to the new job in Helvetia. Her car was packed to the roof. I went to the store for cheese and crackers for our picnic at the park near Bowmansville for the workers at the Home. Linda took us along. It was very wet.

9/11/74 Wednesday
Warm and hazy. I did the ironing. Cut off sweet corn and pulled weeds, sowed spinach, turnips, radishes and lettuce. Picked pickles and limas and put 3 pints in the freezer. Leo Martin called and asked me to take a class of children on Sunday. Sanford called and asked how to prepare raw trype. He has a job pending in Los Angeles, California. Eby mowed yard.

9/16/74 Monday
Fine weather. Warmer. I washed and ironed. Picked pickles and canned one quart. Got in corn and found it too young. Put three pints in freezer. Planted in a lot of flowers.

Joe was here and patched the mortar between stones on front steps. Advertised the farm for sale. Clarence's left for their trip to Europe.

10/1/74 Tuesday
Fine weather. Worked 12-8. Got eggs on way home. Rested and left at 11:20 to go to sew at Ephrata Hospital. Stirred up oatmeal and chocolate chip cookies. Harold Groff brought two baskets of Smokehouse apples. Sue Martin called to plan our trip to Helvetia. Ray called to tell about their trip to Staunton, Helvetia and Jim's.

10/2/74 Wednesday
Cool weather. I baked the cookies. Dug the sweet potatoes. Mice had destroyed a lot of them. Cut off some corn and got 50 dozen off for the freezer. Have 74 pints done. Did the ironing and some mending. Worked at Harvest Drive from 3:00 to 6:00. We went to midweek service.

10/8/74 Tuesday
Left Grace's at 9:00 and arrived in Helvetia about 12:30. Stopped on our way at a store and a lookout. Ate our lunch and looked around the town. Saw the church, the pottery house, restaurant, cheese factory, gift shop and storage barn. After supper we went to visit Mrs. Mailloux, a daughter, and a boy who helps her. Eby and Jay fixed one of the beds. I mended the sofa and we cleaned windows.

10/9/74 Wednesday
Weather was beautiful. Had a good night and carried more water from the stream. Eby, Jay and Dallas worked on the well and got it working. Mary Alice, Sue and I took a walk to the cemetery and got winter garden things. Had chicken corn soup and went to the store. Left for Weaver's at 3:00 and arrived there at 6:00 after a beautiful drive through the mountains. Grace had a good supper.

10/15/74 Tuesday
Partly cloudy with showers. We packed up and left for Edgar's at 7:30. I drove part way. Ate our lunch in the car on the way and got here at 1:00. Rhoda is babysitting for a neighbor who is in the hospital. We bought a bushel of apples and made 15 quarts from part of them. Saw the new room furnished for the first time.

10/16/74 Wednesday
Rained. Helped Rhoda to get Rosa's quilt in the frame and start quilting. Eby brought some of the children home and went with Edgar to a business meeting at the church. Had our tea with Rhoda and Edgar before going to bed.

11/6/74 Wednesday
Clear and cooler. Worked 12-8. Rested a while. Made some food ready and took lunch to Aunt Cora, ate with her and spent the afternoon. She was full of talk and I worked on Marcia's state bird patches while I listened. We went to midweek service at church.

11/9/74 Saturday
Beautiful day. We left for Linda's wedding at 9:00 and she was married at 10:00 in Mechanics Grove Church of the Brethren. 157 attended the reception. All went well. Karen and Kim cried. Milton and Ray took the pictures. Went to their home to see her gifts. Happened on an accident by Octorara Presbyterian Church on the way home. We narrowly escaped when a car hit a steam engine. Milton's came and we had 17 for supper. Mary Alice and Nancy left.

11/11/74 Monday
Fine weather. Edgar's left at 9:30. I washed a big wash. After lunch I went to help clean up the little cemetery where our great great grandmother was buried. Uncle Joe, Elsie, Paul, Elvin and two boys were helping. We made an improvement. Got wash in. Our new roomer, Duke Johnston, came for supper. We went to Meadville. Luke Horst is our speaker. The subject was Relationships.

11/22/74 Friday
Fair. Cleaned things up and stopped at the store, for gas and for bread on our way to Abram's. Chatted a while with Pat. Made supper for Mary Alice and Nancy, who came at 6:00. Got 4 pints of salsify ready for freezing. Girls helped lay out some patches for my quilt. Mary Alice got her hair cut, so the world has lost some of its joy again.

11/30/74 Saturday
Pleasant weather. Eby worked till noon and took it easy. I did up the work and worked at Harvest Drive from 12:00 to 4:00. Becky King was in charge. Made four dozen boxes of potatoes. I finished the pillow cases and stamped them all. Melvin Barge and Paul Wright were here about selling the farm. Melvin Barge called at 11:00 and said farm is sold. An Amish woman hung herself at Jay Hostetter's old farm.

12/11/74 Wednesday
Fine weather. I mixed nine kinds of cookies and put them in the garage refrigerator. Shelled the peanuts, made raisin and date fillings. Cleaned corn fodder off the garden. Went to Clarence's this afternoon and helped with Elizabeth Ressler's crib quilts. Went to John Glick's for the mottos.

12/12/74 Thursday
Shower this morning. Cleared sunny. I did the cleaning. Stirred up two kinds of cookies and popped a big kettle of corn. Framed the mottos and wrapped them. Rested a while. Called Mabel. Watered the flowers and transplanted some thumbergia. Melvin Barge called for the deed and some other papers for the farm.

12/14/74 Saturday
Cloudy day. Worked 12-8. Nancy and I made 100 dozen cookies. Kept us busy. Eby did some collecting for Medical Center and visited Rutter Skiles this afternoon.

Mary Alice called and is living peacefully in Helvetia. Nancy packed up and left at 7:30. I bathed and went to bed.

12/24/74 Tuesday
Partly cloudy with rain this evening. I grated a cocoanut and made more flap jacks. Made peanut brittle. Talked to Mabel. Read this evening. Eby came home at 1:30. I went to the store this forenoon. Levi and Anna Mary brought a big bowl of fruit. Duke gave a box of candy. Alfred gave bakeware.

12/25/74 Wednesday
Fog, clouds, rain, wind and sunshine. We went to Isaac's for dinner. They were all there except Judy. She went to her boyfriend's (John Lentz's) home. They took us to see Judy's school. A real nice school room with pretty decorations and drawings. I called Edgar's and Weaver's this morning. Dale was at Edgar's and Mary Alice and Nancy at Weaver's.

12/28/74 Saturday
Partly cloudy. Worked 12-8. Stopped for bread at Amish store. Made things ready for Sunday dinner. Eby worked till noon. Ray's came about 7:30. They gave us two window frames with family pictures.

12/30/74 Monday
Fine weather. Milton took Mike to New Holland and got his car hose fixed. Doug is vomiting and not feeling well. I finished dolly quilt and cracked some shell bark. Milton did some. Milton and Barbara visited Aunt Cora. I rested with Doug and told him stories. They left for home at 6:20. We had a gripe meeting at Meadville till 11:10. A disturbing meeting. It did not edify.

1975

1/1/75 Wednesday
Damp with rain, sun and wind. Eby went to antique sale at Harry's Auction and to cow sale at New Holland. Made a date to have a hog butchered. Made up beds and put wash away. Cut an apron and sewed some. Mary Alice called and said she is doing well on her new sewing machine. Worked at Harvest Drive from 3:00 to 8:30. Ruth Meck, Dora and Sevilla were working.

1/10/75 Friday
Partly cloudy. Washed some dresses. Did the cleaning. Made up four quarts of Armenian relish from Ed's recipe. Rested and read. Sewed up some patches. Called Aunt Cora. Eby worked late. Two airplanes crashed in California. Ray and Jane flew to California. Isaac's got Laura at the Philadelphia Airport.

1/15/75 Wednesday
Sunny. Ten degrees. Becky called and said Rosa can have a job. I wrote her a letter. Sewed patches most all day. Helen called about the changes coming at the Home. Had our midweek service. Lots of discussion and ended with a Communion service.

1/20/75 Monday
Snowing most all day. No school. I wrote to Nancy and sent her a package. Wrote to Sanford and sent him his baby pictures for the shower. Sewed patches. Talked to Mabel. Jay Martin went to the hospital for numbness in his fingers and hands. Snowmobiles are traveling.

1/25/75 Saturday
A wet day for Levi's sale. Eby went and the heifers and implements brought good prices. Worked 12-8. Slept till 2:30. Called Helen and she is not feeling very well. Menno Eby's are at the home for the weekend. A bomb exploded in a New York restaurant killing four and injuring forty five.

2/6/75 Thursday
Partly cloudy and snow is melting. I went to Sewing Circle. 12 there. Did a pretty quilt for L.M.S. sale to pay for the gym. Roy Kreider died this morning. Called Becky to tell her that Rosa will be able to start working in April. Went to work at 10:00.

2/19/75 Wednesday
Still damp. Did the ironing. Went up to farm and mended ceiling in the dining room. Brought more things from the attic. Got carpet rags ready. Took two boxes of Milton's books to Coy's in New Holland. Stopped at Harry Good's and Shady Maple. A New Holland boy died from a fall after sniffing from an aerosol can.

2/22/75 Saturday
Fine weather. We all went up to the farm to empty the attic. Had it all done in time to have dinner at 12:00. Dale came this afternoon and put up new dining room light. Charlie and Nancy Crawford came to see Mary Alice. Eby worked till noon. He, Robert and Stevie went up to the farm this afternoon. Daylight savings time.

3/1/75 Saturday
Fine weather. Went with Ruth and Esther Clark and Mabel and Mildred to a quilting in Wayne. Had a nice time and got a lot quilted. Eby took the junk to the dump. Went for the hams and took some chairs to have redone. Mary Alice called and said all is well.

3/16/75 Sunday
Warmer and snow is almost gone. Went to Meadville. Had class together with Richard as teacher. We went up to see Aunt Cora this afternoon. She is getting attached to her new Goldie cat. We went to Meadville this evening. Four men gave a report

on going with a shipment of potatoes to Honduras. Aristotle Onassis, one of the world's richest men, died.

3/31/75 Monday
Clear and cold. Eby worked till 8:30 and we went in to the lawyer's office to make settlement for the farm. I did a little shopping and we stopped at Elva Scarr's where I got fitted for a new garment. Finished hemming Marcia's quilt. The siren blew. Sowed flower seeds in hot bed.

4/7/75 Monday
Nice day. Cold. Wash froze. Cleaned Alfred's room. His phone was put in. Did the ironing. Cleaned some cupboards. Called Mabel. Eby went to Board meeting. 800 orphans arrived in the U.S. from Vietnam for adoption.

4/26/75 Saturday
Beautiful day. Eby hauled Christ King's both ways for a frolic. We went shopping to Lancaster. I got a coat at Hagar's for $38.00. Stopped at Harvest Drive and worked till 6:00. Made a lot of potatoes. Edgar's got here a half hour before we did. Had a handy supper and looked at slides and visited.

4/28/75 Monday
Clear morning and clouded over. I did a big wash and made up the beds. Rosa slept late and took a bike ride. After lunch I took her to Harvest Drive to start her new job. I helped Eby put up more pea wire this evening.

4/29/75 Tuesday
Cloudy day. Worked 12-8 at Home and 4-8 at Harvest Drive. Took Rosa to Harvest Drive at 2:00 and visited Issac Smoker's. Jay Martin had some heart spells and was admitted to the hospital last evening. Half undecided about our trip to California. Abram called and said we are to go.

4/30/75 Wednesday
Fine weather. Rosa had the day off. I let her drive to the bank when I went for traveller's checks. I made things ready for our trip. Washed car, planted pickles, limas and some flower seeds. Milton came for supper when he brought some students to L.M.S. for three days. He and Rosa mowed the yard. Saigon surrendered. Had a lot of calls with good wishes.

5/1/75 Thursday
Raining. All packed and Uncle Charlie took us to York to meet Abram's at 8:30. Flew United Airlines from Baltimore to San Francisco at 10:30 and arrived at 1:00 Pacific time. Charlie met us and showed us some places in San Francisco. Took a cable car and a modern railway ride. Ed and Charlie took us for a Chinese dinner and how we did eat the good food. Went to bed at 1:00 E.D.T.

5/2/75 Friday
Sunny, cool and clear. Ed cooked a good breakfast. Went to see the redwoods. Then Abram's left for L.A. by plane. We drove to see some dairying country. Had a picnic lunch high in the mountains by a lake. Ed and Charlie flew their Hawaiian kite. I wrote some cards and called Gary Martin. We took Charlie and Ed out to dinner this evening to the Victoria Station.

5/3/75 Saturday
Had early breakfast and called Rosa. She said Uncle Jay took a turn for the worse yesterday. Called Aunt Mabel this evening and she said he is feeling some better. Charlie and Ed took us to meet our bus and stopped at a redwood park and Golden Gate Bridge park. Rainy. Left Jack Tar Hotel at 9:00 and traveled to Monterey, seeing a lot of interesting things.

5/5/75 Monday
Beautiful weather. Cool. Had breakfast in dining room and bus left at 8:45. One couple was late again. Stopped for Danish baked things and drove over some pretty scenic country. One stop in Century City, one in Hollywood and on to L.A. where Sanford met us. He took us to our motel and then to his apartment for supper. Back to motel and I wrote letters and cards. Called Clarence's and Jay is feeling better.

5/6/75 Tuesday
Fine day. Sanford took us to see dairy country, lots of alfalfa and lion country safari. We went to have a tour of the Queen Mary and to Disneyland where we met Abram's and had rides and saw all the interesting things made up to entertain and get people's money. Had a big day and were ready for bed.

5/7/75 Wednesday
Clear and warmer. Sanford took us to see his office and the Pacific State Hospital. We met Jill Keen and took her out for lunch. Sanford drove through the Chino Valley and we saw the big dairies and thousands of cattle. We met Abram's at Disneyland Hotel and attended the session of the psychiatric convention. 12,000 there. Margaret Mead was the speaker.

5/8/75 Thursday
Sanford called us early and gave us a snack and then took us to meet Abram's and get the bus to go to the airport. Left at 9:00 to leave for home. Stopped at Las Vegas and then on to Baltimore. Abram's took us to Gap from Baltimore and we had a snack before they got on their way home.

5/9/75 Friday
Good weather. I washed for Alfred and Rosa brought it in. She went with me to Linda's place to pick up Ray's meat. Eby went to Amos Bowell's and got bologna, dried beef and doggies and picked up the chairs. Left for Ray's at 10:30 and ate our

lunch in the car under a shade tree. We helped put their meat in the freezer and Eby went with Ray on calls. I cracked shell barks and we made a nut cake and some dressing. Had a good supper of leg of lamb.

5/10/75 Saturday
Some rain and hail. We took a walk and drove to Princeton. Ate lunch and left about 3:00 for home. Ray's went as far as a museum in Doylestown where we spent an hour or more. Very interesting. The car stopped at the intersection at King of Prussia. Got home safely at 8:00. Rosa worked till 11:30. Abe called and said Jay is worse.

5/17/75 Saturday
Sunny and warm. Worked 12-8. Anna Mae not well. Rested and went to Harvest Drive at 10:00 and worked till 1:00. Left for Meadville Sewing School. 22 there. Stopped at Spring Heads for water cress. Almost stepped on a snake. Eby harrowed garden. Jay is still improving. Bathed and went to bed early.

5/19/75 Monday
Fine warm day. Cleaned Alfred's room. Washed and ironed. Hoed some of the garden and it hoed nicely. Rosa slept from 11:00 to 11:00. It is Whitsontide Monday and the Amish are visiting. Did the Home record this evening.

6/23/75 Monday
Warm day. Cleaned Alfred's room. Washed and ironed. Hoed some weeds. Picked last strawberries and first pickles. Called Sanford and he is feeling better. Rosa worked on her rug. Eby tried to harrow garden and it is very hard. Plane crashed at the Kennedy Airport after being struck by lightning and 112 of the 122 aboard were killed.

7/1/75 Tuesday
Clear and pleasant. Worked 12-8. Stopped for 10 dozen dirty eggs for Milton's. He and Barbara went with me to buy a new refrigerator. He helped Daddy bring it home after work and it is doing fine. Worked at Harvest Drive from 10:30-1:00. Milton put a new light in the apartment.

7/2/75 Wednesday
Clear and pleasant. Washed and ironed. Cleaned our bedroom and cleaned up old refrigerator in garage. Rosa went to Witmer's for a cookout as she has the day off. Eby had to make a decision and it was to quit at Keen's. Picked red raspberries. Rhoda is going to the hospital for a hernia operation.

7/3/75 Thursday
Warmer with gust and heavy showers afternoon and evening. I went to Sewing Circle. Eby's first day of retirement. He harrowed and hoed some of the garden. I cleaned and scrubbed garage this afternoon. Eby took and nap and helped. Eby went for milk.

7/7/75 Monday
Partly cloudy and warm. Eby and I picked 31 pounds of gold cherries at Elmer Beiler's at 28 cents a pound. Eby helped to seed and I canned 11 quarts. Hoed some garden, picked the pickles and red raspberries. Art Keen came to get Eby to come back to Atglen to work as it is not going well with Curtis and Debbie.

7/14/75 Monday
A lot of rain. Four inches and some came in basement. Eby burned the trash. Art Keen came to tell Eby to come back to work tomorrow. Finished up Bible School materials. Mary Alice called and things are going well in Helvetia. First night of Bible School.

7/15/75 Tuesday
Heavy showers morning and evening. Some places had ten and eleven inches in the past week. I worked on the apartment and did a big wash and ironing. Eby went back to Keen's at Parksburg and is Art's private secretary. He worked till noon and went to Vintage sale this afternoon.

7/29/75 Tuesday
Sunny and warm. Worked 12-8. Stopped for thread and eggs. Canned some pickles. Made chocolate chip and white cake. Eby went to Lancaster to see about Social Security check. Took out some potatoes. Joe Bechtold was here painting porch. Put the Virginia quilt in this evening. It is a problem.

7/30/75 Wednesday
Real sunny and warm. The Westman's stopped for their pickles and canned things on the way home to Florida. I took Elam King's and another couple to a reunion on Beaver Road near Oregon. Eby brought them home and stopped for groceries. Isaac's baby boy was born this afternoon.

7/31/75 Thursday
Hot day. Mabel, Ellen Groff, Margie and Sue helped to quilt the one Grace sent from Virginia for the Relief Sale. Got a nice lot done. Helen and Aunt Cora called. Isaac came on his way from the hospital and said the baby is not doing so well. I quilted till 9:00. Called Charlie.

8/7/75 Thursday
Cool and pleasant. Worked 12-8. Took Annis along to Sewing Circle. Eleven there. Had a bite of lunch and Joanne, Sally, Karen and Kim took me along to the hospital to see baby Bradley. He now moves some. Eby did some bookwork. Rosa finished her rug. I went to bed early.

8/8/75 Friday
Beautiful day. Worked 12-8. Stopped at Meadville and fixed up library books. Did the cleaning and took a nap. Made a walnut cake. Eby took out potatoes, mowed

the yard, sowed turnips and harrowed some garden. Called Elizabeth. The baby is taking the bottle and off one of the medications.

8/10/75 Sunday
Warmer. Worked 12-8. Went to Meadville. Forty one there. Emma taught and Amos preached on Revelations 3:15. Rosa went with us to Isaac's to see little Bradley. He is doing better. Spent the evening at home. Mary Alice called from Ocean City.

8/13/75 Wednesday
Hot with gust and rain. Rosa took me to Emma Hershey's and I went with Emma and others to Landis Valley Museum to quilt. Helen brought me home. Rosa worked on her quilt after supper. A high school is to open in the old Linville Hill School. Nancy called and said she has a new boyfriend who gave her 25 roses and dinner.

8/24/75 Sunday
Left at 6:30 with Clair Denlinger's for Spruce Lake Camp. Foggy drive. Had a very pleasant day with the morning service, dinner, miniature golf, shuffleboard, walking, visiting and evening service. Rosa went to church at Columbia. Afred moved more things in.

8/25/75 Monday
Sunny and warm. Gusty and rained last night. Had breakfast and a morning service. Did a little quilting. Left at 11:00 and Clair's drove us over the Poconos. Had a snack lunch and boat ride. Ate supper on the way home and got here about 9:00. It was a fine trip.

8/30/75 Saturday
Partly cloudy and cool. Packed up the food and left for Black Rock at 10:15. Used the administrative basement for our reunion. Everyone was there including Judy's boyfriend. Uncle Charlie did not make it. Uncle Mart Groff was our guest. Little Bradley was a good baby for his first reunion.

9/18/75 Thursday
Cloudy with showers. I cut all the grapes. Made jelly, juice and four quarts for pies. Washed up the dishes and put them away. Alfred slept all day. Had a big letter from Rhoda. Called Isaac's and Nancy. She modeled her hands with expensive rings for a Christmas catalog.

9/19/75 Friday
Cloudy and rainy. Worked 12-8. Stopped at Elam King's for rhubarb and put 15 pints in the freezer. Sewed a while and took a nap. Eby worked on the water softener. Found it broken. Patty Hearst was captured in L.A. Bathed, packed and came to the Home. The new heating system is not yet finished. No hot water. No heat.

9/27/75 Saturday
Slept till 8:00 and had breakfast with Stevie and Jennie. We then went to the Augusta Relief Sale. Spent the day seeing all the activity and effort that goes into this project. The quilt sale was very interesting. Highest two sold for $820. and $555. The Staunton ladies' that I helped quilt bought $155. Had a barbecue supper and took the children home. Grace and Robert helped finish up. The sale came to $60,000. Weather was fine.

9/28/75 Sunday
Beautiful day. Went to the Staunton Church. They have made some big improvements. Had a sermon by Pastor Nolt on Ephesians 4. Sunday School lesson was about the flood. Had a good dinner and left for Helvetia at 3:00. Took turns driving and got there at 6:30. They were all done at the restaurant and we had a snack before hearing the Helvetia news and going to bed.

9/29/75 Monday
Fine day. Got up at 8:00 and saw the cheesemaking. Picked the grapes and made jelly. Picked up some apples and made 17 quarts of applesauce for freezing. Had a tour of the restaurant, antique store, and some of the sheds. Eby trimmed the grapes and some of the wild roses. We helped clean it all up for mowing grass. He made a big mistake trimming off the hemlock in front of the restaurant. Got some things for winter gardens.

9/30/75 Tuesday
Fine day. Ate with Mary Alice and Debbie and left for home at 8:10. Had a good night and drove all the way home with one gas and toilet stop. Drove a few miles out of the way with a wrong turn. Got safely home at 5:30. Daddy drove most of the 400 miles on this trip. Made supper and went to bed early. Dale called. Esther left some fresh buns.

10/1/75 Wednesday
Worked 12-8. Wrote to Mary Alice. Tom Denlinger died about midnight from a heart attack. I washed and picked a bushel of limas. Eby mowed yard and helped shell them this evening. Put seven pints in the freezer. Talked to Alice Crouse, Mabel, Sue, Annis, Esther and Helen. Eby told Alfred no more furniture.

10/4/75 Saturday
Fine weather. Worked 12-8. Dale came and went with us to Tom Denlinger's viewing at the Presbyterian Church. We then went to visit Nancy. Spent the day eating, visiting and seeing her place of work. Got home at 8:30. Nancy sent some of Mary Alice's things to store here. Someone stole the Social Security checks from the Home mailbox.

11/10/75 Monday
Cloudy with an inch of rain. I made a cake and pudding. Ray and Jane went shopping for a rocker for John's baby-to-be. The girls stayed with me. This afternoon we went to the Hans Herr House and stopped to see Aunt Cora. Ray and Jane went to visit Kathleen Denlinger.

11/18/75 Tuesday
Fine weather. Got things together and left at 8:00. Stopped in Lancaster and at Kauffman's for apples. Went on to Ithaca. I drove from Hazelton. Got here at 3:30. We made applesauce and got parsley ready for freezing. Visited this evening.

11/19/75 Wednesday
Fine mild day. Slept late and took Rhoda to Ithaca to get a huge carton. Stopped to see Bethel Grove Church. Cut patches this afternoon and evening. Talked. Marcia is practicing music. Conrad is embroidering quilt patches. Edgar went for choir practice.

11/20/75 Thursday
Beautiful day. Left Edgar's at 8:50 and had a good trip home. Stopped in Lancaster and bought Eby two shirts at Garvin's closing out sale and a cashmere coat for me for $79.00. Got home at 4:00. Eby went to Board meeting. I went to bed early. House smells of burned chicken. Alfred went away and left it burn to ashes.

11/26/75 Wednesday
Fine day. Went to Harvest Drive at 7:30 to help cut up 60 turkeys. Got home at 2:30. Stopped for butter, bread and gas. Cut up our turkey, did the sweet potatoes, filling and pumpkin pies. Cooked bones and picked it off. Mopped kitchen. Eby set up tables.

11/27/75 Thursday
Pleasant weather. Got things ready for Thanksgiving dinner. We went to Paradise for services. Clair Eby preached. The text was "Let the redeemed of the Lord say so." Good attendance. Abram's, Isaac's, Jim's, Dale and Nancy were here for dinner. Eby washed up the dishes and I went to bed.

12/2/75 Tuesday
Clear and cold. Worked 12-8. Stopped to pick water cress and at the Dry Goods store. Cleaned apartment. It still smells very much of smoke. Had windows open all day. Eby took lawn mower to be serviced and got all of bologna sliced. Watered the flowers. Had a big letter from Amy. Did some mending and called Mabel.

12/6/75 Saturday
Foggy with some ice. Rained this evening. We all got around and went to Judy and John's wedding at 10:00 at Mechanics Grove Church. Met the Lentz's and lots of

the other guests. Reception was held at Harvest Drive. All went well. Milton's joined the others here for supper. Some did shopping on the way back.

12/10/75 Wednesday
Partly cloudy. I stirred up sand tarts, flap jacks, peppernuts, raisin filled, taylor cookies. Made a date and nut loaf, rice krispies, date balls and haystacks. Went to the store and forgot my list, so I forgot to get oatmeal. Motor went out on the mixer. Dusted and swept. Shelled peanuts and got oranges and grapes ready for fruitcake.

12/11/75 Thursday
Good weather. I stirred up two kinds of cookies and started baking at 8:00. Nancy came at 10:00 and we baked cookies until 5:00. Made a lot, about ten kinds. We went to the Christmas party at the Fire Hall. I took fruit salad and cookies. There was a lot of food and much left over.

12/12/75 Friday
We left Gap at 6:00 with Uncle Charlie to go to the Lancaster Depot and took an Amtrak train to N.Y.C., then changed to a Long Island train and got here to Stony Brook by 12:15. Eby went with Milton to a class. Mike had a wrestling match (his first and he lost) this evening. Milton and Eby went. Doug, Barbara and I stayed here. Went to the dining hall for supper.

12/15/75 Monday
Mild with light rain. Milton had a meeting before breakfast, and Barbara went to the infirmary from breakfast in the dining room. Packed up and Barbara took us to the depot at 10:00. Had a good train ride home. Charlie met us at the depot and we got home at 4:00. Cooked some Long Island potatoes and broccoli for supper.

12/25/75 Thursday
Cold, cloudy with good skating. Eby took me to the Home where I worked 8-4. He came back for a good Christmas dinner. 18 went away. There were only two tables. Sewed up some patches. Did the Home record book. Isaac's had their family all home for dinner.

12/29/75 Monday
Fine weather. Cleaned Alfred's room. Washed. Made buns, graham cracker fluff, cole slaw and other food for supper as Milton's came at 3:30. They had been to MCC to look about a job for their sabbatical year. Eby went to the home and helped Joe finish the bathroom.

12/30/75 Tuesday
Rained. Worked on quilt. Last evening a bomb was set off at Laguardia Airport in N.Y.C. killing 11 and injuring 75. A horrible time. We went to the New Holland Bank to pay some bills for the Home project.

1976

1/1/76 Thursday
Snow and sunny. Worked 12-8. Slept two hours and went to Clarence's for dinner. Menno's, Jay's, Landis', Paul's, Charlie and Mart and Miriam were there too. Had a very good dinner and nice time visiting. Sewed some patches this evening. Ray and Jane called. Started to read Bible through this year.

1/8/76 Thursday
Bad weather and cleared this afternoon. No school or sewing circle. Eby worked this A.M. and stayed home this P.M. I finished sewing the patches on the flower garden quilt. Pat and Jim called to tell us that Jim has a stone that will have to be removed with surgery. Eby went to Medical Center meeting.

1/15/76 Thursday
Fine weather. Went to Sewing Circle. Stopped at Abner's and helped with Esther's quilt for a couple hours. Eby slept propped up and went to work this forenoon. Kept quiet this afternoon and evening. I called to ask about Jim. Called Abram to ask how to proceed with Daddy's pain.

1/19/76 Monday
Clear and cold. Five above zero. Cleaned apartment. Washed. Worked on Nancy's rug. Eby went to the Historical Center this afternoon. Says his fracture is some better. Eby has not found his hearing aid. Doesn't miss it much.

1/20/76 Tuesday
Snowed about two inches. I wrote to Rhoda. Worked on rug all day. Called Aunt Cora. She is making two new dresses for summer. Eby did not go to the Historical Center. Eby's rib is much better. Art is very kind to him.

1/24/76 Saturday
Fine day. Did some cleaning and washed the car. Eby did some reading, sleeping, worked on clothes pole, went to the store and for milk. I made ice cream. Called Jim in Holy Cross Hospital and he is feeling real good. Still has his stone and is hoping it will dislodge and pass out. Abram and Pat were to see him. Dale went to help with Jim's work over the weekend.

2/2/76 Monday
It went from 32 degrees at midnight down to 8 degrees and snowed three inches, blowing it into drifts. No school and the ground hog saw his shadow. I cleaned the apartment. Started a rug for Sanford. Eby worked on his clothes pole. Had Darrell Smoker open drive and he went for milk and paper. I called Esther and Mabel. Minnie and Dale called. 12 degrees below in Perry County.

2/6/76 Friday
Cloudy with a little snow. Worked on rug. Eby went to Historical Center this afternoon. An estimate of 6000 killed in an earthquake in Guatemala, El Salvador and Honduras. Many injured and more tremors reported.

2/8/76 Sunday
Partly cloudy. Worked 12-8. Went to Meadville. 41 there. Emma taught our class. Amos preached on the Holy Spirit. I slept and read this afternoon. Nancy called and said she injured her knee on her desk drawer on Thursday. It is recovering. Abram called and asked if we will babysit a week in May.

2/9/76 Monday
Fine weather. Cleaned Alfred's room. Washed and ironed. Wrote family letter. Washed the car. Eby worked at Keen's this A.M. and took old green bed for repairs this afternoon. Called Margie and Jay is recovering. David was to see him and they asked about Kenneth. They don't know where he is. Mended and rugged.

2/10/76 Tuesday
Sunny and warmer. Washed some dresses and coverings. Made a grape pie. Worked on rug. Sanford called and said he may take a month's vacation and go to help in Guatemala. 17,500 dead. Eby had trouble with the truck coming home from the Historical Center. He went to Board Meeting this evening. I made some valentines.

2/24/76 Tuesday
Weather fine. Worked 12-8. Fannie S. sick all night and vomited twice. Francis B. had a seizure at 6:30. I rested a short time when I got home and we met Isaac's at Guernsey Barn and they took us to Holy Spirit Hospital in Camp Hill to see Jim. His minister and Pat were there too. Had dinner in Camp Hill at the Dutch Kitchen. Dale called and told us about his promotion.

3/1/76 Monday
Mild and sunny. 60 degrees in the shade. Cleaned Alfred's room. Wrote a letter and some stories to Doug. Washed and ironed. Planted the hot bed. Margie called and said Jay went to church and was trimming grapes. Talked to Aunt Cora. Jim called and said he went home this afternoon. He is feeling real good after his surgery.

3/10/76 Wednesday
Biggest snow of the winter. Melted some. Had a quilting party. Mabel, Esther, Annis, Margie Kauffman, Emma and Miriam Hershey. Got a nice lot done. Eby worked this morning and went to Lancaster about income taxes this afternoon. Went to bed early.

3/24/76 Wednesday

Clear and mild. I quilted all day. Eby worked at Keen's and went to Lancaster to have income tax done. Over $13,000 required. Had card and letters from Mary Alice and Debbie and a thank you note from Peter Haile's. Ray's came this evening.

3/31/76 Wednesday

Rainy. Started quilting before breakfast and worked on it all day. Have 85 patches left. We went to Christ King's on our way to Meadville and picked up a $25,000 check as a payment on the farm.

4/8/76 Thursday

Weather cool. I wrote family letter and made up a seed order. Aunt Cora called twice. I cleaned bookcase and desk. Did not feel very well. Planted some flower plants that Margie sent. Philip Ruhl died this afternoon from injuries in an accident Saturday evening near Greensburg.

4/18/76 Sunday

Warmest Easter on record. 95 degrees. Went to Meadville. Had our communion. Washed feet with Nora. A visitor family was there in a large camper. We went to Abram's for dinner. Had ham, broccoli, baked corn, rhubarb, potato salad and cake. Dale, Sanford and Nancy were there. Stopped to see Aunt Cora and she was not at home. Some folks went in creeks bathing.

4/24/76 Saturday

Donald and Linda picked us up at 3:50 and we started for Stony Brook. Stopped for breakfast and got there at 8:15. Had brunch at 10:30 and met some of the folks. Went for a drive and stopped for ice cream. Linda and I walked to the shopping center and greenhouse. Barbara made us a good fish supper. Milton and Donald went for clams for supper. Had some slides and visited.

4/25/76 Sunday

Cloudy with showers. After breakfast we went to chapel service at the school. Daniel Dale, a missionary to Japan, spoke. We had dinner in the dining room, met a lot of the faculty. The Don Gabelien's have resigned and are going to Atlanta, Georgia. Visited till 3:30 and left for home. Got here at 7:30. Stopped for a snack. Nancy and Abram called. Charlie sent a yellow mum for my birthday.

5/4/76 Tuesday

Clear and cool. Did some mending. Made a cake for Eby to share at work to celebrate his birthday. Took Helen Ranck along to The Willows where Willard and Ruth Myers treated us to a dinner. Helped Eby put the balance of the pea wire up and dug up some weeds.

5/6/76 Thursday
Weather fine. Worked 12-8 and Linda followed. I got things ready for leaving for Abram's at 1:30. Eby worked till noon. We got to Abram's at 2:30. They were almost ready for their flight to Florida. Eby went to Linda's for supper and to Board meeting. I took the four children to a music program at the high school. Planted some petunias.

5/7/76 Friday
A few showers. I made rice krispie cake, oatmeal cookies, blueberry buckle and things for supper. Mended Becky's trousers and blouse, Andy's glove, and put some more stuffing in some cushions. Took Andy for his music lesson. Watched T.V. and played games with the children. Becky hurt her ankle. Wrote family letter.

5/8/76 Saturday
Clear and cool. Slept till 7:00. Played with Becky and Sammy. She left for Astronomy class at 10:00 and then went to a horse show. Came home at 4:00. David and Andy went to choir practice. Made some beans in crock pot, red eggs, a cake and apple dumplings for supper. Eby came about 4:00. We put pea wire up. Played jacks with children. Abram called.

5/13/76 Thursday
Clear and warmer. Eby came at 2:00. He and Andy mowed lawn. I washed the children's beds and clothing. Cleaned their rooms. Did some mending. Made a blueberry pie. Took Andy for band and brought him home. Eby took David for music lesson in Lebanon. Helped Becky study her states and capitols. Had a busy day.

5/14/76 Friday
Partly cloudy and warm. Dusted and cleaned the balance of the house. Made a chocolate cake, cupcakes, tapioca, blueberry pie and some snails. Eby ran the cleaner. Did the wash Eby brought from home. Put heart patches on a pair of Becky's pants. Busy day. Got home at 8:20. Did some ironing and came to the Home for the weekend to help with the cooking.

6/7/76 Monday
Fine day. Cleaned Alfred's room. Washed and ironed. Called Aunt Cora and she said she is down in the dumps and there is no help to get out. Mabel and Mildred came to help quilt this afternoon when they brought watches to Harvey. Picked some sugar peas for Linda as hers were destroyed by the hail. Joe Bechtold put ventilators in the porch ceilings. Went to bed early.

6/11/76 Friday
Hot. Worked 12-8 and went to Good's store and waited till it opened at 9:00 and they did not have a hat for Daddy. Got home at 10:00 and picked two boxes of

strawberries and a basket of peas. Cleaned up a bit. Eby worked till noon and helped cover peas. Packed up and came to Robert Weaver's new home by 7:30.

6/12/76 Saturday
Warm day with showers this evening. Spent a quiet day here with the Weaver's. Put some peas in the freezer. Grace, Jennie and I went to the Co-Op and I bought Daddy two new straw hats. Took a walk to the upper end of their farm. Lots of evergreen trees. Watched a T.V. program about an adopted family of twelve.

6/13/76 Sunday
Cloudy and much cooler. Packed up and went to the Staunton Church, where they had their dedication service and a delicious fellowship dinner. After this we left for Helvetia. Got there about 5:00 and ate in the Hutte. Spent a nice evening with Mary Alice, Debbie and Doug.

6/14/76 Monday
Partly cloudy. Had a good fish breakfast. Left for home at 8:30 and had good traveling all the way. Got home at 4:45. Had three detours. Had our supper and I picked a bushel of peas. Eby helped shell them and I put them in freezer.

6/28/76 Monday
Warm day. Cleaned apartment. Left to pick cherries at 8:00 and the sour ones were all picked. Got enough gold ones for seven quarts. Seeded and canned them. Had a long talk with Mabel about their Virginia trip. Washed and ironed. Isaac Kauffman was given three quarts of bean soup from a restaurant. Did some quilting.

6/29/76 Tuesday
Sultry with evening showers. Wrote to Grace with Stevie's card. Leon Denlinger's stopped on their way to the shore to ask about reunion program. I quilted most all day. Eby trimmed some trees. Nancy called and said a lot of farmers are in Philadelphia for a big Holstein convention. Isaac Kaufman ate bean soup for breakfast, dinner and supper.

7/2/76 Friday
Beautiful weather. Cool. Got up at 5:00 and did two freezers of ice cream. Eby went for ice. Went down to the highway with Margaret K. to see the Bi-Centennial wagon train go by. It took a half hour. Jim and Pat came at 9:15 and then went to a big sale at Guernsey Barn. 70 animals sold. I took the ice cream for Home picnic. Isaac, Elizabeth and Bradley came and brought tea. Made ten quarts for freezing and dried the balance.

7/11/76 Sunday
Heavy rain this morning with water going in the basement. Got the firemen to pump it out. Everything a mess. Missed church. Sanford helped clean up. We went

to Hershey's Homecoming this afternoon. Attendance good. Abram's and Sanford were here for supper. Jay and Margie came this evening.

7/14/76 Wednesday
Good fresh air. I hosed the basement rug real good. Finished scrubbing the basement floor. It is drying. I did the mending and canned the pickles. We took Sue along to Bible School. 130 there.

7/17/76 Saturday
Beautiful, cool and sunny. Eby harrowed garden and mowed lawn. I did some cleaning. Made currant and red raspberry jelly and canned pickles. Have 15 quarts. Planted beets, carrots, corn and radishes. Had a letter from Mary Alice and she must quit and leave Helvetia.

7/22/76 Thursday
Partly cloudy and warm. Picked the pickles and canned four quarts. Picked raspberries. Made root beer and popped corn. Cut and started sewing a slip. Put the rug on basement floor. It is very limber and puckered. Dale called and said he is going to California for a vacation. Went to Bible School. My class is getting worse.

7/23/76 Friday
Warm and sultry. Did some cleaning. Eby helped put some beds together. Picked and canned some pickles. Had our last night of Bible School and the class was very disorderly. Dark and cloudy. Eby took me to the Home and I slept on the couch. Sanford is coming for me.

7/26/76 Monday
Fine weather. Cleaned apartment, washed and ironed. Picked pickles and dug a bucket of potatoes. Canned two quarts of small pickles and put some in salt water. Did a gallon of dill sliced. Eby mowed yard. Told Alfred to vacate. Did Home report and other bookwork.

7/30/76 Friday
Sultry. Heavy rain, hail and storm reported from last evening. Worked 12-8. Fannie S. died about 4:00. Milton's left five minutes before I got home. I stopped for peaches and eggs. Picked and canned pickles. Did 13 pints of corn. Made a gingerbread for Bradley's birthday and we went down and stopped for ice cream and pretzels. He is doing real good.

8/9/76 Monday
A wet day. I washed and it did not get dry. Picked and canned pickles and did some soybeans. Picked a bucket of beans. Eby went to Lancaster and bought wallpaper for apartment and got Nancy's baby picture enlargement. Called Grace and she said Mary Alice can stay on in Helvetia till September 15.

8/11/76 Wednesday

Good weather. Left at 6:45 to visit the Clemens'. Eby drove to Scranton and I drove the rest of the way. Ate our lunch on Route 79. Got there by 12:00. All were fine. We had a tour of the premises and got the quilt assembled. Eby went with Edgar to prayer meeting. Rosa had supper with a friend.

8/12/76 Thursday

Had a shower. We decided to make quilt frames and had them done and put the quilt in to start quilting by 1:30. Eby and Fredric went for the needed parts. Darlis helped make a good supper of chicken, succotash, and chocolate cake. Fredric showed his pictures of his fourteen weeks in British Honduras.

8/17/76 Tuesday

Clear and cool. Picked a bushel of limas. Eby, Sammy and Becky shelled them. Canned pickles and made cucumber relish. Ironed. Becky and Sammy made things from cucumbers and played together very nicely. Eby went to business meeting at Meadville. He cut early sweet corn and took some to Elam's.

8/23/76 Monday

Warm. Washed. Picked pickles and a bushel of limas. Eby shelled them this afternoon. I picked off elderberries and made juice. Put some paper up in the apartment. Milton's came about 2:30. Doug is staying with us while they vacation in Maryland. Went to bed early.

8/26/76 Thursday

Hot and sultry. Made a pie, cooked tongue and made meat loaf and four dozen red eggs. Barbara washed and went shopping with Mike. Milton took Doug a ride on the Strasburg Railroad this forenoon. I took Helen along to Bird-in-Hand Restaurant where Raymond Hollinger's treated nurses to dinner for taking such good care of Fannie S.

8/27/76 Friday

Warm. Worked 12-8. Milton's helped get things together and packed for our trip to Jim's for the reunion. Left about 3:30 in Milton's station wagon. Stopped at Benner's restaurant for supper. Got there about 7:00. Everything was shining. Edgar's stayed at a cottage near Belleville and most of the others at the Holiday Inn.

8/28/76 Saturday

Sunny and warm. I went to barn and saw Jim's new stalls and the pony and colt, heifers and cows. Ray came to check the cows. Greg brought the chicken. We went to the camp where the family, all but Joanne and David, came for our reunion. Had a very nice time together. It was a pretty, quiet place. The pool was fun for the children. Guests were Ed Eng and Debbie Zander.

9/7/76 Tuesday
Fine day. Picked a bushel of limas. Eby shelled them, and I froze them. Picked and put two quarts of green beans in the freezer. Made two baskets of grapes into juice. Made catsup. Started some flower slips. Truck went to the garage this evening. Had a card from Charles and Ed. They are seeing Rome and other places in Europe.

9/12/76 Sunday
Beautiful day. Went to Meadville. Went to Amos Hershey's for dinner. We took Sue along to Hostetter Reunion at Paradise Park. An octet sang and Hershey Hostetter spoke on making a contribution to society in our generation. I got two silver dollars for having the most children. Called Abram. They took David to the George School in Newtown today.

9/20/76 Monday
Sunny with rain this evening. Washed and ironed. Repotted some African violets. Called Aunt Cora. She was mixed up. Talked to Mabel. Eby helped with the little family cemetery. Mowed yard when he came home. I slept two hours.

10/4/76 Monday
Clear, sunny and mild. I washed and ironed and mended. Planted in more flowers. Esther came this afternoon. Isaac K got two new shirts for everyday. Eby dug the barberry bush away from the rambler rose and set up the T.V.

10/22/76 Friday
Clear and frosty. Worked 12-8. I gathered some greens for winter gardens. Made up three. Put some flowers in the house. Cleaned some celery. Did the cleaning. Eby went to the shoemakers and got his brief case sewed. He went to the store and took naps.

10/23/76 Saturday
Clear and cool. We took Clarence's along to L.M.H.S. where two bus loads started on a historical tour to Germantown. Saw the first Mennonite Church in America, and old schoolhouse where Christopher Dock taught, the Wyck homestead, an old Brethren Church, the Rittenhouse homestead and the sight where the first paper mill operated. Had a full meal at Conestoga Church. Got home at 8:50.

10/27/76 Wednesday
Frosty. Made 32 sweet potato croquettes. Cut off cannas, elephant ears and pulled cut flowers. Raked some leaves. Eby worked all day. Linda and Donald came to take tool boxes off the new truck. Helped Linda stamp quilt patches. Linda told us we will be great grandparents.

11/3/76 Wednesday
Cloudy. Worked 12-8. Took a nap. Cleaned and processed the salsify for freezing. Got nine pints. Eby was home this forenoon and worked this afternoon. Mary Alice called and said they are settled in Charlottesville. Went to midweek service.

11/25/76 Thursday
Fine weather. Rosa came at 2:00 and is not feeling well. Disturbed too about her training. The children were all here except Milton's and Charlie. Darlis came with Robert's. Mary Alice, Sanford and Nancy served very efficiently. Had a good day and so much for which to be thankful.

11/28/76 Sunday
Partly cloudy and mild. Worked 12-8. Edgar's went to Meadville and they and the Weaver's were here for chicken corn soup, fruit, tossed and vegetable salads. Had strawberry delight. They all left by 2:30. Rosa left for Goshen at 6:30 with Janice Martin. Darlis went with the Weaver's to E.M.C. Spent the afternoon and evening resting and reading.

11/30/76 Tuesday
Clear, cold and white. I did a big wash and ironing. Saw five deer in the field across the road. Went to visit Elsie King this afternoon. Eby shelled walnuts. Esther called and invited us for Sunday. A deer hunter from Ronks drowned trying to get a deer. Two died of heart attacks, one was shot, and one was killed in a car accident.

12/7/76 Tuesday
Rained all night. Worked 12-8. Went to Good's and Shady Maple. Wrote family letter. Rested. Made cranberry jelly and mints. Eby shelled walnuts. Called Sue Martin. We decided to have brothers and sisters on New Year. Finished reading book, My Son, My Son.

12/17/76 Friday
Snow squalls. Took Elam to his home, stopped to get three hams for Ray's. Nancy came and we baked a lot of cookies. Eby went to Elam. Nancy and I went to Flaud's where she bought five plants for gifts. Eby went to the auction and bought a lamp for Isaac K's room.

12/18/76 Saturday
Sunny and pleasant. Worked 12-8. Went to Dorothy Felpel's funeral at Stumptown. Went to Sewing School this afternoon. Stopped at White Horse dry goods for gifts for Sunday School class. Bathed and went to bed early. Jim's Pat called about her flap jacks. Dough is crumbly.

12/21/76 Tuesday
Very cold and windy. Did the ironing and mending. Popped corn and made it into cracker jack. Made haystacks. Eby did not come home for lunch as he went to a

cow sale. High was $1800. for one cow. Donald and Linda took us to a Seafood Restaurant for supper. Ate to our fill. They came in a while.

12/24/76 Friday
Nice weather. Finished things up, packed, bathed and ate early lunch and left for Ray's at 11:50. Got there by 2:15. They are all getting over a bug. Jane's Mother is helping with the work. I bathed and combed the girls. Jane's mother lit candles in bakery bags along the road in the yard. Listened to Christmas programs.

12/25/76 Saturday
Cloudy and we slept late. Had a big time opening gifts. Girls were happy. Had light lunch and a good turkey supper with all the trimmings. Went to Squibb's to see the quilt display and to see the new veterinary hospital. Milton's came to Ray's about 4:00 and we all left for Gap in two cars soon after 8:00. Got home safely.

1977

1/1/77 Saturday
Clear and cold. Had Clarence's, Jay's, Menno's, Landis', Paul's and Charlie. Mart and Miriam were sick.

1/3/77 Monday
Harvey's have had one attic window open all winter with a screen.

1/10/77 Monday
Cloudy and warmer with rain and slush. We all went to the Farm Show and spent the day looking at all the nice things. Had a trained horse show this evening. Got very cold, icy and windy. Daddy coughing very badly. Got home at 10:30.

1/11/77 Tuesday
Nice and sunny. Eby worked all day. I packed lunch for the Weaver's and they left at 10:10. Harvey's put their attic window down. I washed and rested this afternoon. Eby went to a Board meeting at the Home.

1/13/77 Thursday
Sent Aunt Emma Ray a card for her 103rd birthday. Cut some rug rags and started braiding a rug for Sanford. Eby went to a Board meeting at the Medical Center. Isaac K. got his first check.

1/27/77 Thursday
Sunny and cold. Worked on rug. Took Elam to sale in Smoketown. Eby went to bed to sleep warm. Schools closed till Tuesday all over state to save fuel. Amish schools are open. Eby's suit came. Isaac K got a new five-year battery in his car.

1/30/77 Sunday
Worked 12-8. No service at Meadville to save fuel. Went to the chapel. Mark Leaman preached. Helped in dining room. Jay and Margie visited this afternoon. Got home at 6:30.

1/31/77 Monday
Ray called. I called Aunt Cora. Cold. Washed and ironed. Worked on rug. Made a pot of vegetable soup. Eby tried to keep warm with electric heater and in bed. Isaac K ate supper with us after cleaning some snow from the drive. I took Lydia Zook's watch to Harvey's for repair.

2/2/77 Wednesday
Sunny and cold. I washed and ironed and made up beds. Eby went for pork and we put ours in the freezer. Made pig foot jelly. Elaine Eckman has a broken vertebrae in her back from tobogganing. No one has shown for the job at the Home. Some think we should do it.

2/7/77 Monday
Clear and cold. I washed and ironed. Worked on rug. Isaac scraped ice from the drive. He ate supper with us and there was little left. Eby worked at the Historical Center this afternoon. President Carter's 9-year-old daughter Amy was baptized yesterday. Went to bed early.

2/9/77 Wednesday
Warmer. I worked on the rug and made valentines. We went to Millwood Bible School this afternoon. A 16-year-old Amish boy was kicked and killed by a horse on Noble Road.

2/10/77 Thursday
Mild and snow is melting. I made ice cream and had trouble getting the ice cream freezer started. Did some cleaning. Made supper for Milton and two lady teachers from Stony Brook. Had a nice visit with them. Dale called to talk to Milton about anniversary plans. Milton's did not get an assignment for their sabbatical yet.

2/23/77 Wednesday
Sunny and mild. Worked on my dress. Was all ready to go to visit Aunt Cora but she was not home. Eby worked at the Center. They are making trouble about hauling Amish without a special license and insurance. Harvey's are home from Florida. Uncle Charlie came to talk about hauling Amish while he was waiting to take Amish doctor home.

3/4/77 Friday
Wet day. Worked 12-8. Sewed. Took Emma to shop at Petersheim's for groceries and food for meeting on Sunday. Mervin went too. Took a nap when we got home. Eby went to Center this afternoon. I took Annis along to Women's Day of Prayer

at Hershey's. A good number came out. Ray called and said Jane has quilt in and would like some help. I missed the call.

3/7/77 Monday
Sunny and colder. I washed, ironed and mended. Cleaned up garage, tied up papers and scrubbed the floor. Washed some windows on the outside. Trimmed clematis. Eby helped Joe Kershner haul some furniture in our truck. He went with Donald and Linda to take some furniture to have refinished. They visited for a while. Trapped miner was rescued after one week in coal mine. Seven others dead.

3/11/77 Friday
Sunny and warm. I cleaned drawers and cupboards. Made sauer kraut for supper. Went to Clarence's at 12:30 to help with quilt. Eby harrowed the garden. Moslems are making trouble in Washington D.C. I cut Eby's hair this evening. Amaryllis is blooming.

3/14/77 Monday
Got up at 5:00 and Uncle Charlie drove our car and took Mabel, Mildred, Sue and I to Ray's. Left here at 7:00 and arrived at 9:20. Quilted on her king sized cross stitch quilt. Got a good amount done. Ray took us to see the new hospital that is under construction. Had dinner and supper. Started for home at 7:00. Jane's mother was there. Laura went to school this afternoon. Martha did not have to go on Monday.

3/15/77 Tuesday
Sunny and mild. I washed and ironed. Cleaned some flower beds and raked yard. Eby went to Vintage to the sale. I took a short rest. Called Helen and Mabel. Had a letter from Amy and she has had shingles for five weeks. Nancy called and has a foot problem. Dr. says it is a chipped bone and will need surgery. She has a lot of pain and is using crutches.

3/17/77 Thursday
Fine weather. I cleaned closets and drawers. Aunt Cora and Uncle Joe called. He has $1300 for the cemetery fund. Eby went from work to a sale at Gibson's in Chester County. He went to a Board meeting at medical center. Nancy called and said she cannot have surgery till Tuesday. Her foot is painful with infection wearing off. Emanuel King was killed on Gap Hill this morning when hit by a car. Horse killed too. He was 56.

3/23/77 Wednesday
Sunny and windy. Nancy had surgery on her left foot in Center City Hospital in Philadelphia. She called and is happy to have her foot on the mend. Linda called to say she is sick and would I work for her. Had a very busy day. Abner's want to take us out for supper tomorrow evening. I called Abram's and talked to Andy.

3/24/77 Thursday
Cold and windy. Worked 12-8. Had 11 trays for all the sick. Baked a nut cake and made dressing. Esther came with a strawberry and raisin pie and they took us out for supper to Bird-in-Hand restaurant. Had reservations and flowers sent. I slept and washed the car this afternoon. Eby went to a cow sale. Nancy called and said she had to walk a lot today. She will have to stay in the hospital till Saturday. Mary Alice got a job.

3/26/77 Saturday
Fine day. Eby met Fredric at the depot. Some of the others came here. Sanford helped bake pies. We all gathered at the Fulton Inn for our Golden Wedding Anniversary celebration. Enjoyed the dinner and all the guests. Missed Edgar's. Nancy came from the hospital this morning.

3/27/77 Sunday
Clear and pleasant. We called and Rhoda is on the mend. Our whole family except Rhoda attended services at Hershey's. Hershey Hostetter preached on "What is in thine hand?" Everyone made us welcome. Elizabeth made chicken corn soup for all. We had plenty of food.

3/28/77 Monday
Wet day. Washed and ironed. Dried it in the basement. Cleaned up house and put things in order. Talked to Mabel, Aunt Cora and Esther. Dale called and said he is bringing a friend on Friday evening. Eby tried to get caught up on his sleep this afternoon. Fredric left to visit his Grandpa Clemens and Uncle Wayne.

3/29/77 Tuesday
Fine warm day. Worked 12-8. Fredric and I packed up and left for Ithaca at 9:00. Stopped a half hour for lunch and got here at 3:00. I made supper, and Edgar, Fredric and I went to the hospital and found Rhoda real good. She has a little fever and some lung congestion. Marcia is babysitting. I can hear the tree frogs singing.

3/30/77 Wednesday
Very warm. People are in shorts and shirtless. Wrote to Weaver's and sent Jennie's card. Washed all the sheets and clothing. Took Andrea to a birthday party. Went on to the hospital with Marcia and Conrad. Rhoda is feeling better and the fever is gone. Dropped Marcia off for her music lesson. Children had no school. I stuck a few onions in the flower bed. Gusty with rain this evening.

4/1/77 Friday
Weather fine. Made two blackberry pies and twenty four apple dumplings. Fredric and I packed up and left for the hospital at 9:00. Rhoda seemed to be improving. Left hospital at 12:15 and arrived home at 5:15. Dale and his friend Mae were here. Eby had the pork chops in the oven and we ate at 6:00. Eby went to a medical center

meeting, and Dale, Mae, Fredric and I visited till they left at 8:30. I called Nancy and she is working again and getting shots for the infection in her foot.

4/18/77 Monday
Fine weather. I washed and ironed. Put some busy lizzie slips in aquarium and put it in the basement window. Repotted some plants. Eby worked at Atglen till noon, took a nap, worked on his ditch and watered garden. Peas are up. Called Rhoda and she visited her doctor today. He said all is well. Rosa and Jonathan are home and will be leaving for Poland and Honduras on Wednesday and Thursday. Called Nancy and she is better. Stitches out and bandage off her foot.

4/29/77 Friday
Very cool. Worked 12-8. Left at 8:30 for Shady Maple and Good's Store. Stopped for eggs. Made chocolate chip cookies, chocolate cake and tapioca pudding. Took a nap. Eby set the table for Milton, Doug and the eight foreign students he brought for a tour. All ate heartily. Eby went with them to the auction. Doug stayed with me. Milton took the four girls to the Coy's.

5/11/77 Wednesday
Clear and cool. Joe Bechtold painted the living room pineapple color. I painted the windows. Eby and Isaac helped put things in order again. I marked some of the quilt. Ripped hem out of the sheet. Eby mowed and raked some yard. Elizabeth called and said Linda's baby boy was born about 1:00 A.M. Weighed over 8 lbs. and is Benjamin Lee. She had planned to work today.

5/13/77 Friday
Worked 12-8. Stopped for eggs, gift, bread and popcorn. Baked a cake for Doug, bathed and packed. Made a lunch and Eby came home at 11:00. The Coy's came for us at 12:00 and brought us along to Milton's. Arrived by 4:00. The two Chinese girls cooked us a real Chinese supper before they left for NYC. Stony Brook is very pretty with spring green and flowers.

5/16/77 Monday
The weather was beautiful all weekend. We left Milton's at 8:30 and had some slow places around JFK Airport because of some protesting. Stopped for ice cream and got home by 4:00. Isaac K. took good care of things. Doug had to cry when we left. Called Mabel. Rhoda called and said Edgar's father died this forenoon.

5/18/77 Wednesday
Had good showers this evening. I cut an apron and started cutting a new dress that I bought at Sears on Long Island. Eby mowed yard and I made a supper for Linda and Donald. We stopped to see the new baby on my way to work. He is a nice baby. Worked 4-12 as Francis is on vacation. The chapel folks did a song service at the Home. Miriam and I had a long chat.

5/28/77 Saturday
Sunny and cool. Edgar's went to his home after breakfast and came back this evening. I prepared some food and went to Sewing School. 24 there. Abram had an accident on Route 81. Few injuries but the car is ruined.

6/1/77 Wednesday
Cloudy and warmer. Heavy gust and flooding rain. I picked sugar peas for supper. Made a little strawberry preserves. Did the ironing. Quilted this afternoon. Eby worked on rack for morning glories. He got a notion to put a shower upstairs, but it passed off. I wrote to Jim's and sent Greg's graduation gift. Went to midweek service at Martha Hershey's.

6/2/77 Thursday
Cool. Had two inches of rain. Took Annis along to Sewing Circle. Finished a quilt for the Samaritan Home. Eby worked on his trellis. I rested and quilted and went to bed early. Called Mary Alice and she is enjoying her new job with the boys. She and Debbie spent the weekend in Helvetia. John Stoltzfus came to see if Ray could come look at his horses. I called Ray for information.

6/10/77 Friday
Some showers. Did the cleaning. Wed onions, picked strawberries. Quilted and took a nap. Sanford came about 8:00 and I got him some supper. Eby and Isaac Kauffman went with Isaac to get fish down in Maryland. Only seven rockfish available. Did not get home till 7:30. Abram called, said he still has some sore spots from the accident.

6/14/77 Tuesday
Cloudy and raining this evening. I quilted. Trained the limas and hoed them and some flower beds. Dug first potatoes. Picked a dishpan of sugar peas. Took car to garage. Making ready for quilting helpers. A 12-year-old boy in Manheim hung himself. Eby is talking about a change from Meadville.

6/23/77 Thursday
Worked 12-8. Felt dizzy about 4:30-5:00, then got better. Ate very little. Soaked my feet and trimmed my nails. Rested a while and did the cleaning. Got things ready for our Virginia trip. Eby went with Bob Keen and Jay H. to see Dale's Agway store to get some ideas. Watered this evening.

6/24/77 Friday
Fine weather. Packed and left with Jay and Sue and Bertha Shirk at 8:30 to visit Weaver's, Mary Alice and Sanford in Virginia. Took our time and stopped to see Harper's Ferry and had our dinner in Hilltop Hotel. Left Bertha at Jesse Byler's and got to Grace's on a country road by suppertime. Played some games with the children after supper. Stevie and Jennie found a baby bunny that was hurt. Found

the garden doing well in spite of dry weather. Took some pictures with the camera that Nancy and Charlie gave us.

6/25/77 Saturday
Spent a good night and left for Richmond to visit Sanford about 10:00. Pretty drive and got there by 1:00. He showed us his place of work and other interesting sites around Richmond. Had a good supper with beans and meat loaf and lemon sponge pie.

6/26/77 Sunday
Warm day. Had a good night and breakfast. Sanford directed us to Powhatan Church. Art Ranck preached. Went to Mary Alice's for dinner. She and Debbie took us for a drive. Their apartment is comfy and interesting. Got back to Weaver's by 7:00. Stevie and Jennie did some magic supposedly.

6/27/77 Monday
A warm day. Had a good night and breakfast at Weaver's. Grace took us to Valley Paving to see the machinery operating. Left at 10:00 for Harrisonburg to pick up Bertha. Stopped to see Natural Chimneys on the way. Had our supper at a restaurant and got home by 8:00. Found all well. Jay's car is air conditioned and we rode in comfort.

7/8/77 Friday
Very sultry and hot. Worked 12-8. I made a fudge chiffon. Picked a quart of red raspberries and a quart of blueberries. Tried to sleep and read to Doug. Went to the tent this evening. Took Jay and Margie. The Groff boy died who was struck by lightning.

7/12/77 Tuesday
Sultry with showers. Worked 12-8. Had a busy time. Menno passed away about 6:00. Milton's left for camping trip. I slept after hoeing the roses and slept again this afternoon. Eby went to Center and to Board Meeting this evening. I took six passengers to Bible School. Had order problems with my class.

7/13/77 Wednesday
Hot and sultry. I picked and canned some pickles. Did some hoeing and picked stones. Took a nap and did some mending. Eby took it easy. Took our load of nine to Bible School. 127 there. Two of my boys are very unruly.

7/25/77 Monday
Had very good showers, over an inch. I washed and ironed. Picked and canned pickles and put nine pints of corn in freezer. Eby took it easy and cleaned out rain spout. Dale called. He is coming on Sunday. Rhoda called and said Rosa would come here with Don Ranck's from Kennedy Airport on her way from Poland.

7/28/77 Thursday
Fine weather. I worked 12-8. Rested an hour and picked pickles. Got packed up to take Rosa home and left after lunch. Eby and I each drove part way and had a good trip. Arrived at 5:55. Had a good supper and spent the evening visiting. Rosa was happy to be home again.

8/2/77 Tuesday
Fine day. Worked 12-8. Washed six baskets of peaches and they had 25 baskets for canning. I stopped for apples and eggs and made five quarts of sauce. Becky and Sam went to Isaac's with Linda to go to Sandy Cove. I did some trimming in the yard. Picked and canned pickles. Neighbor's new dog barks most of the time. Called Aunt Cora and someone threw a potato through her bedroom window.

8/26/77 Friday
Weather fine. Worked 12-8. Stopped for vinegar and pears. Cooked eggs and put them in juice. Got food all packed up. Bathed, rested and packed. Jay and Sue picked us up at 6:00 and took us to Ray's. Jay's went to a motel. Ray's have everything in tip top shape all ready for our reunion. Jane's mother helped. Tables from church and chairs from neighbors. Games all set up.

8/27/77 Saturday
Weather fine. Ray sliced cold cuts. Everything ready and Weaver's came first. All others came but Charlie and Fredric. Debbie Zander, Mae Bleiler and Daniel Dietzel made our number 55. Everything went well and all had a good time playing, wading and visiting.

9/26/77 Monday
Rained and foggy. Worked 12-8. Invited ten of the guests from the Home for Wednesday. Rested till noon. Washed and ironed. Cleaned two closets and the notion drawer in the kitchen. Got fourth yellow jacket sting this evening on my foot. Eby helped with the railing at the Medical Center. Eby and I have colds.

9/28/77 Wednesday
Beautiful day. I made things ready for dinner for ten guests from the Home. Mabel brought a load because our car was out of order with a broken water pump. Ruth Myer brought a load. All seemed to enjoy their day. Nancy called and said she got back from California at 12:00 last night. Had a good time but has plenty of work waiting to catch up on.

9/29/77 Thursday
Beautiful and sunny. Cooler. I made twenty seven quarts of applesauce. Picked and canned a quart of pickles. Eby mowed the yard. I called birthday greetings to Esther. We took car to garage this morning. Talked to Mabel. Had a letter from Milton's. They may be going to India. Finished reading Francis Nolt's book, The Persecutor.

10/3/77 Monday
Clear, windy and cooler. I washed and ironed. Cleaned the kitchen drawers. Eby went to Medical Center to level off dirt. Has it in the back. His cough hangs on. Brought the Christmas cactus in from the porch. Abram's are coming home from their trip to Sweden, Poland and Finland. Went to bed early.

10/10/77 Monday
County full of tourists. I washed and ironed. I rested a while and had early supper. We took Emma and Miriam along to Akron for apple snitzing. 45 there and we did 33 bushels. There are 320 bushels still to do. An Amish barn floor gave way at a hoe down Sunday night and some young people were hurt.

10/23/77 Sunday
Went to Spring Run Church with Jim's. Enjoyed the service and the Sunday School class. Had a good turkey dinner and went for a drive to the top of the mountain. Leaves are at their beauty peak. Got home by 5:45.

10/27/77 Thursday
Showery and damp. I cleaned the kitchen cupboards and washed the windows on the outside. Called Mabel and got a report on their three-day bus trip. Called Aunt Cora and she asked if I started fire in my cookstove yet. Took Isaac K. along to Meadville this evening. About thirty there.

11/1/77 Tuesday
Weather fine. Went with Mabel to Black Rock where 115 women quilted and did many crafts and ate gobs of delicious food. Brought a crib quilt along to hem. Went to Hershey's Revival. Aunt Emma Ray died at 3:00 P.M.

11/22/77 Tuesday
Damp and rainy. I cleaned celery, radishes, carrots and roasted two 15-pound turkeys. Cut bread for filling. Made four mince pies and four crusts for pumpkin pies. Eby used the sweeper and set up the tables. Peeled oranges. Got a Thanksgiving card from Nancy.

11/23/77 Wednesday
I cut up the turkey and made gravy. I cleaned up kitchen, bathroom, laundry room and scrubbed the porch. Made the pumpkin pies. Damp and rainy. Sanford came for supper, and Ray's brought Abraham Stevens from Amber and were here for the night.

11/24/77 Thursday
Weather mild and partly cloudy. I got things ready for dinner to serve to 36 people. Abraham Stevens was our guest from Nicaragua. Had plenty of everything. Judy's Julianne was born at 11:00. Milton's got a telegram that they are to go to India.

11/28/77 Monday
White with snow. Isaac K. did his first job at the Medical Center. I washed and ironed and dried it in the basement and on the porch. Sowed some thumbergia seeds. Made up the beds. Eby is getting some ideas for removing the partition between the kitchen and dining room. Had a long talk with Aunt Cora. Helen Ranck called about Aunt Emma's will in niece's and nephew's favor.

12/4/77 Sunday
Went to Meadville for our last time. Took Norman and Michelle along. Eby gave his farewell speech. I wrote to Weaver's. Milton called about their Christmas trip plans.

12/5/77 Monday
Dark, cloudy, cold and rainy. I washed and ironed. Dried it in basement. Quilted more than second border. Eby hung the plaque that the Meadville congregation gave us. Isaac K. is eating more meals here. Did not go to the Historical meeting because of the weather. Eby went for milk. I went to bed early.

12/11/77 Sunday
Worked 12-8. Went to Kinzer for our first service. Had oyster soup for lunch. Slept all afternoon. Went to spend the evening with Aunt Cora. She is keeping warm and happy. Victor Groff's new chicken house blew down on Friday evening.

12/15/77 Thursday
Partly cloudy and mild. Worked 12-8. Nancy was here when I got home to help bake cookies. We baked flap jacks, sand tarts, ginger, peppernuts, taylor, raisin-filled, gumdrop and oatmeal. It went good. Nancy invited Beaver for supper. Nancy left at 8:30.

12/16/77 Friday
Clear, frosty and milder. I mixed and baked mince meat and pinwheel cookies. Made date balls, kisses and peanut brittle. Boxed up gift cookies and put balance in freezer room. Eby went to help clean up Victor's blown down pullet house. 100 men were there. Elizabeth called and Bradley talked to me. Cleaned up trays and cookie sheets and put them away.

12/19/77 Monday
Cloudy, dark and drizzled. I washed and ironed. Did a good amount of quilting. Isaac K. looked on a while. Eby peeled potatoes for the first time. I made cracker pudding. Went to bed early. Wrapped some gifts for ladies at the Home.

12/23/77 Friday
Fine weather. Eby and Dale went to Keen's after breakfast to see the store. We left at 9:00 for Edgar's. Stopped for lunch in Binghamton and got there at 2:30. They have a lot of snow. The children are all home from Goshen, and Darlis is busy working in the Donut Shop, cleaning and babysitting.

12/25/77 Sunday
Weather fine. Had some gift opening. After breakfast we all went for a short service to Bethel Grove. Had fruit and nuts and snack foods and a full Christmas meal at 5:00. Had balance of gift opening in afternoon.

12/26/77 Monday
Fine day. 13 degrees at Edgar's. We left for home at 8:00 and got home at 2:30. Stopped for lunch in Morgantown. Dale left soon after we got home to meet Mae Bleiler to go for supper. Read our mail and put things away. Eby went for milk. Went to bed early.

12/29/77 Thursday
Fine weather. I made a peach pie and chicken corn soup for lunch. Milton took his shoes to John Glick. Eby and Milton's went to Keen's for bird seed. Doug and I visited this afternoon. Barbara did some mending. We all went to Abram's for supper and had a nice evening. Got home at 10:00.

1978

1/3/78 Tuesday
Clear, white and cold. I washed and ironed. Took Christ's wife and little girl to Dr. Hess this forenoon. This afternoon we went to see John Reeser at Fairmount Home. Stopped for quilt filler. Linda came and she and Donald and Benjie took us to Akron for a Christmas treat at a restaurant.

1/9/78 Monday
Rain turning to snow and it blew all day. Down to ten degrees this evening. I washed and ironed and mended. Eby stained the French door. No school. Worked on small quilt. A 20-year-old Amish boy was killed in car at White Horse.

1/10/78 Tuesday
Two degrees above. Worked 12-8. Had no trouble driving. Joe Bechtold came and put door between living and dining rooms. Eby helped. I sewed on my chair quilt. Sorted some papers this evening. Eby went to Board meeting.

1/13/78 Friday
Began snowing early. Worked 12-8. Linda had a problem getting up the hill. Plumbers finished moving the lavatory in the apartment. I cleaned the kitchen, dining room and bathroom. Isaac worked on the snow. Eby and I went to Lancaster to have our will brought up to date. I bought a new handbag for $10.60.

1/20/78 Friday
Snow, wind, sleet and drizzle. Most everyone is snowbound. Isaac got to the Center. Eby stayed home. I made some vegetable soup. We did the Home report and watched the snow. Worked on a scrapbook for Bradley.

1/22/78 Sunday
Sunny and cold. Went to Kinzer Church. Isaac went with us and had his beans for dinner. Paul Clark preached on Revelations 2. Called Rhoda for her 50th birthday.

1/25/78 Wednesday
Cloudy, warm and water everywhere, getting in basement. We worked with shovels, sump pumps, shovels and hose. Kept it from getting too deep. Isaac helped and ate supper with us. Went to bed at 12:00 and Isaac kept on.

1/26/78 Thursday
Much flooding and basement is being pumped out by firemen. They had 34 calls. Isaac worked on the water and we went back on the job till Eby went to work. It lessened by noon and we could relax and Isaac slept till supper. Was some stiff and sore. Lots of water stories. Elizabeth called to see if we were all right. Much colder this evening.

1/27/78 Friday
Windy and colder. Eby and Isaac both went to work. I cleaned up the basement room nice and dry. Everything back in place and rug is drying in heater room. Put curtain on new door. The paper is full of stories of high waters, flooded basements and homes and people rescued by boats and helicopters. Firemen are busy pumping water.

1/31/78 Tuesday
Sunny and chilly. I cut patches this forenoon. Joe came and worked on the closet and took off some plaster. Eby helped him. I took Helen along to Harvest Drive where the help and nurses from the Home had a dinner on their own and a pep session for the nurses and the new administrator and his wife.

2/3/78 Friday
Weather fine. Worked 12-8. I slept till 11:30. Helped Eby put shelves in closet and worked on fitting dining room rug. I shampooed it this evening. Nancy called and said she has a promotion—use of a car and a $2000 raise. Charlie called and said he is planning his house.

2/4/78 Saturday
Fine weather. Eby took truckload of junk to dump. I did some cleaning. We met Isaac's at the Guernsey Barn and went with them to John Lentz's for dinner and to see little Julianne. Worked on my picture this evening. Eby got $4000 from Aunt Emma Ray's estate.

2/16/78 Thursday
Sunny and had a little snow. Worked 12-8. Stopped at White Horse Dry Goods for vanilla, shoe polish, metal sponge and rubber bands. I painted closet hooks and rest of pineapple paint. Isaac went to Horning's with Eby for our hutch. I put some things in it. Eby went to Board meeting at Medical Center. I stayed up and served a treat.

3/9/78 Thursday
A cover of snow. Cloudy and warmer. Worked 12-8. Helen and Francis are paying to have the nurses station painted and papered. I did some cleaning and put up new shade in laundry room. Finished hemming Becky's quilt. Margie called. Donald's Pluma has a broken leg from a snowmobile ride.

3/10/78 Friday
Partly cloudy and cleared this evening. I did some cleaning. Made a walnut cake, cooked sweet potatoes, made ice cream, potato salad and other things for company. Made mints and fruit cocktail. Uncle Charlie took us to Abram's for supper and to "The Sound of Music" at Hershey High School, where Sammy had a part. Got home at 12:00.

3/17/78 Friday
Worked 12-8. Very foggy coming home. I slept till 11:30. Cleaned Isaac's room and basement room. Eby took Elam on a shopping trip for lumber and started asking 25 cents a mile. Finished reading "Listen to the Land."

3/25/78 Saturday
Some rain. I prepared food and cleaned up kitchen. The Weaver's came this afternoon and Ray's at bedtime. Eby went to Fire Company Sale and big Relief Sale at Harrisburg. Came to $132,000. Top quilt was $925 for a Hollie Hobbie.

3/31/78 Friday
Mild. Worked 12-8. Had a flat tire. Tim changed it. I cleaned some. Took a nap. Charlie came at 5:30 from a three-day meeting in Washington. Had a nice evening visiting with him. A 21-month-old Amish child drowned in the Pequea Creek near Millwood.

4/26/78 Wednesday
Cloudy, cool and windy. Worked 12-8. Stopped for apples, cider and eggs. Cooked some beef and ground it for mince meat. Took a nap. Cleaned our bedroom for housecleaning. Eby mowed yard and planted cannas and elephant ears. Went to midweek service and had a "try hunger" meal. Even #'s got a full meal and unevens got soup with no dessert.

4/27/78 Thursday
Cloudy and cool. Worked 12-8. Went to Sheep Hill and bought dress fabric. Went to Shady Maple and Good's. Got home by 10:20. Rested and made 10 quarts of mince meat. Eby finished mowing yard. Had first asparagus for supper. Ex-president Ford was in Lancaster today and gave a $2500 speech. Watt and Shand celebrating 100th anniversary.

5/4/78 Thursday
Good showers. I went to meeting at Hershey's this afternoon. Good attendance. We went to services again this evening. Nancy called and said she got the job in Minnesota.

5/14/78 Sunday
Rained lots. Went to Meadville. Amos preached on Mothers. Emma taught our class. Charlie sent a Mother's Day song by Western Onion sung by Ed.

5/23/78 Tuesday
Mild and pleasant. I quilted and hoed garden and flower beds. Eby took truck to garage and nursed his cold. He met Uncle Joe to see about right of way to the little family cemetery. Isaac finished up the sauer kraut and mashed potatoes. He is delighted to be going to a singing this evening.

5/29/78 Monday
Showers in some places. I did a wash of sheets and towels. I quilted till Nancy came at 11:30. Eby brought chicken dinners from Kinzer Fire Company. We all went to buy a set of Noritake for Nancy at Amish China. Nancy left after supper. I quilted till 8:00.

6/12/78 Monday
Sunny. Washed and ironed. Hoed some garden and cleaned flower beds. Took a nap. Eby harrowed garden and Harvey and Margie complained about our garden row on their side. Nancy called and I called Milton's. Still no visas. Eby went to Board meeting.

6/13/78 Tuesday
Rained. Worked 12-8. Called Ruth Coy. Truman is still holding on. Stopped for plants and put in marigolds, eggplant, and yellow tomatoes. Cleaned living room and put in quilt. Took a nap. Milton's called and said they plan to leave tomorrow for their trip to India without their visas.

6/16/78 Friday
Sunny and cool. I picked peas and Eby helped shell and we had enough for ten pints to freeze. I called Charlie and Milton's left for Hawaii from San Francisco at 9:00 last evening. Nancy called and said she is doing fine and they had heavy thunderstorms yesterday and all night. Eby watered the garden. We came to the Home for the weekend.

6/24/78 Saturday
Washed car, helped plant sweet potatoes, hoed limas, cut off daffodils, took a rest, roasted beef and worked at Harvest Drive from 1:00-6:00. Eby put up frame for tomatoes and pickles. Spent evening resting.

6/28/78 Wednesday
Pleasant. Worked 12-8. Stopped for eggs. Made dinner for Jim's. They got here about 11:30 and left at 3:30. Had a nice visit. I slept till 6:00. We went to Midweek service. I called Ruth Coy and Truman is not very good.

7/1/78 Saturday
Clear and cool. Nancy came early for breakfast and stayed for dinner. I finished hemming quilt. Eby stripped back door and put on stain. Had a nice visit with Nancy. Her things left on a van for Minnesota last evening.

7/5/78 Wednesday
Beautiful day. Cool. I did some cleaning. Put moth balls in sweet potato rows. Pulled some weeds. We went to E-Town to get Eby's new suit and shirt, $238.00. Stopped at Bay Window for cards. Went to Midweek service and saw Allen Shirk's pictures of China and Hong Kong.

7/15/78 Saturday
Real nice mild day. Dale came and we all went to Joanne's wedding at Black Rock. Dan's father did the ceremony in the presence of nearly 300 guests. It was a meaningful wedding. Had Abram's, Edgar's and Dale for supper.

7/21/78 Friday
Hot. I prepared food for the weekend. Did the cleaning. Slept this afternoon. Eby washed car and watered the garden. The Clemens' came about 7:30. Darlis, Marcia, Conrad and Andrea came along. The other three are in Indiana. Jonathan in construction, Fredric in therapy and Rosa at the trailer factory.

8/8/78 Tuesday
Hot and sunny. Worked 12-8. I called Ruth Coy and Truman is doing better. Went to Shady Maple and Harry Good's. Slept till noon. Mended. Hoed some weeds. Eby bought a beetle trap and caught 1 1/2 quarts this P.M. The County is full of tourists.

8/9/78 Wednesday
Hot and sunny. I dug balance of potatoes for a total of 2 bushels. Emptied over three quarts of beetles. Westman's visited in Parksburg. Nancy called and asked if we would buy the car she leases in about a year. Got a tape from Milton's. Sent a $12.00 care package to Mike. Postage was $39.00.

8/18/78 Friday
A hot day. Charlie came this morning and we had a nice day together. Eby took him to Rough and Tumble. He went to see Dan and Joanne this evening. Isaac's were there. I took a nap this afternoon and after supper. Visited with Charlie until 11:30 when I went to work. He is taking off at 5:00.

8/26/78 Saturday
Weather was just right for our reunion at Black Rock Retreat. All were there but Milton's, Charlie, David, Andy and Beth. Our guests were Abraham Stevens, his friend Frank, and Debbie Zander. Had good chicken barbecue and lots of goodies. Had twenty for the night.

9/2/78 Saturday
Fine weather. Eby woke up before 4:00 and was dizzy and nauseated. Kept in bed till 8:30 and went back this afternoon. Washed car, went to store and feels better. Made elderberry and pineapple jelly and jam. Did some cleaning.

9/14/78 Thursday
Cool. Worked 12-8. Stopped for pears, peaches and eggs. Rested two hours. Made peach preserves and some beet jelly. Picked limas and Eby shelled them. Electrolux man came to service our cleaner and we decided it was not worth fixing. We bought a new one for $349. He allowed $50 for old one.

9/19/78 Tuesday
Heavy rain at 4:30. Worked 12-8. Wrote to Rhoda and Mary Alice. Slept till 11:00. Got things lined up for the picnic and had the Home folks here this evening. Had a nice time together in the house. Nancy called and said she got her class reunion book and she is the only single girl in her class.

9/26/78 Tuesday
Clear and cool. I did ironing and mending. Straightened up the freezer room. Packed up some canned goods for Mary Alice, Sanford and Nancy. Picked the tiny pickles and canned a quart. Picked over the limas. Eby went to the Vintage Sale. An airplane crash in California killed 141 people. It fell on houses and killed some.

9/29/78 Friday
Clear. Worked 12-8. I got things ready for going to Virginia. Bathed and rested a while and we left in the afternoon and got there by 7:30. The Weaver's were all over at the sale grounds. Sanford came for the night and was helping with the sale supper this evening.

9/30/78 Saturday
A good day for the relief sale and there were around 25,000 there and about $90,000 taken in. Highest quilt price was $1150 and the second one was $1050. Sanford took Mary Alice's furniture in our truck and I went with her to her new place.

10/1/78 Sunday
Nice weather. Went to church with Grace and family and spent the day with them. Mary Alice, Debbie and Meg Lyons came in the afternoon and stayed for supper. Made French braids for Debbie and Meg.

10/9/78 Monday
First frost. I washed and did some hasty ironing. Our tourists left at 10:25. got things packed and ready to go to Camp Hebron. Picked Jake and Elsie Martin up at 1:30 and we got here by 3:00. Met a lot of folks. Had a good sauer kraut supper and had some get acquainted games. Tillman Smith gave a talk on aging. Floyd Hackman gave some memory talk.

10/10/78 Tuesday
Perfect weather. Had a nice day of visiting and went to the store, on a tractor ride to see the camp grounds and a rope show. Had a quiz, a computer supper and a game period. Tillman Smith talked on aging. Did some quilting and had drink and pretzels for a bedtime snack.

10/12/78 Thursday
Another beautiful day. Had a good chapel talk. Helped with quilt and got it finished in the early afternoon. There were cart rides and I did not go. Had a spelling bee. I missed catechism. Words were difficult. Spent a lot of time visiting.

10/15/78 Sunday
Beautiful day. Worked 12-8. Went to Kinzer. Melvin Barge preached. Rested and went to visit Truman Coy. He is glad for company. Could not get an answer from Aunt Cora, so Mabel and I went up and she was the same. She does not get to the phone very often.

10/20/78 Friday
Beautiful day. John Metzler's picked us up at 7:00 and took us to meet the bus at Morgantown. Paul Brubaker drove the bus with 33 passengers to Hickory, North Carolina. We are staying in the Town and Country Inn, a very nice new motel, in room 137. Have a friendly group and are meeting new people. Ate supper at Ma and Paw's Cafeteria.

10/21/78 Saturday
Clear. Had breakfast at the motel and went to Hickory for M.D.S. meeting at the huge Baptist Church. Lunch at church and supper at Ma and Paw's. Session again this evening and back to our motel by 11:00. Everyone seems to be friendly and enjoying the activities.

11/1/78 Wednesday
Mild. I puttied and painted windows and got a lot of sunshine. Eby helped this afternoon. Had our preparatory service this evening. Paul preached on How Much God Loves Us. Seven characteristics. My plate is cracked.

11/5/78 Sunday
Mild and sunny. Went to Kinzer communion. Dale was here for dinner and stayed till 10:00. Is thinking of marriage. Isaac's came this P.M. and looked at Milton's slides. Made part of a tape. Bradley is taking more steps and saying more words. Aunt Cora in hospital after a fall yesterday.

11/21/78 Tuesday
Worked 12-8. Went to Shady Maple for food. Stopped at Coy's for their tape. Truman went back to the hospital yesterday because of bleeding. Roasted two turkeys and had Dale and Mae for supper. He is all ready for his trip to India. Eby got ice cream and oysters. Had a letter from Milton's and finished one to send with Dale.

11/22/78 Wednesday
Nice day. I cut up turkeys and made the gravy, bread for stuffing and got things lined up for dinner. We went to Kinzer for our Thanksgiving Service. Ray's were here when we got home. Eby brought chairs from the Fire Hall. A cult in Guyana murdered some men and several hundred committed suicide by drinking a poison.

11/23/78 Thursday
Thanksgiving. Cloudy and rained this evening. Ray and Jane helped get things ready for dinner. Everyone was here by 12:15 and we served Edgar's, Abram's, Isaac's, Jim's, Weaver's and Ray's. Had plenty of everything. Mary Alice, Sanford and Nancy called from Minnesota. Dale called before going to Kennedy Airport to start for India with Mae.

11/28/78 Tuesday
Snow is melting. I washed and ironed. Put all the celery in and dug some salsify and carrots. Eby finished the walnuts. A mayor in California and another prominent man were shot to death. Ray's left for Barbados for a veterinary convention. Two deer hunters died of heart attacks and one was shot. Went to bed early.

12/14/78 Thursday
I baked cookies all day. 11 kinds. Eby helped with the sand tarts and decorating the icings on some. Wrote two letters. Have a head cold.

12/18/78 Monday
Sunny and not so cold. I washed and ironed. Wrote to Milton's and did some cards. Eby dug balance of the salsify. Invited the brothers and sisters for New Year's dinner. Got some boxes of cookies ready. Watered the plants and treated the busy lizzie for mold. Went to bed early.

12/20/78 Wednesday
Dark and cloudy with sleet, ice and rain. Did some cleaning. Put cookies in containers. Nancy came at 12:00. We made five more kinds of cookies. A woman was killed on the highway and there were lots of accidents. A lady came to check on the apartment for Home Care. Had a sauer kraut supper.

12/21/78 Thursday
Cold and windy. I made a portion of Russian tea cookies. Nancy slept till 10:00 and we went to White Horse Knittery and she bought a gift. Got some water cress at Spring Heads. I cleaned it. Dale called to say he is home from India and is coming for supper. He brought Mae and had a lot to tell about India.

12/22/78 Friday
Clear. Had news from Elizabeth first and then Rhoda of Darlis' plane lost on flight from Phoenix to Amarillo, Texas. Did a lot of phoning and there is no news of the

plane and its four passengers this evening. I cut some rug rags and got some clothing ready for Good Will. Went to bed early.

12/24/78 Sunday
Heavy rain this evening. Went to Kinzer this morning. Good sermon on gold, frankincense and myrrh. Uncle Charlie took us to Abram's, saw his new office, had a good supper, went to their church program. Called Edgar's. No word of Darlis.

12/25/78 Monday
Weather fine. Left at 8:30 for Ray's. Had good driving. Had a nice relaxing visit and good turkey dinner. Daddy, Ray, the girls and I went to see the recrossing of the Delaware and the Washington crossing. Lots of people there. Ray's gave us an indoor/outdoor thermometer. No word of Darlis.

12/26/78 Tuesday
Weather good. Eby went with Ray till noon. Jane was busy with her crafts. Grandma Koerwer was busy knitting. Laura and Martha were knitting through spools and starting embroidery. Their living room is redone with some paneling and new windows. We got home at 3:45. No word of Darlis.

1979

1/5/79 Friday
Sunny and cold. Worked 12-8. Rested till noon. Sent a letter to Milton's. Started a rug for Mary Alice. Cleaned an old cake pan that was Mrs. Stone's. Eby used the sander on it. Went to the auction this evening. Edgar and Rhoda are going to Arizona this evening to meet the parents of the others who were on the plane and to see where Darlis was working in Phoenix.

1/6/79 Saturday
Snowed. I did the cleaning and worked on the rug for Mary Alice. Eby took Isaac to the Medical Center to shovel snow. Made a dish of cracker pudding. A gasoline truck spilled at the end of Route 41 and stalled traffic for some time. No one was hurt. A 12-year-old Amish boy found $10,000 in jewels on Stumptown Road in a plastic bag and called police. He will be rewarded and complimented for his honesty.

1/12/79 Friday
Snowed all day. Isaac K. worked eight hours at the Medical Center. Eby had no trouble driving. I did the cleaning and worked on my rug. Some interested folks had a meeting to take action on the crossroads of Route 41 and Atglen Road. Went to Home early because of the roads. Had no trouble.

1/17/79 Wednesday
Snow. I worked on rug. Took Esther Arment along for Meals on Wheels. It was a little bad with the snowing and no cinders down. Eby mended some chair rungs that were loose. I cut his hair. Had a nice letter from Jonathan. Went to Home early because of the snow.

1/20/79 Saturday
Snow, sleet, ice and rain. I made a cocoanut cake for Fire Hall and one for at home. Made a lemon sponge and cooked sweet potatoes. Helped at Fire Hall from 10-3. The pot pie got sticky and we had to put all on new paper with more flour. Had a busy time. We went at 4:30 to have our own supper of pot pie, dried corn, cole slaw, biscuits, corn bread and jello. Clair Denlinger was taken by ambulance to hospital with heart attack.

1/21/79 Sunday
Rained, foggy and warmer. Went to Kinzer. Sanford Hershey preached on Hell. Dale came for dinner and showed us a lot of his slides from his India trip. Evening service at Kinzer and lots of others cancelled because of weather.

1/23/79 Tuesday
Clear. Worked 12-8. Had letters from Milton and Doug. Worked on rug this afternoon and evening. An article in today's paper says that since 1973 more than six million babies have been killed by abortions. President Carter is giving the State of the Union address this evening. Eby broke his bottom plate in three places eating some sweet chocolate.

1/26/78 Friday
Worked 12-8. Windy with snow flurries. Stopped for apples. Laced a lot of rug and cut strips from skirts that Mabel sent with Clarence from Reusit. Wrote to Sanford and he called this evening about a problem he was having making snow pudding. We went to the auction and got two pounds of English walnuts.

2/6/79 Tuesday
Fine day. I went to Bible School. 167 there and had very interesting class discussions. Eby worked all day. Snow is forecast for tonight. Isaac boiled a head of cabbage for breakfast. Dale called this evening and said he is very busy with meetings. He may get a promotion. Mae too may get a new office.

2/11/79 Sunday
Zero and a nice fresh, sunny day. Went to Kinzer. Paul preached on Jethro, the Man Behind the Scene. Spent the afternoon resting and reading. Wrote to Grace and finished Valentines.

2/12/79 Monday
It snowed most all day and gave six inches. I washed and ironed. Swept the apartment and finished the rug. Dried wash on porch and in basement. When Isaac saw the

snow, he said, "Praise the Lord," and struck out to work at the Medical Center. Was gone all day. Eby washed the dishes and I left for the Home early. Could not make it up the hill, so went by Meeting House Road.

3/8/79 Thursday
Sunny and mild. Wrote to Rhoda and sent Conrad's birthday card. I laced up all the rug. Joe Bechtold brought my two crewel works framed. Eby had him check the doors. We went to Lancaster to get common powers of attorney papers for Abram and Isaac to do our business in case of disability.

3/11/79 Sunday
Colder with snow. Paul preached on Ten Kinds of Faith. Very good. Had a quick dinner and Clarence's came and we took them along to visit Charles Horning's. Had a nice time chatting and listening to Emma and the girls. Abram called and said John Lerch had a heart attack and Pat flew to Florida this afternoon.

3/13/79 Tuesday
Worked 12-8. Had a real good morning. Did a big load of wash and Francis and I had a long talk. I rested and Mary Alice came with her Log Cabin quilt and we started quilting.

3/26/79 Monday
Windy and cold. Went to L.M.H.S. to quilt for sale. Fifteen there and we worked on three quilts. Eby brought Stephen Fisher to repair our dining room table and kitchen table. The cost was $3.00. Went over to Harvey's to get instructions for caring for plants while they are in Florida. Begin, Sadat and Carter signed Pact of Peace between Israel, Egypt and US.

3/29/79 Thursday
Some showers. I quilted most all day. There was a leak at the nuclear power plant on Three-Mile Island in the Susquehanna River. Eby coughed a lot today. Making some moves to stop water from washing the garden and yard.

3/30/79 Friday
Worked 12-8. Had some new victims of the virus at the Home. I wrote to Milton's. Took a nap and quilted. Eby got a notion to plant garden. Put in potatoes, peas, onions, spinach and radishes. Eby is still coughing. Abram called and said he may take the children to Dale's because of radiation fallout. It is making a stir.

4/1/79 Sunday
Went to Kinzer. Paul preached on Five Fools of the Bible. We took Helen Ranck along to Landis Homes. Aunt Cora seemed real good. The nuclear problem is not solved. Abram called and said that Pat and the children went to Dale's place. 50,000 have left Dauphin County. Seems like the experts cannot find a solution. Rhoda

called Abram's and said they could come up there. Spent the evening reading. Many schools are cancelled.

4/2/79 Monday
Cloudy and damp with showers. I washed and ironed and quilted. The nuclear plant is supposed to be under control. The bubble is smaller and it is cooling, for which we are thankful. I talked to Nancy. She came back from California this morning and was tired. Some airlines are on strike and her plane had 350 passengers.

4/3/79 Tuesday
Worked 12-8. Had a good morning. Wrote to Milton's. Rested till noon. Quilted all afternoon and evening. Eby went with Uncle Joe this evening to see about buying a right of way to the old cemetery. The nuclear plant seems to be cooling down and they say the danger is past. Called Minnie. Uncle Joe's Josie's Josie has a little Josie, which pleases him. It is the 4th generation of Josies.

4/5/79 Thursday
Windy and colder. I took Annis along to Sewing Circle. Did one quilt and finished two others. Eby ordered some topsoil from the Stoltzfus sons. Things are calming down at Three Mile Island. I quilted this evening. Eby went to Flaud's for asparagus roots. I watered the Kauffman's flowers as they are in Florida. Judy had a baby girl, Jennifer.

4/14/79 Saturday
Rained and cleared. Eby, Sanford, Ray and Jane went on a shopping trip. The girls stayed with me. I made a peach pie and prepared a sauer kraut dinner. Made buns and pudding. Peeled potatoes for Sunday. Roasted the ham. Did some cleaning. Played some games with the girls and made red eggs.

4/15/79 Sunday
Easter. Had a good day. Ray's went to Paradise, and we went to Kinzer. Had our communion service. Abram's, Isaac's, Ray's, Dale and Mae and Sanford were here for dinner and supper. We went up to Paradise this evening. The house was filled. David went along back to George School with Ray's.

4/25/79 Wednesday
My 74th birthday. I cleaned some kitchen cupboards and cleared off some honeysuckle bank. Transplanted some daisies. Sowed cardinal vine seed. Put rose pellets around roses and trimmed them. Eby took two loads of topsoil from Lapp's to stop water from washing. We went to midweek service. Truman Coy died. Got calls and cards with notes for birthday. Charlie called from Honolulu at 10:00.

4/27/79 Friday
Showers and cleared. I made a cake and fortune cookies for Abner's birthday. We went to Truman Coy's private funeral this afternoon at the United Methodist Church

in New Holland. Stopped at Rubinson's for a few things. Went to Coy's for supper and met some of Barbara's relatives from Ohio. Packed up and came to the Home. The Board is having a meeting to satisfy H.E.W. I called Robert Weaver's where Edgar's, Mary Alice, Nancy and Sanford are visiting.

5/11/79 Friday
I house cleaned the attic, a warm job. Wrote to Pat and to Milton's. Eby harrowed the garden. I thinned the pickles. Took a nap this afternoon. Abram called and said he is leaving for Chicago and they plan to fly Pat's Dad home by ambulance plane with a doctor and nurse. I went to the Mother-Daughter Banquet at Kinzer Fire Hall. Elizabeth was my daughter.

5/15/79 Tuesday
Beautiful day. I washed and ironed. Painted windows in Isaac's room. Eby took car to garage. Hauled an engine to Intercourse for Elam. We put baler twine to one row of peas. Eby is quitting his job.

5/18/79 Friday
Began raining at 1:30. I did the cleaning and made a raspberry pie. We did the Home report this afternoon. I ground a knob down to fit lid on the pitcher I got at Ivan Wick's sale. Had a letter from Milton's. Abram called and said John Lerch died yesterday. Went to bed early.

5/31/79 Thursday
Worked 12-8. Took a nap and packed up for our trip to Ray's with meat. Picked it up at Amos Bowell's and left there at 1:10 and got to Ray's at 3:40. Helped put it in the freezer. Eby went with Ray to hospital and watched him do repair surgery on a dog. Jane is a teacher's aide at school.

6/1/79 Friday
Nice mild day. Ray had the day off. He drove our car to Newtown where David graduated from the George School, a Quaker High School. Abram's whole family was there. We were served a good lunch. I helped Ray clean and plant more flowers in the beds. He mowed and trimmed.

6/5/79 Tuesday
Worked 12-8. Had a real good night. Did a load of wash and made a daisy bouquet. Eby stemmed berries and I put a lot in freezer and made preserves. Washed and ironed and took a couple naps. Eby gave Isaac a pep talk this morning. Had a thunder storm and showers.

6/9/79 Saturday
Worked 12-8. Left here at 9:15 and went to Lancaster to have a correct signing of the title to station wagon. Went to Karen's graduation at L.M.H.S. Held under the trees on bank of Mill Stream. Had lunch at Joanne's with all Isaac's family. I slept

all afternoon. Had a bite of supper and went to Hershey's 100th anniversary service. A good interest was shown.

6/15/79 Friday
Weather fine. Got up at 4:30 and met bus at Historical Center at 7:00. Our bus with forty passengers went to Meadowbrook Community of Brothers at Farmington, Pa. Had lunch with the folks and toured the premises, the school and the toy making shop. Had an information session. I got a sting and swollen hand. Went to Springs Church and met our hosts for the night. We stayed with Harley and Lucille Dietrich. They treated us very well.

6/16/79 Saturday
Fine weather. Had a good night. Served a good breakfast at the Dietrich's and were taken to the bus at 7:45. Went to the museum in Springs. Large collection of very old things. Had a scrumptious dinner at the Casselman Restaurant. Also a tour of the community and Penn Alps. Started home at 2:30, made a rest stop and got home at 7:30. Made supper, picked a few peas and made a sponge cake. Had a big letter from Rhoda.

6/22/79 Friday
Worked 12-8. Had a good night. Hoed the limas and some other parts of the garden. Put some stakes and strings to the pickles. Made some food ready for the weekend. Rested a while. The Weaver's and Sanford came this evening. The gas situation is getting very serious. Had a good rain and a little hail.

6/26/79 Tuesday
Worked 12-8. Stopped to get apples. Rested a while. Had early lunch and started for Jim's at 12:00. Had a good trip out and got there at 2:00. Everything was in tip top shape. Jim had hay in the making and Pat had changed her schedule. Greg is a big help farming and very fastidious. Beth is driving the car. Gas situation real serious.

7/1/79 Sunday
Worked 12-8. Warmer with some showers. Helped with the dining room and cooking. We went to the service at the chapel. Rhoda called about 9:00 and said the plane with Darlis and her friends was found yesterday on Green's Peak in Arizona. Ruth Coy called and said Milton's got to Kennedy Airport last evening and Treichler's met them and took them to Stony Brook by 9:00. We called Milton's and they are busy getting things in order.

7/2/79 Monday
Partly cloudy and a few showers. I took Helen Ranck and Emma King along for cherries at Beiler's. Too many pickers for the amount of trees and ladders. Got mostly gold ones and canned 11 quarts. Did 5 quarts of yellow beans and 6 quarts of pickles. Eby took Ed Umble to the horse sale at New Holland. When he got home he helped

seed cherries and picked the beans. I called Rhoda and they have heard from the Phoenix folks. Memorial services are planned at the Phoenix church for Thursday. The remains of the victims were buried out there. A thorough investigation is being made of the wreckage.

7/3/79 Tuesday
Sunny and breezy. I did a big wash and ironing. Eby had a trip to Lancaster with two Amish this morning and took five to pick over 300 lbs. of cherries this afternoon. He picked a bucketful for us. I put strings to my Emma Horning beans. Rhoda called and said they have set July 29 for memorial service for Darlis in Ithaca.

7/6/69 Friday
Beautiful day. Daniel and Joanne picked us up at 8:45 and we came with Isaac's and all their family but Karen to their cabin at the Mountains. Got here about 2:00 and stopped for a light lunch on the way. Had swimming, games, mowing lawn, eating and plenty of activity. Children are having a lot of fun. Took a drive to spot deer at dusk. The boys put off some fireworks and Benjie did not like them one bit.

7/7/79 Saturday
Beautiful weather. All slept late and had a farmer's late breakfast. A lot of us went up the mountain to see the beaver dams. Some went swimming, pitched quoits, played badmitton, scrabble and cards. Children having a great time. Judy had an asthma attack and John took her to the doctor. Men got the lawn mowed. Had chicken barbecue.

7/13/79 Friday
Very warm and sultry. I did the cleaning. Picked a quart of red raspberries and some pickles. Had a letter from Rhoda with a copy of the program from the Memorial Service in Phoenix. I wrote a note to them this morning. Eby watered the garden real wet. Bathed and went to bed early.

7/24/79 Tuesday
Partly cloudy and sultry. Got up early and packed up to go to Milton's. We picked Barbara up in New Holland. Barbara did most of the driving and we got here by 5:30. Milton had things in hand. After supper we saw some slides of their travels and India. Doug is happy to be home and very much interested in the slides. Milton looks so much thinner.

7/25/79 Wednesday
Very warm. Had a few showers. Slept late and had breakfast at 9:00. Canned the pickles that I brought. Barbara made jam and she and Daddy went to the store. Milton and Mike worked and Daddy and Doug walked over to see them. I got some beans ready that I brought along. Played some games with Doug. Daddy and I hoed the

garden. Milton tied up the tomatoes and trimmed some bushes after he came from work. Looked at more slides this evening. Doug keeps very busy sorting slides.

7/29/79 Sunday
Cloudy with showers at home. Sunshine in New York State. All ready to leave Gap Fire Hall at 7:55 on the M.D.S. bus driven by Marvin Stoltzfus for the Memorial Service for Darlis at the Bethel Grove Church. Picked up Uncle Menno's, Uncle Frank's, and Uncle Bob's at East Petersburg Church and Abram's and Robert's at Lebanon Mall. Stopped to eat our lunches at a roadside rest. Arrived at the church at 1:50. Had a very nice service and well-attended. Were served a nice lunch and left for home at 5:30. All had a sociable time and got home at 11:00. Ray, Sanford, Nancy and Mary Alice stayed for night.

8/15/79 Wednesday
Cool. Eby got 100 ears of corn for Milton's and I froze 35 pints. I made some tea concentrate for the reunion. Had a day of "Try Hunger." I ate very little. Did the Home report and wrote thank you letters for Home gifts. Worked on my printer tray this evening.

8/18/79 Saturday
Rainy, cool and cloudy. I made a casserole and cupcakes to take to the Martin reunion at Lititz. 84 there. We stopped for peaches and to see Aunt Cora at the hospital. She is very weak. Stopped for Doug at the Coy's where he and Mike came by train. He played some games with Isaac and is glad to be here again.

8/19/79 Sunday
Foggy and cleared off. Abram called at 7:30 and said that Andy was hit on his bike by a car on his way home from work and killed instantly when he was almost home. Eby went to church and Doug and I stayed at home. I had dinner ready so we could go to Abram's. They are shocked and in grief. Dale and Mae came to get Stevie Weaver as he came with Becky from Sanford's by bus to spend the week with Dale.

8/20/79 Monday
I washed and canned 11 quarts of peaches. Eby got 100 ears of corn up by Linville Hill and Doug husked it and he brushed it and I put 43 pints in the freezer. Isaac played a game of Parcheesi with Doug. Had a lot of calls today. Sue Martin called from Spruce Lake.

8/21/79 Tuesday
Worked 12-8. A quiet night. Stopped for eggs. Took a nap. Had early lunch and met Isaac's at the Guernsey Barn and went with them to Abram's. They are very sad. A lot of people came and called. Many brought food and they have plenty. Dale and Stevie Weaver came for Sammy. Elizabeth and I did some cleaning. I did the ironing and picked the pickles when we got home.

8/24/79 Friday
Put things in order. Made a cake, red eggs and cole slaw for the reunion. Had some phone calls and cards from sympathizing friends. Charlie and Ed left for Abram's this forenoon and took most of our food along. Daddy washed the new car. Nancy came and drove our car with us to Camp Morehart.

8/25/79 Saturday
Weather nice and warm. All had a good night. Isaac's and Jim's families came and we had early lunch and went to the Derry Presbyterian Church for Andy's Memorial Service. It was well attended. We all came back to camp for supper and also had the Ohio relatives. Had a nice evening together. Milton shared his India slides.

8/26/79 Sunday
Weather good. Grace served a pancake breakfast. Becky stayed all night. Abram's came after the Ohio folks left. We had a song service, Milton spoke and Rhoda had a talk. Had prayers and dismissal. Lots of good leftovers for lunch. Vote was unanimous to use the same place next year.

8/27/79 Monday
Sultry with much rain. Milton's came for breakfast and left at 7:30 for home. Rosa, Jonathan, Mary Alice and Sanford left about 10:00. I picked pickles and canned some. We took Clarence and Mabel along to Aunt Cora's funeral at Strasburg. The boys were all there but Billy and Kenneth. I drove the new car from Strasburg. Went to bed early.

9/4/79 Tuesday
Sultry and hot. I did some trimming and cleaning flower beds. Cleaned wax from car with kerosene. Ironed. Picked pickles and prepared three quarts for chow chow. Joe Kershner stopped in for a short visit and Hansen Poole came to chat. Eby washed car with Comet and mowed yard. I went to Harold Groff's for pears. 502 traffic deaths from Labor Day weekend.

9/7/79 Friday
Worked 12-8. Had two loads of wash. Wrote family letter. Invited ten ladies for next Thursday. Took a nap. Picked some limas for Isaac's. Eby took them down when he went with Isaac to a farm sale. The properties sold for more than $500,000, so Isaac did not buy them. I took David Fisher's wife and boy to Lancaster to Dr. Muhler. Stopped for fabrics and got two dress lengths. Stopped at Eshleman's Store and Nickel Mines Store. Eby went to Gap auction.

9/18/79 Tuesday
Worked 12-8. Had a busy night with a lot of wash. Wrote to Milton's and Grace. Had hair to comb on nine heads. Called my corset lady. Made an angel food cake and took a nap. Canned four quarts of peaches. Dale called and said his new job looks big. He is living in a motel. Eby went to the Vintage sale and mowed the

bank across the road. An 87-year-old Lancaster woman was killed by thieves and her brother critically injured.

9/19/79 Wednesday
Fine weather. I prepared things for tomorrow's dinner. Picked limas and Eby shelled them. Got in corn, tomatoes and celery. Made meat loaves, pealed potatoes, made buns and did some cleaning. Eby scrubbed porch and swept part of drive. The 81-year-old brother of Lancaster woman died. Both died of thirst and starved from being tied and taped.

9/21/79 Friday
A very wet day. Isaac K. here all day. Oh my! I made sandwich spread. I took Ruth Summers with Meals on Wheels in the rain. Eby delivered some grapes for Elam. Gave Isaac a lesson in making a diabetic caramel pudding. Rested this afternoon and went to bed early.

9/30/79 Sunday
Cloudy with showers. Went to Kinzer. No visitors for our host Sunday. Nancy came for dinner and stayed till 9:00. We went to Strasburg Cemetery to get dates on Grandmother and Grandfather Hersh's graves but could not find them. Called Mabel. Abram and Pat called to invite us to go with them to a service in Philadelphia for parents of body donors.

10/11/79 Thursday
Cloudy and cool. I cleaned drawers and cupboards in kitchen. Picked a few limas and green beans. Went with Eby to a specialist in Lancaster. He said he should have tests and xrays in the hospital. Jay and Margie stopped a while on their way from Landis Homes. Called Grace and she said they still have snow from the eight inches that fell yesterday. Had no school, so made snow balls and snow man.

10/12/79 Friday
Wet day. Did some cleaning. Took Meals on Wheels. Eby dug some sweet potatoes. Ruth Coy brought Milton and he ate with Daddy and went along to Book Sale. Barbara and Doug came from Stony Brook and ate with me. I made a bowl of tossed salad with things from the garden. Doug and I played Social Security.

10/16/79 Tuesday
Warmer. Worked 12-8. Finished cleaning the kitchen cupboards and went with Eby to pick up a new coil for the stove and go on to the hospital where he was admitted for his possible prostate problem. I came home by Good's Store and got him some P.J.'s. Spent a quiet evening and got jars ready for applesauce. Eby is to have his specimen tomorrow and wants me to come in.

10/18/79 Thursday
Worked 12-8. Had a busy night with wash, mending and repair on the medical record book. Got things ready for lunch and went to bed. Abram came from hospital and

woke me at 10:15. We ate and left for Philadelphia to go to the memorial service for body donor's families. Abram went on to Washington. I went in to see Eby. He had more tests and seemed groggy, but did wake up.

10/19/79 Friday
Sunny and in the seventies. Cleaned our bedroom and did weekly cleaning. Abram called from Washington after he talked to Daddy's doctor and said his test yesterday showed no malignancy, for which we are so thankful. Clarence's took me along to the hospital this evening.

10/20/79 Saturday
Very warm day. Took my cake to the Fire Hall and helped from 9:00-2:00. Made two pies, a pudding and cooked sweet potatoes. Milton called to say that he and Mike would come around 9:00 after Mike ran somewhere near Albany. Made some buns. Called Eby. Milton put new burner on stove. Mike called his girlfriend near Philadelphia. She is a student at Stony Brook.

10/21/79 Sunday
Warm, in the 80's. Milton and Mike ate breakfast and left for North Carolina after stopping at the hospital to see Daddy. Abe stopped for a couple hours on his way home from Washington. I went to Kinzer and we had our communion. Ate my chicken dinner alone and went to hospital. Dale and Mae came to see Daddy. Came home at 6:00.

10/24/79 Wednesday
Colder and windy. I left at 9:00 for the hospital and stayed in till 9:00. Eby had his surgery at 2:00 and was back in his room by 5:30. Dr. Breslin called to tell me he came through very well. Daddy had a severe backache most of the evening.

10/27/79 Saturday
Weather nice. Slept till 7:00. Brought most of the flowers from garage and put them at the windows. Went to the hospital before 1:00. Sally and Leo were there and Clair Eby. Abram and Pat came and took me to supper at the Kountry Kitchen. Dale and Mae and John and Judy came this evening. Daddy was feeling better, walking a little and on a light diet. Got home at 9:15.

10/31/79 Wednesday
Beautiful day. Eby called and said he can come home and I went for him at 10:30. Went to Christiana for meds. He took a nap this afternoon, ate well and took it easy. I worked in the yard and cleaned up some corners. I went to Elam's for milk.

11/22/79 Thursday
A nice mild Thanksgiving Day. We went to Hershey's Church for service. A good sermon. Abram's, Isaac's, Dale's and Uncle Charlie were here. Karen and Becky helped get dinner on. We had a nice visit. Rhoda called. Daddy took boneset tea.

12/3/79 Monday
Clear and cold. I washed and ironed and baked sand tarts, flap jacks, peppernuts, chocolate chip, and rice krispie date balls. John Hershey was here and installed a heater in dining room. Isaac K. was struck on highway coming home from Coatesville and is in the hospital with a broken leg. Had a lot of calls inquiring about him.

12/4/79 Tuesday
Worked 12-8. Clear and cold. I took a nap, we ate early and took Elam's along to visit Joe Kershner in York County. Had a nice time and good trip. Reuben Stoltzfus stopped after visiting Isaac in hospital and said he is not good. Has broken leg, ribs, and head and other injuries. Mildred Groff left on a tour of Jamaica this morning.

12/8/79 Saturday
Fine weather. Got all packed up and left at 9:35. Stopped to see Isaac Kauffman in the Osteopathic Hospital. He is in intensive care and knew us. Left on our way to Robert Weaver's. Took turns driving and got here by 3:50. Ate a lunch on the way. Had venison steaks for supper. Stevie and Jennie went to a Christmas party and stayed over at E.M.C. for the night. The wood stove in basement is giving good results. Called Sanford to tell him we will stop for supper tomorrow evening.

12/11/79 Tuesday
Clear and warmer. Had a good night, cocoa and doughnuts in our rooms and started out at 8:15. Stopped for our lunch at a restaurant and came on to St. Augustine at 2:15. Took a tour and saw many of the historical places but did not have time to get off to see any. We stopped at the Georgia Welcome Center this morning and the Florida Welcome Center when we arrived. Ate at Fidley's Smorgasbord this evening and stayed at the Francis Motel tonight. $12.00 for two beds. Jay, Sue, Nora and I walked to the Pottery Shop that had everything we did not need.

12/13/79 Thursday
Sunny and warm. Called Westman's and left the motel and headed south. Stopped at Daytona Beach and drove on the beach for some miles. Had brunch at a pancake house. Next stop was the Kennedy Space Center and Cape Canaveral. It is fantastic. Took a two hour tour of the 3000 acres and saw much of the equipment. Drove on to Fort Pierce and are putting up at a Holiday Inn for the price of $28.00. Walter is still talking.

12/14/79 Friday
Sunny and warm. Left Fort Pierce at 8:15 and found the Westman's real easy in Stuart. They served us lunch and supper and we went for a long drive to see the area. Her sister Grace came and we met her and the next door neighbors. A young man walked in who seemed to be a dope addict. We are sleeping at Grace's house, and Walter's and Jay's at Art's house. Very nice and comfortable.

12/20/79 Thursday
Sunny and cool. Left motel at 8:00 and started for Plains. Stopped at a small gift shop before Americus and found Plains, which was a surprise, because it is so small, only about 600 population. Found Davis Brothers Motor Lodge which is very comfortable with a king size bed. All seem to be feeling good. We saw thousands of pecan trees, cotton and peanuts. Country is level but becoming more rolling as we travel north.

12/22/79 Saturday
Partly cloudy and cold. Drove through North Carolina and into Virginia. Stopped to eat two times and to see the Natural Bridge. Eby and I went down to see it as the others had seen it. Arrived at the Weaver's about 5:15 and unloaded our possessions and what we had gathered on the trip.

12/24/79 Monday
Had some rain. Robert and Steve worked on some wood. Daddy shelled a pound of our pecans. I helped Grace to prepare some of the food. Jennie cut the filling bread. Grace packed up some cookies and candy and Robert delivered it to some of their friends and neighbors. Mary Alice, Debbie, Sanford and Nancy came for a supper of vegetable soup, salad and the dessert they brought. Sang carols, Steve and Jennie had a game and we looked at slides.

12/25/79 Tuesday
Christmas at Weaver's. Weather fair. Had a good night and breakfast. Gift exchange began at 8:00 and all got a lot of lovely gifts, including Daddy and me. Had a delicious turkey dinner with all the trimmings. Dale called from Edgar's and we talked to Rhoda too. Worked on a large puzzle and played Scrabble. Mary Alice, Debbie and I took a walk down to the road. Looked at more slides and helped Jennie play with her question game. Some watched T.V.

12/26/79 Wednesday
Fine weather. Had a good breakfast, loaded our car with fruit, luggage and gifts. Said our good byes to Grace, Mary Alice, Sanford, Nancy, Steve, Jennie and Debbie. Robert had already gone to work. Left at 8:45 and got home at 3:00. Stopped at hospital to see Isaac K. He seems real sick yet. Unpacked and made some calls. Eby went for milk. Read our Christmas cards and mail. Marked our trip on the map.

12/27/79 Thursday
Partly cloudy and windy. I did a big wash and it dried good outdoors. The heat was off all night and Eby called the mechanic and he put on a new motor. Charlie brought a shirt for Eby from Abram's. We added up our trip bill and it totalled $896.85. That should suffice for a while. Had a long talk with Mabel.

Baking bread in her kitchen.

The Eighties

1980

1/1/80 Tuesday
A fine day. Worked 8-12. I took a nap. We went to Paul's for dinner. All were there but Jay's and Charlie. They had their family. Had a good dinner and a nice visit. Jay and Margie came this evening. Showed them some slides of our Florida trip and others.

1/4/80 Friday
Cloudy with some snow. I did the cleaning. Rested a while. Had a call for the room from Arnold Cohen in Philadelphia. Forgot my turn for Meals on Wheels, so Ruth Summers did it alone. Eby cracked walnuts. Eby washed the dishes and I went to the Home early.

1/10/80 Thursday
Clear and sunny. Eight degrees. Worked 12-8. Roads are bare and fields are covered. I slept till noon and sewed on my dresses. Eby took Jay along to visit Isaac Kauffman. He is to go to a nursing home tomorrow. Arnold Cohen came to see the room and is coming on Sunday. Eby went to Board meeting at the Medical Center.

1/12/80 Saturday
A nice day. I did the cleaning. Made a lemon sponge cake from one of Art Westman's lemons. Sue Martin called to say they decided to go to California. Spent the evening reading.

1/21/80 Monday
Clear and colder. I washed and ironed and mended. Eby finished the soap, got out turnips and carrots, fixed mirror on the station wagon, brought milk and sprouted the potatoes. Nancy called and said she was ice fishing on Saturday. I went to bed early.

2/3/80 Sunday
Beautiful day. Ten degrees. Went to Kinzer and the text was Peter's faith. Dale and Mae were here for dinner. Said they plan to announce their engagement. We took a drive with them to see new Gap development. Talked to Mabel and Sue.

2/20/80 Wednesday
Mild and sunny. Helped Eby antique the case of drawers, wood box and wide bench. Cleaned and scrubbed basement rooms. Raked some yard. Eby took Christ King's and her mother to Dr. Ruth Hershey. Went to midweek service.

2/22/80 Friday
Worked 12-8. Wet day with snow this morning. I did the dusting and cleaned some drawers and cupboards. Took a nap. Jay Hostetter went with Eby to the Home this afternoon to help with painting. We went up to auction this evening. Bought some writing pads.

3/17/80 Monday
A wet day. Ira Stoltzfus delivered our $95.00 stove and took our old one. It was first installed in 1950 and was just like new. I washed and ironed and did some quilting. Eby hauled some Amish men this P.M. Went to bed early.

3/18/80 Tuesday
Worked 12-8. Cleared mild after good showers. Eby worked at the Home till P.M. and took five Amish boys to Root's auction with rabbits, cats, dogs, pigeons, etc. I napped till noon and quilted. Dale and Charlie called this evening. Charlie is working with the refugees coming into California.

3/21/80 Friday
Rained. Worked 12-8. Bertha fell boom sock on the floor at 3:45. Got her up and she has pains. Stopped at Byler's on way home and got some needs. Slept till noon. Jay Hostetter stopped in and is greatly disturbed about the move to use musical instruments in worship. Eby went to the auction and I quilted.

3/27/80 Thursday
Beautiful day. I quilted all day. Eby sawed a limb from the birch tree and went to East Brook for a checkup. Bought two dozen pansies and he planted them. There is a lot of commotion about Three Mile Island and its nuclear plants.

3/28/80 Friday
Partly cloudy. Worked 12-8. First night to work in new nurses station. It is fine. Rested after I did the washing. Took Meals on Wheels with Ruth Summers. Eby took Jay to Home to help paint. He washed both cars. Mabel came and helped to finish the quilt. Sanford brought his girlfriend, Tera Yoder.

3/29/80 Saturday
Showery. Sanford took Tera on a tour, came back for dinner and went out again. I made some food ready and did some cleaning. Eby worked on the old bed. Looked at some pictures this evening.

4/2/80 Wednesday
Eby drove 112 miles today with hauling. He painted stair steps and worked on bed. I helped with bed. Hemmed more than half of quilt. Eby found the Meadville well information in the 1967 diary. We took Jay and Margie along to Hershey's for Meadville night. The subject was the New Covenant.

4/9/80 Wednesday
A wet day. I cleaned the closets in hall, bathroom and dining room and cleaned some drawers. At 10:00 Bennie Fisher came to visit with wet clothing and a damaged umbrella. Had dinner and Daddy took him home at 3:00. He is 73 and slowing down. Played his mouth organ and took a long nap. Daddy did some patch painting in the living room. Went to midweek. Uncle Paul and Charlie gave us a report on their four years in C.P.S. It was interesting.

4/12/80 Saturday
Beautiful day. Eby cut a bucket of water cress and we left at 8:00 and got to Ray's at 10:00. Laura Koerwer was there and we all had a nice time. Eby went with Ray on calls. Played some games with the girls. Dale came for a Chinese supper.

4/14/80 Monday
Wet day. Washed and ironed. Dried it on porch and in basement. Kathleen came for her seeds. Sally called about her quilt. A 17-month-old Amish girl drowned in a horse trough near Byerstown yesterday.

4/21/80 Monday
Warm and pleasant. I washed, ironed, washed windows on the outside, scrubbed screens and put them in. House cleaned the sink corner. Planted some dahlias. Eby felt sick at 10:30 and went to bed till 2:00. He put wire up for the clematis he bought on Saturday. He planted cannas, elephant ear and sowed grass seed on the north side of house.

4/22/80 Tuesday
Worked 12-8. Had a quiet night. Slept till 11:00. Eby not feeling good and rested often. I helped put mushroom manure on garden. Took manure off roses and pulled some weeds and hoed flower beds. Jay and Sue came this evening to plan for our trip to California. Eby is coughing.

4/25/80 Friday
Eby did a bit of hauling and took it easy. Says he feels better. I cleaned dining room and kitchen. Eight Americans were killed trying to rescue hostages in Iran. Mabel and Abram called with birthday wishes.

4/30/80 Wednesday
Worked 12-8. Had a quiet night. I stayed till noon and helped Linda paper a bathroom. Stopped for plants and my shoes. Cleaned basement room and took a nap. Eby took lawn mower for tuneup. He is not feeling too good. I sponged his neck till 11:30.

5/2/80 Friday
Fine weather. Left at 7:30 with Jay's for Abram's and then on to Middletown Airport for our TWA flight to California to visit Charlie. He met us at the airport in the Chevy

van Nancy rented for us. Came to his new house where Ed was busy after shopping for food. Had a roast beef dinner and visited till bedtime. Eby was very tired and took a long nap before supper. Charlie was called away for a couple hours.

5/3/80 Saturday
Sunny. Had a good night. Helped pack a picnic lunch and after Charlie did some errands we started out for seeing some places. Saw an earthquake fault and an oyster place. Bought some oysters and had them barbecued for our supper. Sue and I helped make some crepes.

5/4/80 Sunday
Sunny and pleasant. Went to Grace Episcopal Church in San Francisco. Had dinner at Hilton Hotel. Had a ride on a cable car and drove down a crooked street. Went to shore and drove on a high mountain road. Spent evening here. Had artichokes, sandwiches and tomatoes. Watched T.V.

5/5/80 Monday
Sunny and pleasant. Eby is feeling better. Slept late while Charlie and Ed went for recreation. Sue and I made a sponge cake for Eby's birthday. A lady from singing telegrams came and sang for him before we had our turkey supper that was roasted in a charcoal oven. We took a drive to the Louis Martin winery and saw thousands of acres of vineyards. Ed worked. Sue and I took a walk to see the new houses and went through one next door.

5/6/80 Tuesday
Weather the same. Charlie went to Laundromat this morning and away on business this afternoon. Sue and I climbed the cliff and did some cleaning. I made some pie crusts and we had two quiches baked for supper. Sue and I counted the rooms in the house next door. Fifteen rooms and seven baths and lots of closets. Sue typed some of Emma Horning's poems for me.

5/7/80 Wednesday
Weather the same. Up early and left at 6:15 for Yosemite National Park. Charlie drove and we saw a lot of God's wonderful creation. The high solid granite mountains and beautiful waterfalls. Had a ride on shuttle bus and got on free because of being senior citizens. Ate the lunch that Charlie packed. Got back at 8:00 and went to bed early.

5/8/80 Thursday
Charlie went to the gym and we were on our own all day. First I made three pie crusts, we ate breakfast and packed some food. Left at 9:30 with Jay as our driver. Went north on 101. Saw redwoods, California geyser, petrified forest, pretty countryside and mountains. Charlie and Ed had a good vegetable soup supper for us with a wonton appetizer.

5/9/80 Friday
An unusual showery day. We spent the day here. I made two lemon pies and Sue got two pineapples ready. Ed was here all day. Charlie was gone this morning and met Abram's and brought them here about 1:30. We took some walks and went through some new houses. Had a good dinner of chicken, salad, pie, dill tuna mold, crackers and pineapples. Went to bed after packing.

5/10/80 Saturday
Left Charlie's at 6:45 for airport. Abram drove and returned the van. Left on TWA at 9:00 and had landings at Chicago and Pittsburgh. Had good flights and got home at 10:30. Stopped at Abram's. It was a good trip.

5/14/80 Wednesday
Nice day. I worked outdoors all day. Hoed and cleaned up flower beds and some garden. Planted morning glories. Eby took Christ King's wife and her mother to Ruth Hershey for treatment. We went to Kinzer this evening. Had a program in song.

5/19/80 Monday
Had a heavy shower at 5:30 A.M. Washed and ironed a big wash. Eby brought the liver, heart and ox tail. I sliced the liver and put it in the freezer. Vernon Yoder brought Isaac Kauffman and he can walk without a cane. Went to bed early.

5/21/80 Wednesday
Wet day. I cut Eby's hair and we did Home report. I made spinach-filled crepes for supper. Isaac had visitors and it gave him a boost. He went to Millwood with Leroy Lapp's. Eby did some hauling and visited Jay this forenoon. I sorted Dale's things for Reusit and washed a lot of shirts and pants.

5/26/80 Monday
A beautiful day. We took Ray's along to Isaac's and saw their beautiful new kitchen and other renovations they had done. Ray did some work on Isaac's cows. After a late dinner they packed up their meat and got balance at Bowell's to take home with them. I washed and got it all dried. Isaac took a walk to visit some neighbors. I planted the passion vine that Ray brought for me.

6/4/80 Wednesday
Clear, cool and windy. Eby washed the cars and mowed the yard and put the radio out to keep the birds from the strawberries. I worked on dolls. Arnold brought two friends after school and took them out for dinner. Isaac sat glum all day. I went to Sewing Circle.

6/18/80 Wednesday
Very fine weather. I picked one bushel of Early Market peas and put 11 pints in freezer. Eby helped shell them. Insurance lady was here to see Isaac and left him in

a bad mood. Eby mowed yard and did 75 miles of hauling. I hoed flower beds and planted two dozen petunias and some marigolds. Made a strawberry pie.

7/10/80 Thursday
Sunny and warm. Eby picked 4 quarts of blueberries and chased the birds. I picked potato bugs morning and evening. Made two gallons of applesauce. Did fourteen of Sally's quilt patches. Ira Buckwalter asked Eby if we would consider a year of V.S. at the Home. Elam King's Barbara was hospitalized after she fell from the hay wagon and was run over.

7/15/80 Tuesday
Sunny and hot and getting dry. I washed and ironed. Did the limas and picked potato bugs. Rested. Eby watered, picked blueberries and went to Vintage. I hoed some garden. I sewed some patches this evening. There have been 654 deaths due to heat.

7/21/80 Monday
Very hot. 108 degrees by 4:30. Had cooling showers by 6:30. Sewed and cut patches. Isaac took a lunch and hopped a ride to visit a friend. Eby took it easy. Nancy called and we had a long chat. I went to bed early.

7/24/80 Thursday
Beautiful day. Canned four quarts of beans and two of pickles. Picked raspberries for the last time. Eby trimmed the strawberries and harrowed them. Eby went for milk. Mt. St. Helens erupted again, sending ash and smoke eleven miles high. I went to bed early. Made cupcakes.

8/3/80 Sunday
Worked 12-8. Hot with a shower last night. Had a quiet night. Went to Kinzer and Eby went to Millwood for ordination. Spent evening at home. Sanford is in hospital for knee problem.

8/13/80 Wednesday
Eby left after breakfast and did over 120 miles of hauling. I helped with picking squash, pickles, freezing corn and limas. Sara Marie came and plans to take Isaac for six weeks. I helped him pack and picked pickles and a bucket of limas.

8/15/80 Friday
Cloudy with good showers. Took it easy visiting and did a couple butterfly patches for Beth. We left Jim's at 12:30 and picked up Abe and Lizzie and Daniel at their daughter's place in Brush Valley. Got home safely at 5:30. Milton called and said Doug was hit by a car and is in the hospital. We were looking for them to come this evening.

8/22/80 Friday
Partly cloudy. Made cole slaw and red eggs and got food packed for our reunion. Eby drove for Meals on Wheels. We left at 1:40 to meet camp director at 3:00. Stopped to

get quilt fabric. Found everything in fine shape at Camp Morehart. All got there by bedtime except Isaac's and Jim's. Abram's had a very long sub, enough for everyone.

8/23/80 Saturday
Partly cloudy. I helped with breakfast. Elizabeth and the girls made the dinner. A photographer came to take pictures. Everyone had plenty to do playing games, taking walks, looking at slides, visiting, reading, drinking root beer and punch.

8/24/80 Sunday
Beautiful weather. Jay's brought Frank Kreider's and Charlie for breakfast. Had a service outdoors. Bible reading, prayers, singing and three poems by Jennie W. After our chicken corn soup and leftovers we all left by 3:00.

9/5/80 Friday
Some showers in early morning. Worked 12-8. Had a good night. Got plums on the way home. Rested after I did some pickles and pear butter. Eby went to see about our new table. I got things ready for chow chow and hoed up the celery. Isaac was in bed until after supper.

9/7/80 Sunday
Fine day. Went to Kinzer. Ben preached council sermon. Because the bus had three seats left, we went on it to the Bowery to take in the service. Paul Clark preached on the Prodigal Son to about 85 alcoholics. Got home at 12:30.

10/14/80 Tuesday
Clear and cool. Worked 12-8 and had a busy night. I went to Metal Crafts and man was not there. Eby helped me can 26 quarts of applesauce. Rested this afternoon. Eby went to Ivan Clark's sale. It sold for $263,520. He hauled Amish from 4-7. Sanford called. He likes his new home and is joining the Quakers.

10/25/80 Saturday
Worked 12-8. Rained all day, over two inches. Got breakfast for M.D.S. guests when I got home. I slept and Eby went to the M.D.S. meeting at Maple Grove. I went this afternoon and then we went to the banquet at Dutch Town and Country this evening. A full dining room. I went to work early. Donald Hostetter died.

10/27/80 Monday
Clear. Washed and ironed. Eby took out the cannas, dahlias, and elephant ear. He cleaned up some of the rubbish. Isaac went out this afternoon. Eby cut off the roses. Nancy called and said she is buying a house. Talked to Mabel and Sue Martin. Made up the beds.

11/14/80 Friday
Mild. Eby raked some leaves and had two hauling jobs. I did some cleaning and took Meals on Wheels. Esther came at noon time. I went to a nurse's meeting at the

Home and Blanche had a good talk for us. Isaac did a lot of moaning and groaning. We went up to the auction a couple hours. Got nothing but cheese.

11/16/80 Sunday
Beautiful day. Went to Kinzer. Harold Book preached on John 17, Our Intercessor. Dale and Mae came for dinner. Mae is wearing a diamond. Went to bed early.

11/22/80 Saturday
Cold and sunny. I got Isaac's lunch ready and left for Warren Hershey's sale at 11:00. Eby had two hauls. Bought a stove for Milton's for $5.00 and paid Dan Kurtz $5.00 to haul it. Isaac spent the day in bed and went to the diner after supper. I spent a quiet evening reading.

11/24/80 Monday
A wet day. Over two inches of rain. Eby left at 8:00 and hauled till 1:30. I washed and ironed. Dried it in the basement. Did some mending. Gave the stove we bought for Milton's a thorough cleaning. Worked about four hours on it. There was an earthquake in Italy that killed 83 people and injured more.

11/27/80 Thursday
Thanksgiving day. Partly cloudy with some sprinkles. Ray, Jane and the girls helped us with dinner. Had 26 at the tables. Abram's, Isaac's, Jim's, Ray's, Dale and Mae. Milton and Sanford called.

11/28/80 Friday
Rainy. I put things away and got the tables back in place. Finished cleaning up Milton's stove. Eby took Isaac along to Ephrata with Abe and Lizzie Stoltzfus to get steam baths. Rested a while. Isaac went to the diner after supper and stayed till 12:00. I went to bed early.

11/30/80 Sunday
Sunny. Went to Kinzer. Milton and Doug came for their stove and had dinner. We went to Dan Dietzel's and he took Elizabeth and us along to Abram's. We shared the graveside service for the burial of Andy's ashes.

12/9/80 Tuesday
Cloudy and mild. I packed up the plants for Sanford. Got lunch early and went to Ephrata Hospital to sew. Eby had two hauls and went to the Board meeting at the Home. Plans to resign as director. I mixed peppernuts and baked and iced them this evening. Isaac, Elizabeth and Bradley brought a coat for Jennie W. this evening.

12/10/80 Wednesday
Packed up and started for Virginia at 9:40. Stopped for lunch and arrived at Grace's about 3:00. Spent a nice evening with them and saw the new sewing room and

woodstove. Robert is working for his brother Jim on the farm. Stevie and Jennie are enjoying school.

12/11/80 Thursday
Weather fine. We left for Richmond to visit Sanford this morning. Found his new home comfortable and inviting. He made dinner for us and Tera came over dinnertime. Got back to Weaver's at 5:00. Mary Alice and Debbie came for supper and spent the evening. Robert and Grace took Jennie to her Christmas program.

12/15/80 Monday
Cold and started snowing at 11:00. I washed and ironed. Baked four kinds of cookies. Peanut butter, date pinwheel, date balls and raisin filled. Had Abram and Pat for supper. Abram had a meeting and an appointment with some Amish after supper. I went to work at 10:15 and had to walk up the hill. Parked at the church.

12/19/80 Friday
Worked 12-8. Had a quiet night. Colder. Washed some dresses and ironed all of them. Took a nap. Eby bought spray paint and tried painting his hat. Jay Hostetter stopped in about Donald's estate and his will. Isaac did a lot of phoning. I sent more cards. Isaac up to diner till 1:00 A.M.

12/22/80 Monday
Weather fine. Clarence took us to the station for the 6:32 train to Stony Brook. Arrived at 12:20 and Milton met us. Doug was home with a cold. Mike and Barbara working. Played some games with Doug. Two of Mike's friends were here for supper. Had good fish and other goodies. I peeled potatoes and got celery and apples ready for Waldorf salad.

12/23/80 Tuesday
Had a nice day. Barbara worked in the P.M. We were invited to the Treichler's for supper. Had all the Christmas trimmings and a good supper. It was snowing. Milton did some shopping. Eby and Milton bought a big turkey.

12/24/80 Wednesday
Snowed and got much colder. Milton, Daddy, Barbara and Mike went to the Christmas Program at the Setauket Church. I stayed with Doug and we colored some of his Christmas country posters and read India diaries until after 12:00. Everything is ready for Christmas and Doug can hardly wait.

12/25/80 Thursday
A white Christmas. Four degrees. Very cold and sunny. Slept late and had 10:30 breakfast. Opened gifts for a long time. They gave us a rake, hoe, gloves, dress hangers, notes and candy. Had a good turkey dinner and played some new games. Jim's called and Abram's were there for Christmas.

12/26/80 Friday
Got things packed up and Eby used the sweeper. I did some mending. Barbara and Mike went to work. Milton, Barbara, Doug, Daddy and I started for Ray's about 2:00 and got there by 4:00. Had a good supper and a nice visit. Left for home about 8:00 and had car trouble and were detained over an hour. Got home at 12:00 with a new generator belt.

1981

1/1/81 Thursday
Cloudy with some snow. Prepared a lunch for Isaac and it was untouched when we got home at 6:00. We started at 10:00 and took Clarence's along to Landis' to visit with all of our family. Had a nice time. I came to the Home by 6:45 because of snow threats.

1/12/81 Monday
Cold all day. Eight above this evening. I quilted all day. Too cold for washing. Wrote a letter to Amy and called Sue Martin. Eby went to the garage and put our road maps in order. I went to bed early. Trying to chuck a cold and sore throat with tea and warmth and hot lemonade.

1/13/81 Tuesday
Worked 12-8. Had a good morning. Zero. Rested an hour and went to Edith Hoover's to knot comforts till 12:30. Picked up Miriam Hershey and went to Bird-in-Hand Restaurant to have dinner with workers from the Home. My dinner cost $4.59 plus $1.00 tip. Eby had two hauls to Leola. Farm Show is in progress.

1/20/81 Tuesday
Eby cleaned some snow from driveway. He had one haul and went to Parksburg to pay the oil. Inauguration for President Reagan at noon today. The hostages were released. I did a lot of quilting. We took Meals on Wheels. Isaac come downstairs to see the quilt and was in bed a lot. I made rice krispie cake.

1/30/81 Friday
Worked 12-8. My last shift at the Home. Stopped for apples. Worked on hemming quilt. Took a nap. Eby had no hauling. Isaac stayed put all day. We went to the auction this evening. Got a dozen cups and candy. I have a bit of a cold. Some wells and springs have gone dry.

2/1/81 Sunday
Went to Kinzer. Paul's text was "Walk." 90 there. We went to Isaac's this afternoon. Bradley and I played Winnie the Pooh. Spent evening at home. Dale called and they are planning a trip to China for their honeymoon. Raining this evening.

2/11/81 Wednesday
A rainy day turning to snow this evening. Eby went to Bible School this forenoon. Abram came for lunch after seeing two patients. I worked on valentines and wrote to Laura and Martha. Linda's baby girl was born this afternoon. We went to midweek. Amos Hershey spoke on "Love."

2/16/81 Monday
51 degrees. Saw wild geese. Washed and ironed and mended. Eby trimmed grapes and emptied the cesspool. Ben Clark and Mildred came and Eby helped audit the books for Kinzer. I wrote to Clemens. Elizabeth called to say that Isaac is to be ordained deacon on Sunday.

2/20/81 Friday
Wet day. Eby ran the cleaner. I made a pudding, pies and Dutch Goose and baked beans. Did some cleaning. Milton's came at 5:30. Eby, Milton and Barbara went to Gap Auction. They got wicker chairs, a wash basket, blankets and an ironing board. I played with Doug.

2/22/81 Sunday
A wet day. We left with Milton's for Mechanics Grove for the service and Isaac's ordination as deacon. Had a nice service and fellowship with good lunch. All their family were there and Abram's. We all went to Isaac's and stayed until 4:30.

2/23/81 Monday
A wet day. Milton and Barbara stopped this forenoon. Doug and I played Aggravation and Social Security. Eby put a handle on the drawer upstairs. Hershey Hostetter was here for an apartment for his son Ed. Milton's left at 3:00. I cleaned the hutch, woodbox and some desk drawers.

3/17/81 Tuesday
Cold and windy. Eby planted sweet peas. I worked on cozy corner embroidery. Eby had no hauls. He drove to Paradise for a freezer bulb and an oven bulb. Eby got some nice turnips and two heads of cabbage from the barrel.

3/27/81 Friday
Cloudy with a few showers. Eby had a haul and repaired the mailbox after a horse bolted and knocked it off. I did some cleaning. Made a roaster of baked beans. Eby took Dan King's to Dad's this evening.

3/28/81 Saturday
Beautiful warm day. I got up at 4:00 and made doughnuts for Fire Company Sale. Eby took them over at 10:00. I did the clean up and was ready to go with him to the sale at 1:00. Came home at 3:00. He bought some lumber. Got food ready for tomorrow.

3/30/81 Monday
Good showers. Washed and ironed and put things in order. I went to Victor Groff's to help quilt with nine others for Locust Grove School. Read this evening. President Reagan and two others were shot. Had a letter from Rhoda. Barn burned yesterday near Lampeter.

4/2/81 Thursday
Beautiful day. Eby had King's to haul both ways. I did a haul to Leola. Took Annis along to Sewing Circle. I read the scripture. Took it easy and read this evening. President is on the way to recovery.

4/3/81 Friday
Warm. Eby hauled the King's this morning. I did the cleaning and made cupcakes and a pudding. Had dandelion salad for supper. I washed the car and Eby did the station wagon and took manure off the roses. I sowed some flower seeds. Bathed and went to bed early.

4/6/81 Monday
Windy and cold. Washed and ironed. Cleaned freezer and heater rooms. Eby put logs on bank to hold the soil. I went to Anna Mary Lapp's Stanley party and got $10.88 worth. Sanford called and said he is to be married in June.

4/10/81 Friday
Beautiful day. Daddy cleaned up the pile of topsoil and I raked a spot for seeding grass. We planted the cannas and elephant ear. Took Meals on Wheels. Eby helped cement tombstones in the old cemetery. He hauled for Ike and went to Book Sale with Clarence this evening. Cleaned our bedroom.

4/14/81 Tuesday
An inch of rain and then cleared this evening. I went with Mabel to sew at the General Hospital. Had a good day. Eby had three hauls. We took Jay and Margie along to Paradise. Ed Hostetter and bride-to-be came to check things out in the apartment and the colors were not so good for them.

4/18/81 Saturday
Warm. Helped with potatoes at Fire Hall till 12:15. Ray's came for dinner and we had takeout Ham Supper here. Helped play croquet with Ray and the girls. Made red eggs and graham cracker fluff to take tomorrow. Eby washed cars and got water cress. Spent evening at home.

4/24/81 Friday
Some showers. I helped make subs at Fire Hall. Made a cake, red eggs, and got potatoes ready for salad. Eby had a haul. Jay stopped in to chat. Sanford and Tera came this evening, the Weaver's and Isaac's. Read some of my book. A three-year-old Amish child was killed when a gate fell on him.

4/25/81 Saturday
Cold and cloudy. Sanford and Tera sorted his cartons of treasures. Mr. and Mrs. Harry Arch from near London came for dinner and went to People Place's this afternoon. Esther came and brought me a birthday gift. Mary Alice and Abram called.

4/28/81 Tuesday
Warmer. Eby helped clean the garage and wash windows and put on screens. I planted flowers out this evening. Eby had three hauls. Isaac stayed put all day except for a walk outside to look at a bird. Trial has started for Zimmerman for murder of Evelyn Fisher.

5/7/81 Thursday
Beautiful day. Cool. Took Annis along to Sewing Circle. Did a big quilt plus five on the machine. Eby had three hauls and mowed some yard. Isaac in bed till supper. He watched ballgame and went to diner. Zimmerman got a life sentence for the murder of Evelyn Fisher.

5/11/81 Monday
Lots of good showers. Worked for Miriam 12-8. Slept till noon. Eby had some hauling and I did some sewing. Isaac's came with some homemade ice cream, and Donald Ibach's, Judy and the two girls bought other goodies to celebrate Grandpa and Benjie's birthdays. It was a nice evening.

5/14/81 Thursday
Beautiful day. Eby had three hauls. I did some weeding, trimming and planting. Isaac took lunch and went to Coatesville for a haircut and to game and diner this evening. I sewed. A teacher is coming to see the apartment. Pope Paul was shot and wounded. Soaked my feet and cut toenails. Had some of Donald Ibach's fish for supper.

5/19/81 Tuesday
Cloudy and cool. Made some shoo fly pies. Repotted the big cactus and planted 17 pots of new ones. Eby had two hauls and he pumped the cesspool and shredded soap. I worked on my dresses till bedtime. Got an invitation to Heidi Denlinger's wedding.

5/25/81 Monday
Fine weather. I washed early and the wringer popped and I wrung it by hand. Eby took it to Reuben and he taught him how to fix it. Did the ironing and some hoeing. We took John Metzler's along to see film of "Trail of the Conestoga" at Bowmansville. Ed Hostetter is moving in this evening.

6/5/81 Friday
Left home with Clarence's and John Metzler's to meet buses at Historical Center at 4:45 to start our tour to Canada. Weather was fine and we saw Niagara Falls,

museums, churches, cities, fertile farmland, highways with lots of traffic and people much like the USA. Have a good group of people, mostly senior citizens.

6/6/81 Saturday
Fine weather. Had a good breakfast and left the college at 9:00. Saw a lot of interesting places. Had supper at Elmira Mennonite Church and saw film afterward. Everyone is friendly and seems to be enjoying the tour. Lots of singing and visiting on the bus.

6/9/81 Tuesday
Showers and got windy. Washed and ironed. Eby had three hauls, the last one to pick up four Amish girls at Sam West Health Meeting in Blue Ball. It lasted till after 11:00. I took eight to Bible School. Had a good lesson on The Law of Liberty. Big class. I went with Eby to Blue Ball and wished I was home in bed.

6/12/81 Friday
Started picking peas at daybreak and took a bushel to huller and put sixteen packs in freezer by 9:30. I made a cake and five pies for Sanford's wedding. I took Elsie Martin along to Bible School. 103 there. Someone treated to popsicles.

6/13/81 Saturday
Warm. Uncle Charlie took us to York, got there at 6:00, met Abram's and went with them to Sanford's wedding in Richmond at the Quaker church. Had a good lunch on the lawn. About 52 at the wedding and at the lunch. Had a nice time.

6/14/81 Sunday
Jim's, Becky and us slept at Sanford's. He and Tera went to her apartment, Abram's to Mary Hulbert's. Had a late breakfast and started home. Got home at 3:10. Stopped for a snack at Burger King and had dessert here. Abram and Becky picked some sugar peas and strawberries.

6/16/81 Tuesday
Very warm. Eby picked the berries and I made eight glasses of jam. He spent Isaac's food stamps. Had a haul this afternoon. Isaac to the doctor all day for his pimple. I worked on cleaning the bank. Made three bottles of tea concentrate. Three Lancaster men died when rescuing an 8-year-old from cesspool where grass clippings formed a deadly gas.

7/18/81 Saturday
Warm. Uncle Charlie and Jay Martin's went with us to Dale's wedding. Took a snack and ate near the church. Edgar's came too. They were married at 1:30 and had a reception at 4:30 at the Holiday Inn. Went to Bleiler's and got home at 10:00.

7/20/81 Monday
Very hot and sultry. Had a gust this evening with over an inch of rain. Washed this afternoon and picked a lot of pickles. Isaac Beiler's ensilage got on fire this afternoon.

I took Christiana and Edna to Lapp's fruit farm. Took Katie King to Dr. at Nine Points and stopped about three places.

7/29/81 Wednesday
Pretty day. Took Sue Martin along to Dietzel's and met Elizabeth and Joanne drove our car to Abram's where we helped clean up their new house. Did windows, drawers and cupboards. Ate our lunches in their screened patio. Carpet, linoleum, painters and so were working. Got a nice lot done and left at 3:30.

7/31/81 Friday
Packed up and met Elizabeth at Linda's and she drove us to their cabin on the mountains where all their family came for the weekend. Stopped for lunch. Got there about 1:00. Isaac and Donald came about 10:30 Friday night. Had a good supper of chicken pot pie. Went for a drive and saw some deer. Played Family Feud and Uno. Everyone happy.

8/11/81 Tuesday
Hot. Canned pickles, tomato juice and beets. Cleaned off all early corn. Eby had three hauls, one to Lancaster and he stopped to see Isaac. He had more surgery. Sanford had his knee operated on again this forenoon. He and Tera called and he has a cast on and is pretty sleepy yet. Did some mending and worked on scrap books. Mildred came for paprika. John Diener went to Mexico for asthma treatment.

8/17/81 Monday
Beautiful, cool and pleasant. We got things all set up for the tour with Martin's in Jay's new van, our car, and Isaac's. Saw Sperry Rand, Cloisters closed, film on Amish at People Places, Strasburg Museum, old cemetery, and some to Hershey cemeteries and home place at Cattail. Elizabeth helped to serve a picnic supper and we visited till 9:00.

8/28/81 Friday
Did some cleaning. Daddy was hauling. I got my food ready for reunion. Red eggs, cole slaw, applesauce, corn and chicken for soup, root beer, tea, etc. Bathed, rested and took off for Camp Morehart at 3:20. Got there by 5:00. Made supper for 34.

8/29/81 Saturday
Had a nice day with the children except Dale, Mae and Nancy. Good food. Jane's mother and Oliver, Sam's friend from Germany, were our guests.

8/31/81 Monday
Showers. Got garden things for Sanford. We visited and they left at 1:00. Eby had several hauls and I did one. Got the apartment ready for Rebecca Rhoades. Had a long talk with Nancy. She will be happy to get the reunion tape that the children made for her. Eby changed insurance to Mennonite Aid.

9/8/81 Tuesday
Eby had three hauls and I did one this afternoon. Made a fudge chiffon cake for Oliver's birthday. Jay took Becky and her friend Jennie, Sam and Oliver on a tour and brought them here for dinner. Rebecca had her first day of school. Had an inch of rain starting about 4:00. Read this evening.

9/14/81 Monday
Very warm. Washed and ironed and made up beds. Milton's left at 9:00 to take Doug to his new school. Eby had three hauls and I did one to New Holland. Bennie Fisher was here when I got home. I took him home at 6:45.

9/16/81 Wednesday
Had almost two inches of rain before noon. We went to Solanco Fair for a chicken pot pie dinner and met Isaac's there. Exhibits were not all judged, so did not see many. Lifetime cookware salesman came and Daddy came home just as I had convinced him of no sale, and Daddy bought $379 worth. Picked pickles and got out beets.

9/21/81 Monday
Fine weather. Washed, ironed and mended. Worked on quilt patches, have nineteen done. Eby had three hauls. Talked to Sue Martin and Mabel. We are eating the thirty-five pound watermelon that Ray sent with Dale last Tuesday.

10/4/81 Sunday
A little bit of frost. Paul preached on "Living in these times." Milton and Barbara were here for dinner. Doug is doing well at his new school. They showed a film on India. Sam stopped with a friend to use our phone. Went to see little Andrew Daniel Dietzel.

10/7/81 Wednesday
Windy. Eby busy hauling. I cleaned drawers, cupboards and closets. President Sadat of Egypt was shot and killed. Anna Slaymaker took me along to Sewing Circle. I wrote family letter and included one of my mother's letters from 1914.

10/13/81 Tuesday
Foggy. A good morning. Packed and took Abe and Lizzie Stoltzfus along to Brush Valley to visit their daughter and family. We then went to Jim's. Pat and I made some quince honey from quinces I took along. I worked some of Beth's patches while we visited. Beth is in college and Greg is helping with farming.

10/14/81 Wednesday
Fine weather and foggy morning. Visited till noon and left after dinner to pick up the folks in Brush Valley. Got home at 5:30. Esther called and said Mabel had an accident in the fog. It happened when she was doing a drive to the hospital with one of Daddy's runs. It was a distressing thing, but no one was hurt much. We had our preparatory and feet washing service this evening.

10/28/81 Wednesday
Pleasant. Eby pumped the cesspool and had two long hauls. I cooked up the sweet potato tails and made quince honey. Rested and read. 33 Haitians drowned off the Florida coast when a refugee boat was sunk by huge waves.

11/13/81 Friday
Coldest morning. Ray's went to Isaac's all day and got back at 11:00. I did some cleaning. Eby hauled the King's and took out turnips, beets and carrots. I started Karen's quilt. Talked to Mabel and she is feeling better and went to Lester Leaman's funeral yesterday. I popped corn this evening.

11/16/81 Monday
Rainy. Washed and dried it in basement. Made a pie and things for dinner as Jonathan came from Philadelphia for dinner and on to Abram's where he will have an interview at Hershey Medical Center tomorrow.

11/23/81 Monday
Cloudy and cold. We packed up and I prepared food for Isaac. We went with a group in John Yoder's van to Paul Brubaker's to get on the bus to start for Toledo, Ohio to see the accumulated corn in the warehouse. Stopped for night in Youngstown, Ohio. Had good traveling and fellowship.

11/24/81 Tuesday
Slept at Best Western Motel. Left at 7:30 for Toledo. Got to dock when the 12:00 service was almost ended. Saw the tons of corn in bags stored in warehouse. Also a large ship by the dock. About 150 persons at the service. Got home at 2:00 A.M.

12/14/81 Monday
Went to help get Dale's house ready in Phoenixville with Mae's parents, sister and Jane. Did not find much dirt. Got home at 3:00 because it started snowing. I made two walnut cakes for the folks who let Eby pick up their walnuts. Eby took Abe Ebersol's to a viewing for a 20-year-old killed in his auto.

12/18/81 Friday
Sunny and snow melted some. I did some cleaning. Eby took me for Meals on Wheels. He had two hauls and met our international student at airport and his suitcase was in Philadelphia so he went back for it this evening. Dan, the student, gave us a pretty Chinese vase for Christmas. I started hemming the tablecloth that Abram's gave us. Jim's had a box of cheese sent to us.

12/19/81 Saturday
Clear and cold. Prepared some food. Dale and Mae came for capons and were here for dinner. They went to order a table. Our Japanese student got here at 6:00. Both students seem to be doing all right.

12/25/81 Friday
Mild. I made fruit cocktail and took bread, celery and pickles for our dinner at Joanne and Daniel's. Had a nice time with Isaac's. We spent the evening looking at some slides with our students. Joanne gave us each a gift of candy. We called the Weaver's and talked with Grace, Sanford, Mary Alice, Nancy and Tera.

12/29/81 Tuesday
Sunny. Students went to shop in Intercourse. Eby shelled a pint of walnuts for Nancy. Abram's called and they are back from Ohio. We took the students to Isaac's for supper and they saw how dairying is done. Nancy went to Lebanon to see Beaver and her child.

1982

1/1/82 Friday
Cloudy. I made fruit salad to take for our dinner at Mart Groff's for all of my family, plus our Chinese and Japanese students. Miriam had a very good dinner and we had a nice visit. She had some games for sharing together. Eby took students along to get John Diener in New Holland and his wife let them see some of their house. Masoa made us a Japanese supper and we liked it very much.

1/2/82 Saturday
Clear. Dan and Samao packed up and left at 10:00. Jay Hostetter came and went along with Eby to the airport. I prepared lunch for Milton's. They came over to do some shopping and go to Ruth Coy's for supper and night. Roasted a capon and made sweet potatoes, filling, celery, cracker pudding and things for Milton's tomorrow. Had a talk with Mabel.

1/5/82 Tuesday
Sunny and windy. I washed and ironed and mended. Had extra sheets and tablecloths. Eby had two hauls and went to Vintage Sale. Vera Mast brought Margie to learn how to lace braided rugs this afternoon. Called to hear if Mary Alice is home from her visit to Charlie and because of much rain and mudslides, she could not get to the airport today and hopes to get on her way tomorrow. Eby is chilly this evening.

1/7/82 Thursday
Cloudy and mild. I took Annis along to Sewing Circle. Knotted a comfort and made a pretty quilt for Maranatha School Sale. Eby had some hauls. He grated soap and cracked walnuts. California is having $100 million dollars in damages from rain and mudslides. I called Mary Alice and she got home last night. Eby got too close to a welding torch and has three sores on his head and a sore left eye.

1/13/82 Wednesday
18 degrees and snowed all day. Eby had two hauls and read. I quilted all day till 10:00. Abe and Pat called to see how we are doing in the cold. I called Joanne and Daniel's father came home from the hospital last Friday. We heard on the news that a 747 plane hit a bridge on takeoff and went into the Potomac River with more than 70 on board.

1/26/82 Tuesday
Sunny, cold and icy. Eby had a haul to Lancaster and elsewhere for Ike. I quilted all day and got a lot done. Eby shelled walnuts. Isaac ate no lunch but ate a large amount for supper, including enough fries for four men. Eby listened to Reagan's state of the union address.

2/2/82 Tuesday
Ground hog saw shadow. Raining this evening. Eby had a haul this morning before we went to Bible School. 150 there. Classes were interesting and good. Snow is nearly gone. Had a nice letter from Jonathan in India. Did some reading. Very little water came in basement. There is trouble in El Salvador and in Poland. Ethiopia has closed some doors.

2/9/82 Tuesday
Snow covered. Eby had a drive till noon. Schools were cancelled but not Bible School. I did not go. Cut patches this morning and made valentines this afternoon and evening. Rebecca cleaned her apartment. A plane crashed near Tokyo and killed 23 passengers. My right knee is not so good.

2/13/82 Saturday
Sunny. Eby had three hauls. I made a Dutch Goose for supper for Sanford and Tera. They helped cut some quilt patches. We went to Shady Maple and Good's. Got apples and stopped for bread at the Stoltzfus girls. We visited and looked at pictures this evening.

2/20/82 Saturday
Some snow late in the evening. I prepared food. Eby had a haul and went to the store. He bathed Isaac and went to the Presbyterian Church to pick up five pounds of cheese for the poor from the government. Edgar's came at 3:00 and Abram's at 4:00. Had a nice visit.

2/21/82 Sunday
Edgar's took Dale, Mae and Rosa along to Neffsville to hear the Goshen Chorale sing. Conrad came here with them for dinner. Dale and Mae took Rosa along to their place and she drove back to Philadelphia from there. We took Conrad to New Holland this evening where they sang again and he came here for the night.

2/22/82 Monday
Cleared. I washed and it dried good outside. Eby had an 11:00 haul and took Conrad to LMHS for their program. I took two of Amos Stoltzfus' to the Osteopathic Hospital. Made some extra stops and got 200 pounds of sugar at Black Sam's. Milton and Barbara came about 8:00 and went to Coy's for the night. They are off to Ohio in the morning with Ruth Coy.

3/11/82 Thursday
Partly cloudy. I quilted most all day. Eby had three hauls. He bathed Isaac and Charles Bauman took him to Lancaster to sign for extra oil money. He stopped at Wagon Wheel and is not back yet at 9:30. Nancy called and she is all set for her trip to Hawaii.

3/15/82 Monday
Cloudy and cool. I washed, ironed and mended. Eby had two hauls. I brought Rebecca back when she took her car to the body shop. Quilted and did some mending. Sent birthday cards to Barbara and Mike. Isaac in bed all day and to diner this evening. Nine teenagers out of ten were killed on a Long Island railroad crossing when the driver tried to beat the train. He drove around the crossing bars.

3/16/82 Tuesday
Cloudy, snow and rain. John Metzler's picked us up and we met the bus at the Gap Diner and two more joined us with dairy farmers on a trip to Montgomery and Berks Counties to visit four super dairies. Saw a lot of dandy cows and stables and traveled in new country. Got our supper at Kempton Fire Hall. Very good food and service.

3/20/82 Saturday
Mild day. Eby had one haul, and he and Ray went for eggs and cheese. We all went to Karen and Ed's wedding at Landisville and the reception at Hostetter's in Mt. Joy. They had a pretty wedding and a lot of people. Dale brought our seeds.

3/27/82 Saturday
Clear and cool. I got up early and made doughnuts for the Fire Company Sale and we took them over and stayed to help till 3:00. Got real cold. Bought some food. I quilted till bedtime. Eby rested. Called Edgar's and Jonathan got back from India last night and has a lot to tell about. Nancy called and said her Hawaii trip went well.

4/3/82 Saturday
Left at 5:30 for Relief Sale at Harrisburg. Took 10 others along with Rebecca. A very large crowd and quilts sold good. A Tree of Life for $1600. Came home through pouring rain. Jane and her mother got their own supper and Isaac's. He went to the diner after playing Parcheesi with Jane and the girls.

4/10/82 Saturday
Sunny and not so cold. Got food ready. I did a big wash of bed clothes and ironed and made up beds. We picked up Sanford's quilt frames and got our licenses updated with our pictures. Eby had one haul and bathed Isaac. Had a good evening.

4/11/82 Sunday
Had our communion service in charge of Paul Clark. All done by 11:30. We had a quick lunch of oyster soup and met at Jay Martin's for our trip to Virginia with Bertha Shirk and Marian Weaver in Jay's van. Weaver's met us in Park View. Had our supper with them and an evening visiting. Weather was good for travel.

4/12/82 Monday
Cloudy and cool. Grace and children have off school. We repotted some plants. Jennie and I cut some patches. Grace got in her sewing cupboards and pulled out some rug wool and a comfort top. So we started knotting it after she went out and bought a sheet. Jay and Sue, Mary Alice, Sanford and Tera came for supper. We had roast chicken, mashed potatoes, limas, cole slaw, cranberries, peach pie and ice cream.

4/13/82 Tuesday
Finished the comfort, played Scrabble, ate a snack of Tera's Maple Nut Pie and left for Park View around 12:00. Picked up the others and got home by 6:45. It rained some good showers. Eby is having a small M.D.S. meeting about a corn shipment to Poland. Isaac did not eat nearly all of the food I had prepared for him.

4/22/82 Thursday
A pretty day, cool. Eby had two hauls. We left at 9:00 with Dale's table and got to Phoenixville by 10:00. Mae showed us the house and garden. We went to Dale's store and bought two roses and a trowel. Had lunch with Mae and got home by 2:30. I planted the roses. Eby went to Bowell's for three trypes, the liver and the heart. Eby went to Smoketown for the corn project. I cleaned trypes for three hours.

5/6/82 Thursday
Nice day. Annis took me along to Sewing Circle. We did two quilts and two comforts. Seventeen there this morning. Eby had some hauls and mowed yard. I planted the begonias out and some cannas. Finished hemming Beth's quilt. Esther came this evening and brought Eby some donuts, a big jar of salted nuts and some buns. Great Britain and Argentina are having war over the Falkland Islands. Each lost a ship.

5/10/82 Monday
Windy and cool. Eby had two hauls. I washed and ironed and mended. Cleaned and cut some dead branches from the backyard. Sanford called this evening and said they are all ready for their trip to England tomorrow. I called Mabel. The British and Argentines are still fighting.

5/13/82 Thursday
Weather fine. We did some cleaning. I made chicken corn soup for early lunch and we packed and left for Abram's and got there at 1:00. Came with them to Edgar's and arrived at 5:30. They stayed for supper and left for a convention in Toronto. They planned to stop in a motel for the night.

5/14/82 Friday
Fine day. We slept late and quilted most of the day. Looked over the garden and flowers and visited. Eby looked at some books, took a walk and some naps. Andrea showed us the things Jonathan brought from India. Marcia had a cleaning job and a babysitting job.

5/17/82 Monday
Some showers. Packed up and Rhoda took us to Ithaca at 8:55 to take the Greyhound bus to come home. Changed in Binghamton and stopped in Scranton and Wilkes Barre and got to Harrisburg at 2:20, where Becky met us and took us to our car. We came on home. It was a good trip. Eby watered this evening. A young Amish boy was killed in a car crash early Sunday and two others injured. War continues with Britain and Argentina.

5/19/82 Wednesday
Had good showers. Eby had a haul and washed station wagon and mowed half of yard. Joe Bechtold was here all day patching some cracks in the wall. I washed sheets and attic beds. Swept some of attic. Isaac had to sit up all day because of his bed. We went to midweek. Had a film on women from the world by Victor, Flossie and Dean Groff. Nancy called and said she is getting married June 5.

5/20/82 Thursday
Showers this evening. I made some peppernuts. Eby washed car and finished mowing. Jay's took us along to Kinzer for Ascension Day meeting. B. Charles Hostetter and Myron Dietz were speakers. Mary Alice called and is in the process of buying a house in Charlottesville.

5/27/82 Thursday
Sunny and warm. I prepared dinner for twelve ladies from the Home. Helen Ranck helped and we brought them in two cars. They enjoyed the day and I did too. Eby had several hauls. Helped Eby put in bean poles. I hoed most of garden. I stopped for plants at Flaud's and planted them this evening.

5/31/82 Monday
Fine warm day. Eby is putting an air conditioner upstairs. I picked a pint of sugar peas for Joanne and Dan. We went up there for a cookout. The family was all there but Leo. Had a nice time. Sanford called this evening and they got back from England Saturday evening. Had a good trip. Worked on my dress this evening.

6/1/82 Tuesday
Showers this evening. I washed and ironed. Eby had one haul and I did one to Medical Center. Did some hoeing in the garden and flower beds. Susan Kauffman called and wants the apartment for next term. I read More With Less Living.

6/7/82 Monday
Partly cloudy and cool. I washed and ironed. Put seven pints of sugar peas in freezer. Eby had three hauls. Isaac's came a while this afternoon and brought us a couple boxes of huge strawberries. Took out more tulips. Nancy called and said her wedding went off real good. Weather was fine and about 40 there. Mary Alice came back from Minnesota today.

6/15/82 Tuesday
Sunny and warm. Eby had one haul, and I picked some strawberries and put some in freezer. Hoed and tied up limas. Cleaned pea row. Gene Petersheim came to ask for information on Bennie Fisher. We had very little to share. Eby cleaned and washed station wagon. Nancy called from L.A. and I talked to Gary.

6/22/82 Tuesday
Fine weather. Eby had one haul to the hospital. I picked three quarts of blueberries and one of black raspberries. Picked two buckets of peas and put ten pints in the freezer. Eby helped shell them. I hoed flower beds and did lima beans. Nancy called and they bought a townhouse in L.A.

6/23/82 Wednesday
A pleasant cool day after rain last night. We left at 8:30 for Clarence's and went to Jay Martin's where we met the others and went on our tour for the day. First to Weaver's egg plant, to F&M Museum and to Oreville Home, where we visited a lot the guests. Came to Clarence's and had our supper and visited till after 9:00. Had a nice walk in the Park of the Five Senses. Ate our lunches in the Pavilion. A very good day.

7/5/82 Monday
Pleasant. I washed and ironed and mended. Hoed the garden and flower beds. Had a little talk with Isaac about helping himself from the refrigerator. Had chicken barbecue dinner from Kinzer Fire Company. Doug called from home for 4th of July. Milton and Barbara talked too. She and Jean Soderstrom are coming here after taking Doug back to school.

7/13/82 Tuesday
The corn is growing very fast. United Parcel picked up Nancy's china this afternoon. Hope it gets to her as it left. Eby had three hauls. I canned 8 quarts of pickles. I did some sprinkling this evening, picked and washed pickles.

7/19/82 Monday
Hot with evening showers. I washed, picked pickles and canned five quarts. Put blueberries in freezer. Eby had three hauls. A funeral was held for two of plane crash victims at Hammer Creek. Nancy called and said the china arrived in perfect condition.

8/7/82 Saturday
Warm. Eby had two hauls and washed both cars. Laura and Martha helped me clean the insides. The tourists Milton sent left after breakfast. Washed and made up beds. An Oklahoma couple rented the apartment for three weeks. Cleaned and made some food. Sanford called and said that they have news, we are to be grandparents again. Played with the girls.

8/13/82 Friday
Beautiful day. Eby had three hauls. I did the cleaning. Made two cakes and cut a ham and cooked an end. We took Anna Slaymaker along to the Kinzer Church picnic. I took a fudge chiffon and ham salad. Most everyone was there. Lots of good food. Fredric and Carol came for the night and I gave them dessert.

8/19/82 Thursday
Pretty day. I canned 13 quarts of peaches and did 5 quarts of dill tomatoes. Picked a bucket of snap beans and almost a bucket of pickles. Cleaned the pickle seed. Eby had some hauls and pumped the cesspool. Isaac got contrary over a peach. Had a mute peddler. Eby picked the tomatoes.

8/20/82 Friday
Sunny, cloudy and showers this evening. Eby had four hauls, two beyond Hammer Creek. I did the cleaning and canned 12 quarts of tomatoes. Had a long talk with Mabel. Her treatments are going better. Isaac in room all day. Said he would eat the peaches for supper, but I chucked them out. Conrad came this evening after bringing Marcia for a wedding and rehearsal.

8/21/82 Saturday
Good weather for the 34th Hostetter Reunion at Intercourse Park. 51 there. Lloyd Kreider was appointed vice president and Isaac is president for 1983. Rosa came and she and Conrad were here for supper and left about 7:00 to pick up Marcia and go home. Finished reading Buggies, Blizzards and Babies.

8/27/82 Friday
Partly cloudy. Did some cleaning. Packed our foods for reunion and were ready to leave with Dale and Mae for Camp Morehart. Left at 3:15 and got there at 5:30 and only Becky was there. Mae and I made chicken corn soup for supper for 32. Had cookies and punch for Nancy and Gerry.

8/28/82 Saturday
Beautiful day. Dinner was made by Virginia folks. Our meals were prepared and served by captains and helpers. Had quoit games and scrabble for evening along with Dale's China slides and popcorn. Got better acquainted with Gerry. Some played volleyball.

8/29/82 Sunday
Beautiful day. Cool. Had a hearty breakfast and plenty of leftovers for lunch. Had some songs and reminiscing. Visited and cleaned up after lunch and packed up and got on our way home. Had a flat tire near Elizabethtown and were detained for an hour till a garage man got us on our way.

9/6/82 Monday
Fine weather. The tourists left at 8:10. I did a big wash and ironing. Eby had several hauls. After supper he was called to bring Christ King to Elam's after little 18-month-old Gideon was killed under the wheels a the tobacco wagon. I went up and helped what I could. Peeled some pears to cook for the meals and brought some along home to can for Emma.

9/8/82 Wednesday
Cloudy. I put canned things on shelves. Canned two quarts of pickles. Eby had a haul. We went to the funeral of Gideon King at 12:30. Got home at 2:30. It was a very large funeral and all in German. 24 wagons went to cemetery. We went to Midweek service. John Winters is teaching Zachariah.

9/20/82 Monday
A wet day. Got up early and washed and ironed. Dried it in the basement. Eby had two hauls and went with Jay Hostetter to assemble chicken cages for a wind-destroyed house this afternoon. Eby brought 12 large chickens from Petersheim's at 70 cents per pound. I cut up four and cooked bony pieces. Have pain in right shoulder and arm. Worse today.

9/21/82 Tuesday
Cloudy. Eby had two hauls. I got vegetables ready for Isaac and to take along to Virginia. Made chicken corn soup and chili. Dug some sweet potatoes. My shoulder and arm hurt real bad. Picked half bucket of limas for Sanford. The Amish are frolicking the second barn fire in southern part of the County. Suspicious.

9/22/82 Wednesday
All packed up and started for Virginia at 8:30. Eby drove to Virginia and I drove on to Charlottesville. After unloading and seeing the house we began work on the yard. Ellen borrowed a mower and we got busy. Mary Alice cooked us a good supper.

9/23/82 Thursday
Pretty day. We had a good night and got to work on the yard after breakfast. Mary Alice started fire in her woodstove. We raked, trimmed, mowed and moved and stacked a lot of wood. Cleaned up and left for Sanford's at 4:45. Got there for 6:00 and met him on Parham Road. He guided us to Wilmington Avenue. Had a tour of the garden and yard. Both looking fine. Tera had a good supper for us. My shoulder and arm are feeling real good. Sanford showed us his slides of England.

9/24/82 Friday
Partly cloudy. Eby mowed Sanford's yard. Tera left at 7:30 for a meeting and got back at 2:30. She fixed a tuna noodle casserole for our lunch. Sanford and I rigged up the new quilt frames and we put a quilt in and I started to quilt. We had more than one border done by bedtime. Sanford did some painting. Seven deaths from poisoned Tylenol tablets.

9/25/82 Saturday
A pretty day. We had a light breakfast and left Sanford's at 6:30 for the Relief Sale. Had our breakfast and got good seats, then looked over the quilts. It was a good sale and the proceeds were $125,000. Mary Alice and Ellen were there helping. Had our chicken barbecue at Robert's for supper.

9/27/82 Monday
Clear and pleasant. Had our breakfast and left Weaver's at 7:30 and got home by 12:45. I drove through Virginia and we came by Harrisburg. Eby took some Amish ladies to Shady Maple. I talked to Mabel and Martha Stoltzfus. John Crouse died and his funeral was this forenoon.

10/25/82 Monday
A cold rainy day. Eby finished hulling walnuts and had some hauls. Was held up with a car and buggy accident. Horse killed and driver taken to the hospital. I made 23 quarts of apple sauce. Uncle Charlie stopped with my baking pans. I worked on photograph album this evening. My arm feels real good.

11/5/82 Friday
Cold and windy. Eby had two hauls. We dug the celery. It is very nice. I cut a bucket of spinach, some broccoli and parsley. I cooked some scrap celery, carrots and onion for V-8 juice. I sent three birthday letters. We went up to auction at 6:00 and got home at 11:00. Bought some homemade baked goods.

11/23/82 Tuesday
Cloudy. Eby pumped cesspool and had several hauls. I cleaned celery, made buns, doughnuts, and sweet potato croquettes. Cut filling bread. Did the ironing. Mabel called. We got Christmas money in envelopes for children, grandchildren and great grandchildren.

11/24/82 Wednesday
Cleared colder. I roasted the turkey and made the filling and got food ready. Did some cleaning. Eby had a lot of hauling and bathed Isaac. Ray's came this evening and brought us a dollhouse which he made

11/25/82 Thursday
Beautiful. Ray and Jane helped get things ready for dinner. Abram's, Isaac's, Jim's, Dale's, Ray's, Dietzel's, Donald, Benji and Betsy were here. Had a nice time together. Charlie called and said Ed's father died last week. He and Ed are going to Hawaii for a week's vacation.

11/29/82 Monday
Foggy and cleared. Eby had several hauls and had the station wagon serviced. I washed and ironed. Dried it in basement. Milton and Barbara came for supper and left for home. A 50-year-old Amish girl was murdered by an 18-year-old boy in the basement of his home on Saturday evening. Eby bought himself two sets of underwear at the White Horse Dry Goods Store. I read this evening.

12/2/82 Thursday
Cloudy and mild. Eby and Dave Clark left here at 5:00 to pick up Leon Summers and get the bus to go to Atmore, Alabama for an M.D.S. meeting. Annis took me along to Sewing Circle. 16 there. Worked on some Round the World quilts. Very pretty. Started reading I Lift My Lamp. Sue came down to talk and read this evening.

12/9/82 Thursday
Colder. I did some cleaning. Stirred up some sand tarts. Eby had several hauls and stopped at Shady Maple for cocoanuts and some other needs. Isaac went down to the garage this evening, the first time out of the house since Sunday. Mary Alice came about 5:15. We cut quilt patches and visited. Pat and Becky stopped on way from an interview at Ursinus College.

12/10/82 Friday
Cloudy. Eby had some hauls. Mary Alice helped make the sand tarts and went along to take Meals on Wheels. I went with her to Intercourse and bought fabric for Marcia's quilt. We stopped and got Kathleen Denlinger's rug cutter and cut a lot of Mary Alice's fabrics into strips. Elam brought a load of manure.

12/11/82 Saturday
First snow. Mary Alice sorted the balance of her books and we had time for visiting. Eby had two hauls. Mary Alice left after lunch and we got the room ready for Roger. I stirred up flapjacks and cream cakes. I scolded Isaac because he did not eat his supper for an hour and a half.

12/25/82 Saturday
Cloudy and mild. We left for Dale's at 9:00 and got to their place in Phoenixville by 9:50. Had a good turkey dinner and a nice visit with them and Mae's parents. Got home at 5:00 and gave Isaac his supper. He was in bed all day.

12/27/82 Monday
Mild with drizzle. I washed and ironed. Put quilt in the frames. Made a pot of stew. Eby had some hauls and did some walnuts. Washed Isaac's bed so he was up all day. Donald's and Daniel's took us to Family Restaurant near Lincoln this evening. Had a good dinner and overate. They spent some time here when we came back.

1983

1/1/83 Saturday
A beautiful day. I quilted till 10:00 and we went to Clarence's for our annual New Year dinner. It was a good one. All were there but Josephine. She was not well. Landis and Paul brought Amy and Menno along as Menno does not drive any more because of his eyes.

1/7/83 Friday
Mild and sunny. I did the cleaning and took down the Christmas cards. Washed some lousy plants. Eby had some hauls. I am more than half finished with quilt. We turned it around. Eby's T.V. cost $95.00 for repairs.

1/15/83 Saturday
Snowy day. Had a nice day with Sanford and Tera. Showed them how to do braided rugs. Milton's and Doug came this afternoon for supper and left at 7:30. Eby had no hauling.

1/16/83 Sunday
Fine day. Snow off the roads. Went to Kinzer. John Winters preached on Love. Sanford and Tera went for church only. Had lasagna for dinner. I got all packed and off with Sanford's at 2:00 and arrived in Richmond by 6:00. No problems. Had a light supper and saw some slides. Eby was all set to take over his responsibilities at home.

1/17/83 Monday
Sanford and Tera had off work and I helped them quilt all day. Colder. Mary Alice and Grace called to see if I got here. They plan to come on Friday. Tera cooked good meals.

1/21/83 Friday
Cloudy. Got started to quilt early. Robert brought Grace, Jennie and Mary Alice to help quilt. Got here about 10:00. Tera worked till noon and Sanford took the day

off. Did not get quilt finished. Another day needed. Got to Mary Alice's house by 5:00. Ellen had supper ready. We started lacing her rug and got to bed late.

1/22/83 Saturday
Cloudy with wet snow turning to rain. Slept till 9:00 and had a day lacing rug. Abram and Pat came about 11:00 and Mary Alice had a treat of plucket and coffee. We all went to the dollhouse store and Abram bought me some treasures. After the wedding at 2:00 and the reception at 4:00 we started for home at 6:55 and arrived safely at 11:50. Abram's stayed here for the night.

1/28/83 Friday
Fine day. Did some cleaning. Cut Eby's hair. He cracked some nuts and bought a 1975 station wagon for $995.00 from Rohrer's at Smoketown. I went along to bring it home. He did not have any hauling all day. Called Dale and his tests came through good. Baked two nut cakes, one for bake sale.

2/4/83 Friday
Windy and colder. Eby had some hauls. I cut and picked out patches for Kim's quilt. Put balance in better order. Called Margie for her birthday. Called Mabel. Very quiet evening with everyone gone. Fire department called out two times. Found that my eye and physical exams are overdue for my license.

2/5/83 Saturday
Beautiful day. Did some cleaning. Eby bought a hog for 55 cents a pound. I went to New Holland for my eye exam and had no luck at two places. Called Abram and had him fill out my paper for physical exam. Blood pressure was 170-90. We stopped at green stamp store and had 19 books redeemed for a clock, blanket, sheet and pillow cases. Eby had one haul. Baked a walnut cake for Abram's. Read and bathed.

2/7/83 Monday
Snowed enough to cancel school. Eby took me to Medical Center for eye examination for my driver's test. Ordered new glasses. Test cost $28.00. Washed this afternoon. Went to bring Fisher girls from doctor at Intercourse. Eby had other hauls. Put Christmas cards away.

2/12/83 Saturday
Sunny and bright with 12 inches of snow. We were snowed in till noon when the snow plow opened our drive for $15.00. I shoveled both porches. Made a nut cake and did some cleaning. Eby cracked walnuts till noon. I called Dale's. He is feeling better and they had burglars in his store last night who took three chain saws. Finished little rug for dollhouse. Gave Roger lunch for shoveling snow.

2/28/83 Monday
A nice day. I washed and ironed. Put Kim's quilt in the frames. Made chicken and waffles for supper. Eby cracked walnuts and had some drives. Faucet still leaking in

apartment. Amy was to have some tests in the hospital today. Gasoline is getting cheaper.

3/3/83 Thursday
Fine day. Mild. I took Annis along to Sewing Circle. Eby had some hauls and finished the walnuts. I quilted this evening. A second man was arrested for the murder of the Amish girl in New Holland. I called Nancy and she said they are having an awful lot of rain. She said Aunt Emma called her today from June's.

3/8/83 Tuesday
A wet day, colder. Eby had some hauls. I brought John Diener and his nephew home. Eby went to have his eyes examined and he may have a cataract. I did some quilting. Some thunder and lightning this evening.

3/11/83 Friday
Cloudy and colder. Eby had plenty of hauling. I made a mince pie to take to Abram's. I did some quilting. Met Uncle Charlie at 5:00 and he took us to Abram's for supper and then to Becky and Sam's high school to see and hear the play "Brigadoon." It gave a full house and we got home at 11:20. The play did not have a good moral.

3/19/83 Saturday
Cloudy with showers. I made food ready for supper as Milton's came with both boys. Eby had some hauls and has $236 for the week. I soaked my feet while I quilted. Nancy called this evening and all is well with them. Uncle Frank's are visiting them tomorrow.

3/22/83 Tuesday
Windy and cold, freezing. I washed and ironed, hung some on line and porch. Eby was real busy hauling. Wrote to Nancy and sent Gerald a birthday card and gift. Eby got new glasses for $99.00. Sent my application for driver's license for $21.50. This is for four years. Dr. Clark died after 112 days on an artificial heart.

3/27/83 Sunday
Very wet day. Went to Kinzer. Amos Hershey preached a good sermon. We had a hasty lunch of chicken corn soup and went to pick up Uncle Charlie at 12:00. He drove us to Hershey where Abram drove our car to Messiah College to hear a concert on the creation. It was very good for those who like this kind of thing. We got home safely at 7:00.

4/10/83 Sunday
Wet day. Went to Kinzer. Ralph Graham preached. The topic was "Purpose." Dale and Mae came for dinner and supper. We went to the Gap Fire Hall for the celebration of Dr. Beacher's 50 years of service to our community. Nancy called and said they had a slight earthquake this morning.

4/12/83 Tuesday
Some sunshine and cool. I took John Diener and Ivan to New Holland. Ann Slaymaker took Emma Metzler, Ella Zimmerman, Kathryn Graham and me to the General Hospital to sew. Five others were there. Sanford called at 8:00 and said 6 lb. 4 oz. Jacob Lynn came about 7:00. All are fine.

4/19/83 Tuesday
Snowed all day and everything is covered and still snowing and blowing at 11:00 P.M. John Yoder came and took Isaac to the hospital. He was admitted. Eby had a few hauls. Eby is coughing and full of cold. I cut and sewed some patches for an around the world quilt for dollhouse bed. Cleaned the basement room. Jim and Pat stopped in on the way home from a road supervisor's convention in Philadelphia. They did not stay long as it was snowing faster.

4/25/83 Monday
Cloudy and cool with rain. I wrote to Charlie and he called this evening. I left at 10:15 and stopped at Rohrer's Mill for wheat germ and flour and got to Joanne's by 10:35. She had her mother and sisters and six children. Had a baby shower for Judy and birthday party for me. Got home at 3:45. Esther came and brought me a birthday gift. Eby had hauls.

4/28/83 Thursday
Beautiful, sunny and warm. I did some cleaning and lined up the meals for Eby and Isaac. I am taking the Greyhound to Sanford's this P.M. Eby took me to the bus in Lancaster and I got to Richmond at 9:15 where Sanford met me. I got to see Jacob before he went to bed. He is a sweet baby.

4/29/83 Friday
Nice day. I helped to rake up some garden and helped plant some vegetables. It was all ready for planting and Tera put in a lot of the plants she had started in the house. I cut some rug strips from a big bag full they bought. They took me to the park to see the azaleas. There were so many and they were very beautiful.

4/30/83 Saturday
Warm day. I held Jacob and cut more rug strips. Sanford did some washing and we had early lunch and they took me to the bus at 12:15 and I got started home. Waited almost two hours in Washington to change buses and changed again in York. Eby met me in Lancaster and we got here by 8:00. Nancy and Gerald sent me flowers from Hawaii for my birthday.

5/7/83 Saturday
Nice day, windy. Eby took a load to a funeral in Lebanon County. I took Christ Blank's to four places and the Stoltzfus girls to a sale at Morgantown. Eby pumped cesspool. James Lee Lentz was born to John and Judy.

5/27/83 Friday
Pleasant weather. I did the cleaning. Took Meals on Wheels with Edna Stoltzfus. Eby had some hauls. I took out daffodils and tulips and got the corner bed ready for planting. Sowed some heavenly blue morning glories. A man drowned at Ocean City rescuing two Amish women.

5/28/83 Saturday
Fine day. Showers late evening. I went to Flaud's for plants. Spent $9.40 for flowers because Daddy wants pretty beds. Went to Fire Hall at 9:00 and helped make 100 subs. We went to Karen and Ed's for dinner with all of Isaac's family. Had a good dinner and nice time. Spent evening at home.

5/29/83 Sunday
Rainy day. We left at 6:30 and went with Uncle Charlie to Abram's and on to Juniata College in two cars for David's graduation. It was the largest class ever. Had our dinner after baccalaureate and before the commencement at 2:00. Got home by 7:30.

6/3/83 Friday
Sunny with showers this evening. I did the cleaning. Eby harrowed the garden and had some hauls. He had a weak spell. I got supper for Milton, Barbara and Doug. They came for a niece's wedding in New Holland.

6/20/83 Monday
Good showers. Eby pumped cesspool. He had some hauls and I did one this afternoon. I washed, ironed and mended. Cleaned up garage. Made chicken and waffles for supper. The Amish girl who almost drowned in May died. Jim Herr got a life sentence for the murder of Naomi Huyard. Got family letter and a picture of Jacob.

7/7/83 Thursday
Beautiful day. Eby had plenty of hauls. I went to Sewing Circle alone. Picked and canned ten quarts of yellow and green beans. Eby harrowed some of the garden. Sanford called last evening and said Tera's father passed away and was found outdoors. They were getting ready to go at once.

7/10/83 Sunday
Pretty day. Went to Kinzer. Bill and Judy Hoover gave a talk on their work in Belize. Had a quickie lunch and went to the Samaritan Home to give a program. Visited some of the guests and saw the new furniture in the sitting rooms. Called Sanford. Tera and her sisters stayed at Big Island to work on the house.

7/23/83 Saturday
A fine day. We got up early and met Isaac and Donald Ibach and he took us up to their cabin for the weekend. Some of the family went up Thursday and some came

on Saturday. Elizabeth, Joanne and I went to an antique place nearby and bought a few things. Saw a snake there.

8/6/83 Saturday
Sunny, hot and dry. I picked and canned pickles. Made a cracker pudding. Cleaned basement room. Went to the Vietnamese wedding at Kinzer. Had more than they expected. Eby was real busy hauling and bathed Isaac. Isaac found his razor at the drive-in and he is all hepped up. Thinks he should celebrate.

8/13/83 Saturday
Partly cloudy and cool. Eby had one haul and he shelled the limas I picked. Put five pints in freezer. Made five quarts of applesauce from harvest apples. Picked and canned pickles. Abram called and said Mary Alice was raped and the man was caught last evening. She and Ellen went to visit in West Virginia. Eby did the sweeping and I did the cleaning.

8/15/83 Monday
Beautiful day. I washed, ironed and mended. Canned four quarts of tomatoes. Picked the pickles. Eby had some hauls. I called Mary Alice and she is feeling better since the man whose victim she was is in prison. She is still staying at a friend's house.

8/23/83 Tuesday
Partly cloudy and sultry. I picked and canned the pickles and made cucumber relish. Picked limas and put eight pints in freezer. Eby was busy hauling and mowed the yard. Put some geranium slips in as it is full moon. Called Ray about reunion. Nancy called and said Charlie is coming with them.

8/25/83 Thursday
Warm day. Eby had some hauls. I picked and canned pickles and tomatoes. Did the cleaning and got supper for Nancy and Gerald, Charlie and Sanford's. Jacob's first visit.

8/26/83 Friday
A hot day. Eby took Sanford and Gerald to Rough and Tumble. Tera and Nancy helped me make cole slaw, red eggs, dried beef and things ready for Isaac. Packed all up and left for Camp Morehart at 3:15 and got there at 5:00 just after Becky got there. Had 23 for a chicken corn soup supper. Sanford's took Jacob to Abram's for the night in Hershey.

8/27/83 Saturday
A warm day with showers. Had a good night. Had a quoit game and lots of visiting. Captains and helpers did a good job serving all the good food. Weaver's got here in afternoon and Sam, David and Oliver later on. Played some games with Doug. The family helped Mary Alice buy a burglar alarm.

8/28/83 Sunday
A hot day. Jay, Sue and Uncle Charlie brought Landis, Josephine and Paul this morning. We had some singing and reminiscing. Visited and had our lunch. All packed up, cleaned up and left for home at 2:15. Got here by 4:00. Dale and Mae took Charlie to the Philadelphia Airport. Nancy and Gerald went to Virginia to spend a few days.

9/2/83 Friday
Nice warm day. Prepared food for lunch and supper for the Westman's. Eby went for them at 10:00 and we had a nice day together. Art went with Eby on some hauls and looked for a little barn for Bubby. Rhoda called and said Fredric's got their Korean baby on Monday.

9/14/83 Wednesday
Sunny and cool. I picked tomatoes and pickles. Gathered things and made vegetable soup. Eby brought ten chickens and I put them in the freezer. Cut up two and cooked the bony pieces. Went to midweek service and had a session for writing letters to Russian Christians in prison. A fifteen-year-old-Amish boy was killed filling silo.

9/22/83 Thursday
Sunny and cool. Had an inch of rain. Eby had some hauls, 100 miles. I went to the store and to Clarence's for a bushel of grapes. Mabel helped me pick some off while we talked. She has a problem with tired spells. I made 18 quarts of grape juice. Picked limas and Eby helped shell them.

10/1/83 Saturday
Cloudy with showers and warm. I did the cleaning and made a walnut cake, oatmeal cookies and potato salad. Eby was busy hauling and has over $400 for this week. Loren Dietzel died yesterday morning. Had a letter from Mary Alice and she is doing better but may sell her house.

10/21/83 Friday
Sunny and pleasant. I did the cleaning and made pies, a cake, buns, sweet potatoes, waffles and cole slaw. Cleaned celery and radishes and picked off all the peppers and nice tomatoes. We covered the celery in case of frost. Milton's came about 8:00 and Ray's got here about 10:00. Had a treat of pie and ice cream. Ray brought a corner cupboard for the dollhouse.

10/22/83 Saturday
Had our first frost. Had a late breakfast. I went with Ray's to Strasburg and to an antique place and dollhouse store. Bought some canisters for new corner cupboard. Ray's left about 3:00 for Baltimore. Eby had some hauls and bathed Isaac. Spent the evening reading.

10/29/83 Saturday
Pretty day. Eby bathed Isaac. We left at 9:30 for Jim's and stopped in Clay to buy a railroad book for Eby. Stopped at a restaurant for a snack and got to Jim's at 2:30. Pat made a turkey dinner. Had a nice time visiting. The leaves are at their peak of beauty.

11/3/83 Thursday
Partly cloudy with showers. Annis took me along to Sewing Circle. 18 there. Eby was busy hauling. He bathed Isaac. Vernon was here and got the story of Isaac's bad behavior. I made the second pair of curtains for our bedroom. Wrote some birthday letters. An earthquake in Turkey killed over 1000 people.

11/9/83 Wednesday
Sunny, mild and calm. 78 degrees. I brought Sadie to school. Sewed up some garbage bags to carry leaves. Eby helped with cleaning yard and rain spouts when he did not have any hauls. I worked in yard most of the day. Planted tulips and daffodils. Stirred up two kinds of cookies. Nancy called and said Sanford's left for home today after a visit with them.

11/24/83 Thursday
A wet Thanksgiving day. We had 12 of Isaac's family, 5 of Abram's and 3 of Jim's. All had a nice time visiting and eating. Abram's stayed for a little supper

11/25/83 Friday
Rain, snow, wind and sunshine. I took teachers and a boy to a farm on Running Pump Road. Eby had some hauls and went for our pork. I put it in the freezer and cooked pig feet. Sugar cured hams and bacon. Put flowers from garage to pole in living room. Called Sally and told her we did not trust the weather to come to their house for dinner. I read this evening, started The School of God.

12/4/83 Sunday
A wet day, mild. Went to Kinzer. Ben Clark preached. We had Frank Kreider's and Robert Neff's for dinner. Irvin's did not trust the weather. Went to Old Road where Jay and Margie celebrated their 65th wedding anniversary. Spent evening at home.

12/6/83 Tuesday
A wet day. I took Annie to and from school. Did the ironing and quilted. Eby went to Dr. Breslin and he said he is in good health for his age. He had a lot of hauling.

12/16/83 Friday
Nice weather. I took Annie both ways. Eby was hauling till 9:30. Milton's came about 10:45 and had Ruth Coy along to go with them for the holidays. Had cow in the garden for Doug's favorite dish. Washed the car and dug carrots, beets and salsify. Finished the quilt at 9:00 and gave Eby's knee a treatment.

12/20/83 Tuesday
Sunny and cold. I baked cookies—sand tarts, flap jacks, taylor, peppernuts, date pinwheels and raisin filled. Put icing on a lot of them this evening. Finished hemming quilt this evening.

12/22/83 Thursday
A wet day. I could not go for teachers because of the icy roads. Eby did his hauls. I got up early and put the potato salad together. Baked two kinds of cookies. I filled two pig stomachs to take along to Clemen's. Did some cleaning.

12/23/83 Friday
Weather fair. I took Annie to school. She gave me a box of goodies. Eby took his men to work and gave some cookie boxes. Packed up and went to Dale's at 11:30 and on to Edgar's where we arrived about 5:00. Had a ham supper. All the children are home except Fredric. Weather and driving were good.

12/24/83 Saturday
Cloudy day and began snowing after dark. Had a good night. Peeled apples for pies and dried a tray on the woodburning stove. I baked the two pig stomachs that I brought along for supper. Dale, Mae and Jonathan went shopping, and Edgar and Andrea to clean church. Did some skippers on the quilt. All went to Christmas program at the church except for Daddy and me. Jonathan started Daddy on aspirin for his knee. Zero tonight. Opened some gifts.

12/25/83 Sunday
Christmas. Snowed all day. Zero and up to six degrees. We went to church in two cars. Had our turkey dinner at 2:00 and dessert at 7:00. Jonathan showed us his slides of India and Nepal. Had two sessions of gift giving. We got an electric corn popper, sprayer, magnifying glass, mugs and gloves. Isaac called to ask if our house was ready for zero degree weather. Had a nice time visiting.

12/26/83 Monday
A cold day, six below zero. Had a late breakfast and packed up and left at 9:45. Roads were bare from Binghamton on home. Dale and Mae did good driving and we got home at 3:00. House was warm and we took it easy. Talked to Mabel and she said Bobby Martin had an accident and is in the hospital and badly injured. This is Menno's golden wedding anniversary.

12/31/83 Saturday
Clear and cold. Eby had some hauls and refused some. He bathed Isaac. I made mince pies and roasted the pork. Got some food ready for Monday. Isaac's came with Bradley this P.M. Eby's knees are feeling better with taking aspirin. More chicken flocks have the Asian flu. M.D.S. is called to help clean poultry houses.

1984

1/1/84 Sunday
Went to Kinzer. Paul preached on "Maturing Through Trials." We spent day at home. Paul's came in mistake for tomorrow. We had two kneeling prayers this morning. I did some writing. Isaac snitched food from the refrigerator this morning.

1/2/84 Monday
Cloudy and not so cold. Took Annie to school and home. Eby took men to work and home. I got the food ready for New Year dinner. All the family members came plus Miriam Hess and Paul Martin. Had a nice visit. Some thieves are active in our area. Had a quiet evening.

1/9/84 Monday
Fine weather. Took Annie both ways. Washed and ironed. Sorted some fabric and made a doll dress. Repaired some dolls. Isaac discarded his ragged shirt and pants. He was in bed all day. Eby was busy and made over $80.00 today. Did some hand washing.

1/12/84 Thursday
Clear and cold. Roads still icy from yesterday's snow. Eby took his regular hauls plus Annie and Ike. I made curtains and a fireplace for the dollhouse. I cut some patches. Eby is coughing.

1/13/84 Friday
Took Annie this morning and she went home with parents. Eby busy hauling and I took the men from Simmontown. Made food ready and did some cleaning. Sanford's got here at 5:30 and Jacob is a fine baby. Had chicken and waffles for supper. Snowing this evening.

1/14/84 Saturday
Sunny and warmer. Eby did no hauling. We visited with Sanford's. I went with them to Dutchway, Leisure Crafts, and Lengacher's. Dale and Mae came this afternoon and left about 8:00. Jacob is real friendly and can creep and stand up at chairs. Roads are getting bare again.

1/15/84 Sunday
Fine day. Went to Kinzer. Sanford's came for church. They left at 1:50 for home. David Thomas preached on The Holy Spirit. We rested this afternoon. Jay and Margie took us to Kinzer this evening for last session of David Thomas' Holy Spirit series. He gave us plenty of food for thought.

1/17/84 Tuesday
Partly cloudy with light snow. I took Annie both ways. I started a braided rug. Eby had his regular hauls and shelled a pint of walnuts. Eby bought 12 dozen eggs

for $10.00 from Steve Stoltzfus as his chickens will be doomed tomorrow. Flocks continue to get the flu. I put a hanging lamp in the dollhouse.

1/18/84 Wednesday
Snowed all day, total 8 inches. Eby took John Diener both ways this forenoon and men to Simmontown. I took Annie to school only. Worked on rug. Put onion poultices on Eby this afternoon for his cough. It is better. Had drive plowed open. Eby bathed Isaac. Nancy called and said she is having some physical problems and is going to the hospital next Thursday.

1/25/84 Wednesday
Icy, foggy, mild, sunny and cleared. Eby took John both ways, bathed Isaac and worked on his income tax. I left at 10:00 for Joanne's for Sister's Day. Elizabeth, the five girls and children were there. Joanne taught us candlewicking and served a good lunch. Had a baby shower for Karen. I stopped for wheat germ and oatmeal at Rohrer's Mill and Clarence's for Mabel's rug braiders.

1/26/84 Thursday
Clear and up to 58. I worked on rug from 7 to 9 this evening and for a while this forenoon. Eby drove for Ike and his regulars. Washed both cars and the garage. Tried to do some candlewicking.

2/2/84 Thursday
Beautiful day. Warmer. I took Annis along to Sewing Circle. Got home at 2:00 after our quilt was finished. I went to Dutch Way and stopped at Leisure Craft and got some candlewicking thread. Eby had some hauling. We went to business meeting and had first move for making a covenant. All went smoothly. Moved to repave and make drive in cemetery and add a $500 piece of land. The M.D.S. bus got off to California. Groundhog saw shadow.

2/10/84 Friday
Clear and up to 66. Eby had hauling and cracked some walnuts. I took two teachers home. Worked on my rug and it is 36x18. Isaac did not need breakfast as he ate a lot of jelly eggs. Vivian Westman came for the box of canned things for Art and Dorothy in Florida. Got Nancy's Dresden plate quilt in mail.

2/23/84 Thursday
Partly cloudy and raining after dark. I had a quilting party with nine. They got a lot quilted on Nancy's quilt. I quilted till 11:00 as Isaac was not here and I didn't know if he wanted supper. The Bubble Boy died at twelve years.

2/24/84 Friday
Fine day. 66 degrees. I started quilting at 6:00 and stopped at 10:30. Eby had a lot of hauling and I did one. Rhoda called to say that Fredric's little boy was born this morning.

2/27/84 Monday
Cold east wind. I washed and ironed. Quilted most of the time. Eby was busy hauling from early till late. Isaac went with him to Christiana to take his pants to dry cleaner. Some Amish men went by bus to California to visit a relative who is serving a life sentence for the murder of his second wife.

3/5/84 Monday
A rainy day. Eby had plenty of hauling. I washed and ironed and mended. Put Becky's quilt in the frames and got one border quilted. Have it in the living room. Isaac went to Senior Citizens at New Holland and it was not what he was expecting but he plans to go five days this week.

3/11/84 Sunday
Fine cold day. Went to Kinzer. Paul preached. Went to Margie Hershey's funeral at Hershey's and the house was almost filled. Nancy is to go to the hospital this evening. Eby had a weak spell on the way to church.

3/16/84 Friday
Cloudy. I did some cleaning and quilted. Dug some salsify and it was very muddy. Roasted pork and got potatoes ready. Eby had hauling. Politicians are voting to get prayers back in schools.

3/23/84 Friday
Partly cloudy with snow flurries. I trimmed quilt and sewed on some binding. Eby had some hauls and I took the teachers home. I went with Clarence's to Maple Grove for the viewing of Esther Byler and came home before the service. The first time for this procedure and I hope it will be the last. Did some cleaning this afternoon. Went to the Fire Hall at 7:00 and helped till 9:00 for the sale tomorrow.

3/27/84 Tuesday
Cloudy with rain this evening. Got up at 3:00 to watch the placing of the steel beams for the new bridge over the railroad tracks. I took John Diener to and from work and a boy to the doctor in Intercourse and his mother to a quilting. Cleaned the top cupboards in the kitchen. Teresa and Frank did some arguing. Called Mary Alice and she has a bid on her house. She is packing for her trip to visit Nancy.

3/29/84 Thursday
A very snowy day, with some schools closed. Eby did his regular hauls. I cleaned three closets, the woodbox, desk and dry sink. Eby cracked walnuts. Teresa and Frank are arguing a lot. Anna Mary Lapp invited me to her Stanley party. Hemmed a side of Becky's quilt. Wringer repairs cost $78.87.

4/5/84 Thursday
Cloudy with gusty showers this evening. Took Annis along to Sewing Circle and did some pretty quilts. Eby had some hauls. No Frank. I sent for Feathersprings for foot relief. Eby tried rubbing his knee with vinegar.

4/8/84 Sunday
Fine day. Went to Kinzer. Paul preached on "Looking." Milton's and Treichler's were here for dinner and we had a nice visit. Eby was called to take a young woman to Osteopathic Hospital at 6:00 to have her first baby. I went along.

4/18/84 Wednesday
Clouds, sun and rain. Eby was busy hauling. I cleaned two bedrooms and took a rest this afternoon. Mabel called. We went to Passion Week service and took Anna along. George Brunk preached to a full house. Reuben's dog is not scaring the chickens off.

4/25/84 Wednesday
Cleared and cool. Eby busy hauling and I took Naomi to Paradise and brought her home. Washed and ironed. Did basement bed and washed curtains and cleaned living room windows. Got cards and letters. Took Anna along to midweek service and Tom and Sue Martin and Richard Buckwalter talked on church covenants.

4/29/84 Sunday
Beautiful and warm. Went to Kinzer and had a service conducted by the Mountain Anthems. Was very good singing. They were served dinner. We spent afternoon and evening at home. I filled out a questionnaire about Aunt Cora for Jennie Weaver and wrote to Weaver's. Sanford called and they celebrated Jacob's first year yesterday having twenty friends for brunch. He said Mary Alice is buying a house. I called Mary Alice.

5/3/84 Thursday
Eby got up at 4:00 and started preparing for our takeoff. We left home at 7:00 and picked up Jay and Sue and went on to Abram's. Flight was delayed till 10:25. We changed planes in St. Louis to a real big TWA with over 300 capacity. Arrived in L.A. by 5:00 Eastern time. Nancy met us and we came here to their house. Sue and I cut some quilt patches and after supper Jay's went to Joe Croft's (June Kreider's). Had a good flight and plenty to eat.

5/4/84 Friday
Beautiful day. Got up late and had breakfast. Jay and Sue found their way back and Nancy took us on a drive to see some homes of wealthy people and to Marineland to see the dolphin show and whales and others. Saw lots of Redondo Beach beauty. Sue hemmed a quarter of the quilt and we cut more patches. Nancy made us a good

salmon supper with fresh apple pie and ice cream. Gerald showed us some pictures of his travels.

5/6/84 Sunday
Beautiful day. Jay and Sue came for breakfast. Gary and Nancy took us to the Glass Cathedral where Robert Schuller is the pastor. It is very beautiful and has 10,000 members. Had a lunch here and some TV this afternoon and evening. Abram and Pat came for supper and Jay and Sue bought the ice cream birthday cake. Spent the evening together. I got cards ready to send.

5/7/84 Monday
We left Nancy and Gary at 9:15 and started for Sequoia National Park. Had a nice drive by orange, lemon, olive, nut, vineyard, grain, alfalfa, oil wells and barren mountains. Very interesting drive and pleasant weather. In the park which is as big as some states we saw the giant redwoods and the beauty of the mountains from the high places at 7000 feet and some less. Found a six unit motel at Squaw Valley next to a restaurant where we ate a good supper and settled in for the night at $22 each.

5/8/84 Tuesday
Beautiful day. We started from Squaw Valley Motel at 8:00 and drove through miles of the best farm land in the world. Grapes, peaches, oranges, apricots and many vegetables. There are large dairies, one we went into with 1600 cows. Went to see the earthquake damage at Coalinga and to see the St. Luis Dam where we saw a film show how it is used. Came on to Seaside where we have checked in at the Gateway Lodge Motel. Had our supper at a next door restaurant and signed off for the day at 6:30.

5/9/84 Wednesday
Same weather. Left Seaside and took 17 mile drive around the peninsula. It is very beautiful. We continued up the coast and stopped to see points of interest. Saw more farm land. Stopped at a food market and bought tomatoes, artichokes, cauliflower, etc. Had a little bit of a problem finding 7 Acorn Court. Got here at 4:30 and Ed was here. Charlie came about 5:15. He made us a good supper and Jay and Sue bathed in his outdoor heated pool. We are to sleep in his king sized bed.

5/10/84 Thursday
Weather fine. After a good breakfast we made pie and tartlet shells and left for the Civic Center where we had a guided tour of the place by a volunteer guide. After this we had a good picnic on the park grounds and then back to Acorn Court. Charlie and Ed prepared us a very good fish supper with potatoes, salad, and three kinds of pie. They gave Sue and me plants and gifts from the Marshall Islands. Packing to go home.

5/11/84 Friday
Weather good for flying. We had a good breakfast and left for airport about 10:00. Left car at National, met Abram's and said good by to Charlie. Our flight was at 1:00. We changed planes at Pittsburgh and got to Abram's at 10:00. John Lerch's got there a short time before and surprised them. Jay drove our station wagon to their place and we got home by 12:00. Found things as we left them. The garden grew.

5/18/84 Friday
Cloudy and cool. Eby had hauls and I took Christiana to and from Ruth Hershey and brought John Diener home. Eby brought our half of beef. I put it in the freezer, cured the dried beef and cooked two trypes. They cost $32.00 and I was shocked at such a price. Mabel called and we had a long talk.

5/29/84 Tuesday
A wet day with three inches of rain. Eby had hauling. I cleaned garage and took two boys to Dr. Blank. I asked Isaac about his visit to basement and eating all the jelly eggs. He is very mum. I told him he can go to Sara Marie. I wrote her a letter.

6/1/84 Friday
Clear and cool. I swept basement room and washed up kitchen. Had a call from Rachel at Senior Center complaining about Isaac being too dirty and smelling bad. A man from the office on aging is coming to have an interview next week.

6/9/84 Saturday
Very warm day. I made pies and picked first sugar peas for dinner. Abram's and Mary Alice were here. Had a nice visit and Mary Alice went to 20th class reunion at Dutch Town and Country. Eby had no hauling and did some sprinkling this evening.

6/29/84 Friday
Nice warm day. Wrote to Weaver's and Sanford for birthdays. Did some quilting. Eby had hauling and finished the yard mowing. He harrowed up the pea patch and I planted 79 celery plants that some Amish gave to him. Planted corn, beets and carrots. Soaked my feet and trimmed nails. They finished paving Chestnut Street.

6/30/84 Saturday
Cloudy with heavy showers. Eby was busy hauling and I took Ike's to a party and home again. Did the cleaning and made oatmeal cookies. Picked black raspberries and blueberries. Garden is doing well and celery had an easy day. The filmmakers left the County and "Witness" is being criticized by some.

7/1/84 Sunday
Had almost five inches of rain this morning. We were kept busy sweeping water in basement until church time. Flooding in many places. We spent day at home

resting and reading. Finished reading Robert Schuller's book. He is pastor at the Crystal Cathedral.

7/9/84 Monday
Pretty day. I washed and ironed. Picked black and red raspberries and a quart of blueberries. Made a half portion of red raspberry jelly. Replanted corn and planted some beans. Picked some for supper. Hoed weeds. Eby had hauling and got my dental plate mended for $5.00 at Dr. Caldwell's. A young woman came over from the ball game to call cops about a reckless driver.

7/15/84 Sunday
Nice warm day. Went to Kinzer. John Winters preached a harvest sermon. I wrote to Amy and Landis' and just then they came to see us. Had a nice visit. Jay went to the hospital yesterday for his heart and is in intensive care. Jay and Margie came about 5:30 and went with us to Kinzer where Landis Homes gave program. Sue called and said Jay is comfortable.

7/18/84 Wednesday
Showers and clearing. Eby had hauling. I picked the beans and pickles. Jay had open heart surgery and Sue called to report. Abram called to get the report.

7/22/84 Sunday
Nice day with some showers. Went to Kinzer and John Winters taught the combined classes. Paul preached a good sermon on "Gifts." Abram and Pat stopped in on their way to Valley Forge for a wedding anniversary celebration. They stopped to see Jay in the hospital and he is recovering normally. I wrote to Conrad in Nicaragua. James Hershey's little boy drank poison and is in Medical Center.

7/23/84 Monday
Warm day. I washed and ironed and helped Eby put pea wire around the tomatoes to keep our neighbor's chickens out. Eby had some hauling. I finished the quilt at 11:40 P.M. Went to Ruth Clark's house to help make out prayer calendar for August. Sue called and told me Jay is doing well.

7/26/84 Thursday
Fine day. I ripped Mary Alice's stuff for rugs. Eby brought Kathleen's cutter, but it doesn't work good. Eby mowed the yard and had some hauls. Harvey's are getting their eggs from the neighbor's chickens.

8/8/84 Wednesday
Warm day. Isaac picked us up and we left Lancaster Depot at 6:42 by Amtrak for a visit with Milton's. Got there by 12:30 and visited and he took Isaac and Brad and Elizabeth along when he took Mike to do his lawn work. Barbara came home from her job in the afternoon. She prepared us a good fish supper and we ate on the patio. Milton took all but Daddy on a tour of the school this afternoon.

8/9/84 Thursday
Not so warm at Stony Brook. Barbara and Mike went to work. Milton served us breakfast at 10:00. Elizabeth and I washed the dishes and I shortened a pair of trousers for Doug. Barbara and Mike came home at noon to say good bye and we left at 12:55 on Long Island train and got to Lancaster at 6:20. Had good train travel both ways. Donald and Linda and Benji and Betsy came to depot and we went for supper to a restaurant.

8/17/84 Friday
A warm day. I picked a big bucket of limas. Eby helped shell them. Made a cake and cupcakes, a pudding and prepared for Jonathan for supper. Eby busy hauling. I brought John home and stopped with Kathleen's rug cutter. We took Jonathan along to visit Uncle Jay Martin after supper. He seems good.

8/24/84 Friday
A beautiful day. Eby did his regular hauls earlier and we got started for Camp Morehart at 4:45. Milton's did some shopping and came back about 3:00 and helped pack things in our station wagon and we all went in it with Milton driving. I took things for chicken corn soup and Abram cooked it for supper. Charlie came with Abram's.

8/25/84 Saturday
Fine weather. We had late breakfast and some quoit games. Had a Hostetter trivia quiz. By 5:00 49 arrived and some went home. Had jig saw puzzles, some games and picture-taking. Mae prepared some calico barbecue for dinner and it was good. Had baked potatoes and lots of good things. Elizabeth, Judy and Karen brought pies. Had cold things for supper. Plenty of visiting and caring for babies.

8/26/84 Sunday
Fine weather. We had a good night and breakfast. Had teams doing a Bible game hunt. A service with Fredric led the singing, Jennie Weaver read Psalms 119:1-6, Rosa had prayer, Conrad told about his Honduras and Nicaragua summer, and David his work with the Merton Center. Got home at 3:40 with Milton as driver.

9/29/84 Saturday
Partly cloudy and cool. I went to Fire Hall at 7:00 to help prepare food for a table at Gap Sale. Got home before 10:00. Eby brought John Diener and Isaac came to try to solve our basement water problem. Eby had hauls. I made pies, cupcakes and cooked chicken for soup. Got vegetables ready for fellowship meal. Jay and Margie stopped in for a short visit from Kinzer pig roast. Grace called and said they had a good Relief Sale in Virginia. Mary Alice got one of my rugs for $135 and Sanford the other for $200.

10/1/84 Monday

A rainy day. I made some applesauce. Took Ben Glick's wife to seven different places this afternoon. Took Anna Mary this morning and evening. Got potatoes ready for a gallon of potato salad for the meal tomorrow. Margie passed away about 10:30 this morning. Three people killed in a car accident down by Isaac's.

10/4/84 Thursday

A beautiful day. I made potato salad in case of company for lunch. Isaac and Elizabeth took us along to Margie's funeral at Old Road. They had a nice service for a full house in charge of Clair Eby and Richard Buckwalter. A lunch was served at White Horse Fire Hall for over 100. I trimmed raspberries this P.M.

10/10/84 Wednesday

Mild day. Took Anna Mary to and from. Made vegetable soup. After fog was cleared I got cheese for Ray's, ordered shoes for myself and went to Bowell's for lard and they had no small containers. Got two hams for Ray's. We ate supper and started for Ray's at 5:45 and got there at 7:45. All went well and they served us dessert. Ray showed me his pretty woodworking.

10/12/84 Friday

Fine warm day in the 70's. Took Mary Anne to and from. Made 26 quarts of applesauce. Eby was busy hauling and mowed the yard. Got Mrs. Thomas' quilt in the mail today. Rested a while and picked the limas. James and Pat were awarded the National Soil Conservation Award.

10/15/84 Monday

Fine day, mild. Took Anna Mary both ways and the King girls to their schools. Washed and ironed and mended. Eby picked up walnuts and did some hauling. I picked limas and we shelled them. I am trying to memorize Romans 12 for our Sunday School.

10/31/84 Wednesday

Beautiful day and very warm. I took Anna Mary both ways and Mrs. Christ King to and from her daughter near Churchtown. Got wheat germ, oatmeal and flour at Rohrer's Mill and stopped at Clarence's to give Aunt Mabel some quince for her birthday. Got home at 10:20 and raked leaves. Eby helped an hour and it's all done but the back yard.

11/1/84 Thursday

Cloudy and mild. No hauling for me. Annis took me to sewing circle. We did an endless step quilt and knotted a comfort. Got home at 2:20 and raked leaves till 4:00. Eby was busy hauling and cleaned the rain spouts. Indira Gandhi, the ruling lady in India, was assassinated.

11/9/84 Friday
I took Anna Mary both ways. Went to Sam's new store and got paint to finish floor in heater room. Cleaned the hall carpet. Finished cleaning raspberries and tying them up. Eby had hauls. We went to a program for Relief Sale at the Martin sales building. A good turnout. Offering was $618. It was much too cold and the quartet sang too many numbers.

11/20/84 Tuesday
Coldest yet. Twenty degrees. I roasted three turkeys and dug and cleaned celery and made carrots ready. Got things lined up. Eby pumped cesspool. An oil explosion in Mexico killed 262 people and injured many more. Put electric heater in garage to keep flowers warm. Eby made a table for food in garage.

11/22/84 Thursday
A fine day. We had a good Thanksgiving with Edgar's, Isaac's, Abram's, Jim's, Ray's, Dale's and Sanford's. We ate in two shifts. Girls played with little ones in basement room. Baby Fae with the baboon heart died after two weeks.

12/4/84 Tuesday
Fine day. At 6:00 A.M. I took Elam's and Dan's to their homes for a wedding. Took Anna Mary to and from. I cleaned celery and made carrot curls. Quilted some. We went to Airie King's wedding to a Lapp. Had a very interesting time. 350 people there and lots of food. Rachel Blank, who is Mrs. Aaron Lapp, wants Rhoda to visit her. She lives in Bartville.

12/6/84 Thursday
Cleared colder. Took Anna Mary one way. Worked on the Relief Sale dinner and served 15 people. All seemed to eat hearty and enjoyed an evening visiting. More than 1000 people in India have died from a Union Carbide leak and many more are suffering from the effects.

12/13/84 Thursday
Mild weather. Took Anna Mary both ways. Stopped at Flaud's greenhouse and bought three busy lizzies. Baked cookies, sand tarts, flap jacks, raisin filled, gum drops, chocolate drops, date pinwheel, peppernuts and rice krispie date balls. Iced some this evening. Eby had some hauling and shelled peanuts and put them on the sand tarts. McDonald's opened their new restaurant in Gap.

12/18/84 Tuesday
Damp and mild. Took Anna Mary both ways. Brought Susie to the wedding on Ike Eby farm. Made up some cookie trays and went to Dutchway to get a turkey for Abe Stoltzfus and took it out. Stopped with Esther's cookies and chicken and she was not home. Took Kathleen a try of cookies and she was not home. Took some

to Annis and she was not home. Washed the car and moved celery to the garage as it is too warm in the basement.

12/20/84 Thursday
A sunny day. Took Anna Mary both ways. Packed some cookies and quilted a lot. Eby was busy hauling. Lady called to try to sell us new windows for the house. Eby has a hunch to buy a little barn. We went to a program at Spring Garden School. It was well done. Had a big letter from Rhoda. Conrad has mono and needs rest.

12/23/84 Sunday
Fine sunny day. Went to Kinzer. Paul preached. Ceramic candles were lit and music from records was played. Carolers sang a few songs. Roy Witmer gave pencils and candy canes. Spent afternoon and evening at home. My cold is hanging on.

12/25/84 Tuesday
Beautiful day. Spent a quiet morning and then went to Isaac's and had a real Christmas with lots of gift giving and a real good ham dinner with plenty of many things. All of their family were there. Frank and Teresa gave us a box of goodies. Ike and wife stopped and gave us a fruit tray.

12/30/84 Sunday
Nice mild day. Went to Kinzer. Had a Christmas program on other country's Christmas customs. Paul preached. Had Isaac's, the Dietzels, Ibach's and Haug's for dinner. Had a nice visit with all of them. Eby started reading The Reaper's Song. No hot water this evening.

12/31/84 Monday
Mild and drizzly. Took Anna Mary both ways. Eby had his regular hauls and read his book. Had plumber repair hot water heater. I quilted most of the day and rolled twice. We got a card from Abraham Stevens. He is in med school in Mexico. We had a good year healthwise and otherwise.

1985

1/1/85 Tuesday
Mild, cloudy and drizzly. I did some quilting this morning and evening. We went to Clarence's for our family get-together. All were there plus Miriam and Paul Martin. Had a very good dinner and a nice time visiting. Three of their Vietnamese friends came. Eby finished reading The Reaper's Song.

1/2/85 Wednesday
Mild and cloudy. Washed and ironed. Dried it in the basement. A man came to put in the new phone that the children gave us for Christmas. Jay stopped in to chat on

his way to see David. Eby had some hauling. Three heifers were hit and killed on the highway this evening.

1/10/85 Thursday
Cold and snowing this afternoon. I took Anna Mary this morning and Eby did this evening. I quilted all day and it is getting less. Elam brought a load of manure. Mabel called this evening. Abram Mellinger donated four million dollars to charities.

1/24/85 Thursday
Fine day, mild. Took Anna Mary both ways. Finished ripping the wool pieces. Got Kathleen's cutter and started cutting strips for rugs. Eby had hauling most all day. Got a check for my quilt and Eby took the quilt to United Parcel. Read The Reaper's Song till 11:00.

1/31/85 Thursday
Snowed about four inches. I took Anna Mary one way. Eby did his regular hauls and took it easy. He is coughing a lot. I bunched the wool strips and hung them all up and cleaned the basement room. Frank and Teresa had a loud argument and he left with some luggage. She was silent all day.

2/2/85 Saturday
A lot more snow and rain. Edgar's decided to miss the wedding as the roads were bad and no signs of snow stopping. Edgar took Rhoda, Jonathan and me to see where Jonathan will be working and to Dutchway for groceries. We worked on my rug. Eby did not have any hauling. He is coughing all the time.

2/5/85 Tuesday
Snowed from 3:00 on. Took Anna Mary both ways. Her sister spent the day with her. I worked on braided rug. Took Eby to the garage two times as station wagon got repairs. Eby had extra hauling. His cough is better. It is good to be in the warm tonight with snow falling. Made out seed order.

2/11/85 Monday
Sunny, in the forties. Eby had some hauls and roads are not all opened. I washed and ironed. Made up beds. Worked on braiding and have color problems. Frank came back last night and apologized this morning for his conduct Thursday a week ago when he left. Teresa went to Ephrata on her job for three days. Frank cleaned some snow from drive.

2/14/85 Thursday
Fine day. Took Anna Mary and her sister both ways. Worked on rug and cleaned inside of car. Got Mother's shawl out of cedar chest and cleaned and aired it and gave it to Lizzie for inspection. Eby was busy hauling. Called Mabel. Sam Stoltzfus dug our mailbox out of deep snow for $10.00.

2/18/85 Monday

A fine day. I took Anna Mary both ways and Susie to Green Tree. Worked on rug and finished it and started a second one for Relief Sale. Stopped at Abe Stoltzfus' and Lizzie took Mother's shawl and gave me $45.00 for it. Eby had some hauling. Called Helen and we had a long talk.

2/21/85 Thursday

Fine weather. Eby took Anna Mary as he had time this morning. Worked on rug all day. Ordered some flower seeds from Burpee. Eby cracked walnuts and had some hauls. It was good to be home all day. Milton's went to California to visit Charlie and Nancy. Snow banks are sinking.

2/28/85 Thursday

A fine cool day. Transmission went out on the station wagon and Eby did all the hauling and was kept real busy. I worked on rug. I went to Fire Hall at 5:30 and helped till 9:00. It was a banquet for Senior Citizens. Had a nice letter from Doug. A 15-year-old girl from Hempfield High School died from a poison she worked with at school.

3/12/85 Tuesday

Very windy day. I took Anna Mary both ways. Eby pumped cesspool. I finished marking quilt and quilted a while this evening. Went to Dutchway. Prepared some fruit and vegetables. Martha Burkholder had surgery for a tumor on her bowel. She is very sick. Eby had hauling.

3/13/85 Wednesday

Real nice day. Took Anna Mary to school. Made food ready for my quilters. Eby had some hauling. I did some cleaning and made buns. We went to midweek. Jeff, a mountain climber, gave a talk about he and his buddy being lost, almost frozen before their rescue on Mt. Washington three years ago.

3/14/85 Thursday

Partly cloudy and mild. Took Anna Mary in morning only. Had a quilting for Jennie's quilt. Aunt Mabel, Amy, and Sue, Annis, Esther, Miriam Hess, Mary Shearer and Dorothy Martin. They got a lot done. Ray was at New Bolton Center for some classes and came for supper. Eby is having a cold. I quilted some this evening.

3/23/85 Saturday

A damp day with showers. Milton was here for breakfast and Eby took him to Manheim to pick up his new car and drive it home. I went to help at Fire Hall at 9:30 and came home at 2:00. It gave a big sale and lots of food was served. Looks like Frank left with T.V. and clothing.

3/30/85 Saturday
Had a good night in Jennie's room in Staunton. Mary Alice, Sanford's, Nancy and Gerry came about 11:00. Grace served a turkey dinner with all the fixings. Had Christmas gift exchange after dinner with visiting. The folks all left about 7:30. Robert played some old round records this evening.

3/31/85 Sunday
Cloudy, rainy and cool. Went to Staunton Church with Robert's and on to Mary Alice's where Nancy and Gerry and Sanford's came for dinner. Saw all of Mary Alice's new property. Came back with Robert's to spend the night.

4/1/85 Monday
Clear and cool. We ate breakfast with Robert and Grace and left about 6:50. Picked up Bertha at Jesse Byler's and got home at 1:30. Stopped at a roadside rest to eat the lunch Grace packed for us. Eby drove all the way. He did his evening hauls. I went to bed early as I did not sleep last night. Had too much on my mind.

4/4/85 Thursday
Sun and showers. Took Anna Mary home only. Went to Sewing Circle alone as it did not suit Annis. Eby had hauling. We went to Passion Week service at Hershey's. A full house. Paradise had the opening with some unpleasant piano music and choir.

4/10/85 Wednesday
Clear and cold. Took Anna Mary both ways. Brought plants from bedrooms. Transplanted some pepper plants. Cleaned Isaac's drawers and closet and closets in our room. Got three boxes ready for Goodwill. The U.P.S. brought a cloth stripper for rugs from Grace, Mary Alice, Sanford and Nancy.

4/24/85 Wednesday
Cloudy and cool. Eby took Anna Mary both ways and was busy hauling all day. I cleaned the bathroom and woodbox. Sorted papers and magazines. Jonathan had a busy day looking into his new job and trying to find a place to live. I started work on the piece Elizabeth gave me last birthday. Jonathan came back at 6:00 and is looking at house ads.

4/25/85 Thursday
Partly cloudy. Eby did all the hauling. I celebrated my 80th birthday making cupcakes, oatmeal cookies, cleaning the kitchen window corner. Esther came and gave me a dish drainer and tray. Jonathan took us out for supper to the Gap Diner. Isaac's and Bradley came and brought ice cream, cake and drink. Jonathan looked at some houses.

4/26/85 Friday
Fine weather, dry. Eby had some hauling. I made two pies. Jonathan took Eby to East Petersburg for the car. It cost $360 for paint job and repairs. He went to see

Irvin and got a desk light at stamp store. Mary Alice got here at 4:00. She, Jonathan and I went to the Gap Auction. She bought a green pitcher.

4/28/85 Sunday
Fine day with a few sprinkles. Went to Kinzer after getting Mary Alice packed up. She left at 9:00 to get back for a wedding. Paul preached on Justification by Faith. Spent the evening at home. Reread my 27 birthday cards and letters.

5/4/85 Saturday
Sunny and pleasant. Eby mowed the yard, had hauling and bathed Isaac. I made cookies for Fire Hall and a cherry pie. Washed the car and worked on rug. Swept basement room. Barge's called and said Jonathan got his house for bid of $50,000. Jay Hostetter called and said Abram is on T.V. if we want to see him.

5/13/85 Monday
Had a little rain and then a sunny day. Took Anna Mary this morning and then took Susie to Green Tree. Washed and ironed. Mildred Fisher came to fit me for foundation. Bill was $213.50. Too expensive. Eby cleaned the rain spouts and had some hauling. I made rhubarb sauce. Isaac K is complaining about the hot weather. I did some rug this evening.

5/15/85 Wednesday
Fine day with a few showers. The oven unit went out and the turkey did not roast so nicely in the small oven. Tried baking a nut cake and it did not bake even. Made sweet potato pudding and filling balls. Hope Clark gets oven fixed for tomorrow. Eby harrowed the garden. Worked on rug.

5/16/85 Thursday
Cloudy with showers. No hauling and I got off to a good start with dinner and Clark Electric came at 9:30 and put a new unit in the oven and my problems were solved. Had a nice time visiting with our company and the dinner turned out real good. Put everything in order and went to Paradise for the Ascension Day meeting. Poor attendance.

5/29/85 Wednesday
Cloudy and cool. Eby was busy hauling. I took the Glick's to and from a potato chip making. Went to Dorothy Martin for coverings and no one was there. Took my Bible to have it repaired and on to visit Ruth Coy. I went to Provident Bookstore to spend Christmas certificate and on home. I called Mabel to share Amy's letter. Greased the sewing machine. Bottled the tea and put it in freezer.

6/1/85 Saturday
Fine weather. Eby did some short hauls. I washed the car. We packed up and left for Jim's at 10:15, stopped at Benner's Restaurant for lunch and got to Jim's by 2:30.

Jim and Greg were putting haylage in the silo. Jim showed us their slides of last summer's trip to Europe.

6/2/85 Sunday
A nice day. Went to Spring Run Church with Jim's. I went in the old ladie's class with five others. Greg showed me his many chickens on our way home. They look great at three pounds. Pat had a good roast chicken dinner. We left at 3:30 and got home at 6:15. Jay Hostetter came this evening.

6/3/85 Monday
Partly cloudy and pleasant. I went to help quilt at Anna Kurtz's for a Meadville girl. Came home at noon and picked peas for supper. I brought Bradley from school and he was here for supper and the night. He saw a ball game and did not like the thunder storm. I let him call home.

6/7/85 Friday
A pleasant day. I took Katie to Dutchway. Started picking peas at 5:00 and got almost two bushels. Eby took them for hulling and I put 29 pints in the freezer by noon. We went to the dispersal sale for Isaac's cows below Quarryville. Highest one brought $1150.

6/9/85 Sunday
Cloudy with a few showers. Went to Kinzer. Glen Hershey preached on The Sabbath Day. Spent afternoon and evening at home. Rhoda called to say she will be coming with Jonathan next weekend. Called Mary Alice and she and Jennie plan to fly to California on Friday.

6/17/85 Monday
A fine sunny day. Jonathan looked after a lot of things. I took Rhoda along to his new house and we did a lot of cleaning. Found a lot of dirt. I came home at 5:00 and they came home at 8:00. Eby had plenty of hauling. I picked a quart of strawberries.

6/18/85 Tuesday
Partly cloudy. Washed and made a dinner to take to Rhoda and Jonathan and we ate it with him at his house before they went home. Planted two tomato plants for him. I picked six quarts of raspberries. Eby had hauling and went to Rutt's with a load this evening. I seeded the cherries that Naomi and Lizzie gave me.

7/8/85 Monday
Some showers. Took Katie to work. They have started to build new store at Dutchway. Eby had his regular hauling. I picked pickles and red raspberries. I did a lot of quilting. Eby cut off the irises and the marigolds will have more show. Jay Hostetter stopped in to ask how to make sauer kraut.

7/16/85 Tuesday
Real nice day with good rain. Eby had some hauling. He helped with corn and I put 59 pints in freezer. Was done till 2:00. Rested and quilted. Turned it around to work the other side. Jay H. stopped in to pay his bus ticket. A farmer in Springville found his seven horses dead this morning when hit by lightning. Reagan's surgery found cancer.

8/2/85 Friday
A fine cool day. Eby was busy hauling all day. I picked two baskets of lima beans, shelled and put in freezer. Milton's came about 2:00 and helped pick the balance of the beans and helped shell. Did 20 pints. Had a talk with Teresa about Frank. Milton's went to the auction for a short time. Milton brought us a lot of fish.

8/8/85 Thursday
Sunny and sultry. Eby busy hauling and mowed some yard. He is bringing Ike and Anna home with their new baby. I canned 5 quarts of peaches. Made 3 quarts of tomato juice. Worked on my pillow top this evening. Made some wrapping yarn balls. Called Annis and Clair's back pain is caused by bone cancer. He is getting two kinds of treatment.

8/11/85 Sunday
Sultry and warm. Went to Kinzer. Ben Clark preached. George Beacher visited and had part in the service. We went to Robert Westman's for dinner in Leacock. The Westman's, his parents, came from Florida last Sunday. I started reading the Paradise anniversary book this evening.

8/23/85 Friday
Fine day. Took Katie to work. Did the cleaning and washed the car. Made a sponge cake for Mary Alice's birthday. Charlie came for lunch from Philadelphia. Uncle Jay H. stopped to see him. Packed up our food. I made four dozen red eggs. Started for New Holland at 3:30 and Milton drove our car to Camp Morehart for our 6th reunion there. I made chicken corn soup for 25 and three more came later when it was all gone.

8/24/85 Saturday
Nice mild day at Camp Morehart. Had some wool rug cutting, a spelling bee and pitching rings. Some played trivia and scrabble and other games. Jacob, Matthew, Andrew and Bradley were the little ones. All had a nice time visiting.

8/25/85 Sunday
Showery and mild. After our breakfast and some visiting we had our worship service in charge of Edgar and Rhoda. Sang some songs of praise and some were suggested. Jennie Weaver read from Psalms. Edgar read a poem and we had some talks on the different persuasions by Dale, Sanford and Rosa, and after that we had sharing of

experiences and plans. All shared good lunch food. Cleaned up and checked out. Clair Denlinger passed away yesterday.

8/27/85 Tuesday
Fine day. I washed and ironed. Picked a bucket of pickles and some tomatoes. Pulled a lot of weeds. Went to Clair Denlinger's funeral this afternoon. They had a nice funeral. Isaac's were there and stopped here a while. Eby had some hauling. I did some candlewicking this evening. Mabel called.

9/1/85 Sunday
Cloudy and pleasant. We went to Kinzer. We had rabbit for dinner. Went to the hospital to see Irvin. The nurses were walking him. He is very weak. Next we went to see Sue H. at the Mennonite Home. She did not respond at all. Spent evening at home. Called Nancy and she said they are going to Hawaii for vacation instead of coming to Virginia.

9/6/85 Friday
Sunny and warm. Took Katie to work. Made apple dumplings and got food ready. Went for Westman's at 9:00 and took them on a tour to see some places of interest. Had a nice time visiting with them. Bubby's came for supper. Eby took Art along to do some hauling. He does not look very well and Dorothy is getting more feeble.

9/8/85 Sunday
A warm day. Gust and rain at noon. Went to Kinzer and had Council Meeting. Had our lunch and left for the 38th Hostetter reunion at Habecker's Church. The interest seemed better. We went to the Hostetter-Miller cemetery to dedicate the memorial stone that Daddy paid for.

9/17/85 Tuesday
Beautiful day. I went to Elam's for milk. The carpenter Amos Zook was here all day doing repairs. Eby was busy hauling. I cleaned some cupboards, drawers, and bathroom closet. Teresa came back and said she plans to move out in October and get a job with Hallmark cards.

9/21/85 Saturday
Sunny and warm. I took Naomi, Lizzie and Abe to Emma Esh and home again. Went to Dutchway for food and got barbecue for supper. Picked over a bushel of limas and gave Elizabeth a basket when she, Kim and Bradley came to mow the yard. Teresa came back this evening and I was sleeping and did not say good bye.

9/22/85 Sunday
Cloudy, warm, calm and fine day for our service and fellowship at Intercourse Park. Most everyone was there and the food was good and plentiful. We got home at 3:15 and spent a quiet evening at home reading. Sanford called and said we are to be grandparents again.

9/27/85 Friday
Had four inches of rain and the basement is getting water. Called Sanford and he said Richmond weather is good. We ate breakfast and packed off for depot after Eby took men to work. Left Lancaster at 7:30 and changed trains in Philadelphia after an hour wait and arrived in Richmond at 2:20 where Sanford and Jacob met us. We looked at all the improvements in gardens and lawn. Had a nice evening and Tera made us a good supper. Did a little quilting.

9/29/85 Sunday
Slept late and had a good breakfast. Went to Friends Meeting at 11:00 where a good number came for worship. From there they took us to the depot for the 1:20 train. Tera packed us a lunch to eat on the train. We got home by 9:00. All went well.

10/5/85 Saturday
Cleared nice and sunny. Milton's did some shopping and Eby did some hauling. I took Katie to work. We packed up and went to Isaac's for a chicken barbecue dinner with their family, Milton's and Jonathan. Had a nice time. They made ice cream for supper. Jay H. stopped to see about living with us.

10/10/85 Thursday
Nice warm day. I washed bed things from apartment and attic. Scrubbed rugs and porch. House cleaned two bedrooms and five closets. John Hershey worked all day on lights for apartment. Eby busy hauling and had car trouble in New Holland and I had to take men and teachers home. I could not go with Clarence's to Menno's and Landis' because of the electrical work. Was disappointed.

10/14/85 Monday
Very foggy morning, sunny and rained. Took Katie both ways. Did a big wash of sheets, pillow cases and towels. Cracked balance of '84 walnuts and picked out a quart. Eby helped finish after supper. Isaac came at 12:00 and drove our car to go to Irvin's funeral. Saw all the family and some grandchildren.

11/3/85 Sunday
Cloudy and cool. Went to Kinzer and to Kinzer Fire Hall where the Helping Hands class served the Oldsters a good dinner. I had a short reading. Went to Jay Martin's and Issac's, Jonathan and Uncle Jay's went to Derry Church in his van for a farewell reception for Samuel. It was a good evening. Jim and Pat came too.

11/7/85 Thursday
Beautiful day. I took Katie and Rachel to and from a wedding. Eby washed the station wagon and did some hauling. I did some quilting. Called Grace and Virginia is having flooding with 42 deaths and some missing. Millions in damage.

11/19/85 Tuesday
Partly cloudy and mild. Eby took Katie to work. I quilted till 10:45 and got ready to go with Clarence's to Menno's. They left me off and went on to other visits. Amy and I had a nice visit. Menno is real feeble and Amy gets around slowly. Got home at 5:00 and quilted after supper till late.

11/24/85 Sunday
A nice day. Went to Kinzer. Paul preached on Romans 12:1-2. We spent a quiet afternoon at home. Jay came for a couple hours this evening. I called Charlie at noon and talked to Sam just a half hour before they were taking him to the airport to fly to Korea.

11/30/85 Saturday
Very rainy day. Eby had some hauling. I hemmed quilt on three sides. Did a big wash and ironing. Milton's got here about 8:30. Viola Lawrence had sale of her stock in the store today.

12/4/85 Wednesday
Partly cloudy. I took Katie and her mother to work. Went up to Elam's for milk. Went to Clarence's to go along to M.C.C. to help make soap. We did 200 pounds and got home at 12:00. I buried the carrots and the beets in the hot bed. Smoke washed the dried beef and cut some rug strips. Eby bathed Isaac and told him his old shoes are doomed. Jay is in the hospital for his back.

12/6/85 Friday
White this morning but most melted. Eby busy hauling. I made vegetable soup. Put 10 packs of carrots in the freezer. Washed 10 dozen eggs. Made a sponge cake for Fire Hall Christmas Bazaar. Washed the car. Heated and strained grease for soap making. Got oil tank filled. No word from Jay. Eby burned Isaac's old shoes and sweater.

12/8/85 Sunday
Went to Kinzer. Had lasagna for dinner. Went to Fire Hall at 2:00 where a reception was held in honor of Viola Lawrence's 86 years and more than 60 keeping store and restaurant. Jay came this evening to chat for a while.

12/14/85 Saturday
Colder and windy. Eby had two hauls. We tried to fix the waffle iron but it did not last. Eby broke his glasses and took them to New Holland to get fixed for $30. I did the cleaning real good. Started a rug for Sanford. Had last fresh spinach for supper.

12/15/85 Sunday
A fine day. 18 degrees this morning. Went to Kinzer. Took Jay along to see Aunt Sue Hostetter. She is poorly. Stopped at Robert Neff's and they are as usual. Robert is losing out. This evening we went to Kinzer for a Christmas program. Jay was not

going to Old Road as they had a tree and a drama. Sue called and Jay was able to go to church.

12/17/85 Tuesday
Fine weather. Eby was busy hauling. I went for milk only. Baked two kinds of cookies. Now have more than 800. Worked on Sanford's rug. A school teacher came to look at the apartment. Aunt Sue Hostetter died last night.

12/21/85 Saturday
Clear, snow-covered and cold. Eby had two hauls. Isaac and Elizabeth took us to the funeral for Sue Hostetter at Hershey's and a lunch at Old Road. All the 8 children, 45 grandchildren and 82 great grandchildren were there except for the two in Africa and one in California. I took Kathleen and Esther cookies and neither were home so I came home and worked on rug. Joanne gave birth to Angela Marie.

12/25/85 Wednesday
We left at 8:00 for Jim's and had a good trip except it was a bit sloppy in places. There was less snow in Mifflin County. Got there at 10:30. We had a good ham dinner and lots of good things. It got real cold and we went out to see the milking. Beth fixed supper. Pat went to work at 3:00 and returned at 11:00. Had a nice quiet day.

12/31/85 Tuesday
Partly cloudy and mild. I was home all day. Finished Sanford's rug. Had just enough brown to finish last row. Eby was busy hauling. He brought some groceries when he took Katie home. I did a cocoanut that he brought. Eby bought me a diary at Gordonsville Bookstore for $8.00. There was a stabbing in Lancaster. Elam paid off $6000 on the farm.

1986

1/1/86 Wednesday
A beautiful day. Eby had a couple short drives. We went to Jay Martin's for our annual family dinner. We had a nice time visiting and Jay seemed his usual self, but Sue said that he sleeps a lot. He did nap a few times. Had a good ham dinner. Played Bible trivia to use their Christmas gift.

1/5/86 Sunday
Light snow and pleasant. We got things lined up for dinner. Went to Kinzer church. 73 there. Milton's went to Bellevue. Sanford's went to the old Quaker Church. 5 there. Had Milton's, Sanford's, Isaac's, Mart Groff, Miriam and Jonathan for dinner. Jacob was disappointed that Bradley did not come. Sanford's left for home at 3:30 and Jacob was happy. Doug complains about going back to school after a two week vacation.

1/13/86 Monday
Sunny and snow flurries. I washed early and hung it on the line. It dried good. At 9:00 I took Nancy's quilt to Intercourse for the third time and Sara was not at home again. Inquired of the neighbors and found out she went to spend the day with her daughter. So I stopped at Stoltzfus bakeshop for bread and buns. Asked if they knew of anybody who marks quilts and one of them does, but after she saw it she said it was too difficult. Came home and decided to do it myself. Have it all done but patches and panels. Eby had hauling and picked out some walnuts.

1/17/86 Friday
Fine weather. I made doughnuts. The Weaver's got here about 11:00 and we had time for visiting before lunch. Isaac and Elizabeth came to visit and brought Bradley from Linville Hill when school was out. He had a good day with 100% in spelling. The Weaver's went to Ebersole's to order a chair. We all went to Green Dragon after supper and bought some food and other things.

1/18/86 Saturday
Nice mild day. Eby had some hauling and Robert went along on one. I made things ready for dinner. I peeled my pineapple and cooked a quart. Grace gave me a new quilt pattern and did two yards of quilting. They left for home at 3:00 and I quilted till bedtime. Talked to Mabel and she said Amy went back to her home and is planning to go to The Home in February. They visited Menno on Thursday and he seemed real good.

1/26/86 Sunday
Some snow and rain. We went to Kinzer. Paul preached from Romans 15. Jay Hostetter was there and came here for dinner and visited this afternoon. I finished reading Betrayed. Mabel called and said she talked to Rachel and Menno is fine and can leave Heatherbank as soon as they can get him in some place. They plan to have sale and go to the Home.

1/28/86 Tuesday
Snow drifted and roads plowed. Eby did his regular hauling plus a few extras. No school because of the roads. I did a lot of quilting. Eby helped turn it around. A space craft exploded at nine miles up. I called Sanford and they plan to move on Thursday and are busy packing.

1/29/86 Wednesday
More snow and cold. Eby had some hauling and quit about 3:00 because the roads were getting slippy. I quilted all day. Did 30 yards. Paper is full of the space explosion. Seven persons lost their lives, five men and two women. No trace has been found.

2/4/86 Tuesday
Snow turned to rain. Eby did no hauling this morning. We were doubtful about the weather to go to help get ready for Amy and Menno's sale, but Uncle Charlie took us to Mt. Joy and helped to get the barn, little house, cellar and attic ready. Mabel and Sue helped sew tags on their clothing. Got home at 4:10. I ripped a bag of wool after supper.

2/22/86 Saturday
Cloudy and mild. We left for Virginia at 7:30 and arrived at Weaver's at 1:50. Drove in some snow and ate our lunch in a rest area. Nancy and Gary came from Sanford's about 3:00. Had some fog and snow. We had a nice time visiting. Jennie worked her evening shift. We went to bed late.

2/23/86 Sunday
Sunshine most all day. Had a recorded sermon from last Sunday. No one went to services. Sanford's came about 10:30 and had a good trip. Mary Alice came later. We had a good turkey dinner with many extras. Had a Christmas gift exchange this afternoon. We got a flashlight, candy, letter holder, two rug books, writing paper and a dollhouse set.

2/24/86 Monday
Cloudy with some snow. Robert went to work early. Grace and Jennie took the day off. We left for home at 10:00. I drove to rest area in West Virginia where we ate the turkey sandwiches that Grace made. Got home at 3:30. I cut 33 butterflies from the patches Grace and Nancy gave. Mabel called and said I am to help with Menno's sale.

2/27/86 Thursday
Cold and cleared. Eby had hauling. I washed car in garage so it would not freeze. Braided some rug. I called Zelma in the hospital and she seems resigned. People are saying that Jay is going to live with us.

3/3/86 Monday
Partly cloudy. Eby had hauling. I washed and ironed. Braided rug and wet all the yard wool and dried it outside. Jay was here and he hopes to sell his house and come to our apartment.

3/14/86 Friday
Very wet day. I did some cleaning and made sherbet and mints. Our freezer is not keeping things frozen properly. Eby looked at some new ones. He got a new burner for the stove and had hauling. Made a walnut cake. Caught three mice. Worked on rug after supper.

3/18/86 Tuesday
Fine weather. Eby was busy hauling and I took the King's to the foot doctor for a 5:00 appointment. The Stoltzfus Associates delivered our new Amana freezer which cost $499. They took the old one along. We moved all the food. I cleaned some yard and sowed the hot bed. Burned some trash and braided rug.

3/22/86 Saturday
A beautiful day. We took Clarence's to Jay's and he took us all to Mt. Joy for Menno's sale. A lot of relatives were there and they had a very good sale. Corner cupboard sold for $7000. Property sold for $68,400. Mary Alice and Ellen were there and Jonathan. Mary Alice got Grandma Martin's four kitchen chairs.

4/8/86 Tuesday
Partly cloudy and cooler. I cleaned the attic. Scrubbed most of floor. Eby had some extra hauling. There are two nice white leghorn roosters coming to visit. Peas are up.

4/10/86 Thursday
Cold and cloudy with snow flurries. I cleaned all the kitchen drawers and cupboards. A big job. Did the cleaning. Eby used the sweeper and had some hauling. I cooked some chicken for corn soup. Cut a bouquet of daffodils and narcissus.

4/13/86 Sunday
Cloudy and cool. Went to Kinzer. 85 there. Took Clarence's along to Samaritan Home for a program this afternoon. The Home is looking better each time we go. Sanford called and said the twins came at 5:30 and 5:45. Luke Tanner and Micah Yoder. All are well and he is excited. I called Elizabeth, Edgar's, Sue, Esther, Jim's to tell the news.

4/25/86 Friday
Fine weather. I cleaned the living room. Put the plants out. Eby busy hauling. He marked out the garden. I planted beans, limas, corn, pickles, salsify, beets, dill, lettuce, peppers and marigolds. We went to Abner's for a birthday dinner. I got gifts, candy, cake, napkins, tea towel, and soap lady.

5/2/86 Friday
Sunny and windy. Eby was busy hauling. I took Barbara home and the girls from Dutchway. I defrosted and cleaned the refrigerator. Elizabeth, Bradley, Joanne, Donnie and Linda, Ed and Karen and Matthew came with cake and ice cream and all the goodies for Daddy's birthday.

5/9/86 Friday
Clear and cool. Eby had hauling and harrowed some garden. I braided rug most all day. Tried to persuade Isaac to behave more sensible. Have a man overnight who came to Rough and Tumble. Rug measures 41 inches.

5/13/86 Tuesday
Weather just right. I hoed roses, trimmed some flower beds and hoed blueberries. Anna and Rosa brought some things for Jay. Sue called to say that Landis is going to have surgery for his colon. Sanford called and said Luke had his hernia surgery and seems to be doing well. I braided a lot of rug. Eby busy hauling.

5/15/86 Thursday
Cloudy and cool. Eby went to the store and had some hauling. I took Sadie and four girls to her home. Frank Weidman's and Lloyd Kreider's helped Jay move more of his things in. Eby brought Amos to work out a safe way for the stairs. I finished the third rug and started another one.

5/16/86 Friday
Warmer and dryer. I hauled some pupils and a teacher. Worked on rug. Vera helped Jay bring more things. He said he feels like running off. Eby busy hauling. Rodena called for help at Fire Hall. Called Sanford and Luke is doing good. The second railroad bridge was torn away tonight.

5/24/86 Saturday
A beautiful day. I worked on rug this forenoon and finished it by 8:30. We took Jay along to Ronks Fire Hall for the Senior Citizen Banquet. It was filled with many hungry oldsters. Eby had some hauling.

5/30/86 Friday
Fine warm day. Eby pumped the cesspool. Baked oatmeal cookies and a sponge cake. Made baked beans and lasagna. Boiled ham. Made strawberry preserves and did the cleaning. Picked a big pan of sugar peas. Sanford's came at 10:15. The twins slept all the way. They are two sweet little boys.

5/31/86 Saturday
The twins did not sleep too well and their day was not so quiet. We had a nice time visiting. Eby had some hauling. We picked six boxes of strawberries. Sanford and Tera took Jacob for a ride on the Strasburg Railroad. They took all three to the farm to see Elam's.

6/10/86 Tuesday
Pleasant day. I washed and ironed. Did some quilting. Eby had hauling. Jay took Clarence to MCC for the day. He picked up a catalogue for Pat at Hornings. I made a walnut cake and we took it and some ice cream for Jonathan's birthday this evening. His landscape job is an improvement.

6/12/86 Thursday
Cloudy and wet with two inches of rain. Eby had hauling all day. I did some weeding and planting at wheels. Planted the impatients in plastic containers. Planted marigolds at different places. Made oatmeal cookies and sent some to Jacob with Abner's. I

took rugs up this evening for them to take to Weaver's. Did some quilting. Called Jonathan about his picnic table. Karen's baby girl was born yesterday.

6/15/86 Sunday
Fine warm day. Went to Kinzer. Glen Hershey preached on Balaam and Balak. Went to Clarence's for dinner. Jay and Anna Slaymaker went with us to Kinzer this evening to see a film on the family by Dr. Dodson.

7/4/86 Friday
Fine weather. Eby had hauling. I was home all day. Eby harrowed the garden and I hoed it. Made a pot of vegetable soup. I did some quilting. Rhoda called and said they are all set to fly to England tomorrow.

7/6/86 Sunday
Very warm. Went to Kinzer. Paul preached on peace. We spent the afternoon at Betty Hoover's funeral at Old Road. She was 94. Had a quiet evening and did not go to see Dr. Dodson's film at Kinzer. A three-year-old Amish boy had his foot trampled and Clarence took him to the hospital.

7/10/86 Thursday
Beautiful day. Cooler. I quilted most all day after we found the piece that was lost from Eby's hearing aid. Eby had hauling. I picked almost a bucket of pickles. Esther helped me quilt this evening. Eby put the sprinkler on the pickles.

7/14/86 Monday
Breezy, hot and dry. Milton's left soon after 9:00 so that Doug can be back at school by 11:00. I picked pickles and got corn off for them. Eby had hauling and I washed and ironed. Sue Martin called and we made plans to go to Sanford's. Called Sanford and the dates suit. Had a letter from Sam and I wrote him one this evening.

7/17/86 Thursday
Partly cloudy and sultry. I wed the tea. Did four quarts of beets. Eby took corn to Esther, fish to Clarence's and bought quilt batting at Georgetown and got wheat germ at Rohrer's Mill. He had some hauling. He tried to silence the stove clock and stopped it and broke the timer. I put Mrs. McCasson's third quilt in and got some quilted.

7/24/86 Thursday
Sunny and warm. I mended Eby's hat. Cleaned Isaac's room. I picked lima beans and put five pints in freezer. Picked the pickles and canned two quarts. Eby harrowed the garden and I hoed most of it. Abram called and said they are going to Korea August 6. Milton's and their group are leaving for India tonight.

7/27/86 Sunday
A hot day. It rained a lot last night and flooded the new part of the Mennonite Home with 27 inches on the ground floor. Guests were evacuated. Went to Kinzer

and took a harvest sample. Paul preached a harvest sermon. We had a quick lunch and packed up frozen foods. Jay and Sue came with Uncle Charlie and we left for Richmond and found our way safely in 4 ½ hours. Found them fine and had a good supper. Jacob was happy to see us.

7/28/86 Monday
Still very warm. We enjoyed holding the twins and Sue helped bathe them. Had a nice morning and I made cow-in-the-garden for dinner and Tera made poppyseed cake. We left for Weaver's soon after 2:00 and got there at 5:30. Grace had a good supper for us. Had a nice evening visiting.

8/1/86 Friday
Very warm. Eby had some hauling. I did some cleaning and washed the car. Prepared some meals for Jay to serve Isaac and packed a lunch for us. Jonathan came here and put his car in our garage and we left for Edgar's. Stopped in Binghamton to eat our lunch. Drove through very heavy rain and got there by 8:00. Found them all in good health and they gave a good report on their trip to England.

8/3/86 Sunday
Sun, rain and pleasant weather. Went to Bethel Grove for services. Rhoda served us a good dinner and we left for home at 2:30 and got here non-stop at 7:00. Abram and Pat called and said they are ready to leave for Korea Wednesday to visit Sam.

8/9/86 Saturday
Sunny and warm. Eby hauled Ike and others. I cleaned off some garden to cultivate for late planting. Did some quilting and a little cleaning. Sue Martin called. Steven Benson got a life sentence for the murder of his mother and adopted brother.

8/19/86 Tuesday
Warm and sultry. I was home all day. Eby had hauling. I washed and ironed. Made oatmeal cookies. Scrubbed the little rugs. Cleaned the basement room. Sorted the papers for tying up. I picked almost a bushel of limas. Eby sowed the turnips. Had a long talk with Mabel. Abram called from San Francisco and said the flights are overbooked and they will have to wait to come home until tomorrow.

8/23/86 Saturday
A fine day for reunion at Camp Morehart. Big rain after dark. Had a good night. Family members kept coming in the forenoon. Our dinner was cow-in-the-garden, cole slaw, applesauce, baked potatoes, drinks, pie and ice cream. All had plenty. Had a good time and the new babies were Angela Dietzel, Susanne Miller, and Luke and Micah. A total of 65 were there. Played quoits, trivia games and others.

8/24/86 Sunday
Beautiful and cooler. All had a good night. Fredric's went to Jonathan's and Sanford's and the Gourley's to a motel. Grace made mush for breakfast. It was the first mush

and milk for some. Ray was in charge of our devotions, which was good. Had some reports from those who were in England, Korea and India. Had plenty of food left for lunch. Everyone on their way by 1:50.

9/7/86 Sunday
Fine weather. Cooler. Went to Kinzer. Ira Nafziger preached and they came here for dinner. Had a nice visit. I read the book on bishop Jonas Martin. Pat called and said we should be at the church for Greg's wedding by 10:15.

9/13/86 Saturday
Beautiful day for Greg's wedding. Isaac and Elizabeth came at 7:00 and he drove our car. The wedding was held at a Catholic Church in Lewistown and the reception was held at the Belleville Mennonite School. We stopped at Jim's a short time on our way home. Weaver's had car trouble after 80 miles and had to miss the wedding. Abram's, Isaac's, Milton's, Ray's, Dale's and Edgar's were at the wedding.

9/21/86 Sunday
Fine weather. Took Jay along to Kinzer this morning and evening. Had a Gideon speaker from New Jersey and groups from Hershey's, Paradise and Mt. Pleasant to sing special with some instruments this evening. Ladies had no coverings and wore earrings and necklaces. Some congregational singing.

9/25/86 Thursday
Cloudy and warm with some showers. Eby busy hauling. I baked oatmeal cookies before breakfast. I worked on the bank and got it finished. Looks better. Eby trimmed the mimosa tree. He has an idea for landscaping the bank for $3000. I got stung by a yellow jacket. Finished reading the book about Jonas Martin and church split in 1893.

9/27/86 Saturday
Eby had little hauling. Milton's went to New Holland and went shopping with Mother Coy. Came back about 8:00. I made pies and things ready for tomorrow. Grace called and said Virginia had a good Relief Sale. My rugs came to $910 and the quilt sale totalled $65,000.

10/9/86 Thursday
Sunny and warm. Eby had hauling. I cleaned some cupboards before breakfast. Cleaned the dining room and bathroom. Made sandwich spread. Pulled down some lima bean poles and shelled about two pints. Eby got two bags of walnuts from Katie and Lydia. Mabel called and said she could not find a coat for her price and style. I got a $200 check for the quilt I did.

10/28/86 Tuesday
Fine weather. Eby busy hauling. I washed and ironed. I boiled the cider I bought from Dayton Hostetter because it was dirty. Painted the board with house number

and used up the can of white paint to touch up some spots in the house. I worked on Mary Alice's rug wool. Amos Hoover dropped off 24 nice quinces.

10/29/86 Wednesday
Beautiful day. Eby busy hauling. Went to Linville Hill School for Grandparents Day. I was the oldest Grandparent. It was a nice thing with the classes singing. Stopped at Clarence's and gave Mabel some quinces. Went to Dutchway and got $38 worth of groceries. Finished cutting Mary Alice's rug wool.

11/2/86 Sunday
Cloudy day. Went to Kinzer. Paul preached on Stone Throwing. The "75 and older" were served a very good dinner in our new basement with kitchen. Pictures were taken of us and Linford Hershey did a drawing and his wife talked. Sanford called and said their trip is off because of Aunt Florence's death.

11/16/86 Sunday
Nice mild day. Edgar's went to Akron Church where Jonathan goes. We went to Kinzer. Had Jeanne Hershey give her near drowning experience. Edgar's and Jonathan were here for dinner before they left. Spent evening at home. Called Amy.

11/25/86 Tuesday
Sunny and mild. Got started early roasting the four capons. Had them roasted by noon and some cut up. Had them all done and things ready to take along when Mae came at 4:30. She ate supper and we packed things into her car and were off to Dogwood Road with capon, gravy broth, celery, limas, corn, pickles and some pots and tableware. I got a call that Dorothy Westman is hospitalized with a tumor on her lung.

11/27/86 Thursday
A pretty day, mild. Dale and Mae had everything well organized and the food was ready by 1:00 to serve to 36 family members. Had a nice time and Sanford's came here afterward.

11/28/86 Friday
Good weather. Sanford and Tera had a quiet night. They went to Dutchway and to see Kathleen Denlinger. This afternoon Sanford and Jacob went to the Strasburg Railroad Museum. This evening they all went up to Elam King's. Esther came to see the twins this evening. I mended Jacob's blanket and helped with Micah and Luke.

11/29/86 Saturday
Fine weather. Eby had hauling. Sanford's started for home at 10:00. The babies were fine this morning. I packed a snack for them. Tera washed up the dishes and put the bedrooms in order and more. I did some cleaning and washed the car.

12/6/86 Saturday
A fine day. Harold Groff picked us up with Clarence's at 6:30 and took us to the depot for the train to New York. Changed for Long Island and arrived at Stony Brook at 2:15. Milton met us and we had a nice visit and a good supper. They invited the Soderstrom's too. Doug called up and we had a nice talk with him.

12/7/86 Sunday
Pleasant weather. Had our breakfast and went to church at Setauket. The pastor's sermon was on Fear. Had a nice service. They took us to the water and then home for dinner. We ate at the school. Saw the Treichler's, Peter Hailes and many others. Folks were friendly. Took the train to Penn Station and got home at 9:45. Mildred met us at the depot. We were confused on the way from Philadelphia because of riding backwards.

12/10/86 Wednesday
Sunny and mild. Eby busy hauling. I went to the store and brought Lena from New Holland. Worked on my patches. We went to Midweek. Ralph and Katherine Graham talked on the parable of the talents. And Ralph mentioned eating out on Sunday, the devotional covering, and the communion cup. An egg plant burned at Ephrata with more than a million dollar loss.

12/17/86 Wednesday
Fine weather. Eby had hauling. I went to Dutchway for cocoanuts and got them ready. Went out to Christ Glick's for a diary. Worked on flapjacks and date balls and rolled some dough in balls. Isaac, Elizabeth and Bradley came this evening. They are planning their new house in three years.

12/18/86 Thursday
Cloudy. Eby not so busy. I was very busy baking cookies. Did more than 1000. They got real nice. Eby put the peanuts on the sand tarts. Charlie sent me a solid maple cutting board and Daddy an umbrella and two pairs of socks. I finished Christmas cards and letters this evening.

12/20/86 Saturday
Cloudy. I did the cleaning. Eby had some hauling. I made apple dumplings for supper. Gave Jay three. Cut 42 panel patches for Martha's quilt. Got word this morning from Olga Link that Dorothy Westman died last night. Talked to Mabel.

12/25/86 Thursday
A cloudy, mild Christmas. Had an easy morning and left for Abram's at 10:15. Had a hearty welcome and a delicious dinner of chicken breasts, blue fish, potato filling, salad, cranberries, gingerbread with applesauce and frozen topping, four kinds of candy and nuts. They showed us slides of their Korean trip. They gave Daddy a sweater and flannel pajamas. I got a framed picture of me, Christmas notes and dollhouse table and stove. Got home at 5:30.

12/29/86 Monday
Sunny and mild. Eby did his morning hauls and spent three hours in bed before the evening runs. Then he went to bed again at 6:00 feeling very groggy. I put some onion poultices on till 10:00. Milton worked on his books for information. I washed and ironed and worked on quilt.

12/30/86 Tuesday
Cloudy and some sun. Milton did Eby's hauls and took three women to Dutchway and then drove our car to the Historical Center to do some research. I came home and gave Mabel the peas and sauer kraut for New Year's dinner. Barbara and the boys came about 2:15 and left to shop. Eby did a drive this forenoon and is back in bed with a temperature of 103.

12/31/86 Wednesday
A fine mild day. Eby in bed till 5:00. Got up, shaved and ate supper at the table with Milton's. I made a lemon sponge pie and ham for supper. Did some cleaning. Caseworker came to interview Isaac. Eby's temperature is down to 101 this evening.

1987

1/1/87 Thursday
Cloudy and began snowing at 4:30. Eby slept well and his fever is down to 100. He was up most of the day. Ate better. I went to Clarence's alone. All were there but Eby. Had our first carry in dinner. It went well.

1/3/87 Saturday
Clear and in the 30's. Eby got up and went for the paper and to the bank. He took containers to the butcher for our pork. Spent the balance of the day resting, sleeping, coughing and eating a little. I did a little cleaning and some quilting. Talked to Mabel.

1/4/87 Sunday
Fine weather. I went to Kinzer alone. Eby is still coughing. He ate dinner and feels good so far. Went to bed at 7:30. I read and wrote letters. Jim called and said they have a lot of drifting snow and he got a 9 point deer. Nancy called to ask about Daddy. She said National Car has sold for $410,000,000. Dale called and said they have the flu. Picked it up at the Weaver's at Christmas.

1/10/87 Saturday
Snow, rain and slush. Eby had hauling. Isaac's left Bradley here while they went to Hershey Kurtz's sale. Jonathan brought his girlfriend this afternoon. I made apple dumplings and rice pudding. Quilted after supper and studied Sunday School lesson. Charlie called and said he will start on last trip to Pacific Islands tomorrow.

1/22/87 Thursday
Snowed. Eby did his morning hauling and stayed in the rest of the day watching it snow. I got milk at Elam's and quilted the rest of the day. Mary Alice called and said they are snowed in, so won't be coming this weekend.

1/24/87 Saturday
Clear and cold. Some roads are not very well opened. Eby did only one haul. He used the cleaner. The $98.00 repair makes it clean better. I did some quilting.

2/3/87 Tuesday
Fine day with the snow melting. Eby was busy hauling. I did some quilting. Vernon was here and he is in the process of moving Isaac to the Samaritan Home. Minnie called and said Robert Neff is very low. Nancy called and said they have bought a new house and sold theirs for a nice profit.

2/12/87 Thursday
Cloudy with snow flurries. Eby had hauling and I took his lunch. I washed and ironed. Made a cherry pie and a sweet potato pudding. Did some quilting. Isaac seems pleased about going to the Home.

2/16/87 Monday
Nice day. Sunny and cold. Eby had a good day hauling. I brought Barbara home and stopped to have her glasses fixed. Helped Isaac pack and Vernon took him to the Samaritan Home. I put half the binding on Martha's quilt. We burned Isaac's mattress and I took some things from his room.

2/23/87 Monday
Snowed and we have 19 inches. Drive was not opened till 12:30. Eby had some hauling this afternoon and evening. I washed and ironed. I put some new pictures in the window frames in the kitchen. Did some odd jobs. Called Rhoda to hear about Andrea's back. No surgery or brace.

2/25/87 Wednesday
Fine day. Eby had hauling. I took Jake King, the painter, home. I did a lot of odd jobs cleaning some corners. Esther came to take a picture of Martha's quilt. Sue called and said Abram was to be on T.V. this evening about the Amish study they are doing.

3/1/87 Monday
Showers and March winds. I washed and ironed. Dried on porch and in basement. Eby had an accident in Willow Street when he took Gideon Stoltzfus to get his meat at the butcher's. He called me to take Amos Beiler and his little girl to Dr. Rutt's. Eby has a bumped knee and Gideon some cracked ribs. The station wagon is a wreck. I am shook up. Eby's back is not so good. I put a bandage around it at bedtime. We are so thankful that no one is seriously injured.

3/5/87 Friday
Nice day. Eby did his regular hauls. We took Clarence's along to John Noll's funeral at East Petersburg. I repaired a dress and started quilting Laura's cushion. Cleaned up spring coils from ashes of Isaac's mattress.

3/9/87 Tuesday
Cold and windy. Eby had some hauling. I finished the cushions for Laura and Martha. Got the ten birthday cards for March ready for mailing. Cleaned the sewing machine drawers.

3/11/87 Thursday
Sunny and cold. Eby had a busy day driving. I cleaned the stove and refrigerator. Scrubbed eight rugs. Raked some leaves and burned them. Made a pan of baked beans. Cut some patches and have cramps in both legs. Four New Jersey teenagers committed suicide.

3/15/87 Monday
A fine day. I washed and ironed. Cut first ham and bacon. Made a jelly roll and an apple pie. Eby had hauling. He sold the wrecked car for $100. Nancy got here about 7:00 and we had a few hours for visiting.

3/17/87 Wednesday
A beautiful day. I made doughnuts. Nancy worked some on a wallhanging. Joanne and the children came for some pussy willows. Nancy and I took a drive to Intercourse to see quilts at People Place's and the Country Store. Nancy and I looked at pictures.

3/20/87 Saturday
Daddy did no hauling. Leroy disced the garden. Eby put lime on the garden. I finished cleaning and Sanford's got here by 10:00 and had lunch. Weaver's and Mary Alice came at 2:00. All the family came to Bird-in-Hand Restaurant where we had an Anniversary Celebration. Ate a good meal and had a nice time visiting with an interesting program. Charlie and Ed are spending the night here.

3/21/87 Sunday
Fine weather. Charlie and Ed had breakfast with us and left this forenoon for Washington after we left for church. We went to Kinzer. 101 there. Some of Edgar's, Sanford's, Rays's and the Weaver's came here from the Harvest Drive Motel for dinner. They had table set up and a good vegetable soup with cold cuts and cheese ready when we got home. Milton's came from Coy's. Everyone was gone by 3:00. Had a quiet evening.

3/22/87 Monday
Sunny and warm. I washed and worked in the garden all day. Eby helped with the pea wire and I planted peas, onions, potatoes, radishes, spinach, beets, carrots, six roots of asparagus and the rose Charlie brought. Eby went to the eye doctor and has a cataract. He went to a sewer meeting this evening.

3/25/87 Wednesday
Fine warm day. I worked on Becky's wallhanging while I watched to keep the chickens off the garden this morning. I finished raking the back yard and bagged the junk. Eby had hauling. Jay cut meat at Byler's.

4/6/87 Monday
Everything is white and it's still snowing. Daffodils are peeping above the snow. I washed and ironed and worked on the wallhanging. Eby had very little hauling except his regulars.

4/12/87 Sunday
A nice April day with some showers. Went to Kinzer. Had our footwashing service. Mark Leaman preached on forgiveness. Isaac's came for lunch and took us to see Ed Miller's this afternoon. Had a tour of their 25 greenhouses.

4/21/87 Tuesday
I hoed and planted all day. Beans, corn, limas, pickles, salsify, dill, onions, elephant ear, etc. Temperature in the 80's. Eby had some hauling. Landis had a colostomy today. Eby is coughing.

4/25/87 Saturday
Eby took the girls to work. I cut a dress and started to sew it. We decided to visit Landis at Good Samaritan Hospital in Lebanon. He is not feeling so good yet. Met Milton's at Yoder's Restaurant in New Holland. Mother Coy came too and we were treated to a delicious dinner. Milton's and Doug were here for the night.

4/29/87 Wednesday
Windy and cool. I went to Elam's for milk. Eby hauled Ike and his regulars. Jay cut meat. Landis is still in Intensive Care and his doctor said he has terminal cancer. I cut the rug wool and started braiding.

5/2/87 Saturday
Showery and mild. I made pies and beef macaroni for lunch. Bathed and got ready and had lunch for Charlie. He got here at 12:00. We ate and left for Bancroft School to visit Doug. We drove around and saw Haddonfield. Took all out for dinner to Denny's. Got home in good time and Charlie got some big stones and water cress.

5/5/87 Tuesday
Cleared and is cool. I washed and ironed. Eby had some hauling. I braided some rug. It is one yard long. Elizabeth called to say they are bringing supper up for Daddy's birthday. Ham and gravy, mashed potatoes, peas and carrots, salad, ice cream and cake.

5/9/87 Sunday
Beautiful day. We went to Kinzer. Paul preached a Mother's Day sermon, "6 Mothers from the Bible." Spent a quiet afternoon and evening. My eye is the same. Landis still in the hospital. Emma passed away at 11:30.

5/13/87 Thursday
Good weather. Had breakfast at 5:30 and Eby got done hauling by 8:00. Isaac's came for us and drove our car to Emma's funeral at Manheim. Burial at East Petersburg. Had a big lunch at the Church. Ray came to the funeral and took me to Samaritan Hospital to visit Uncle Landis. Abram, Pat and Sam went too and got us in off visiting hours. He is very sick but plans to go home tomorrow. Braided some rug.

5/14/87 Friday
Some sun and showers. Did some braiding. Eby had hauling. I had an appointment with Dr. Stoltzfus for an eye checkup. He said I have an ulcer in my cornea and gave me drops.

5/17/87 Sunday
Pretty day. We left at 6:30 for Abram's to go along to Becky's graduation at Juniata College. All went as planned. They took us to a restaurant for our dinner and Pat had a pan of lasagna for our supper when we stopped. Got home at 8:15. Dwight Groff and Jay Meck were in the lot at Kinzer and the lot fell to Jay. Called Josephine from Abram's and she said all is planned to move Landis home tomorrow.

5/19/87 Tuesday
Wet and cool. I worked on rug all day. Landis passed away at 4:30 this morning. I called most of the children. Did a lot of phoning.

5/20/87 Wednesday
A wet day. Had a poor night. I made cracker pudding for Josephine. Did up work and went to eye doctor. He looked it over and said to come next Tuesday. Picked Mabel up and went to Jay's, and Uncle Charlie took us all to Landis'. James and Paul were helping Josephine to keep busy.

5/22/87 Friday
We took Clarence's to Jay's and we all went in their van to Landis' funeral at Stauffer's Church. Abram's, Isaac's and Jim's were there along with many cousins and friends. Frank Zeiger preached a good sermon on Psalms 90. Had a nice lunch for a lot of people. Got home at 3:20. Braided some rug. Kim mowed the yard.

6/2/87 Tuesday
A warm day. Eby had hauling most of the day. I finished up the corner and planted some flowers. Cut the tea and made a pot of concentrate. Put four pints of strawberries

in the new freezer. Went to doctor for my eye. He said it is better, but come again. Braided some rug.

6/6/87 Saturday
A beautiful day. Eby's eye is real good after his cataract surgery yesterday. He can see better with the operated eye than his good one. Elizabeth and Bradley stopped in to see how Daddy is doing. I did cleaning, some trimming and made a cake. Picked four quarts of strawberries.

6/8/87 Monday
Fine day. Worked on rug. Picked four quarts of berries. Elizabeth took us to doctor's office and he is very well pleased with Daddy's eye. He can drive. The hook on Jay's door fell through the eye and they tried to get the door off in vain. He took the ladder and went in through the window.

6/11/87 Thursday
Eby busy hauling. I made two shoo fly pies for Boston sale and an apple pie for supper. Picked sugar peas. Braided some rug. Mike came for supper. He is having vacation before starting his job as a lawyer. Grace called and said Steve got a job near Washington.

6/13/87 Saturday
Good weather. Eby had some hauling. I did some cleaning and prepared for company. Sanford got here soon after 10:00. We had a nice day visiting. Sanford and Jacob took a ride on the Strasburg Railroad. Jacob had a time catching fireflies.

6/18/87 Thursday
Fine day. I took Sue Diener to Beiler's for dark sweet cherries. I picked 11 lbs. Picked off the peas and pulled them out. Put 7 pints in freezer and 2 pints of sugar peas. Putting cesspool on the garden. Braided some rug. Eby went to eye doctor and got a good report.

6/22/87 Monday
Very warm and we had a lot of rain. We took the pea wire out and Eby worked up the ground. I planted sweet corn, pickles and beets. Trained the limas. Eby had hauling. We got word this evening that Bradley was injured when run over by the tractor when Isaac was making drain field. He is in the hospital. I called Abram's. I finished second rug.

6/24/87 Wednesday
A fine warm day. I canned five quarts of blueberries and raspberries. Went to Dutchway. Did some cleaning. Went up to Dietzel's and went with Joanne to visit Bradley. He had therapy and some liquids. Elizabeth was there all day. Mary Alice came at 4:00.

6/25/87 Thursday
Warm day. Eby had hauling. Mary Alice and I went to Georgetown Store and she got fabrics for wallhangings. I got some notions. Eby and Mary Alice went to cemetery to check lots. Mary Alice took me along to the hospital to visit Bradley. He was brighter and is getting food.

6/30/87 Tuesday
Pleasant. Eby had hauling. I picked the black raspberries. Worked on rug and got a few rings added. Hoed the garden. This evening we met the gravestone man from New Holland and ordered our gravestone. Becky left for Austria.

7/13/87 Monday
A warm sunny day. Eby had some hauling and he cut off weeds from the bank. I washed and ironed. Picked blueberries and red raspberries. Planted beans, dill, beets and carrots. Hoed some garden and thinned late corn. Bradley came home from the hospital after three weeks.

7/18/87 Saturday
Fine weather. Eby had a few morning hauls. Grace and Robert got here about 10:45. After dinner we went to Maggie Hershey's sale. It was very good. Next we went to Isaac's and saw all their family. They were having a chicken barbecue supper. We went on to Longwood Gardens and ate a snack, saw some flowers and their fountain show. It was very pretty.

7/23/87 Thursday
A hot day. I went with Eby to have his eye checked. All was well and the doctor took three warts off his eyelids. I drove home. Had a letter from Milton in Pakistan. I braided rug this forenoon.

8/4/87 Tuesday
A hot day. Eby did his drives and brought the painters. Rhoda and Edgar picked us up at 8:30 and took us out to Jim's. I took a bushel of limas along and we shelled them before dinner. Pat had a good dinner for us. Greg and Cindy were there. We stopped on the way home at Benner's Restaurant. Edgar's went to Jonathan's for the night. Nancy called and we had a long talk. She is looking for a new job.

8/8/87 Saturday
Hot and sultry. I went with Clarence, Mabel and Esther Clark to the Hans Herr House for quilting at their Craft Days from 9:00-12:00. Went to Granville Clark's funeral this afternoon. Canned two quarts of pickles.

8/15/87 Saturday
Warm. Eby had some hauling. We attended the 40th reunion of the David Hostetter family at Intercourse Park with 35 attending. Had frankfurters and finger foods.

The ice cream truck did not make it in time. Milton called and said he came home from India this afternoon and had a tomato sandwich.

8/17/87 Monday
Very hot. I washed and ironed. Fredric's have their baby from India. Eby busy hauling. I picked tomatoes, pickles and yellow beans. An airplane crash in Detroit killed 156.

8/20/87 Thursday
Nice weather. Eby busy hauling. I cut the soy beans and he helped pick some off and cleaned up the stalks. Jay helped pick some out and I put twelve pints in the freezer. Jonathan left a large head of cabbage on porch on his way home from his Grandma's funeral. Rhoda sent it.

8/28/87 Friday
Eby did hauling till 1:30. I baked two cakes and got the food loaded in our car. We got ready and left for our reunion at Camp Morehart. Stopped at Lancaster Court House to pick up a paper for Elam King. Becky and Sam were on hand when we got there and we got things going for supper. Had a nice evening.

8/29/87 Saturday
Had a quiet night. Mike was met at the airport in the night. Had chicken and beef pot pie for dinner. It was liked and all consumed. 54 at the reunion. Isaac was not feeling well and could not eat. Ray blew bubbles for children, had quoit pitching, some table games and ball. Lots of talking and sharing. Abram, Milton and Sam gave reports on China, India and Korea. Nice sunny day, cooler. Some went home after supper.

8/30/87 Sunday
Fine weather. Had a good night. Breakfast and lunch were served with some food left over. Our service was in charge of Dale and Mae. Jonathan had our devotions with a responsive reading. Sang about four songs accompanied by Rosa and the keys. Some historical facts by Dale and reports on the lives of Bishop Isaac Eby and Grandpa Martin. Rosa drove our car to Jonathan's and we were home by 4:00. Nancy called for a reunion report.

9/5/87 Saturday
Good weather. I made things ready for company. Scrubbed the porches. We went to Ada Buckwalter's funeral this afternoon at Hershey's. Went out to the cemetery to see our gravestone that was put up last week.

9/25/87 Friday
Fine weather. Eby did his morning hauls. Had our breakfast and packed up for our Virginia weekend. Started at 9:30 in Dale's car. Stopped at a rest stop and ate our lunch and arrived in Charlottesville at 3:20 to visit Mary Alice. Had a nice time.

Left for Expoland at 5:30 and had our supper, looked at the quilts and went on to Robert Weaver's for the night. Nancy and Gerry came there too.

9/26/87 Saturday
Had a good night and got off to the sale by 7:15. Had breakfast and marked our seats. Looked over the quilts and the other things set up for sale. The sale was good. My four rugs came to $690. Had plenty to eat and met some folks. It was a good day. Had supper at Weaver's with Mary Alice, Ellen, Nancy and Gerry and Dale's. An evening of visiting. Sanford's all came to the sale.

10/1/87 Thursday
A fine day. We left Ray's this morning and stopped at a museum and the Boehm factory and showroom in Trenton. Saw the beautiful things that are too expensive for us. Went on to Surf City to Dr. Stoltz's house. Went out for dinner and had supper at the house. Took a walk on the beach and just took it easy watching the Atlantic Ocean. Helped Jane with her crib quilt. California had an earthquake. 6.1 on the scale.

10/3/87 Saturday
Cloudy with showers. Martha went with Ray to work at the hospital. I watched T.V. with Laura. Eby went with Ray to do some horse surgery. I helped Jane with dinner. Jonathan and Ruth came for dinner and to take us home. We left at 2:30 in the rain. Found all well here. I called Mabel and Clarence is doing well. I called Nancy and they were shaken and scared with the earthquake but had no damage

10/15/87 Thursday
White frost and sunny day. I was home all day. Eby had hauling. I made 102 sweet potato croquettes. Richard asked to borrow $2.00 for gas so I asked him if he'd like to work it out doing some garden work. He carried off the lima poles and took down the pea wire. Victor Groff is in the hospital for a heart problem.

10/16/87 Friday
Fine sunny day. I made about four gallons of sauer kraut. Did some cleaning. Washed the car. Cleaned off some of the garden and picked flower seeds. Eby had hauling. Rescuers are working to rescue a baby from a dry well in Texas.

10/20/87 Tuesday
Cloudy. Eby was hauling and I was home all day. He had new tires put on the station wagon. I planted some flowers and put the cactus in our bedroom. Trimmed some bushes. Had a letter from Nancy and they are selling their house and looking for jobs in Virginia. Wrote a big letter to Nancy.

10/31/87 Saturday
A beautiful day. Eby took the girls to work and we left for New York on the 8:30 train from Lancaster. Arrived at Penn Station where Milton met us. He, Barbara, and Debbie, the school nurse took us to have a boat ride on Circle Line to see the City

from the water. It was a nice relaxing way to see and hear about all the important places. Next we saw Rockefeller Center, a cathedral where a Catholic wedding was in progress. From there we met Jane Wai, who invited us to share in a dinner for her granddaughter's birthday at a Chinese Restaurant where we had eight courses of fine food. Saw Doug's new place on our way to Stony Brook.

11/1/87 Sunday
Beautiful day. Had a good night and went with Milton's to Setauket for a 9:00 service. Heard a good sermon on Stewardship from their pastor. Had a good dinner at the school. Milton showed us some slides of Pakistan, and an Indian neighbor and her two children came for a short visit. Had a very good day. Saw Milton's garden and lawn with flowers.

11/8/87 Sunday
A mild day. Went to Kinzer. Spent afternoon and evening at home reading. Jay chatted a while. Charlie called and plans to go to Hawaii tomorrow for six days and then to Australia for a week to teach doctors who are in health programs and will be serving in the Pacific Islands.

11/16/87 Monday
I washed. Eby had hauling and Jay went to the Horse Sale. I raked a lot of leaves and Margie called from next door and said she could not take the smoke when Eby burned them, so he watered it out. Esther came to quilt and invited Pearl Lapp and she came and did five patches while I did two. We took Anna Slaymaker along to a meeting at Kinzer. Had a talk on astronomy. Eby did not care for it.

11/25/87 Wednesday
Eby had hauling. I got the turkey, croquettes, limas, celery, pickles and a few other things ready when Linda came for me and we found our way to Dale's after some missed turns. Mae had everything under control and I had an easy afternoon. We went to see the Christmas lights and they were not turned on.

11/26/87 Thursday.
Had a good night and helped Dale and Mae set up the tables for Thanksgiving dinner. I made the gravy and Mae got things put in place and dinner was ready to serve at 1:15. The Weaver's got here first. Abram's were a little late because they had an Amish wedding at Shippensburg. Had plenty of good food and nice visiting. 35 people in all. Got home by 6:20 and quilted.

12/5/87 Saturday
Colder. I made a cake for the crafts sale at the Fire Hall. Helped from 10:00 to 12:00. Took it easy till Dale and Mae came to take us out. Kathleen Denlinger took us all to Willow Valley for a good meal and to the Hans Herr House for the Christmas tour. It was a real treat and we got home by 9:30.

12/25/87 Friday
Dark, cloudy, mild and drizzly. Had an easy morning and went to Donald Ibach's for dinner. Had a nice time and a good dinner with Isaac's family. Got home at 5:30. Had a chat with Jay.

12/28/87 Monday
Cloudy with some snow. Eby had a couple hauls and chickened out by afternoon. I washed and ironed. Worked on crib quilt. Put balance of cookies in freezer. Called Milton's and Doug is moved home and will be going to his new place next Monday.

12/31/87 Thursday
Sunny and not so cold. Snow is melting. I did the cleaning. Sorted the sweet potatoes as some have dry rot. Eby had some hauling. I got all the carrots out that were buried and got some ready for tomorrow.

1988

1/1/88 Friday
Cloudy and mild. Eby had off and we spent the day at the Mennonite Home where Menno and Amy had reservations for our annual New Year dinner. I took peas and carrots and cookies. Miriam had prepared good pork and sauer kraut. All family members were there. Menno was not so good. We had a nice time.

1/8/88 Friday
We are snowed in. Eby went for paper and to bank. He had the day off. Jay was in too. I finished the third quilt top for Sewing Circle and started another one.

1/10/88 Sunday
Sunny and cold. Went to Kinzer. Had Jonathan, Ruth Keidel, Abram, Pat and Sam for dinner. Had a nice visit. Jay visited at the Home. Spent the evening reading. Jay visited for a while.

1/13/88 Wednesday
Clear and not so cold. Jay went early with Ken Mast's to the Farm Show at Harrisburg. Very icy and Eby did no morning hauling. He took his driver's test at 1:30 and failed. Did his runs this evening. I worked on scrap book. Made a pan of baked beans. Cleaned snow off the front porch. Cleaned the car with warm water in garage.

1/19/88 Tuesday
Partly cloudy in the forties. I finished the fifth comfort top. Worked on the counted cross stitch that Charlie gave me. Too icy for driving this morning. Eby took his second test and failed. I am some disappointed.

1/22/88 Friday
Good weather. I did some cleaning. Eby had hauling this forenoon and evening. This afternoon he took his driver's test for the third time and passed on everything. It was an answer to my prayers. We both felt a big relief. Isaac's came this evening. Bradley has a lot of pain.

1/23/88 Saturday
Fine weather with snow showers. I made some pies. Sanford's came about 10:00 and we had a good time with Jacob and the twins. They took a drive this afternoon and I went with them to see the rug that Kathleen Denlinger is making for them. Eby had a couple hauls and had a restful day. They took the boys to Elam's.

2/1/88 Monday
Mild day. Snow is almost gone. I washed and ironed. Finished hemming crib quilt. Cleaned up bedroom. Had a long talk with Mabel. Made two quilt patches. Jay left for Florida at 2:30 A.M. Jennie Weaver went to Hawaii.

2/10/88 Wednesday
A beautiful day. I sorted the sweet potatoes and made 45 croquettes. Sprouted the potatoes. Cleaned the freezer room. Gave molding the third coat. Bradley went to the Hershey Medical Center.

2/11/88 Thursday
Nice day and began snowing at dark. Eby did some hauling. I worked on sorting and cutting patches all day. Isaac's stayed with Abram's overnight and Bradley was in the operating room for four hours. They did work with instruments and put off surgery for six weeks. He may come home tomorrow. Amy called to say Menno is not so good and has been moved to intermediate care.

3/14/88 Monday
A fine day. Eby had a busy day. Mary Alice and I went to Lebanon to Dale's Agway Store and bought seeds and lime and fertilizer. Dale showed us his house and we stopped to visit Aunt Josephine. She seemed fine. Got home at 5:30. After supper we marked some of Mary Alice's wallhanging.

3/17/88 Thursday
Clear and cold. I made a pan of soap. Cleaned drawers and bottom cupboards in kitchen. Worked on rug. Eby busy hauling. Had a card from Charlie in Hawaii. Sue had her surgery and was in the O.R. from 11:00 till 3:45. Abram called.

3/23/88 Wednesday
Sunny and warmer. Eby had hauling this afternoon. I worked on rug. Cleaned the bed in our room. Sue fell and broke her hip. Abram called and said they would like to take us out to eat for our anniversary.

3/24/88 Thursday
A fine day. Warmer. I cleaned six closets. Leroy disced our garden. Eby had some hauling. Martha Burkholder called to say Sue was having surgery to repair her hip. I braided some rug. Abram and Pat came from a meeting in Philadelphia and took us to Gap Diner for our anniversary. Very good.

3/28/88 Monday
Sunny and cool. I washed and ironed. Stirred up some oatmeal cookies. Eby had some hauling. The Mennonite Home called and said they have a room for Jay. I trimmed the raspberries and cleaned the chick weed from the red ones. Sam called and said he would meet us at the Philadelphia depot on Monday. Braided some rug.

3/31/88 Thursday
We left Lancaster depot at 7:15 for Richmond. Sanford, the boys, Nancy and Gerry met us at 2:15 in Richmond. Tera had a good supper for all of us and we went with Nancy and Gerry to spend the night. We did some planting for Sanford's. Put in asparagus and he has azaleas and pansies to plant tomorrow. His yard, fence and patio are very pretty.

4/1/88 Friday
Sanford and Jacob took us to Mary Alice's in the forenoon and Nancy and Gerry came around noon. We had a good time planting asparagus, peas, onions, lettuce, carrots and potatoes. She and Ellen served us lunch and we went to Nancy's for the night. We put Mary Alice's wallhanging in the frame. Looked at the Abe Lincoln film for a while.

4/2/88 Saturday
I started quilting before breakfast and Nancy worked on it too. Robert, Grace, Jennie, Charlie, Nancy, Gerry, Mary Alice, Daddy and me were all at Sanford's for a cookout on the new patio. Had a nice time together. Charlie left for Washington and we went with Nancy and Gerry.

4/3/88 Sunday
The Weaver's and us stayed at Nancy and Gerry's. Robert and Gerry went to the Sunrise Service and Robert took Nancy and us the Methodist Church for the Easter Service. We all had a good dinner of ham, turkey, new potatoes, carrots, green beans, salads, ice cream and bunny cake made by Ellen. Luke and Micah got real tired. This evening we watched balance of Abe Lincoln film.

4/4/88 Monday
Nancy took us to the 9:15 train and Sanford and the boys were there to see us off. Ate Nancy's good lunch in Washington. Sam met us in Philadelphia and took us by taxi to see his room and campus and helped us board our train and we arrived home by 6:00.

4/12/88 Tuesday
Cloudy and cold. Eby had a full day of hauling. I cleaned the windows and washed the curtains. Bradley had his surgery at Hershey Medical Center for eight hours and the surgeon is pleased with results. Braided some rug. I called Mabel and she said she took some food for Jay's. Sue is doing her best, very pale.

4/15/88 Friday
Cool with evening showers. Eby had hauling and mowed some yard. I did some cleaning. Went with Joanne to visit Bradley at Hershey Medical Center. He seemed real good. Ben, Paul and Fay Clark came to serve us communion because we were in Virginia on Sunday.

4/21/88 Thursday
Sunny, cool and windy. Eby hauling all day. Braided rug. Eby harrowed garden. Got a certificate from Charlie and Ed saying they put a tile in the Golden Gate Bridge for the Rainbow Project in our honor.

4/25/88 Monday
Sunny, windy and cool. I washed and ironed. Mended Eby's sweater. Planted corn, beans, pickles, salsify and rutabaga. Eby harrowed. I braided some rug. Eby had some hauling. Esther came and brought me lots of jelly eggs for my birthday and fruit cake and dried fruit. Grace, Mary Alice and Sanford called. Bertha Shirk called and sang Happy Birthday.

5/3/88 Tuesday
Good weather. I did some rug and planted limas. Eby had hauling and tried to pull a tree from the window well and thinks he cracked a rib. I took King's both ways and stopped at Flaud's for plants, peppers, tomatoes, alyssum and begonias. Planted them. Soaked my feet.

5/5/88 Thursday
A very wet day. Eby had a bad night with his chest. I bandaged it at 4:00 A.M. He did his hauling and brought Steve Fisher with two drawers all done with rollers. I braided rug. Esther came this evening with two pieces of peach pie.

5/8/88 Sunday
A beautiful day. We went to Kinzer. Paul preached on the 7th Commandment. We went to Isaac's for Mother's Day dinner prepared by Kim. Very good. Ed Miller's and Joanne and the children came this afternoon.

5/9/88 Monday
Sunny with rain this evening. I washed and ironed. Worked in the garage. Put flower pole in the corner with plants. Eby had some hauling. He took five drawers to Steve Fisher. Isaac's took Bradley to Medical Center for Xrays and pain relief. Eby is moaning about his rib cage.

5/12/88 Thursday

Ascension Day. A beautiful warm day. I prepared a dinner to take to Jay Martin's and share it. Sue seems to be gaining and is able to walk with her walker. Went to Kinzer for Ascension Day service. Eby's side is better.

5/19/88 Thursday

Very wet. Pipe was stopped up and we had water in the basement. Pulled rug back and swept water for four hours. Dried real good by evening. Eby had only regular hauling. I cooked two chickens and got meat ready for corn soup. Jay bought a cow for $1000 at the sale last evening. Got a rug ready for children to sit on at the park.

5/20/88 Friday

A wet day with a bit of sunshine by times. I did the cleaning and took a rest. Edgar and Rhoda came at 12:30 for lunch. I helped with getting food ready for supper for Jonathan's prenuptial party at a church in Lancaster. Clarence and Mabel came over this evening to see my rugs.

5/21/88 Saturday

Edgar's came for their forgotten suitcase and brought some leftover food. Eby had a couple morning hauls. I washed the car. Isaac's and Bradley came at 1:00 and drove us to Jonathan's wedding at Refreshing Mount Camp. Nine of our children were there, plus Laura and Martha. I mixed up meat loaf for tomorrow when we got home.

6/10/88 Friday

A beautiful day, cool. Sanford's took me with them and we stopped at Clarence's a few minutes and then to Strasburg Railroad for a ride. Stopped at Uncle Jay's a few minutes and then on home for lunch. We went to Dale's Agway store and to his house and saw the new kitchen. It is very pretty. Had our supper. Sanford and Jacob went to Elam's.

6/13/88 Monday

Sunny and warmer. I washed and ironed. Picked three quarts of sugar peas. Made a batch of strawberry jam. Jay sat on the porch and chatted before going to Lloyd's. Rosa got a box of his things. Eby had hauling. I took Mrs. Joe Stoltzfus to Rhoad's locker and had car trouble, something with the brakes.

6/18/88 Saturday

Sunny and warm. Getting dry. I prepared things for lunch. Nancy and Gerry got here about 11:45. We worked on marking the quilt Nancy pieced for the Relief Sale. They went to Byerstown Bakery and to a class reunion at Holiday Inn this evening. Jay stopped for a chair to use at a sale. I ironed the apartment things.

6/19/88 Sunday

A sunny day. Nancy and Gerry went for a drive. Had 64 at Kinzer. Dale and Mae were there. We had dinner and visiting. Nancy and Gerry left at 3:00 and Dale and Mae at 5:00. I called Charlie and he got home from Sweden last evening.

6/27/88 Monday
Clear, windy and dryer. I washed and ironed. Did some quilting. Picked two quarts of black raspberries and two quarts of currants. Eby had hauling and pumped the cesspool on the garden. Picked a few pickles. Yesterday an Amish family was struck by a drunken driver and some are in serious condition.

7/6/88 Wednesday
Sunny and dry. Eby had hauling. We did some sprinkling. I did some quilting. Went to Sewing Circle alone as Anna was going elsewhere. Elam King's premature baby was twelve hours old and died. They had the funeral today.

7/13/88 Wednesday
Sultry and warm. I dusted the limas and hoed and trained them this evening. Eby had hauling and harrowed garden this evening. I went to the store. Brought Barbara and Lena home at 5:00. Finished Mary Alice's log cabin quilt today.

7/20/88 Wednesday
Had good showers in the night and more this evening. Cloudy most all day. The sewer is finished and we cleaned up most of the dirt. I papered some of the apartment. Eby had hauling. Bradley had more work done at the Medical Center yesterday. A report that John Stoltzfus sold to K-Mart.

7/25/88 Monday
A fine day. Rhoda and I did some quilting. Had an early lunch and went to Ray's. He took off work and showed us all their improvements. Took us for a drive to see all the development and Princeton. Martha's boyfriend came to have supper with us and then they went to a movie.

7/30/88 Saturday
Sunny, warm and humid. I did the cleaning. Scrubbed. Eby had hauling. Did some quilting and made Oh Henry's and rice krispie cake. Brought in some vegetables. Isaac's and Bradley came this evening. It was his 13th birthday.

8/4/88 Thursday
Sunny, hot and getting dry. I canned pickles and did weekly cleaning. Eby took folks to Lancaster and took his lunch along. Milton's came at 7:00 and brought a lot of frozen fish. Jonathan and Ruth came this evening and showed us their pictures. We treated to ice cream, etc.

8/6/88 Saturday
Partly cloudy with good showers in the Ferguson Valley. Milton drove our car and took us, along with Barbara and Douglas, to Beth's wedding at Spring Run Church of the Brethren. It was a pretty wedding with a reception at the Holiday Inn for 180 guests. Went back to Jim's for a while and stopped at Abram's.

8/7/88 Sunday
A pleasant day. Milton's left this morning for Washington D.C. to treat Doug to some places of interest. We went to Kinzer. Jay Meck preached on God's Blacklist. Spent balance of day resting and reading.

8/15/88 Monday
Sunny, hot and dryer. Eby had hauling and sprinkled garden and picked two buckets of tomatoes. Put seven pints of corn in freezer. Quilted a good strip. Mike called to say that he is engaged to Jan Mines.

8/26/88 Friday
A pretty day. I got things finished up for going to Camp Morehart. Eby hauled till late lunch. We packed the food and quilt in station wagon and met Milton's in New Holland. He drove and took Daddy and Barbara took Doug and me. We had supper of vegetable soup and other things.

8/27/88 Saturday
A fine day. The others came this forenoon and we had 65 for dinner. Isaac's family provided a very good dinner of chicken barbecue, applesauce, cole slaw, pies and baked potatoes that Bleiler's brought. We worked on Nancy's quilt and finished it by 10:00. Had a good supper made mostly by Ray and Jane. Some went to motels for the night.

8/28/88 Sunday
Warmer and pleasant. Had a nice worship service by the Virginia branch of the family. Had a good lunch and signed off and Sam drove our station wagon and David took me to Abram's. We got home by 4:30. Jay stopped in for a chat.

9/6/88 Wednesday
Clear and cool. Eby busy all day, $117.00. Picked some limas. Had 11 at Sewing Circle. Rhoda called and said Marcia has announced her engagement.

9/23/88 Saturday
Cloudy with showers. Went with Grace to the Relief Sale at 6:00. Ate our breakfast with tables full of others. Marked out seats and walked to the far end of the grounds where Grace had her stand of handmade articles. Bought some fresh doughnuts and went back to main building. Got our seats and sat most all day watching the sale. Highest quilt sold for $5000 and a lot of others for high prices. My braided rugs brought $975. The highest was $450 and least was $75. We bought chicken barbecue and had it here at Robert's with the rest of the Virginia family.

9/24/88 Sunday
A cloudy wet day. We went with Robert and Grace to Springdale Church. After the service Robert took us for a drive to see different parts of Virginia. Very pretty. Had

a turkey dinner at 1:30 and spent the afternoon visiting and watching the Olympics and listening to the presidential candidates on T.V.

10/6/88 Friday
Partly cloudy and cool. Eby had hauling. I did the cleaning and prepared food for supper. Samuel came this afternoon to get help with rug braiding. He did well. Mary Alice and Ellen came about 5:00. All three went to Gap auction.

10/7/88 Saturday
A real nice day. Eby took girls to work. We left early for Mart Groff's sale. He had a good sale with a lot of things. The farm sold to an Amish man for $303,000. Ray's came and Mary Alice and Ellen went. Ray took us all to Gap Diner for supper. A big day. We got a floor lamp for $5.00.

10/26/88 Wednesday
A fine day. I went to Grandparent's Day at Bradley's school. It was nice and well-attended. After that I went on to Georgetown and bought fabric for a dress. Varnished the wood for kitchen and swept our bedroom. Bronzed the kitchen radiator and stool this evening. Eby had hauling.

11/5/88 Saturday
Cloudy with showers and lots of water. Sanford's went for a drive this forenoon and I made lunch. This afternoon I went with them to the Toy Train Museum at the Strasburg Railroad. Edgar and Rhoda got here about 5:00. Eby had a few hauls and is not feeling good.

11/6/88 Sunday
A fine day. Sanford's and Edgar's left by 8:30. Edgar's were going to Jonathan's commissioning service. Daddy is still not feeling well so we stayed home all day and missed the over 70 fellowship meal. I had the Sunday School lesson to myself.

11/9/88 Wednesday
Good weather. Eby had hauling. I made a cake for the Firemen's Meeting this evening. Cut my dress and worked on it. Had a card from Charlie in Hong Kong. Jonathan and Ruth were leaving for Kampuchia.

11/19/88 Saturday
Cloudy with rain. Uncle Charlie came at 7:30 and took us to Isaac's and he had Lloyd Kreider's van and took nine of us to David and Susanne's wedding in Washington. It was held in a Unitarian Church and the reception at a nice restaurant. Ed Miller drove us home and Edgar's are staying here for the night.

11/23/88 Wednesday
A fine day. Eby had hauling. I carved the turkeys. Did some cleaning. Anna Kreider brought Jay to tell us he is going to the Mennonite Home December 1 and will be

rooming with Mart Groff. We got the Christmas money gifts ready this evening. I did some quilting.

11/24/88 Thursday
Thanksgiving day. A fine day. Daniel Dietzel's came and took us to Ed Miller's for a good dinner. We took turkey, croquettes, celery and pickles. A very good dinner. Charlie brought us home and he and Weaver's are here for the night.

12/7/88 Wednesday
A mild day. I ironed. Went to Gordonsville for cards, a diary and things for cookies. Replanted some raspberries and rhubarb. David Stoltzfus dropped Jay off and we visited all afternoon. He likes the Home. Anna took me along to Sewing Circle.

12/8/88 Thursday
A nice mild day. The three landscapers were here working all day and got a lot done on the bank. Destroyed nearly everything including my currants and tea. I mixed cookies all day and have about 13 kinds. Eby had hauling. Mabel called.

12/22/88 Thursday
A fine day. Eby had some hauling. I quilted most all day. Our new roomer was here all day. A 737 plane crashed in Scotland and killed all 258 passengers and set fire to forty houses. A 7-year-old Amish boy was hit and killed. Put onion poultice on Eby and gave him boneset tea.

12/24/88 Saturday
Foggy, mild and cloudy. I did some cleaning and quilting. Eby hauled for Ike. We went to Isaac's for our Christmas dinner. All their family was there. We got a lot of presents.

12/25/88 Sunday
A fine mild day. Went to Kinzer. Had a program instead of sermon. Candles at windows and special music. We had apple dumplings for lunch and spent a quiet afternoon and evening.

12/26/88 Monday
A fine sunny day. We had second Christmas. Uncle Charlie took Jay and Sue and us to Abram's for dinner. David and Susanne brought a quilting chair from the Weaver's, Charlie, Ed, Mary Alice and Ellen. I tried it out quilting this evening. Works very well.

1989

1/2/89 Monday
Foggy, mild and cleared. I quilted morning and evening. We went to Clarence's for our annual New Year's dinner. All were there but Josephine. Menno came for the

first time out of skilled care. Had a good dinner and visiting. Richard's car window was smashed this morning and the cop came.

1/4/89 Wednesday
Snow caused two hour delay for schools and our Sewing Circle was cancelled. It was my turn to drive. Ivy was in her room all day. I quilted. Eby helped turn it to the other side. New chair is fine. Eby went only for the paper today. He did not trust the roads.

1/6/89 Friday
Snowed most all day. Eby did not go for paper or mail. In all day. I quilted and made apple dumplings for lunch. Had radio on all day and learned a lot. Eby washed the dishes.

1/8/89 Sunday
Cloudy and mild. Snow is melting. Went to Kinzer. Paul preached a good sermon on Micah 6. Spent afternoon writing letters. Eby thinks he will stop hauling Amish. Ivy quiet and out of sight.

1/13/89 Friday
A fine windy day. I did some cleaning. Took the King's home. Eby hauled Ike most all day. Mary passed away this afternoon. I put some pictures in the new album this evening.

1/16/89 Monday
Cleared and a nice day. I washed and ironed. Eby had hauling this forenoon. Isaac's came at 12:30 to take us to Mary's funeral at East Petersburg. The children were all there, but not all of the grandchildren. They served a good supper and we got home at sundown. I took the tacks from the quilting frames. Called Milton's to say we will not be going to Mike's wedding.

1/21/89 Saturday
A fine cold day. Eby had a few hauls. I made cracker pudding and roasted two chickens and made filling balls. Had an easy day. Elizabeth called and said they would bring cheeseburgers for supper. They brought fruit too and I had salad and ice cream. Jim and Pat stopped in on their way from taking things to Beth. We set the table for eight.

1/24/89 Tuesday
A fine mild day. Eby had hauling and I took the King's home. I made a slip and cut white patches. Richard is out of money and food. I gave him sausage, sweet potatoes and cracker pudding.

1/26/89 Thursday
A cloudy day with showers. Eby had hauling. I went for milk. Had a letter from Jonathan. I cleaned most of the heater room. Eby gave Richard a lecture about

his lifestyle. I gave him supper and he went away. Soaked my feet and read this evening.

1/27/89 Friday
A fine mild day. Eby had hauling. I did the cleaning and made some food ready for Sanford's visit. They got here about 4:30. Jacob, Luke and Micah were full of pep. Richard paid some of his rent.

1/28/89 Saturday
A fine mild day. Eby did a few hauls. Sanford's took a couple drives. Jacob stayed with me and helped make doughnuts and we played Social Security and Blind Man's Bluff. They went to the Park and up to Elam's. Eby dug the salsify. Jacob suggested strawberry shortcake for lunch and we had it. I made chicken pie for supper.

2/13/89 Monday
Partly sunny with snow and showers this evening. I washed and ironed. Took Christianne to White Horse Dry Goods and I bought a comfort bottom for Sewing Circle for $2.39. Got a quilt from Christianne to put binding on. Did half of it. Braided some rug. Eby had some hauls. I gave his feet reflexology for his cold.

2/14/89 Tuesday
Cloudy and mild. Eby had some hauling. His cold is better. Repeated the reflexology. I worked on the rug, 40 inches. Finished binding the quilt. No rent from Richard. Eby laid down the facts this morning.

2/18/89 Saturday
A fine sunny day. Eby did one haul. We went to Clarence and Mabel's 60th wedding anniversary at Harvest Drive Restaurant. About 38 there. Had a good dinner and nice program and fellowship. Jay and Sue came this evening. I called Pat and Jim had his eye done and all seems well. I fell.

2/19/89 Sunday
A fine day. Edgar's went with us to Kinzer. Conrad came for dinner. They all left about 4:00. I took a nap. My soreness is better. Abram called to offer to see about doing something for Daddy's shaky problem.

2/26/89 Monday
Sunny and cold. School called one hour late because of ice. Eby did not do his morning drive, but had some later. I washed and ironed. Richard has not come back for his things. Eby has his third cold.

2/28/89 Wednesday
A fine cold day, lamb like. I took Anna Slaymaker to Sewing Circle all day. Worked on an appliquéd quilt for Kansas sale. Eby had hauling. Barbara called and they plan to leave early in the morning for China. I worked on rug this evening.

3/2/89 Saturday
Cloudy with drizzle. Made some food ready. Mary Alice and Nancy got here about 11:00. We put Nancy's crib quilt in frames and mostly finished it. They went for a walk in the Gap Park. We had a nice time visiting. Eby had very little hauling.

3/11/89 Saturday
A beautiful day. Eby had some hauling. I did some cleaning and made a cherry pie. Worked on last row of rug. Nice weather for Gordonsville Sale. Richard came for his things in the garage and said he will be back to pay his rent.

3/14/89 Tuesday
Cloudy and mild. Eby had hauling. I cleaned some cupboards, drawers, closets and kitchen shelves. Worked on third rug. Went for milk. Rhoda called and things are shaping up for the wedding. Had letter from Milton's in China. The space shuttle is having problems.

3/21/89 Tuesday
Cloudy and colder. Eby had hauling. I worked on rug. Lennie and Marian brought some clothing. I transplanted red begonia and some thumbergia. Had a lot of radio, some tiresome.

3/22/89 Wednesday
Fine day, colder. Eby had hauling and took his lunch. Christanne stopped to pay for hemming her quilt. Worked on third rug all day and had it done all but a foot when I ran out of black strips. President Bush got to Conestoga School and the Penn Johns Elementary this forenoon.

3/25/89 Saturday
A fine day for the annual Gap Sale. I made a walnut chiffon cake and took two cakes for the sale. It gave a big crowd with a lot of things to sell. I helped a while from noon till 2:30. Eby hauled some people. Spent the evening reading.

3/27/89 Monday
A fine day. Eby had no hauling for second Easter. He cleaned some garden and put up new wash line. Brought Amos to cut down our diseased white birch tree. I washed and ironed. Started fourth rug. Lennie and Marian brought a couple boxes. I raked some garden.

3/29/89 Wednesday
A fine warm day. Eby had some hauling and helped clean trash off the garden. I cleaned the attic and Lennie and Marian Shales said they would move in the apartment tomorrow, but they came at 11:00. So I had to quit. Worked on rug. The huge oil spill in Alaska is creating a lot of problems.

4/3/89 Monday
Rained and cleared warm. Eby had hauling. I washed and ironed. Emptied the upright freezer for defrosting and made a pot of vegetable soup. Have a lot of vegetables. The Shales went out for lunch and dinner. Donald came for the white birch wood. Mrs. Fisher, the corseteer, stopped in.

4/8/89 Saturday
Sunny with showers in the evening. Eby had some hauling. He took me to Quarryville to have my picture taken for license. We went on to Groff's Orchard for strawberry plants and they did not have them in yet. He put fertilizer and lime on garden that he bought at Agway. I hoed the long flower bed and planted a snowball bush. Made a cherry and an apple pie.

4/13/89 Thursday
Sunny and cool. Eby had hauling. He bought a new garden tractor for $454.74. He used it on the garden with good results. He planted a row of potatoes and I stuck the onions and planted red beets and 25 strawberry plants, Jerseybelles. I did the cleaning and made a nut chiffon cake.

4/15/89 Saturday
We went with Isaac's to Friendly's for our breakfast and back to Motel to get dressed for Marcia's wedding. Got to Bethel Grove Church and soon Abram's, Ray's, Mary Alice, Milton's, Weaver's and Dale's arrived. They were married at 11:00 and we then went to the Holiday Inn for the reception. Had a very good dinner and lots of visiting. Left for home at 3:30 and got home by 8:30.

4/22/89 Saturday
A fine day. Eby did some hauling. I made some food ready for today and tomorrow. Charlie got here about noon. He brought an azalea and two peonies and helped plant them and put our pine tree in a new pot. Charlie went for a drive and for water cress after supper.

4/25/89 Tuesday
Fine weather. Eby had hauling. I washed windows on the outside. Planted the geraniums. Did some cleaning in the living room. Esther came and brought me a box of candy for my birthday. Mabel and Mary Alice and Ray called to say Happy Birthday. Got lots of cards.

4/26/89 Wednesday
Sunny and warmer. Eby had hauling for Ike. I cleaned the garage and washed the car. Eby bought Michigan peat moss for the flower beds. The Schales come and go. Sanford called and the boys sang, "Happy Birthday, Grandma." I got more letters and cards.

5/5/89 Friday
A very wet day. I finished putting Angela's quilt in and got some quilted. Made a peach pie for Eby's birthday and liver for supper. Esther came and brought him a card and a peach pie. I gave Lennie and Marian each a piece. Eby had some hauling.

5/14/89 Sunday
Mother's Day. Good weather. Took Lennie and Marian Schale along to Kinzer. Sanford's went to Friend's Meeting and came for dinner. Abram's came too and we had a nice visit.

5/15/89 Monday
Some sun and showers. I washed and ironed. Did some quilting. Eby had Whit Monday holiday. He took papers to Christiana and got some lemons and sugar for tea. He met Elizabeth at Linville Hill School and she had two big bags of spearmint tea. I made a lot of concentrate.

5/20/89 Saturday
A fine warm day. I finished the cleaning. We took Marian along to John Metzler's sale. We left at 11:30 to meet Milton's at Mother Coy's. We all went to Yoder's to celebrate Doug's 25th birthday. Eby had two hauls. I roasted a chicken, made sweet potato pudding and baked corn ready for the oven and a lemon sponge pie. Chatted on the porch with Marian.

5/21/89 Sunday
A beautiful day. Went to Kinzer. Hershey Hostetter preached on Hell. Ray and Jane came for church and here for dinner. They took us to Isaac's this afternoon. We had a tour of their new house. It is getting more and more ready. Ray's ate a snack and left at 6:30. Chatted on the porch with Schale's. Did some reading.

5/24/89 Wednesday
Some rain. Eby had trouble with the station wagon and I brought him from Turkey Hill. It was soon fixed. I am more than half done with quilt and Eby helped turn it. I did some mending. Someone told Eby that glass jars will keep rabbits away so I put four by the peas.

5/26/89 Friday
Sunny and a little shower. Eby had hauling. I quilted most all day. Went for milk this morning. The new mattress makes good sleeping. The Schale's were away this afternoon and I had a chat session on the porch this evening. The peas look poor with the rabbit topping.

6/13/89 Tuesday
Sunny and showers. Eby had hauling and took his lunch. I finished Angela's quilt with the binding. Eby is trying to get help to get rid of the rabbits. Today is Laura's

high school graduation. Sat on the porch and chatted with Marian. Made a portion of strawberry jam.

6/14/89 Wednesday
Cloudy and a few sprinkles. Eby had hauling. I hoed some garden. My front tooth came out when I was eating lunch. I prepared supper for Abram and Pat and they went to Kinzer where he gave a talk on mental health.

6/19/89 Monday
Sunny and warm. Eby had hauling and took his lunch. I washed and ironed. Took my plate to Dr. Caldwell in Leola and he put my tooth on in short order for $8.00. We put lima bean poles up and Eby harrowed the garden. I hoed some and picked a half bucket of peas and shelled them while Marian chatted.

6/20/89 Tuesday
Sunny with a few showers. I hoed the garden and tied up tomatoes and replanted the limas. Eby got some peas given to him and I put yesterday's with them and put five packs in freezer. Took Kathryn King and two children home from Ruth Hershey and got bumped when I crossed the highway.

6/21/89 Wednesday
Humid and showers. Eby hauled Ike till noon. We took the peas and wire out. I got about a quart of shelled peas. Got some information about car repairs. Marian got me potatoes at Dutchway. I feel a little better today. We called Abram's.

6/22/89 Thursday
Warm with scattered showers. Eby had some hauling and I did some hoeing. Kim mowed the yard. Elizabeth took Bradley to Hershey Medical Center. The insurance adjuster came. Abram called about his car for sale.

7/8/89 Saturday
A fine day. Eby had some hauling. I baked oatmeal cookies, a lemon sponge, tapioca, ham and cole slaw. Tied up the tomatoes and limas. Picked three tomatoes and some wax beans. Did some cleaning. Marian showed her picture album and chatted. Anna Mary Lapp was killed last evening in New Jersey.

7/18/89 Tuesday
A fine day, foggy morning. Eby had hauling. I picked and put eight pints of beans in freezer. Read and rested a while. Planted some coleus and geranium slips. I ripped some rug wool and chatted with Marian on porch. Abram called. Sam is going to China and Becky to Alaska.

7/25/89 Tuesday
A warm day with good showers this evening. Eby had a busy day. I washed, ironed and mended. Gave Marian a tray of vegetables and eggs for her birthday. The Schales got

some money and went out to eat. I got only seven pickles. They are not producing. Called Rhoda and they had a good trip to Guatemala.

8/5/89 Saturday
A warm day. I made a custard. Eby had a few hauls. The Schales went out to eat. Milton's were going to a pig roast for Barbara's school reunion at noon and they were driving home later. I worked on Bradley's quilt top.

8/10/89 Thursday
Nice cool weather. Eby had hauling. I baked oatmeal cookies for the reunion. Baked two pounds of beans. Picked pickles and some green beans and dug potatoes. Samuel came to say good by before going to China on August 20. Marian is ready to let Lennie go.

8/19/89 Sunday
Fine weather. Took Lennie and Marian along to church. Sanford and the boys got here about 12:00. They had a busy time. Went to Gap Park and to Elam's. Dale came to get Jacob for the week. Milton came with a bus load of foreign students who stayed at Benner's.

8/20/89 Monday
A warm hazy day. Eby had hauling. Milton left with Stony Brook van to go with foreign students for the day and they all came here this evening to drop him off. Dale and Jacob left for their day of fun. Sanford picked up his braided rug that Kathleen did and they left at 10:30. I put the quilt in that Nancy and Tera did and got some quilted.

8/24/89 Friday
A nice day. Eby had a few hauls. Sanford's went to the Park and got potatoes. We had late lunch and got things packed up and met Milton's and he drove our station wagon to Camp Morehart. We had only twelve for supper and less overnight. We put the quilt in and did some quilting.

8/25/89 Saturday
A beautiful day, cool. We started quilting before breakfast and quilters kept at it off and on all day. We wrapped it up at 6:30 for me to bring home to finish. Had about 53 for dinner provided by the Virginia folks and Elizabeth and the girls made pies and ice cream. It was all very good and plentiful. Had a good time visiting.

8/26/89 Sunday
A fine day, warmer. Had a good breakfast prepared by Dale and Mae. The worship was in charge of Milton. We sang and had a nice program with some members sharing milestones of the past year. Had a good dinner with a big variety of good food. Put everything in order and had our farewells and left by 12:20. Conrad drove our station wagon and took the Pontiac.

9/5/89 Wednesday
Nice weather. Eby hauling for Ike all day. I quilted. Put 59 ears of corn in the freezer and the limas Eby shelled last evening. I went to the store and stopped to get my glasses fixed. First time alone in the new car. Marian went to bank, store and Slender You.

9/14/89 Friday
A nice warm day. Eby had hauling. I did some garden work and flower beds. Eby ate his lunch here. My upper plate broke in half when I ate a piece of a pepper. I read a while.

9/28/89 Friday
Eby took his men this morning and Ray's came at 9:00 and we started for Virginia. We ate the lunch I packed at a nice rest stop. Went to Weaver's and from there went to the P. Buckley Moss Museum and saw all her pretty drawings and dollhouse. Next we went to the Holiday Inn and got our motel rooms. We went back to Expoland and had supper with Walter Weaver's. Saw a lot of pretty quilts and many other things. Went back to motel and turned in for the night.

9/29/89 Saturday
Got up early and went to the sale. Picked our seats and looked around. Had doughnuts and looked at the many interesting things. The sale was well attended. My rugs came to $800 and Tera and Nancy's quilt brought $750. Highest quilt was $3600. Sold lots of food. Had a sprinkle of rain early and was good weather after. Went to Mary Alice's for supper and had sale food and other good things. Went through thick fog to motel and got there safely. Quilts totalled $73,000.

9/30/89 Sunday
A wet foggy day. Slept late and had our breakfast in rooms. Left for Sanford's and got there by 11:00. Found them all fine. Had a good dinner and nice visit. The rug Kathleen made for them looks very nice and they have done some papering. Next we went to Nancy's and had a good supper and a nice visit. Gary kept T.V. on for the men folks. The screened deck is nice and they have lots of pretty things. Brandy is contented.

10/14/89 Saturday
A fine warm day. I prepared some food for Sunday. Jim and Pat came at 11:20 and took us to visit Ted and Beth in Dover, Delaware. Had a good trip and nice time. Got home by 8:00 and visited a while. Beth had a good dinner and her house is very clean and nicely furnished.

10/18/89 Wednesday
A wet day and mild. Eby had a busy day with Ike. He saw two accidents. I cleaned cupboards and put a third wallhanging in the frames. Made four quarts of applesauce.

275 were killed in the earthquake in California. I called Charlie and he said they had no damage. I looked at some of it on Marian's T.V.

10/20/89 Friday
Lots of rain and cleared colder. I prepared dinner for Becky, who left for Reading at 2:30 and is leaving for Alaska on Tuesday. Eby had all day hauling. I quilted and Marian chatted. Jim's Pat called and said Jim fell and sprained his wrist.

10/24/89 Tuesday
A fine sunny day. I grated the horseradish that Clarence gave. Eby had some hauling and harrowed the garden. I made things ready for the new stove. It came at 10:00 and they took the old one to Isaac's new basement. Cost was $581.94. I dug the salsify, some beets and carrots. Did the ironing. Quilted this evening. Becky went to Alaska today.

11/3/89 Friday
Cleared after the rain. Eby hauled Ike and others. I made pies, a cake and more food ready for the weekend. Did some cleaning. Marian got some good news and found $100 she had laid back. Mary Alice and Ellen came for supper. They went up to the auction and we had nice visiting.

11/4/89 Saturday
A frosty morning and sunny day. We went to David and Minnie's sale at 8:45. Mary Alice and Ellen and Ray and Jane came too. House sold for $67,000 to a young Amish man. Eby bought a hose rack with some hose. Ray and Mary Alice did more for the sale. We had supper here for Ray's and the girls and Abram stopped by on his way from Philadelphia in time for supper.

11/8/89 Wednesday
Cloudy with showers. Eby hauled Ike till 2:00. I dug red beets and carrots and cleaned off some trash. Planted balance of the tulips and daffodils. Cleaned some basement drawers. Marian met Lennie at the airport and they are living together again. Had a card from Becky and wrote back this evening.

11/11/89 Saturday
Nice weather. Eby had some hauling. I did some cleaning and got some quilting done. Germany no longer has a wall between east and west, so people are free to go and come.

11/23/89 Thursday
Thanksgiving Day. All is covered with snow but sun shone all day. Kim came at 10:00 and took us to Ed Miller's for our Thanksgiving dinner. 42 there. Had a nice time and a good dinner. Robert and Grace brought us home and are staying for the night.

11/24/89 Friday
Clear and cold. Snow did not melt. Eby had hauling for Ike this afternoon. He visited with Robert this forenoon. Grace and I quilted and talked. Steve got a deer on Wednesday. Robert and Grace left for home at 2:30.

11/26/89 Sunday
A fine day. Went to Kinzer church. Paul preached and had balloons with six things God wants us to have. We got one for being the longest married. Had a quiet, restful afternoon and evening. The Schales did not go to services and ate out and shopped.

11/28/89 Tuesday
Rain, snow and wind. Eby had a few hauls. He put treads on the apartment steps and picked up sticks in the yard. He thinks we should put our names in at The Home. I quilted most all day. Christanne called to say she has quilts ready for me to do.

12/1/89 Friday
Partly cloudy. Eby had hauling most all day. I quilted. Made two cakes, one for the Fire Company sale. I dug up the corner for strawberries. Marian and Lenny are low in funds and cannot pay rent on time. Mother Teresa was having a pacemaker put in today.

12/2/89 Saturday
Seasonable weather. Eby had a few hauls. I did some cleaning and prepared food as we invited Jay's and Charlie for tomorrow. David died at 1:00 today after having pneumonia. I did some quilting. Called Abram's and Isaac's.

12/3/89 Sunday
Sunny, cold and windy. Went to Kinzer. Jay Meck preached on "Lead us not into Temptation." We had Jay's and Charlie for dinner. After dinner Charlie took Jay's home and then took us to Mennonite Home to visit Minnie. She is reconciled. I called ten of the children to tell them of David's death.

12/5/89 Tuesday
Very cloudy all day. Eby had hauling. Christanne had a bad pain in her neck and wanted a ride to the doctor. It was better by the time Eby got home. I quilted and had radio all day. Called Mabel and she is ready for her cataract surgery tomorrow.

12/6/89 Wednesday
A cloudy day, warmer. Eby had his morning and evening hauls. Isaac and Elizabeth took us along to David's funeral at Hershey's. Real good attendance. We were served lunch with about 40 others. I did some quilting. Anna Slaymaker took me to Sewing Circle. Marian said she doesn't think Lenny is going to stay.

12/8/89 Friday
Snowed all day, six inches. Eby did morning hauling before it snowed. We spent an easy day. I canned the sauer kraut and hemmed Bradley's quilt. Lenny and Marian got social security checks, paid the rent and went shopping. Called Mabel and she is taking it easy and her eye is scratchy.

12/11/89 Monday
Sunny and warmer. Eby did no hauling till afternoon. I washed and hung it in basement. Hemmed half of Christanne's quilt. Called Mabel and Sue. Got some cards and letters. Worked on our cards till 11:00. Titus Martin's son was murdered in Florida when he and his wife were taking a school bus to be shipped to their daughter in Costa Rica.

12/15/89 Friday
Sunny, cold and snowing this evening. Eby had a full day of hauling. I made date pinwheels, chocolate balls, peanut brittle, hay stacks and coated crackers. Mike and Jan sent us a fine book of historic places in Georgia. Beautiful.

12/18/89 Monday
Cold and sunny. Plumber came to fix circulator. I packed a box of cookies for Sanford's and Eby sent them UPS. Packed some for Isaac Stoltzfus and family, and Eby took them with a chicken. They gave a fine tray of fruit. I worked on family papers for Nathan Hess.

12/20/89 Wednesday
Sunny and cold. Eby hauled for Ike. I put most of cookies in freezer. Wrote to Grace for her birthday. Made elk for supper, and it was good. One of Eby's men gave it to him from Colorado hunting. I called Mabel.

12/23/89 Saturday
Sunny and cold. Eby had some hauling and I did some cleaning. Made a dessert and roasted a turkey and made kisses. Elam King's house caught fire from an overheated stove while they were having a family Christmas dinner. It burned the apartment very badly. We went up as the fire engines were leaving.

12/25/89 Monday
Christmas Day. Real nice day. Dale and Mae and Ernest and Mildred Bleiler had Christmas day with us. They brought homemade ice cream and cookies. Dale's brought a book on China and a car for Daddy.

12/26/89 Tuesday
A few degrees warmer. Eby had no hauling for second Christmas. I washed and ironed. Checked greetings and addresses. We went up to Elam's at 4:00 to see fire damage. Very bad.

12/27/89 Wednesday

Partly cloudy with snow after dark. Eby had some hauling. I cleaned some drawers and the hutch. Sorted some cards and Eby helped put Dale and Mae's picture in window frame. Kathleen called and said Elam's are tearing the whole house down.

12/30/89 Saturday

Partly cloudy and warmer. Eby not feeling good at night. Better today. Started to braid a rug. Isaac's came and brought supper and ate with us and spent the evening. I gave Bradley his quilt and he was pleased. Eby and Isaac went up to Elam's to see the progress on the house.

12/31/89 Sunday

Icy, foggy and rained. We neglected to turn on the radio and did not hear the cancellations. Went to church and found no one with the doors locked so came home and spent a quiet Sunday. Mabel called. Talked to Rhoda and she said there was a murder at their neighbor's when someone shot a father, mother and two children.

Ruth and Eby Hostetter on a spring outing, 1996.

The Nineties and 2000

1990

1/1/90 Monday
Clear and windy, in the 30's. I worked on rug till 10:30. Eby had a haul to Honey Brook, and we left for Jay's at 11:15, where Charlie served us a good dinner of roasted goose and lots more. All were there but Menno and Josephine.

1/13/90 Saturday
A fine day. Eby had hauling this A.M. Sanford's went for a drive and up to Elam's. I finished hemming the quilt. Played figmill with Jacob and Sanford. Had a nice time visiting with Sanford and Tera.

1/14/90 Sunday
A fine day, warmer. Went to Kinzer. Paul preached on God's Inspired Word. Sanford's went to meeting. I went to the Park with them for a while. The boys had fun. They started for home at 4:30. Had a quiet evening. Sam called from Hong Kong this evening.

1/20/90 Saturday
Snow, rainy and foggy. #12 snow. Made some food ready. Nancy and Gerry got here at noon. About 3:00 we went to Isaac's and stopped at Georgetown Store for quilt materials. Saw Isaac's in their new home for the first time. Everything is very nice.

1/22/90 Monday
Nice weather. I washed and ironed. Found the lost book just where I put it. Worked on rug and it is almost big enough. Eby had very little hauling. Edgar's left for Florida.

1/25/90 Thursday
A wet day. Eby had a few hauls. I hemmed Christanne's quilt all day and got done at 8:00. I called Grace and Mabel. Ray called and said rabies are getting close and Jane is having root canal work done and Martha has not decided on college. Their neighbor Millie is still smoking.

2/6/90 Tuesday
Fine day. I made a pudding, cake, and cooked a chicken. Eby had some hauling. I took a nap. Edgar's came about 2:00 from their Florida trip. We took them up to see Elam's new house. Visited this evening.

2/12/90 Monday
Nice weather. Eby had a full day. I washed and ironed. Quilted on second half. Called Sue. Had a letter from Rhoda. They have some murder suspects at Ellis Hollow.

3/1/90 Friday
Good weather. Eby had hauling. I finished quilting the king size quilt. Did one side on Christanne's quilt. Had rabbit pot pie from the one Eby caught in a cage.

3/13/90 Tuesday
A warm day. 80 degrees. Eby had some hauling and he cleaned up grape trimmings from pruning. I cleaned the kitchen cupboards and hall closets. Planted lettuce in hot bed. Many gardeners are planting.

3/19/90 Monday
Partly cloudy. Eby had some hauling. I washed and ironed. Cleaned the beds and did some cleaning in the two bedrooms. Finished reading the third Lindbergh book and am convinced that Hauptman was an innocent man.

3/24/90 Saturday
White with snow. #18. Our 63rd anniversary. The Gap Fire Company Sale. We went at 9:00 and I started my shift at 12:00 and got home at 6:00. It was a busy day. Cut Eby's hair.

4/7/90 Saturday
White with snow, #19, and quit by 9:00. Jim Fry brought the new station wagon and they got legal work done. Eby gave Ike's Anna a free trip to the store. I did a bit of cleaning and quilted. Had some sunshine this P.M.

4/10/90 Tuesday
Real nice weather. Eby had hauling and we managed to get some garden planted. Ground was in good shape. I did some quilting. Marian gave a bouquet of fresh flowers. I finished reading Elmer Hershey's book.

4/17/90 Tuesday
Cold with rain and cleared. I quilted all day. Marian was here a lot. Lenny got a job as Security Guard at Apple Car Sales. Eby had a little hauling.

4/19/90 Thursday
Fine day. Eby had no hauling except regulars. I did some quilting. Ed and Marcia came for supper and to spend the night. Had a nice visit. Nancy called and said the quilt arrived safely. I wed the strawberries.

4/24/90 Tuesday
A fine warm day. Eby had hauling and I did some housecleaning. Worked up a fresh cocoanut. Dale called and said to watch for Thursday T.V. program.

4/25/90 Wednesday
A warm day. I cleaned the kitchen and dining room. Went to the store. Marian came down to chat. Esther brought a birthday gift. Had our group of 12 for Bible Study. Abram, Mary Alice and Ray called. Got cards and letters for my birthday.

4/26/90 Thursday
A warm day. Elizabeth came and gave me help with housecleaning. Screens, windows, porches and woodwork. A big lift. I did the bathroom and cleaned roses this evening. I watched T.V. with Marian and saw Ruth and Jonathan.

4/28/90 Saturday
Nice warm day. I made food ready. Mary Alice and Ellen got here about 1:00 for lunch. They went to the Eby sale above us and Mary Alice bought a Sewing Machine for $4.00 and a floor lamp. We had a nice evening visiting.

4/29/90 Sunday
Some rain and much cooler. Went to Kinzer. Mary Alice and Ellen came for church. Had our dinner and they left about 1:30 in the rain. I started reading the book Mary Alice gave me. Eby read and slept. Marian chatted after taking Lenny to work.

5/7/90 Monday
A fine day. Edgar went with Eby on drives. Rhoda put binding on quilt. Conrad came this evening to tell about his time in Cambodia and to show his pictures.

5/24/90 Thursday
A fine day. Ascension Day. Isaac's came about 6:30 this morning and we left for Jim's. Stopped at Benner's for more breakfast and got there by 9:40. Had a nice visit and a good dinner. Got home by 7:00. Sanford and the boys called and said they will come for the weekend.

5/26/90 Saturday
A very wet day. Sanford's came about 10:30. We had a good day. Daddy and Sanford went to George Kramer's sale and I went with Tera and the boys to the Park.

5/27/90 Sunday
Cleared and a nice day. Went to Kinzer. 44 there. Stella Newswanger gave a talk on her experience with the hurricane. Sanford's went to Quaker meeting. Abram's came for dinner. Pat, Tera and I went to the Park with the boys. Eby, Abram and Sanford went to the cemetery. We went to Isaac's this evening.

6/5/90 Tuesday
A fine day, cool. I dusted some vegetables. Washed and ironed. Eby had hauling. Worked on rugs. There is trouble about midwives for Amish without proper credentials. I called Mike and Jan. They are fine.

6/25/90 Monday
A fine day. Eby had driving. I did some trimming and picked raspberries. Edgar's got here about 2:15. We visited and went to Isaac's for supper, a good one. Saw a video of Jonathan and Ruth in Cambodia.

6/26/90 Tuesday
Fine weather. Edgar's left at 9:00 to shop at Zook's and drive to Weaver's for Sister's Day tomorrow. I washed and ironed and picked some raspberries. Planted 50 celery plants and started hemming a quilt.

7/1/90 Sunday
Fine day with evening showers. Went to Kinzer. Paul preached in a long necktie. We took Clarence's along to Tel Hai. Visited John and Emma and Alice.

7/4/90 Wednesday
A warm day. Eby had hauling for Ike. I defrosted and cleaned the refrigerator. Dale came for dinner and I canned pickles for Becky and made her a box of food for them to take to her in Alaska. Dan and his mother picked us up and took us to Isaac's for a picnic this evening.

7/12/90 Thursday
A wet cool day. Eby had driving. I worked on rug all day, 47 inches. Kim mowed yard between showers. There is opposition about developing the Stoltzfus farm off Newport Road near Intercourse.

7/19/90 Thursday
Wet and sunny. Eby had a little driving. I helped make over a thousand subs at the Fire Hall this morning. Eby harrowed garden and I hoed it. Beetles on sweet corn. The Schales are looking for an apartment.

7/21/90 Saturday
Warm with fine showers this evening. Front door was locked and broken. Got Amos to put a new lock on it. Eby had a little drive. He had a weak spell and took the afternoon easy. I prepared food for company. Had a quiet evening. Set the table.

8/4/90 Saturday
Sunny and warm. I did some cleaning and picked over the limas. Eby helped shell them. Got corn, potatoes, tomatoes, etc. ready for Sunday dinner. This afternoon I went shopping. Miriam Horning called and said Emma is in the hospital with a broken hip.

8/10/90 Friday
A wet day. I canned four quarts of tomatoes. Did some cooking and putting jars on shelves. Did some cleaning. Picked and shelled some limas, but it was awful muddy and I almost got stuck.

8/18/90 Saturday
Sunny and warm. Eby had a couple drives and got hit at the intersection and ruined the station wagon and has a bruised shoulder. I made lasagna for lunch for Milton and his friends. We all went to Intercourse Park for the Hostetter Reunion. Abram talked on their trip to China. Isaac brought us home and visited a while.

8/20/90 Monday
Cloudy and wet. I washed and ironed. Canned 7 quarts of tomatoes. Picked a bushel of limas and Eby shelled them. Put 11 pints in freezer. Eby did a little driving. The adjuster came and said the station wagon is not worth repairing.

8/21/90 Tuesday
Cloudy and drizzled. I washed the towels and our bed. Picked tomatoes and limas. Eby helped shell them. He did some driving. He was tough with Marian for her remarks to the Amish about his accident. She went up early this evening. I soaked my feet.

8/23/90 Thursday
A very wet day. Eby did a little driving. I made a nut cake. Did some cleaning. Sanford's came for supper. Boys are fine. We played some games and had an ice cream treat.

8/25/90 Saturday
A fine sunny day for the reunion. The family all got there and a lot of grandchildren and five great grandchildren. Virginia folks prepared the noon meal with Elizabeth doing the pies. Food was very good and so was the fellowship. Some pictures were taken.

8/26/90 Sunday
Fine sunny day. 26 for worship and breakfast and lunch. Clemens in charge of the worship. Very nice. Charlie brought us home and we stopped by Abram's to see Becky's video and at the Mennonite Home to see Uncle Mart and Jay and Aunt Amy. All as usual.

8/30/90 Thursday
A fine day with morning fog. Eby had some driving. He bought a station wagon for $5000. I picked a half bushel of limas and froze four quarts. Made vegetable soup. Jay stopped for chatting.

9/6/90 Thursday
Very foggy and warm. Eby had driving. I did five quarts of grape juice and picked a bushel of limas. The Schales rented Victor's trailer and are happy. Kim mowed the yard.

9/7/90 Friday
Sultry. Eby had driving. He harrowed some garden. I canned four quarts of tomatoes, five quarts of grape juice and put seventeen pints of corn in freezer. Hoed some garden. Abram and Becky called from Barrow, Alaska.

9/10/90 Monday
A mild day. Eby had all day driving. I did fifteen quarts of grape juice. Made some food ready for Greg. He got here about 7:00 for late supper. Had a nice visit with him. Marian has some concerns about the future.

9/15/90 Saturday
Eby took John to work. Got milk and paper. I did the cleaning and Kim came at 10:00 and took us to John Lentz' for a good chicken barbecue dinner with all their family. Isaac's brought us home. I finished Christanne's quilt. Called Rhoda and all is well with Jonathan's in Cambodia.

9/30/90 Sunday
Nice mild day. Went to Kinzer. Had an MCC film instead of Sunday School. It was so so. Had David, Ben and Paul Clark's for dinner. Good company. Jim Martin stopped while making a survey of Gap to find Presbyterians.

10/3/90 Wednesday
A fine day. Eby drove for Ike. I washed all the apartment things and ironed scarves. Mended some and did some much-needed cleaning. Marian stopped to find her salad fork. No luck. Shampooed my hair. Grace called and said the Relief Sale came to $195,000.

10/4/90 Thursday
Partly cloudy with rain. Eby drove for Ike. I worked on the apartment and went to Levi Esh's at 11:30 to help with a bus load of important folks that Abram was hosting for a dinner in an Amish home and farm. Hemmed a side of Christanne's quilt this evening.

10/8/90 Monday
Fine warm day. Eby had a date for his eyes with Dr. Stoltzfus. I washed and took off the screens and washed all the windows and put storm sash on the front door and scrubbed the front porch. Put basement windows in. Hemmed one side of quilt.

10/11/90 Thursday
A wet warm day. Amish Fast Day, so Eby had off. He put the walnuts to dry and put two storm windows in. I quilted most all day. Lenny brought the key and said he would like to live in our apartment alone.

11/4/90 Sunday
A fine warm day, no coats. Went to Kinzer and Jay preached a Stewardship sermon. Had extra song time. Isaac's took us to Dale's for dinner. Abram's were there too.

Had a good dinner and nice visit. Abram's and Dale's gave me new Alaskan fur house slippers for Christmas.

11/12/90 Monday
A cold windy day. Eby had a few drives. I washed and ironed. Finished hemming Christanne's quilt. Eby delivered them. Put the flower pole in the small bedroom with plants. Read a lot of Angkor Wat book Ray gave. Esther stopped in with some sweet petal.

11/19/90 Monday
A fine day, cold. Eby drove for Ike. I washed and ironed. Dug and cleaned the celery. The mice ate most of the hearts. Made vegetable soup. Isaac's and Bradley came this evening. A dead baby was found in a bag on Mascot Road.

11/20/90 Tuesday
Clear and cold. Eby had the day off. He brought the two turkeys and I roasted them. Pat and Becky came this afternoon for supper. We had a nice visit. Got the Christmas money ready this evening. I started reading Ice Palace.

11/22/90 Thursday
A fine Thanksgiving Day. Isaac's came and took us along to Ed Miller's with turkey, croquettes, celery and pickles. Others brought food too and we had a good dinner. 31 family members were there. Robert and Grace brought us home and are staying till Saturday.

12/10/90 Monday
A fine day. I washed, ironed and mended. Eby had driving. I cracked some walnuts. Did some quilting. Dale called and said they will come for Christmas. Worked on cards and notes. Got a box of fancy pears from Milton's.

12/12/90 Wednesday
A fine day, mild. Eby had driving. I baked 750 cookies. Eby helped with sand tarts. The man came to see the apartment, but he is a smoker. Mike and Jan sent us a nice ham ready to eat.

12/15/90 Saturday
Icy and turned to rain. Eby hauled this morning. Anna sent a nice basket of goodies. Isaac's took us to Clair Kreider's funeral in Hershey. Abram's and Dale's were there. We had supper at Abram's and got home in good time.

12/17/90 Monday
Partly cloudy. Eby drove for Ike and others. I washed and quilted. Have over 100 yards done. More troops are being sent to the desert. Gas came down five cents. An 11-year-old Amish boy was struck and killed on his scooter on Quarry Road.

12/20/90 Thursday
Pleasant weather. Eby hauled John to and from and took Christanne to doctor. He brought two wallhangings for hemming. Rhoda called for some food preparation information. I quilted. Got cheese and other goodies from Jim's and dates and figs from Abram's.

12/25/90 Tuesday
A fine day and cold. Dale and Mae came and took us along to Isaac's for Christmas. Lots of gifts and a good dinner. I quilted this evening. Ray called and they had a good Christmas.

1991

1/1/91 Tuesday
It was a beautiful day. We had our annual New Year dinner. We had a nice time and all enjoyed the dinner. Paul seemed better and took part in conversation. Menno thought he could come along till this morning and then gave it up. I hemmed two sides on the quilt for Christanne.

1/3/91 Thursday
Eby had a drive and made things ready for dinner, and Ray came at 10:30 and we left with him in his new car at 2:00 for Hopewell. Had a good trip. After supper they took us to see the Christmas decorations. Martha was at work at the small restaurant where she works part-time.

1/5/91 Saturday
We slept late in the bed with an electric blanket. Saw a lot of deer from the window. Isaac's came about 10:30 and had no trouble finding the way. Relaxed and visited till noon. After lunch we went to see the Lindberg estate which is three miles away and had a tour with a boy who lives there with 17 others. He showed us the whole house and told us what he knew about the kidnapping. Ray took us for a drive to see places of interest. Had a good dinner of lamb roast and left for home at 7:00.

1/8/91 Tuesday
Eby took John to work the last time. Ira Nafziger will pick him up on his route. Eby drove for Ike this afternoon. I did a lot of quilting. Have ten patches left. Snow is not melting. It is real Farm Show weather. War clouds continue to hang over the Persian Gulf with thousands of troops stationed over there in the desert.

1/11/91 Friday
Eby was home all day because of the bad travel. Many schools were closed. There were not so many at the last day of the Farm Show. I quilted most of the day. Made a chocolate cake for the dinner at Maggie's funeral. Abram and Pat called this evening.

They are well and said that Becky has it cold in Barrow. A polar bear killed a man there. War is threatening in Saudi Arabia. We had a sauer kraut supper. The power was off and on this evening. Eby drew some water.

1/16/91 Wednesday
Eby drove for Ike today. I quilted and have two patches left. War has started with the dropping of bombs and missiles on Baghdad. We listened to President Bush give a talk at 9:00. Got the invitation to Kim and Mark's wedding.

1/21/91 Monday
Eby drove for Ike in afternoon. Some schools closed for snow. I washed and dried it in the basement. Bound a large star quilt for Christanne. Got done at 9:30. Daddy's cousin Lillian Denlinger died at more than 103 years. Fighting continues in Saudi Arabia. Eby's shoulder hurt by spells as a result of the fall he had at the porch step a week or more ago.

1/25/91 Friday
Eby drove for Ike all day. I did some cleaning. Baked bread, a cake, apple crisp, tapioca and Amish fellowship bread. Marian stopped in this morning to weigh herself on our scales. I took it easy for a while as Sanford's did not get here till 4:30. We had a nice evening. Played Social Security and hide the button. The boys were very active and had an interesting time at the aquarium in Baltimore. Sanford fixed our new light.

1/26/91 Saturday
Eby drove for Ike a while. Tera and Jacob learned to make little boxes from cards and it went well for them. They took the boys to the Park after lunch and then we went with them to Rohrer's Mill and the Strasburg Railroad and Uncle Jay's. The boys are having fun. We played games and they went to Elam's to see the milking and the new baby, Emma, that came yesterday. Played hide and seek, figmill and a trick game. Weather is fine.

1/28/91 Monday
Eby drove for Ike a short trip. I washed and put it on the porch and in the basement. I went to Dr. Stoltzfus for an eye examination. Tested 20-30 and will get new glasses. I cracked all the walnuts and Eby helped pick out, almost a quart. I cut some greeting cards for candy boxes. Dale called from Washington when they returned from their trip to Africa. He said that all went well. There is a meeting at Kinzer this evening in the interest of the unchurched in Kinzer.

2/3/91 Sunday
We went to Kinzer. Paul preached a Peace sermon. Got counsel questionnaire. Went to Clarence's this afternoon. I took Mabel some of the fabrics Kathleen brought for Sewing Circle. Read Ice Palace this evening. It is about Alaska. Milton called and they spent the day with Douglas. Went to his church and to a museum with him this afternoon.

2/6/91Wednesday
Eby drove for Ike all day. He brought the meat this morning before he went to Ike's. I went to get my shoes and they cost $61.00. Stopped off at Kinzer for Sewing Circle. Stayed till 3:15. At 3:30 Carl Denlinger came to tell us that his sister Mary is critical in the hospital after surgery for cancer. He did not think she would live till morning. I put most of the pork in the freezer and cooked the pig legs. I called Elizabeth to tell her about Mary. Abram and Pat called from Florida to tell us they are grandparents. David's little Benuel was born at 5:00 and all is well.

2/9/91 Saturday
No driving today. Isaac and Elizabeth came soon after 9:00 and drove our car to the funeral for Mary Martin at the Grace Baptist Church in Lancaster. It gave a big crowd. Carl and Leon both spoke. The burial was at East Petersburg Mennonite and they served lunch in the basement. We took Isaac's out for lunch and went to visit Robert. He was real alert. Elizabeth was not back from the burial. We had popcorn, apples and chocolate milk for supper. I made rice pudding for Uncle Charlie as I invited him for dinner tomorrow.

2/11/91 Monday
Eby drove for Ike for a few hours. I washed and ironed and cut my dress. Got some sewed up. Marian stopped in for a chat. Abram called this evening to say they saw the new grandson, Benuel David, and he is a nice baby. Mary Alice called to say she may come next Monday to help with her quilt.

2/12/91 Tuesday
Eby had a short drive this afternoon and had an easy day. Fixed the door on the wardrobe. I worked on my dress. Called Josephine for her birthday. She seems to be doing fine making noodles and gathering eggs. I called Mabel this evening and she is braiding a rug. We did some reminiscing about the early 1900's. Last evening there was a barn fire near the Strasburg Railroad.

2/16/91 Saturday
Cold and windy. Eby stayed in all day and nursed his cold with hot drinks and honey and lemon juice for his cough. Rhoda called this forenoon and we had a long chat. She said Andrea may stay in Indiana after her graduation. Her boyfriend lives out there. I did some cleaning and put a hem in my dress. Made a cake and rhubarb sauce and some other food. Mary Alice called and said she is coming tomorrow. I sewed the backing on the quilt frames.

2/18/91 Monday
Eby drove for Ike this afternoon. Had late supper. Mary Alice and I marked the quilt and put it in the frame by noon. We did some quilting this afternoon and visited this evening. Three persons were murdered in Landisville.

2/19/91 Tuesday
Eby home all day on his chair. Mary Alice and I quilted and got one end of border done and I did a row of patches this evening. She left at 1:45 to visit friends in Baltimore and spend the night before going home tomorrow. The paper reported that the Weaver's 14-year-old adopted son murdered his parents, Dr. and Mrs. Weaver, and his adopted sister. L.M.S. and Locust Grove schools are shocked as the two were students there. Eby changed to Mennonite Insurance.

2/22/91 Friday
Eby brought the hams and pig stomach from the butcher. He drove for Ike. I cut up the turkey, made gravy, filling balls, fruit cocktail, mince and cherry pies. I have a bit of a cold and am forcing the liquids. Did some cleaning and quilted. The tulips are up and the wild geese are flying. There is a prospect of peace on some terms.

2/25/91 Monday
Eby did not have any driving. He took the garden tractor and lawn mower for tune ups. He had an easy day working on his income tax. I washed and ironed and did some quilting. My cold is hanging on. My nose is like a fountain. Had a nice letter from Jonathan. They should be packing up for the flight home. Eby brought Barr Realty to see the apartment and gave it to them to rent.

2/28/91 Thursday
Eby had driving for Ike. He took the shirts Kathleen gave back to Goodwill and bought himself a hat. I cleaned the last closets and put the fabrics in drawers. Clarence brought Mabel to get some fabric for making school kits and crib comforts. We had a nice letter from Martha. She may stay in Philadelphia this summer. The news says the war is over and it makes the Kuwait people very happy. I washed salt from the bacons.

3/1/91 Friday
Eby drove for Ike this P.M. He put lime and fertilizer on the garden this morning. I am wearing my new shoes to break them in. I quilted a lot today. I called Edgar's and Jonathan and his family arrived in Ithaca at 5:00 this evening after their flight from Cambodia. They had a good flight with Carla and Christopher.

3/8/91 Friday
Eby had driving for Ike. I made sweet petal, cracker pudding, chocolate syrup. Got some vegetables ready, etc. Did some cleaning and had things ready for our overnight guests. The Weaver's, Edgar's and Nancy and Gerry all got here by 10:00.

3/9/91 Saturday
Beautiful day. The folks all got around for breakfast and ready to take off for Kim's wedding by 9:00. Had no problem finding the Hopewell church. The wedding was a beautiful celebration with everyone doing their assignment. The guests all seemed to

enjoy the fellowship and the delicious catered meal in the huge decorated dining room. Some of the family came back this evening and we had a pleasant evening together.

3/20/91 Wednesday
Eby had a big day with Ike. I cleaned the bathroom closet and cupboard under the sink. Did weekly cleaning. Cleaned some yard next to the porch. Went to store and bought a lot. Bill was $73.24. A pint of vanilla was $12.75. Marian came about 3:30 and took time to chat till 5:00. She is feeling good, but not good enough to do yard work. I did some quilting. I got a book on Helvetia from Mary Alice and the red fabric to hem her quilt.

3/21/91 Thursday
Eby had driving for Ike. I did some quilting and made food ready for Jonathan and his family. They got here about 12:45 and all were doing fine. The children were friendly with no problems. Jonathan showed us his album of pictures. They had an invitation to visit a friend in Lancaster for supper.

3/28/91 Thursday
Daddy drove for Ike. We planted the peas after he came home at 4:00. Jonathan and his family left this morning for Ithaca. I washed the towels and beds and they dried so fast. Ironed and made up the beds. I made 8 quarts of mince meat. I moved the flower pole and the plants to the garage. Wrote to Rosa and soaked my feet.

4/4/91 Thursday
Eby drove for Ike. Jonathan and Ruth took Carla to court for the adoption procedure. I kept Christopher and he was good. They had dinner invitations this evening. Eby harrowed the garden. Jonathans are staying at some place for the night to be on hand early for a meeting. I did some quilting this evening.

4/5/91 Friday
Eby drove for Ike. He brought pansies and a quilt from Christanne. I planted the pansies and stuck a row of onions. Raked and picked up some stones. I roasted a duck and made a strawberry dessert for Sunday. Washed for Jonathan's and dried it in the basement. Jonathan's were gone all day.

4/8/91 Monday
Very warm. Eby had regular drives and one to the Dr. at Blue Ball for all six of Ike's family. I sent Jacob's birthday card. Did the washing for Ruth. Jonathan left at 5:30 for Washington and meetings. He is not back at 10:00. Eby harrowed some garden and we put in potatoes, beets, radishes, cabbage, spinach, carrots, lettuce, cauliflower, broccoli, peppers and strawberries. I made doughnuts. Ruth is packing up.

4/9/91 Tuesday
Eby had regular drives. I did some quilting and cleaned the weeds from asparagus and strawberries. I put some mulch on flower beds and pulled out the old hot bed.

Jonathan's got all packed up and left for Philadelphia at 9:20. The babies had a good night and were in a good mood. I took a snap shot of them. I am wearing my old glasses to heal my nose. Mervin put mulch on the bank and mowed the yard. Eby harrowed balance of garden.

4/18/91 Thursday
Eby drove for Ike and took lunch. We put wire netting around the peas to keep the rabbits out. Saw three of them looking for breakfast. I quilted but still have more to do. Kim called and said she will mow tomorrow. Invited Clarence's for Sunday and Mabel is not feeling so well this evening. I shampooed my hair.

4/25/91 Thursday
My 86th birthday. Eby drove for Ike in the P.M. Mary Alice's quilt is all done. I put Christanne's in the frame. It looks nice, an around the world. I planted some thumbergia at the porch. Put the big Christmas cactus on the porch. Esther brought a fancy cake for my birthday. She and Abner gave us dinner at the Country Garden Restaurant.

4/28/91 Sunday
Went to Kinzer. Jay Meck preached on H E L P. Mary Alice and Ellen went to the Quaker Church. They took us to The Home this afternoon and we visited Minnie, Jay, Menno and Amy. Jay Groff called this morning to say Mart Groff died about midnight from a heart attack. Jim called this evening and said Ed and Marcia visited them for two days and had a great time with his turkey calls.

5/1/91 Wednesday
Eby drove for Ike until 11:00. Isaac's came up and took us along to the funeral for Mart Groff at Stumptown at 2:00. The church was well-filled. We stayed for the lunch in the basement. Some of the cousins were there. Elizabeth called this evening and said Ed and Karen have a baby girl.

5/3/91 Friday
Cooler. Eby drove for Ike all day. I finished cleaning the kitchen and bathroom by 12:30. Took a blow and washed the windows on the outside. Amos Blank came to look at the windows this evening and will give an estimate on replacing them. I cooked a tongue and soup bone. Got some photos from Jonathan. They should be in British Columbia with her folks. They think 100,000 may have died in the typhoon in Pakistan. I turned the quilt three times and have one border done.

5/12/91 Sunday
Went to Kinzer. Jay preached a Mother's Day sermon. The fathers went up front and sang. Had some instrumental music. We had our dinner and read this afternoon. I finished reading Plain and Simple that Mary Alice gave and started reading Cambodian Witness.

5/23/91 Thursday
Sunny and pleasant. Eby had some driving. I washed and ironed. Did some quilting and hemmed half a big quilt for Christanne. Eby did some watering this evening. There is a cholera epidemic in Cambodia. Jonathan's should be there by now.

5/25/91 Saturday
Very warm. Eby had a drive for Ike and John. Got some food ready. Sanford's went to Dutchway and bought a rose and helped Daddy plant it. For supper we had Sanford's, Isaac's and Dale's. The boys had fun playing. Called Rhoda this evening. They are well and have had no word from Jonathan's.

6/1/91 Saturday
Warm day. Eby took John to and from work. We started picking peas at 6:00 and had 31 pints in freezer by 10:00. Eby was first at the huller. I made three portions of strawberry jam and put four pints in freezer. We picked peas after supper and put them in refrigerator in garage.

6/2/91 Sunday
Went to Kinzer. 64 there. We had an afternoon and evening at home except for going out for John Diener's viewing. I read Cambodia Witness. The bite I got on my leg picking peas is red and sore.

6/5/91 Wednesday
Eby drove for Ike. We pulled some weeds on the bank. I wed the round flower bed and did some quilting. Went to the store at noon. Jean took me to Sewing Circle. I called Rhoda to tell her that Diane Gehman came this morning to tell us that Jonathan's got safely to Cambodia before she left to come home, and they were all feeling at home again.

6/12/91 Wednesday
Eby drove for Ike. I did some quilting. Picked some blueberries. Cleaned up for our meeting. 11 here. I did not feel good and laid down a few times. Dale called to ask when Robert is coming to do the driveway.

6/15/91 Saturday
Eby drove for John and Amos. We brought the cauliflower in and I processed eight packs for the freezer. I did some quilting and took some rests. I just have no pep. Eby sprinkled this evening.

6/16/91 Sunday
We did not go to church as I was not feeling able. Had a dinner of pork chops, peas, etc. Isaac's and Abram's came this afternoon. My pulse is down to 36 and I am not feeling very spry.

6/17/91 Monday
I took it easy this morning and Eby took me to 11:15 appointment. Dr. Hartley said off to the hospital in the ambulance. This was done and the whole bit and I was admitted and had a trial part put in. Got plenty of nursing attention. Elizabeth brought Eby in.

6/18/91 Tuesday
Things are going as usual, getting lots of nursing care. Elizabeth and Isaac brought Eby in. I had terrible cramps this forenoon.

6/19/91 Wednesday
Elizabeth brought food for Eby. Edgar and Rhoda came. I had a pacemaker put in today.

6/21/91 Friday
No going home as the monitor did not work and I have to put one on for 24 hours. Edgar's and Daddy came in. Abram called. Very good nursing care.

6/22/91 Saturday
Am put in the hospital for another day because of too much redness at the incision. Eby and Edgar's came in this afternoon. Had some odd T.V. characters hopping around. Quiet evening. Read several chapters in Ezra.

6/23/91 Sunday
Morning procedures as usual after a good night. Heard a service from the Crystal Cathedral in California. A man told me I can go home after I got more instructions. No one came and the regular nurse did the job and called to tell them to come for me and I got home by 4:00. Took a rest and had a nice time visiting with Dale's and Abram's when they stopped in. Lots of calls. They set up a new portable phone for me.

6/25/91 Tuesday
Pleasant weather. Eby did some driving for Ike. Rhoda defrosted and cleaned the refrigerator. She made a rhubarb cake from Aunt Sue's recipe. Rosa came about 11:00 and left at 4:00. Had a nice visit with her. Eby did some sprinkling.

6/27/91 Thursday
Eby was busy hauling Ike. Nancy took me to County Line for blood test. Elizabeth took me to Dr. Kirschner, the surgeon. He said my incision is doing well. Rhoda, Grace and Nancy did some changing the rooms. Grace did some weeding in the flower beds. Mildred brought Clarence and Mabel to visit this evening. Grace called to say that she and Nancy got home safely. Had Nancy's meat loaf and Grace's peach pie for supper.

6/29/91 Saturday
Eby had a drive for Ike and the rest of the day off. Rhoda helped me shower and shampoo. Charlie and Edgar came for lunch. Jim, Pat, Beth, Ted, Abram, Isaac, Elizabeth and Bradley came this afternoon. I stayed up all day and felt real good. Charlie helped Rhoda make a pot of vegetable soup. She did a lot of cleaning. Eby scrubbed the porch.

7/1/91 Monday
Eby took John two ways and had the rest of the day off. Edgar and Rhoda left at 7:30 and she called to say they had a good trip home. Our new tenant, David Fuller, moved in this evening. Charlie made early lunch and left at 12:00 for Washington to fly back this evening. Eby and I washed this afternoon and the Maytag was sold and taken away this evening. Charlie went to the store and bought a Whirlpool automatic.

7/5/91 Friday
Eby drove for Ike all day but came home for lunch with Jane, Laura and Martha. They brought chicken barbecue and more goodies. Jane took me for my 10:30 doctor's appointment. Jane left at 2:25. Uncle Charlie brought Amy and Mabel for a visit, which was very nice. I made the breakfast and supper.

7/8/91 Monday
Eby had driving for Ike and Christanne. Barbara King came to help today. She processed the soap I had made earlier. Eby took the dried beef to get sliced at Dutchway and bought a box of sweet cherries for $34.00. I canned ten quarts, froze one and kept plenty to eat fresh. We had a bean supper. Kim called to say she is coming to do pickles. Sally called to say she and Linda are bringing supper on Thursday night. Eby helped me shower.

7/12/91 Friday
Eby drove for Ike. Barbara came today. She wed the bank, tied up the tomatoes, pulled some corn for the refrigerator, combed my hair and washed the dishes. Mary Alice came about 3:00. We had leftovers from last evening and Mary Alice took Barbara home before supper. Conrad called and said he is coming tomorrow.

7/13/91 Saturday
Three inches of rain. Eby had day off. Mary Alice and I made cracker pudding, a sponge cake, and cole slaw. Her friend Anne came from Philadelphia and they went out for lunch and did some touring in the County. Conrad came to visit this afternoon on his way to a friend's reception. Mary Alice quilted this evening.

7/15/91 Monday
Pleasant. Eby took some folks to New Holland sale. Blank came and put some new windows in. Elizabeth cleaned them. She picked limas and shelled them. I gave

them to Mary Alice. She packed up after combing my hair and doing a few other things and left at 10:20. I took a rest and got dressed to go with Elizabeth to the Cardiovascular Associates. I called Becky to say belated happy birthday.

7/18/91 Thursday
Very warm. Eby drove for Ike. I had no girl today. Took it easy and read a lot. Dale and Mae came this afternoon. They were touring in the County to celebrate their wedding anniversary. I planted some beets and dill this evening. Eby harrowed the garden.

7/23/91 Tuesday
Eby took Anna and Levi to the doctor and to do some shopping. I had the day to myself. Cleaned some cupboards and put things in order. Put a zipper in Eby's pants. Cleaned some drawers. They called from County Line and said my blood check was good but cholesterol is 211. Had a good shower about 5:30.

7/26/91 Friday
Eby drove for Ike and Christanne. I made some peach butter. Grace and Jennie went shopping this afternoon and got home just as the storm came with rain. Robert got here before lunch. I made a cake. Grace and Jennie picked limas for tomorrow dinner. Robert got the drive cleaned spotless for the cover job.

7/27/91 Saturday
Cooled off. Had early breakfast and Dale brought the sealer and Isaac and Bradley came to help and they all worked on the driveway and had it done by 10:30. It looks perfect. We made peach pies, cherry and caramel custard. I took the cherry and caramel custard to the Martin reunion with some sliced tomatoes. We took Clarence's along and there were 63 there. Grace made a blueberry cake for the 9:30 snack with lemonade.

8/5/91 Monday
Cooler and dry. Eby had a few drives. He did some watering and brought the crib from the attic. I washed and ironed and hemmed the balance of the quilt. Picked the pickles. Abram and Sam called. Sam got home from China yesterday and is recovering from jet lag.

8/6/91 Tuesday
Cooler. Eby had driving for Ike. I picked limas and put seven pints in freezer. Eby helped shell them. I took a rest and Eby got lunch on the road. I did some mending and ripped a coat for rugs. Eby did some watering this morning and evening. No sign of rain. A drunken driver hit an Amish wagon in Ohio and killed six members of a family and injured others.

8/14/91 Wednesday
Showers this evening. Eby had a full day of hauling for Ike. I did some yard work this forenoon. Did flower beds and trimmed some. Cut Harvey's bush by our asparagus.

Hoed strawberries. Took an hour rest and read the newspaper. Canned some pickles and cleaned off turnip patch for sowing. My heart tested 71 beats this evening.

8/21/91 Wednesday
Eby drove miles for Ike. I washed our bed clothes and did some cleaning. Made a cake. Went to the store. I picked the pickles and got all the corn off and put it in the refrigerator. Dug some potatoes. Sanford's got here about 8:00 and the boys are full of action. Played Figmill with Jacob.

8/24/91 Saturday
Weather pleasant for the reunion and we kept the fans going. Rhoda and the little boys were in charge of breakfast. The Saturday guests kept coming till noon. Had 65 for dinner. Martha made a special casserole and Charlie had some new things filled with a salad mixture. All ate well. There were a variety of good pies with ice cream from Isaac's family. Had a nice time visiting. Thomas Hines was here for the first time and he and Rosa announced their engagement. Had a Scrabble game and Sam showed a lot of interesting China slides.

8/25/91 Sunday
We all had a quiet night and a good breakfast with some of Grace's good buns, fruit juice and cereals. Joanne and Karen were in charge of the our worship period. Joanne had a responsive reading and there was singing and reminiscing. Had a lot of good leftovers for lunch. Cleaned up and put the place in order. All packed up and gone by 2:00. Had a good trip home with Edgar and Rhoda. Put things away and retired early.

9/4/91 Wednesday
Eby drove for Ike all day. I made two peach pies and took one and a glass of peach butter to Harvey's. Cleaned up the mess a rodent made in the basement with my violets and the dollhouse. Replanted some healing plants. Put some slips to sprout in water. Made eggplant casserole for supper.

9/14/91 Saturday
Had over an inch of rain. Eby had driving for Ike till 2:00. I made apple dumplings and cooked a chicken for pie and soup. Did the cleaning. Rhoda called and we had a long talk. They are considering a trip to Cambodia. I got corn in and ready for soup. Some Amish children came selling Stanley and Watkins products for their school. Glen Hershey called to ask if I could tell him about the Russian families that came in 1921. I had no definite memories.

9/17/91 Tuesday
Very warm with good showers this evening. Eby had a full day for Ike. I sewed some patches. Had an antique buyer. I got ready for Elizabeth to take me to the hospital for a pacemaker checkup. Karen, the nurse who did my checkup, said that I was doing very well.

9/18/91 Wednesday
Eby had all day driving for Ike. I made a big chicken pie and got other food ready for our dinner with Emma, Charles and Miriam Horning. Clarence and Mabel came at 9:15 and we went to their home. Mabel took cole slaw and apple crisp. We all enjoyed the dinner. Emma had much difficulty talking and looks sickly. Charles was quiet as usual. We stopped at Weaver's Store on the way home and I got dress fabric, thread, underwear for Eby and a lunchbox. I was glad we got to visit them.

10/11/91 Friday
Good showers. Eby not feeling well and it was Amish Fast Day so he took it easy. The plumber came and corrected the leak in the laundry room. I got up early and washed clothes. Made 56 sweet potato croquettes. Did some cleaning.

10/23/91 Wednesday
Mild. Eby drove for Ike. I did some cleaning. Cleaned my closet and checked my dresses. Some worn out. I sat on the porch to peel turnips and potatoes for supper. Had midweek service here in charge of Jay Meck.

10/24/91 Thursday
Foggy morning. Eby drove for Ike all day. I did some odd jobs getting ready for winter and our trip. I had an appointment with Dr. Hartley. He said my blood pressure is up and he gave me some pills, and he said my hearing is not so good. He had the nurse wash out my ears with thirty years of hard wax. I bought some drops and more pills like I was taking. The hearing aid man brought Eby's new aid this evening. I mixed some cookies.

10/26/91 Saturday
Very foggy. Sanford and Micah stayed overnight and Micah did not sleep so well and had a little fever. Sanford got him some medicine. We packed up and had early lunch of apple dumplings, potato salad and dried beef. Left for Virginia at 12:20 and got to Nancy and Gerry's at 4:50. It was sunny in Virginia. Had a good supper and Eby and Gerry watched ball games this evening. Nancy and I planned a crib quilt for one of her friends having a baby.

10/27/91 Sunday
Had an easy day, a T.V. sermon by Robert Schuler's son from the Crystal Cathedral in California. At noon, after a farmer's breakfast, we left for a drive and went as far as Norfolk and the tunnels and bridges. Saw a lot of Virginia we had not seen before. The leaves were beautiful and the weather pleasant. Had a good supper. Watched the World Series on T.V.

10/28/91 Monday
Nice weather. Sanford took off work most of the day. I went with Tera to visit Luke and Micah's school this forenoon. It was very interesting. Tera read them a story

while they ate their spider crackers that we helped them make. Tera worked this afternoon. Sanford dug the salsify and I processed it for freezing. Eby helped Sanford with leaves. Played games with boys this evening.

10/29/91 Tuesday
Pleasant. Had our breakfast together. Sanford had the day off and cleaned up the leaves. He took us to visit school and we went to Jacob's room and he read them two stories. Tera worked part of the day and brought the boys home early. I cut quilt patches off and on all day. Played some games.

10/30/91 Wednesday
Frosty. Nancy came for us at 7:30 and took us to Mary Alice's in Charlottesville. Visited this morning and she took us for a drive to see some points of interest, the place where she works, the Kluge estate, etc. Had a good supper of chicken pot pie and then she and Ellen took us on to Weaver's. Abram called Mary Alice last night and said the Gap School was burning from 7:00 to 11:00. Isaac called here at Weaver's and said all was well after the efforts of twelve fire companies.

11/1/91 Friday
Weather is fine. Grace finished my dress and took the day off. Robert came home at noon and we went to the Clothes Line Store and I bought fabric for a dress. There was a fire we passed on our way to visit Herman Burkholder's. We found Ruth very disabled and getting around with a cane. They were very sociable and seemed to enjoy our visit. We had a nice evening. Jennie made us popcorn and we watched the news.

11/14/91 Thursday
Eby had some drives for Ike. He has a cold and not much pep. I made sweet potato croquettes for Thanksgiving. Have 120 frozen. Worked on rug. I cooked the bony chicken pieces and cut it off. Grace called and said she has my dress almost done. Ray called and said Millie Anderson is still in the hospital. Their trip to Italy is scheduled for December 29-January 7.

11/17/91 Sunday
Fine weather. Went to Kinzer and Robert Zook preached, a very active speaker. Went to Isaac's for Thanksgiving dinner with their family. We got home before dark. I finished reading A Whisper in a Dry Land.

11/20/91 Wednesday
Pleasant, in the 70's. Eby drove for Ike. Got the oil tank filled. I processed some horseradish. Sat on the porch to grate it. Planted the small roots. Worked on rug. No action at the schoolhouse. Nancy called and they will be bringing Goldie along for Thanksgiving. She said it is so warm there that her bulbs are coming up.

11/27/91 Wednesday
Cold and calm. Eby drove for Ike. I cut up the turkeys and cooked the bones and skin for broth. Made up the bed for Gourley's. Did the cleaning. Milton called this morning to ask how to remedy his overcooked sweet potatoes. He was preparing them for Mike and Jan's visit. Edgar's were leaving for Fredric's for the holiday weekend.

11/28/91 Thursday
It was a real nice day for our dinner at Donald and Linda's. We took the turkey, gravy, croquettes and celery. We had plenty of the usual goodies. They had everything well planned and prepared for eating with tables in their basement room for 29 of the family. The Weaver's and Gourley's came here for evening and night. Sanford and the three boys called. They had a good Thanksgiving.

11/29/91 Friday
Eby drove for John and Ike. The Weaver's and Gourley's went to the Hans Herr House and other places of interest this forenoon. I made a cake and roast beef for dinner. The roast pan sprung a leak but I managed to save the gravy. Eby thinks he can have it mended. The Gourley's went down and asked Mr. Vincent for 13 bricks as they are tearing the schoolhouse down. He gave them kindly.

12/5/91 Thursday
Cold. Eby had a couple drives. I went with one and we stopped at Dutchway for my cookie things. I stirred up five kinds and got two cocoanuts ready to grate. The one I bought was not good and Eby took it back and got two in exchange. We stopped at the Little Store on our travels and got the things Dutchway did not have. We sent Stony Brook $1100.

12/14/91 Saturday
Mild. Eby had some driving. I made up some cookie plates and boxes. Worked on the cards and notes. Abram called to see how we are doing. He thinks we should have flu shots. He was going to Washington. The Christiana Bank was robbed a second time.

12/18/91 Wednesday
Snow flurries. Eby drove for Ike. I braided rug. Went to the store and the bill was $53.00. Bought three chickens. Took a box of cookies down to the Vincent's and did not find anybody, so left them at the trailer door. Found a box of grapes on the porch from Milton's. I called the hospital and had my appointment changed because Elizabeth has a sore foot and I did not want to ask her to drive. Rhoda called this evening and said Jonathan and Ruth have a little son, Andrew.

12/22/91 Sunday
Fine day. Went to Kinzer. Had a big lot of extras. Piano music, choir singers, readings, giving out paper bells to write our praises for 1991. We had Lenny and Marian for

dinner. They seemed to eat well and be glad of the invitation. Made out real good eating with my damaged plate.

12/25/91 Wednesday
We had a nice quiet day. Isaac, Elizabeth and Bradley came and brought a good salad and dessert. We had chicken, filling, croquettes, corn and limas. We all ate well. I laced some rug. Ray's called. They had Christmas with Grandma Koerwer.

12/29/91 Sunday
Went to Kinzer. Jay Meck preached. We had Clarence and Mabel for dinner. She is very forgetful and had some coughing. I read Pioneer Kansas Women till late. Sanford and the boys called. Dale called and said he will bring their international student on Tuesday.

12/31/91 Tuesday
Eby did some drives for Ike. I prepared lunch for Dale and the international student they are hosting for the holidays. She came from Taiwan and is a very nice 25-year-old who is a university student in Illinois. After lunch we went to the Mennonite Home, where Dale had never been, and visited the relatives and Esther Groff. Came home by some landmarks, the Hatville School, Cattail Homestead, water wheels, etc. The girl said in her country older parents are cared for by their children.

1992

1/1/92 Wednesday
Eby had the day off. We put up new calendars. Uncle Charlie came for us at 11:15 with Uncle Clarence, Aunt Mabel, Uncle Menno and Aunt Amy. He did not tell us where he was taking us for dinner, but we went to Hershey Restaurant on #896, where the rest of the family met us. We were served a good dinner. We went along to take Uncle Menno's back to the Home as it was a hassle getting him in and out of the van. We then came back to Uncle Jay's for visiting. Spent a quiet evening reading.

1/3/92 Friday
Eby drove for Ike this afternoon and cleaned beans from the gutters this forenoon as I held the ladder. I finished reading Pioneer Women of Kansas. I spent a lot of time cleaning and putting my desk in order. Sorted letters and clippings. Spent some time cleaning my old aluminum pan. Rhoda called and they are thinking about their trip to Cambodia.

1/9/92 Thursday
Eby drove for Ike this afternoon. I worked on rug all day. Tried to reach Dr. Calwell to see about getting my plate repaired, but there was no answer. President Bush is in

Japan and got sick and vomited at a dinner. John gave Eby some deer sausage and we had some for supper.

1/18/92 Saturday
Cold. Eby had a drive for Ike and John. I cut up the turkey and made a fruit and vegetable tray. Set up the table and Ray's came about 10:30. Nancy and Gerry got here around noon and Abram soon after. Isaac's came about 1:15. They all told us that they have decided to have a family dinner on March 21 for our anniversary.

1/19/92 Sunday
Cold. Nancy and Gerry had breakfast and started for home with Goldie soon after we left for church. We went to Clarence's. Mildred made a good dinner. We had a nice visit. Mildred had a box of old letters and cards and valentine's that we enjoyed. There were letters our mother wrote to our father in their courtship days.

1/22/92 Wednesday
Eby had driving for Ike all day. I worked on rug and have 16 rows done. I called Mabel and she did a lot of repeating. Called Sue and Jay was at the doctor on Monday. He said it takes a long time for the nerves to heal. Jay has pain and has very little use of his hands. This is Rhoda's birthday and she is celebrating in Cambodia. I made a sausage casserole for supper.

1/23/92 Thursday
Eby had only John to haul today. He put the mailbox up again. It was blown down last week. I worked on rug. We went to the doctor this afternoon. Eby had a driver's physical. I had a little checkup. He sent me to the drugstore and two bottles of pills cost $74.48. Eby had to call hearing aid man for more information.

1/31/92 Friday
Eby had driving for Ike and Christanne. I cleaned the rug rags from the basement closet and there is a lot of it. I sewed up some strips and cut some. Mary Esther called and said Victor Groff fell at the farm. An hour later she called and said he died on the way to the hospital. Later Mabel called to tell me. I called Abram's and Isaac's.

2/4/92 Tuesday
No driving. Milton, Barbara and Ray came before 10:00 to take us along to Paradise for the viewing and funeral for Victor Groff. The church was filled. We did not go to Kinzer for the burial. It was a good time for visiting. Abram's, Isaac's, James, Milton's, Ray and Dale's were there. They served lunch in the fellowship hall to 168 people. After this there was time for eulogizing on a tape. We stopped at Ben King's on the way home for the poem Nancy had done in Fractur by Lydia Anne.

2/5/92 Wednesday
Eby drove for Ike all day. I had a quiet day and fasted at lunch. Have both quilts bound and bagged and ready for Christanne. I called Mabel and she said Victor's

eyes and some skin were donated. I called Charles Horning's and Emma is the same. She tries to talk and knows when she has company.

2/8/92 Saturday
Eby had a short drive for Ike and Sanford went along. He went to Elam's for milk. The boys had a lot of fun in the snow. They kept very active and went along to Dutchway with Sanford and Tera. Jacob bought a game much like Scrabble and we played one game. Made some card boxes. Isaac's and Bradley came this afternoon. We had early supper and Sanford's left at 5:50. We listened to Sunday School meditations.

2/26/92 Wednesday
Eby drove for Ike. I braided some rug. Went to the store and picked up my coat at Beiler's. Cost was $10.00. Put balance of pudding in the freezer. Watt and Shand sold out both their stores to a company in York after it was in the family for 114 years.

2/28/92 Friday
Eby brought the hams and bacons and drove for Ike. I cleaned bathroom closet and cupboard and scrubbed the floor for the new linoleum. Scrubbed the kitchen and put glow on it. Eby went out the front door for the mail and he fell up the steps when he came in. I did some rug.

3/5/92 Thursday
Eby had a full day with Ike. I did some preparing for our company. Did some planting for Jacob. He wants cactus. The girls who murdered Dr. Show's granddaughter may get the death sentence.

3/7/92 Saturday
Eby drove for John and Ike. I baked bread and roasted the meat. Made a dish of caramel fluff. Got water cress salad ready. Made sausage casserole ready for supper. Edgar's got here at 3:00. We heard a lot about Cambodia and they showed us a lot of photos. Eby hung the new picture that Mary Weber drew for us.

3/8/92 Sunday
Edgar's went with us to Kinzer. Abram's, Sam and Melissa, Dale and Mae were here for dinner and to hear about Cambodia this afternoon. Edgar's showed their slides. Abram's have a new Mercedes and I talked to Milton on their car phone. They came back from Hawaii on Thursday.

3/16/92 Monday
Eby drove some for Ike. It was white with snow this morning but it was soon gone. I did not sleep last night so I took a nap this morning. Washed, ironed and mended. Bagged some rug strips. Watered plants. There were eight barns burned in Big Valley and most were set.

3/21/92 Saturday
Eby had a haul for John and one for Christanne. Had a nice time with Sanford's and Ray and Jane came for lunch. Sanford brought Barbara King to stay with the boys and we left at 4:00 for the Hollinger House for our 65th anniversary celebration with all the family plus Abner and Esther. We were served a good meal after the photographer took pictures. Jean Thomas served fruit cocktail, ham loaf, scalloped potatoes, limas, salad, pickles, cake, ice cream and mints that Jim's Pat made. Had a time of sharing memories and visiting.

3/22/92 Sunday
Went to Kinzer. 52 there plus our 29. Had a big surprise when they all came in at 10:00, plus Uncle Jay's and Uncle Charlie. All went to Isaac's for dinner where Donald, Linda, Mark, Kim and Karen served appetizers in dining area. Later we went to the basement with two large tables set up with primroses and pretty napkins and cups. We had nice buns, stuffed chicken breasts, baked potato casserole, peas and carrots, frozen fruit salad, apple and Quaker town pies with ice cream, nuts and mints in cups. All was very good. Had a nice time visiting before everyone started leaving for home.

4/6/92 Monday
Eby had a drive for Ike and John. He harrowed the balance of the garden. I helped put up wire netting to keep rabbits out. I washed and ironed and worked on scrap books. Pat sent a clipping of Greg at his job. I made out a seed order. Nancy called. Gerry is going to room with Steve. We had Dean come for dinner. He does not eat sweet potatoes or peas. I had both. He does like meat and beans and filling balls.

4/12/92 Sunday
We went to Kinzer. Ruth taught our class and Paul preached. The choir sang a few numbers they practiced for Passion Week. We went to the Samaritan Home for the program this afternoon. I finished a letter to Abram for his tribute album.

4/13/92 Monday
Eby had regular drives. I washed and ironed. Got living room windows ready for cleaning. Put flower pole in garage. This afternoon we took my letter for Abram to the Cattail girl to have it made pretty. Then we went on to New Holland for a bathroom light and to Plank Road for pansies. I planted three dozen. Jim called and another farm was fired in Big Valley. The fire bug has not been caught.

4/16/92 Thursday
Eby had some driving. This afternoon he took me to Lydia King to pick up the letter for Abram's album and then to Dutchway for groceries. I was taking a break and reading some lent scripture when Gerry walked in on a trip from Washington to Lancaster. I wired Sue some cut flowers. The rain is making the grass look good after Elizabeth's raking.

4/19/92 Sunday

Went to Kinzer. Had our communion service with some changes. Unleavened crackers shared with partners holding hands and looking in eyes. With feetwashing practicing the holy kiss with a hug. Jay Meck's topic was "The Incomparable One." We had Elizabeth Ressler, Uncle Jay and Uncle Charlie for dinner. Had a nice visit and Jay went to the hospital and Sue's doctor said that her recovery is ahead of schedule.

4/23/92 Thursday

Eby had driving for Ike. He took the baby to the hospital with yellow jaundice. I washed the bed clothes and Eby helped clean the bed and put things back on. I worked in the yard. Cleaned the raspberry row and did some trimming. Mildred stopped for Mabel's coverings and we chatted a while. Eby mowed the back yard this evening. I ripped some of the wool that Kathleen brought. Abram's called this evening. Sam is accepted at Brown in Rhode Island and David has been accepted for his PH. D.

4/25/92 Saturday

My 87th birthday. Eby drove for Ike and Christanne. I cleaned the kitchen windows. Got down twice to answer the phone. Rhoda called and we had a nice chat. Sue called and she is doing real good. Mary and Esther Clark called and sang Happy Birthday. Esther called. Eby harrowed the garden and I hoed some of it and put paper between the pea rows. Sanford and the boys called this evening. Aunt Amy called and Charlie called from New Orleans. Jacob played Happy Birthday on his horn. Grace called and we had a long chat. Milton and Barbara called and said they are to be grandparents.

5/2/92 Saturday

Eby had no driving but he brought Levi Esh to put our counter in the bathroom. I gave him a check for $435.79. The plumber will finish next week. I started a rug for Marcia. Eby made the rows and I planted limas, corn, pickles, dill, parsley, and radishes. Just as I got done Isaac's came on their way from helping Kim and Mark. It got warm this afternoon and the sun went behind a bank. We gave Bradley $10.00 as the school will be picking up trash and he needs sponsors.

5/5/92 Tuesday

Eby had driving for Ike. I cleaned the refrigerator and helped at the Fire Hall this afternoon. We had a nice time. Esther came before I left and brought Daddy a peach pie and bread. Marian left candy and a card. I called Sanford's and Jacob played Happy Birthday on his little horn. Talked to all the others. Milton and Barbara called to say happy birthday.

5/24/92 Sunday

Went to Kinzer. 52 there. Spent the afternoon at home. I called Ray's for their 23rd anniversary. They had just gotten home from meeting Laura at the airport when she came home from her trip to Austria, Italy and Germany. Martha left on her camping trip this morning. Mildred took us to Kinzer this evening. It got colder and is raining.

5/31/92 Sunday
Had our picnic program and dinner at the church. A good number there with some tourists. My salad and pies were eaten. We had lots of good things. There were lots of testimonies and singing. We left early and got ready to go to Abram's Tribute dinner. Uncle Charlie picked us up here and took us to the Marriot Hotel in Harrisburg. We were first there and it gave over 200. The program was interesting and Jim's, Dale's, Ray's, Edgar's and Charlie were there from our family. Got home at 10:45.

6/4/92 Thursday
Eby had a drive this afternoon. He harrowed the garden and we put the lima bean poles up and I hoed most of the garden. Planted some yellow, white and green tomato plants and 75 sweet potatoes. Eby put strings up for the thumbergia vines and I wed the round flower bed. I sent Ray some salsify seed. Soaked my feet and started reading Surviving Without Romance. Put three packs of spinach in the freezer and made a salad for supper.

6/16/92 Tuesday
Eby drove for John only. He mended the hose and did some sprinkling without leaks. He sharpened the butcher knife. I washed the bedclothes and ripped the balance of wool pieces that Jane gave. I called Aunt Elizabeth this evening and she said Robert asked for Eby today and it was the first he said anything for weeks.

6/22/92 Monday
Very cool. Eby had his regular hauls. He bought a new latch for the porch door and could not understand the installation. We picked two bushels of peas and he took them to the huller. I put 26 pints in freezer. I picked the sugar peas and put 12 pints in freezer. Put 2 pints of strawberries in freezer. Trained the limas. Finished reading Surviving Without Romance. It was very informative. Eby helped nip the sugar peas. David put the new door latch on.

6/25/92 Thursday
Eby had some drives for Ike. He harrowed the far side of the garden. We planted cabbage, broccoli, cauliflower, corn, green and yellow beans and carrots. I worked on rug. The summer cactus is full of beautiful flowers. Grace, Mary Alice and Nancy were driving to Edgar's today for the annual Sisters' Day.

7/7/92 Tuesday
Eby drove for Ike and brought Barbara to mow the yard. I washed and ironed. Made red raspberry jelly and cookies. Picked the black raspberries and blueberries. Nipped the pansies. Big article and pictures in the paper about closing the Samaritan Home. Carpenters are busy on Vincent's project at the schoolhouse. Our beef is ready at Dutchway.

7/10/92 Friday
Eby had no driving. I finished things up and packed for trip to Edgar's. Made cole slaw to take along with the beef, cookies, beans and rice krispie cake. Tom and Rosa came and we were packed up and left at 1:00. Rosa drove and Tom entertained me in the back seat. We got better acquainted. We had a good trip with one rest stop. Fredric's came on Monday and are well adjusted.

7/12/92 Sunday
We went with Edgar's to Bethel Grove services. There is a large congregation. Had a good dinner of cold beef, potatoes, peas, cole slaw and buns. Had ice cream, cookies, and popcorn later on. The children played ball and kept active till bedtime. Carol quietly gathered things up and started packing. Tom and Rosa left about 3:00 and Ed and Marcia a little later.

7/13/92 Monday
Fredric's family got all packed up and left at 7:00. It got very quiet with only Andrea left. I hemmed a wallhanging for Rhoda this forenoon and evening. After lunch Edgar's took us to visit Ed and Marcia in their log cabin in DeRuyter. Saw their chicks, four pigs, Reba the dog, Yoder and Katie the cats. Andrea stayed for the night and will take the plane back to Goshen in the morning.

7/14/92 Tuesday
Started home with Edgar's at 8:00 and had a good trip. Stopped in Lebanon at Agway but Dale was out for business. Ate our dinner at Kreider's Restaurant on the way home. Read the news and relaxed. There was rain here and things have grown. There were four killed in auto accidents while we were gone. Rhoda and Edgar worked on getting garage doors ready for painting.

7/15/92 Wednesday
Eby drove for Ike. I washed and ironed and cooked. Edgar and Rhoda painted the garage door two coats and it looks like a good job. They do not think it is a good color, but Daddy is pleased. Rhoda and I looked over the garden and found first tomato and picked some beans for them. Picked some big pickles and washed them.

7/16/92 Thursday
Eby had no extra drives. Barbara mowed the yard. Edgar's left at 7:30. I made a peach pie, bread and buns. Made things ready for supper. Grace and Jennie got here about 4:00. The brought two packs of venison and some fancy bread. Eby got a 24 lb. box of apricots at Kauffman's for $15.95.

7/20/92 Monday
We took John to work, then loaded Isaac Stoltzfus' family and went to Schafferstown and to a nearby lake and fishery for a day of fishing. It was a good day. Ike and the

boys and Anna caught 32, I caught 3 and Eby 1. Had our picnic lunch. I made the sandwiches and drink. It was interesting to see the process. I washed and ironed.

7/28/92 Tuesday
Eby had some drives for Ike. He cultivated the garden and I hoed some of it this afternoon. Elizabeth took me for an appointment with Dr. Small. He checked me out good and said I was fine but must have a blood check and take two pills a day for blood pressure. I got the births and marriages listed for our historian, Betty Meck. Eby pulled a basket of beets and I washed them.

8/4/92 Tuesday
Eby took me to the Medical Center for a blood test only. I got sixty pills at the drugstore for $49.95. 5.50 off for senior citizen. I started braiding Jennie's rug this afternoon. A box was delivered and it was new shoes for walking from Nancy. I put them on and wore them till bedtime.

8/11/92 Tuesday
Eby did morning and evening drives. Abram and Pat came at 9:00 and took us to the Philadelphia Zoo. We had a good day and there were lots of people there. The zoo has been changed so much since we were last there some 30 years ago. Animals, birds and reptiles are very interesting and well kept. We got in heavy rain coming home. Isaac's came this evening. They brought eggplant and gladiolas.

8/29/92 Saturday
It was a cool day for our reunion at Camp Morehart and we spent most of the time indoors visiting. The children played outdoors and some went down to the pool. Little Ben and Stephanie had a good time running all around. Ed Ludwig was missing because his hogs and chickens had to be butchered. Others had reasons for their absences too.

8/30/92 Sunday
Had a good day at Camp Morehart. Ray was in charge of our worship service. Edgar was our chorister and Laura had a story for the children. Had some Christmas memories and scripture reading with prayers. I came home with Barbara and Eby with Milton. Sanford's came here about 5:00. Spent a nice evening visiting, playing and looking at photos.

8/31/92 Monday
Eby had driving. Sanford and Tera suggested that we take a lunch and go for a ride on the Strasburg Railroad and have lunch in the park by Cherry Hill Station. The weather was perfect and there were many people riding the train and eating at the park. Next we went to Mennonite Home to visit the relatives and Esther Groff. Had a nice evening with Sanford's after they made their visit to Elam's.

9/24/92 Thursday
Colder. Eby drove for Ike. I washed some windows on the outside. I picked two big buckets of tomatoes. I went to the store and the bill was $51.21. I made some tea concentrate. The trial is on for the three involved with the Show girls murder. Eby helped empty the trough and put new dirt in for the hen and chicks. Someone was here while I was at the store and put a chair by the door.

9/25/92 Friday
Eby had driving for Ike. He dug some sweet potatoes for Sunday. I cut all the grapes and he picked some off. I made 14 quarts of juice in half gallon jars. Got celery, carrots, broccoli, radishes, turnips, etc. for a salad platter. Called Clarence's this afternoon. Cut some rug strips. Had a Crop walk letter from Sanford. Miriam Hess called this evening and said Amy has been in the hospital with a heart attack since Tuesday. She is out of constant care now.

9/27/92 Sunday
Went to Kinzer. Mark Leaman preached our counsel meeting sermon. Had our footwashing service. Greg and Cindy came for dinner. We had a nice visit with them. Cindy is weak and tired but has gained some weight. Milton called and Doug was home for the Jewish holiday. A new headmaster will be announced soon. I started reading No More Shacks. It is about Habitat for Humanity.

9/28/92 Monday
Eby had drives for Ike. I washed and ironed. Elizabeth took us to Lancaster to have our wills updated this afternoon. Barbara mowed the yard and cleaned up some leaves. I called Sue and asked about Amy and she did not call her today, but Rachel said she is still in the hospital. I cleaned dry sink cupboard and made an order to National for stockings.

10/14/92 Wednesday
Eby drove for Ike all day. I housecleaned the dining room. Put the flower pole and plants in sewing room. Scrubbed the porch and raked some leaves and got ready for our midweek service. We began the study of Ecclesiastes. Sanford called and I talked to the three boys. They raised almost $1000.00 for the Crop walk.

10/20/92 Tuesday
Heavy frost. Eby drove for Ike. I washed. Put porch chairs down. Took out the dahlias, elephant ear and coleus. Put geraniums on window sills and put some plants in basement. Covered tomatoes. I mended Eby's old coat. Dale called to say he has to move his job to Western Pennsylvania in three weeks.

10/25/92 Sunday
Went to Kinzer. 57 there. Jay Meck preached. He hit on nonconformity for a change. Kathy and her mother read scripture and played unfamiliar music. Had a quiet afternoon and evening. Jim's picked up their chairs on the way home.

10/30/92 Friday
Eby drove for Ike. We took Clarence and Mabel along to the funeral for Elmer Martin at the Fairview Church. It gave a house full, about 550 people. Got home at 2:10. I made quince honey from some quince that Ray brought. It started raining after dark. No word from Amy. Got things lined up for our trip to Jim's tomorrow. Eby fell on his wrist and it is hurting.

10/31/92 Saturday
Isaac's came at 7:00 to take us to Jim's. We left Bradley off at Ed Miller's. Stopped at McDonald's for breakfast and got there by 10:30. Pat had a good dinner for us and she took us to an antique place at Reedsville where they had a huge collection of all kinds of things. Cindy went with us. I bought an antique washboard for $27.00. We got home by 7:30. Rhoda called to say they will come on Friday afternoon. Sue called to say that they will do bypass surgery for Amy on Monday.

11/4/92 Wednesday
Eby drove for Ike 100 miles. I varnished the kitchen chairs and the table with five table boards. They are still sticky this evening. We ate supper at the card table. Jean took me to Sewing Circle. Mabel has a cold and did not want to go. The new president is Clinton. Amy was to leave the hospital by ambulance today.

11/7/92 Saturday
Eby took John to work. Edgar and Rhoda took us to Philadelphia to visit Thomas and Rosa. We had no problem on the way down but some leaving Philadelphia. Had a nice visit and a good lunch. They have a nice comfortable home and very clean. Spent the evening visiting. Called Miriam and she said it would be best not to visit Amy tomorrow.

11/10/92 Tuesday
Eby had vacation for weddings. We raked the yard and burned a lot of leaves. I did some cleaning and watered the plants. Made a pot of vegetable soup. Wired Amy some flowers. Called Mabel for her 86th birthday. The children all visited her. I called Miriam and she said her mother seemed some better on Sunday. Mary is coming in from Bemidgi, Minnesota. We put the kitchen table and chairs back in the kitchen.

11/11/92 Wednesday
Eby drove for Ike till 11:30. Sanford and Jacob came about 9:30 and had time to relax before dinner. We left with them about 1:00 and got to Richmond by 6:30. Tera had a good supper and the boys were ready for visiting. Jacob tried braiding a rug and did real good. We stopped to see if their table was being made at a Kurtz place and asked for Samuel Stoltzfus. He was close by and we stopped for a short visit.

11/12/92 Thursday
Had a good day. Sanford cleaned up some leaves. Daddy took it easy. Tera had her quilt ready to mark and we got it in and I began quilting and got a nice start on it. She went to work at 9:00 and got home about 4:00. Sanford served us lunch and took us to visit the boys' school. We saw some slides, did some quilting and started Jacob on braiding a rug this evening. We saw Sanford's outdoor railroad project. Luke was busy braiding some string.

11/14/92 Saturday
After we had a good breakfast with blueberry muffins I did some quilting and it is more than half done. Gerry and Nancy came and she helped to quilt and they took us to their house for lunch. Eby helped put some storm sash on and I went with Nancy to get some pansies and some winter plants like cabbage. Spent some time watching TV. Everything is in order and real clean. Goldie is well-behaved.

11/15/92 Sunday
Had a good night at Nancy's. Gerry stayed back and Nancy took us to Staunton in time for the 10:30 service at Staunton Mennonite Church. The pastor Richard Weaver preached a good sermon on the power of the Holy Spirit. Met a lot of the folks. I called Jay Martin's on Nancy's car phone. Had a good dinner and time for visiting. Nancy took us to see the lot in Fishersville where they hope to build a house sometime. Jennie and Steve came this afternoon and evening.

11/16/92 Monday
Mary Alice came in time for breakfast. Steve went out early to hunt for deer. Nancy, Mary Alice and us started for home at 7:10. Had good driving in Nancy's Pontiac and got home at 11:45. They had a snack and started back at 12:30. Nancy called at 4:45 and said they were driving up Weaver's driveway. We read the back news and mail. Put linoleum under the flower pole and set up the clothes rack that Sanford gave for my rug strips. Marked Laura and Martha's cookbooks.

11/23/92 Monday
Eby drove 100 miles for Ike. I washed and dried it in the basement. Did the ironing and mending. I got the celery ready and put the outside stems in the freezer. Made

three quarts of cranberry jelly. Mike called this morning to tell us that Erica Lynn came early this morning. She weighs six pounds and is twenty inches long. Mother and baby are both well. Milton called this evening and they are well pleased with their granddaughter. I sewed some rug strips.

11/26/92 Thursday
I made the gravy and packed up turkey, croquettes, celery and cranberries. Isaac's came for us at 9:20 and we went to Ed Miller's. Had a good dinner and good visiting. We went home with Ray's. All went well and we had a nice evening.

11/27/92 Friday
Still cloudy and we had a good night. Ray's gave me a 1993 diary and Daddy a chocolate locomotive. They took us for a drive to see some of the extra fine houses where the wealthy live north of Princeton. After lunch they took us to Trenton where Daddy found a coat in an outlet store for $100.00. Laura's boyfriend, Glenn, came for supper. We had a nice evening. Martha called from London.

12/8/92 Tuesday
No driving as Amos was married today to Reuben King's daughter. We left for the wedding at 8:30. Took in the singing, two sermons and testimonies. Had a good dinner. We visited and heard more singing and had more eats. Came home at 4:00. I did some patches this evening.

12/13/92 Sunday
Went to Kinzer. Jay Meck preached. Had a hasty lunch and took Clarence's to Jay's and Charlie drove us to the 60th wedding anniversary for Elmer and Susan Shirk. Had a nice time with friendly people. Abram's stopped by for supper on their way from Washington. I made a quick one. Lydia Martin called to say that Emma Horning died this afternoon. I called Mabel, Jay's, Amy and Paul's.

12/24/92 Thursday
Eby had driving for Ike. He picked up a gallon of oysters for the Esh's. I worked on rug off and on. Ted and Beth stopped a little while on their way to Jim's. They brought a pretty bouquet. Esther came and brought about ten pounds of gum candy and jelly eggs and a piece of cheese. We got a nice greeting from Leo.

12/25/92 Friday
Had a nice day. Went to Daniel Dietzel's with some of the rest of Isaac's family. Joanne had a lot of pretty decorations and their newly-decorated basement is plush. They gave us gifts. Isaac's gave Daddy a shirt and me a box of Tide washing powder. Linda gave a quilt box and a lot of crackers, cheese, sausages and party mix. Sally gave a pretty scented candle. Mark and Kim stopped in this evening on the way to Isaac's and gave us a big poinsettia, sausage and scrapple.

1993

1/1/93 Friday
The New Year came in sunny with lots of wind clouds. We set up the table for eleven guests. Amy called and said she has not been feeling so well for a couple days. At 9:00 Pauline called to say that Paul was sore from a hernia and polyp that he had done, so they are not coming. Next we took two boards out and four places off. I got food all ready and cooked less of some things. Jay's, Charlie, Clarence's and Miriam Hess were all that came. We had a nice time visiting. Mabel seemed real good.

1/6/93 Wednesday
Eby drove for Ike. Mildred took me to all day Sewing Circle. We did a quilt for the Samaritan Home. Had a good day of fellowship. Mabel was there all day. Martha Clark was there. I did not know her as it was about seventy years since I saw her last and she has aged. Made a sauer kraut supper.

1/14/93 Thursday
Eby had driving most of the day. We had some sunshine. I worked on rug. I called Edgar's and he had a lot to tell about his week in Florida helping with reconstruction. He said it is difficult to describe the destruction from Hurricane Andrew. Rhoda is doing a quilt for Rosa. She teaches a Russian woman English.

1/18/93 Monday
Eby had only his work men. He had an easy day. Tom and Rosa came about 11:30 and were very interested in our old things. Tom was very talkative. He enjoyed the dinner, especially the mashed potatoes. He ate so many he had no room for dessert. Rosa was pleased with the chair.

1/20/93 Wednesday
Eby drove nearly 200 miles for Ike today. I made 30 sweet potato croquettes, 2 jelly rolls, some fluffy puffs and rhubarb sauce. Went to the store and the bill was $89.86. My first time this year. I read this evening. Got an invitation to quilt at the Fire Hall. President Clinton went into office today.

1/22/93 Friday
Eby drove for Ike this afternoon. I cut up turkey, made gravy, filling balls, fruit cup and cooked the bones. Eby ran the cleaner. He caught the end of my rug thread spool and it wrapped and got the cleaner tight. I worked on it about three hours and finally got it real good after 2:00. Eby had car trouble when he went for John and left it at the garage. I rolled ice cream in the jelly roll cakes.

1/23/93 Saturday
Eby had a holiday. He helped set up the table for our guests. This was our turn to have Ike Stoltzfus' family and his workmen. Also his brother Amos and his bride

Lydia. I gave her the rug I made for her. Everyone seemed to enjoy the turkey dinner. Uncle Charlie brought them in his van and took them home. He came back and I gave him some leftovers. It was a good day.

1/27/93 Wednesday
Eby drove for Ike. I watered the plants. Did some small odd jobs that were waiting. I worked on rug this afternoon with radio for company. Made a half portion of root beer and sliced some bacon. President Clinton has passed the abortion law and homosexuals can serve in the armed services. Kinzer business meeting was this evening but Eby needed the rest.

1/28/93 Thursday
Eby drove most all day for Ike. I worked on rug most of the day. Marian came about 3:30 and we got into some scripture and she is going to live her way. She knows how a Christian should live. I showed her Lev. 20:13 and Deut. 22:5. A Florida man shot and killed three men who were responsible for him losing his job and he then shot himself. Talked to Mildred about the business meeting. It lasted late. They are concerned about Kinzer's young.

1/30/93 Saturday
Eby had a drive to New Providence. I got food lined up for dinner and supper. Sanford's got here about 10:30. The boys were rested and happy. It was first time in their new car. Tera took them to the Park for a while and they went up to Elam's when they were milking. They had a large frog picture to color that Mary Alice gave them. We played games, checkers, figmill, snap cards, hide the button and more.

2/5/93 Friday
Eby drove for Ike from 10:30 till evening. 286 miles for the week. I made the souse and put the pudding in the freezer. Worked on relaxing the rug and got a lot done. They called for the fourth time to remind me of my Monday appointment with Dr. Stoltzfus. Two cards and two calls.

2/11/93 Thursday
Eby had a drive for Ike this morning. I made a pig stomach for lunch. Ray and Jane came about 11:30. They brought a rocker to have caned. We took it to an Amish woman on Quarryville Pike. We stopped at Georgetown Store and bought a few things. Jane showed us photos from their England trip. I made chicken and waffles for supper.

2/18/93 Thursday
Eby had an easy day. He brought eggs and milk and some things from Dutchway. I made some Jogger in a Jug and we each took a dose. Worked on rug. Have 18 rows done. Had some radio. Snow did not melt as it was too cold.

2/21/93 Sunday
It began snowing before daylight and kept it up most of the day. Many services were cancelled, but not Kinzer. Jean said there were 46 there. We spent the day at home reading and having radio sermons. Rhoda called and said that Marcus Austin Hines was born at noon today.

2/26/93 Friday
Eby was put all day. He did the income tax papers. I finished the fourth rug. Sewed up some rolls of rug strips and oiled the sewing machine. I called and talked to Tom Hines, Rosa and Rhoda. The baby is good and all is well. Philadelphia had a small quake today. A bomb did damage at the Board of Trade in New York.

3/6/93 Saturday
Eby had no driving. He ran the sweeper. I did some cleaning and prepared food for the Clemens'. We bathed and got all ready. I rolled some strips. Put up the rollaway bed for Marcia. They got here about 5:00. I made cow in the garden for supper. They brought a good report from the Hines'. Tom has a good job.

3/13/93 Saturday
We are having the blizzard of the century. Traffic is almost at a standstill. Visibility hinders road plows. Strong winds and much snow. David and his boys stayed put all day. Power went off a few times, but not too long. I called Abram's and Isaac's to cancel Sunday dinner. Milton called to say they got home by midnight. Rhoda, Abram, Isaac, Charlie and Sanford called. I called Dale and Jim. All are snowbound. Radio reports that more than 400 church services are cancelled and lots of other things. I sewed rug strips and watched the storm.

3/14/93 Sunday
We spent the day at home. Had radio sermons and music, watched the snow removal and traffic, and read. Had a lot of phone calls. A bobcat opened our driveway. It had a lot of snow.

3/15/93 Monday
Eby had no driving. Roads are getting opened and used. Eby got the drive salted and made a bare path to the road. No mail, but we did get a Monday paper with a lot of blizzard news, the worst one of this century. It is getting icy this evening. Schools and many other things are cancelled for tomorrow. I washed and sewed my rug strips. I called Amy and she is sick, vomiting and dizzy. Is to have Xray.

3/17/93 Wednesday
Eby stayed put all day. The snow melted a lot and there was water only in the freezer room. I sewed strips all day. Mail carrier went today. We sent $25.00 to help pay the Esh quadruplets' hospital bill. I called Miriam Hess and she said Amy is very

sick. She and Rachel took her for an Xray and she has bronchitis and is not eating or drinking. It snowed a little this evening.

3/20/93 Saturday
Eby took Anna for groceries and spent the balance of the day in his chair. I did some cleaning and cut patches from some fabric pieces that Kathleen gave. A murder in the paper named an Amish man who murdered his wife in northwestern Pennsylvania. I made a Quakertown pie. I called Marian and she said that Lenny was sent home last night because he was sleeping and may lose his job.

3/25/93 Thursday
Eby had driving for Ike and came home for lunch. I made a sausage casserole for lunch and Ray and Jane came about 11:30. We ate lunch and went to L.M.H.S. for the quilt show. Met Joanne and Elizabeth and had a good time seeing all the antique quilts and friends who were there. On way home we stopped at Flaud's for seeds and fertilizer and at White Horse Dry Goods for quilt backing. Ray's left for home at 7:30. It was a good day.

3/26/93 Friday
Eby drove for Ike. He had diarrhea and ate little. I worked on my rug and rolled up all the strips on Elizabeth's roller. Have a lot of variety. Saw the first robins and a lot of noisy birds. A crocus opened by the porch. I called Amy and she is feeling better. I cleaned up the holly leaves off the porch. Had a letter from Jacob. He needs rug thread. Micah wants to make one too. Made a pecan chiffon cake for the Gap Sale.

4/2/93 Friday
Eby helped put ham in the freezer and he picked up sticks in the front yard and drove for Ike. I cooked a piece of ham, baked a cake and made some food ready. Did some cleaning. Called Sue and we had a nice chat. Talked to Charlie first. He said there is an idea that footwashing is on the outs.

4/4/93 Sunday
Went to Kinzer. Paul Clark preached. Had our spring footwashing. Martha Burkholder, Ellen Groff and Kathryn Graham did not practice this custom this time. Mary Alice and Ellen went to Quaker meeting. They left at 2:00 and I washed up dishes after they were gone. We read and had a restful afternoon.

4/11/93 Sunday
We spent the day at home because I got sick in the night. Woke up about 1:00, sweated, dizzy, giddy and nauseated. Eby helped me to the bathroom and it went both ways. Maybe it was food poisoning from Saturday dinner or a bug. I stayed in bed till noon and Eby did not go to church as he did not feel normal. Had a quiet

day. Milton called to say his peas are planted. I had some good naps and ate toast and milk, feeling much better. Read this evening.

4/14/93 Wednesday
Eby drove a lot of miles for Ike. He helped put up pea wire before he left and I planted the peas and onions. I raked on side of the drive. Burned the trash pile. Did some cleaning and made turnips for supper. Abram called to see how we are doing. I feel better but appetite is still not normal. Had our last midweek meeting on the book of Ecclesiastes.

4/23/93 Friday
Eby drove for Ike most of the day and came home for dinner. Ray's came with their friends Hugh and Gertrude White. They brought Laura's quilt and had left a patch for me to do. I got it done just as they came home from a tour of the County. Ray brought me a strip roller that he made. It is very nice and he did one for Elizabeth. I braided rug this evening.

4/24/93 Saturday
Eby drove for Ike till noon. I braided rug and bathed and dressed for Abram's visit to take us to Country Gardens for my birthday dinner. They came about 5:00 and we had a lot of good food and a nice evening visiting. I called Ruth Coy at Brethren Village and she is well-satisfied with her living there. Abram called Becky and Sam from his car and they are both fine. I got eight birthday greetings today.

4/25/93 Sunday
Went to Kinzer. Paul preached a good sermon on things we have no control over. They sang Happy Birthday. We went to visit David Clark's this afternoon. He is recovering from shingles. Micah called and I talked to all three boys and Sanford. Their ground is too wet for gardening.

4/28/93 Wednesday
Eby drove for Ike all day, 177 miles. I put balloons on the pea wire to keep the birds off. I did some rug braiding. Harvey is busy with his spring work. I started reading Isaac's book on Nickel Mines history. Charlie and Ed sent an orchid for my birthday by Federal Express.

5/13/93 Thursday
Eby drove for Ike. He gathered up my weed piles from yesterday and planted two raspberry plants. I finished cleaning living room and worked on the bank for an hour till it rained. Took a rest. Went to the store. Bill was $51.38. Got a lot of things. I transplanted my big fern and started one for Clarence. Nipped old pansies off. Made a batch of tea concentrate. Snow balls are blooming, and it is cold.

5/16/93 Sunday
Went to Kinzer. Richard Buckwalter Sr. preached about people and how important we all are. Mabel was not there. Had a quick lunch and Isaac's came for us to take us to Laura's graduation from nurses training at University of Pennsylvania in Philadelphia. After the two programs were done our car would not start. Had to get AAA to check and they were slow while we ate a snack on Laura's porch. Got home safely at 8:30. Car worked fine. Mother Koerwer was going to dinner with Ray, Jane, Laura and Glen.

5/18/93 Tuesday
Very cool. Eby had a drive for Ike. At 1:00 we picked up Anna, the little girls, her mother and sister Elizabeth and her little ones and went to see the rose greenhouses in Christiana. There are thirteen greenhouses full of rose plants. Beautiful. He gave us each 25 roses. Eby got carrots at Dutchway and I made a gallon of sticks ready for Aaron Martin's funeral meal at Old Road. Emma Witmer picked them up this evening. I mended a porch chair.

5/22/93 Saturday
Eby had a drive for Ike. He got his new hearing aid this afternoon and it is very good, $550.00. He harrowed the garden and I hoed most of it. The birds have been rough on the peas. Potato bugs are here. Mildred called and said they took Mabel to the doctor and he put her on a respirator. I dug the tulips and Eby brought marigolds and I planted them in the long flower bed. I took a bath while we had Sunday School meditations.

5/29/93 Saturday
Had a nice leisurely morning with Sanford's. We packed a lunch and went to Ebersole's chair shop and to Horning's to check on chairs for Sanford's. Then we stopped at a fish pond south of New Holland and the boys enjoyed fishing for a half hour. They each caught two and cost was $2.25 each plus lines and bait. Caught two for us. We ate our picnic lunch at the Pequea Church. Sanford cleaned the fish and we had a chicken and waffle supper. I played croquette with the boys. Luke won. It was a good week for haymaking.

5/30/93 Sunday
Fine day. Went to Kinzer. No adult classes. Had singing, poems, etc. Sanford's went to Quaker Meeting. We got home first and had cold ham, new potatoes, creamed corn and a variety of desserts. Sanford's gathered up their things, fish and all, and left for home at 1:30. Mabel called this evening and she talked real good. I called Sue and Jay was able to go to church. I took a nap and read.

6/2/93 Wednesday
Eby drove for Ike. I finished the fourth rug. Did some weeding, hoeing and planting. I called Marian in the hospital and she is having a lot of problems and does not know

when she can come home. Bennie Fisher died. Jean took me to Sewing Circle. We knotted a quilt for folks in Alabama. I wrote off some recipes. Arlene said Lengacher's are not making any more butter, so there will be no buttermilk.

6/5/93 Saturday
Cool. Eby had the day off. I made a blueberry pie. Picked three quarts of strawberries. Worked on recipes and may call it done. Abram called and Becky had a few words. She is moving home and plans to get a car. Did a little cleaning. Charlie called and he had a lot of news. Will be going to the Marshall Islands before too long. Has an architect to advise about his renovations. I called Nancy for their anniversary.

6/6/93 Sunday
Fine weather. Went to Kinzer. 60 there. Had some visitors. Had Uncle Charlie for dinner and he took us to see Marian in the hospital and to the Mennonite Home to see Jay and Menno's. Charlie came in and said the car would not start. Eby went out and found he had the wrong car. Then Eby thought he had left his hat in the Home and Charlie went in to get it. Eby found he was sitting on it in the car and called him back. I called Mabel and read The Last Days of Pompeii.

6/9/93 Wednesday
Eby drove for Ike. I went to the store and got two tongues for curing. Just as I got back and had things put away Charlie came with Sue, Lois, Esther and Paul. We had two hours of real good visiting and it was so good to have Lois and Esther share their experiences.

6/23/93 Wednesday
Eby drove for Ike. I went to the store. The bill was $44.67. I did some cleaning and scrubbed the porch. Made a cake and got some lettuce ready. Made some tea concentrate. Edgar's got here before 8:00 and we had time for visiting before the three Virginia girls came about 9:00. We had an ice cream treat before going to bed.

6/24/93 Thursday
Edgar went with Eby for a drive and took some things to Reusit in White Horse. The girls got busy on the recipe book. They had all the equipment and were well organized to put it all in order and put it in the backs.

6/25/93 Friday
Eby had some driving for Ike. Had late breakfast and the girls got all packed up and visited before going to Uncle Jay's at 10:00. Uncle Jay is not so good, but did some work with the hose on the porches. Mary Alice and I came home and had lunch with Daddy. She went to do some shopping this afternoon.

6/26/93 Saturday
Eby had the day off. Mary Alice took her morning run in the Park before she ate breakfast. She helped pick blueberries. We took it easy until her two friends came

with five-month-old baby Sarah. They picked her up to take a tour and go to Country Gardens for dinner, so they took off after an hour.

7/5/93 Monday
Eby had a drive for Ike. I did some cleaning. Made a pie and cake. Got food ready for supper. Barbara came about 3:00 and Michael, Jan and Erica came about 5:00 from Pittsburgh where they visited her sister. Erica travels very well. She is friendly and happy. Barbara King mowed the yard and Barbara took her home as it was so hot to ride the scooter up the hills.

7/17/93 Saturday
Pleasant. Eby had the day off. He cultivated the garden and did some hoeing. I did some cleaning. Got some food ready for Sunday. Rhoda called this evening to say that John Edmund Ludwig was born today, 8 lbs. 12 oz. Eby planted some corn where he took the red potatoes out.

7/30/93 Friday
Eby drove for Ike. I finished the fifth rug this afternoon. Rhoda called to say they will be going to Tom and Rosa's and getting there this evening. We had a thank you from Marcia for the baby gift. Also a nice letter from Mae. I did the sprinkling and soaked the celery. Read the Alaska magazine that Becky gave us.

8/1/93 Sunday
Went to Kinzer. Paul preached. The Armenian women from New York were there again. We went to Paul's this afternoon. Paul joined in the conversation and looks better. I read Last Days of Pompeii this evening. Abram called and he thinks we should go to Goshen with them when he gets his award in October and Daddy is not in favor.

8/6/93 Friday
Eby drove for Ike this afternoon. We had more than two inches of nice rain today. Did not run off and is so good for everything. I canned two quarts of pickles. Worked on my dress. Called Grace and they were getting a good rainfall. All is well with them. Jay came home from the hospital this afternoon and is feeling real good with his pacemaker. Mary Alice called and she came home on Tuesday from New Mexico where she spent a week after the week she spent in Charlie's home.

8/20/93 Friday
Eby drove for Ike this afternoon. He silked corn for me this morning and I put twelve pints in the freezer. It is nice Silver Queen. I trimmed some yard after Barbara mowed. Made party mix, chocolate syrup and rhubarb sauce. Cooked a piece of beef and a tongue. Had a gust and heavy rain this evening. The Siamese twins were supposed to be separated today in Philadelphia hospital.

8/22/93 Sunday
Went to Kinzer. Paul preached. Had a birthday celebration for Charlie, his 75th. Uncle Jay and Aunt Sue, Clarence and Mabel, Miriam brought Aunt Amy, Paul and Pauline, Isaac's and Abram's. All enjoyed the dinner and Jay laid down some of the afternoon. We did some reminiscing and Abram taped it for Uncle Menno. Mabel did real good with her respirator. Abram took some pictures.

8/27/93 Friday
Eby drove for Ike till noon. Dale and Jacob left at 10:00 and Charlie came soon after 12:00 in a rented car from Abram's. After we ate he loaded our portion of food for the reunion, 5 gallons of root beer, beans, red eggs, things for chicken corn soup, cookies, cake, peaches, cucumber slaw, tea concentrate and roses. Got to Camp Morehart soon after five and had 22 for supper. Had a nice evening.

8/28/93 Saturday
A very warm day. The family kept coming and the Virginia folks were in charge of the noon meal, which was ham, beans, potatoes, cole slaw and pies from Elizabeth and Joanne. Had some new games and the girls made a partner game quiz that was interesting. A number left on Saturday evening. It dropped a little rain toward evening. Ray's were in charge of supper and had clam soup. It was good with plenty of vegetables.

8/29/93 Sunday
Pleasant. Uncle Charlie and Jennie Weaver came for breakfast. The dishwasher was a problem and we were sparing with dishes because of hand washing. Jonathan's family shared the upstairs with a divider and it worked fine. Dale and Mae were in charge of our worship service. Milton, Jonathan, Ruth and Sam gave some of their experiences with other people's religions. Everyone packed up and said our good byes and left for our homes. Spent the evening resting up.

9/12/93 Sunday
Went to Paradise Community Park for our service and fellowship dinner. We took two pies and a succotash casserole. There was special singing, scripture, prayer, poems, verses, etc. About ten missing. Abram called and said he has all plans made for the trip to Goshen.

9/17/93 Friday
Eby drove for Ike this afternoon. He went to Rhoad's Store and got banner lye, callous pads, syrup and shaving cream. Stopped for eggs and red peppers. I made Oh Henry's. Finished Eby's pants and worked on my dress. Getting things lined up for our trip to Goshen.

9/22/93 Wednesday
Eby drove for Ike. I did some cleaning for our midweek service. David had his boys and did not go out this evening. Eby scrubbed the porch. Mrs. Vincent brought a basket of apples and gave them free. She stayed for a nice long visit and told about her many experiences. We listened to President Clinton's speech on health care. Stirred up two kinds of cookies.

9/25/93 Saturday
Eby had no driving. He raked leaves in front yard. I made some rhubarb tarts and a jelly roll for ice cream. Cooked sweet potatoes. Jonathan's came this P.M. on their way to Philadelphia to visit Rosa and Tom and he is to preach at a Cambodian church tomorrow with an interpreter. I treated them to the rhubarb tarts. Today was the Relief Sale in Virginia. I cut Eby's hair.

9/27/93 Monday
Eby had a drive for Ike. I washed and ironed. Made a three gallon crock of sauer kraut. Cleaned corner of the garage and scrubbed the rug. I put buttons on two pairs of Eby's trousers for suspenders. Did some work on one of my dresses. Grace called and she is busy but the Relief Sale being done is a big job done. It was a rainy day, but the sale was good, raised about $175,000. The highest quilt brought $7900, a white one that the same sisters make each year.

9/30/93 Thursday
Got up at 4:00, had breakfast at 5:00 and Uncle Charlie picked us up and then Aunt Sue and took us on to Abram's at Hershey, where we left for Goshen. Stopped for rests, lunch and dinner and got here to Holiday Inn at 8:45. Have a very nice room. Pat was good company and the car was driven safely by Abram. Charlie and Sue were going to stop and see Josephine after dropping us off.

10/1/93 Friday
Got up in a hurry and had a light breakfast in dining room and first we went to a program at the college and then to the church for meeting the award winners and a snack. Met a lot of folks from Goshen College graduates and their families. We had a lunch here with ourselves as Abram's had other invitations. Later they took us for a drive to see the huge retirement center and parts of Goshen. Later they went with us for dinner. We spent the evening reading. No word of Charlie yet. We called Fredric's and are to go there tomorrow afternoon.

10/2/93 Saturday
We had an interesting day. Breakfast, lunch and the banquet this evening. There were a lot of people and the three award winners all spoke and Peter Dyck was the

main speaker. 800 ate. We all went to see Fredric's this afternoon and Andrea came too. Sanford and Luke and Charlie came this forenoon.

10/3/93 Sunday
We ate breakfast in the dining room with Abram's, David's, Samuel and Melissa, Becky, Charlie, Sanford and Luke. Charlie paid the bill. We went to church at the college auditorium where the attendance was 1000. Met a lot of friendly folks. Ate lunch at the college dining room. Left for Ohio after lunch and came to the Comfort Inn for the night. Ate at Wendy's. Had some T.V. and bedded down.

10/4/93 Monday
Had breakfast at the Comfort Inn and left Youngstown for Dale's. Got there before 10:00. We had a tour of his big business and his pretty house. Left a little before 12:00 when he had to meet someone. Drove off a bit to see Horseshoe Curve, which is an interesting place. Rode to the top and saw an Amtrak train go by. Went through the museum. Had a pretty drive to Hershey. Becky served us a snack and brought us home by 8:00. I gave her corn, limas, pickles and cookies. Read the news before going to bed.

10/9/93 Saturday
Eby went to Elam's for milk. I made a pumpkin pie, bread and things for dinner. Ray, Jane and Laura came about 11:00. Ray trimmed the bushes, pussy willow tree and some holly. Laura helped clean up the trimmings. Isaac's came after mowing the little cemetery. Had a nice time visiting. Eby went with them to get peppers. Jane brought a bag of woolens for rugs. It was a mild day for trimming and we could sit on the porch.

10/20/93 Wednesday
Eby drove 200 miles for Ike. It was a dark wet day. I cleaned the living room. They called for my pacemaker and said it was perfect. Esther came for a chat. I cleaned the onions and finished the English walnuts. Put balance of cauliflower in the freezer. Watered the plants with rain water. Worked on picture albums till after 10:00.

10/23/93 Saturday
Fine weather. Eby and Isaac formed the new cement walk from the porch. They were done soon after dinner. After I had the dishes done Marian came and left at 3:40. I raked some maple leaves and some blacktop before dinner and planned to do backyard, but did not get it all done. Took an early bath and read till Sunday School meditations. Lesson about Abraham and Sara with birth of Isaac. Eby bought a pair of high shoes at Knapp's for $84.00 and he says they feel comfortable.

10/29/93 Friday
Eby drove for Ike. I polished the kitchen cupboards. Made 65 sweet potato croquettes. Burned some garden trash and it is getting less. Got some broccoli and celery ready for

Jim's. Popped some corn in case Halloween may give some beggars. Called Sanford's and talked to Tera, Jacob and Sanford. Bathed and went early to bed.

11/7/93 Sunday
Pretty sunny day. Went to Kinzer. 60 there. I called to offer to stay with Mabel and she said she is going to church and does not need anyone to stay with her. Mildred brought her for the church service. She did alright. Spent the afternoon reading Rachel, a new book in the Kinzer selections. Mary Alice called and she may come next weekend.

11/13/93 Saturday
Eby had day. He and Edgar went to Peachy's sale for a short time. We took them to Fisher's Furniture Store in Georgetown and they bought two tables. Mary Alice got here while we were gone and she went to the sale for a while. She brought her rug wool and we got her started on a long rug. We had time for visiting.

11/14/93 Sunday
We went to Kinzer. Edgar's left at 8:00 for Landisville for a visit with Rohrer and Mabel Eshleman. Rhoda got sick on way here about 7:30 and went to bed early. Mary Alice went to Quaker Meeting and there were 25 there. She left at 1:30. We read and rested. Charlie called and he came back from Hawaii on Friday. He will be coming to Washington this week. I called Jim's and they are doing well. Greg has a new job as extension agent. His chickens go tonight. Clarence and Mabel were not in church.

11/24/93 Wednesday
Eby had an extra drive for Ike. I cut up the turkeys and cooked the bones. Cleaned up for our midweek meeting. Nancy called and said they sold their house in Mechanicsville and will we moving December 1. Kathleen brought a bag of woolen skirts for rugs.

11/25/93 Thursday
Thanksgiving Day. I made the gravy and packed up turkey, croquettes, pickles, limas and celery and we left for Joanne and Daniel Dietzel's at 10:00 and were the first ones there. Joanne had everything in order ready for the guests, which totalled 37. I came home with Jane, Laura, Martha and Glen, and Ray drove our car. They came in a short time. Robert and Grace came here for the night. We had a nice visit this evening.

11/26/93 Friday
Eby had over 100 miles for Ike. He took it easy this forenoon. I ripped the five skirts that Kathleen gave and sewed some strips. Robert and Grace left about 10:00 for Baltimore to help Jennie move to her new place. Grace gave me some advice for rug braiding.

11/30/93 Tuesday
Eby had only one workman to haul. I did the small ironing. We finished the English walnuts and did all the black walnuts. I used the nut cracker we borrowed from Isaac's and it did a real good job. We have a big quart of kernels. I read this evening. Ray called and said Jane's mother is very sick after gallbladder surgery.

12/17/93 Friday
Eby had driving for Ike this afternoon. I made some date and nut candy and peanut brittle. Packed up some cookies for Ike Stoltzfus, mail carrier and Vincent's. Caught two mice in the basement. I took a nap in P.M. Called Sue and Jay came home at 4:00. Seems to be breathing better and ate well at supper. He is very sleepy.

12/18/93 Saturday
Eby had an easy day. He ran the cleaner. I did some cleaning and prepared some food. Eby put Vincent's cookies at their mailbox and they said thanks when I called. Bathed early before Sunday School meditations. I weighed 155 lbs.

12/21/93 Tuesday
Eby had only his regular drives. I mixed four kinds of cookies and got food ready for dinner. Milton and Barbara came at 12:00 with forty packs of fish. They left at 2:30 to spend the night with Bob Kurtz' and take Mother Coy along to Stony Brook tomorrow for Christmas. I baked the cookies this afternoon. Eby went to Dutchway and got a few things I needed.

12/22/93 Wednesday
Eby drove for Ike most all day. I did four more kinds of cookies. Got a tray ready for David and his little boys. Also one for Kauffman's and one for Jay's. Called and Jay answered and he sounded normal. Sue called later and said he is still sleeping a lot and his appetite is not good. I invited my family for a New Year's dinner. Wrote my Christmas memories for Sunday.

12/25/93 Saturday
I made oyster soup for Eby's breakfast. We got things ready and left soon after 10:00 and stopped at Jay's to give them cookies, salsify and fish. Jay was able to go to Frank's in Columbia for dinner. We went on to Donald Ibach's for dinner. I took cookies, pickles, celery, carrots and turnip stars. The Dietzel's, Mother Mary, and Isaac's were there. We had a sumptuous dinner. Fruit cocktail, buns, ham, capon, filling, mashed potatoes, peas, carrots, scalloped oysters, ribbon salad, cranberry salad, vegetable tray, two ice cream pies, mints and cookies. Isaac's, Joanne and Linda gave us gifts, $20.00 and $10.00 cards and goodies.

12/26/93 Sunday
Went to Kinzer. Jay preached. Had some Christmas memories by about six, including me from the early 190-s. Had a quick lunch of salsify soup and spent the afternoon looking at Verna Graham's scrap books.

12/31/93 Friday
Eby did not do any driving because of the cold and snow. He ran the cleaner in the living room and dining room. Got van filled with gas and took it easy. I did some cleaning. Cooked meat for kraut and did a pre-cooked ham for two hours. Mildred called and said that Mabel is a little better but not able to come tomorrow.

1994

1/1/94 Saturday
Weather was pleasant. We set up the table for 11 guests. Had Jay, Sue, Charlie, Paul, Pauline, Amy, Miriam Hess, Abram and Pat. Served raw fruits, ham, mashed potatoes, peas, salsify casserole, sauer kraut, vegetable plate with celery, lettuce, olives, turnip and carrot snowflakes, applesauce, pickles, ice cream, cookies and candy. All ate well and we had a nice day. Mabel was not able to come. Spent the evening reading.

1/2/94 Sunday
Went to Kinzer. Paul preached and the text was Light. As we pulled into the garage I felt very sick and stayed sitting a while and Eby helped me to a rocking chair and then to bed. Slept till 3:00 and then felt better. Ate some toast and milk and spent the evening reading.

1/8/94 Saturday
Icy and everything is glistening. Eby called Isaac Stoltzfus to say we can't drive to their dinner and he said Paul Martin will come for us. So at 11:15 he came and took us with no problems. We had a nice visit and a good dinner. There were 14 at the table. Amos and Lydia had their new baby too. Paul brought us safely home. I did some braiding and Elizabeth called to see if we were all right.

1/10/94 Monday
Ice is still hanging on and it is cold. Eby went to bank and Dutchway and ordered a quarter of beef. I did a small wash and worked on rug. I wrote to Martha. When she was coming home a man threatened her at gunpoint and took the car when she was parking it for the night. I called Charlie. Andy was helping with supper. Charlie has his 54th birthday.

1/14/94 Friday
Some melting, but turning colder. Eby went for milk and the mail. Spent the day reading and eating. I worked on Mary Alice's questionnaire and wrote a lot. Looked at some scrapbooks and picture albums.

1/16/94 Sunday
Went to Kinzer, 47 there. Clair Eby preached a good sermon on the Woman Who Touched the Hem of His Garment. Went to Clarence's this afternoon. Mabel was dressed and out in the room. We talked about the old days. I called Ray and Jane

is home but going back to her Mother in Perkasie tomorrow. I am reading Daniel, a book on an Amish family.

1/17/94 Monday
Many things were closed today for the holiday and weather. I washed and ironed and started a rug. Did Eby's toenails this evening. It snowed a lot and rained and sleeted. Is snowing again at 10:00. There is not much traffic. I called Sue and Jay is sleeping most of the time and needs a doctor. But the snow is bad for travel. I read more of Daniel and Eby is reading it too. An earthquake in California killed 24 and injured many. 6.4 on the scale.

1/19/94 Wednesday
Very cold. Nine below zero and sunny. Eby stayed in. I worked on rug. I called Sue and Jay did not go to the doctor. Grace called and they are icy with no school all week and Robert no work. Steve has a broken ankle. Dale called and it was 25 below zero with 30 inches of snow. He is warm and the river is frozen. Rhoda called and they have two feet of snow and below zero. It is supposed to be the worst cold spell in 100 years.

1/24/94 Monday
Temperatures got to forty and melting. I washed and ironed and braided some rug. Eby went to bank and has decided to quit driving. Last night at 11:20 a call came from the Police Department in New Orleans asking for Ray's phone number. It was about his stolen car. I called and Jane said their car is found and that the police found our number in Martha's address book. They will have more details later. I talked with Sue and Jay has a doctor's appointment.

1/25/94 Tuesday
Smucker's mended the broken spouting and Abner's man came and cleaned some of the deep snow from up by the house. Eby worked on the frozen drain under the porch and it is not open yet. About 22 women did a lot of quilting at the Fire Hall. Elizabeth called to see if we need anything. Eby thinks he will stop driving for Ike.

1/28/94 Friday
It was a hectic day with ice and rain and water coming in basement and we kept dipping it to the sump pumps. It was more than they could pump. So by 1:30 Eby called our plumber. He did not have a pump so next he called the Fire Company and they were busy on other basements and said they would come next and they did with eight men. They pumped the basement and worked on the frozen pipe under the porch. Darrell came with backhoe and made some ditches to drain and Eby used some hot water with hose the firemen left and it opened and was the answer for the dammed water. It got very foggy and the heater is on and the pumps are running and the moon is shining very pretty at 10:00. The plumber came and checked the sump pumps.

1/31/94 Monday
Nice weather. Lots of ice not melted. I washed and ironed a small wash. Eby did some work in basement to help it dry and broke up some ice chunks on drive. Miriam Hess came this afternoon with some old photos and we had a good time looking back. She called at 8:00 and said her father (Uncle Menno) died at 5:00 this evening. I called and told Isaac's. I braided rug.

2/4/94 Friday
Charlie picked us up with Clarence, Mildred, Paul and Pauline, Florence and took us to the Mennonite Home for the funeral service for Menno Hess. All their family was there and some grandchildren and greats. They had a nice service and the burial was at Kraybill's Cemetery. Next was a luncheon at Mt. Joy Church. It was very good. Got home by 3:00. I wrote a letter to Josephine about the funeral. I called Sue and she said Jay hurts all over and his feet are swollen.

2/6/94 Sunday
Went to Kinzer. 55 there. Ralph Graham preached on Where is God, a good message. Robert Metzler was anointed with oil. Paul Clark and Ben were in charge of the anointing. We had Lenny and Marian for dinner. They left by 3:00 and we had time for reading. Ray and Jane called and they are doing well. Mother Koerwer is better and they may get their car back soon. Mary Alice called and we had a long talk.

2/8/94 Tuesday
It started snowing at 9:00 and gave about four inches. Rained and sleeted. Our revival service was cancelled and a lot of schools dismissed at noon. Eby got milk at Galen's. Luke called and wanted an old story for his class. I told him about Sam Plank's bake oven fire. Worked on rug and Mary Alice's papers.

2/10/94 Thursday
Eby went to the bank and did some reading. He sold the van to Mr. Zerby for $2000. It went to Delaware. I made a nice lot of pig foot jelly. Worked on rug. Reports say more snow tonight and Friday. We got a beautiful valentine from Dale and Mae.

2/16/94 Wednesday
Snow is melting slowly. I worked on Mary Alice's papers. Sorted some fabrics for Sewing Circle. Eby is reading Isaac's book. Becky called and said she will stop in tomorrow for dinner. I reviewed some diaries from way back. Had a pacemaker call and she said there were some skipping beats.

2/21/94 Monday
It was very foggy all day. Warm with snow melting and sump pump in basement well pit keeps running. Mary Alice and I tried to correct her braided rug with poor results. She went to do some shopping and started for home after lunch. Martha

called to say Sue has been sick all day and last night. Charlie took her to doctor. I called Clarence's and Paul's and told them.

2/24/94 Thursday
Eby took charge of the sump pump. I worked on rug. Sue went to a specialist and was put in the hospital. I called Jay and he said she has pleurisy. Martha called and she said it is jaundice. Abram called and he said it is pretty serious.

2/25/94 Friday
Had a sunny day. Eby brought the ham and bacons and we put them in the freezer. I worked on rug and have 34 rows. We had an appointment with the eye doctor and both got new lenses. He said my glaucoma is better than last year. Charlie stopped in to tell us about Sue. He called this evening and said he took Jay in this evening and Sue was sitting out and was cheerful.

3/11/94 Friday
Nice mild day. I watered the plants. Did a little rug. Baked a nut cake. Marian came this afternoon and has a lot of problems. She said she is afraid to die. Eby ran the cleaner this afternoon. I called Sue and she is feeling better but has little pep. Jay is some better but sleeps most of the time.

3/25/94 Friday
Fine sale day. Eby and Sanford went over to the sale and bought chicken barbecue for our dinner. Tera, the boys and I had a nice morning. She took the boys to the Park. I made a sweet petal. Sanford took Tera and I to the Sale and the boys to the Strasburg Railroad. We saw a lot of quilts sold and a mob of people shopping. Sanford trimmed the maple tree and Tera and the boys picked up the sticks. After supper we played some games and looked at photos and visited.

4/1/94 Friday
Eby sat still all morning. I fasted and read the Gospel accounts of Good Friday and had a quiet day. Started a rug this evening. David finished the porch with metal strips. It looks good. Mud is drying up. There was a man killed when his car fell into a sinkhole twenty feet deep.

4/9/94
Eby went to Graham's at 8:30 and Gerry and Nancy came at 9:30 and took me along to Amos Hershey's sale. They had a big crowd and nice things to sell. Nancy bought six chairs for Sanford's and a chair for them. We got home at 12:30 and went to Graham's sale. The house brought $74,500. They took Goldie to the Park. Had a nice evening.

4/17/94 Sunday
Went to Kinzer. Mary Esther invited us for dinner but we were having John Winter's and David Clark's. Had a nice time visiting. Charlie called and said Jay passed away

at 7:20. I called Abram's, Issac's, Jim's and Clarence's. Amy called and said she could help Sue if needed.

4/18/94 Monday
I washed and ironed and dried it outdoors. Eby mowed some grass. We went up to see Sue a while this afternoon. She seems to be accepting her loss. Charlie is taking off the rest of the week. I called Grace, Dale and Barbara. Abram called Aunt Sue while we were there and I talked to him too.

4/20/94 Wednesday
Fine weather. Eby gave me a treatment and my throat is much better today. I ironed the sheets and made up the bed. Made potato salad and cole slaw and sour cream cookies and cooked a chicken. Eby cleaned up the strawberries and harrowed the garden corners. Esther called to offer to take us to the viewing. The call came for my pacemaker and she said it is fine.

4/21/94 Thursday
Got some things ready for supper and Ray's stopped for us at 9:30 to go to Jay's funeral at Paradise. A lot of relatives and friends came for the service. Fred Martin had a good sermon on Psalms 139. A sextet sang Whispering Hope that was one of Jay's favorites. After the burial about 135 ate in the church basement. 8 of our children and 3 grandchildren were there.

4/22/94 Friday
I worked on Mary Alice's rug and it is 5 feet x 2 feet. Eby went for pansies and I planted the round flower bed full and have some left. She gave extras. Called Sue and she is having the day with Charlie doing some quiet jobs. Got a birthday card from Abram's and one from the Clinton's at the White House.

4/25/94 Monday
Very warm. I washed and ironed. Shampooed my hair. Esther came for my birthday and brought gifts and a beautiful birthday cake. About 5:00 the old stone house was on fire and is badly burned out. The Clark girls called and sang Happy Birthday. Nancy called with birthday greetings and Gerry started his new job today. Charlie stopped this morning for a chat.

4/29/94 Friday
Few evening showers. We painted the porch and front walk with a green cover. Eby took me to Dr. Hartley for a six month checkup. He said a patient like me don't help pay his bills. The nurse took a blood test. Eby put mulch on flowers and roses. I worked on Mary Alice's rug. My pills cost $127.00.

5/4/94 Wednesday
Eby put dried blood on the peas. I braided rug and finished it this evening. Joanne and Linda came for us at 11:00 and took us to Country Gardens to celebrate

our birthdays and they picked up Aunt Sue too. We had a nice time and good dinner.

5/18/94 Wednesday
I housecleaned the balance of windows and the window corner in the kitchen. Eby harrowed the garden and I hoed most of it. Planted pickles and Eby planted the tomatoes. He bought alyssum and petunias. Got some asparagus roots from Burpee and I planted them. Eby is complaining of pain in back.

5/23/94 Monday
I washed and ironed. I planted a row of corn and some beans and pickles. Betty Meck called and said her father passed away after being an invalid for many years. I burned the trash. Eby put fertilizer and mulch on the garden and flowers and watered the new grass.

5/25/94 Wednesday
I polished the cupboard doors and all the doors. Did the bathroom tile and the tub. Had early lunch and Elizabeth took us to the funeral for Robert Neff at Calvary Home Chapel. We did not go to the cemetery at Willow Street Mennonite Church.

6/11/94 Saturday
Milton mended our light in dining room and curtain rod in our bedroom. They did some shopping at Dutchway and got plants at Ken's Gardens. Abram's came this afternoon and took us to Country Gardens for Father's Day. Milton's left at 4:00 on a bus for Philadelphia to take a boat ride on the Delaware River to celebrate Barbara's 40th anniversary from New Holland High School. I made a pan of lasagna for Sunday dinner.

6/15/94 Wednesday
Warm and sultry. Got ready by 9:30 and Eby took me to the cardiologist for pacemaker check. A young girl did it this time. Then we went to Long's Park to eat our picnic lunch and on to the Mennonite Home to visit Amy, Jay and Minnie. Went to Dutchway on way home for groceries. Marian called and said Lenny is leaving her and would we have a room for her. I emptied the refrigerator to correct the leak after it is defrosted. Rhoda called and we had a long chat. They are getting ready for their family's annual visit.

6/18/94 Saturday
We picked over the peas and I put nine pints in the freezer. Eby picked three quarts of strawberries and I put three pints in the freezer and had shortcake for supper. Made a gallon of spearmint for drinks. I picked a quart of blueberries. I made new arm covers for Eby's chair. Marian called and said peace has been restored. Did some ripping.

6/27/94 Monday

Lots of good showers. Eby hoed weeds and did some sprinkling before it rained. He got broccoli, cabbage and cauliflower and we planted it before it rained. I sowed dill seed for the third time. Picked a quart of blueberries and all the currants. Made three glasses of jelly and kept some to dry for an experiment. Judy King called to ask for my great grandmother's name. It was Magalina Oberholtzer who married Joseph Martin. Pat called for an article a woman wants.

6/28/94 Tuesday

I washed and ironed and mended. With a half inch of rain Eby did not need to do sprinkling. He did some cleaning in the yard. We looked in the papers for the article Pat asked for. I asked Marian for her evening papers from last week and she did not care to oblige and I got too upset.

7/11/94 Monday

Cool, bright and sunny. Eby sprinkled all morning and again this evening. He mowed the new grass and went to the Little Store for sugar and when he got home found it was 25 lbs. of salt, so he took it back and the clerk did not even say she was sorry for her mistake. I washed, ironed and mended. Made root beer and braided rug. Picked pickles this evening and washed all I picked so far.

7/13/94 Wednesday

Eby sprinkled and scrubbed the porch. I did some cleaning. Got cleaned up and Elizabeth came at 2:00 to take me to Dr. Small. He said I do not need to come again. All was well. I made a casserole for Elizabeth and one for us. Had our meeting here this evening.

7/17/94 Sunday

Went to Kinzer. 53 there. Went to Isaac's this afternoon. Bradley was home and we had a nice visit. Abram and Pat called. They are going to a condo in N.H. on Thursday with their family. I called Grace and she said Nancy and Gerry were there on Saturday canning pickles. I called Jim's and had a nice talk with Pat. She said Beth's dog gets its test next week to see if it passes to be a seeing eye dog.

7/20/94 Wednesday

Very hot. Milton worked on the garden irrigation and got it well set up. He adjusted the receptacle at the table. I made a bean dinner and the burner was not connected at first, but it was cooked by 12:00. Milton's left at 1:30 to visit Mother Coy. I took a rest and had my call for pacemaker and forgot to put the phone back on and it was a flop. The refrigerator seems too warm and I am sending the bra back that is too small.

7/31/94 Sunday
Had some rain. Went to Kinzer. 45 there. Had a film of refugees leaving for Paraguay in the 40's. Went to Sue and Charlie's for a good turkey dinner and Charlie took us in our car to the Mennonite Home to visit Amy and Jay. Caleb Hess and his four children were there. Aaron, Benjamin, Abram and Emily. I called Nancy. She is having medication and starts therapy for her back on Tuesday.

8/7/94 Sunday
Pleasant. Went to Kinzer. Came home and quickly had our lunch and packed up as Abram's came to bring us to Nancy's at Ashburn in their new house. Had a good supper and Sanford and Micah came for us and had dessert with us before Abram's left for home. We got to Sanford's by 9:30 and had a while chatting before going to bed. It was a big day.

8/8/94 Monday
Fine day. We knotted a comfort that Tera covered. Sanford worked and came home for lunch. Mary Alice came for supper and Tera cooked a good one. She brought a wallhanging that is partly done and we got it basted and ready to finish for quilting. Eby took it easy. Jacob is raising three little toads from tadpoles. Jacob learned to knot comforts.

8/9/94 Tuesday
Got up early and left for Weaver's and spent the day there. Sanford had a meeting at Fishersville for most of the day. Jacob went along and had a good day. Everything at Weaver's was in tiptop shape. We got back to Sanford's by 9:00 and went to bed.

8/11/94 Thursday
Sanford and Tera went to work. I sewed binding on one side of the comfort and helped Jacob with his quilt top and he got it all together and basted for the quilting. Luke and Micah's music teacher came. Sanford and I canned 8 quarts of tomatoes. Tera made up a good lasagna for supper. The carpenters are supposed to come tomorrow to work on their Florida room.

8/12/94 Friday
Sanford worked and came home for lunch. Tera had off. I hemmed a side of the comfort before breakfast. Then I helped Jacob with his quilt. I helped Micah start a nine patch. Tera and the boys left with us to come to Nancy and Gerry's. Stopped at Roy Rogers in Warrenton for our supper and got here by 6:00. After Tera saw the house they started on their way home.

8/14/94 Sunday
A half inch of rain and strong winds. Went to Kinzer. Paul preached with his full face of whiskers on The Rich Man and Lazarus. We spent the afternoon reading and resting. Had calls from Rhoda, Ray, Mildred and Esther. I called Jim and

he is alone while Pat, her mother, sister and daughter and Beth are at Rehoboth Beach.

8/19/94 Friday
Eby shocked all the corn that is done and finished doing the bank for the season. I mixed two kinds of cookies and made a chocolate cake for the reunion. Cooked a big chicken and made it ready to freeze for the chicken corn soup for the reunion. Did almost two rows on the rug. Marian came and I darned Eby's stockings while she chatted. She said that Lenny does not wear darned socks.

8/20/94 Saturday
Pleasant. I baked oatmeal and sour cream cookies. Cleaned a little. Made a salad basket for the reunion and took a cake. Eby did some trimming and scrubbed the porch. We left at 3:30 and spent the evening at Intercourse Park with 35 family members. Had plenty of good food and a nice fellowship. Robert and Jeannette were there. Minnie is improving. It was decided to discontinue our reunion after having about 50.

8/27/94 Saturday
Reunion Day at Camp Morehart. Edgar's were in charge of breakfast and the Virginia group was in charge of the noon meal. Had pork, baked potatoes, fresh vegetables, turkey, cole slaw, pickles, applesauce, pies and ice cream. Ray's were in charge of supper. It was clams, corn on cob, olives, pickles, cheeses, buns, cantaloupe, watermelon, cookies. There was picture taking, sharing, puzzles and a good time with 60 people there for lunch.

8/28/94 Sunday
Dale and Mae served breakfast. Cereals, juice and pancakes. Sanford's boys helped. Sanford's were in charge of our worship session. It was good. There was plenty of good food left for dinner. All the good byes were done by 2:00. Ray and Daddy came home in our car and Martha drove theirs with Jane and me. Got here at 4:00. I called Amy and read.

9/19/94 Monday
Washed and ironed. Canned a quart of pickles. Made apple dumplings and an apple pie. Did some phoning. Eby started coughing at 4 A.M. and kept it up till 6:00. He took it easy all day and is coughing less. Read this evening. Called Mary Alice and she came home from her vacation last evening. The refugees have moved into the house their Friends Meeting made ready.

9/23/94 Friday
Eby cleaned some twigs and leaves from drive. I cleaned cupboards and drawers in kitchen. Put the flower pole in the garage and put some plants on it. Called Grace to see when they are coming in October. She will be helping get ready for the Relief

Sale this evening. Got a notice to renew my driver's license and must have a physical and eye exam, so I decided to quit driving.

10/3/94 Monday
I washed and ironed. Made a portion of sandwich spread. Eby dug the sweet potatoes. Got a bushel of nice ones and a basket of smaller ones. Tried an onion poultice for Eby's cough.

10/4/94 Tuesday
Ruth Hershey took me to Sewing Circle. Had nine and we did three quilts. Eby cut up the sweet potato vines. I gathered the cactus all by the porch ready to get them winterized. Called Miriam Hess and had a long talk. She said her mother is getting more mixed up.

10/8/94 Saturday
Sunny and mild. Isaac and Elizabeth came at 6:50 and we started for our visit to Jim's. Stopped at Benner's Restaurant for breakfast. Got there at 10:00 and had a nice day with them and Greg and Cindy. Pat took some photos. Eby's back hurt him real much. Bradley had a barn party this evening.

10/10/94 Monday
Pleasant. I washed and ironed. Washed the windows on the outside. Esther came and we had a chat session. Eby brought the walnuts from Ike Stoltzfus and hulled half of them. His back is hurting. I raked a lot of leaves in the backyard for mowing. I called Sanford and they are fine. Boys like their new schools. Their new porch room is almost finished. Milton called for directions to make sweet potato croquettes.

10/12/94 Wednesday
Cool. I pulled the beets and made three quarts and made four pints of Harvard beets. Eby finished the walnuts and put all in the heater room away from the squirrels. Marian called to say a man on T.V. said there is no God. And a law in a N.J. town fines anyone for swearing. Had turnips for supper.

10/16/94 Sunday
Pleasant and a little frost. Went to Kinzer. Had our communion service. Mark Leaman preached a good sermon and served the emblems. We had a light lunch and Abram and Pat came after 3:00 and stayed for supper. Mildred called and said Mabel has gone into a coma. Abram's stopped on their way home and he called and said he thought she had a massive stroke. Mildred called just before 10:00 and said she is gone. Daddy said his back is feeling better.

10/17/94 Monday
I washed and ironed. Made up a six layer casserole for Clarence and Mildred. We went over this afternoon and they seem to be accepting the loss of Mother. Almeda

was there and left soon. I called to tell a lot of the cousins and called most of our children this evening. I picked a five quart kettle of nice green beans and Eby nipped the ends.

10/19/94 Wednesday
A fine mild day. Ray and Jane came at 9:00 and we went to Kinzer for viewing before the funeral service for Mabel. The church was filled. Jay and Paul had the service, which was well done. Ten of our children were there and Micah. Miriam brought Amy and Rachel helped. Edgar's were here for the night. Milton's stopped for a while. Manny's tree service came at 2:30 and the dead pin oak was down and piled up by 5:00. Daddy had some back pain this evening.

10/22/94 Saturday
Amos Zook and his boy put up a new grape arbor at the end of the yard. I made a pan of cold water soap. Eby took it easy and did not take his pain pills till bedtime. I raked leaves in the backyard and a lot were down. I burned them. Canned a quart of V8 juice. Amos balanced the old freezer in the garage. I called Clarence and he is getting company.

11/5/94 Saturday
Eby scrubbed the porch, ran the cleaner and raked some leaves. I prepared food for tomorrow. Ray called and they are packed to leave Monday for Hawaii. Their renovations are getting done. The girls are keeping busy. Charlie called and they are having rain and he is keeping busy and has flown 185,000 miles this year. Had Sunday School meditations about King David.

11/7/94 Monday
Pleasant and mild. I washed and ironed. Brought some magazines from the attic. Eby cleaned trash from the garden and pulled the turnips. It is ready to be plowed. Barbara mowed the yard for the last time. Marian came and we had a real discussion. She said she could not live with Eby two weeks. I cut and sewed some strips and oiled the sewing machine. There was a driller doing places in the field across the road all day.

11/16/94 Wednesday
I worked on rug all day. Eby shelled the bean seed. I called Sue and Amy. Eby talked to Jay. The morning paper said a shopping center is to be built next spring in our corn field.

11/19/94 Saturday
I prepared food and did some cleaning. Eby raked some leaves and did the sweeping and scrubbed the porch. I bathed and soon Marian came and a bit later Mary Alice. She did some shopping in Intercourse later. Isaac and Elizabeth came and Mary Alice was typing the family record I made for David Martin.

11/20/94 Sunday
Went to Kinzer. Mary Alice went to Quaker Meeting. They had 8. She was home before us. Her friend Anne from Philadelphia came to spend the afternoon and they went for a drive. We went to the 50th anniversary for Harvey and Margaret Kauffman at Maple Grove. We had a nice time and saw a lot of old friends. Mary Alice did some more typing this evening.

11/24/94 Thursday
Got up at 6:00 and made 28 croquettes so as to have enough. Got everything loaded and got off before 10:00. Picked up Sue and went to Donald and Linda's. She put the turkey and croquettes in for heating. Laura and Glen were there. Ray drove our car home. Jane gave me a diary for Christmas.

12/5/94 Monday
A dark, wet day. I washed and ironed. Blocked the rug I made for David. A beautiful bouquet came from a Parksburg florist from Mike, Jan and Erica. Worked on cards this evening. Called Amy and she seemed real good.

12/8/94 Thursday
I worked on the cookies all day, have more than 300 done. Mixed up more and got a cocoanut ready this evening. Eby went to the store and got some things for making goodies. Esther called to tell me that Kathy Denlinger died of a heart attack this morning. Marian called and said she hopes she does not see another Christmas. There are so many problems with them.

12/13/94 Tuesday
I baked four kinds of cookies and coated some graham crackers. Rhoda called and said she was having a problem making sweet potato croquettes. I tried to give her advice. Esther came with the funeral program. We set up for our meeting.

12/18/94 Sunday
Went to Kinzer. Paul preached on the Incarnation. We had Ralph Graham's and Arlene Denlinger for dinner. Had nice visiting. Joanne called to say a group from Ridge View would come to sing for us. By 8:00 about a dozen came and sang beautiful carols and visited for a while.

12/22/94 Thursday
Eby went to the store and got some things we need. I used up the coating chocolate. Made a fourth portion of flapjacks and baked them as soon as they were mixed. They got nice. I made up some cookies for the Vincent's and Eby took them to Gloria and we got a poinsettia from them. Kathleen brought a big bag of fabrics. Charlie sent us a smoked salmon by Federal Express.

12/25/94 Sunday
A fine mild day. We went to Kinzer. Had three special singers with three songs and the scripture of Christ's birth. We went to Daniel Dietzel's for a big turkey dinner. We had a nice time and got gifts. Later Isaac's took us to see the great lights in Oxford on Jim Herr's property. Ray called. Laura and Glen announced their engagement.

12/26/94 Monday
Beautiful day. Abram and Ben came for us at 10:00 and took us to Hershey for second Christmas. Jim's, Dale and Mae, Sam and Melissa, David and Becky were there. We had a good dinner cooked by Sam and Becky. It was mild and some of us took a walk down by the creek. Abram and Pat brought us home. I read this evening.

12/31/94 Saturday
Grace called this morning and they are well and keeping busy. Mildred and Clarence came for us and they took us to meet Charlie and he took us all with Paul and Pauline in his van to Lapp's Restaurant to be treated to our annual New Year dinner. Rachel brought Amy. After dinner we all went to Sue's and had a nice time together.

1995

1/2/95 Monday
I washed and ironed. Ripped and sewed up strips from suit that Abram's gave. Eby took his watch for repairs and made a date to have the pork butchered. Minnie called and said Amy was looking for me. I called her later and she talked real normal.

1/4/95 Wednesday
I roasted the turkey and made 34 sweet potato croquettes. Marian came and we did some serious chatting. She is not happy with us using the word ain't and others. I worked on my desk this evening. Eby brought eggs.

1/13/95 Friday
Eby took me to Dr. Stoltzfus for my annual eye test and I did not pass for driving. I have cataracts in both eyes. I worked on knotting the camp quilt. I made some food ready for supper. Marian spent some time here this afternoon and laid on the davenport to sleep.

1/14/95 Saturday
Eby went to Turkey Hill for milk because it was foggy. I got things ready for lunch and Sanford's came at 10:30. We had time for visiting before lunch. I gave them the camp quilt I finished yesterday. Tera took the boys to the Park a while and Sanford took them to Elam's. We had a nice evening. I quilted on Micah's quilt.

1/17/95 Tuesday

Eby leveled the upright freezer and I cleaned it and put food back. Worked on scrap book page all the rest of the day. Roofer here all day. I called Mary Alice. She had a good week in Vermont in the snow. She got home yesterday. Earthquake in Japan.

1/21/95 Saturday

I worked on rug. Took a rest and Josephine called and had a lot to say. She is doing real good. Isaac's came and he trimmed the maple tree. After I was finished with the dishes Abram's came after being in Ephrata. They think I should have cataracts removed. Isaac's were having their family for a farewell party for Judy and Karen going to Russia.

2/1/95 Wednesday

I worked on Valentines and made a birthday card for Benuel. Cleaned the chest freezer. Nancy left soon after 8:00. She has some pain in her shoulder yet. We worked on the pole that Nancy gave for Christmas with a peace banner.

2/2/95 Thursday

The groundhog saw his shadow. Now we know there will be more winter. I started a rug for Beth. David helped to put up the peace banner and it looks pretty. Eby pulled the flowering cabbage out.

2/4/95 Saturday

It snowed about 10 inches. Abner cleaned our drive this afternoon. Roads are bare, but freezing and blowing tonight. I made a dutch goose for supper. Worked on rug. Sue called and said Bobby died.

2/8/95 Wednesday

Eby went for the hog meat. It was 330 lbs. and cost $219.00. I put pork chops, ribs, roasts, and sausage in the freezer. Cooked the legs for pig foot jelly and picked it off this evening with some giblets. Cooked the bony ribs. We went up to see Sue this afternoon. Annis called this evening and said Bobby lived in same house with John Plastino.

2/9/95 Thursday

I made the pig foot jelly and did some cleaning. Sent Betsy's birthday greeting, a homemade one. Isaac and Elizabeth came to take us to the memorial service for Bobby Martin at Paradise. There was a good number came and we had cake and drink with good fellowship.

2/15/95 Wednesday

I worked on rug. Eby took income papers to be done. Abner and his men worked on Vincent's cleanup all day. He was forced to have it done. A man was killed on Gap Hill in an accident. I called Amy and she talked almost normal. Had pacemaker checkup on phone. All is well.

3/5/95 Sunday
Went to Kinzer, 35 there. We had plenty of time to get dinner for Jonathan, Ruth, Carla, Christopher and Andrew Clemens. They got here after 2:00. The children are very busy and we had nice visiting. Dale called and said Agway laid off 600 men. Abram and Pat called and Becky goes for Outward Bound to Baltimore March 16.

3/15/95 Wednesday
Beautiful and warm. Eby burned some of the bank and some of the sticks he picked up in the yard. I cut the old coat into strips and sewed them up. The sewing machine did not work well and tried my patience. Call came for pacemaker check. Made an appointment with Dr. Small. Helped with tax papers. Sent four birthday letters. Marian called and apologized for her conduct on Saturday.

3/20/95 Monday
I washed and ironed. Eby bought three dozen pansies and I planted them in the round bed. I called Amy, and Miriam called later and said her mother could not tell her later anything I said. I worked on stories for Mary Alice. Josephine called and talked a long time. She says Pat does so much for her health.

3/22/95 Wednesday
Eby went to Clarence's and took his taxes back and then went to the store. We worked on sewing machine and gave up. I called a repair man and he will come soon. I set up the portable machine and used it to put a zipper in Eby's pants. Worked on rug. Tried to call Amy. Miriam called and said they took her phone because she was making odd calls.

3/25/95 Saturday
Daddy took my nut cake over to the Fire Hall before breakfast. I cleaned the closet in my craft room and put things in order. Daddy went to the sale early and Mary Alice did not get here till 11:30. We went over and joined the mob. It was full of people. Lots of food was bought and quilts did not bring high prices. Mary Alice got some window sash for a donation. Had chicken barbecue for supper. Had a nice evening with Mary Alice.

4/1/95 Saturday
Did some cleaning and made a custard. Eby went to Dave Clark's sale this afternoon. He bought some rope. Abram called and said they will take us to Andrea's wedding and we are to decide soon. Isaac's took us to Ed Miller's to see the Russian slides from Judy and Karen.

4/4/95 Tuesday
I worked on scrap book page and it is so difficult. Had early dinner and Elizabeth took me to my appointment with the cardiologist. Had blood check, urine specimen and Xrays. Got home by 3:00 and had early supper after my fast. Eby got car filled

with gas and is reading a book Clarence gave him. Worked on scrap book page all evening.

4/7/95 Friday
Eby finished putting the mulch on places and cleaned it up. He got the tire fixed that had a nail. I washed some of Kathleen's rug strips and sewed them all up. Took most of day. Barbara called after 9:00 to say Mike and Jan's son was born at 7:00. Clayton Thomas.

4/10/95 Monday
I washed silence cloth and linen table cloth and they dried outside. Washed and ironed. Did some checks for Eby. I sent for stockings. Mailed Jacob's homemade birthday greeting. Sanford called and we had a long chat. He may get a new job as state jobs are getting shaky.

4/17/95 Monday
We uncovered the peas and Eby harrowed garden. Peas are up. I hoed what is planted. Washed and ironed a small wash. Burned trash and four old tires and it made a lot of smoke. Did some work on summer dress and some rug. Got the family letter and one from Clinton's.

4/20/95 Thursday
Eby helped to wash the windows on the outside. We planted the bulbs this afternoon. I wed the strawberries. Christ King mowed the yard. I braided some rug. A car bomb in Oklahoma wrecked a federal building and killed children and adults. It was horrible. Charlie sent me a beautiful apron from Guatemala.

4/25/95 Tuesday
Beautiful day. My 90th birthday. Eby marked the balance of the garden and we planted limas, pickles and corn. Ground was in very good shape. I made oatmeal and sugar cookies. Eby did some sprinkling. Abner came for us at 6:00 for a birthday supper. Florence Groff, Esther Glick, Jean Hershey and Isaac and Elizabeth were there to share in a good supper. Mary Alice called this morning to say happy birthday. Mary and Esther Clark called and sang. Charlie called from Newark, N.J.

4/27/95 Thursday
Eby went to the bank and sprinkled. I got letters off to Mike and Jan and Fredric. I did some weeding on the bank and burned the trash. Mildred called. I counted my cards and have 75.

4/29/95 Saturday
Beautiful day. Milton helped Daddy take the metal junk to Galen's. After breakfast he took Daddy along to Annis' sale before going for the students at Charles Groff's. There were eight of them to spend the day seeing things in the County. Ray

came later and took Mary Alice and me to Annis' sale. There was a good number of people. Eby bought a swivel chair and I bought a grater and dish. Dale's and Jim's came and the sale was through in good time. House sold for $133,000. Paul White's stopped by a short time with Mildred Horst. Later on Dale and Abram took us for a drive. When we got back everything was set up for a birthday surprise. The table was set for 20. It was beautiful with two bouquets and a huge salmon, asparagus, casserole, potato salad, tomato salad and three kinds of pies that Isaac's brought, plus olives, pickles, nuts, candy and more. Everything was cleaned up and put in order for more visiting after supper. Milton and Mary Alice stayed for the night.

5/3/95 Wednesday
I had no food or drink since yesterday supper. Elizabeth came at 9:30 and took me to Medical Center for cataract surgery. All went well and we got home at 2:00 with a patch on my left eye. Elizabeth brought a casserole for supper. Abram, Esther and Sue called. I spent the time reading. I have no pain in my eye yet.

5/4/95 Thursday
Had a real good night. Elizabeth came early and took me to the new hospital campus for 8:15 appointment. Had patch taken off and Dr. Reich said all was well. We got home in time for Daddy to have the car to go to Roy Witmer's funeral at Kinzer. I slept while he was gone and took it easy all day. Esther brought a peach pie for Daddy's birthday. Abram called to check on me.

5/14/95 Sunday
Went to Kinzer. I read the poem "Two Temples" and Donna talked about being a mother. Had dinner to ourselves as there were no guests. Read this afternoon and evening. Milton, Dale, Jim and Charlie called. Charlie said they had a sad service because a 28-year-old member of their church jumped from the Golden Gate Bridge and Andy is in the hospital.

5/26/95 Friday
Had a good rain last night. We did some cleaning and prepared for Sanford's visit for the weekend. Lee Brown and the new man came to get our final plans in order. Sanford called and said they would come Saturday afternoon. Eby picked a few strawberries and covered them to keep birds off.

5/27/95 Saturday
Pleasant. I got some food ready and Sanford's came about 2:00 after getting lost in the southern part. We drove to Lengacher's for cheese and met three of their family. Went on to Cattail Homestead to show the boys the water wheel and the premises. After supper Sanford took the boys to Elam's and stopped at the Park to see a ballgame.

6/3/95 Saturday
We went to the funeral service for Elva Clark at the Presbyterian Church and to Bradley's graduation from L.M.H.S. this afternoon. Dan Dietzel came for us. We went to Isaac's with them for a party with their family this evening. Kim and Sally brought us home.

6/8/95 Thursday
Elizabeth took me for my last appointment for my eye. Dr. Raich said 20/20 vision at 90 years was good and I should recommend him to my friends. Eby picked three quarts of strawberries. I made a slip this afternoon. I made an appointment for glasses.

6/13/95 Tuesday
Wash dried and put away. We picked a bushel of peas and I put 18 pints in freezer. Eby did some shopping. Got a new broom. I picked some sugar peas for Esther. Braided some rug. Trained the limas. Called Mary Alice and she had a good week in San Francisco. I finished reading Amish Women, the book that Verna Graham loaned me.

6/17/95 Saturday
We got off to Charlie and Sue's by 9:30 and started for Derry Church for Samuel and Melissa's wedding. All was well planned and the guests were friendly. We ate at the Country Club. 10 of the children were there, all but Charlie and Sanford.

6/20/95 Tuesday
Eby set up garden sprinkler. Marked out and planted corn and picked three quarts of blueberries. Cleaned the blueberry bank. Trimmed the round flower bed and planted marigolds and trimmed the long bed. I planted more pickles. Did some rug. O.J. Simpson murder case still in session.

6/23/95 Friday
We got all done and ready at 11:00 when Abram's came. Got here to the Hampton Inn at 10:00. Driving went well and we stopped for supper in Turusburg, Ohio. I enjoyed the scenery.

6/24/95 Saturday
Had our breakfast in the dining room free and we left for Goshen and drove some country roads and saw the homes and farms. Got to the church in good time for Andrea's wedding as pictures were being taken. Met family and friendly guests. Had a luncheon and Abram's brought us to our hotel.

6/25/95 Sunday
We had free breakfast at the hotel and left about 8:00 with Milton's. Gave a good bye earlier to Abram's when they left for Smithville for the Myer reunion. Had a good drive and got to Jim's about 5:00. Had a nice evening visiting with Pat and Greg and Cindy after we had finished a good snack in their nice cool porch room.

7/15/95 Saturday
Hot. We tried to keep cool. I canned pickles and picked them this evening. They are doing good. I made tomato aspic. Did a little cleaning. I washed bed clothes. I called Nancy. Gerry's knee is healing. Some chickens and cattle are dying from the heat.

7/19/95 Wednesday
Eby went to the store and got everything right. He worked on getting the drive ready. I baked 100 oatmeal cookies, a nut cake, cupcakes and five gallons of root beer. Pacemaker lady called to check and said all was well. More that 600 died from heat and a million chickens. I picked a few pickles. Called Sue and she had her cataract surgery.

7/21/95 Friday
Mary Alice, Nancy and Grace got here by 10:30 and we took lunch to Aunt Sue and Uncle Charlie. He did a good job of the table and dishwashing. Next we went to the Mennonite Home and visited Aunt Minnie and she was fine. We found Uncle Jay resting but very alert. Aunt Amy is wanting to leave the Home, but she did visit. We did not find Esther Groff. Got home in time to prepare a cooked supper. Mary Alice and Nancy left at 7:30. Edgar finished the painting job.

7/26/95 Wednesday
After breakfast we picked the balance of the limas and Eby and Sanford shelled them. Micah helped me blanche and pack them. Put 14 pints in the freezer and all done by 10:30. This afternoon Daddy went with them to Georgetown and Sanford bought an Express wagon. They went to Elam's and the Park for a while this evening.

8/5/95 Saturday
Hot. Eby went to the bank and did the sweeping. I did some cleaning and scrubbed the porch. Decided it was too hot to invite company. Worked on rug. Picked pickles. I called the Weaver's and Fredric's are there as they were having car problems and glad to have a place.

8/13/95 Sunday
Went to Kinzer. 39 there. Emma Witmer invited us for lunch, a good one. Jay Meck's and Flossie were there. We had a nice visit. Spent the evening at home reading. I called Grace and she is able to use her arm more. Jennie is home for the weekend and is looking at wedding books.

8/14/95 Monday
We went to the funeral for Charles Horning at 9:30 at Springville Church. The house was filled and the service was long. Stopped at Yoder's for vinegar and I canned pickles this afternoon. Eby took a bushel of tomatoes to Ike's Anna and took her to Kauffman's for peaches at $8.99 a basket. She gave us eight.

8/26/95 Saturday
After a good night and a clear morning we were all packed up and left for Camp Morehart for the reunion. Sanford, Eby and Jacob in our car and Tera and the rest of us in theirs. We arrived safely at Camp by 8:50 and got the potatoes started baking. The others arrived to have dinner by 12:00, about 49 in all. We had good visiting and some left to go to motels and some went home.

8/27/95 Sunday
After a good night Dale and Mae served breakfast. Mary Alice was in charge of our worship service with Jacob, Luke, Micah, Robert and Gerry having part and some with everyone helping. Edgar's, Abram's and me were in charge of noon meal. I made corn pudding and tomato salad. Ray drove our car back, and they spent some time here before going home.

8/28/95 Monday
Had some rain last night. Did morning work and got things ready for dinner. Charlie and Ed came at 10:30. Daddy took them on a short tour. We ate at 12:30 and visited till almost 3:00 when they left for Harrisburg Airport for their 4:15 flight. I canned 15 quarts of peaches that Eby got.

8/29/95 Tuesday
Eby did sprinkling morning and evening. I washed and ironed. Made V8 juice from yellow tomatoes and a variety of things. I sowed some radishes and lettuce. I sent a pickle recipe and some dill to Ed Ludwig. I called Clarence and there was not anything special from Kinzer. I did some rug this evening.

9/21/95 Thursday
Eby went to the bank. He helped scrub the hall carpet and it dried real good. He brought the Kauffman woman from the Nickel Mines nursery and she planted a small evergreen in the front yard. I did 24 quarts of applesauce. The hearing aid man brought Eby's hearing aid all repaired for $129.00.

9/26/95 Tuesday
Stopped raining long enough for Sanford and me to pick a half bushel of limas and get broccoli and sweet potatoes to bring along. We packed up and ate an early snack and left for Richmond at 11:45. All went well and we got here by 5:20. Tera had a good supper after Eby helped shell the limas. We worked on Jacob's quilt till bedtime and it is almost done. It rained off and on most all day. I called Rhoda and they got home last evening from trip to Seattle.

9/27/95 Wednesday
Beautiful day. First Sanford and I finished the quilt Jacob made for the Relief Sale. Tera worked. After lunch we got to making applesauce. Did 28 quarts. Jacob came

home at noon to help and later went for his music lesson. Micah and Jacob practiced this evening. We chatted till after 10:00.

9/28/95 Thursday
Tera worked. Sanford and I mended and turned the braided living room rug. Nancy stopped for a half hour on way from a meeting. Sanford took us to Grandparents' Day at Luke and Micah's school. It was nice and we got a free lunch. Micah made an applesauce cake and we had a ham and bean supper. Worked on Mary Alice's video this evening.

9/30/95 Saturday
We got off the Relief Sale by 7:30. Jacob went with us and Tera brought the two boys and her niece Amy later on. It was a big sale with lots of pretty quilts and other things. Highest priced was $7000. After the sale we went to Weaver's for barbecue dinner with Ray's, Nancy's, Sanford's, Jennie and her boyfriend, and Mary Alice. We went to Nancy's with Jane and Gerry. Nancy went with Ray to show him the way. It was a big interesting day. Ray's things brought over $900.

10/1/95 Sunday
Had a good night at Gourley's with breakfast. After visiting and seeing the yard and flowers, we started for home. Steven joined us for breakfast. Had a good trip and got here by 1:00. I made chicken corn soup. Jane washed the dishes and we had a nice time till they went home about 5:00 after their twelve-day vacation. We read the news. Jim and Pat stopped on way from Beth's where they spent the weekend. Gave them ice cream.

10/5/95 Thursday
It rained most all day. I did some cleaning and got some food ready. Mary Alice came around 3:00 and she had her wallhanging along and some papers for the video. Her friend Jan got to the motel and she went there this evening. Eby went to the store.

10/6/95 Friday
Had three inches of rain. Mary Alice and Jan met at the motel and travelled to get the photos they needed and came here for lunch. Did some of the interview work with us this afternoon. Jan went to rest at her motel and came back after 7:00 to work on photos. Isaac and Elizabeth came this evening.

10/7/95 Saturday
Mary Alice and Jan got on the job by 9:30 and got a lot done before lunch and more done this afternoon. They went back to Jan's motel to work and came back for 6:30 supper. The girls left after supper to work at the motel again. I called Miriam Hess and she is not pleased with the care Amy is getting.

10/8/95 Sunday
Pleasant. Mary Alice and Jan had some photos this morning and came back. They left by 10:30. I called Mary Alice this evening and she made it home with no problems. We went to Kinzer. Had footwashing. Esther Clark and I went together. I read a while. Pope John Paul is in Baltimore today and thousands were there to hear him.

10/23/95 Monday
I prepared food for dinner. Samuel came at 12:00 for a visit before leaving for his new home in Albuquerque. We enjoyed the time with him. I did the washing after he left.

11/4/95 Saturday
Very cold. We left for Clarence's sale at 8:00 and got good parking. Had a good crowd and things sold very well. I did not get anything for Miriam Hess as they went too high. Ray's and Milton's were there and Ray helped the sale. They all came here for supper of cow in the garden, red eggs, applesauce, cole slaw and apple and Quakertown pies and ice cream. Jane washed the dishes and they left at 7:00.

11/11/95 Saturday
Eby polished the cupboards and the wainscoting in the kitchen. I cleaned the sink corner and scrubbed the floor and waxed it. Isaac came and trimmed the snowball bush by the garage and met Bradley here when Kim brought him after being there several days. We went to Sue and Charlie's for dinner with Paul and Pauline. He had an Ox Roast dinner for the benefit of Black Rock. It was good and Paul seemed better.

11/14/95 Tuesday
Eby shelled nuts and has a lot done. He helped me clean our bed. I finished cleaning our room and did the laundry room. Jim called and said he is staying indoors as it was snowing yesterday and today. It was dark all day. Last week five houses were robbed here in our corner.

11/20/95 Monday
Grace called this morning and said Gerry's mother died last night and Nancy and Gerry are on their way to Missouri. Nancy called to say they were almost there. I washed and cleaned the celery. Burned the lima vines this afternoon. Went to bed early.

11/21/95 Tuesday
Mild. Eby did some work in the yard. He went to Rhoad's Store for smoke salt to do the dried beef and tongue. I roasted two big turkeys. I called Steve Weaver and got the number for Gerry's home and later got the information to send a sympathy bouquet for the viewing and service.

11/23/95 Thursday
Thanksgiving Day. Got everything packed up and Charlie and Aunt Sue picked us up at 9:00 and took us to Ed Miller's for Thanksgiving dinner. Five of the children were there and grandchildren and greats, a total of 41. Becky's boyfriend Kenneth was there. Robert and Grace brought us home and we had a nice evening with some rain. Nancy called and they got home this afternoon.

12/4/95 Monday
I washed and ironed. Processed two cocoanuts. Eby cleaned the vines from the porch wire and put fertilizer on some sod. He got a knee support at the drug store and thinks it will help. I called Paul for his birthday. He seemed good and made conversation. I made some checks for charities.

12/6/95 Wednesday
I stirred and baked flap jacks and sand tarts. The mixer quit when it pulled too hard. Eby put peanuts on the sand tarts. Charlotte Snowdon called and we had a long chat. She and her daughter Suzanne are living in the County now and are coming to see us. Had a thank you from Jennie Weaver.

12/11/95 Monday
I washed and dried it in the basement. Made some cocoanut puffs. I made some family gift checks and wrote letters and did cards. Frank Kurtz was killed last evening when a horse landed on his car.

12/18/95 Monday
I did the morning work and stirred up some cookies. Charlie came for me at 11:00 and took me for my semi-annual pacemaker checkup. All was well since June 1991. I packed cookies for the Vincent's and Ike Stoltzfus' and Eby delivered them. Kim stopped on way to take Elizabeth for cataract surgery and gave us a nice dressed chicken. Started snowing after dark.

12/19/95 Tuesday
Sleet. I washed and ironed and worked on rug. Current was off and on this afternoon and stayed on after 6:00. It is icy and Eby did not get the mail. Most schools were cancelled. I called Josephine and invited them for New Year's. Marian called and thinks we should be reimbursed for power failure. Elizabeth is doing well and did not risk going to the doctor.

12/25/95 Monday
A bit of sunshine. Donald Ibach came for us and took us for dinner. We had a nice time and Isaac's brought us home. I read the book Linda gave. We got an amaryllis, candy, party mix, and a pretty trinket. Dale sent an Agway truck.

12/26/95 Tuesday
I made food ready for dinner. Abram, Pat, Becky, David and Ben came at 11:00 and we ate at 12:00. They visited and left about 2:30 to visit Aunt Sue. A few minutes after they left Milton's came. We had a nice time and they took us to Diener's Restaurant for supper. We had a nice evening with no dishwashing.

12/28/95 Thursday
We had late breakfast and Milton's left at 10:00. Made up bed and a sausage casserole for freezing. Nancy came around 3:00 and stayed for the night. She had a meeting at Harrisburg Airport. They plan to go to Missouri next week to get Gerry's mother's house ready to sell.

12/31/95 Sunday
Went to Kinzer. 39 there. Had a video with Chuck Colson. Had an afternoon and evening reading and relaxing. I called Dale and they are well. I am reading Chicken Soup for the Soul that was a gift.

1996

1/1/96
I got up at 5:00 and got food ready for our New Year's group, Clarence and Mildred, Miriam Hess, Sue and Charlie, Paul and Pauline. The dinner was appreciated and we had a nice time together. Miriam did not think it wise to bring Amy, and Josephine cannot make long trips. I started to read the Bible through.

1/7/96 Sunday
Snowbound. No service any place. It snowed hard all day. Galen plowed the drive but it is filled again. I read most all day and am at Exodus10. Had calls from Isaac, Milton, Dale and Marian. I called Jim's, Charlie and Esther.

1/8/96 Monday
Snow stopped this afternoon. All business was ordered closed and no one on roads but for snow removal. Fined if caught. David cleaned the porch and his car. Galen plowed the drive about 4:00 and David left. I cut and sewed some strips and started a rug. Bradley called and said he had an interview at Quarryville Home. Nancy called and they are getting Gerry's mother's house ready to be cleaned tomorrow.

1/9/96 Tuesday
I worked on rug. It began snowing at 3:00 and gave about three inches till 7:30. Abram called from Pittsburg where they are staying till they can get a flight home. Paul Martin picked us up at 5:30 with Isaac Stoltzfus and family and took us to a Chinese restaurant for our annual dinner with Isaac and his other employees, about 25 in all. Got home safely at 8:15. No school or mail. Got two newspapers this afternoon. Snowmobiles are going past on the street. It was a nice evening.

1/10/96 Wednesday
A bit warmer. I worked on rug and have 12 rows done. Abram called and said they got home at 6:00 and all is well. Mary Alice called and she worked today for the first this week. The boys at the Home are shoveling snow for folks in the area and are happy with the pay. Mail went today.

1/24/96 Wednesday
More melted. I decided to skip quilting at the Fire Hall this year. I did more knots on the comfort here. Anna Kreider called to say that Junie was taken to the hospital on Sunday evening and is real sick. I called Elizabeth Neff and told her. We got set up for our midweek service and had everyone here.

1/27/96 Saturday
Heavy rain. We spent time visiting and playing games. Had chicken corn soup for lunch and cow in the garden for supper. Sanford took us for a drive to see high waters and to get goodies at Stoltzfus'. Sanford showed me how to do counted cross stitch. Boys played games, a lot of jacks.

2/7/96 Wednesday
More snow last night. I put the pig foot jelly together. Worked on scrap book page for Mrs. Cox all day. Some young Morman men came and we had an interesting half hour visiting. Eby missed them as he had gone to Dutchway for casters. He scrubbed the porch. An airplane fell into the Caribbean Seas with 189 German tourists. No survivors.

2/13/96 Tuesday
Eby got up giddy and took it easy all day with light diet. He is feeling better this evening. I did some cleaning and treated some plants. Finished the rug for Conrad. David put casters on the stand for the video. Got a pretty valentine from Dale and Mae and I sent Doug a valentine. An accident in Italy on a foggy highway caused 11 deaths and involved 300 cars.

2/16/96 Friday
Have a lot of snow. Road was plowed, Highway is good. I made some food ready. Charlotte called and said they are back from Scranton. I called Mary Alice and she will not know till morning if she is coming. I called Vera and she said Junie may not last today and she called two hours later and said he is gone. Eby kept the porch swept and ran the cleaner. I washed the floors.

2/17/96 Saturday
A nice day. Mary Alice called to say she will come and got here by 2:30, just as Charlotte and Suzanne got here. Later the video was set up and we got to see it for the first time. It is well done. We had supper at 6:00 and they stayed till 9:30 and seemed to enjoy the evening. I did some food for tomorrow.

2/20/96 Tuesday
Had a short forenoon with early lunch. Isaac's took us along to the funeral service for Junie Hostetter at Maple Grove. The house was filled and 700 attended the viewing last evening. It gave some folks sharing memories and a lady did some high singing. Isaac's took us to Harvest Drive for a good dinner. They came in and spent the evening.

2/21/96 Wednesday
Mild and the snow is going. I mended some rugs. The hooked acorn rug was a problem on the border. Eby rubbed the hams for the third time. He could not get the video to work with all of Mary Alice's good directions. Minnie called for funeral news. I called Elizabeth Neff and gave her a report. Pacemaker lady called and said all was well. Got a real B&B note from Charlotte Snowdon.

2/23/96 Friday
Very foggy all morning. Eby worked on the porch chairs. He got the video started and we ran it off. David showed him some buttons and he watched it this evening. Eby took me for my annual eye checkup and the left eye has 20/20 vision and the right one a cataract. We stopped at Elam's for milk. I invited Sue and Charlie for Sunday. I sorted a lot of greetings.

2/25/96 Sunday
Sunny and pleasant. Went to Kinzer. Paul preached on Psalms 127:1-2. Had Uncle Charlie and Aunt Sue for dinner and Mildred and Uncle Clarence to see the video. They liked to see it. We spent the evening reading. I called Mary Alice and she will have a different week as there was a fire at the Home and the sprinkling system did more damage than the fire.

3/1/96 Friday
Calm and cold. I cleaned some cupboards. We took the chairs to John Stoltzfus and picked a cover. He said it may take five weeks. Worked on rug. I am wishing I had given some better answers to Mary Alice for the video.

3/7/96 Thursday
Colder. Eby went to the store with many others stocking up for bad weather. Soon Vera Mast came while Ken was getting a haircut. We had a nice visit. I made doughnuts. Had a sick spell this afternoon and laid down. Soon felt better and finished things up. It is getting icy. I called Mary Alice. They are back in the Home with all the water damage corrected. I braided some.

3/10/96 Sunday
Went to Kinzer. 39 there. Spent afternoon and evening at home. I wrote to Doug and read. Ray and Milton called to say they got home this evening and all went well with their trip to Turkey. They have lots to tell. I called Isaac's and Bradley started his job with pigs. Isaac had his first week with new job.

3/20/96 Wednesday
I worked on rug. Eby went to the store. I set up for pacemaker check but I got sick and could not have it done. Vomited and was very weak, slept till 8:00 and felt much better. Eby got his own supper. Eby brought some things from the attic for the sale.

3/24/96 Sunday
Pleasant. Edgar's went with us to Kinzer. 48 there. Jay preached. Our anniversary was mentioned. Edgar's left about 1:30 and I read till time for popcorn. Isaac's came this evening. Jim called and he had no news from Beth yet.

4/1/96 Monday
I washed and ironed. Eby took a box of hand rags and jelly eggs to Isaac Stoltzfus and got seeds at Flaud's. I finished the rug. Jim stopped in on his way from Dover to tell us that Beth's little boy was born this morning and Pat was staying down for a week. His name is Colton James.

4/7/96 Sunday
A dark wet day. Sunrise service was held in the church. We had communion and footwashing service. Jay preached. I washed with Esther Clark and Hattie Engle. We had Charlie and Sue for dinner and an afternoon of visiting. Josephine called and they had a covering of snow and still snowing.

4/16/96 Tuesday
Had more than three inches of rain. I worked on dress and call it done. It is a problem and I am not pleased with it. We both got birthday cards from President Clinton and his wife Hillary.

4/21/96 Sunday
Went to Kinzer. 42 there. Had a quick lunch and went up to Charlie and Sue's and he drove our car to Manheim Church for Frank Kreider's funeral. It was well attended. Spent a quiet evening. I called Jim's, and Pat came home from Beth's this evening. Charlie called and they are moving back to the renovated home.

4/25/96 Thursday
Isaac and Elizabeth picked us up to go to Chambersburg for the funeral of Verna Denlinger at the Cedar Grove Church. Saw a lot of the relatives and stopped for dinner on our way home. I have 17 birthday cards. Had calls from Abram's, Ray, Sanford and boys, Mary Alice and Sally. I called Nancy. Charlie called after 9:00 to say he sent a gift. I looked and found a big box on the glider with three dwarf roses.

4/28/96 Sunday
Went to Kinzer. Jay preached. He called this morning and invited us to take a drive this afternoon. Left at 1:00 and got home at 5:30. Saw Lloyd Weaver's big tulip farm, lots of pretty country down to Pequea and the river hills where some went on the trails. Our last stop was at Gochenouer's new log house that they built themselves.

5/2/96 Thursday
I did the bathroom. Eby went to the store. He cultivated some of the garden and I hoed the peas and onions and strawberries. Nancy came about 4:30 and after supper we went to Buyerstown greenhouse and got some plants. She went to the bake shop and I visited with Mother Stoltzfus for a short time.

5/6/96 Monday
I washed and ironed. Made cracker pudding and cupcakes and covered some marshmallows. Eby went to the store. Elizabeth called and said they will bring supper for Daddy's birthday. They came with a big dinner of stuffed chicken breast, new potatoes, asparagus, apple sauce, buns, cherry pie and peach ice cream. They brought candy and Bradley sent some car cleaner.

5/7/96 Tuesday
Began raining after 5:00. I made meat loaf and got food ready for Sam and Becky. He came about 11:30 and it did not suit Becky, so we had a nice time visiting with Sam. He will be graduating from Brown in Rhode Island. I trimmed some yard this evening. John Stoltzfus brought our porch chairs all nicely done for $150.00. Charlie and Ed sent some cheese cakes for Daddy's birthday.

5/11/96 Saturday
We got started for Jennie's wedding at 7:45 and got there just as the photos were being taken. It was a nice simple wedding, about 90 there. I met Paul's Grandma and she was friendly. After the reception we went to Jonathan's for a nice visit. It began raining and kept it up all the way home.

5/12/96 Sunday
Milton's left about 8:00 for Great Neck. We went to Kinzer. We had the Colton family from New York for dinner with their four boys. Very friendly folks and we enjoyed their visit. Rhoda called and said Hana Renee was born last night.

5/16/96 Thursday
Ascension Day. We took it easy and had holiday with the Amish. Some young folks were walking by, the girls with white bandanas and the boys with no hats. I cooked the pig stomach for trype. Did some reading. Mildred and Clarence took us along to Old Road Church this evening.

5/24/96 Friday
I got the cactuses ready and Eby hung them on the maple tree. I cleaned some corners in the garage. Eby did some sprinkling. Some strawberries are turning red. Eby burned the trash. The Gap bank robber has not been caught yet. My throat is a bit better.

5/26/96 Sunday
Went to Kinzer. 49 there. Paul preached. Michael and his family came about 12:30 and were tired from their Saturday wedding. We had a nice time with the children, Erica and Clayton. They slept in the middle room.

5/27/96 Monday
Had nice showers and the children slept will. We had late breakfast and early lunch and they left at 12:15 for the Philadelphia Airport for their flight to Atlanta. Uncle Charlie called and said he will take us to the Mennonite Home and we left at 1:30 and visited Amy and Jay. She was real good and Jay had severe back pains by spells.

6/2/96 Sunday
A pleasant day. Went to Kinzer. Jay preached. Jim's and Ted's were here when we got home. I made a quick dinner and they left with Pat by 12:30 with the new little grandson Colton. He did very well. Jim stayed a while longer. Soon after he left Abram and Pat stopped on the way home from Norristown. And later Miriam and Martha Horning came for family history. Ray and Jane called and all is ready for the wedding.

6/8/96 Saturday
Isaac's picked us up at 8:45 and took us to Ray's where we had lunch and saw the renovations and went on to Hopewell Church for Laura and Glen's wedding at 2:00. It was well planned and all went well. Micah was ring bearer and all the attendants stood in line. It was a good ceremony and the Girls' Choir sang very well. Went on to the Boys' Choir School for the reception. It was pretty and well planned with catered good food. Guests were friendly and socialized enjoying each other. We got home safely before 11:00. It was a good day.

7/12/96 Friday
I baked oatmeal cookies and watered the limas with water running down the middle. Picked the pickles and worked on rugs. Had a letter from Mary Alice and she is invited to spend a week's vacation with friends who rented a cottage on Cape Cod. Eby did some sprinkling.

7/13/96 Saturday
Over three inches of rain. It was a dark day. John Esh brought a big box of nuts and we shelled a lot. I braided rug part of the time. Minnie called after 3:00 and said that Jay passed away after a long illness. Vera Mast called to tell me too. Isaac and Elizabeth came this evening. Bradley stayed home alone.

7/16/96 Tuesday
Beautiful day. We did morning work and were ready for Isaac and Elizabeth to take us to the funeral service for Jay at Old Road. He had planned most of the service. Pastor Ginder preached on his chosen text John 3:16. James and Dale came of our family. Many were served lunch at White Horse Fire Hall. After we got home we set up and shelled balance of walnuts for Levi Esh.

7/18/96 Thursday
I cleaned and cut the rhubarb and put Sanford's in the freezer and had Elizabeth's ready for the freezer. She took us to have Eby's eyes checked for cataract surgery. I picked and washed the pickles and canned five quarts. Read this evening. Charlie called and wants us to visit him in September. A plane exploded off the coast of Long Island and fell into the Atlantic with 230 passengers lost.

7/19/96 Friday
Over an inch of rain. Worked on rug and did the round flower bed and some trimming. Christ mowed the yard. I picked a few pickles. Invited Charlotte Snowdon and Suzanne to our reunion and she invited us to go out to dinner August 8. We looked at the Olympics till 10:45 and didn't hear President Clinton speak so we gave up.

7/31/96 Wednesday
Elizabeth came at 7:30 and took us for Eby's cataract surgery. It went well and we got home by 1:00. He rested and felt real good. Nancy came for supper and overnight.

8/3/96 Saturday
Got up early and did up the many jobs preparing food and cleaning. Cared for Eby's eye. Took a rest and looked for Fredric's and they got here after 4:00 and we had supper at 5:30. The children had no room for dessert. I played some games with Zachary and Kevin. Carol and Peter did the dishes. They left around 7:30 for a motel near Hershey.

8/8/96 Thursday
Hazy and hot. Eby did some cultivating. I did some cleaning after I had a dizzy spell. I planted some peas where the onions came out. Elizabeth called to see if we need any help. I rested and got ready for Charlotte and Suzanne to take us to Yoder's for a treat to dinner. Got home by 7:45. They were kind and friendly.

8/23/96 Friday
Very warm. Eby sprinkled and scrubbed the porch and did the sweeping. I made a birthday cake for Mary Alice and got food ready for supper. Sanford's came this afternoon and we got things lined up for tomorrow to leave by 8:00 for Camp Morehart. The boys slept in their sleeping bags. Sanford and Daddy went for the potatoes and Sanford washed them.

8/24/96 Saturday
Got up early and got thing ready and loaded after breakfast and started at 8:00. Sanford and Daddy went in our car and Tera drove theirs with the rest of us. Had a good trip and got to Camp Morehart by 8:30, the first there. The caretaker stayed for a while. All the children were there and some grandchildren and some greats. There were two babies, Hana and Colton. Had a good day together with plenty of good food. Our guests were Charlotte Snowdon and Suzanne and Ernest and Mildred Bleiler.

8/25/96 Sunday
Dale and Mae were in charge of breakfast and our worship. Milton's, Ray's and Edgar's gave reports of their trips to Turkey and the Holy Lands. Very interesting! Had plenty of leftovers and good things for lunch with some to divide. Ray brought me home in our car and Jane drove theirs and dropped Charles off at the airport for his flight. They stayed here for a nice time chatting. Glen, Laura and Martha did not come this year.

8/27/96 Tuesday
I pulled corn and Eby silked it. I put 15 pints in freezer. Canned four quarts of tomatoes. Picked two buckets of limas and we shelled them. Clarence called and said they will take us to the meeting at Kinzer this evening in regard to homosexuals. I got an appointment for my feet tomorrow evening.

8/28/96 Wednesday
Eby cut grapes and helped pick them off. I made 8 quarts of juice. Put 10 pints of limas in the freezer. Took a rest and had early supper. Eby took me to the Medical Center and I had my first foot treatment. It feels fine.

9/12/96 Thursday
We got things packed up and had early lunch. Jane took us to Dr. Raich for Daddy's eye appointment. It took a long time with waiting. We got home and got ready to leave for Ray's. He had supper waiting when we got there safely. Had a nice evening in their clean, tidy home.

9/13/96 Friday
Ray had the day off and we went to the hospital and saw his productive garden and Dr. Stoltz doing an operation on a dog and met some of the hospital folks. Went on to see Glenn's store and next to their home. Had lunch and visiting in the quiet of their pretty home. Had a good supper and nice visiting in the evening.

9/16/96 Monday
I washed and dried it in the basement. Eby set poison for the bugs. Elizabeth was getting her second cataract done. I did the ironing and sewed some and cut rug strips. I called Grace, and Steve and Silvia's wedding went well.

9/27/96 Friday
I got awake early and we got ready for Uncle Charlie when he came to take us to Abram's. He drove to the airport and we flew to Chicago and changed planes for San Francisco. Charles and Ed met us in the van they rented for our travels. Next we arrived at their renovated place. It is beautiful and comfortable plus modern. Abram's stayed at a hotel. The trip was not tiresome.

9/28/96 Saturday
Foggy in morning and cool. Went to the market that lines both sides of a street with very much food of many kinds with a multitude of shoppers. Charles and Ed bought a good supply and we got big dates and quinces to bring home. Next project was preparing food for the evening guests. Abram and Pat came from their meeting. Andy and a friend and some others. Total 11. Andy played some good music. All were served well and enjoyed the good food.

9/29/96 Sunday
Had a relaxed morning and were taken to services and met at the curb from the entrance by the pastor with a hearty welcome. The service was good with a visiting pastor. It was followed by a fellowship meal in the Hall with most everyone very friendly. Charlie and Ed brought three elderly ladies from a retirement home. Next we saw more of the city driving to a beach picnic area where they had prepared a good lunch. Had a pleasant evening.

9/30/96 Monday
After a good breakfast we went with Abram and Pat and Charles and Ed on more sightseeing to the museum for the cable cars. They have been in operation for many years. Next we saw more of the city and stopped at the orchid greenhouse, one of the largest in the world. It is beautiful. Charles brought me one to bring home. No problem on the plane. Got back to Charles' place and had a good supper and evening. Packed up for flight home.

10/1/96 Tuesday
Had a snack and left for the airport at 7:00 with Ed and Charles. Had a good flight to Chicago. After a rest we continued in our wheelchairs to next flight for Harrisburg. Both were comfortable and Abram drove to Hershey where Uncle Charlie and Aunt Sue met us and drove us home. Found all well here. Charles called soon after we got home.

10/3/96 Thursday
I washed and ironed. Eby went to the store and cleaned up, putting the hose in for the winter. I talked with Mildred and Elizabeth. Ray and Rhoda called. Rosa's twin girls were born this morning. We picked most of the tomatoes and peppers. Did some banking this evening. Had first turnips for supper.

10/25/96 Friday
I cleaned some dining room carpet till dew dried off celery and we took it all out and put it in the old freezer in the garage. I pulled radishes, carrots and a turnip for vegetable tray for Sunday. We took the old fern down and put up a hearty plant. I called Charlotte Snowdon and we had a good chat. Digging continues across the road.

11/21/96 Thursday
Eby watched the progress across the road and went for a battery for my pacemaker check. Had a good report. I got birthday cards ready and wrote to Doug. Isaac and Elizabeth came this evening. Made some checks for charities. Sanford called to say Micah is in the hospital for an asthma attack.

11/22/96 Friday
Cold. Eby watched progress from the window. I watered plants and did some cleaning. Got the carrots processed and in the freezer. Soaked my feet as I could not get an answer from Helen the foot doctor. Called Sanford and they had all been at the hospital with Micah. He is better but will stay till Sunday.

11/28/96 Thursday
Got up at 6:00 and put turkey in the oven and got croquettes ready. Got packed up and Ray came before 9:00 and took a rest before taking us to Ed Miller's for our Thanksgiving Day with 35 family members. It snowed and driving home was not so good. We passed by some accidents. Ray had tea and a rest before he started home. Jane called at 8:45 and said he was safely home. Becky's friend was there.

12/5/96 Thursday
We did some cleaning. Eby used the cleaner. Charlotte Snowdon and her daughter Suzanne took us to Sight and Sound for the Christmas program. It had a full house with a lot of pretty lights and music. The took us to Diener's Restaurant for a good supper. Got home by 5:00 and spent the evening on cards. Abram called later. Becky's boyfriend is special.

12/21/96 Saturday
Pleasant and cold. I did some paint patching and cleaned the bathroom. I called Sue and she was moving to Landis Homes and will go to stay on Monday. No work on project all day. We got a box of oranges and grapefruit from Nancy and Gary.

12/24/96 Tuesday
I roasted the chicken and made caramel sponge. Uncle Charlie came and made a visit and told us about his accident yesterday. He had a finger bruised and his left arm bumped. The pickup that hit him was on the wrong side of the road going more than 50 miles an hour. Next Abram and Pat came with an armful of gifts. Candy, videos, calendar, puzzle and tea set. Isaac and Elizabeth came this evening.

12/25/96 Wednesday
Fine day. We set the table and I got all the food ready to serve by 2:30. Dale and Mae came about 1:00 and Milton's and Doug around 2:00. The Virginia folks were all going to Weaver's plus Charles and Ed. Abram's were having David, Ben, Becky and her friend. Isaac's were going to Dietzel's, James with family. Ray and Laura were working. Edgar's were with a few of their family.

12/31/96 Tuesday
I cut up the turkey and made food ready for the New Year's dinner. Eby swept the drive and the dining room. The men had to stop on the mall project because of too much rain.

1997

1/1/97 Wednesday
It was a good day with no fog, ice, snow, rain or wind. Had a dinner of turkey that Uncle Charlie gave. Aunt Pauline brought good cole slaw and Mildred brought graham cracker fluff. Uncle Charlie brought Aunt Sue from the Home. Aldus and Judy King stopped a while as they knew Paul's were here. We did some reminiscing.

1/5/97 Sunday
Went to Kinzer. 41 there. Paul preached a New Year's sermon. Eby is feeling better. I took a nap and had a quiet afternoon. I wrote a letter to Charles for his birthday. Dale called and said Marcia had a baby boy. He talked to Rhoda.

1/19/97 Sunday
Fine cold day. Went to Kinzer. Hershey Hostetter preached on Glory. Sanford's went to Quaker Meeting. We had Victor and Sally, Vic and Jit, Sanford's and Uncle Charlie for dinner. Tera was such very good help and we had special visiting while Tera, Sally and Sanford did up the dishes. Uncle Charlie went to see Aunt Sue. Had a nice evening with Sanford's. Rhoda called and she came home on Wednesday after her stay with Marcia helping with Daniel James.

1/20/97 Monday
Cold. Had late breakfast and Sanford's got packed up and started for home at 9:30 after a good weekend. I took it easy watching the inauguration of Clinton's second term. Big event. Washed a load this afternoon and dried it in basement. Eby is keeping quiet on his chair and sleeping most of the time and went to bed for a while. I started reading the books about Tera's Yoders.

1/22/97 Wednesday
Top soil was hauled at the mall project all day. I worked on rug. Ray called and said they will come tomorrow. Eby took me to the foot doctor and got my nails cut and corns trimmed. Eby swept and set the table for our Bible study.

1/25/97 Saturday
David worked on kitchen light and it is the wrong kind. I tied off Rosa's rug and sewed up the strips that came from Jane's fabric and rolled them up. Finished reading the Old Testament that I started in 1996.

1/29/96 Wednesday
Pleasant. I got things ready for dinner. Betty Meck brought her Mother Elizabeth for dinner and a visit. She seemed real good and we had a nice time. Yesterday Sight and Sound had a 15 million dollar fire.

2/1/97 Saturday
Eby washed the car and porch. I prepared food for Sunday. Did some cleaning and braided rug. Called Charlotte Snowdon and she had a lot to say. Nancy called to say the children are planning a 70th Anniversary celebration for us March 22.

2/6/97 Thursday
I worked on the pork all day and it is all done and in the freezer. Could not get any oil of cloves for the pig foot jelly. Eby brought most of the meat from garage and took it to the freezer when ready.

2/9/97 Sunday
Went to Kinzer. Jay preached. Charlie came for dinner and took us to Landis Home to visit Sue. She seems good. Ronnie and his wife and Martha Burkholder were there. Charlie gave me a book about Bennie Fisher's life and I read till 12:00.

2/11/97 Tuesday
I worked on rug most of the day. Eby took me to Dr. Hartly and he suggested a new bone drug and gave me samples and an appointment in two weeks. I am undecided about such an unhandy pill. I think he needs patients. Men worked on roof all day.

2/13/97 Thursday
I started the bone pill and one for blood pressure. Eby went to the store and got a big order as snow is forecast. I worked on rug and wrote some letters to Amy, Doug and Robert and Grace. Eby rubbed hams.

2/22/97 Saturday
I got things ready for supper. Mary Alice came about 3:00 and we visited till Charlotte and Suzanne came. Then Mary Alice and Suzanne went to Intercourse for shopping. Daddy, Charlotte and me did some visiting and had our supper at 5:30. The girls did the dishes and we had nice visiting. They left soon after 9:00. Miriam called to say Amy is not so good.

2/24/97 Monday
I washed and ironed and dried it outdoors. Jim came this afternoon and brought a new toilet seat and visited a while before going on to Dover to bring Pat home

after a week in Cancun, Mexico with her sister's family. I called Miriam and Amy is on oxygen and not eating. Eby trimmed some of the maple tree. Lots of action on mall project.

2/25/97 Tuesday
Did usual morning work and Eby took me to Dr. Hartly for appointment. All was well with the new bone pills. I worked on rug and had time to watch the dirt haulers with three trucks keeping busy. Eby trimmed some maple tree. Did some checks this evening.

2/27/97 Thursday
I cleaned bathroom closet and hall closet. Eby took me to Dr. Stoltzfus for my annual eye exam. I have a cataract forming on my right eye but got no change in glasses. Some dirt hauled in late afternoon. Helped with income tax this evening and did some rug. Called Nancy and she has things lined up for March 22.

3/1/97 Saturday
Three loads of dirt hauled before it rained. Eby cracked a lot of nuts. I cleaned the hutch. Planned to have Charlie take us to the Home tomorrow to visit Amy, and Miriam called and said she passed away at 8:00. I did some calls and Sanford called to see how we are doing. We are just three left now.

3/3/97 Monday
Have a good cover of wet snow. I washed and dried it in basement. Abram called from Hawaii and said they are about to leave for their flight home. Minnie called to sympathize for Amy's parting. I got sick after lunch and did not have a good afternoon. Daddy did some kind nursing and I ate some toast this evening and feel much better. Snow plows had some work today.

3/4/97 Tuesday
Eby took me to Sewing Circle. Had eight and got a lot done. Mildred brought me home. Eby worked on the nuts. Kim brought some hoagies for Isaac's to pick up and two for us. Milton called to say they will be going to the funeral and will bring us home from Mt. Joy.

3/5/97 Wednesday
Milton's left for home after 8:00. I took it easy and did not take any medication since Monday. Worked on cards and rug. Called Annis and had a long talk with her. Eby took it easy and took nuts to Levi's.

3/10/97 Monday
I washed and the washer stopped so we had a repair man come and there was sand in the hose. Got it going and dried but not ironed. I got a sick spell soon after 9:00 and was slowed up till about 3:00 when I helped Eby finish the nuts.

3/15/97 Saturday
I got things ready for dinner and Tom and Rosa came with Marcus and the twins for a first visit. They were very good and did not take any naps or cry and were pleasant. We had a nice visit and they went home about 3:00. I washed the dishes after they left. Braided balance of rug this evening. Invited Uncle Charlie for tomorrow but he has plans.

3/17/97 Monday
I washed and ironed a small wash. Dried it outdoors. David made holes in the trash barrel. Marvin and Ruth stopped in for information for the songs on Sunday. Had a shampoo. President Clinton is recovering from knee surgery.

3/19/97 Wednesday
Snow is all melted. I cleaned the refrigerators and made rhubarb sauce. Eby washed the turnips and they are not all good. He scrubbed the porches and some windows. A water truck hosed the dirt off the road to the highway. I sorted some magazines. Rubbed Eby's back. Had call for pacemaker and all is well.

3/21/97 Friday
I did the hardboiled eggs. Eby is having a problem with his back and constipation. He took it easy all day. I did some cleaning. Jim called and wants to find an express wagon for Colton. Beth and Ted have flu and will not be coming on Saturday evening. Sue called and she is confused. I massaged Eby's back.

3/22/97 Saturday
Got things ready and Jim and Pat came and we went to buy a wagon for little Colton. Nancy brought some food on way to New Holland where we all got together at 6:00 to celebrate our 70th Anniversary. All the family, some relatives and friends totalled 81 guests for dinner and a pleasant evening together. Isaac's brought us home and we had no overnight guests. It was a good evening.

3/23/97 Sunday
Beautiful day, cool. Gerry, Nancy and Tera came just before we left for church and put food and things in place. They all came to Kinzer for the service. We had them all here for lunch, about 35. Had a nice time together. They all got on their way home before 4:00. It was a very special weekend and we spent the evening relaxing and thinking how special it all was.

3/28/97 Friday
Eby had a good night and stayed in bed till noon. I cut and sewed some strips and did nursing care. Got more anniversary cards. A cult of 39 people were suicides in California. Isaac offered to do our garden today but it is not cultivated and too wet.

3/31/97 Monday
Unpleasant. Got food ready for dinner and Jonathan and his family came for dinner. Ruth took three of the children to see the chickens at Orpha's home. She lives near them in Baltimore. We had dinner at 12:30. Jonathan kept Hana and stayed here and got some family history. Jonathan's left soon after 2:00. It started snowing by 1:00 and has a half foot by 9:00 and still coming down fast. Eby is feeling better and I rubbed his back.

4/2/97 Wednesday
Snow is melting. I did the ironing and cleaned the toy cupboard. Sorted some cards and did some reading. I called Sue, Paul and Charlotte Snowdon. Eby went to Blank's to pay for snow removal. I like the book that Jonathan's gave about Mennonite Women.

4/8/97 Tuesday
Edgar painted the living room and some wall spots on other rooms. We put the muslin on the peas and swept and put things in place. Edgar planted the rose that Charles and Ed sent. We took Edgar and Rhoda to Country Garden for supper and drove by the old Eby house near Buyerstown on the way home. Saw the Longwood Gardens video when we got home.

4/11/97 Friday
Eby cut the red seed potatoes and helped put up the strings. I planted potatoes, carrots, salsify and beets. Eby went for strawberry plants and I planted 25. Eby's back is hurting badly. I put the heat to it and he took pain and laxative pills.

4/17/97 Thursday
Eby went to the store and got a big order. I planted the elephant ear and some dahlias. The peas are up and strawberries are up good. Wrote a note to Mike and Jan and explained missing one of Clayton's birthdays. More poles were put up at the mall. The Lambert girl is out of jail and not guilty of murder.

4/22/97 Tuesday
I made a cherry pie. Read the news and the paper was full of the five-year-old murder of Laurie Show, and Michelle Lambert was set free after five years in jail. Eby filled the birdfeeder and looked at the garden and fell down. Dale left soon after 7:00 this morning and came back at 5:00 and put mulch around some of the plants. Isaac and Elizabeth came this evening and harrowed the garden and burned the trash.

4/25/97 Friday
I worked on rug till noon. Worked on trash pile and it is getting less. Eby went to Flaud's and got more mulch and some asparagus roots. I dug and planted 8 roots. Abner came for us at 6:00 and Esther had a dinner for my birthday. Very good. We saw her beautiful quilt and the video from her trip to the Holy Lands. Sanford's

sent a beautiful bouquet of cut flowers. Nancy called and Charles was there, and I talked to him too. Ray and Jane called.

5/8/97 Thursday
I ripped some skirts for rugs. Planted some flowers and nipped the pansies. Eby watched the robins from the peas with B.B. gun. Lots of men on project.

5/11/97 Sunday
Very pretty cool day. Went to Kinzer. Jay preached and there was scripture about mothers read. We had our noon meal alone. Took a nap and wrote letters. Dale, Jim, Milton and Charles called, so it was a good Mother's Day.

5/16/97 Friday
Dale had the day off and he put mulch on the flower beds. I did some ripping and have a lot done. This afternoon Dale took us to Georgetown to see chairs and on to Quarryville to a chair shop and we bought one for Daddy that seems to fit him. Isaac's brought the chair this evening and we had time to visit. A lot of dirt was moved today.

6/6/97 Friday
I baked two kinds of cookies. Made a nut cake for Saturday sale and Jean picked it up and two heads of lettuce. Set two mouse traps as there is some snitching. Eby wed some of the peas. More blacktopping was done today.

6/10/97 Tuesday
We went to Rohrer's in Smoketown for lima seed. I replanted them again. We stopped at Knapp's shoes for their selling out sale and each got a pair of shoes. Eby sprinkled again this evening. I planted some healing plants. Josephine called and she is having a lot of health problems, but keeps talking to Pat. I made some birthday cards.

6/12/97 Thursday
I did some hoeing and planted beans and more salsify and dill. Cleaned and burned trash pile and picked some stones. All 8 asparagus roots are growing. The three sisters from Virginia drove to Edgar's today for Sisters' Day.

6/18/97 Wednesday
Eby went for milk. Elizabeth took me for my semi-annual pacemaker check, and it was OK. She brought some strawberries and I put three pints in freezer and made seven glasses of jam. Put two packs of sugar peas in freezer. Eby hoed some garden. I called Nancy and she said Sisters' Day went very well. We had first hull peas for supper.

6/21/97 Saturday
We had late breakfast and got ready to go with Isaac's, and Victor and Sally guided us to visit his folks in Paoli. We had a hearty welcome and good dinner and visiting.

His sister came too. Got there by 1:00 and got home at 7:00. It was good and warm for the pool.

6/24/97 Tuesday
We got up early and pulled and picked all the peas before breakfast. We shelled them and I put three pints in freezer. Eby brought the sliced dried beef and I put it in packs for the freezer. He brought three boxes of strawberries and I put three pints in freezer and made a portion of jam. Eby sprinkled this evening. They used up all the topsoil pile and it is level.

6/27/97 Friday
Eby had hose on limas and potatoes and sprinkled this evening. I did a few odd jobs. The new Weis Store had open house this evening and a lot of cars filled the parking lot. It was a very nice evening. Eby brought milk from Elam's.

7/3/97 Thursday
Eby went to the store and bought Oxheart cherries and I canned 13 quarts and kept 2 quarts for fresh. I did some trimming and David mowed this evening. Isaac and Elizabeth came this evening and we had a nice visit. Abram called and said Josephine is very sick. Joanne invited us to the family gathering tomorrow evening.

7/21/97 Monday
Some clouds but no rain. I washed and ironed. Eby cultivated and I hoed a lot of the garden. Did some braiding. I called Pauline and they will go along to visit Josephine on Thursday. The new road is opened and 897 is shut off from Route 30.

7/24/97 Thursday
I got first corn off but it is too young. We went over to the Weis Store for the first time and I got flowers for Josephine and some other things. Had early lunch when Abram came to eat with us and then picked up Paul and Pauline and took us to visit Josephine at Polyclinic Hospital in Harrisburg. She was glad for our visit and did a lot of talking. We got home at 5:45 and had late supper.

7/26/97 Saturday
I made a casserole for the reunion and we got everything ready to leave at 11:00. Clarence went with us. We had a nice time visiting with 44 relatives. Had plenty of food. Got home by 5:00. I braided some rug this evening. I was the oldest one at the reunion. There are older cousins, but they were not there.

8/5/97 Tuesday
We finished the first corn. Did fourteen packs today. Eby did the silking and we had it done by noon. I picked pickles. Isaac's came this evening and he pulled the corn out by its roots. Eby did some sprinkling.

8/23/97 Saturday
All up and had breakfast and packed, leaving at 8:10 for Camp Morehart. Got here first and the caretaker soon left and we put everything in place. Had a good day together and Abram took Rhoda and me to visit Aunt Josephine in the hospital. She did not respond and Mark and David came back here and visited with the cousins for a while. Some went elsewhere to sleep.

8/24/97 Sunday
Dale and Mae served breakfast to our group and to those who came back. Had a nice worship period. Sanford's boys did some music. Dale was in charge. Doug read some scripture and Edgar led in prayer and had remarks. Had a few songs. There was plenty of food and leftovers were served for lunch and taken home. We had our farewell and came with Edgar's to their home at Ellis Hollow. Abram called to tell us that Aunt Josephine had died and her funeral is on Thursday.

8/28/97 Thursday
We had a quick breakfast and got off to Stauffer's for Josephine's funeral. We had no problem finding it. There was a good number in the church for a good sermon. All the family was there even though some not on the best of terms. After burial a good lunch was served to a lot of family and friends. Rhoda's, Abram's, Isaac's, James' and Ray's were there. Ray's brought us home and stayed till 5:00. Edgar's left for home from Stauffer's. It was a busy day.

8/29/97 Friday
I did a big wash and held it over. Picked a lot of limas and Eby shelled and I put twelve pints in freezer. Rhoda called and she got the tomatoes done that they took along. They had a good trip home. Dale called and said that Mae's father passed away after colon surgery.

9/13/97 Saturday
I worked on rug most of the day. Eby did some odd jobs. David mowed the yard. I called Jim's Pat and Barbara. Milton was away for the weekend and Jim was still at work. I put two bleachers on the celery. Eby pulled some red beets for tomorrow's giveaway. Abram called from Washington to ask about Aunt Sue.

9/25/97 Thursday
I did some cleaning. Gathered things together for our trip to Virginia. Did some broccoli and cauliflower for the freezer. Got corn off to take along. I cleaned the window corner in the kitchen and Daddy could not notice the difference.

9/26/97 Friday
We got up early at 5:00 and made things ready for our lunch and all of a sudden I got a sick spell and was in bad shape for our trip when Ray and Jane came to pick us up at 8:30. Instead an ambulance was called and they sent me off to the hospital.

I got a lot of tests and was soon feeling better. It was disappointing to miss the trip. Ray and Daddy came in to the hospital, and Ray and Jane got started for Virginia by noontime.

9/27/97 Saturday
Had a real good night in the hospital. Got a lot of tests and good nursing care. Had calls from Charles and Dale. Isaac's and Abram came to visit. Isaac's brought Daddy along in. The food was not so good.

9/28/97 Sunday
I got dressed and washed for breakfast. The doctor came and said I can leave and said good bye. No help from nurse. Abram came and brought me home at 11:00. He stayed for an hour before he went on to Lititz for lunch. We had good chicken corn soup that Elizabeth brought. I rested and Eby did the dishes. Isaac's came at 4:30 and Abram's came back and had some talk with Daddy. Had calls from many of the children.

9/30/97 Tuesday
I did the meals and a quart of V8 juice. Eby brought an Amishman to measure for the washroom and he made a hole for dryer fuzz. Isaac's came this evening and helped move refrigerator into kitchen. Sanford, Ray, Milton and Rhoda called.

10/1/97 Wednesday
I did the cooking and ripped several woolen pieces that Jane brought. Very nice wool. Eby worked hard cleaning the garage and it looks so much better. Isaac came this evening and helped put plants in the garage because it may give frost. He had some good ideas for the laundry room and it may be made better. Spent evening reading.

10/5/97 Sunday
Went to Kinzer. Paul preached on envy. It is not right. Went to Mildred and Clarence's with Charlie and Esther Clark. Had a nice visit. Spent the evening quietly. Ray called and they just came home from a week's vacation at Cape May. He was hoarse from a cold. James called and they are well and harvesting alfalfa and corn. They saw two bald eagles in their field eating a ground hog.

10/9/97 Thursday
After chores I picked balance of limas and helped Eby shell. Put six pints in freezer. Eby went to the store and I was ready to go for my toenail cutting when he got back. After supper and dishes I got a bit woozy. Abram and Sam called from Albuquerque to say they are doing well and went for a balloon ride.

10/20/97 Monday
Good wash day and I washed but did not iron. I picked the limas and Eby took the poles down and pulled the vines out. I picked some tomatoes. I called Mildred and they were putting flowers on Victor's and Mabel's graves at 2:00.

10/25/97 Saturday
Eby took his 11 lbs. of nuts to Ivan Stoltzfus and then did the sweeping. I did the dusting and the floors. Jim's, Beth and Colton came about 1:00 and met Theodore here and they left about 3:00. Colton cried when he left Jim and Pat. Doug and Milton's called. Doug had been to Florida with his housemates.

11/3/97 Monday
I washed and ironed, cooked and strained the cider that Lois brought. Made a jar of V8 juice. Eby took papers to Amos and got eggs and a few things at the store. Uncle Charlie took us to see Sue, and he has a tumor in his throat that he will be getting removed soon.

11/4/97 Tuesday
I worked on sweet potatoes and made 77 good sized croquettes. Put them in the garage to cool overnight before putting them in the freezer. Uncle Charlie was getting Xrays today. Abram called and said Grace has a breast problem and will be getting treatment. I called Grace and we had a long talk.

11/6/97 Thursday
I worked on birthday cards and have November done. Abram called and said he talked to Uncle Charlie's surgeon and the problem is serious. I called Grace and she has started on her treatment. Eby shelled the vine bean seed and took it easy. Wendy's is making progress and is being rolled for paving.

11/9/97 Sunday
Went to Kinzer. Jay preached and seven young people of the YES team put on a show that had no meaning. I felt very disappointed. Uncle Charlie and Abram's were here for dinner. Abram helped Charlie with some things before going to the hospital.

11/11/97 Tuesday
Nice weather for Amish weddings. Grace was having her first treatment. I did some mending and put a cover on Eby's white shirt collar. I cleaned the flower bed in the corner. Men were planting some plants between the trees. I wrote to Daniel Hess and sent him our children's names and addresses.

11/12/97 Wednesday
I made some applesauce from the apples Lois and Melvin Harbold brought. Pat came on her way to Beth's and had a rest stop. I called Grace and she said her treatment was better than she expected. I called Uncle Charlie and he is ready for tomorrow's surgery. Had our Bible Study here this evening.

11/13/97 Thursday
I cleaned some drawers. Uncle Charlie had surgery for the tumor in his neck. Abram talked to the surgeon afterwards. He was in his room and able to write that he felt comfortable and is able to eat. There was more digging across the road.

11/17/97 Monday
Pleasant and colder. I washed and ironed, dried some in dryer. Eby raked some leaves. I did some mending. Grace called and she was pleased with the anointing service last evening. Her next treatment is December 4. Got some checks ready for banking.

11/23/97 Sunday
Went to Kinzer. 185 there for our celebration. Noah Hershey preached a good sermon. The 1950 quartet sang three songs. We had lunch at the Fire Hall and came home after seeing more in basement. Abram and Pat came about 3:30 and we had supper. The call came that Aunt Sue passed away. Abram's took us to evening service. It was well attended and had a good message on Isaac Eby. Abram called from his car phone to say that Aunt Sue's service is at 11:00 on Wednesday.

11/26/97 Wednesday
Isaac's took us the funeral for Aunt Sue at Paradise. The service was well planned and attended. A full lunch was served to a lot of people. Two of Bobby's daughters were there and two grandsons. Uncle Charlie did not come. Abram and Isaac were pallbearers. Milton's, Jim's, Mary Alice and Nancy and Gerry were there.

11/27/97 Thursday
Beautiful day. Isaac's took us along to Ed Miller's for our Thanksgiving dinner with about 36 family members. Ray roasted and brought capons and others brought food. We made croquettes, celery and pickles. Martha and her boyfriend were there. Spent the evening reading. I called Rhoda at Jonathan's in Baltimore. They plan to come here tomorrow.

11/29/97 Saturday
Edgar's spent the day and did some cleaning. Edgar's took us to visit Uncle Charlie and he seemed in good spirits, but was in bed. After cleaning some celery for Rosa we had our supper and spent a nice evening visiting.

11/30/97 Sunday
Edgar's left for Philadelphia at 8:00. We went to Kinzer. Had a dinner of leftovers and spent time resting and reading. Grace called and she had been to church and seemed real good. Abram called and does not hear much progress with Uncle Charlie. I called Ray's to ask about Jane's mother. She is staying with them now and is not doing so well.

12/3/97 Wednesday
Sanford helped with cookies after breakfast and Mary Alice, Nancy and Gerry came later with a lot of cookie dough and we baked cookies and got a lot done. They left for home at 6:00.

12/8/97 Monday
I did some more goodies, haystacks and coated some little pretzels and candy. Eby cracked nuts and has a lot done. Abram was visiting Uncle Charlie and called me to talk with him, but he does not have any interests. I checked the Christmas cards this evening as we are getting some.

12/17/97 Wednesday
Had a sick spell early this morning and feel much better. Eby went to the store and I made cranberry for New Year and took it easy. Got a pretty bouquet from Nancy and Gerry. Plumber came to check job in laundry room. Business is good at the mall.

12/22/97 Monday
Sleet and snow and rain. Cinder trucks were busy. Carpenter brought the new cupboards for the washroom and was done by noon. Bill was $1000. Plumber did not get here for his job. I got some cleaning done and got some cookies ready for New Year's. Linda called and invited us for Christmas. Got a box of pears from Charles and Ed.

12/25/97 Thursday
Had a nice morning and Mark and Kim took us along to Donald Ibach's where some of Isaac's family spent Christmas Day. Had a delicious dinner and many gifts were given. Isaac's brought us home. Ray and Dale and Rhoda called. Rhoda said Andrea and Ian will come Saturday.

12/26/97 Friday
I made ready for Charles and Ed's visit. Eby did the sweeping. They came at 12:00 after visiting Uncle Charlie at the Mennonite Home. He was dressed and in his room. Abram called from New Mexico to see how we are doing and gave us his number. We had a nice visit with Charles and Ed before they left for Nancy's. Spent the evening reading.

12/30/97 Tuesday
I got celery, carrots and turnips ready, roasted the turkey and cut up bread for filling. Did some cleaning. Eby did the sweeping. Rhoda and Abram called. Abram's got home from New Mexico today. Had a good time with a lot of skiing for the young folks. Edgar's had two feet of snow.

1998

1/1/98 Thursday
Fine cold weather. Got food from the garage and ready for dinner. Miriam came first and we got food in the oven and dished some things. Had Clarence and Mildred, Paul and Pauline, Melvin and Lois Harbold, Esther and her friend, Anna Martin

and James Martin. All ate well and seemed to enjoy the visit. We felt it was well worth the effort.

1/3/98 Saturday
Eby took papers to Isaac and got eggs and went to the bank. We cleaned up leaves by the porch. I spent the day doing the fabrics that Jane gave for rugs. It is very nice. Clarence called about Charlie and I got the latest from Abram. No more isolation or fever. Abram went to see him and took him for a walk in the hall.

1/4/98 Sunday
Went to Kinzer. Paul preached. We had leftovers for dinner. Spent a quiet afternoon and evening. I called Grace and Mary Alice. Grace had a good day and went to church. Her blood count is very good. Ray and Jane called and Martha announced her engagement.

1/9/98 Friday
We ordered trousers for Daddy and sent for license. I worked on the rug. Got a book from Mary Alice and read a lot this evening. The title is Any Given Day. There were 52 divorces listed in today's Intell for the past week.

1/13/98 Tuesday
I worked on rug and got food from basement. Eby swept the room and I dusted for our company this weekend. I called Irene Noll and gave her a report on Uncle Charlie. Got checks ready for banking and Eby took them. I finished reading Any Given Day and liked it very much.

1/15/98 Thursday
Rained and mild. I cleaned the flower pole. Cut Eby's hair and toenails. Baked a cake. Cleaned celery and made a pot of vegetable soup. Grace called and she had a session with her surgeon and he gave her a good report. Surgery is scheduled and she is in good spirits and friends are good to her.

1/16/98 Friday
I did some cleaning and Daddy did the sweeping. Made a mince pie, red eggs, filling balls and roasted a chicken. Got a big letter from Fredric's with thanks for our Christmas gifts. Sanford's got here at 8:45 all doing fine and grown a few inches since we saw them last. We had a treat and went to bed after visiting.

1/23/98 Friday
I worked on rug most all day. Eby went to the bank. Lena Clark died. Paul called and remembered her as one of his teachers at Hatville. I read the Weaverland Church History till 10:00. It is so interesting. It is foggy this evening.

1/29/98 Thursday
Eby is feeling better and brought the paper in and put letters in mailbox. I worked on rug. President Clinton is making the news for some misconduct. The Lisa Lambert case is still making news. She claims innocence in the Show murder.

2/5/98 Thursday
Cloudy, wet and mild. I made 66 doughnuts. Did some cleaning. Lisa Michelle Lambert was taken back to prison in a N.J. prison for women. I did my toe nails this evening. Eby had a better day.

2/7/98 Saturday
I got food ready and set up for lunch with cow in the garden. Robert and Grace came with Jennie and Paul. Grace seemed real good but did lose some weight. They took the high chair and the dollhouse along. Abram and Pat called. He had seen Uncle Charlie and he gets a few tests next week. I called Kathleen and she is getting hip surgery soon.

2/9/98 Monday
Fine sunny day. I washed and did some mending. We sent some rug thread to Jacob, Luke and Micah. Eby took it to the post office. I called Richard Vincent and he gave me a report of Gloria's surgery. She is paralyzed on the right side. I worked on birthday cards this evening. Called Mary Alice and she is going to West Virginia for a four-day vacation.

2/12/98 Thursday
Eby stayed in bed all day. Came out for supper. I massaged his back twice and he tried Charles' treatment with his feet up. I made an onion poultice at bedtime. Called Grace and she is doing good, made cookies and visited the school where she taught and has her house in order. I worked on rug and was nurse for Eby.

2/13/98 Friday
Pleasant weather. Eby got up and dressed and got the water started as it was off and the plumber came later and put in a new part so it should not happen again. The barn burned on Clair Denlinger's farm and made a lot of confusion. Eby had a doctor's appointment. He had Xrays and got new meds and orders to take it easy. Miriam Hess came this afternoon for a nice visit and information on the good old days. Brought some pictures she had enlarged from old prints.

2/16/98 Monday
I washed and cleaned the bed. Eby had breakfast in bed and got up and dressed at 10:00. Rested two hours after lunch and is feeling some better. I put onion poultice on at bedtime. A couple were burned to death on top of the hill this morning. Grace

called and she is feeling real good and they were going to Jim and Ruth's for Robert's birthday. Rhoda called and they are all well and Marcia and the boys are there for the week. I did some pictures and drawers.

2/18/98 Wednesday
Mild and wet. Eby had breakfast in bed after a good night. Mildred took us to the doctor and he got some things to do, an enema and milk of magnesia. He got both with good results. Had pacemaker check on phone and all is well. I cleaned some drawers and cupboards. Read this evening. Mildred brought chili con carne for supper. Aaron Mark Weber was born after midnight, so his birthday is February 18.

2/20/98 Friday
Eby came out for breakfast and was up all day. He went to the bank and brought the mail. Men put the gas heater in the basement. I scrubbed the porch and did some cleaning in the basement. I made an onion poultice this evening and Eby went to bed at 8:30. Abram called at noon from Puerto Rico to ask about Daddy. I called Grace and she is feeling good. I read this evening.

2/21/98 Saturday
I did the cleaning. Eby was up all day and was feeling real good. Kathleen came for pussy willows and I helped her get a lot for someone. Isaac's and Bradley stopped on the way home from seeing the new grandson. Jim and Pat stopped on way home from seeing Beth. Colton wanted to come home with them. Pat's mother had a stroke and is in the hospital. Ray called and he has a hearing aid.

3/3/98 Tuesday
Grace had her surgery and all was well when Robert called and said she was resting and the surgeon gave a good report. I worked on rug and called Irene. She said Jay is doing well after his prostate surgery.

3/5/98 Thursday
I worked on rug. Washed some pants for Eby. He took some papers to Ike Stoltzfus and got eggs. I called Grace and she came home today. Nancy came and is staying with her. We got a photo of little Aaron Weber. We packed Milton's coat that he forgot and sent it U.P.S. Ray called to tell us Jane's mother had a spell and is in the hospital unconscious.

3/6/98 Friday
We cleaned and emptied the dining room, ready for a cleaner coming at 12:30. Had our lunch and they came on time. One man got on the job and made a good job of cleaning the rug and it was done by 2:30. It was all free for an advertisement. We put everything back in order.

3/8/98 Sunday
Dark, cloudy and rained. Went to Kinzer. Mark Leaman preached. Had our lunch and cancelled our visit to see Charlie with Isaac's. Spent a quiet day reading, resting and phoning. Ray called and said Jane's mother died yesterday. I called Grace and we had a long chat. She is feeling good.

3/17/98 Tuesday
I did the washing and used the dryer. Worked on rug. We exchanged the mattresses on middle room and basement. Big job, but bed is ready for our next guests, Edgar and Rhoda. I called Charlotte Snowdon and we had a very long talk. Spent the evening reading.

3/21/98 Saturday
Cold, windy and damp. Got ready to go with Isaac's to Sue's sale. There were a lot of things to sell and a good number of buyers. Some things sold very well and there were a lot of bargains. Abram's brought us home and Laura and Jane came for a visit. We got the mailbox and not much more. Saw a lot of friends and relatives.

3/24/98 Tuesday
Edgar's spent the night and we had a nice morning together. At noon they took us for our anniversary dinner at the Country Garden. It was very good. Next they packed up and left for home. I got started on a clean-up of the sewing room. Jay Meck called to say God bless our anniversary.

4/8/98 Wednesday
I got things ready for dinner and Nancy and Silvia came about 11:45. We did some chatting and ate soon after 12:00. They went to Buyerstown Greenhouse and bought a load of nice plants. Came back and relaxed a while and left for home at 3:00. They brought geraniums and impatients for me. Silvia brought a pretty bouquet. I did some rug this evening.

4/10/98 Friday
I spent the morning reading the gospels about the crucifixion and Eby took it easy and read and went for milk. Had late lunch and I ripped skirts this afternoon. They are very nice. A tornado killed 30 in Alabama. The Lambert case is coming up again. I wrote for Jacob's birthday.

4/18/98 Saturday
Eby scrubbed the porch and did some sprinkling. I made rice pudding, a sponge cake, red eggs and roasted an eye roast and made other foods for tomorrow. Grace called and she is getting her treatments each day and is doing real good. The hearing aid man came to fix Eby's aid. Charlie called from San Francisco and we had a long chat.

4/25/98 Saturday
Did a bit of cleaning. I called Grace and she is doing real good but got dizzy when she was trimming yard. I took it easy and got more cards. Esther Clark called and sang Happy Birthday to me. Milton and Barbara called this evening. Ray and Jane called and they were going to New York with Martha today.

4/29/98 Wednesday
Eby worked on rows and I planted limas, salsify, beans and spinach. I sewed some strips from Nancy's skirts. Eby cut some mulberry twigs from bushes. The Lisa Lambert case is on again in Lancaster court. I read Silver Threads this evening.

5/7/98 Thursday
Pleasant showers this evening. I did some braiding. Cleaned the bed by garage. Eby spent a quiet day and finished reading Silver Threads. Pauline called and said they visited Charlie and he seemed real good and said thanks for coming. Judy is soon to start her treatments. I finished Minnie's book, Why Christians Get Sick. The Lambert case is setting her free. I called Charles and he just came home from Montana.

5/8/98 Friday
Daddy did the sweeping and I made a nut cake and braided rug and cleaned. Got cards and two books from Mary Alice and read 113 pages in one this evening. Mudslides in Italy killed 55 people.

5/16/98 Saturday
Very warm. Eby cultivated and we planted four rows of corn. I did the sweeping and Eby scrubbed the porch. I made food ready for Sunday. Too warm to work. Arlene Hostetter called this evening to say that Minnie passed away. I called Grace this morning and she is doing real good.

5/18/98 Monday
I washed and put half in dryer. Hoed the roses. We covered the strawberries so the birds can't eat them. A roofer mended the roof. Eby harrowed the unplanted garden. Vera Mast called to ask the cause of Aunt Minnie's death. I called Nancy and they had a good vacation in the rain. She injured her good foot two weeks ago.

5/20/98 Wednesday
Pleasant. Elizabeth took us to the funeral for Aunt Minnie at the Mennonite Home. Don Augsburger and Dorcas Martzell were the speakers. A good number attended. The family was real small. Robert, Jeannette, Arlene and Minnie's sister Verna's daughters. They were all pallbearers. Only a few went to the burial at Hershey's. Sam's Emma Ruth was born.

5/23/98 Saturday
Fine weather. Sanford's had a good night and we got ready for Isaac's to come for us by 9:00 and go to Derry Church in Hershey for Becky and Ken's wedding. It

was well planned and all went well with service at 11:00 and the reception at the Country Club immediately following for 120 guests. Guests were friendly and did a lot of socializing. An evening picnic was held at Abe's for a lot of the guests, but we left for home. Isaac drove a nice way to see pretty county.

5/25/98 Monday
I mended Eby's trousers after the morning jobs and got ready for Isaac's to pick us up at 11:30 to take us along to Victor and Sally's for a day with Isaac's family. Had delicious food and lots of visiting. Sally has a lot of beautiful flowers and a house full of pretty things. Isaac drove in some pretty country and we had a good evening. Ed Miller's gave a passion vine.

6/5/98 Friday
I did some hoeing in the garden. Eby got milk at Elam's and he complains of his leg hurting. Abram called and he talked to Charlie's nurse and she said they think he had a slight heart attack but is resting good today and ate his meals. I invited Isaac's and Jay Ranck's for Sunday dinner.

6/13/98 Saturday
I prepared food and did the weekly cleaning. Mary Alice came this afternoon and went to do some shopping at Intercourse. We had time for nice visiting. She went to the drugstore and got a walker for Daddy to use. His leg is lame.

6/15/98 Monday
I washed and put it in the dryer. The rug roll rack broke and all went down. Eby helped fix and put it all back. I ripped the good skirt from Nancy and put it on a roll. The rolls are all mixed up. I picked two quarts of blueberries this evening. Eby is using his walker.

6/24/98 Wednesday
Had good rain in night. I canned six pints of blueberries and made currant jelly. Did some trimming this evening and David cleaned up the trimmings when he mowed. Some Amish boys were caught selling drugs.

6/30/98 Tuesday
Partly cloudy and showers. Had wind storm and rain this evening and a new tree blew off the bank and fell on road. I worked on rug and got a lot done. I picked a quart of red raspberries. Eby tied up the tomatoes. Galen Blank's son is in a Philadelphia prison because of drug problems.

7/5/98 Sunday
Beautiful day. Went to Kinzer. Paul preached. The Clark told us about her year that is planned in China starting soon. We gave a hundred dollars to help pay her trip. Milton and Ray called when they got home from Ireland. They enjoyed the trip. Little Benjamin arrived this evening to Andrea and Ian Zeurcher, the 31st great grandchild.

7/9/98 Thursday
Eby went to Rhoad's Store and got 25 lbs. of sugar for $10.95. I picked the pickles and did the limas and transplanted the red beets. Eby got cauliflower and broccoli plants. I finished the N.J. rug and started one for Nancy from her skirt material. David mowed the yard. Abram called on the way home from his car after a visit with Charlie. He is comfortable.

7/17/98 Friday
Did some cleaning and got packed for our weekend at the Clemens reunion. Ray's got here soon after 11:00 with lunch for us. Ray did some weeds on the bank and we got started soon after 1:00 and got to Jim's in time for Ray to help milk. Jane and me went to Greg's and had a nice visit with them. When milking was done we took Jim out for supper. Then we went to the Christian camp where the Clemens' were gathering. All were there but Andrea, Ian and little Benjamin and Andrew Ludwig.

7/18/98 Saturday
Fine weather. Had a good breakfast, lunch and picnic supper served by the folks here. Had a good time visiting and playing with things here. The activities were taking walks, doing photos, etc. The picnic was in the pavilion up on the hill and later a scavenger hunt. Beds and rooms were real comfortable and clean. We decided to stay for Sunday.

7/20/98 Monday
Warmer and humid. I washed and ironed and mended. Eby sprinkled all morning. I canned apricots and pickles and worked on rug. I used horse lineament on Eby's knee that Ray brought on Friday. I spent the evening reading.

7/29/98 Wednesday
Eby sprinkled morning and evening. I hoed the roses and some garden this evening. I called Almeda and they will bring Charlie on Sunday. I got back on pills today, ran out for two weeks. Garden is doing well except for the pickles.

8/3/98 Monday
I washed and put it away. Eby cultivated some garden. I mixed some oatmeal cookies. I got a spell when baking them, took a rest and got better to finish the job. Esther came while we ate supper and chatted. Eby picked first ripe tomato.

8/7/98 Friday
Clear and warm. Sanford and Jacob went to Hershey Park and spent the day using the fun things. I washed the floors and did the sweeping. Eby had an easy day and did some sprinkling morning and evening. I got an appointment for my nose and called Elizabeth. Sanford and Jacob gave a good report on their day at

Hershey. He called Tera. It is full moon tonight. I massaged Eby's leg as I have done for weeks.

8/12/98 Wednesday
I washed our bed things. Measured the rugs for the Relief Sale and called the Weaver's so it could be put in the sale book. Eby picked a bucket of ripe peppers and gave them to David to take to his meeting for folks with no gardens. I called Sanford's and they are all home again. Micah sent a note about his good time at camp. Got a letter from the plastic surgeon. I am scheduled for my nose spot.

8/22/98 Saturday
Had breakfast at 7:00 and all packed up when Ray's came at 8:00 and took us to Camp Morehart for our 20th reunion. About 45 made it for a good lunch provided by the Virginia group. Had a good time visiting and some went home by evening and some to motels for the night. Daddy slept in the men's room and me in the women's to avoid the steps.

8/23/98 Sunday
Sunny and warm. Dale and Mae were in charge of breakfast and all was ready for the worship service that was in charge of Gerry and Nancy. The topic was Prayer and it was very well planned and appreciated. There was plenty of food served for lunch with more time for visiting before cleaning up and saying our good byes. Ray's brought us home and relaxed a while before leaving for home. We spent a quiet evening reminiscing.

8/27/98 Thursday
Sunny and a bit cooler. We cleaned and set up for our midweek study of Job. Eby did some sprinkling. Elizabeth came and took us for my 1:00 appointment with the plastic surgeon. Dr. Arthur gave me the facts and made it very serious and did not seem to think surgery was wise. So I decided to skip it and we came home with no results except to live with it.

8/28/98 Friday
Clear and humid. Eby helped get down grapes and pick them off. Did 13 quarts of juice concentrate. Cleaned mess up and had a good rest. Eby sprinkled morning and evening. He picked five cantaloupes. I picked some pickles and oiled the sewing machine. Abram called and asked about my Dr.'s appointment and Charles called and asked how it went.

9/14/98 Monday
Clear and warm. I canned two quarts of V8 juice. Picked and washed the pickles. Called Uncle Charlie and he is doing well and we had a nice chat. Isaac's came this evening and had a problem from Rhoda about our bed not being good for sleeping.

9/15/98 Tuesday
Eby pulled and washed the beets and I canned nine quarts of pickled beets and put a quart in freezer for buttered beets. Cleaned up the colorful mess and had a quiet evening.

9/28/98 Monday
I washed and ironed and made up the beds after a new queen sized bed was delivered and the others changed to other rooms. Called Betty Meck and asked her to bring Elizabeth next Tuesday. Hurricane George is still doing damage. I picked the red raspberries. New bed cost was $702.78.

10/5/98 Monday
Cloudy and mild. I washed and put some in dryer and some on porch. Eby went for a flu shot. Abram's called on way to take Benuel home to his Mother after they took him to Goshen to visit his Daddy. Grace called this evening and she is doing real good. Grace sent a Relief Sale book. My rugs brought $860. I called Karen and they will have the Thanksgiving dinner one more time.

10/6/98 Tuesday
Cloudy and mild. Minnie took me along to Sewing Circle. We did a nice lot of comforts and they were pretty. Mildred brought me home. We did some reading and discussing this evening. I took a walk around the yard and saw a lot of work to do.

10/18/98 Sunday
A beautiful day. 80 degrees. Went to Kinzer. Jay preached a good sermon. Had a quiet afternoon. I read the book of Revelations. Ray called and they are doing the turkeys for Thanksgiving. Martha and her friend will be coming with them. I called Grace and they are excited about flying to California this week. Mary Alice called and she had a good day having everyone for Sisters' Day.

10/24/98 Saturday
Beautiful warm day. I made a cake, cracker pudding and other things ready for Mary Alice and her friend Terry. They came this afternoon. Isaac and Elizabeth came and did some trimming. Mary Alice and her friend went shopping and left after supper to go to friends for the night. David mowed the yard.

10/30/98 Friday
I set up for company. Ray's got here first at about 10:30 and Ian and Andrea and Benjamin came soon after. We had time for visiting before dinner. Baby was very good. After they left for Philadelphia to visit Tom and Rosa, Ray and Jane took us to Intercourse to do some shopping at Zook's. Ray's ate a snack and left at 5:30. Jane left her pretty quilt for me to hem.

11/10/98 Tuesday
Very dark and cloudy. I worked on Ray and Jane's quilt hem all day. Had black thread and black lining and used two lights. Eby set up for our midweek service. Eby did English walnuts.

11/11/98 Wednesday
I worked on Ray and Jane's quilt all day and it is more than half done. Eby worked on walnuts and is tired this evening. There is much suffering in Central America from the storm and rain damage and many are going to help with relief projects. An Amish barn burned while the family was at a wedding.

11/24/98 Tuesday
Nice weather. Got things set up for company. Sam and Melissa came with little Emma for dinner. She was very good and they stayed till 3:30 and went on to visit Becky and Kenneth in Baltimore for supper and on to Hershey for the night. Had our Bible Study this evening.

11/26/98 Thursday
Rained over an inch in the night. We got things ready and Isaac's came for us soon after 10:00 and took us to Ed Miller's for the fourth year for Thanksgiving dinner. We took sweet potato croquettes and quince jam and limas. Isaac's brought us home by 5:45. Spent a quiet evening and the day went well. The Miller's had everything set up perfectly for dinner for forty.

12/1/98 Tuesday
Eby went to the store again and exchanged bad cocoanut. I cleaned the car windows and one in garage. Did the cocoanut. Eby shelled the peanuts. I watered the plants and did some cleaning. Decorations are showing for Christmas and much advertising to make business. Tobacco is not looking like a good crop to farm. Some of last year's crops are not sold yet. I called Pauline and Judy is doing better and will soon be getting radiation treatments.

12/4/98 Friday
Grace, Mary Alice and Nancy came and baked a lot of fine cookies and were all done and left at 3:30. Mary Alice went to the Gap antique shop and a bought a colored glass window to place in one of her windows. I put the cookies in cold storage and quit for the day.

12/19/98 Saturday
Did the morning chores and got things ready for Isaac Stoltzfus and went at 11:30 for dinner with all his help. Had a very good dinner and afternoon treat and a big box of fruit to bring home. Had a nice time visiting with the folks. Had a quiet evening. Had Sunday School meditations. President Clinton was to be impeached today.

12/25/98 Friday
Cold and sunny. Daniel Dietzel came for us soon after 12:00 and we had a delicious dinner with their family. Everything was made pretty for the celebration. Isaac's brought us home. Grace called and they had a nice time with the Virginia folks. Milton called and they had a nice day with some guests from Douglas' house. We got some nice gifts, two blooming plants and some goodies.

12/29/98 Tuesday
Dark, cloudy and foggy. Got all set for company. Grace, Robert, Nancy and Gerry came about 11:00. They brought dinner from Wendy's. I made fruit cup. Milton's came later and stayed until nearly 8:00. Nancy took the two chairs she had repaired. We got a box of goodies from Charles.

12/31/98 Thursday
Flurries and colder. I roasted two chickens and cut them up. Made filling balls and peeled potatoes. Got things ready for New Year's guests. I called Charlie and told him to be ready at 11:00. A dozen new chickens came and they are hungry and cold. They may belong to Richard Vincent. Clinton's impeachment is on hold. Mildred is making a pudding for tomorrow dinner.

1999

1/1/99 Friday
Partly cloudy and cold. We had a good day with company. Clarence and Mildred, Miriam Hess, Harold and Lois Harbold, Uncle Charlie, Uncle Paul and Aunt Pauline, Esther and her gentleman friend and her daughter Barbara. Had a lot of visiting and bringing up old times. Miriam had game papers to work on and an interesting album with old photos that they did enjoy. The girls seemed to enjoy visiting with the relatives. Paul seemed feeble and quiet. Charlie was pleasant and enjoyed the day. It was a busy day.

1/2/99 Saturday
Colder with snow flurries. The poor chickens are cold and hungry. They say Richard Vincent is sick in bed. I took it easy and tore and made some woolen rolls for rugs. Eby took it easy and stayed warm. I started reading the Bible and did five chapters. We have had our New Year's family dinners since 1976 at Uncle Clarence's. We had leftovers today.

1/3/99 Sunday
We did not trust the weather as many services were cancelled. We stayed home all day. Rhoda called and gave a report of their holidays that went well. I called Melvin Meck's and Betty was not home but Melvin said that Elizabeth has gone into skilled

care because she is confused. David's boys fed Richard Vincent's cold hungry chickens some bread crumbs and they ate it quickly.

1/9/99 Saturday
Damp, foggy and dark. We looked in scrapbook for some information about the Kreider family who were murdered by Albert Bomberger years ago. Found it for a Lititz woman. Abner came for us before 12:00 and took us to their house for dinner. He brought us home and we had a quiet evening.

1/10/99 Sunday
Went to Kinzer. Jay preached and got along well. Had a quiet afternoon and evening. No word of Richard Vincent. I wrote information to Lancaster Farming about the murder of the Kreider family July 7, 1993.

1/14/99 Thursday
I worked on rug. I finished reading Christ Beiler's book and the book of Genesis. The Vincent chickens are still hungry. Kathleen said she will give them a home. I finished the letter for Douglas. David brought our mail in this evening.

1/18/99 Monday
I did a small wash and used the dryer and put it all away. We tried to get the chickens in the garage, but no good. I worked on rug and it got cold because the heater went off. Called the trouble man. Lou Ann Good called to say thanks for the answer I sent to the question about the Kreider family murder July 7, 1993.

1/21/99 Thursday
Verna Graham took me to Fairmount Home to visit Elva Engel. She seemed real good and we ate with her in a private dining room. Got home soon after 1:00 and Eby went to the store in the rain. He is planning to catch the eight chickens some way. I soaked my feet and Eby did his too.

1/22/99 Friday
Dark and cloudy all day. We got seven chickens in the garage and put them in a crate and Kathleen came for them this evening with Stephen King to help. The pretty rooster got away and he was killed crossing the road. We will miss the pretty chickens. I did some cleaning and made cracker pudding. Eby went to the new bank. This is Rhoda's birthday #71.

1/24/99 Sunday
Cloudy all day. We went to Kinzer. Paul preached from Galatians 5. Sanford's went to Quaker Meeting and left for home soon after 3:00. Abram called and they are doing well. Ray's got home from Mexico last evening after a week and had a nice time. David caught another rooster.

1/29/99 Friday
Eby got milk and swept the garage where the chickens had made it dirty. I recooked the scrapple as it was too mushy. Worked on rug. There are still some little chickens. President Clinton's impeachment is on hold. I called Isaac and he saw the article I sent to Lancaster Farming about the murder of the Kreider family.

2/8/99 Monday
I washed and used the dryer. I braided some rug and did some writing for Eby doing his taxes. I finished the letters to the Jonathan Clemens clan and got Betsy's ready. I called Irene Noll and she is getting better slowly from her broken hip. We had the good fish that Ray's brought for supper.

2/11/99 Thursday
Sunny and mild. Eby trimmed the grapes and cleaned the garage. I made 70 doughnuts. Braided some rug. Grace called and she has good reports from her tests and Xrays. Steven and Silvia are on vacation to Costa Rica. Isaac and Elizabeth came this evening. Bradley was working late.

2/12/99 Friday
Eby got eggs and took some papers to Isaac Stoltzfus. I roasted some pork and made a walnut cake. Had a pain in my left back side. There are still some chickens in the woods by the mailboxes. I gave David and his boys some doughnuts.
(On 2/14/99 Ruth Martin Hostetter suffered a dissecting abdominal aneurysm. After a brief hospitalization, she was referred to a hospice facility for palliative care and given only days to live. After thirty days, she needed to leave the Hospice Center and was moved to Fairmount Retirement Home. She was initially placed in skilled care and later moved to assisted care, where she joined her husband Eby. Their home and many of their possessions were sold at an auction in May, and both of them continued to live at Fairmount.)

3/28/99 Sunday
Our company was Becky and Ken, Abram, Esther Martin and her friend for a foot massage, Ray, Jane and Laura and Isaac, Elizabeth and Bradley. A good day.

4/1/99 Thursday
Ray and Jane came and brought tulips.

4/2/99 Friday
Isaac and Elizabeth came and helped Daddy with some desk work. We ate in dining room.

4/5/99 Monday
I went to devotions. We heard the Springville chorus sing this afternoon. I took a long walk.

4/7/99 Wednesday
Edgar and Rhoda came. Esther and her friend brought Loda. Esther did my feet. Charlie called from home. Took some walks.

4/8/99 Thursday
Grace, Mary Alice and Nancy did a good job cleaning and getting ready for the sale.

4/24/99 Saturday
Sunny and cool. Had the Sunday School lesson taught by Phares Weaver. I read the book that Mary Alice sent today. Notes on the Kitchen Table. It is very good.

5/29/99 Saturday
Ray, Jane, Laura, Martha and Lucas came while we were hearing the violin family and we had a nice visit and he took us all for big drive to see some country. Later Abram and Pat came and then Isaac and Elizabeth for the evening. Lucas weighs 10 lbs. and is a good baby. Martha is ready for the wedding and we have decided to miss it.

6/2/99 Wednesday
I had a tub bath. We had a game this forenoon. Sat on the porch in the fresh air this afternoon. Got a refrigerator in the room. Went to the chapel to hear the Weaverland singers this evening. They were good.

6/4/99 Friday
Had exercises in the activity room. Esther Martin and her friend came for a visit and she gave my feet a good treatment. Isaac and Elizabeth came this evening for a nice visit. Abram and Mary Alice called.

6/6/99 Sunday
Pleasant weather. Abram and Pat came and took us to Kinzer for church services. It was good to see all the folks there again. We had dinner here in our own room. We went to the chapel to hear the chorus from Weavertown. Had a quiet evening.

6/9/99 Wednesday
Eby had a nurse bring him ice cream and a quart of strawberries.

6/11/99 Friday
Eby and Abram met the buyer and they settled for the house payment. I called Charlotte Snowdon and we had a long chat. I walked to the end of the hall and sat outside for some fresh air. Uncle Charlie called and we had a nice talk.

6/16/99 Wednesday
Jay and Ruth Meck came and served Elva Engle and us our spring communion. Jay is having eye problems and is getting a bit feeble. Esther and her friend came and she gave my feet a good treatment. Rhoda called and we had a nice long chat.

6/18/99 Friday
We had exercises and trivia about Pennsylvania this afternoon. The world's oldest woman died in Texas at age 118. I walked in the hall and visited with Lizzie Martin. We are looking for Sanford's this evening. They were here at 9:00 and all in fine looks after their trip from Richmond. Had a nice evening and they went to New Holland for the night.

6/20/99 Sunday
Pleasant weather. Nancy and Gerry brought Mary Alice and we had a nice visit before they were on their way home after the wedding. James and Martha were married at 5:00 and all went very well for the outdoor wedding. Jim and Pat stopped in a while. All the family was there except Rhoda and Edgar. Had a quiet evening. I called Ray and they are getting rested. Called Isaac's and talked to Bradley.

6/28/99 Monday
Had exercises in morning and spent a quiet afternoon. I took a walk to the end of the hall and sat with Lizzie Martin. Had a driver take us to Dr. Stoltzfus for my eyes to be checked. Should get a new lens.

7/6/99 Tuesday
We had exercises in the morning and bowling this afternoon. Sat at end of hall with Lizzie Martin. Ray called and said they will come this weekend and bring a picnic lunch. No glasses yet.

7/9/99 Friday
Pleasant. Had exercises. Ray, Jane, Laura and Baby Lucas came with a delicious lunch that we ate in New Holland Park at a picnic table. They took me for my glasses and they are good. They were here till 4:30. Little Lucas is doing real good and knows his Grandpa.

7/12/99 Monday
Milton and Barbara came at 9:00 and took us for a nice drive as far as Berks County and to see a big lake and pretty country. Stopped for ice cream at Lapp's and they bought plants and corn and cantaloupes. Got back at 2:30 and they soon left for home. I wrote to Douglas and read Henry Martin's book, Circle of Love. Grace called and said it was raining all day there. She is doing real good.

7/15/99 Thursday
Abram and Patricia took us for a drive to Hospice where I was for a few weeks before coming here and to Mennonite Homes to see Uncle Charlie, Zelma and Anna Mary Martin. Took us out for dinner and back here by 3:00. I called Rhoda and they are enjoying the visit with Fredric's family.

7/20/99 Tuesday
Got ready for our big day with Miriam Hess' heritage tour. 25 joined in the interesting places we visited. All went well as we visited cemeteries, home places and friends as

far as Strasburg, Intercourse, Cattail and others. Miriam did a good job and folks were well pleased. The King's on the home place were so friendly. They served root beer.

7/30/99 Friday
Had exercises. Mother and daughters with violin this afternoon. I walked hall and sat out on the porch. I called Pauline and she is to have more cataract surgery next week. Isaac's went to their cabin for the weekend. There was a shooting in Atlanta and 19 were killed.

8/3/99 Tuesday
We had bowling and sat on porch. Mary Alice called and she is working on my old diaries and goes to her Writer's Conference next week. I called Rhoda and Rosa and the children are there for a week. I sat outside with Lizzie and a single lady.

8/12/99 Thursday
Same weather. Still dry. Sat on side porch and Paul Eby's wife came after the others left. Eby worked on the desk. Ray and Jane came and took us for a long drive and we saw the corn looking like a sad crop, short and drying from the bottom and without any ears yet.

8/24/99 Tuesday
Pleasant. Had sharing and Janet Gehman was in charge. Rhoda called and her one foot is better. She is listening for news from Andrea. The 104 year old man from upstairs died.

8/27/99 Friday
Cloudy and good rain. We had exercises and devotions. Charles came this afternoon. He came to Abram's last night after a late flight. Getting set for tomorrow and the reunion. I called Uncle Charlie and invited him to our reunion and he said "no way." He could not take it. Naomi is still living.

8/28/99 Saturday
Charlie came and took a half hour in bed as he did not sleep last night in New Holland. We started for Camp Morehart for our last reunion there. Had a good trip. There were 49 for dinner and not that many for supper. All the children and spouses were there. We had plenty of good food and a good time visiting. Charles brought us here by 8:00 to spend the night and he went to New Holland.

8/29/99 Sunday
Charles came for us and took us back to Camp Morehart. Ray's family was in charge of the worship service. The we had more visiting and lunch with plenty of good food. Got things put in order and had our good byes and all left for their homes. Charles left to get his 3:00 plane to California. Abram brought us back after dropping

Patricia off in Hershey. He took us a nice drive to pretty places in Hershey and to Phil Haven and more. Abram stayed till after 5:00. It was a good weekend.

9/2/99 Thursday
Played shuffleboard and had a Bible session. I wrote to Becky and Ken and sent a baby gift to the Zuercher's in Goshen. Rhoda called and she is going to help Andrea with Isaiah.

9/8/99 Wednesday
Had a game of ping pong. Had a quiet afternoon and devotions. Grace called and she sent two nighties. Had a group of good singers this evening. My upstairs nurse friend is getting married in April.

9/9/99 Thursday
Pleasant and showers at night. Had exercises and devotions. Things are getting moved for the sale. Three tents are set up. Clarence and Mildred came this afternoon. The earthquake in Greece reports many dead. We did not go out to hear the men singing.

9/11/99 Saturday
A beautiful day. Had the annual sale of many things that were brought in. We bought barbecue dinners for Abram and Pat, Issac and Elizabeth, Bradley, Ray and Jane, Glen and Laura and Lucas. There was a lot of people here for the day. The highest quilt sold for $900. Tents were all down by dark.

9/19/99 Sunday
Pleasant day. Had a restful morning. Had service by Weaverland. Had a surprise when Jim, Pat, Beth and Colton came this afternoon on way from Delaware to Jim's. All are doing well and Colton was happy to go to Grandpa's. I sat with the group at the side door this evening.

9/23/99 Thursday
Pleasant weather. Had trivia with the letter J. A murder suicide happened in Leola. Eby had Martha in for ice cream this evening. We had a birthday party for Raymond. I walked the hall. The 106-year-old woman upstairs died yesterday.

9/29/99 Wednesday
Cloudy and drizzle. Had my weekly bath and then our ping pong. I wrote the family letter. My feet have been swelling and I set with them up. I walked the hall and I like the small wheels on my walker.

10/8/99 Friday
Had exercises. Milton, Barbara, Ray and Jane came this afternoon on their way home from travels since the Relief Sale. They gave a good report and Ray's are going home this evening. Milton's were staying in New Holland as they are retired. They had a lot to share.

10/16/99 Saturday
Had our Sunday School lesson in the chapel. Clarence and Mildred came for it and we gave them dinner in the private dining room. They visited for a while and then Kenneth and Becky came and we had a nice visit. The pill nurse gave us cider from her own trees.

10/22/99 Friday
Had our Sunday School lesson in the chapel this morning. Isaac and Elizabeth came this afternoon. I finished reading the book Abram gave, Birch Hollow School Ma'rm. Very good.

10/24/99 Sunday
Esther and Abner came for us and took us to Kinzer Church and to Mildred and Clarence's for a good dinner. Verna Graham was there too. Mildred brought us back here by 3:00. We took it easy and after supper Abram came and we had a nice evening.

11/2/99 Tuesday
Edgar and Rhoda came at 9:00 and we went to Landis Homes and visited Irene Noll and Kathryn Gersinger. Had a nice time and came on to the Amish Shoe Store near Gordonsville. I got new shoes for $49.50. Then we came here and Edgar's stayed till we went for supper and they went to their motel in New Holland. Milton called this evening and they are doing well.

11/22/99 Monday
Mild. Had exercises. Had our blessings written on the board. More than 100 were mentioned. I wrote to Douglas. Myrtle gave me some horseradish sauce.

11/25/99 Thursday
Abram and Pat came and took us to Issac's for Thanksgiving dinner and brought us home at 6:00. We had a delicious dinner, fruit drink, buns, turkey, filling, sweet potato croquettes, scalloped oysters, cranberries, pickles, celery, pies, ice cream, baked corn and candy. Spent a quiet evening. Had 25 for dinner.

11/28/99 Sunday
Milton, Barbara, Douglas, Dale and Mae came here and we all went to Kinzer for the service. Paul preached and we met a lot of the folks. Came here and ate in the small dining room, then we spent till 5:00 visiting here. Had a singing group this evening.

12/5/99 Sunday
Had a quiet morning. Had our service in the afternoon with the Gap Amish Church. Becky's baby boy was born yesterday, Nicholas Allen. Called Grace and told her of Becky's baby's birth. Mary Alice and Nancy plan to be with her on Monday for a cookie bake.

12/12/99 Sunday

Pleasant weather. Had a quiet morning. Devotions and worship service this afternoon in the chapel. Frank and Lydia Martin came this evening for a nice visit. Abram called and Becky and baby are doing well. Some singing children passed in the halls. Ray and Jane are leaving for a trip to Costa Rica this morning with a touring flight. I read this evening.

12/15/99 Wednesday

Cloudy with rain. Bath morning. Played bingo. Farmerville School, all 8 grades, sang in the chapel. They were very good and many filled chapel. They used risers. Had a quiet evening. Isaac called and gave a report of Mark's cow sale today. His entire herd, nearly 100 cows, sold well. Highest over $3000.00. Spent the evening reading. Had pacemaker check.

12/18/99 Saturday

Had a good Sunday School lesson. Had Bible quiz and Lutheran Church sang Christmas carols this afternoon and another group in evening. Esther Smoker called and we had a long chat. Mike's roses are beautiful and Nancy's cactus is too.

12/25/99 Saturday

The Dietzel's came for us at 11:30 and we had a delicious dinner with Linda's and Kim's families. Isaac's and Bradley brought us home by 6:00. Milton called and Douglas. Had a good evening catching our breath. Charles called at 7:45 and they were having dinner at Andy's.

12/29/99 Wednesday

Bath and horse shoes. Robert and Grace and Nancy and Gerry came for dinner in the small dining room. Had nice visiting and they left to see the Cloisters.

12/31/99 Friday

We had a good day. Sam, Melissa, Emma, Becky, Kenneth and little Nicholas came to visit. It was good to see them all. Emma is walking and talking. Little Nicholas is a nice baby. They left for Abram's at 4:30. We had a quiet evening. The year is almost gone and 2000 is soon here.

2000

1/1/00 Saturday

The New Year came in very quietly and the day was pleasant. We had a sauer kraut dinner. Had our Sunday School lesson in the morning and a Bible quiz in the afternoon. Dale called.

1/8/00 Saturday
Had Sunday School lesson on Prayer. Sam, Melissa and Emma came for lunch and we had a nice visit with them. Emma was so good. Sam and Emma were flying home today and Melissa was having some interviews for work in this area. I took a walk and we had a quiet evening. Mary Alice called and she is doing well.

1/11/00 Tuesday
Had sharing in the chapel with Debbie. Had the lady with music on her lap. Spent evening reading. Eby is reading Edith Hoover's book.

1/24/00 Monday
Cold. We had exercises and devotions. Had popcorn to lace on thread to make strings to feed the birds. Had a long evening for reading. An Amish friend and her two grandsons came in. Our rose is blooming again, the one Mike gave for Christmas.

1/28/00 Friday
Had exercises. Jonathan, Ruth, Carla, Christopher, Andrew and Hana came soon after 11:00 and had lunch with us in the small dining room. The shared the violin music and left for home by 3:00. The children kept active but were well behaved. We had Martha make them a bag of popcorn to eat on the way home. We had a nice long evening for reading.

1/30/00 Sunday
Began snowing at 2:15 and kept it up till dark. We had a restful morning and our service this afternoon by the Weaverland group. Milton called and they are going to an island for a week. Ray called and he said Lucas is creeping.

2/4/00 Friday
Cloudy and snowing a little. I called Milton's and talked to Barbara and they are going to a southern island tomorrow. Had exercises and a halfway party this afternoon. Winter is half gone. We had a quiet evening reading.

2/5/00 Saturday
Had the Sunday School lesson. Mary Alice and her friend Terry came for a visit. Then Abner and Esther and Isaac and Elizabeth. Isaac had a pack of old letters that came from Mother, Granny and Aunt Cora. So I had reading for the evening.

2/14/00 Monday
I had a normal morning with devotions and exercises. Took my walk and worked on puzzle, then I felt very sick and was hot and nauseated. I spent the day in bed, vomited and was very uncomfortable. Ate very little. Abram called and said that Daddy will likely have it too. My temperature and blood pressure were checked often. Bed felt good.

2/15/00 Tuesday
Daddy is feeling sick, but not like I was. He stayed in bed till noon and we ate in our room. Abram called from Florida. Daddy is feeling better, but it was both days for me and the nurses had Daddy see how a bubble bath works. Had Mennonite school pupils here to play games. We played marbles. This evening we helped do shell barks for someone's mother.

3/4/00 Saturday
We had exercises and Miriam Hess came for a nice visit before noon. She had the news from Stumptown. We had Bible study this afternoon. Miriam brought a lot of Strasburg newspapers.

3/14/00 Tuesday
We had bowling and devotions. Bensinger's came for income papers. We got a very nice anniversary card from Dale and Mae in Mexico. The windows were housecleaned today inside and out.

3/22/00 Wednesday
It rained and made a lot of flooding. The doctor was here and gave Eby an exam and looked at my nose. Ray called and they are all home from Mexico and had a good trip. We will hear more later. Dale and Milton called later.

3/24/00 Friday
73rd Anniversary. Abram and Pat took us to Elsie Martin's funeral at Hershey's and we saw a lot of relatives. Nancy and Gerry sent us cut flowers. Got some cards. Isaac and Elizabeth came this evening. It was a big day.

3/27/00 Monday
Had our devotions and morning exercises. Esther called and we had a good long talk. I sorted some papers. Our home in Gap was sold again for $148,000 and folks have moved in.

4/2/00 Sunday
Milton and Barbara came and shared some of their photos from their trip to Mexico. They were very interesting. Robert, Grace, Jennie and Paul came and had dinner with us in the little dining room. They left for home at 2:00. It was a nice visit. We heard singers this evening. Bradley called this evening.

4/3/00 Monday
We had exercises and devotions. The tulips Jennie brought are still very pretty. Milton's came back this afternoon before going home.

4/4/00 Tuesday
Had a sick spell and had nurses come in the night.

4/5/00 Wednesday
Bath and bingo. Rested in P.M. Had Weaverland singers this evening. A larger patch on my nose this evening.

4/6/00 Thursday
Devotions and shuffleboard. Abram came and had a nice visit. Isaac and Elizabeth were here this evening and we had a nice evening. I called Uncle Charlie and he is the same. No more nose treatment.

4/7/00 Friday
Had exercises and Ray and Jane came at noon and took us to Lititz to see a wheel chair. Ray stopped for plants. Uncle Paul's Judy was here when we got home. Rhoda called this evening and we had a long chat. We saw a lot of pretty country. Martha brought me a cup of popcorn. Laura sent a pretty bouquet. It was a good day.

4/8/00 Saturday
Had our Sunday School and we talked about a room change and when we came back it was all rearranged the way we wanted it. Becky, Kenneth and Nicholas came at noon and we had a nice visit. Nicholas weighs 16 lbs. and he was good. Spent the evening at the small group.

4/11/00 Tuesday
The nurses had a yearly seminar. We watched the bottle game. Charles called and we had a good talk. Mrs. Oberholtzer gave me some Vitamin E oil for my nose as it healed hers. I have it on tonight.

4/15/00 Saturday
I read Jimmy Carter's book. We went to Sunday School in the chapel. Paul called and we had a nice long talk. No company.

4/18/00 Tuesday
Sharing with a woman's questions. Census was taken in the dining room. Next was bowling. Had some rest time. Got family letter. Singers came from Blue Ball Brethren Church. Got birthday card from the Clinton's.

4/20/00 Thursday
Had a good morning and a good Easter sermon. Steve Weaver and Silvia came at noon and we had a visit. Silvia is a very nice person. Steve still has his long hair. I read this evening. We had a fire drill at 7:00. Ray and Jane called. Lucas started walking today. The sore on my nose is getting less with the Vitamin E oil.

4/21/00 Friday
Sanford's came this afternoon and went to Abram's to spend the night. It was good to see Sanford's. They are spending Easter with Becky and Kenneth.

4/23/00 Sunday
Donald Ibach came for us and took us to Mechanics Grove Church for the service and then to Isaac's for a very delicious dinner with most of their family. Donald brought us home and Dale and Mae were here for a visit. We had a good day.

4/24/00 Monday
Had devotions and exercises. A party for seven with April birthdays. Bertha gave me a card with $10.00. Got a pretty plant from Charles and Ed and cards.

4/25/00 Tuesday
I have been keeping quiet and reading Jimmy Carter's book. Had the telephone put back in service. Esther and Abner came this evening and we had a nice visit. Mary Alice called and Ray and Jane and Abram.

4/26/00 Wednesday
Bath morning. I have some dizziness and Dr. saw me. I stayed in bed all day with meals in room.

4/27/00 Thursday
Abram was here and I was sleeping from the pill I took. We went to the service this afternoon.

4/28/00 Friday
Had exercises. Isaac's came this evening. Ray, Jane, Laura and Lucas came this afternoon and Lucas is almost walking.

4/29/00 Saturday
Went to Sunday School. Rhoda called and we had a nice chat. Frank and Lydia Martin came this afternoon. Abram called.

Epilogue

My mother died on May 2, 2000. The pen was still clipped to the cover of her last diary when I received it, and remains there still. My father died on April 28, 2006, just a week before what would have been his 100th birthday. As I have read all those years of diaries, combing through and selecting details of their long and productive lives to include in this book, I have looked for nuggets that would represent both the ordinary and the extraordinary of their days. My filter has been, as all filters are, imperfect. Others might well have chosen differently what to include, what to exclude.

My mother once said, after reading some of the Little House on the Prairie series, that she too would have stories like that to tell, and she started a list of the topics she might write about. She always welcomed requests from grandchildren for an "old time story" they might need for a school assignment. She told us stories while she ironed, lining us up on the long bench facing the ironing board. She never wrote all those stories, but what she did was spend hundreds of hours over the course of a lifetime "keeping track" with her diaries, and those combine to weave a richly textured story of a life, the story she may have believed she never got around to writing.

This book is, I hope, a way for her to share her stories, remind us of a heritage, and bear witness to what it meant to be alive during this time: to raise a family, to tend a farm, to wake up each day and make the best of it, and then, thankfully, at the end of the day, to reflect and take note. She offers us endless records of bales and bushels, quarts and crocks, lathes and shocks, but she knew, and we know, that the measure of a life both includes and transcends those details.

M.A.H.

Made in the USA
Monee, IL
21 August 2020

38788258R00360